SURVEY OF
American Industry and Careers

SURVEY OF
American Industry
and Careers

Volume 3

Food Services—Local Public Administration

The Editors of Salem Press

SALEM PRESS
Pasadena, California   Hackensack, New Jersey

Editorial Director: Christina J. Moose   *Research Supervisor:* Jeffry Jensen
Project Editor: Rowena Wildin   *Photo Editor:* Cynthia Breslin Beres
Manuscript Editors: Stacy Cole, Andy Perry   *Design and Layout:* James Hutson
Acquisitions Manager: Mark Rehn   *Additional Layout:* William Zimmerman
Administrative Assistant: Paul Tifford, Jr.

Cover photo: ©Image Source/CORBIS

∞ The paper used in these volumes conforms to the American National Standard for Permanence of Paper for Printed Library Materials, X39.48-1992 (R1997).

Library of Congress Cataloging-in-Publication Data

Survey of American industry and careers / The Editors of Salem Press.
    v.   cm.
   Includes bibliographical references and indexes.
   ISBN 978-1-58765-768-9 (set : alk. paper) — ISBN 978-1-58765-769-6 (vol. 1 : alk. paper) — ISBN 978-1-58765-770-2 (vol. 2 : alk. paper) — ISBN 978-1-58765-771-9 (vol. 3 : alk. paper) — ISBN 978-1-58765-772-6 (vol. 4 : alk. paper) — ISBN 978-1-58765-773-3 (vol. 5 : alk. paper) — ISBN 978-1-58765-774-0 (vol. 6 : alk. paper) 1. Business—Vocational guidance—United States. 2. Industries—United States. 3. Occupations—United States. 4. Vocational guidance—United States. I. Salem Press.
   HF5382.5.U5S87 2012
   331.7020973—dc23
                                  2011019601

First Printing

PRINTED IN THE UNITED STATES OF AMERICA

Contents

Complete List of Contents

VOLUME 4

VOLUME 5

VOLUME 6

List of Tables and Sidebars

SURVEY OF

American Industry and Careers

Food Services

©George Muresan/Dreamstime.com

INDUSTRY SNAPSHOT

General Industry: Agriculture and Food

Career Clusters: Agriculture, Food, and Natural Resources; Hospitality and Tourism

Subcategory Industries: Airline Food Services; Cafeteria Food Services; Caterers; Food and Beverage Carts; Food Concession Contractors; Food Concession Stands; Food Service Contractors; Industrial Caterers; Lunch Wagons; Mobile Food Services

Related Industries: Airline Industry; Beverage and Tobacco Industry; Criminal Justice and Prison Industry; Food Manufacturing and Wholesaling Industry; Food Retail Industry; Hospital Care and Services; Public Elementary and Secondary Education Industry; Restaurant Industry; Spectator Sports Industry; Travel and Tourism Industry

Annual Domestic Revenues: At least $8.15 billion USD (Datamonitor, 2010)

Annual International Revenues: At least $84.3 billion USD (Euromonitor International, 2007, and Datamonitor, 2010)

Annual Global Revenues: At least $92.5 billion USD (Euromonitor International, 2007, and Datamonitor, 2010)

NAICS Number: 7223

INDUSTRY DEFINITION

Summary

The food services industry provides nourishment to consumers eating in a variety of settings, including schools, hospitals, military bases, recreational sites, work sites, commercial transportation carriers, and prisons. Constituting a leading global industry, food services are available from numerous sources, including cafeterias, caterers, mobile carts, booths, and concessions. Services are adjusted to comply with the different cultural protocols regarding food in different countries. Many food service businesses supply large quantities of food for crowds, while contractors frequently provide food services for businesses, industrial sites, and other establishments. The industry employs people to fulfill diverse roles at various levels, often providing teenagers and other workers their first jobs.

History of the Industry

Because food is an essential aspect of life, humans have depended on food services for several thousand years to sustain them when they are not in their residences. Historical records refer to ancient Egyptians, Greeks, and Romans serving quantities of food to groups of people assembled for religious ceremonies, so-

A young girl gets her lunch at a school cafeteria. (©Monkey Business Images/Dreamstime.com)

cial celebrations, and sporting events. By the Middle Ages, crowds gathered at monasteries, castles, and colleges relied on staffs of cooks and workers to prepare their meals. Abbeys and royal households cultivated vegetables, fruits, and grains and maintained large kitchens.

Food services have fed workers throughout history, from ancient eras onward, whether those workers were hired, apprenticed, or enslaved. During the nineteenth century Industrial Revolution, Robert Owen, a Scot, established a dining room and kitchen for his mill workers to prepare meals or buy food at affordable costs, often subsidized by him. Considered a pioneer in workplace food services, Owen realized that investing in nutritional resources enhanced his workers' productivity.

Other employers adopted food service plans for workers to receive complimentary meals or foods priced at less than market cost. Workplace food services expanded in the twentieth century, enabling workers to obtain nourishment from on-site cafeterias or machines vending food and drinks. Food

service carts often assembled near workplaces at lunch time to sell workers foods. During the 1970's, food services businesses, especially caterers, began bringing workers' orders to their workplaces.

California restaurants developed the cafeteria concept to feed miners quickly during the mid-nineteenth century gold rush. Instead of being served by waiters, patrons gathered their food choices from displays. Cafeterias became fundamental to many types of food services, especially those provided by schools to feed simultaneously large groups of students, faculty, and staff. Many prisons also incorporated centralized food services to feed inmates.

Food services have been associated with education for centuries. In the mid-nineteenth century, schools provided meals that students' families might have been unable to afford, as an incentive for attendance. College students often acquired food from social clubs they joined or boarding houses where they roomed. By the early twentieth century, nutritional science developments helped educators realize that food choices were crucial to the functioning of children's brains and their learning processes. Many communities adopted food quality standards for school lunchrooms. The National School Lunch Act of 1946 and the Child Nutrition Act of 1966 provided funds to incorporate meals and milk distribution into school schedules.

In the nineteenth century, hospital food services recognized that serving nutritional foods to patients could help improve their health. Soldiers injured in 1850's Crimean War benefited from Florence Nightingale's insistence on supplying nutritious foods to hospitalized troops. Military forces worldwide developed food services to feed troops and their dependents during peacetime and wartime. This nourishment is often credited with boosting troop morale.

Transportation food services have provided meals for passengers on railroads since the mid-nineteenth century. In the 1940's, J. Willard Marriott was supplying box lunches for passengers on some airplane flights. By the mid-twentieth century, the International Foodservice Distributors Association aided suppliers in that industry. The 1970 founding of Sysco Corporation altered the food services industry by uniting distributors to dominate the market, selling $415 million worth of products soon after being established.

The Industry Today

Modern food services represent a significant aspect of many people's lives worldwide, both as a source of nourishment and as a source of employment. Consumers have come to both appreciate and expect that food will be conveniently available in or near most public social and employment settings. About half of the U.S. population frequently uses food services when they are not eating at home. One-fourth of people in the United States often consume meals in their residences that have been prepared by some form of food services business.

Twenty-first century commercial and noncommercial food services represent the greatest source of retail employment, hiring almost 10 million people in both nonrestaurant and restaurant food services. Many modern food services occupations resemble their precedents, such as cooks, nutri-

tionists, and servers, with changes reflecting technological advances and improvements. Food services remain essential to the operation of schools, hospitals, military bases, long-distance transportation, prisons, and basic institutions common to most world cultures.

Twenty-first century food service providers evaluate consumers' demands and interests, especially regarding popular types of cuisines—often ethnic or gourmet foods—and fads in taste, in order to retain and gain more customers. They also attempt to address the dietary concerns of specific groups, such as consumers who are diabetic or who keep kosher. To be competitive, modern food service providers strive to recognize potential new markets and products they can exploit to expand their enterprises and increase their profits. Twenty-first century cruise ships promote food services as part of their brand identity, emphasizing the quality

Company cafeterias can be very attractively designed. (©Sandra Howard/Dreamstime.com)

and variety of the meals they serve as incentives for people to choose specific cruise lines for vacations.

Modern food service providers recognize that consumers' cultural backgrounds, lifestyles, and attitudes regarding food shape their dietary and nutritional expectations. Some providers also try to satisfy clients concerned about animal welfare and the environment. They may purchase food supplies from local farmers or sell organic foods whose ingredients have not been exposed to chemicals, hormones, or antibiotics. Green food services strive to use cage-free poultry eggs, recycled packaging, and foods without monosodium glutamate (MSG), high-fructose corn syrup, or partially hydrogenated fats.

The economic recession of 2007-2009 affected both food services businesses and their clients. Food services managers endeavor to deliver goods

Caterers, who often provide food and beverages for wedding receptions, are an important aspect of the food services industry. (©Dreamstime.com)

that meet the budgets of their clients, especially those of large institutions. Some of them seek wholesome foods to fulfill contracts, considering such issues as rising food prices. Food services companies prepare meals for people to cook at home, providing the convenience of prepared foods more economically than restaurants can. Some companies cook for customers in their residences.

Many twenty-first century food services companies take advantage of resources available on the Internet, such as professional and marketing networks, and create Web sites to publicize their services. Some food services vendors maintain blogs that discuss their activities, achievements, ratings, and reviews. Social networking sites, including Facebook and Twitter, enable mobile service providers to transmit their current and future locations to their client base, alerting potential customers of their availability. Customers often promote or critique their food services experiences online.

Medical food services providers also incorporate technological innovations, including computers and robots, to improve their performance. Food services companies supply day-care centers, tending children and adults unable to function independently. Mobile food services, such as Meals-on-Wheels, deliver prepared meals to housebound people. Wholesale warehouse stores, such as Sam's Club, provide extensive food services, issuing catalogs for customers operating restaurants and other food-related businesses to acquire essential supplies, ranging from bulk quantities of food to individual pieces of equipment.

According to the U.S. Department of Agriculture (USDA), American schools served 30.1 million lunches and 9.8 million breakfasts in 2007. The USDA under the Barack Obama administration sought to improve and modernize the nutritional requirements for public school lunches to address a growing childhood obesity crisis. In 1993, the U.S. Food and Drug Administration (FDA) began to publish updated Food Codes at four-year intervals. These codes (including a 2007 supplement between the 2005 code and the 2009 code) emphasize food safety and establish guidelines for food services and other food industries. Although not compulsory, this system encourages uniform food service practices in diverse geographical areas. In June, 2005, the Association of Food and Drug Officials stated that forty-eight states and U.S. territo-

Meals on airlines are prepackaged by food service companies. (©Tyler Olson/Dreamstime.com)

ries utilized aspects of the FDA Food Code to monitor food services.

In the twenty-first century, the U.S. federal government expanded funding for military food services, specifically the Army and Air Force Exchange Services (AAFES). The AAFES feeds not only troops but also children attending school on military bases. The U.S. Department of Defense has authorized expenditures of $465 million annually for military food services to hire disabled employees, many of whom are wounded veterans.

In February, 2010, the U.S. General Services Administration (GSA) announced plans for improved food services, incorporating fresh and organic foods grown by local agriculturists, for federal employees at workplaces throughout the United States. U.S. State Department employees in Washington, D.C., were the first to experience these revised government food services, which will be extended to over 350 cafeterias for which the GSA contracts food services.

Food services industry personnel benefit from participation in professional organizations. Many such groups maintain Web sites that provide members access to resources and apprise them of industry news. Message boards and listservs enable industry members to interact and share ideas, experiences, and employment opportunities. Some organizations post podcasts of speeches by industry leaders. Members may also participate in Webinars that offer educational information related to food services.

INDUSTRY MARKET SEGMENTS

Food services businesses vary greatly in size. Many food trucks, carts, and other small vendors are sole proprietorships or employ at most three to five people. Other businesses are large corporations that run the concessions at multiple sports arenas and convention centers or that provide food to prisons or schools throughout the country.

Small Businesses

Caterers, food-preparation businesses, and mobile carts and trucks represent food services that usually serve meals to small groups or help customers assemble ingredients to cook in their homes later. These businesses sometimes are affiliated with hotels, grocery stores, schools, malls, or other establishments that can supply steady streams of clients.

Potential Annual Earnings Scale. According to the U.S. Bureau of Labor Statistics (BLS), the average annual income of a worker who both prepares and serves food, such as a food cart worker, was $20,810 in 2009. Food service cooks earned an average of $25,790, head cooks and chefs earned an average of $45,340, and nonrestaurant food servers earned an average of $22,740. PayScale.com, meanwhile, estimates that caterers, 70 percent of whom are self-employed, can earn around $50,000 annually.

Clientele Interaction. Most small food vendors depend on returning customers. Owners and managers seek ways to develop customer loyalty, such as creating programs offering discounts or other re-

Street vendors, like this peanut vendor in New York, take food anywhere people gather. (©David Smith/Dreamstime.com)

Amenities, Atmosphere, and Physical Grounds. Small food service providers often operate in buildings adjacent to the owners' or managers' homes. Most state and local laws prohibit food prepared in private residences from being sold to the public, so mobile service providers are often affiliated with restaurants, delis, or similar businesses and use those establishments' kitchens to cook and package food items.

Many caterers create functional food services facilities with spacious kitchens they design to provide adequate preparation and cooking areas and supply with necessary utensils and equipment. Their storage spaces include freezers, refrigerators, and shelves to hold ingredients and foods, both before and after they are prepared for customers. Food services facilities often include areas where customers can consult with employees regarding their food requests or events. Many small food services businesses include dining areas for clients and guests in their facilities, decorating them with artwork, flowers, and other aesthetic items. Some caterers and small food service providers operate from historic properties that may appeal to customers. Outdoor dining sites adjoining small food services facilities are usually attractively landscaped.

Small food vendors offering meal assembly and food preparation provide clients with large tables where they assemble and prepare ingredients they have gathered from bins, refrigerators, and other storage areas according to recipes and instructions provided by employees. Small food services buildings emphasize functionality and food hygiene, while striving to create a welcoming atmosphere.

Typical Number of Employees. Approximately two-thirds of food service providers are small businesses employing twenty workers or fewer. They hire workers to perform various tasks, ranging from baking, to serving, to cleaning up. Staff size depends on owners' financial resources, as owners often perform the majority of the work. Some small food service providers hire temporary employees

wards, including free food or beverages, to customers who purchase a specific amount of items or services. Small food vendors often seek to emphasize the uniqueness of their businesses and products, such as trendy ethnic or health-conscious menus, compared to the uniformity of products often served by larger franchises. Vendors stress their willingness to design and deliver customized foods and services to meet individual expectations. Small food vendors often supply foods for exclusive groups in skyboxes at athletic events and other social activities and are expected to be discrete regarding any celebrities they serve.

Many small food vendors have Web sites where they describe their services, post coupons, or enable customers to order online. Some print brochures or send electronic newsletters, updating clients regarding changes in menu items and other news. These businesses sometimes host open houses or participate in local celebrations to advertise their services to their communities. Customer recommendations to friends and positive reviews by professional and amateur food critics also aid in increasing business. Small food vendors' owners and managers realize that all guests at events they serve are potential customers and endeavor to impress people with the quality, efficiency, and convenience of their services in the hope of securing more clients.

during peak event times, such as spring months when many graduations and weddings occur or months of major holidays. Employee levels fluctuate in college towns, where food service workers are frequently students seeking temporary sources of income during school sessions or are studying food- or hospitality-related curricula and want to acquire professional experience.

Traditional Geographic Locations. Small food service businesses can be found throughout the United States. Urban areas host a diversity of such businesses, ranging from those offering commuters meals during work breaks to social-event caterers. In rural areas, small vendors often provide foods for special occasions, including cakes for celebrations, snacks for community activities, and other foods not easily acquired from distant cities. Some vendors accept short-term food services contracts from visitors; they may, for example, provide catering for film or television productions filming on location in their communities. Caterers and other small food vendors also occasionally travel to work at events outside their communities.

Pros of Working for or as a Small Food Vendor. Many small food vendors' owners oversee their daily business operations and have the freedom to make essential decisions regarding menus and facilities. Owners and managers often hire relatives or friends as staff, enhancing workplace morale and cohesion. Their work is frequently satisfying because they can connect with and attempt to satisfy individual customers, who often contract their services in conjunction with emotional life events, including weddings and funerals. Employees in small food services sometimes receive extra pay for the long hours, weekends, and holidays they must work and for preparing customized products such as elaborately designed cakes. Although many small-business owners and chefs have completed culinary or other specialty schools and courses, such educational experiences usually are not mandatory, especially if employees are talented and willing to learn as they work.

Cons of Working for or as a Small Food Vendor. Employees of small food service providers often are expected to work for extended periods, setting up for events, serving food throughout the events, and cleaning up afterward. They also must often work on weekends and holidays. The long hours can exhaust employees and interfere with

their familial, educational, and other commitments, discouraging some people from continuing their employment. Employees work with knives, hot stovetops and ovens, and other kitchen hazards that can cause injuries. The enjoyment of creating beautiful foods for special occasions can be diminished by business necessities. Owners are often distracted from their food activities by concerns associated with customers' accounts, licensing, inspections, and maintaining kitchens and equipment, including delivery vehicles.

Vendors' familiarity with many of their clients may pose problems if those clients' demands are unrealistic or if they expect vendors to make unreasonable financial or performance exceptions for them. Some customers may insist that vendors or their employees attain credentials or acquire special skills, such as preparing exotic foods, that require investments of time and money.

Costs

Payroll and Benefits: Most small food business owners compensate employees with hourly wages or by the project. Benefits are often not offered. Owners of small businesses and self-employed vendors pay themselves out of their companies' profits, only after all financial obligations—including employee pay—are met. If a business realizes no profits in a given month, the owner will not be paid in that month.

Supplies: Small food service providers require basic equipment, appliances, and furniture associated with preparing and serving food. Plates, glasses, and utensils utilized by many of these businesses often are of a higher quality, including china and silver, than are those utilized by larger providers because small providers often serve smaller, more socially important events. Related supplies include linens, electronic devices such as computers and stereos, and materials to clean equipment, kitchens, and public areas.

External Services: Small food vendors may contract cleaning services to clean their equipment or they may clean it themselves. They may also contract the cleaning and maintenance of their facilities. Some vendors rent rather than own plates and serving utensils, passing on the cost of the rentals to their customers. Vendors may also contract accounting, business management, collection, or advertising services, as well as consultants to ensure that they are properly licensed and pass all health code inspections. Insurance agents provide food services with various coverage contracts for liabilities and losses. Some small food services invest in floral, landscaping, photography, and pest control services.

Utilities: Small food vendors usually need electricity, gas/oil, water, sewage, telephone, and Internet access. Food services renting their business properties might have those costs included in their leases.

Taxes: Small food vendors must pay local, state, and federal income taxes. Those owning kitchen and dining facilities must also pay property taxes. Those operating motor vehicles, such as vans to deliver or sell food, must pay the taxes associated with vehicle registration and licenses. They must collect any applicable sales taxes from their customers.

Midsize Businesses

Midsize food vendors usually provide meals for such institutions as nursing homes and elementary and secondary schools with several hundred students. They also run cafeterias and businesses' dining commons, and provide food service on various modes of transportation. Such midsize businesses often function as contractors, fulfilling specific fixed-term or per-project requests for service from other businesses.

Potential Annual Earnings Scale. According to the BLS, institutional and cafeteria cooks employed by food service companies earned average salaries of $24,990 in 2009. This average salary was greater than the average salary of cafeteria cooks employed directly by elementary and secondary schools ($22,290) but less than the average salary of those employed directly by hospitals ($26,620). Food servers in the industry earned an average of $22,740.

In the same year, food service managers earned $56,460 per year, on average, while general managers of food service companies earned $83,320. Purchasing agents—who are responsible for obtaining ingredients—earned average salaries between $37,660 and $48,510 per year, depending on the types of ingredients in which they specialized. Salaries at midsize companies are likely to be somewhat below these national averages.

Clientele Interaction. School food service workers prepare and serve food on a regular basis to the same group of diners, including students, teachers, and staff. Most of these clients interact with people monitoring buffet lines of foods, usually limited to specific items scheduled to be prepared according to standardized menus, and with cashiers. Cooks usually remain in the kitchen and do not have much direct interaction with clients, although they may be asked to meet with parents or teachers' representatives to discuss concerns over menus' nutritional content or variety.

School food service workers often are aware of special dietary needs of specific students and ensure that they do not consume any foods that might trigger allergic reactions or violate religious restrictions. Nursing home food service staffs similarly consider potential conflicts with medications and other health concerns when planning and serving meals. They often become aware of diners' food preferences and accommodate requests for substitutions or supply favorite foods when possible.

Workplace food service workers interact with office employees and visitors in company dining rooms and in cafeterias that cater to multiple businesses located in the same building or area. As in school cafeterias, buffet-line workers and cashiers interact regularly with customers, while cooks experience much less interaction. Workers may get to know regular clients and become aware of their food interests.

In commercial cafeterias, food service companies attempt to cater to local food preferences. In the South, for example, they may feature home-style meals or regional favorites such as fried catfish. Food service vendors for airlines, trains, and ships provide snacks, meals, and beverages that the carriers sell or distribute based on travel duration and class of service. Many such vendors prepare foods at commerical kitchens to be distributed by employees of the carriers and never interact with passengers.

Amenities, Atmosphere, and Physical Grounds. Most midsize food service companies feature utilitarian work or production spaces full of the industrial equipment used to prepare and store foods efficiently and quickly for several hundred people. Serving areas are often utilitarian as well. Foods are usually offered in buffet lines and stations featuring metal serving pans in which they are kept warm or chilled, sneeze guards, and shelves of presliced and other individual items covered in plastic wrap. Vending machines sometimes are available for customers to buy drinks or snacks.

Eating areas often feature uniform tables, chairs, or booths, as well as stations with trays of condiments, seasonings, napkins, and utensils. Bussing stations include trash receptacles and repositories for dirty trays and dinnerware. Instead of repositories, some cafeterias have conveyor belt systems that move dirty trays and utensils directly to dishwashing stations.

School lunchrooms often are painted in bright colors and decorated with mobiles and images that appeal to children and convey educational themes. Workplace dining commons and commercial cafeterias have more mature decorations, including artwork and plants. Food on trains and ships may be served in dedicated dining rooms or cars, or it may be sold at concession stands and snack bars. Meals on all vehicles, including airplanes, is often delivered to economy passengers in functional, shrink-wrapped trays accompanied by plastic utensils. First-class passengers are served meals on plates with metal utensils and linen tablecloths.

Midsize school, workplace, and commercial cafeterias often have attractive patios or other landscaped areas where patrons can eat meals outside. These outdoor areas tend to duplicate elements of their adjacent indoor spaces for design continuity. Museum, theater, botanical garden, and zoo food services often provide dining areas that merge into other architectural elements of those establishments.

Typical Number of Employees. Midsize food vendors generally employ between twenty and one hundred persons, though most employ less than fifty.

Traditional Geographic Locations. Midsize food services are typically located in populated areas with school systems, sizable business communities, government buildings, or other potential clients. Those that supply transportation carriers typically locate themselves near transportation hubs, including airports, train stations, and ports of call.

Pros of Working for a Midsize Food Service Company. Midsize food service vendors that are able to secure long-term or reliably renewable contracts with schools or businesses can offer their employees greater job stability than is available to

small catering firms' staffs. Many workers are able to develop relationships with recurring patrons and enjoy interacting with them, forming a relaxed, friendly community atmosphere in dining areas. Working hours and salaries are usually stable, and employees are not expected to work overtime or on holidays unless they agree to do so. Some companies follow standardized menus that meet government nutrition requirements, eliminating the potential stress of planning more creative offerings. By contrast, companies that contract for cruise ships and other expensive venues may be expected to offer exotic foods, giving employees the opportunity to work with fine cuisine.

Cons of Working for a Midsize Food Service Company. If a midsize company loses or fails to renew a contract, employees may suddenly face layoffs, reassignment, or reduced hours. Midsize food vendors contracting with schools must find alternative sources of income when school is not in session, and those contracting with transportation carriers face the potential of decreased demand for their services when the demand for travel decreases. Kitchen work can be dangerous, involving sharp knives and extreme heat. Employees sometimes suffer injuries and burns from kitchen tools and equipment. Some employees become bored by routinely dealing with the same customers or are unable to avoid unpleasant recurring clients. Other workers sometimes dislike immature patrons, especially schoolchildren, or other difficult consumers who complain about their food or are picky eaters. Many employees consider the uniform nature of some institutional menus and procedures to be tedious and unchallenging. Conferences can be stressful for food service workers if the organizers decide to offer diverse dietary options, ranging from vegetarian to gluten-free meals, to participants.

Costs

Payroll and Benefits: Wages for employees at midsize food service vendors may be hourly, weekly, monthly, or yearly, and they may be tied to a specific contract. Employees usually receive benefits including health insurance, vacation, and sick time, especially if they are employed through a government contract. Some companies provide their employees with meals and other food perks.

Supplies: In addition to ingredients and industrial cooking and serving equipment, midsize food service vendors require bulk quantities of trays, plates, cups, and utensils. They may also need furnishings, computers, and cleaning materials.

External Services: Midsize food service companies may contract services such as interior cleaning and maintenance, uniform and linen laundering, exterior landscaping, pest control, accounting or tax preparation, advertising or public relations, or government relations consulting. At conferences, they may also hire musical performers and technical personnel to operate technological equipment to display visual entertainment.

Utilities: Midsize food service companies usually need electricity, gas/oil, water, sewage, telephone, and Internet access.

Taxes: Most midsize food service companies pay local, state, and federal income taxes and property taxes as applicable. Commercial food services collect sales taxes from retail customers. Those providing meals as wholesalers for transportation carriers and others to resell are not responsible for sales taxes.

Large Businesses

Large food service companies provide meals and snacks for hospital patients, military bases, schools, universities, sporting venues, prisons, and transportation carriers. The largest such companies—such as Sysco, Aramark, and U.S. Foodservice—usually participate in several different food-related industries. That is, in addition to providing food services, such as workplace coffee carts or cafeterias, they may act as food wholesalers, providing ingredients to retail groceries and restaurants, as well as running their own chains of restaurants or grocery stores.

Potential Annual Earnings Scale. According to the BLS, institutional and cafeteria cooks employed by food service companies earned average salaries of $24,990 in 2009. This average salary was greater than the average salary of cafeteria cooks employed directly by elementary and secondary schools ($22,290) but less than the average salary of those employed directly by hospitals ($26,620) or by the federal government ($39,760). Food servers in the industry earned an average of $22,740.

In the same year, food service managers earned $56,460 per year, on average, while general managers of food service companies earned $83,320 and chief executives earned $131,250. Purchasing agents—who are responsible for obtaining ingredients—earned average salaries between $37,660 and $48,510 per year, depending on the types of ingredients in which they specialized. Salaries at large corporations are likely to be either equal to or greater than these national averages.

Clientele Interaction. Employees in large food services experience varying degrees of contact with varying types of clients. Dining area personnel and cashiers interact with diners, while sales and marketing personnel and executives interact with purchasers and decision makers at contracting companies and institutions such as airlines and prisons.

Amenities, Atmosphere, and Physical Grounds. Large food service companies exist in multiple venues. Corporate headquarters resemble the headquarters of any large company, occupying commercial office space or entire buildings in urban centers. Production and operations facilities generally include manufacturing, cooking, or assembly areas in which products such as airline meals or coffee pods are created. Many such facilities produce ready-to-prepare foodstuffs that are then shipped to cafeterias and other kitchen facilities for cooking and assembly.

Kitchens located at venues being served, including schools, military bases, and prisons, resemble those used by midsize companies: They are utilitarian and designed for optimal efficiency and food production on an industrial scale. Serving areas are similarly functional, and those in penal cafeterias are designed for security and efficient control of prisoners rather than for attractiveness. The interiors and exteriors of many collegiate food service areas are designed to be compatible with campus architecture.

Large companies serve venues of varying size. They serve massive sites, such as major convention centers and schools of thousands of students, but they also serve the small venues served by midsize companies. Such venues allow diners to choose from among foods presented buffet-style in metal bins that keep them either warm or cold as appropriate. Plastic shields protect food from airborne contaminants. Stations are stocked with standard dining items, including utensils, condiments, straws, and napkins. Automated systems may be used to move used trays, plates, and utensils to dishwashing areas. Some venues maintain outdoor areas to encourage patrons to move from crowded indoor spaces to other eating sites to ease the flow of diners, especially at peak meal times.

Typical Number of Employees. Large food service companies employ more than one hundred people, and many employ workforces in the tens of thousands. For example, Gate Gourmet, an airline catering corporation, has twenty-two thousand employees. At many of the largest corporations, food services such as industrial catering form divisions within the company rather than representing the mandate of the entire company.

Traditional Geographic Locations. Large food service corporations are national and multinational entities. They have corporate headquarters in major urban centers, as well as regional offices throughout the United States and the world. The sites operated by these corporations can be located anywhere, from urban to rural schools, to prisons, military bases, hospitals, and elderly care centers. Corporations serving the airline industry operate at every major and regional airport, while those providing coffee service to businesses operate everywhere such businesses exist.

Pros of Working for a Large Food Service Corporation. Many employees of large corporations appreciate the stability and consistency of their jobs. Depending on their assignments, employees may enjoy being affiliated with schools, universities, hospitals, or other institutional clients—such as government agencies and entities—that sometimes offer perks and that may encourage employees of contractors to feel as though they are part of their communities. In addition to job security, many food service employees receive benefits associated with working for large corporations, which often give employees stock dividends or gifts. The latter are frequently emblazoned with the corporations' logos, enhancing employees' sense of belonging. Large employers often recognize workers' loyalty by providing service awards, noting anniversaries of their employment, and providing opportunities for educational improvement and professional advancement.

Cons of Working for a Large Food Service Corporation. The atmosphere and corporate culture of large companies often seem impersonal, and employees sometimes feel anonymous and underappreciated as they perform their duties for often changing crowds. Employees with long-term assignments at smaller venues may avoid this feeling to a certain extent, but they may feel a disconnect between their assigned venues and the larger corporations for which they work. Food service workers in universities are vulnerable to school schedules that include semester breaks in which food services are not required. Safety is a concern of food service employees in prisons, as well as at military bases, which have become terrorism targets in the twenty-first century. School violence is another potential risk large food service employees face. Workers also risk injuries from equipment and tools used to prepare and serve food. Large conventions and trade shows hosting a thousand or more participants can overwhelm food staffs striving to meet the numerous and often unrealistic demands of organizers.

Costs

Payroll and Benefits: Large food service companies may pay hourly wages or annual salaries. They often provide salaries because staff can be transfered from one venue to another when contracts expire, so it less likely that they will be underutilized. Large companies usually provide employees with sick leave and vacations, and they often provide health insurance. Promotions and perks reward employees' extraordinary service.

Supplies: Large food services require bulk amounts of food, equipment, and materials used to prepare, package, ship, and serve food. They also need cleaning supplies for kitchens and indoor and outdoor dining areas, as well as computer and telecommunications equipment, office supplies, and shipping vehicles.

External Services: Many large food service companies contract with cleaning services to wash dishes, utensils, linens, and other equipment used to prepare and serve food. They may also contract custodial and pest-control services to keep dining and kitchen spaces clean and free of vermin. While they may have their own advertising staffs, even the largest corporations often hire dedicated advertising or public relations firms to create or consult on major advertising campaigns.

Utilities: Large food services need electricity, gas/oil, water, sewage, telephone, and Internet access.

Taxes: Food service corporations must pay local, state, and federal taxes, as well as applicable taxes in other countries. Commercial food services at many universities, hospitals, cafeterias, and arenas collect sales taxes from customers. Taxes for large noncommercial food services affiliated with some public schools, military bases, and prisons are paid for by governments directly. Large food services owning kitchen and dining facilities and vehicles also pay property taxes and vehicle registration and license taxes.

ORGANIZATIONAL STRUCTURE AND JOB ROLES

Food service businesses must perform the same basic tasks, whether the business in question is a sole proprietorship or a multinational corporation. At small catering businesses, a single owner may perform almost all tasks and contract out the rest, while large companies generally institute division of labor, assigning a single job role to each employee.

The following umbrella categories apply to the organizational structure of businesses in the food services industry:

- Business Management
- Customer Service
- Sales and Marketing
- Facilities and Maintenance
- Security
- Technology, Research, Design, and Development
- Cooking and Food Preparation
- Operations
- Distribution
- Groundskeeping
- Human Resources
- Information Technology
- Administrative Support

Business Management

Managers include small-business owners, as well as corporate executives. Whatever the scope of the operation, the management staff monitors all aspects of it, as well as of the industry sector or subsector in which they compete. Managers may perform diverse tasks, ranging from preparing business plans to cooking food, and they are accountable for all aspects of their departments or businesses. Food service managers provide leadership for their employees and underlings: They set goals and ensure that their businesses function efficiently. As the ultimate decision makers, they must ensure that their businesses comply with safety and health regulations, either by personally securing licenses and enforcing regulations or by delegating those tasks to others.

Managers at midsize and large companies need significant work experience or internships in food professions, and some employers seek further qualifications, such as degrees from culinary schools, community colleges, or four-year institutions in food-, hospitality-, or business-related fields. Individuals may start their own businesses without any specific training or background, but they generally require relevant credentials or other proof of competence and likelihood of success if they wish to receive business loans to cover their start-up costs.

Significant work experience or internships in food professions or other businesses is often sufficient for employment as a manager in many food services, but some employers seek managers who attended a culinary school or earned an associate's or bachelor's degree focusing on food, hospitality, business, or related fields. Food service managers earned an average annual salary of $56,460 in 2009; general managers of food service companies earned $83,320, and chief executives earned $131,250. Promotions, bonuses, and perks are presented to managers to recognize their professional contributions.

Business management occupations may include the following:

- Owner
- President/Chief Executive Officer (CEO)
- Food Service Manager
- Food Service Department Manager
- General or Operations Manager
- Chief Financial Officer (CFO)

Customer Service

Customer service personnel interact with existing clients to determine how to improve services. Those clients may be individual customers of catering firms, diners at cafeterias, institutional contract

OCCUPATION PROFILE

Food Service Manager

Considerations	Qualifications
Description	Plans and coordinates the preparation and serving of food and beverages and handles all associated tasks.
Career clusters	Business, Management, and Administration; Hospitality and Tourism
Interests	Data; people
Working conditions	Work inside
Minimum education level	High school diploma or GED; high school diploma/technical school; junior/technical/community college; apprenticeship
Physical exertion	Light work
Physical abilities	Unexceptional/basic fitness
Opportunities for experience	Apprenticeship; military service; volunteer work; part-time work
Licensure and certification	Recommended
Employment outlook	Slower-than-average growth expected
Holland interest score	ESR

Note: See volume 1, "Publisher's Note," for an explanation of the Holland interest score.

supervisors and purchasing agents, or even the heads of other companies and institutions. Customer service staff consider clients' suggestions for different menu items and other requests. They also handle complaints and attempt to resolve grievances. They sometimes work with marketing and sales personnel to develop strategies to convince potential customers to try their services, and they survey existing customers' opinions of those services, presenting the results to managers as appropriate.

Customer service personnel's qualifications usually include studies in public relations, hospitality, business, or food-related fields at vocational schools or universities. Previous work experience or internships involving food are beneficial. Most customer service jobs require personnel who can communicate well.

Customer service occupations may include the following:

- Customer Service Director
- Customer Service Representative
- Public Relations Representative

Sales and Marketing

Marketing personnel promote their companies' services to existing and potential clients. Sales personnel interact with customers to determine what food services they need and how best to provide them. They often work closely with customer service personnel to identify ways to attract customers. Sales and marketing staffs create publicity and Web sites to advertise food services. They use coupons and other promotions to increase sales. They also attend events, such as bridal fairs, to promote their companies' services.

Most employees hired for sales and marketing positions in the food services industry have bachelor's degrees in marketing or business. Employers also seek sales and marketing personnel with food science or nutrition degrees, especially those with business or communications minors. Photographers, graphic artists, and Web designers often find work in food services sales and marketing departments.

Sales and marketing occupations may include the following:

- Vice President of Sales and Marketing
- Sales Director
- Senior Sales Manager
- Marketing Director
- Senior Marketing Manager
- Sales Representative
- Marketing Representative
- Market Research Analyst

Facilities and Maintenance

Facilities and maintenance personnel monitor the technical systems used by food service companies and seek to ensure minimal disruption to their operations if problems occur. They regularly check and fix malfunctioning machines and the equipment that provides businesses with such necessary resources as water, electricity, refrigeration, and heating, ventilating, and air-conditioning (HVAC). Many maintenance personnel have specific assignments based on their technical qualifications. Some of them specialize in delivery and freight vehicles. Custodial workers ensure that commercial and industrial facilities are clean. In some companies, custodial personnel launder employees' uniforms. Facilities personnel may also be responsible for pest control.

Facilities and maintenance workers in food service companies have varied educational and professional qualifications. Most positions require vocational school training or college degrees in engineering or technology-related fields. Many also require relevant licenses. Entry-level workers usually receive hourly wages.

Facilities and maintenance occupations may include the following positions:

- Chief Engineer
- Facility Manager
- Heating, Ventilation, and Air-
    Conditioning (HVAC) Engineer
- Electrician
- Plumber

- Mechanic
- Custodian/Janitor

Security

Security personnel protect employees, clients, and food. Some patrol food services facilities, observing customers and employees inside dining areas and kitchens to prevent them from contaminating food or committing acts of bioterrorism or theft. Others monitor surveillance cameras placed both inside and outside buildings. Food service companies often deploy sensors capable of detecting various hazards, including chemicals and carbon monoxide, and some employ guards to control access to restricted areas, checking employees' identification and inspecting their bags or vehicles for possible food contaminants, weapons, or stolen property.

Food service companies seek security personnel with both training and experience in public safety. They generally prefer to hire candidates who have studied criminal justice or related fields at vocational schools or universities. Security personnel often are military veterans or former police officers or firefighters. They frequently have certification in first aid, use of firearms, and operation of security technologies.

Security occupations may include the following:

- Security Guard
- Food Safety Inspector
- Biohazard Specialist
- Firefighter

Technology, Research, Design, and Development

Diverse personnel contribute to the creation of products and equipment sold and used by the food services industry. Food scientists test ingredient combinations to produce new flavors and textures to please clients. Nutritionists often contribute to recipe development to provide new foods with marketable nutritional profiles. Food engineers help design food service facilities and plan the placement of equipment and furnishings to facilitate more efficient preparation and serving of foods. They also devise better machinery to improve food services. Cake and pastry decorators attempt to create original designs to attract customers.

Food service companies' scientific and technical employees usually have university degrees in food science or engineering, nutrition, or agricultural engineering. Some have advanced degrees. Many have studied at culinary schools or interned with pastry chefs.

Technology, research, design, and development occupations may include the following:

- Vice President of Research and Development
- Food Engineer
- Food Scientist
- Nutritionist
- Biochemist
- Food Laboratory Technician
- Quality Assurance Specialist
- Cake Designer

Cooking and Food Preparation

Cooking jobs vary widely between social and institutional caterers and food service providers. Premium providers, such as wedding caterers, may seek chefs who can prepare elaborate cuisines, and such chefs may be owner-operators of catering businesses. Caterers in particular must be flexible and creative because they must be able to design menus and recipes to customers' specifications. Institutional caterers and similar companies, by contrast, require cooks who can produce large amounts of basic foods efficiently and consistently, with little variation. These lead food preparers are often supported by assistants with varying degrees of skill and experience, who sometimes aspire to become chefs or head cooks themselves. Culinary students sometimes gain credentials by interning in such positions.

Caterers have varied credentials. Chefs usually have studied at culinary schools and acquired recognition and occasionally certification for their talents preparing foods. Cooks may also have attended culinary schools or have taken food-related courses or home economics at trade schools, community colleges, or universities. Some food service cooks have experience in military food service occupations.

According to the BLS, food service chefs and head cooks earned mean yearly salaries of $45,340 in 2009, slightly higher than the mean salary for all chefs and head cooks of $44,240. Those in the tenth percentile of earners in this occupation earned $22,860, while those in the ninetieth percentile earned $69,560. Cafeteria cooks employed directly by food service companies earned mean salaries of $24,990, again slightly above the mean salary for all cafeteria cooks of $23,870. Tenth percentile earners earned $15,820, while ninetieth percentile earners earned $34,030. Food preparation workers (that is, workers with food preparation duties other than cooking) earned mean salaries of $18,090, below the occupation's cross-industry average of $20,420. Tenth percentile earners earned $15,380, and ninetieth percentile earners earned $28,280.

Cooking and food preparation occupations may include the following:

- Caterer
- Chef
- Sous Chef
- Head Cook
- Cook
- Cafeteria Cook
- Assistant Cook
- Baker
- Pastry Chef
- Line Cook
- Food Preparation Worker

Operations

Both commercial and noncommercial food service providers need a variety of supervisors and entry-level personnel to function. Operations staff set up mobile providers' equipment at venues; carry food from kitchens to serving areas; serve food to diners; clean up after meals and events; wash dishes; stock stations with utensils, dinnerware, and trays; staff buffet lines; bus and clean tables; assist customers; and collect payments. Supervisors may take part in any or all of these tasks, or they may monitor and instruct front-line workers as needed.

The average annual income for food service operations managers in 2009 was $34,530, which was higher than the cross-industry average for supervisors of food preparation and serving workers, $31,460. Tenth percentile earners earned $19,180, while ninetieth percentile earners earned $47,420.

Food service companies often arrange for entry-level employees to receive initial job training and provide additional instruction when new technologies or techniques are introduced. Most entry-level workers receive hourly wages, as low as the federal minimum hourly rate, $7.25, set in 2009. The average hourly wages of cafeteria attendants employed directly by food services companies in that year were $9.40, or $19,540 per year. Food services employees often receive uniforms and food free or at discounted prices.

Operations occupations may include the following:

- Food Preparation Supervisor
- Serving Supervisor
- Logistics Supervisor
- Cafeteria Attendant
- Cart Attendant
- Server
- Cashier
- Table Busser
- Bartender
- Dishwasher

Distribution

Distribution personnel deliver foods and other products to customers. Distribution managers schedule shipments, assign them to drivers and vehicles, and oversee all other necessary logistics. Distribution personnel maintain records and invoices, documenting dates and distances that products are transported. If food services products are shipped overseas, distribution managers typically arrange for permits, customs documents, and tariff payments. They also complete any paperwork associated with transporting food across state lines.

Many food service distribution personnel are entry-level workers whose employers provide all necessary training. Distribution personnel operat-

---

OCCUPATION PROFILE

Food and Beverage Service Worker

Considerations	Qualifications
Description	Takes customers' orders, serves food and beverages, cleans tables, and welcomes customers.
Career clusters	Business, Management, and Administration; Hospitality and Tourism
Interests	People; things
Working conditions	Work inside
Minimum education level	No high school diploma; on-the-job training; high school diploma or GED; high school diploma/technical school
Physical exertion	Light work
Physical abilities	Unexceptional/basic fitness
Opportunities for experience	Part-time work
Licensure and certification	Usually not required
Employment outlook	Average growth expected
Holland interest score	CRE; CSR

Note: See volume 1, "Publisher's Note," for an explanation of the Holland interest score.

ing motor vehicles are required to have licenses, including commercial licenses if they drive large trucks. They may have to undergo additional training and certification to obtain credentials and learn to operate equipment such as forklifts. Some distribution employees may be required to maintain physical standards necessary to lift heavy weights.

Entry-level distribution workers typically earn hourly or yearly wages depending on the work they perform. Employers pay some drivers by the mile. Most food services distribution managers earn yearly salaries.

Distribution occupations may include the following:

- Distribution Manager
- Heavy Truck Driver
- Light Truck Driver
- Freight Loader/Unloader
- Warehouse Worker
- Shipping and Receiving Clerk

Groundskeeping

Groundskeeping personnel perform various tasks for both safety and appearance purposes. They keep exterior areas around buildings clear of debris and other hazards, preventing employees and clients from suffering injuries. Groundskeeping workers also perform landscaping duties, designing attractive grounds for employees and customers to enjoy. They occasionally create butterfly gardens, gazebos, walking trails, or other outdoor sites for employees and customers to use. These aesthetic details usually benefit food service companies by appealing to clients who associate a location's visual appearance with the quality of food served there.

In addition to obtaining gardening experience, some groundskeeping personnel working for food service companies have studied horticulture or botany in high schools, vocational institutions, or universities. Groundskeeping personnel earn hourly to yearly wages, based on their credentials.

Groundskeeping occupations may include the following:

- Head Groundskeeper
- Groundskeeper
- Landscaper

Human Resources

Human resources personnel recruit, hire, and fire employees. They sometimes use Internet resources to find potential employees who have posted resumes on social networking sites, blogs, or other Web sites, and they also recruit employees from culinary schools and other food-related educational programs. Human resources personnel also train employees or secure training for them, administer payroll and benefits, and respond to employee grievances. Most human resources positions require bachelor's degrees in human resources management or similar business fields. Experience or education in food-related fields is also helpful in obtaining human resources jobs in the food services industry.

Human resources occupations may include the following:

- Human Resources Director
- Human Resources Manager
- Human Resources Generalist
- Benefits Specialist
- Payroll Clerk

Information Technology

Information Technology (IT) personnel procure computers and related equipment; maintain, repair, and troubleshoot that equipment; and acquire and perform hardware and software upgrades. They check computers for viruses, malware, and spyware and install firewalls and antivirus programs. They often manage employees' e-mail and Internet services. At companies employing automated production or distribution machinery, IT personnel write the code to drive and monitor such equipment. IT technicians may also manage and operate audiovisual systems used by food service companies.

Most IT staff have college degrees in computer science or vocational school certification and training in IT specialties. They often have advanced degrees or training as well.

IT occupations may include the following:

- Information Technology Director
- Computer Programmer
- Computer Technician
- Computer Security Specialist
- Computer Networking Technician

- Help Desk Staff
- Webmaster
- Multimedia Technician

Administrative Support

Administrative workers perform clerical duties and otherwise assist in all aspects of running the day-to-day business operations of a company. They assist food service managers, file invoices, answer telephones, and prepare correspondence. Receptionists welcome customers and schedule appointments. Many food services administrative workers begin as interns or in temporary or entry-level positions. Requirements vary by employer, but administrative personnel often receive training after they are hired, learning about office technology and procedures—particularly the computer software used to manage food inventories and orders.

Administrative occupations may include the following:

- Administrative Assistant
- Receptionist

INDUSTRY OUTLOOK

Overview

The outlook for this industry shows it to be on the rise. Food services form a dynamic industry that is common to a diverse set of cultures and income levels and experiences consistent demand from individuals and institutions. As populations worldwide increase, so will the need for varied institutional food services to supply students, workers, prisoners, and other institutional populations, as well as caterers and other mobile service providers for special occasions and convenient everyday meals. Social and institutional catering represents the fastest-growing sector in the food services industry.

The global economic recession of 2007-2009 slowed demand for some food services, as consumers with reduced budgets adjusted their spending habits. Food services contractors providing foods for schools, military bases, hospitals, and prisons did not experience significant decreases in their businesses, but caterers, cafeterias, and other independent food services did. Some of these businesses lost customers, while others adjusted menus, ser-vices, and prices to accommodate and retain clients, decreasing their profits. As economies recover in the 2010's, industry analysts expect food services to thrive.

Food service companies typically account for 5 to 6 percent of the overall employment in the larger restaurant, drinking places, and food service industry. In 2008, there were approximately 28,954 nonrestaurant food service companies operating in the United States, representing 5.3 percent of businesses in the larger category. These companies employed approximately 547,200 people, or 5.7 percent of the overall restaurant and food service industry. Almost 2 percent of food service employees either belonged to unions in 2008 or benefited from union policies. While many food service companies employ twenty people or fewer, others have many thousands of employees. Sodexo, for example, employs 110,000 people in its food services division in the United States.

According to the Society for Foodservice Management, its members secure more than 16,500 contracts internationally each year, with sales exceeding $20 billion. In 2009, *Food Management* reported that the leading food service equipment managers in North America and globally included Compass Group North America, Aramark Corporation, and Sodexo. Notable industry supplier Sysco achieved 2008 sales of $37.5 billion. The International Foodservice Distributors Association (IFDA) reports that its members achieve $110 billion in yearly revenues. In 2009, the Tyson Food Service Group was named IFDA Supplier of the Year, an honor it received four consecutive years.

Food services that begin as community businesses often expand into national franchises. By 2006, Dream Dinners, established in the previous decade, operated at 235 sites in thirty-three states and earned $57 million in annual revenues. That business and other food service companies secure contracts from other corporations to provide their employees with food services, especially meal preparation, as an employment benefit.

In winter of 2010, Continental Airlines announced changes in its economy class meal services. It started to charge economy passengers separately for food in the fall of 2010 instead of including the cost of meals in their fares. Continental's Chelsea Food Services maintains kitchens at five of that airline's hubs, including Newark, New

Jersey, and Houston, Texas. Annually, Chelsea Food Services serves over 31 million meals and employs twenty-three hundred people. Continental also contracts with food service companies operating in several international airports to produce and deliver in-flight snacks and meals. Chelsea Food Services, meanwhile, prepares first-class and business-class meals for other domestic and foreign airlines.

Employment Advantages

The BLS anticipates a consistent need for food service employees in the twenty-first century. It projects that employment in entry-level food service positions will grow by 7.7 to 10 percent between 2008 and 2018. Moreover, a high turnover rate in the industry increases the number of available positions. Entry-level food service jobs are often people's first source of employment. Two-fifths of food service employees work part time, double the proportion of part-time employees in other industries. Many part-time employees prefer this status because it permits time for other activities and commitments.

The BLS projects that food service manager positions will increase by 17 percent by 2014, noting an increasing demand for food service managers in health care institutions such as hospitals and retirement homes in particular. This increase, due to growth in geriatric populations, reveals a consistent trend: As a given class of institution—such as nursing homes, schools, or prisons—experiences increasing populations, it will also experience an increased demand for food service workers, since its members need to eat. Food services thus offers opportunities for managerial positions to candidates who may have difficulty finding similar positions in other industries harmed by the recession. White-collar workers seeking employment would do well to consider this industry, which will require people with business degrees and experience, whether or not they have prior employment in food-related businesses. The food services industry will continue to grow as the baby boomers retire.

PROJECTED EMPLOYMENT FOR SELECTED OCCUPATIONS

Food Services and Drinking Places

Employment		
2009	Projected 2018	Occupation
2,214,270	2,517,700	Combined food preparation and serving workers, including fast food
513,090	569,100	Cooks, fast food
791,780	846,900	Cooks, restaurant
599,450	645,900	First-line supervisors/ managers of food preparation and serving workers
1,997,710	2,169,600	Waiters and waitresses

Source: U.S. Bureau of Labor Statistics, Industries at a Glance, Occupational Employment Statistics and Employment Projections Program.

Annual Earnings

The food services industry is difficult to quantify because its revenues are often included in overall restaurant and drinking places statistics and because large corporations often include food service divisions alongside other food-related divisions. Euromonitor International in 2007 estimated global restaurant and food service revenues at $1.85 trillion, of which nonrestaurant food services generated approximately $92.5 billion. In 2009, Global Industry Analysts projected the combined restaurant and catering industries to achieve $2.2 trillion in revenues by 2015, approximately $110 billion of which would come from nonrestaurant food services.

According to Datamonitor, total North American restaurant and food service revenues in 2008 were $191.2 billon, including $163 billion in the United States. Assuming that nonrestaurant food services accounted for 5 percent of those revenues, those services generated $9.56 billion in North America and $8.15 billion in the United States. International revenues were at least $84.3 billion. The G8 nations (United States, Canada, Germany,

France, United Kingdom, Italy, Russia, and Japan) experienced revenue growth in the restaurant and food service industry of 3.7 percent between 2004 and 2008. Their 2008 revenues totaled $366.9 billion, which suggests $18.3 billion in nonrestaurant food service revenues at a rate of 5 percent. Datamonitor projects that 2013 G8 revenues would reach $427.5 billion ($21.4 billion for nonrestaurant food services).

RELATED RESOURCES FOR FURTHER RESEARCH

ASSOCIATION FOR HEALTHCARE FOODSERVICE
455 S 4th St., Suite 650
Louisville, KY 40202
Tel: (888) 528-9552
Fax: (502) 589-3602
http://www.healthcarefoodservice.org

CATERSOURCE
2909 Hennepin Ave. South
Minneapolis, MN 55408
Tel: (612) 870-7727
Fax: (612) 870-7106
http://www.catersource.com

INTERNATIONAL FOODSERVICE DISTRIBUTORS ASSOCIATION
1410 Spring Hill Rd., Suite 210
McLean, VA 22102
Tel: (703) 532-9400
Fax: (703) 538-4673
http://www.ifdaonline.org

NATIONAL ASSOCIATION OF COLLEGE AND UNIVERSITY FOOD SERVICES
2525 Jolly Rd., Suite 280
Okemos, MI 48864-3680
Tel: (517) 332-2494
Fax: (517) 332-8144
http://www.nacufs.org

SOCIETY FOR FOODSERVICE MANAGEMENT
15000 Commerce Parkway, Suite C
Mount Laurel, NJ 08054
Tel: (856) 380-6829
Fax: (856) 439-0525
http://www.sfm-online.org

ABOUT THE AUTHOR

Elizabeth D. Schafer received a Ph.D. in the history of technology and science, specializing in agricultural history, from Auburn University in 1993. Her research focuses on agricultural engineers' work to develop more efficient machinery, equipment, and techniques to cultivate and harvest food and fiber crops. It also examines the role of veterinary science in controlling and eradicating animal diseases that cause public health risks by contaminating food and dairy supplies. She has contributed articles on food science and technology, nutrition, and veterinary history to numerous publications.

FURTHER READING

Birchfield, John C. *Design and Layout of Foodservice Facilities.* 3d ed. Hoboken, N.J.: John Wiley & Sons, 2008.

Borges, Manuel P., ed. *National School Lunch Program Assessment.* Hauppauge, N.Y.: Nova Science, 2009.

Bright, Saunya N., et al. "Institutional Foodservice Benchmarking: Survey of Administrators' Attitudes and Practices in the USA." *Journal of Foodservice* 20, no. 3 (June, 2009): 123-132.

Buzalka, Mike. "*FM*'s Top Fifty Foodservice Management Companies—2009." *Food Management.* September 1, 2009. http://food-management.com/business_feature/fms-top-management-0909.

Chmelynski, Carol Caprione. *Opportunities in Food Service Careers.* Foreword by William P. Fisher. Rev. ed. New York: McGraw-Hill, 2006.

Engelund, Eva Høy, Gitte Breum, and Alan Friis. "Optimisation of Large-Scale Food Production Using Lean Manufacturing Principles." *Journal of Foodservice* 20, no. 1 (February, 2009): 4-14.

Farkas, David. "Finding Tomorrow's Foodservice Leaders Today." *Foodservice Equipment and Supplies* 62, no. 3 (March 1, 2010): 18.

Fenich, George G. *Meetings, Expositions, Events, and Conventions: An Introduction to the Industry.* 2d ed. Upper Saddle River, N.J.: Pearson/Prentice Hall, 2008.

Katsigris, Costas, and Chris Thomas. *Design and Equipment for Restaurants and Foodservice: A*

Management View. 3d ed. Hoboken, N.J.: John Wiley & Sons, 2009.

Manask, Arthur M., with Mitchell Schechter. *The Complete Guide to Foodservice in Cultural Institutions: Keys to Success in Restaurants, Catering, and Special Events.* New York: John Wiley & Sons, 2002.

Mattel, Bruce, and the Culinary Institute of America. *Catering: A Guide to Managing a Successful Business Operation.* Hoboken, N.J.: John Wiley & Sons, 2008.

Millstone, Erik, and Tim Lang. *The Atlas of Food: Who Eats What, Where, and Why.* Foreword by Marion Nestle. Rev. ed. Berkeley: University of California Press, 2008.

Payne-Palacio, June, and Monica Theis. *Introduction to Foodservice.* 11th ed. Upper Saddle River, N.J.: Pearson/Prentice Hall, 2009.

Plunkett, Jack W., ed. *Plunkett's Food Industry Almanac, 2010: The Only Comprehensive Guide to Food Companies and Trends.* 7th ed. Houston, Tex.: Plunkett Research, 2010.

Strianese, Anthony J., and Pamela P. Strianese. *Dining Room and Banquet Management.* 4th ed. Clifton Park, N.Y.: Thomson/Delmar Learning, 2008.

U.S. Bureau of Labor Statistics. *Career Guide to Industries,* 2010-2011 ed. http://www.bls.gov/oco/cg.

_____. "Food Service Managers." In *Occupational Outlook Handbook,* 2010-2011 ed. http://www.bls.gov/oco/ocos024.htm.

U.S. Census Bureau. North American Industry Classification System (NAICS), 2007. http://www.census.gov/cgi-bin/sssd/naics/naicsrch?chart=2007.

U.S. Department of Commerce. International Trade Administration. Office of Trade and Industry Information. Industry Trade Data and Analysis. http://ita.doc.gov/td/industry/otea/OTII/OTII-index.html.

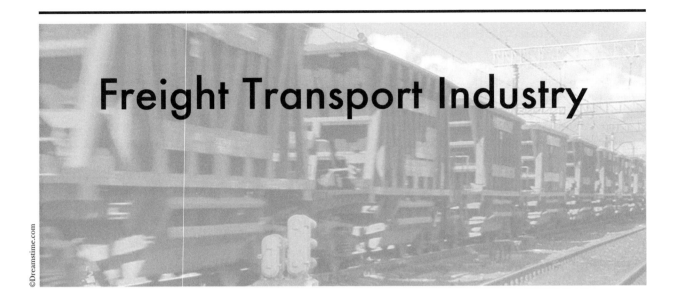

Freight Transport Industry

INDUSTRY SNAPSHOT

General Industry: Transportation, Distribution, and Logistics

Career Cluster: Transportation, Distribution, and Logistics

Subcategory Industries: Deep Sea, Coastal, and Great Lakes Water Freight Air Transportation; Freight Transportation; Freight Transportation Arrangement; General Freight Trucking; Inland Water Freight Transportation; Pipeline Transportation; Rail Transportation; Specialized Freight Trucking; Support Activities for Transportation; Warehousing and Storage

Related Industries: Airline Industry; Highway, Road, and Bridge Construction Industry; Mass Transportation Vehicles Industry; Passenger Transportation and Transit Industry; Petroleum and Natural Gas Industry; Postal and Package Delivery Services; Shipbuilding, Submarines, and Naval Transport Industry; Travel and Tourism Industry; Warehousing and Storage Industry

Annual Domestic Revenues: Freight transportation, $1.8 trillion USD (Plunkett's Research, 2008); oil pipelines, $9.6 billion USD (RITA, Bureau of Transportation Statistics, 2001); gas pipelines, $102 billion USD (RITA, Bureau of Transportation Statistics, 2005)

Annual International Revenues: $66,395,000 (U.S. Bureau of the Census, 2010)

NAICS Numbers: 481112, 481212, 481219, 482, 48311, 483113, 493211, 484, 486, 4881-4885, 4889

INDUSTRY DEFINITION

Summary

The freight transportation industry is among the most important industries in the global economy. Its primary purpose is to move raw materials and finished products across distances. It moves goods from manufacturers and wholesalers to retailers, among various manufacturers, and from sources of raw materials to industrial refiners. It does so via road, air, and rail transportation and by inland, coastal, and deep-water ship transportation. Bulk liquids are moved through pipelines. In addition, the industry includes logistics and warehousing. This highly diversified industry is the circulatory system of the modern global economy.

History of the Industry

Early regular bulk cargo transportation began during the Bronze Age, although Stone Age people were known to have transported large objects over long distances. Merchants using rowed galleys plied the ancient Mediterranean Sea, transporting grain, olive oil, and metals as well as luxury goods. Inland waterways also were used for transportation in ancient times. Shallow draft river vessels were common in ancient Egypt and China. The Chinese empire undertook massive canal-building projects that served to enhance water transportation as well as providing irrigation and flood control.

Until the nineteenth century, most bulk cargo was transported by water. Trade by land or water often was hazardous because of natural disasters, poor facilities and infrastructure, disease, pirates and bandits, and few laws protecting merchants from excessive tolls and taxes. Roads were few and poorly maintained, and moving large quantities of goods using horses, oxen, elephants, camels, or human labor was rarely cost-effective. Long-distance trade over land thus generally dealt with high-value and easily transportable goods. The Silk Road, which connected China with Europe and the Middle East, was a major trade route in ancient and medieval times. Another trade route took gold and salt from West and Central Africa to various points north.

The modern transportation industry has its roots in the Middle Ages, with the first stirrings of modern capitalism. Italian city-states provided shipping transportation for the Crusades (eleventh through thirteenth centuries) and reaped the benefits of bulk trade with the Middle East. At the same time, trading cities on the Baltic and North Seas formed the Hanseatic League, which encouraged the growth of shipping and the development of ports as major trade hubs. This development was aided by new technology. Portuguese mariners developed new navigation techniques in the 1400's that were enhanced by advances in sails and rudders. Port cities built new docks and cranes. The medieval Zuraw crane, still visible in the port of Gdansk, Poland, dates from 1367 and is one of the few extant examples of this tremendous period of growth.

A container ship makes its way down a river. (©Peter Neychev/Dreamstime.com)

European migrations to the New World, beginning in the late fifteenth century, brought a great burst of exploration, and transportation of bulk goods expanded dramatically. Europeans became the leaders in world transportation by the late sixteenth century; the trade empires of Spain, Portugal, the Netherlands, and Great Britain connected China, India, Africa, and the Americas. Sugar, tobacco, indigo, and other crops poured into Europe, along with gold and silver from American colonies. The dark side to this growth was the trade in slaves brought from Africa to the New World to work on plantations.

After the American Revolution, New England merchants took a growing part in the transportation industry. By the middle of the nineteenth century, Americans had become major players in global sea trade. The famous Yankee clipper ships could travel from China to London in as few as 130 days, carrying valuable cargoes of tea.

The development of steam power revolutionized transportation. Steamships no longer depended on wind and currents, dramatically increasing the potential for water transportation. In America and Europe, extensive canal building allowed for cheap bulk transportation far inland. The opening of the Erie Canal in 1825 helped make New York a major trade hub and allowed midwestern wheat to flow to Europe in vast amounts. The greatest revolution in transportation, however, was the development of the railroad, which ultimately conquered the tyranny of space. Railroads extended transportation and logistics into the vast

Inputs Consumed by the Truck Transportation Industry

Input	Value
Energy	$65.4 billion
Materials	$12.6 billion
Purchased services	$86.5 billion
Total	$164.5 billion

Source: U.S. Bureau of Economic Analysis. Data are for 2008.

hinterlands of North America far from navigable rivers, opening up the West for settlement, farming, mining, and logging. By the late nineteenth century, a quarter of all steel in America was being used to make rails. Transportation bound the young United States together, allowing the growth of large-scale industry that relied on raw materials from distant sources.

Air transportation began in earnest during World War II, when huge numbers of transport aircraft were used to supply island outposts around the Pacific in a timely manner. Until the 1970's, this part of the freight transportation industry remained limited because of government regulation, and most cargo flew on commercial passenger planes. This changed in 1977 with airline deregulation, which removed restrictions on the routes operated by all-cargo airlines. Companies such as FedEx grew apace, offering overnight package delivery worldwide.

The pipeline transportation industry has its own separate history. During ancient times, Roman engineers developed aqueducts to supply cities with water from distant mountain sources. Some of these ancient structures remain serviceable today. The first known industrial pipeline was built in 1595 and used to transport brine 40 kilometers between Hallstadt and Ebensee, Austria. Oil and natural gas transportation by pipeline began after World War II but did not take off until the 1970's and 1980's.

The Truck Transportation Industry's Contribution to the U.S. Economy

Value Added	Amount
Gross domestic product	$125.6 billion
Gross domestic product	0.9%
Persons employed	1.443 million
Total employee compensation	$76.8 billion

Source: U.S. Bureau of Economic Analysis. Data are for 2008.

The Industry Today

The freight transportation industry today is a crucial part of the global economy. Indeed, the development of the industry and increasingly efficient movement of large quantities of goods and materials makes possible and profitable the creation and distribution of the goods and services on which consumers and societies rely. Despite the economic downturn of the 2000's and the concerns raised over port security in the wake of the terrorist attacks in New York and Washington, D.C., on September 11, 2001, the freight transportation industry remains strong. According to 2006 Census statistics, the freight transportation sector employs more than 2 million Americans.

The modern freight transport industry has been transformed by several major innovations. The first and most important was the development of intermodal shipping containers. These humble boxes allows shippers to efficiently carry a wide array of cargo. Containers are especially important for shipping high-value but potentially fragile products such as electronics but can be used for nearly any cargo that can fit within their dimensions. Containers can be easily and quickly moved among various modes of transport—from ship to train to truck—without unloading the cargo inside. Today, 90 percent of nonbulk cargo shipping is carried out using containers. This has led to numerous innovations, such as the development of container ships and more advanced port, rail, and truck terminals. The old method of freight shipping—called "break bulk"—has fallen out of use but still is necessary in some less developed regions that lack modern port facilities. Bulk cargo shipping—shipping of raw materials in an unpackaged form—remains a significant part of the industry. A second major innovation has been the use of computerized tracking and distribution systems.

Trucks transport containers filled with a wide variety of finished and manufactured goods to ports. (©Dreamstime.com)

Using simple bar-code scanners, workers can track containers and their contents at every stage of the transportation process. The information can then be relayed to customers. The system does away with a large amount of paperwork, speeds cargo through international customs, and reduces delays and loss of cargo. Information on the location of containers also can be coded via the Global Positioning System (GPS). Computerized control systems are especially critical for pipeline transportation, allowing for greater safety, security, and product monitoring throughout the transportation process.

There are six major sectors of the freight transportation industry: sea-borne shipping, inland waterway shipping, air, rail, truck (tractor trailer), and pipeline.

Sea-Borne Shipping. Sea-borne shipping carries the greatest quantity of goods and materials based on both volume and dollar value. Oceangoing ships carry the largest and most valuable car-

Air cargo carriers transport smaller, high-value cargo, particularly consumer and business packages and bulk mail. (©Mike Kwok/Dreamstime.com)

goes the greatest distance at the lowest cost. There are several major types of cargo delivered by marine transportation. Automobiles and other vehicles are shipped using special "roll-on/roll-off" (RORO) ships. Bulk cargo shipping moves raw materials in large unpacked quantities. Bulk carriers include oil tankers and ore carriers. Containers ride the waves in special container ships. Containers are ideal for a wide variety of finished and manufactured goods including food, textiles, electronics, and spare parts. Because of outsourcing and the wide dispersal of manufacturing facilities to take advantage of lower labor costs, container shipping is the fastest growing segment of the market. The growth of high-volume shipping has led to the massive expansion of port facilities worldwide. Singapore tops the list as the world's busiest port in terms of ship tonnage served, transshipment, container traffic, and bunkering (that is, the supplying of fuel and other necessities for cargo vessels). Shanghai, China, is the second busiest port and is

first in terms of cargo tonnage handled. Rotterdam, Holland, is the busiest port in Europe, and Los Angeles/Long Beach, California, tops the list in North America.

Inland Waterway Shipping. Inland waterway shipping is similar to marine shipping, but here the emphasis is on bulk cargo transported in barges using special river tugboats for motive power. This type of shipping is slow but highly cost-effective because it has significantly lower energy costs. A typical river barge can hold the contents of fifteen railroad cars or sixty trucks. This method of shipping is particularly suited to moving bulk cargo domestically either for local consumption or for transshipment globally at ports that handle both river and ocean traffic. Grain, ore, and coal are the most common loads found on barges.

Air Cargo. Air cargo is another important segment of the freight transport industry. Using specialized cargo aircraft, air cargo carriers transport smaller, high-value cargo, particularly consumer and business packages and bulk mail. The overnight package industry is perhaps the best-known example of this type of transportation, and Memphis, Tennessee-based FedEx is the world's largest air cargo shipper. This segment of the industry continues to grow dramatically.

Rail Cargo. The rail cargo transportation industry is a major part of the domestic cargo shipping industry. Trains provide inexpensive shipping (based on tonnage per mile) for both containers and bulk goods. Container trains have become a common sight, utilizing both single- and double-stack flat cars especially designed for this purpose. Bulk cargo is handled in special hopper or gondola cars. Live animals also are transported by rail in specially designed cars.

Truck Shipping. Truck transportation is a vital part of the freight cargo supply chain. In the United States, truck drivers account for 45 percent of all freight transportation industry employees. Trucks can carry containers, bulk goods, and live animals, as well as smaller loads. The trucking seg-ment of the industry, for example, handles most of the business-to-business (B2B) freight traffic, using large tractor trailers or smaller delivery vehicles. Most truckers operate either independently (working directly for the client) or through freight carriers or shipping agents. Some big companies (such as grocery store chains) operate their own internal trucking operations. Some road transportation is done on regular routes or for only one consignee per run, while others transport goods from many different loading stations/shippers to various destinations. On longer runs, only cargo for one leg of the route is known when the cargo is loaded. Truckers may have to wait at the destination for the return cargo.

Pipeline Transport. Pipeline transportation is a special branch of the freight cargo industry. Pipelines transport bulk liquids, primarily oil and natural gas, although pipelines also are used for public water supplies, especially for urban centers in more arid regions. There are three main types of pipelines. The first are gathering lines, which move

Trains provide inexpensive shipping (based on tonnage per mile) for both containers and bulk goods. (©Dreamstime.com)

raw material from a wellhead or production point to processing or refining facilities. The second type are longer-distance transport pipelines. These move the material from the production or processing site to further processing or transportation facilities. The trans-Alaska pipeline, which moves oil from the North Slope of Alaska to ports such as Valdez, is a well-known example. Finally, there are distribution pipelines, which move finished or processed bulk liquids to the end users. Natural gas pipelines, which distribute natural gas for home heating, are a good example. Each of these types of pipeline relies on a complex series of pumping and monitoring stations that ensure the viability and safety of the system. Natural gas pipelines are an important growth segment of the industry because of rising demand worldwide and the development of cost-effective liquefied natural gas (LNG) facilities, which allow transportation of gas by bulk carrier.

Ancillary Services. In addition to these major segments of the industry, there are important ancillary parts of the freight transportation industry. These include support and logistics, maintenance and repair, port and terminal facilities, warehousing, and tracking.

INDUSTRY MARKET SEGMENTS

Small Businesses

Small businesses in the transportation industry range from individual owner-operators to small start-up firms. The trucking industry is the most common venue for small businesses. There are also independent tugboat operators working coastal waters and ports. The railroad and oceangoing freight transport businesses and the pipeline transport industry are dominated by large firms, although individuals and small consulting firms do provide specialized services to some of these bigger companies.

Potential Annual Earnings Scale. The average owner-operator of a truck can earn in the vicinity of $52,000 per year, although most truck drivers—including individual contractors—make a median salary of about $39,000, according the U.S. Bureau of Labor Statistics. Most drivers are paid by the mile, usually about $0.35 per mile, and average

twenty-five hundred to three thousand miles per week. Drivers cannot exceed thirty-five hundred miles per week by law. Pay rarely covers load times, which can be a couple of hours or more. Some companies will pay drivers extra to wait more than two hours for a load. Having a load does not always guarantee that a driver will have a return load either, and a driver may need to wait until a load is available or drive empty to a third location.

Federal rules restrict the number of hours a driver can work per week; a truck driver can work for fourteen hours per day, but only eleven hours can be actual driving time. A truck driver also must take thirty-four hours off after working seventy hours in a week. This time includes load and drive time. This time off is referred to as thirty-four-hour restart, and after this, a driver can begin a new workweek.

Other factors may affect weekly pay. Driving in heavy traffic, for example, takes time but does not add to paid mileage. Drivers working for small and start-up firms usually are contractors, and those running smaller firms often double as drivers. In some family businesses, for example, it is common for one spouse to drive and manage other contractors while the other manages the business and keeps the books.

Clientele Interaction. Clientele interaction is very important for small companies and owner-operators. They rely on good relations with customers and suppliers to keep running. Owner-operators also must be able to interact well with fellow drivers because networking is a good way to find jobs and avoid problems such as heavy traffic, poor road conditions, and construction.

Amenities, Atmosphere, and Physical Grounds. Truckers live on the road and as such usually are away from their families for extended periods of time. Truck stops are necessity for drivers; many are open twenty-four hours a day and offer food and showers for truck drivers. Many cabs have small sleeping compartments that allow drivers to park and sleep when needed. Drivers work in nearly any kind of weather unless it is so harsh that major roads are closed. This type of life can be difficult. Experience and reputation count, especially for owner-operators. Although drivers compete with each other, experienced drivers are respected, and there is a sense of community among drivers on the road.

Typical Number of Employees. Most small businesses in this industry consist of a single owner-operator, although small firms employing a few drivers also exist.

Traditional Geographic Locations. Over-the-road truckers can be found anywhere in the continental United States and Canada, from major cities to the smallest communities. Owner-operators of tugboats are found on major inland waterways such as the Mississippi River or in major ports.

Pros of Working for a Small Freight Transportation Company. Smaller transportation companies often allow for greater flexibility. The individual strengths and weaknesses of any employee are immediately clear. Greater control over working conditions is another advantage of a small-firm setting. Finally, there is greater potential to develop close working relationships and camaraderie in smaller companies.

Owner-operated companies and those in which most or all of the employees are family gives one the feeling of independence and self-reliance. The firm rises and falls on the owner's decisions, skills, and work ethic. Many independent truckers enjoy having no boss but themselves.

Cons of Working for a Small Freight Transportation Company. The industry is dominated by large companies that set the pace for change, influence many of the rules and practices, and provide economies of scale that can price smaller companies and owner-operators out of some markets. Owner-operators in particular are often on the margins, especially during difficult economic times or when fuel prices are especially high. In smaller companies, benefit packages are almost always smaller and, as with many smaller and individually owned firms, finding affordable health insurance for employees often is tricky and expensive. For owner-operators, the amount of work needed to run the business can be daunting. With more freedom comes more risk and exposure.

Costs

Payroll and Benefits: Average yearly gross pay ranges from $40,000 to $60,000. Benefits at small firms tend to be sparse, and owner-operators often buy individual insurance or rely on a spouse for insurance.

Supplies: The main recurring cost is diesel fuel. In late 2010, the average price was between $2.90 and $3.00 per gallon. An average tractor trailer will consume about $10,000 a year in diesel fuel. However, many independent truckers work on contracts with larger companies in which the contracting company pays for fuel and oil costs. Oil and tires are other expenses and can cost several thousand dollars per year, although some of these costs may not be borne by the operator.

External Services: Cleaning and repair are the major external services needed by small transportation firms, although many operators do their own basic maintenance. Major repairs can cost more than $10,000.

Utilities: Unless the small transportation firm owns its own facilities, utility costs generally are minimal.

Taxes: Most small firms are taxed as Type S corporations, while owner-operators are usually treated as self-employed. There are additional licenses and fees that can cost between $200 and $500 a year, depending on the state.

Vehicles: The capital costs of trucks can be a major cost for small firms. An average "big rig" costs about $100,000. Small firms and owner-operators will be need to calculate financing costs for this expensive but necessary equipment.

Midsize Businesses

Midsize businesses in the freight transportation industry conduct a wide range of activities. There are midsize trucking and delivery firms, smaller air cargo carriers that serve a particular region, tugboat operators, and regional freight railroads that serve a limited geographic area. Midsize firms often develop a niche or specialization that larger companies in the industry do not have or do not find profitable. These niches often include service to specialized areas or industries. By providing flexible, lower-cost service, they can hold their own against larger, better-funded competitors.

Potential Annual Earnings Scale. Because midsize firms have a greater range of services and more employees than smaller companies, salaries vary widely. Truck drivers, for example, work on a pay scale similar to their small-firm and owner-operator counterparts, although they may enjoy better benefits. Flight crews on cargo aircraft earn rates based on experience and position. Pilots earn between $80 and $105 an hour, first officers between

$54 and $72 per hour. Most air cargo companies also pay crews per diem if they have to spend time on layovers away from home. According to the Bureau of Labor Statistics, the median salary for all air crew is $107,000 per year. Cargo and freight agents working for the airlines earn on average $37,000 per year. For those working in the water transportation field, salaries average $100,000 or more per year for managers, $68,000 for skilled captains, and $35,000 a year for sailors. For midsize companies in the pipeline transportation business, most workers earn $45,000 to $60,000 per year on average.

Clientele Interaction. As with smaller firms, clientele interaction is a crucial part of the business. Freight transportation is primarily a service, even if customers are other businesses rather than the general public. Face-to-face contact still is important, although most companies in this category communicate with existing clients and find new customers using modern marketing and communications tools, ranging from specialized Web tools for clients to social-networking media.

Amenities, Atmosphere, and Physical Grounds. Truck drivers, sailors, air cargo crews, and railroad train crews may spend a significant amount of time away from home with all of the advantages and disadvantages of travel. Those working in the trucking industry will experience settings familiar to their counterparts in smaller and owner-operated firms. Inland water freight transport crews tend to work in smaller tugboats with a crew of a few fellow sailors and relatively close living quarters. Air cargo flight crews that experience regular layovers stay in hotels close to the airport. Those employees who work in management, warehousing, logistics, and maintenance do not experience frequent travel; they work in offices, warehouses, and shops appropriate to their tasks.

Typical Number of Employees. Midsize companies in the freight transportation sector can vary widely in size depending on the type of transportation used. Trucking companies can be economically viable with a smaller number of drivers, whereas other forms of transportation require greater overhead and thus more people. On the lower end, companies of ten employees are not uncommon and larger companies in this segment can have one hundred employees or more.

Traditional Geographic Locations. Midsize freight transportation companies can be found all over the United States and Canada. They also are found worldwide. Some midsize companies in this sector are large enough to have multiple locations, including offices in major international transportation hubs such as Singapore or Rotterdam.

Pros of Working for a Midsize Freight Transportation Company. In some ways, employees in midsize freight transportation companies have the best of both worlds. They tend to enjoy greater job security and better benefits than their counterparts in smaller firms without the bureaucratic overhead and the hierarchy. Midsize companies can provide a sense of belonging and camaraderie to employees while giving them better material rewards. As with all companies in this sector, there is a significant opportunity to travel, which is attractive to some people.

Cons of Working for a Midsize Freight Transportation Company. Compared with larger firms, benefit packages in midsize firms can be less attractive (although this is not always the case). In addition, there may be less opportunity for individual advancement within a midsize company. Employees in midsize firms that operate within a particular market niche and interact with a limited number of clients may also find this limiting. Finally, as with any company in this business, workers who do not like to travel or who have families will be displeased with the frequency of time spent away from home.

Costs

Payroll and Benefits: Warehouse and support personnel average less than front-line crew in most of the industry. Experienced air cargo pilots earn an average of $105,000 per year in salary and benefits, while freight handlers in warehouses may earn a third of that.

Supplies: The main recurring cost is diesel fuel. In late 2010, the average price was between $2.90 and $3.00 per gallon. An average tractor trailer will consume about $10,000 a year in diesel fuel. Tugboats and other inland cargo craft also consume a significant amount of diesel, although in terms of moving cargo, they are highly efficient in tons moved per gallon. DC-10 cargo aircraft, one of the mainstays of the industry, use more than 2,100 gallons of fuel per hour at cruising altitude. In late 2010, aviation fuel cost about $2.27 per gallon, so that hour of flight would expend some $4,700 in fuel alone. Most of these costs are borne by the company and passed on to consumers. Employees may be responsible for some specialized uniforms or work-related clothing, but this varies from company to company.

External Services: Midsize companies may use a wide range of outside services, from business consulting to outsourcing particular business functions such as human resources or payroll.

Utilities: Utility costs are incurred in warehouses, offices, and operations centers and include the usual light, heat, and water as well telephone and high-speed Internet.

Taxes: Midsize companies are taxed at the standard corporate rates. Companies that handle foreign trade also may be subject to taxes and fees in other countries if they have operations overseas.

Training Services: Many positions, especially air cargo crew; sailors, deckhands, and captains; and train crew need specialized training and certifications. These often need to be upgraded and renewed with refresher courses and recertification. These services cost, though employees may be reimbursed by their employers. Those entering training programs may be eligible for various scholarships and apprenticeship programs.

Large Businesses

Large businesses in the transportation industry are fewer in number but have many more employees and a global presence. Many, if not most, are multinational companies. Many freight transportation companies are headquartered overseas but have major operations in the United States and Canada, such as Hanjin and Maersk. Large businesses hold a dominant place in the world's oceangoing freight business, in both bulk cargo and container shipping. Large companies also hold a critical position in pipeline transportation, air cargo, and rail freight transportation. Trucking companies, at least within North America, tend to be more diversified, but here again large companies are quite important.

Potential Annual Earnings Scale. Most salaries in large companies are comparable with those in midsize companies because they often compete for the same pool of employees. Truck drivers, for example, work on a pay scale similar to their small-firm and owner-operator counterparts, although

they may enjoy more or better benefits. Flight crews on air cargo aircraft earn rates based on experience and their position. Pilots earn between $80 and $105 an hour, first officers between $54 and $72 per hour. Most air cargo companies also pay crews per diem if they have to spend time on layovers away from home. According to the Bureau of Labor Statistics, the median salary for all air crew is $107,000 per year. Cargo and freight agents working for the airlines earn on average $37,000 per year. For those working in the water transportation field, salaries range from an average of $100,000 or more per year for managers to $68,000 for skilled captains to around $35,000 a year for sailors. In the pipeline transportation industry, most workers earn between $45,000 and $60,000 per year on average.

Clientele Interaction. Because of the global reach of large companies in the freight transportation industry, being able to work with an international clientele is critical. Foreign-language skills and sensitivity to other cultures are definite advantages in this business, especially for workers in management roles. Understanding foreign business models, legal systems, and formal and informal regulations also is important.

Amenities, Atmosphere, and Physical Grounds. Large companies have operations across North America and around the world, so while many employees will be found in corporate office buildings, warehouses, ports, and terminals in the United States and Canada, others will be found in places such as Hong Kong, Singapore, Rotterdam, and Osaka. Because of this, atmosphere, amenities and physically surroundings can vary widely depending on the type of freight transportation involved, the company, and the location. As in small and midsize companies in this industry, workers who help operate cargo planes, trains, or ships will experience a great deal of travel. Crews on large oceangoing vessels, for example, will live and work on board and may experience new ports of call every month.

Typical Number of Employees. Large companies can have hundreds or thousands of employees. Many international companies have employees at major shipping centers worldwide.

Traditional Geographic Locations. Large freight transportation companies can be found all over the United States and Canada. They also are found worldwide. Most large companies in this sector have multiple locations around the world, especially in cities that are major seaports and road, rail, and air cargo hubs. High-profile multinational delivery companies such as FedEx have offices in many smaller communities as well.

Pros of Working for a Large Freight Transportation Company. Large companies have a global reach, so there are opportunities to work overseas and meet colleagues from other cultures. Wages are competitive with midsize companies, though benefit packages may be better (each company is different). As with small and midsize firms

in this industry, those who like to travel and to work around and in trains, ships, trucks, and aircraft will enjoy the fast pace of working for a large international freight transportation company.

Cons of Working for a Large Freight Transportation Company. The downside of working for a large company in this industry, as with many large companies, is that many individual employees can feel their individual needs are overlooked. Large firms tend to have more standardized and bureaucratic personnel policies. There is less flexibility and consequently a lower degree of employee loyalty toward large companies. As with

---

OCCUPATION SPECIALTIES

Rail Transportation Workers

Specialty	Responsibilities
Crane operators	Operate heavy equipment that lifts and transfers intermodal containers and other freight containers from one vehicle or location to another. They facilitate the loading and unloading of trains with self-contained, preloaded containers.
Freight loaders	Load and unload freight from individual train cars and containers, either by hand or using forklifts and similar devices.
Locomotive engineers	Drive electric, diesel-electric, and gas-turbine-electric locomotives; monitor the operation of the engine; oversee the function of the entire train; and maintain prescheduled timetables.
Passenger car conductors	Coordinate the activity of train crews transporting people on passenger trains, maintain timetable schedules, and comply with orders from the train dispatcher.
Passenger train brakers	Inspect equipment prior to, during, and after service; assist passengers entering and exiting the train; operate all climate control equipment in the nonlocomotive sections of the train; and assume responsibility for all nonlocomotive-related functions of trains.
Tower operators	Operate switching equipment from a control tower centrally located within a railroad yard. These operators are responsible for the proper sequencing of switching equipment according to a prearranged schedule.
Yard conductors	Supervise and coordinate all activity related to the movement of cars inside the railroad yard.
Yard tenders	Perform most of the physical work related to coupling and uncoupling railroad cars in a train yard.

midsize and smaller firms, those who do not like to travel or who have families may find aspects of this industry difficult; large firms may expect to transfer employees to far-flung locations worldwide as needed.

Costs

Payroll and Benefits: Pay and benefits in large companies vary according to position and experience. Experienced ship captains and air cargo crew can earn $100,000 per year or more. Major corporate officers can earn several times that amount. Warehouse and support personnel average less than front-line crew in most of the industry, generally averaging $35,000 to $40,000.

Supplies: Most of these costs are borne by the company and passed on to consumers. Employees may be responsible for some specialized uniforms or work-related clothing, but this varies from company to company.

External Services: Large companies may use a wide range of outside services, from business consulting to outsourcing particular business functions.

Utilities: Utility costs are incurred in warehouses, offices, and operations centers and include the usual light, heat, and water as well telephone and high-speed Internet.

Taxes: Large companies are taxed at the standard corporate rates. Because nearly all handle foreign trade, they also are subject to taxes and fees in other countries.

Training Services: Many positions—especially air cargo crews; sailors, deckhands, captains; and train crews—need specialized training and certifications. These often need to be periodically renewed with refresher courses and recertification. Costs for these programs may be reimbursed by employers. Those entering training programs may be eligible for various scholarships and apprenticeship programs.

ORGANIZATIONAL STRUCTURE AND JOB ROLES

Employment opportunities within the freight transportation industry are varied but tend to fall primarily into several main categories. The most notable and visible are those directly involved in transporting freight—the truck drivers, train crews, ship crews, and air cargo crews. However, there also are support and maintenance personnel, warehouse staff, management, sales, security, and logistics and operations, just to name a few. In smaller freight companies, one person may play several roles. In larger freight transportation companies, specialists are much more common. Companies that specialize in certain types of transportation may have materials specialists. A good example is the pipeline transport sector, which needs engineers and scientists who are able to measure and monitor the factors related to the flow rate or temperature of crude oil or natural gas. Research and development also may be important. Because new developments in the freight transportation industry are so often driven by new and emerging technologies, most large and midsize companies need a wide range of specialists, particularly in information technology.

The following umbrella categories apply to the organizational structure of businesses in the freight transportation industry:

- Business Management
- Customer Services
- Sales and Marketing
- Facilities and Security
- Technology, Research, Design, and Development
- Operations
- Distribution
- Human Resources

Business Management

Business management employees in freight transportation companies direct the overall business and its daily and annual operations, develop and execute business plans and strategies, assess the effectiveness of operations, evaluate employee performance, and interact with the board of directors or owners.

Occupations in the area of management include the following:

- Top Executive
- Middle Manager
- Logistics and Operations Manager
- Regional Manager

- Accountant
- Auditor

Customer Services

In the freight transportation industry, customer service personnel assist customers in preparing and shipping orders using phone and Internet communication. Webmasters maintain tools that allow customers to track orders, and specialists handle overseas shipping by interfacing with customers and customs and border officials in several countries in order to ensure that paperwork and documentation is in order so that shipments arrive as rapidly as possible.

Occupations in this category include the following:

- Customer Service Representative
- Customer Service Specialist
- Webmaster

Sales and Marketing

Sales and marketing employees in the freight transportation industry interact with customers, maintain existing accounts, find new accounts, and ensure customer needs are being met. Some occupations in this area are salespeople who market the company's services, employees who create marketing materials (both paper and electronic), and creative staff such as graphic designers who help develop brand identity and test market examples, and conduct surveys.

Occupations in sales and marketing include the following:

- Salesperson
- Marketing Specialist
- Art Director

Facilities and Security

Facilities and security are important sectors of most midsize and large freight transportation companies. Facilities employees maintain warehouses and terminals. They provide maintenance and repair for many modes of transportation—trains, trucks, aircraft, boats, ships, and barges. In pipeline companies, they play vital roles in creating and maintaining all pumping and flow as well as monitoring pressure, flow, and temperature gauges/transmitters for the pipeline at injection or delivery stations, pump stations (liquid pipelines) or compressor stations (gas pipelines), and block valve stations. Security is equally important. Transportation security workers maintain the physical safety of facilities, responding to and preventing accidents and preventing, stopping, and investigating cases of theft, vandalism, fraud, and terrorism. Many transportation companies maintain cyber security offices that prevent data theft and penetration by viruses and worms. This is particularly critical for pipeline transport companies, whose operations are heavily computer reliant and are particularly vulnerable to cyber attacks, especially against oil and natural gas pipelines. An emerging area of security in the freight transportation industry involves the screening and monitoring of shipping containers. Because of the threat of terrorist attacks, there is renewed importance in ensuring that the many thousands of containers moving about on the world's oceans, rivers, railroads, and roads are safe and secure.

Occupations in this area include the following:

- Security Guard
- Cyber Security Personnel
- Facility Worker
- Maintenance and Repair Worker

Technology, Research, Design, and Development

Only larger companies in this industry engage in research and design, since the main function of freight transportation is to distribute existing products and materials rather than to come up with new ones. Many companies will contract or partner with outside engineering firms, think tanks, or universities when they need new technologies. Nevertheless, implementing new technologies, new software, and methods to streamline distribution are important. Technical and information technology (IT) staff play critical roles in maintaining and upgrading existing technology for internal and external customers.

Operations

Operations is the most critical sector of the freight transportation business. Operations personnel are directly responsible for moving freight to appropriate destinations. In air cargo companies, these employees include air crews, especially

OCCUPATION PROFILE

Ship Loader

Considerations	Qualifications
Description	Loads and unloads freight, moving it from transportation vehicles to storage areas.
Career clusters	Manufacturing; Marketing, Sales, and Service
Interests	Things
Working conditions	Work outside
Minimum education level	On-the-job training; high school diploma or GED
Physical exertion	Medium work; heavy work
Physical abilities	Unexceptional/basic fitness; may be required to lift heavy objects
Opportunities for experience	Military service
Licensure and certification	Usually not required
Employment outlook	Decline expected
Holland interest scores	RES; RIS

Note: See volume 1, "Publisher's Note," for an explanation of the Holland interest score.

pilots, flight engineers, and first and second officers who operate the aircraft in a safe and effective manner. Loadmasters oversee the proper stowage of air cargo loads along with handlers, who ensure the integrity of the contents of each flights. Ground crews service and assist air cargo craft on terminals, hangars, and runways. In the trucking industry, drivers are the critical component, but they are supported by warehouse and terminal personnel who load both freight and bulk cargo and complete bills of lading. Bulk cargo and container ships are sailed by a captain who is assisted by officers, radar and radio operators, deckhands, oilers, engineers, and cooks. The number and range of tasks will depend on the size and nature of the ship. Freight trains also demand a variety of operations personnel. There are switchmen or brakemen who work as on-the-ground traffic control. Conductors are responsible for the train, the freight, and the crew, and the locomotive engineer actually operates the locomotive. Pipeline companies employ a wide range of industrial and fluid engineers as well

as maintenance, monitoring, and control technicians; safety and environmental engineers; and repair and construction crews.

Occupations in this category include the following:

- Pilot
- Flight Crew
- Loadmaster
- Ground Crew
- Truck Driver
- Warehouse Worker
- Ship Captain
- Sailor
- Train Conductor
- Switchman
- Locomotive Engineer
- Pipeline Engineer

Distribution

Distribution jobs within freight transportation companies usually involve internal logistics. These employees are often responsible for bunkering of supplies, especially large quantities of fuel required for oceangoing vessels, air cargo craft, and trains. They oversee the acquisition of supplies for crews and vessels and ensure that appropriate supplies are in distributed to locations worldwide and are available as needed.

Human Resources

Human resources employees in the freight transportation industry perform many of the same functions as human resources employees in other industries. They recruit and retain employees, maintain job descriptions, assist employees with benefits, manage payroll, monitor compliance with workplace regulations, handle employee complaints and grievances, and maintain employee personnel records.

Occupations in this category include the following:

In the United States, truck drivers account for 45 percent of all freight transportation industry employees. (©Chad Mcdermott/Dreamstime.com)

- Human Resources Manager
- Human Resources Generalist
- Benefits Specialist
- Administrative Assistant

INDUSTRY OUTLOOK

Overview

This industry is on the rise because of the growth of globalization. Although the industry is highly sensitive to economic fluctuations, and the world economic situation has affected shippers and freight handlers across the board, the long-term prospects for freight cargo shipping look bright.

The global economy and national economies worldwide have become highly dependent on systems of distributing goods, services, and information. Freight cargo is a critical component of these networks. Indeed, without freight transportation, the global economy as whole and most major industrialized economies would grind to a halt. In the United States, there is a continuing push to ex-

port American products. Likewise, other economies are dependent on exporting finished goods. This means that the long-term prospects for freight transportation are very good, especially in international and container shipping. Companies such as FedEx that distribute business cargo in large quantities every day around the world also appear posed for steady growth.

In the air cargo industry, according to the Bureau of Labor Statistics (BLS), job opportunities for pilots and flight engineers are expected to be best; opportunities will continue to exist for those pilots who choose to work for air cargo carriers because of the increase in global freight demand. Opportunities should be favorable for aircraft and avionics equipment mechanics and service technicians, reflecting the likelihood of fewer entrants from the military and a large number of retirements. However, mechanics and technicians will face more competition for jobs with large airlines because the high wages and travel benefits that these jobs offer generally attract more qualified applicants than there are openings. Applicants who have experience and who keep abreast of the latest technological advances should have the best opportunities. Opportunities also are expected to be good for those seeking unskilled, entry-level positions, such as baggage handlers and aircraft cleaners, because turnover is high in these jobs.

The BLS also foresees good prospects in the

trucking industry: It notes that opportunities for truck drivers are especially favorable because of high turnover linked to the lengthy periods away from home. Strict requirements for obtaining and keeping a commercial driver's license also result in attrition. New restrictions on the hazardous-material license endorsement also should increase opportunities for those able to pass the criminal background checks now required. A 2005 study commissioned by private industry showed that there is a large projected shortfall in future over-the-road heavy truckers in the next ten to twenty years. It urged increased efforts to recruit new, younger drivers and to improve working conditions for existing and future drivers as a way to enhance recruitment efforts. Opportunities for diesel service technicians and mechanics also are expected to be favorable, especially for applicants with formal postsecondary training. Growth in the truck transportation and warehousing industry should prompt an increase in office and administrative support employment. More dispatchers, stock clerks, and shipping, receiving, and traffic clerks will be needed to support expanded logistical services across the country. Opportunities for those with information technology skills should be excellent.

Prospects appear equally good for the pipeline transportation industry, which is in constant need of trained engineers. Although new crude oil pipelines are fewer, there is major growth in natural gas pipelines in the United States and Canada as well as in Europe, where three or four major lines are in the planning stages. In addition, as the demand for natural gas increases worldwide and the technology of liquefied natural gas (LNG) becomes ever more cost-effective, there will be demand for new pipelines to serve LNG plants.

Employment Advantages

Jobs in the freight transport industry often are in high demand and provide many skilled, well-paying positions. They demand a wide variety of skills. Travel is a frequent perk of the business, although schedules can be demanding. Ship and barge crews, train crews, and long-haul truckers frequently log tens of thousands of miles per year traveling across the country or around the world. Ship's officers in the transportation industry have an especially exciting and demanding job, as they are charged with operating huge multimillion-dollar container ships or oil tankers with valuable cargo through all types of weather, navigating everything from the open ocean to canals and crowded container ports. This is an ancient and honorable profession with traditions stretching back hundreds of years. Transportation industry jobs in security and logistics demand high-level computer and organizational skills. These posi-

PROJECTED EMPLOYMENT FOR SELECTED OCCUPATIONS

Truck Transportation

Employment		Occupation
2009	Projected 2018	
41,950	46,800	Bus and truck mechanics and diesel engine specialists
31,030	33,500	First-line supervisors/managers of transportation and material-moving machine and vehicle operators
103,570	105,700	Laborers and freight, stock, and material movers, hand
756,010	943,100	Truck drivers, heavy and tractor-trailer
56,460	61,800	Truck drivers, light or delivery services

Source: U.S. Bureau of Labor Statistics, Industries at a Glance, Occupational Employment Statistics and Employment Projections Program.

tions are charged with maintaining the safe and efficient movements of products worldwide and in countering threats that range from environmental hazards to terrorist threats to computer hackers. Large multinational companies often dominate this industry, providing employees with a degree of stability and security. At the same time, there is room for smaller businesses and even individual owner-operators, most notably in the trucking industry.

Annual Earnings

In 2005, the U.S. trucking industry earned $272 million, railroads $52 million, domestic water freight more than $6 million, oil pipelines more than $9 million, and gas pipelines $102 million. Projections are for these numbers to continue to increase.

The freight transportation industry is strongly influenced by trends in the global economy. Short-term prospects during an economic downturn are mixed. However, even with a slow-growth model for the world's major economies, the freight transportation industry in set to grow over the long term, and large, midsize, and small companies will benefit from this trend. Container ship demand is expected to rise at least through 2012. The International Air Transport Association expects Asian cargo volume to surge 33 percent, but growth may slow in 2011. North American airlines are forecast to earn $3.5 billion in 2010 compared with the previously forecast $1.9 billion because rising cargo and passenger traffic enable carriers to post bigger increases in yields than in other regions. Freight transportation is a leading indicator in global economic trends, and while the outlook for the world's economy remains uncertain, the importance of freight transportation is such that steady long-term growth will win out over any temporary declines.

RELATED RESOURCES FOR FURTHER RESEARCH

AMERICAN TRUCKING ASSOCIATIONS
950 N Glebe Rd., Suite 210
Arlington, VA 22203-4181
Tel: (703) 838-1700
http://www.truckline.com

AMERICAN WATERWAYS OPERATORS
801 N Quincy St., Suite 200
Arlington, VA 22203
Tel: (703) 841-9300
Fax: (703) 841-0389
http://www.americanwaterways.org

ASSOCIATION OF AMERICAN RAILROADS
425 3d St. SW, Suite 1000
Washington, DC 20024
Tel.: (202) 639-2100
Fax: (202) 639-2558
http://www.aar.org

INTERNATIONAL FREIGHT ASSOCIATION
P.O. Box 655
Lane Cove, NSW 2066
Australia
Tel: 61-2-9420-9817
Fax: 61-2-9247-7419
http://www.ifa-online.com

NATIONAL MOTOR FREIGHT TRAFFIC ASSOCIATION
1001 N Fairfax St., Suite 600
Alexandria, VA 22314
Tel: (703) 838-1810
Fax: (703) 683-6296
http://www.nmfta.org

U.S. DEPARTMENT OF TRANSPORTATION
1200 New Jersey Ave. SE
Washington, DC 20590
Tel.: (202) 366-4000
http://www.dot.gov

U.S. MERCHANT MARINE ACADEMY
300 Steamboat Rd.
Kings Point, NY 11024
Tel: (516) 773-5000
http://www.usmma.edu

ABOUT THE AUTHOR

John Radzilowski is an assistant professor of history and geography at the University of Alaska Southeast. He received his Ph.D. in history in 1999 from Arizona State University. He is the author or coauthor of thirteen books and numerous articles for academic and popular readers, with work appearing in such publications as *American Heritage of Invention and Technology, Minnesota History,* and *The Public Historian.* His main areas of research specialization include immigration and ethnicity, Polish and Polish American history, and the development of the American Midwest. He writes and teaches on the impact of transportation and infrastructure on urban and rural communities, with a particular interest in how railroads helped to transform and colonize the North American Great Plains.

FURTHER READING

Donovan, Arthur, and Joseph Bonney. *The Box That Changed the World: Fifty Years of Container Shipping—An Illustrated History.* East Windsor, N.J.: Commonwealth Business Media, 2006.

Global Insight. *The U.S. Truck Driver Shortage: Analysis and Forecasts.* Study prepared for the American Trucking Associations, May 2005. http://www.cdlschool.com/_pdf/ATADriverShortageStudy05.pdf

Heitzman, William Ray. *Opportunities in Marine Science and Maritime Careers.* New York: McGraw-Hill, 2006.

Plunkett, Jack W. *Plunkett's Transportation and Logistics Industry Almanac, 2008.* Houston, Tex.: Plunkett Research, 2008.

Research and Innovative Technologies Administration, Bureau of Transportation Statistics. *National Transportation Statistics* (2010). http://www.bts.gov/publications/national_transportation_statistics/.

U.S. Bureau of Labor Statistics. *Career Guide to Industries,* 2010-2011 ed. http://www.bls.gov/oco/cg.

———. "Transportation and Material Moving Occupations." In *Occupational Outlook Handbook,* 2010-2011 ed. http://www.bls.gov/oco/oco1011.htm.

U.S. Census Bureau. North American Industry Classification System (NAICS), 2007. http://www.census.gov/cgi-bin/sssd/naics/naicsrch?chart=2007.

———. *U.S. International Trade in Goods and Services.* July, 2010. http://www.census.gov/foreign-trade/data/index.html.

U.S. Department of Commerce. International Trade Administration. Office of Trade and Industry Information. Industry Trade Data and Analysis. http://ita.doc.gov/td/industry/otea/OTII/OTII-index.html.

U.S. Department of Labor. "High Growth Industry Profile: Transportation." http://www.doleta.gov/BRG/Indprof/Transportation_profile.cfm.

Funerary Industry

INDUSTRY SNAPSHOT

General Industry: Personal Services

Career Cluster: Human Services

Subcategory Industries: Animal Cemeteries; Cemeteries; Crematories; Embalming Services; Funeral Homes; Funeral Services; Memorial Gardens; Mortuaries; Undertaker Services

Related Industries: Landscaping Services; Personal Services; Public Health Services; Waste Management Industry

Annual Domestic Revenues: $14 billion USD (U.S. Department of Labor, 2009); $20.7 billion (U.S. Funeral Market, 2009)

NAICS Number: 8122

INDUSTRY DEFINITION

Summary

The funerary industry provides places and services to facilitate the final disposition of the remains of and the dignified mourning of the deceased. These services vary widely among cultures. In the United States, funerary services are most commonly provided by local funeral homes. While these services are commonly thought of as applying to humans, a growing portion of the industry deals with the disposal and mourning of deceased pets. The ideal and most profitable constellation of services includes funeral services, cremation services, pet services, mausoleums, refrigeration, and cemetery services.

History of the Industry

Ritual funerary practices date back at least as far as the Stone Age. The area around Kassel, Germany, contains evidence of gravesites created during the late Stone Age, between about 3500 and 1600 B.C.E. The graves themselves consist of slabs of sandstone. A large hole in the center of one of the end slabs must have taken some effort to create with simple tools. In folk lore, these holes are known as "soul-holes" and are believed to be openings left for the nonmortal parts of the dead.

Ancient Egyptian culture is notable for its elaborate ideas of death. Huge pyramids and elaborate burial sites with thoroughly embalmed bodies, burial vaults, burial chambers, and sealed rooms characterize that culture. Whether these elaborate places for the dead were built by slaves or by honored experts with their own special tombs near the noble dead is a matter of conjecture and scholarly debate. Experimentation with embalming came about in the United States during the Civil War, when remains of soldiers were shipped home and needed to be preserved.

Some cultures have eaten their dead. The Anasazi, forebears of the pueblo dwellers, may have eaten all or part of their dead; the Agoris, contemporary followers of Shiva, still eat their dead. Zoroastrianism required disposal of the dead by feeding sacred birds atop tall towers. Some Native Americans buried their dead in mounds; others left them to dry on wooden structures. The cultural common element in most practices seems to be a desire to respect and honor the dead in some fashion, whether in anticipation of a continued existence in an afterlife or in anticipation of finality and a return to the environment.

An excellent overview of sepulchral culture is available also in Kassel, Germany, where coffins from Ghana are sold in the shape of cars, fish, and other lively and colorful objects that may have had strong meaning to the deceased. Similar products

have been sold as Crazy Coffins by Vic Fearn & Company in England since the 1860's. In a cemetery in Daytona Beach, Florida, one person is buried in an automobile that he did not want to part with in death.

Europe's sepulchral culture began in the seventeenth century for those who could afford coffins. Until well into the nineteenth century, poor people would conduct funeral services using coffins fitted with gates in the bottom. The gates would open to let each body fall into the grave beneath it, and the coffin would be reused. Tin or lead were used by more affluent families to contain their dead. Coffins constructed from these metals cost about fifty times as much as simple pine boxes. Some religions, notably Islam, call for bodies of the deceased to be interred without vaults or coffins. In such cases, reusable coffins may serve to transport bodies between places of worship and funeral homes. Some religious groups bar funeral directors from altering deceased bodies at all.

As recently as the beginning of the twentieth

American cemeteries are often vast expanses of lawn and subdued markers. (©Ken Cole/Dreamstime.com)

century, the deceased were often washed, dressed, and placed in coffins by relatives at home. Caskets might remain in the home for viewing of the deceased without embalming or other preparatory steps. The average dwelling was also more likely to be near a cemetery than they are today. Even today, however, some rural cemeteries are reminiscent of a time when the living and the dead existed in closer proximity to each other. The growth of the funerary industry is likely to have been a direct result of increasing distance in modern culture from the end-of-life experience, representing a kind of collective denial, although many people visit cemeteries to find solace in contact with the deceased and interred. Some modern markers make such contact easier by displaying pictures of the deceased.

Use of the term "churchyard" for cemeteries indicates that communal burial sites were once close to the world of the living. Situated near, around, and frequently (for particularly respected persons) inside churches, these burial places affirmed community. Gravesites in Denmark and northern Germany are carefully marked with the deceaseds' professions, defining their role in the community when they were alive. Population densities push some cultures to reuse graves. Typically in such cultures, a grave remains for as long as there are relatives willing to rent the site. In the United States, where churches may fail fiscally, churchyard burial is a bit precarious because the fate of churchyards becomes uncertain if their churches fail. Privately owned cemeteries provide greater assurances of burial plots lasting for eternity because their grounds' upkeep must be financially insured by trust funds, the nature and solvency of which are governed by state regulations.

A closer proximity to death is also typical for the culture of Mexico. El Dia de los Muertes, or the Day of the Dead, is a an event celebrated in Mexico with *pan de muerto* (death bread) and various customs, including polishing bones and dressing up as skeletal figures. The celebration may move the living toward a more accepting stance toward their own demise.

Having life take prominence over the immediacy of death is another value as central to Irish wakes as to the funerary practices of many continental European cultures. Such practices are often accompanied by eating, drinking, and visiting members of the bereaved family. Celebrating the life of the deceased is often the theme of formal meetings of friends and relatives. Light and often humorous remarks, reminiscences, and occasional tearful recollections characterize such celebrations. Church services may vary from serious to light-hearted.

American culture appears to be averse to direct contact with death. Cemeteries are typically located relatively far away from residential and commercial areas and, except for some holidays, appear to be generally deserted. While, particularly for rural Europeans, cemeteries may be places for meeting and chatting, American cemeteries are often vast expanses of lawn and subdued markers (although at least one cemetery in Hollywood, California, hosts outdoor film screenings and other events).

For practical reasons, cemetery directors prefer to hire groundskeepers to mow their properties rather than relying on relatives of the deceased to maintain each individual plot. Cemetery licensing requires that new cemeteries have at least thirty acres available for expansion. Some cemeteries, such as St. Louis Cemetery Number 1 in New Orleans, Louisiana, contain mausoleums and surface vaults that vary in structure and appearance. Religious beliefs and traditions are largely responsible for these variations. Families may own cemetery mausoleums, which may be worth up to $700,000. Such structures may contain up to a dozen bodies in sliding drawers that hold one or two bodies each. In Europe, nobles are the most likely to own such mausoleums, while in the United States, wealthy families are the most common owners. A burial plot may cost $2,400. In American cemeteries, plots may be owned indefinitely; in Europe, they are usually rented for about twenty-five years. When a rental term expires, a family may renew its plot rental or abandon its plot, in which case it is leveled and made available for rental by another family.

In the Far East, some religions and traditions employ open funeral pyres. Some Eastern religious traditions teach that the heavenly sphere is coextensive with the world of the living, and pyres may be symbolic of a merging of the dead with that ubiquitous heavenly sphere. Scattering of ashes as ritual goes back thousands of years in Far Eastern cultures. Large pictorial representations of the

Funeral homes tend to be family businesses and rarely hire outsiders, except ad hoc, temporary workers. (©Dreamstime.com)

dead may remain in the family home for meditative or even communicative purposes.

The Industry Today

The modern American funerary industry relies heavily on Christian traditions; statuary in cemeteries, for example, often depicts angelic figures or good shepherds. As American culture becomes increasingly diverse, however, its funerary traditions are becoming equally diverse. Muslims must bury their dead within twenty-four hours of death; however, many jurisdictions require a longer period before interment to ensure that cause of death is properly determined. Florida, for example, requires forty-eight hours before burial to allow time for coroners' reports to be issued. Laws in some jurisdictions also place restrictions upon the locations and manner in which ashes may be dispersed after cremation. Hindus and some other Far Eastern cultures require open-air cremation, which also clashes with common American laws.

Eating of the dead, as practiced by Agoris, would be unthinkable by contemporary Western cultural standards. Some of these limits are set by religious and cultural traditions and habits, although American culture also pays tribute to some levels of diversity. Funeral services, for example, may be practiced where women's presence is not permitted or where no mortician may touch the body. American funeral directors are becoming increasingly sensitive to cultural diversity but may also recognize some limits to cultural tolerance.

Similar culture clashes characterize the funerary industry in other countries. China, for example, is slowly losing the strong taboos that Chinese people tend to associate with the industry. Traditionally, the subject of funerals was not to be talked about, and funeral work was among the lowest-paid and least socially acceptable types of work in China, performed by some of its least educated citizens. Today, however, attitudes are changing.

Families attempt to secure low prices for funeral servcies, and they seek bargains. Funeral homes tend to be family businesses and rarely hire outsiders, except ad hoc, temporary workers. Peripheral industries, such as floral industries, grave contrac-

About 1.8 million caskets are sold each year in the United States. (©Laurin Rinder/Dreamstime.com)

tors, and providers of funeral accessories, are also developing. Some of these services may be offered as part of the diversification of funeral homes.

The relatively high cost of burial has motivated an increase in the use of the cheaper cremation. The percentage of funerals employing cremation increased from 3.6 percent in 1960 to 41.8 percent in 2007. In that year, cremations accounted for 25.2 percent of funerals in New York and 36.8 percent of those in Connecticut. In many other parts of the United States, the rate of cremation is greater than 50 percent. Funeral directors may find that this trend decreases the profitability of the funerary business.

To maintain profitability, crematories may require clients to purchase shrouds. Funeral homes seeking to minimize losses may diversify to include both crematories and cemeteries, as well as a variety of related businesses such as flower sales, jewelry sales, and catering. Flowers sold by funeral homes are most commonly artificial, but they are generally removed after about a month, necessitating new purchases. Casket sales stand at about 1.8

million each year in the United States. Caskets may be purchased from retailers not affiliated with funeral homes.

In most jurisdictions, funeral homes are required by law to accommodate families that buy caskets elsewhere. Special financial support from the state or federal government is provided to help pay for the funerals of veterans and paupers. Veterans are entitled to plots in national cemeteries, when they are available; however, an increasing number of relatives are requesting disinterment from national cemeteries for reburial nearer the family. Paupers' funerals are no-frills arrangements, paid for by local government or religious agencies.

Funeral directors set prices in conference with the family of the deceased. While directors may display great sensitivity to the needs of the family, such pricing arrangements also allow for abuse if a director attempts to sell more services, or more expensive services, than are necessary. On the other hand, funerary services may not vary prices. State, county, or federal agencies conduct reviews of funeral homes to find whether stated pricing is being adhered to from one service to the next. This institution of governmental oversight has remedied some egregious abuses that occurred in the early twentieth century, when funeral homes made up prices as they went along, selling the same casket to different families at different prices.

A new orientation toward environmentally friendly burials may be found in the Neptune Society, which offers cremation and ecologically sound disposal of the ashes, including a submarine cemetery. Neptune Societies abound in Florida, in Texas along the Gulf Coast, and along the Pacific coast. The corporate office of the Neptune Society is in Plantation, Florida, near Ft. Lauderdale. The British Natural Death Centre advocates for alternate methods of cremation, specifically open pyres rather than crematories.

Some businesses provide services to smaller funeral homes, such as organizing transfers of remains, as well as embalming, shipping, cremating, interring, disinterring, and refrigerating them. These businesses support small establishments that cannot provide a full range of services themselves, especially services not in frequent demand. Ancillary businesses may also consist of crematories, cemeteries, or chapels. Most businesses claim no particular religious orientation, though some make a point of listing their orientation. Funerary businesses are regulated by the Federal Trade Commission, the Occupational Safety and Health Administration (OSHA), and various state and local entities. All facilities are subject to inspections and to review of their contracts, as well as comparisons among the prices listed on pricing schedules, contracts, and invoices to ensure that they all match.

Shipping services are particularly in demand. These involve a variety of services, rules, and regulations. Interpreters offer their services for country-to-country transfers. The country from which remains are shipped and the country receiving the remains may each have a variety of rules and regulations governing such shipping. In some cases, specific airlines may impose rules of their own. For example, Germany does not require any particular shroud for human remains, but Lufthansa German Airlines requires a wooden box. An international funeral service exists to handle such issues. Some services focus on issues that typically arise during

transfers between two adjacent countries, such as Mexico and the United States. For these two countries, services may also include overland transportation. Shipping requires consular approvals and inspections, flight and document arrangements, and specialized shipping containers. The U.S. State Department publishes specifications for shipping the remains of U.S. citizens abroad. Consular approval is required for shipping to other countries. States have different rules and regulations regarding the issuance of death certificates.

Specialized services exist to help scatter ashes at sea or in the mountains. Some are associated with funeral homes; some act on a freelance basis. All must abide by the laws that govern the scattering of ashes within their jurisdictions. For example, one may travel with an urn and ashes, but one may not carry these as part of carry-on luggage on airplanes.

INDUSTRY MARKET SEGMENTS

The funerary industry tends to present itself as comprising small, family-owned businesses, but its businesses range in size from such small operations up to large corporations that operate multiple venues. The largest of these corporations is Service Corporation International, headquartered in Houston, Texas.

Small Businesses

The industry tends to present itself as small with one establishment in a city, town, or village, depending on the size of the population of the service area. Many funeral homes or cremation centers, thus, are small and local. Some may be without competitors in small towns and villages.

Potential Annual Earnings Scale. According to the U.S. Bureau of Labor Statistics (BLS), the mean annual income of all workers in the funerary industry in 2009 was $35,700; the median hourly wage was $13.25 and the mean hourly wage was $17.16. Funeral directors earned an average of $60,230 in that year. Workers such as greeters, drivers, and caterers in small establishments are likely to be hired on an ad hoc basis at minimum wage.

Clientele Interaction. Although it is often the assets of the deceased's estates that pay for funerary services, the clientele of a funeral home are best thought of as the family and friends of the deceased. Funeral homes seek to meet the grieving needs of those who survive deceased persons within the context of their religious and cultural practices. Great seriousness and dignified comportment are essential to the behavior of employees, from directors to greeters, information providers, phone answerers, drivers, cooks, and servers. Cultivating the trust of clients increases the likelihood of repeat business. Funeral directors may also need to interact with local banks and other financial entities when funerals are paid for by long-term certificates of deposit or other financial accounts of the deceased. In the case of paupers' funerals, they may be competing with relatives of the diseased to access those accounts. While special interactions are required for dealing with veterans or military personnel, a small local funeral home or cremation service is less likely to encounter such special cases.

Amenities, Atmosphere, and Physical Grounds. Small funeral homes attempt to cultivate a sense of dignity reflected in the curb appeal of their facilities, although those in small towns may attempt to blend into the ambience of their towns. Interiors are generaly decorated in a tasteful, understated fashion in keeping with the somber mood displayed by employees. Physical grounds of both cemeteries and funeral homes must generally be well maintained and ordered; signs of decay or disrepair may harm the impression of potential clients and decrease business. The work atmosphere at funerary businesses is affected not only by the need to maintain a somber mood for the sake of the bereaved but also by the fact that workers interact with and manipulate dead bodies. This job function almost certainly colors the experience of all funeral workers, but its effects may be radically different for different people.

Typical Number of Employees. Small funeral homes are typically staffed by a single family. They are often owned by parents who employ two or three offspring in the family business. Crematories may employ only an administrative assistant and a cremation operator, since such facilities do not typically provide religious services. In addition, these businesses are likely to hire groundskeepers, drivers, and other support staff on a temporary basis, usually at minimum wage.

Traditional Geographic Locations. Funeral homes are located close to the communities they serve. Because all communities require their services, they exist within all communities.

Pros of Working for a Small Funerary Business. Family ownership often sets the mood of small funerary businesses. When clients are not around, the atmosphere at such establishments is likely to be a bit more relaxed and informal than that of a large corporation. The mode of decision making and problem solving is likely to be one of mutual adjustment among collaborators.

Cons of Working for a Small Funerary Business. A small, family-owned business is also likely to be patriarchal in orientation. Grievance procedures, consultations with one another, and collective reflections about the work environment are less likely to be fully evolved. The work environment is much more dependent on goodwill and congenial personalities than at larger firms. Additional workers are likely to be hired on an ad hoc basis, as independent subcontractors, and to be paid minimum wage without benefits. These workers also have little say in the daily operation of the business.

Costs

Payroll and Benefits: In small family businesses, all members of the family are likely to have some role in the business and to share in profits as family income. Temporary additional workers may be hired on an as-needed basis, usually at hourly wages.

Supplies: Funeral homes require embalming chemicals and makeup; protective clothing, body bags, and other equipment for handling and transporting the dead; automobiles and fuel; gardening supplies; and office supplies and equipment. They may also require either premade coffins, urns, and headstones or the materials and tools necessary to construct them.

External Services: Funeral homes may contract casket, urn, and headstone design and engraving services, as well as maintenance and equipment repair, groundskeeping, landscaping, cleaning, or security services as necessary. They may also contract printing, accounting, automobile customization, and private autopsy services.

Utilities: Funeral homes generally pay for electricity, gas or oil, water, sewage, trash collection, telephone, and Internet access.

Pet cemeteries are increasingly common. (©Jason Rothe/iStockphoto.com)

Taxes: Funeral homes and cremation services pay local, state, and federal corporate and property taxes, but family businesses may not pay these taxes themselves. Rather, the owners and their family members may claim and pay this income on their personal returns, in which case they must also pay self-employment taxes.

Licenses: An embalmer's license may be issued by the appropriate state and may be reexamined and reissued periodically. Funerary businesses must keep their licenses current or face additional fees and penalties.

Midsize Businesses

Midsize funerary businesses generally operate multiple facilities, provide diversified services, and maintain their own cemeteries. These businesses are able to enjoy some economies of scale, since their different facilities can share resources such as vehicles and laborers. They may also provide pet cremation or burial services.

Potential Annual Earnings Scale. According to the BLS, funeral directors earned an average of $60,230 in 2009, while general managers of funerary businesses earned an average of $95,040. Embalmers earned an average of $41,150, and funeral attendants earned an average of $23,890. A story published in 2009 in the *Vancouver Sun* indicated that the average salary of all Canadian industry workers was about $40,000, or roughly $38,500 USD.

Clientele Interaction. Although it is often the assets of the deceased's estates that pay for funerary services, the clientele of a funeral home are best thought of as the family and friends of the deceased. Funeral homes seek to meet the grieving needs of those who survive deceased persons within the context of their religious and cultural practices. Great seriousness and dignified comportment are essential to the behavior of employees, from directors to greeters, information providers, phone answerers, drivers, cooks, and servers.

Cultivating the trust of clients increases the likelihood of repeat business. Funeral directors may also need to interact with local banks and other financial entities when funerals are paid for by long-term certificates of deposit or other financial accounts of the deceased. In the case of paupers' funerals, they may be competing with relatives of the diseased to access those accounts. Midsize businesses may be better prepared than are small businesses for the particular requirements of veterans' and military personnel's funerals. Some may even specialize in such services.

Midsize businesses' funeral directors are often actively involved in their communities. Particularly in geographic locations where the population has a high percentage of retired and elderly persons, funeral directors may formally present information about preparing for end-of-life decisions. Veterans' benefits, forms of services, disposal of ashes, forms of interment, death certificates, templates for newspaper publication, and living wills may all be subjects about which a funeral director can offer useful guidance and information. While some elderly people may react with discomfort to the presence of a funeral director, conducting informational sessions may help directors build relationships with their communities that can greatly benefit both those communities and the directors' businesses. Future clients may appreciate a funeral director's aid in planning details of their services ahead of time. It is even possible to arrange and pay for one's funeral in advance. Such contractual agreements may be more reliable when made with midsize businesses than with small businesses.

Amenities, Atmosphere, and Physical Grounds. Midsize funerary businesses attempt to cultivate a sense of dignity reflected in the curb appeal of their facilities, as well as elaborate landscaping and well-kept surroundings. Interiors are generaly decorated in a tasteful, understated fashion in keeping with the somber mood displayed by employees. The work atmosphere at funerary businesses is affected not only by the need to maintain a somber mood for the sake of the bereaved but also by the fact that workers interact with and manipulate dead bodies. This job function almost certainly colors the experience of all funeral workers, but its effects may be radically different for different people.

Elaborately luxurious hearses and limousines, as well as antique cars and vehicles, are likely to be part of the inventory of a midsize funeral home. (©Andy Heyward/Dreamstime.com)

Contemporary audiovisual technology is becoming incorporated into many funeral services, so most funeral homes must include such equipment and expertise. Elaborately luxurious hearses and limousines, as well as antique cars and vehicles, are also likely to be part of the inventory of a midsize business. Some funeral homes, for example, offer carefully maintained antique military vehicles to honor veterans or motorcycle-drawn hearses for motorcycle enthusiasts.

Typical Number of Employees. Midsize funerary businesses may employ twenty or more workers. They generally employ larger and more specialized full-time staffs at each funeral home than are employed at single homes by small businesses. For example, many employ full-time groundskeepers, drivers, and other support staff, usually as salaried employees. These establishments also employ several full-time office staff, possibly including audiovisual experts. Some employ full-time chaplains as well.

Traditional Geographic Locations. Funeral homes are located close to the communities they serve. Because all communities require their services, they exist within all communities. Midsize businesses may operate funeral homes almost anywhere, although their branches must be located near one another if they are to share resources effectively, so they are more likely to be found in regions with large enough populations to support multiple branches.

Pros of Working for a Midsize Funerary Business. Diversified midsize funerary businesses are more likely to achieve financial stability and to provide job security than are small businesses. Midsize businesses are often still small enough that a collaborative, family atmosphere may characterize the relationships among employees. Because these businesses are often somewhat decentralized and lack headquarters, each branch may be afforded freedom to make some business decisions for itself.

Cons of Working for a Midsize Funerary Business. The work environment of a midsize business is still dependent on goodwill and congenial personalities. While such businesses are decentralized, they do have supervisory staff who monitor and instruct other employees, introducing a measure of formality and bureaucracy into the workplace.

Costs

Payroll and Benefits: Midsize funerary businesses may pay information providers, greeters, drivers, chaplains, and similar personnel under contract, while others receive salaries. Larger companies are more likely to provide benefits.

Supplies: Funeral homes require embalming chemicals and makeup; protective clothing, body bags, and other equipment for handling and transporting the dead, including refrigeration facilities; automobiles and fuel; gardening supplies; office supplies and equipment; and audiovisual equipment. They may also require either premade coffins, urns, and headstones or the materials and tools necessary to construct them.

External Services: Funeral homes may contract casket, urn, and headstone design and engraving services, as well as maintenance and equipment repair, groundskeeping, landscaping, cleaning, or security services as necessary. They may also contract printing, accounting, advertising, technical support, automobile customization, and private autopsy services.

Utilities: Funeral homes need standard utilities such as electricity, gas, water, sewage, telephone, and Internet access. Crematories and refrigeration units may increase the costs of electricity or gas by up to $50,000 per year.

Taxes: Funerary businesses must pay local, state, and federal corporate and property taxes, as well as sales taxes and payroll taxes as appropriate.

Licenses: An embalmer's license may be issued by the appropriate state and may be reexamined and reissued periodically. Funerary businesses must keep their licenses current or face additional fees and penalties.

Large Businesses

In North America, only one large funerary business exists: Service Corporation International (SCI). This chain owns funeral homes all across the United States and Canada. Subchains within the larger chain include Stanetsky, Dignity Memorial, National Cremation, Advantage Funeral & Cremation Services, Funeraria Del Angel, Making Everlasting Memories, and Memorial Plan. Like midsize businesses, each of these subchains is able to distribute resources as necessary among its branches, and SCI is able to distribute resources among all of its various businesses as necessary.

This ability is somewhat restricted, however, by the variation in license requirements among the various states. For example, a funeral director licensed in one state may be unable to work in any other states without obtaining additional licenses.

Potential Annual Earnings Scale. According to the BLS, funeral directors earned an average of $60,230 in 2009, while general managers of funerary businesses earned an average of $95,040. Embalmers earned an average of $41,150, and funeral attendants earned an average of $23,890. The top 10 percent of funeral attendants earned more than $33,350, and the top 10 percent of funeral directors earned more than $94,050. A story published in 2009 in the *Vancouver Sun* indicated that the average salary of all Canadian industry workers was about $40,000, or roughly $38,500 USD.

Clientele Interaction. Although it is often the assets of the deceased's estates that pay for funerary services, the clientele of a funeral home are best thought of as the family and friends of the deceased. Funeral homes seek to meet the grieving needs of those who survive deceased persons within the context of their religious and cultural practices. Great seriousness and dignified comportment are essential to the behavior of employees, from directors to greeters, information providers, phone answerers, drivers, cooks, and servers.

The local face of SCI, or any corporation, is the manager and staff of a particular branch. Cultivating the trust of clients increases the likelihood of repeat business for that branch. SCI is in a position to provide all special interactions for dealing with veterans or military.

SCI's funeral directors may be actively involved in their communities, at their own discretion. Particularly in geographic locations where the population has a high percentage of retired and elderly persons, funeral directors may formally present information about preparing for end-of-life decisions. Veterans' benefits, forms of services, disposal of ashes, forms of interment, death certificates, templates for newspaper publication, and living wills may all be subjects about which a funeral director can offer useful guidance and information. While some elderly people may react with discomfort to the presence of a funeral director, conducting informational sessions may help directors build relationships with their communities that can greatly benefit both those communities and the directors' businesses. Future clients may appreciate a funeral director's aid in planning details of their services ahead of time. It is even possible to arrange and pay for one's funeral in advance. Such contractual agreements may be more reliable when made with a large corporation such as SCI than with a smaller business.

Amenities, Atmosphere, and Physical Grounds. The dignity of SCI's establishments usually is reflected in their curb appeal. Elaborate landscaping and well-kept surroundings are typical. The work atmosphere at funerary businesses is affected not only by the need to maintain a somber mood for the sake of the bereaved but also by the fact that workers interact with and manipulate dead bodies. This job function almost certainly colors the experience of all funeral workers, but its effects may be radically different for different people. Contemporary audiovisual technology is likely to be featured at all SCI franchises. SCI makes its own travel arrangements for the transfer of bodies.

Typical Number of Employees. SCI has more than thirteen thousand employees.

Traditional Geographic Locations. SCI operates more than fifteen hundred funeral homes and four hundred cemeteries in forty-three U.S. states, eight Canadian provinces, and Puerto Rico.

Pros of Working for a Large Funerary Business. The greatest possible diversification in the funerary business and the greatest possible financial solvency is likely to provide employees of SCI with job security.

Cons of Working for a Large Funerary Business. SCI has been a subject of several well-publicized controversies involving alleged body switching, leaky caskets, political-influence peddling, and storing decomposing bodies—including those of veterans—in an unrefrigerated garage, among other irregularities. The fact that these various incidents took place in different states at different facilities with different names may highlight the difficulty for a large corporation of policing all of its various branches. It is possible for any branch of SCI to be tarnished by these incidents, even if it has no direct involvement in them.

SCI is a large corporation with a large corporate bureaucracy. Employees, even those who never travel to corporate headquarters or interact face-to-face with corporate heads, may feel less engaged in their work than they would in a smaller business.

Canadian employees of SCI have gone on strike, perhaps indicating a problem with working conditions in at least some locations.

Costs

Payroll and Benefits: SCI's pay rates may vary significantly by location, but the company tends to pay annual salaries and to provide benefits.

Supplies: SCI funeral homes and facilities require embalming chemicals and makeup; protective clothing, body bags, and other equipment for handling and transporting the dead, including refrigeration facilities; automobiles and fuel; gardening supplies; office supplies and equipment; audiovisual equipment; and materials and tools necessary to construct caskets, urns, and headstones.

External Services: SCI is a largely self-sufficient company, but individual branches may sometimes contract security, groundskeeping, or other ancillary services.

Utilities: Funeral homes generally pay for electricity, gas or oil, water, sewage, trash collection, telephone, and Internet access.

Taxes: SCI pays local, state, and federal corporate and property taxes, in addition to other standard taxes, including sales taxes on sales and services.

Licenses: SCI employees must secure the necessary embalmers' and funeral directors' licenses within each jurisdiction. Such licenses are usually issued by states and may be reexamined and reissued periodically. Funerary businesses must keep their licenses current or face additional fees and penalties.

ORGANIZATIONAL STRUCTURE AND JOB ROLES

The staff of most funeral homes is small. Many bill themselves as family businesses. While some may be part of a large corporation such as SCI, the emphasis is always on the family orientation of the business, since the service itself is geared to families. Funeral directors may pride themselves on having inherited the business from parents or other family members and continuing in their families' traditions. In such small businesses, each owner and employee is likely to fulfill several different job roles. As in other industries, larger businesses are more likely to be compartmentalized and to assign a single job role to each worker.

The following umbrella categories apply to the organizational structure of businesses in the funerary industry:

- Business Management
- Customer Service
- Sales and Marketing
- Facilities and Security
- Operations
- Human Resources and Administrative Support

Business Management

Business managers oversee the operation of a single funeral home or a chain of such homes.

Small businesses generally have only one manager each, while larger businesses may have several. Managers are typically responsible for all activities associated with operations, customers, staff, facilities, and financials in a particular location. The primary responsibilities of general managers include daily management of business and finances, tracking of sales and targets, marketing and program development, selection and training of staff, oversight of staff, and community engagement.

Business management occupations may include the following:

- Owner
- President/Chief Executive Officer (CEO)
- Chief Financial Officer (CFO)
- Chief Operating Officer (COO)
- General Manager
- General Counsel

OCCUPATION PROFILE

Funeral Director

Considerations	Qualifications
Description	Arranges and directs all services associated with a funeral, including body transport, arranging service details, and transporting mourners.
Career cluster	Human Services
Interests	Data; people; things
Working conditions	Work both inside and outside
Minimum education level	On-the-job training; junior/technical/community college; apprenticeship; bachelor's degree
Physical exertion	Light work
Physical abilities	Unexceptional/basic fitness
Opportunities for experience	Part-time work
Licensure and certification	Required
Employment outlook	Average growth expected
Holland interest score	ESR

Note: See volume 1, "Publisher's Note," for an explanation of the Holland interest score.

Customer Service

Service is the core activity of the funerary business, whose focus is the satisfaction of mourners. Virtually all positions in the funerary industry focus on service in one way or another. The guiding principle of a funeral home is providing service to mourners in a style that must adapt to the mourners' social, ethnic, and religious backgrounds.

Funeral directors oversee all customer service and funeral arrangements. They plan all details and handle all logistics of each service in consultation with their clients. Often, they not only provide services themselves but also act as an interface with any other service providers, such as florists or engravers, whom the clients wish to engage. They must be aware of all common cultural and religious traditions in their area, as significant differences exist among, say, Hispanic funerals, Italian funerals, and Irish funerals.

Funeral homes may offer food and drink on premises to accommodate mourners. They generally include kitchen areas for food preparation and adjacent sitting areas for eating. While funeral directors may have their own religious beliefs, they must cater to the customs of each set of mourners unless they are committed to serving a specific religion.

Customer service occupations may include the following:

- Funeral Arranger
- Funeral Director
- Funeral Attendant
- Chaplain
- Grief Counselor

Sales and Marketing

Sales and marketing operate slightly unusually in the funerary industry, as a central goal of sales and marketing personal is to convince families to plan before they need funerary services. Even when a death has occurred and services are needed immediately, sales personnel make every effort to convince the family to plan for their later needs.

The costs of funerals are a matter of planning between funeral director and family. Ethical directors must be careful to avoid exploiting bereaved loved ones and selling them services or frills that they do not need. Directors lacking ethics may be able to realize high profits by appealing to family members' sense of guilt and loss while negotiating prices.

Many funeral homes maintain Web sites for contacting families seeking their services. Others rely on word-of-mouth advertisement. For example, if a funeral home has managed to accommodate, say, a particularly well structured Hispanic funeral, members of that community are likely to continue seeking the services of that funeral home. The same is true for religious groups and economic strata.

Sales and marketing occupations may include the following:

- Sales Representative
- Family Services Counselor
- Marketing Representative
- Web Designer
- Webmaster

Facilities and Security

Facilities and security personnel oversee the care and maintenance of buildings and physical grounds, as well as protecting them from theft or vandalism. They may also maintain and repair funeral home vehicles. Facilities staff keep interior rooms presentable and help clean them after a ceremony in order to prepare them for the next ceremony. They also help maintain behind-the-scenes areas, such as embalming stations. Groundskeepers maintain exterior grounds, mowing grass and otherwise maintaining the appearance of cemeteries and other landscaped areas. Guards protect buildings and grounds from vandals and from curious children and other relatively innocuous interlopers.

Facilities and security occupations may include the following:

- Groundskeeper
- Mechanic
- Custodian/Janitor
- Security Guard

Operations

Operations staff perform all central tasks at a funerary business not related to customer service. They transport, embalm, dress, bury, and cremate bodies. They apply clothing and makeup to the deceased to make them appear more alive, especially if there is to be an open-casket ceremony. For victims of severe accidents, this preparation may even entail rebuilding destroyed or disfigured portions of the features, replacing them with wax or other substances. Embalming may also become complicated, depending on chemicals or medications to which the deceased may have been exposed. Specific embalming chemicals are used to counteract excessive bloating associated with life-support systems, for example.

Funeral homes must have mobile hearses, as well as limousines to accommodate mourners. These vehicles are generally relatively rarely used, but they still require some regular maintenance. In the case of small, family-owned businesses, they are likely to be vintage automobiles. Hearses too may be vintage automobiles or even motorcycles. Larger businesses have dedicated drivers and may even have full-time dispatchers to assign pickups and deliveries to those drivers. Businesses that do have dedicated dispatchers and drivers utilize them not only for decedent transport but also for transportation of supplies such as caskets and cremation containers.

Operations occupations may include the following:

- Wax-Model Artist
- Embalmer
- Makeup Artist/Dresser
- Crematorium Operator
- Refrigeration Technician
- Driver
- Dispatcher
- Gravedigger
- Undertaker

Human Resources and Administrative Support

Human resources personnel recruit, hire, train, and fire employees, as well as administering payroll and benefits. At small funerary businesses, these tasks are usually performed by the owner. Larger businesses may have at least one dedicated staff member to oversee benefits and pay. Midsize businesses may assign such tasks to administrative staff. Most midsize businesses and even some small businesses employ at least one dedicated administrative assistant to run the office, maintain files and paperwork, oversee invoicing, and take care of other clerical tasks necessary to maintaining a business.

Human resources and administrative support occupations may include the following:

- Owner
- Human Resources Generalist
- Administrative Assistant
- Receptionist
- Payroll Clerk
- Benefits Manager

INDUSTRY OUTLOOK

Overview

The outlook for this industry shows it to be on the rise, or stable relative to the overall economy. The BLS projects that, between 2008 and 2018, the number of U.S. funeral director jobs will increase by 12 percent, about the same as the average for all occupations, and prospects are particularly good for directors who are also licensed embalmers. Mourners have begun to spend less on each funeral than they once did, but the number of deaths per year will increase in the United States as the population both increases and ages in the coming decades. Thus, demand for funeral services is almost guaranteed to increase, even if the profit margin associated with each client decreases.

Employment Advantages

People with good relationship skills are in demand in the funerary industry. Contact with mourners requires sensitivity, compassion, and tact. While embalmers may not have any contact with mourners, funeral directors must rely on their relationship skills to satisfy clients by arranging ceremonies that are as meaningful and satisfying as possible. Persons with both compassion and event-planning skills are particularly well suited to careers as funeral directors.

Annual Earnings

Various sources indicate annual revenue in the U.S. industry between $14 billion and $20.7 billion. U.S. Funeral Market estimates the average cost of a traditional funeral with burial plot and services at about $8,000.

RELATED RESOURCES FOR FURTHER RESEARCH

FAMILY FUNERAL HOME ASSOCIATION
585 Liverpool St.
New Westminster, BC V31 1K5
Canada
Tel: (888) 683-4533
Fax: (604) 736-2668
http://www.familyfuneral.org

NATIONAL FUNERAL DIRECTORS AND MORTICIANS
ASSOCIATION
3951 Snapfinger Parkway, Suite 570
Decatur, GA 30035
Tel: (800) 434-0958
http://www.nfdma.com

NEW YORK STATE FUNERAL DIRECTORS
ASSOCIATION
426 New Karner Rd.
Albany, NY 12205
Tel: (518) 452-8230
Fax: (518) 452-8667
http://www.nysfda.org

SELECTED INDEPENDENT FUNERAL HOMES
500 Lake Cook Rd., Suite 205
Deerfield, IL 60015
Tel: (800) 323-4219
Fax: (847) 236-9968
http://www.selectedfuneralhomes.org

SERVICE CORPORATION INTERNATIONAL
1929 Allen Parkway
Houston, TX 77019
Tel: (713) 522-5141
http://www.sci-corp.com

ABOUT THE AUTHOR

Reinhold Schlieper teaches English, literature, philosophy, and professional and practical ethics at Embry-Riddle Aeronautical University. He holds a Ph.D. in literature, an M.A. in English, and an M.A. in philosophy from Ball State University. He also holds a graduate certificate in practical and professional ethics from the University of New South Wales.

FURTHER READING

Bowman, Leroy. *The American Funeral.* New York: Paperback Library, 1964.

Bryce, Robert. "The Dying Giant." *Salon,* September 29, 1999. http://www.salon.com/news/feature/1999/09/29/sci/index.html.

Hafenbrack Marketing. *Report: Analysis of Funeral Home Industry.* Dayton, Ohio: Author, 2007. Available at http://www.independentadvantage.com/assets/ReportHMC-FuneralServicesIndustryAnalysis-100207.pdf.

Hoovers. "Industrial Overview: Funeral Operations, 2010." http://www.hoovers.com/funeral-operations/—ID__55—/free-ind-fr-profile-basic.xhtml.

Laderman, Gary. *Rest in Peace: A Cultural History of Death and the Funeral Home in Twentieth-Century America.* New York: Oxford University Press, 2005.

Michaelson, Jo. *Step Into Our Lives at the Funeral Home.* Amityville, N.Y.: Baywood, 2010.

Morton, Brian. "Vancouver Funeral Workers Strike: Average Workers' Income Is About $40,000 a Year." *The Vancouver Sun,* June 11, 2009, p. A3.

Papagno, Noella C. *The Hairdresser at the Funeral Home: Desairology Handbook Questions and Answers.* Hollywood, Fla.: J. J., 1981.

U.S. Bureau of Labor Statistics. *Career Guide to Industries,* 2010-2011 ed. http://www.bls.gov/oco/cg.

U.S. Census Bureau. North American Industry Classification System (NAICS), 2007. http://www.census.gov/cgi-bin/sssd/naics/naicsrch?chart=2007.

U.S. Department of Commerce. International Trade Administration. Office of Trade and Industry Information. Industry Trade Data and Analysis. http://ita.doc.gov/td/industry/otea/OTII/OTII-index.html.

U.S. Funerals On-Line. "U.S. Funeral Market." http://www.us-funerals.com/funeral-articles/usa-funeral-market.html.

Wolfelt, Alan. *Funeral Home Customer Service from A to Z.* Shippensburg, Pa.: Companion Press, 2001.

Furniture and Home Furnishings Industry

INDUSTRY SNAPSHOT

General Industry: Manufacturing

Career Cluster: Manufacturing

Subcategory Industries: Blind and Shade Manufacturing; Furniture and Home Furnishings Stores; Furniture and Related Product Manufacturing; Furniture Stores; Home Furnishings Stores; Household and Institutional Furniture and Kitchen Cabinet Manufacturing; Mattress Manufacturing; Office Furniture (Including Fixtures) Manufacturing

Related Industries: Electrical and Gas Appliances Industry; Household and Personal Products Industry; Textile and Fabrics Industry

Annual Domestic Revenues: $150.7 billion USD (MarketResearch.com, 2008; includes home appliances)

Annual International Revenues: $534 billion USD (*Business Horizons*, 2009; includes home appliances)

Annual Global Revenues: $685 billion USD (MarketResearch.com, 2008; *Business Horizons*, 2009; includes home appliances)

NAICS Numbers: 337, 442

INDUSTRY DEFINITION

Summary

The furniture and home furnishings industry manufactures and markets functional and decorative goods to furnish the spaces people inhabit. In addition to furniture, these goods include floor coverings, window treatments, mattresses and bedding, and outdoor furnishings. Goods are sold in furniture stores, department stores, and specialty stores, including antiques shops and shops that specialize in single products, such as mattresses or patio furnishings. They are also sold by mail order, either through print catalogs or online.

History of the Industry

People have furnished their homes since at least 3000 B.C.E. The wealthy had slaves to build their tables and seating, while the less privileged paid or bartered with craftspeople. Over the ensuing centuries, European countries, most notably England and France, emerged as trend setters. Asian styles developed as well. Those with the financial means wanted their homes to reflect both their personal taste and their position in society.

In America, the early colonists built crude furnishings for their homes using pine and oak from the abundant forests. In the cities, cabinetmakers honed their skills and began producing fine pieces in what would later be called the "colonial

The Furniture Manufacturing Industry's Contribution to the U.S. Economy

Value Added	Amount
Gross domestic product	$30.2 billion
Gross domestic product	0.2%
Persons employed	484,000
Total employee compensation	$22.5 billion

Note: Includes home furnishings and other related products.
Source: U.S. Bureau of Economic Analysis. Data are for 2008.

style." Such early American pieces are now highly sought by collectors, and many are in museums. New England, Pennsylvania, and Virginia led the field of furniture makers, and the high cost of importing, coupled with the colonists' growing preference for domestic goods, drove the industry to grow. By 1775, seven master craftsmen operated furniture shops in Williamsburg, Virginia, alone. The inevitability of the coming revolution turned the preference for domestic goods into a full-fledged boycott of English imports, as the colonies prepared for war.

As more Europeans immigrated to the New World, they plied their trades in the growing number of furniture factories on the East Coast and in the Midwest. They trained apprentices, so the ornate carvings and other embellishments they valued would continue to be produced by the next generation of furniture makers.

In 1876, the Centennial Exposition in Philadelphia put Grand Rapids, Michigan, on the map as the U.S. capital of furniture manufacturing, a distinction it would hold for more than a century. Buyers for retail establishments from all over the country came to Michigan for its semiannual furniture markets. Eventually, however, Grand Rapids' factories needed rebuilding, and North Carolina, particularly Hickory, was able to usurp the former city's status as the nation's furniture capital by offering lower taxes and cheaper labor to manufacturers. In the twenty-first century, most furniture is

produced in Asia, but the largest of the semiannual furniture markets are still held in North Carolina.

Department stores and mass marketers have competed for customers with furniture and home furnishing stores. The most aggressive of the mass marketers was Sears, which began its rise to prominence when Richard Sears and Alvah Roebuck released their first mail-order catalog in 1888. The company enjoyed tremendous growth, and among its many offerings were not only home furnishings but also, for a few years, houses in which to place them.

Styles have changed over the years. In the early 1900's, the style associated with late Victorian England went out of fashion, replaced by the mission style, the arts and crafts style, and other plain, modern designs. Five brothers named Stickley operated successful furniture factories. Three remained in New York, while two, Leopold and John George, settled in Grand Rapids. Their company, L. and J. G. Stickley, still manufactures furniture in New York state, at one of the dwindling American manufacturing facilities.

Gradually, retail furniture chains appeared, such as Ethan Allen, Haverty, and La-Z-Boy. Their size gave them a buying advantage over individual retailers, and they were able to purchase wholesale

Inputs Consumed by the Furniture Manufacturing Industry

Input	Value
Energy	$0.8 billion
Materials	$31.4 billion
Purchased services	$12.7 billion
Total	$44.9 billion

Note: Includes home furnishings and other related products.
Source: U.S. Bureau of Economic Analysis. Data are for 2008.

goods from manufacturers and importers for lower prices. This development put an end to the furniture departments in most department stores. Some retailers have since failed, while some have responded to economic troubles by closing their least profitable outlets.

Fine furniture produced in Europe and the United States fell out of favor with consumers who no longer sought furnishings built to last a lifetime and then be passed on to one's heirs. Instead, consumers came to expect furniture to be more disposable, requiring periodic replacement. A desire for novelty—and for the freedom to buy replacement furniture in the future—spurred the growth of companies selling less costly pieces and harmed those selling more expensive pieces that required significant investment to purchase. Those contemporary consumers seeking more expensive, long-lasting, finely crafted pieces primarily patronize either antiques stores or craftspeople who build custom pieces.

The Industry Today

While some furniture is still manufactured in the United States, most is made abroad, primarily in Asia. North Carolina remains the American furniture center, still hosting semiannual furniture markets for buyers from individual and chain retail establishments. By far the largest domestic manufacturer of home furnishings is Furniture Brands International, which markets many of the bigger industry brands, including Thomasville, Broyhill, Henredon, Drexel-Heritage, and Lane. The company is based in St. Louis, Missouri, and only about 25 percent of its products are manufactured abroad. Emerging trends, such as the increased use of renewable resources such as bamboo, help keep the industry vital.

The Stickley company in New York still produces its own line and has taken over the Widdicomb line as well. Both brands have loyal followings. The Netherlands-based IKEA, in 2009, opened a factory in Danville, Virginia, though the vast majority of its products are still made abroad. Ethan Allen operates six domestic factories.

The retail furniture industry consists of more than twenty thousand companies, many of which are single proprietorships or partnerships. IKEA, Ashley Furniture Industries, Ethan Allen, La-Z-Boy, and Pottery Barn are among the chains in the

forefront of the industry today. It is estimated that the fifty largest companies command more than 30 percent of the market share, so the industry is relatively fragmented. Some manufacturers, such as Furniture Brands International's Thomasville and Broyhill companies, operated their own retail stores, but they were forced to close some of their less profitable locations as a result of the recession of 2007-2009. Former retail giants Wickes Furniture and Jennifer Convertibles have shut down completely. New furniture is an expenditure that is put on hold when jobs are lost, and furniture sales are also closely related to home sales, which have been markedly below average in recent years. The industry is expected to grow slowly until the economy stabilizes and consumer confidence is restored.

Furnishings sales in the early twenty-first century may be categorized as follows: Some 38 percent are of wooden case goods (primarily bedroom pieces), 39 percent are of upholstered pieces, 17 percent are of mattresses and bedding, and the remaining 6 percent are of metal pieces (primarily porch, deck, and patio furniture). In a fiercely competitive industry, small companies hold their own by specializing in merchandise for a particular and clearly identifiable market. Doing better than the basic furniture retail stores are those specialty companies that cater to a specific niche, often high end, that is not as likely to be influenced by the economy. Kindel Furniture in Grand Rapids, Michigan, builds custom pieces for a select clientele that is located worldwide. Kindel is the only remaining manufacturer from the Grand Rapids glory days.

Independently owned furniture stores can succeed by offering something different. The Gallery Furniture store in Houston, Texas, holds its own against larger businesses by offering superior service, a wide selection of moderately priced furnishings, same-day delivery, and over-the-top promotions, including chef-prepared dinners for shoppers. The Gallery has reported over $150 million in annual sales and enjoys a loyal customer base.

The Nell Hill store in Atchison, Kansas, did not have the advantage of being in a big city but still managed to attract clients from all over the Midwest by offering unusual furnishings not found anywhere else. Word-of-mouth and aggressive marketing have driven the store's success. The owner, Mary Carol Garrity, has written magazine columns on decorating, as well as several books. Her legendary success propelled her to open a second store in Kansas City. Along with an eclectic array of case goods and upholstered pieces, she stocks antiques and original oil paintings.

Industry giants such as IKEA and Pier 1 Imports do well because their goods are lower priced than those of other stores and their styles appeal to young people furnishing their first homes or apartments and whose tastes have not yet evolved. These buyers often want what is already deemed popular, as opposed to developing their own styles. Mall fixtures such as Pottery Barn, Restoration Hardware, and Z Gallerie attract younger buyers as well.

One consistently successful market niche serves parents furnishing their children's rooms, as well as prospective parents furnishing nurseries. Parents want the best they can afford, and often grandparents help with the cost of baby furniture or buy

pieces as gifts. Another key to success, especially for single-store companies, is awareness of the needs of the surrounding community. A big-city retailer may cater to loft owners, who may want glass, brass, and leather furnishings. Suburban retailers typically serve clients seeking more traditional styles.

Shopping, even in bad economic times, has been called the United States' national pastime, and Americans continually look for new and better ways to shop. Buying clubs and members-only outlets attract large numbers of eligible members, and home furnishings are just a small part of what they offer. Mail ordering has come a long way since Sears and Roebuck mailed their first catalog, and despite high shipping costs, it is once again popular. Most of the catalog companies, such as Pottery Barn, also maintain traditional stores, but some are catalog and Internet only, allowing them to offer lower pricing. Internet furniture sales have been steadily increasing and produced more than $4.6 billion in 2008.

The retail furniture industry consists of more than twenty thousand companies, many of which are single proprietorships or partnerships. (©Alex Varlakov/Dreamstime.com)

INDUSTRY MARKET SEGMENTS

The furniture industry is fragmented: The top fifty manufacturers control only 30 percent of the market. Thus, manufacturers and retailers of all sizes compete successfully. Small businesses in the industry include individual craftspeople and small shops, whereas the largest companies are multinational corporations that may manufacture furniture, sell it, or both.

Small Businesses

Small furniture businesses include craftspeople operating small workshops, restorers, upholsterers, freelance designers, and single retail stores. Small retail businesses include locally owned furniture stores; specialty shops that focus on a single category, such as hand-crafted Amish furnishings, or that specialize in a single product, such as patio furnishings; and antiques and consignment shops. The global economic downturn has helped second-hand retailers seeking to compete with those selling new furnishings.

Potential Annual Earnings Scale. According to the U.S. Bureau of Labor Statistics (BLS), the average annual salary of all workers in the furniture manufacturing industry in 2009 was $35,390. Industrial engineers earned an average of $62,570, and commercial and industrial designers earned an average of $51,200.

Clientele Interaction. Furniture makers work alone most of the time but interact with their buyers. They may perform custom work for individual clients or sell to small stores. Either way, they sell themselves along with their products, so they need to establish trust.

Retail owner-proprietors have high levels of clientele contact, as they do virtually everything from advertising to buying merchandise to staffing the sales floor. Good people skills are necessary, including the ability to listen attentively in order to gain insight into a customer's taste, needs, and budget. Being able to offer decorating advice is helpful. At the very least, being knowledgeable about the local community can help salespeople and proprietors refer customers to drapers, upholsterers, and other industry-related professionals. Acting as this sort of resource beyond their own stores can help small-business owners cultivate repeat business and community loyalty. Furniture retailing is an industry in which customer service can make or break a small business.

Amenities, Atmosphere, and Physical Grounds. A furniture workshop should be clean, bright, and well-organized, especially if clients visit. Because furniture makers often work alone, they have no other requirements, as long as their workshops are conducive to working comfortably and efficiently for long periods of time.

Retail stores should be aesthetically appealing, with merchandise arranged to give customers an idea of how it will look in their homes. Wood surfaces must be dusted, glass sparkling, and pillows fluffed. Extras such as china on the tables and books or decorative objects on shelves add a cozy feel. Because furniture buying is time-intensive, retailers who offer coffee or other refreshments, encouraging prospects to linger, may enhance the chances those prospects will buy something. Retail outlets should be large enough to display merchandise in an uncrowded manner. Multistory stores often group pieces by manufacturer, and they may put bedroom suites on upper floors, with basements reserved for sale items.

Typical Number of Employees. All types of small furniture businesses are usually one- or two-person operations, with a few part-time employees to help during busy hours or seasons. A furniture maker might have an apprentice. Store employees can include delivery, clerical, and sales staff. Retail stores are typically open days, evenings, and weekends, so part-time workers are essential.

Traditional Geographic Locations. Workshops can be located anywhere and are often separate buildings on their owners' residential properties where zoning laws permit. Furniture stores are found in cities and in suburban mall areas. Ample parking adds to the attraction of a suburban location, but it is not always an option in congested urban centers. Chain stores are found in malls, strip malls, and on the commercial strips where other franchises are located.

Pros of Working for a Small Furniture Business. Small-business owners have complete control of their businesses. Manufacturers can work as much or as little as they choose. Retailers can enhance their business by determining their clients' tastes and preferences and buying accordingly, unbound by corporate dictates regarding inventories.

For example, they can add complementary lines such as carpeting as they see fit.

On the employee side, selling furniture may be fun for anyone interested in learning to build furniture, an art that is fast disappearing. Potential retailers with an interest in home decor have a good opportunity to learn the business from the ground up before opening their own businesses. If benefits are not needed, the flexibility of part-time hours appeals to retirees, college students, or mothers of school-age children. A commissioned sales associate with good people skills can earn a good living.

Cons of Working for a Small Furniture Business. Self-employed business owners may need to work long hours. Customer orders have to be filled, and the bulk of every task falls upon an owner's shoulders. Stores traditionally do most of their business during evenings and weekends. An employee in such a business is limited in earnings, as there is no corporate ladder to climb. Also, full-time work is not always available.

Costs
Payroll and Benefits: Small-business owners pay themselves out of their profits. If there are no profits, they do not get paid. Small furniture businesses often pay their employees hourly wages. Full-time employees may receive benefits, such as paid sick leave, vacations, and health care, along with discounts on merchandise. If part-time employees receive benefits, they are often prorated in accordance with the number of hours worked.

Supplies: Supplies are a major item for furniture builders and can include wood, hardware, tools, fabrics, and wood-finishing products, as well as a limited amount of office supplies and equipment. For retailers, supplies are a relatively small expense and include office supplies and equipment, including consumables such as printer cartridges, business cards and flyers, coffee, paper towels, and toilet paper. A range of furniture polish, glass cleaner, metal polish, and fabric spot remover is also necessary to maintain display merchandise, as are general cleaning supplies for the rest of the store.

External Services: Small furniture businesses may contract legal counsel, accounting and tax preparation, cleaning, maintenance, landscaping, and snow removal. Some store owners hire free-lance window- and interior-display specialists, though most find designing displays themselves to be an enjoyable part of their work.

Utilities: Utilities in the small furniture workshop or retail store include heat, gas, water, electricity, telephone, and Internet access.

Taxes: Small furniture businesses must pay local, state, and federal income, property, and payroll taxes, as well as collecting sales taxes on retail sales and obtaining necessary business licenses and permits. Owners may report their income on their personal returns, in which case they must pay self-employment taxes.

Midsize Businesses
Midsize businesses include single factories, as well as small retail chains that are usually local or regional, with from two to ten stores, and larger single-store operations. Midsize retail home furnishings companies offer more opportunities for employment, with more full-time jobs, as well as greater opportunities to advance within the company. They are less likely to specialize in a single style or single type of product, and they can offer their customers extras that are cost-prohibitive to many smaller companies, such as interior decorating assistance and company financing of purchases.

Potential Annual Earnings Scale. According to the BLS, the average annual salary of all workers in the furniture manufacturing industry in 2009 was $35,390. Industrial engineers earned an average of $62,570, and commercial and industrial designers earned an average of $51,200. The most common production jobs had average salaries between $25,000 and $30,000, and the average salary of all production workers was $30,020. Production supervisors earned an average of $49,190, and production managers earned an average of $82,530. General and operations managers earned an average of $106,980.

Among manufacturers, sales managers earned an average of $109,010, sales supervisors earned an average of $80,770, sales representatives earned an average of $61,270, and retail salespersons earned an average of $36,740. At retail stores, sales managers earned an average of $96,590, sales supervisors earned an average of $49,640, and retail salespersons earned an average of $36,360.

Clientele Interaction. Clientele interaction in a furniture factory is low and is limited to personnel in marketing, customer service, and delivery, as well, in some cases, as clerical staff. Retail employees experience high levels of clientele interaction. Other than positions in warehousing and visual merchandising (designing window and interior displays), there are few behind-the-scenes jobs in midsize retail businesses. Sales personnel need good people skills, and clerical and delivery workers need to excel at customer service. From the person who first greets a customer to the clerical support staff who process payments, all must make sure each sale is a positive experience so clients will become repeat buyers and refer acquaintances to the store. Every employee has a responsibility to work toward enhancing the company's reputation within the community.

Amenities, Atmosphere, and Physical Grounds. A midsize factory works best on a single level, arranged so materials come in one door, are moved through various workstations until the products are complete, and then go out another door to the loading dock. It must also meet all government health and safety regulations regarding saws and other tools and equipment, as well as chemicals such as paints and varnishes. Good ventilation is a must. Where necessary, employees should use masks, safety glasses, and other protective items.

A midsize company's physical store must meet all the requirements of smaller businesses, but it has the advantage of a larger space in which to display merchandise. Midsize stores generally have more sample rooms and more opportunities to show decorative accessories. They strive to make customers feel both welcome and comfortable. Parking areas and sidewalks should be kept clean and well lit to ensure safety.

Where there are multiple stores selling the same merchandise mix, they should have similar atmospheres so that regular customers shopping in different branch stores will have a feeling of familiarity, so they trust the level of service and quality to be as high as at their regular branch. If a building is multistoried, bedroom pieces may be on the upper floor, with sale pieces in a scratch-and-dent basement room. Clearance sale pieces are usually displayed on the main sales floor and are intermingled with those pieces not on sale.

Typical Number of Employees. A midsize factory usually employs from fifty to three hundred

people, depending on the degree of automation used in manufacturing and the company's needs for administrative and office staffs. Factory workers may be unionized, as may delivery people, if the company employs its own delivery workers.

Depending on the number of stores, the number of employees at midsize retail businesses could number from about thirty to two hundred or more. These employees perform the same roles as the employees of small retail companies but in greater numbers. Midsize companies generally have a greater mix of full- and part-time employees. Delivery personnel may work out of individual stores, out of central warehouses, or both. Company offices are likely to be centralized in an original or flagship store.

Traditional Geographic Locations. Factories can be located anywhere, but newer facilities are likely to be in suburban locations. Irrespective of the size of the company, furniture stores are traditionally located both in central urban areas and in suburban retail hot spots, near similar stores. Many customers prefer suburban stores for the ease of parking and safety.

Pros of Working for a Midsize Furniture Business. Midsize companies are able to offer employees more opportunities and higher financial compensation than are small companies. They provide employees with a good overview of the industry, helping build foundations of experience and insider knowledge that can serve them in future careers, either as employees of large companies or as business owners. With fewer layers of management than are typical of larger firms, midsize businesses provide employees with greater access to decision-makers. Job descriptions can overlap, so ambitious employees are more likely to assume greater responsibilities and can even offer input into the running of the company. Because employees play vital roles in the overall success of midsize companies, they gain more visibility and more hands-on experience. As in any retail situation, employee discounts are an advantage.

Cons of Working for a Midsize Furniture Business. Midsize businesses are more structured than small businesses, but they lack the flexibility of large businesses. Conventional retail hours can be inconvenient for part-time staff, though full-time employees with seniority can usually choose their preferred hours. A commissioned salesperson may lose a sale, along with income, if a customer makes several visits but finally makes a purchase on the employee's day off. While some view indistinct job descriptions as a plus, others may prefer greater structure and resent being asked to perform tasks beyond the scope of their regular duties.

Costs

Payroll and Benefits: Midsize furniture and home furnishings factories have both salaried and hourly employees, and all employees are usually full time. Salaried employees often receive benefits, including retirement plans, health insurance, sick and vacation pay, and sometimes flexible scheduling. Hourly employees may receive benefits as well. If they are represented by collective bargaining units, their benefits and salaries will be negotiated by their unions.

Midsize stores have mostly salaried employees, along a few who generate sales and are paid on commission. Full-time employees are often given sick leave, vacation, and other benefits, while part-time workers may also receive such benefits at the discretion of the owner or manager. Vacation and sick days are often prorated for part-time staff.

Supplies: Midsize businesses require office supplies and equipment, including ink cartridges, toner, and other supplies for electronic machinery. Retailers require furniture polish, glass cleaner, and metal polish, and other cleaning supplies. Factories require tools, machinery, raw materials, and safety supplies. Both businesses may require delivery vehicles, as well as the tools and supplies necessary to maintain them.

External Services: Midsize businesses may contract accounting and legal services, insurance, cleaning and janitorial services, merchandise and window display design, trash removal, and snow plowing.

Utilities: Midsize businesses must pay for telephone, Internet access, electricity, water, gas, and heat.

Taxes: Midsize furniture businesses must pay local, state, and federal income, property, and payroll taxes, as well as collecting sales taxes on retail sales and obtaining necessary business licenses and permits.

Large Businesses

While furniture manufacturing in the United States is not the big business it once was, there are still opportunities for those wanting to work in the industry. Thomasville, Henredon, Drexel-Heritage, and Lane—all components of Furniture Brands International—are the largest manufacturers. Some of the others are Ethan Allen, La-Z-Boy, Flexsteel, and Stickley.

Large businesses in the retail furniture and home furnishings industry include chains such as IKEA, Ethan Allen, Rooms to Go, Pier 1 Imports, La-Z-Boy, Ashley, and Pottery Barn, as well as mass merchandisers such as Sears, Walmart, Babies R Us, and Target, which include furniture among their product lines. Their volume gives them the buying power to offer goods at affordable prices.

Potential Annual Earnings Scale. According to the BLS, the average annual salary of all workers in the furniture manufacturing industry in 2009 was $35,390. Industrial engineers earned an average of $62,570, and commercial and industrial designers earned an average of $51,200. The most common production jobs had average salaries between $25,000 and $30,000, and the average salary of all production workers was $30,020. Production supervisors earned an average of $49,190, and production managers earned an average of $82,530. General and operations managers earned an average of $106,980.

Among manufacturers, sales managers earned an average of $109,010, sales supervisors earned an average of $80,770, sales representatives earned an average of $61,270, and retail salespersons earned an average of $36,740. At retail stores, sales managers earned an average of $96,590, sales supervisors earned an average of $49,640, and retail salespersons earned an average of $36,360.

Clientele Interaction. As in the midsize segment, manufacturing employees have limited clientele interactions, unless they are employed in specific client-oriented divisions such as marketing or customer service. Retail employees have much greater clientele interaction, though large companies employ more behind-the-scenes support personnel. Good interpersonal skills are key to success for all employees who sell or who deal with the public. Sales associates must learn to walk the tightrope between friendly customer service and aggressiveness. Furniture buying is a slow, personal process, and a hard-sell approach may send a prospect else-where. A good sales associate learns to read people and determine which customers need assistance and which will bolt if they are not left alone to browse at their leisure.

Amenities, Atmosphere, and Physical Grounds. The ideal factory has an efficient traffic flow to receive materials and discharge finished products. It should contain the latest in technology and tools, have sufficient light, and be well-venti-lated. Most important, employee safety should be considered in all phases of production, with strict compliance to Occupational Health and Safety Ad-ministration regulations.

Branches of chain stores are decorated similarly to one another no matter where they are located. This consistent decor fosters a feeling of familiarity to customers moving around the country. Display furniture must never be allowed to become dusty, and all glass surfaces must sparkle. Manager and franchise owners should strive for an atmosphere of comfort and well-being, as clients often visualize the pieces they are considering in their own homes. Decorative accessories add a cozy touch when not so overdone as to look cluttered. Good traffic patterns make it easy to go from display to display.

Retail stores can be sprawling one-story build-ings or, more likely in cities, occupy several stories, with the main floor reserved for living- and dining-room furnishings. Ample parking is usually avail-able, except in large city retail areas, and should be well-lit and monitored with security cameras.

Typical Number of Employees. Employees of large furniture companies can number from several hundred to tens of thousands or more, in-cluding those employed in factories, stores, ware-houses, and corporate headquarters. IKEA em-ploys nearly 130,000 people globally, making it the world's largest home furnishings company. Con-necticut-based Ethan Allen operates six factories, maintains stores in the United States, Canada, and Great Britain, and employs about 5,000 people.

Traditional Geographic Locations. Factories can be located anywhere, and sites are often cho-sen because of favorable tax regulations, a ready pool of workers, low costs, and ready access to transportation infrastructure. Furniture stores that are part of large corporations are usually located in suburban retail malls, strip malls, and the so-called

franchise rows where similar businesses have out-lets in every midsize to large city. Most cities have downtown furniture districts as well.

Pros of Working for a Large Furniture Busi-ness. Large companies offer greater opportunities to advance. They employ hundreds, if not thou-sands, and have multiple levels of hierarchy in mul-tiple locations. Thus, they provide ample opportu-nities for advancement or geographic change. Motivated employees can start at the bottom of a department and work their way up, or they can move from department to department to learn the entire business before striking out on their own if that is their goal. Large companies also tend to pay higher wages and offer better benefits than smaller companies.

Once employees attain a certain degree of se-niority, the large staffs of large retail stores make it easier to arrange more flexible work schedules. Employees may enjoy working in furniture stores if they are interested in home decor. Unlike some other retail businesses where the commodities are more disposable or less personal, sales employees in the furniture business can build long-term rela-tionships with their clients. Employees may also re-ceive discounts on their merchandise.

Cons of Working for a Large Furniture Busi-ness. Some people are frustrated by the multiple layers of management and other bureaucratic structures common at large businesses. Those working in the lower tiers of such an organization can feel anonymous and insignificant. Workers who like to make decisions and see them imple-mented immediately are likely to be happier in smaller venues where each employee's contribu-tion is both more important and more visible. Em-ployees may need to work long hours, which may be particularly inconvenient for newer employees. Managers are more likely to face unionized em-ployees.

Costs

Payroll and Benefits: Large companies generally pay a mix of hourly wages and annual salaries de-pending on the position. Sales personnel may be paid on commission. Most large companies pay full benefits to full-time employees, including sick and vacation pay, holiday pay, various types of insurance, and retirement plans or profit sharing. Part-time employees may not qualify for benefits. Union members' compensation and benefits are arranged through negotiations conducted by collective bargaining units.

Supplies: Large businesses require office supplies and equipment, including ink cartridges, toner, and other supplies for electronic machinery. Retailers require furniture polish, glass cleaner, and metal polish, and other cleaning supplies. Factories require tools, machinery, raw materials, and safety supplies. Both businesses may require delivery vehicles, as well as the tools and supplies necessary to maintain them. Large companies often also require food and food-preparation supplies for staff break rooms and cafeterias.

External Services: Legal, auditing, advertising, and insurance services are usually contracted and managed by a large company's corporate headquarters. Individual locations often contract directly for local services such as cleaning, routine maintenance, and snow removal.

Utilities: Large companies require all the basic utilities: electricity, gas, water, telecommunications, and Internet connections.

Taxes: Large furniture companies must pay local, state, federal, and international income, property, and payroll taxes, as well as collecting sales taxes on retail sales and obtaining necessary business licenses and permits in each jurisdiction. They must also pay any applicable tariffs or other import and export fees.

ORGANIZATIONAL STRUCTURE AND JOB ROLES

The various tasks required to conduct a furniture business remain the same irrespective of a company's size. In a small operation, the owner handles all or most of the responsibilities, acting in roles including chief executive, advertising executive, sales associate, accountant, window dresser, janitor, and coffee brewer. Midsize companies have employees charged with various, often overlapping, job descriptions. Large companies have whole departments devoted to each function, such as accounting or marketing. Job descriptions at such companies are more rigid than they are at smaller firms, and they are sometimes frustrating for employees who enjoy performing a variety of tasks and encountering new challenges.

Many of the jobs available in the furniture industry exist in many other industries, while others, such as furniture designer, wood carver, upholsterer, carpet installer, and interior decorator, are specific to furniture and home furnishings companies. Not all companies require all positions, as a production operation's needs differ greatly from those of a retail business. Within the industry as whole, however, there is a wide range of job opportunities.

The following umbrella categories apply to the organizational structure of businesses in the furniture and home furnishings industry:

- Business Management
- Customer Service
- Sales and Marketing
- Facilities and Security
- Technology, Research, Design, and Development
- Production
- Distribution
- Retail Sales

Business Management

Business managers oversee companies. Managers may be sole proprietors answerable only to themselves or chief executive officers (CEOs), who are accountable to boards of director or shareholders. A midsize operation typically has one person, usually the owner, calling the shots with input from employees with various responsibilities. The larger the company, the more layers of management. Those with decision-making authority plan their companies' activities and oversee the execution of their plans.

With the possible exception of those sales staff earning commissions, the top managers are the highest-paid employees of a given company. Generally speaking, the larger the company, the more educational credentials and experience that are required for management positions. Managers most often have degrees in business management, accounting and finance, or sales and marketing, including M.B.A. degrees. Smaller companies' owners or managers may overlook the lack of formal degrees and choose applicants with solid industry track records coupled with enthusiasm and proven ability to achieve goals. The smallest businesses, especially those with limited budgets, are more likely to train applicants with no experience, since such candidates command lower salaries. In the furniture and home furnishings industry, important decisions include what to produce or, in retail situations, what to sell and from whom to purchase inventory; how to finance purchases of equipment or inventory; and how large a workforce is needed.

Business management occupations may include the following:

- Owner/Sole Proprietor
- Partner
- President/Chief Executive Officer (CEO)
- Chief Financial Officer (CFO)
- Vice President of Sales and Marketing
- Vice President of Business Development
- Controller
- Sales and Marketing Manager
- Human Resources Manager

Customer Service

Customer service is often the standard by which customers judge the efficiency of a company. People working in this capacity work in concert with sales departments. In manufacturing companies, they expedite orders, arrange shipments, authorize returns, and, in general, anticipate and solve problems to keep customers happy and to keep them coming back. Succeeding in this job requires product knowledge, good communication skills, organizational skills, tact, and patience. Small manufacturers and craftspeople are their own customer service staffs, so they must do whatever they can to make sure their customers are happy with their purchases.

Some retail stores offer interior design services to their customers, often free of charge, to help them make design choices. Interior design specialists assist customers in assembling ensembles of furniture, custom window coverings, rugs, and other accessories that will complement one another and create desired effects in their homes. Large retail sellers of home furnishings may have corporate customer service departments, but their in-store sales associates are the first ones to whom customers come if they experience problems. In small stores, the owner answers customer complaints.

Interior decorating makes use of wall coverings such as wallpaper. (©Dreamstime.com)

Customer service occupations may include the following:

- Customer Service Manager
- Customer Service Representative
- Expediter
- Returned Goods Coordinator
- Interior Decorating Consultant

Sales and Marketing

Sales and marketing are the lifeblood of a company and of the whole furniture industry. Manufacturers sell to wholesale buyers for resale. They display coordinated suites of furniture and individual pieces and accessories to furniture markets, where buyers place orders based on anticipated customer demand. Long before these pieces reach furniture markets, a company's marketing department will have created a plan based on past performance, new trends, and the health of the economy.

A crucial part of marketing is advertising. In the furniture industry, advertising comprises catalogs, billboards, newspaper and magazine advertisements, and—for those companies large enough to afford them—television commercials. Most forms of advertising are expensive and consume a large portion of a company's marketing budget. Advertisements are placed by both manufacturers and retail outlets. Stores advertise locally to announce sales. Large companies have their own advertising departments, midsize ones often use agencies, and small companies' owners may run advertisements in local newspapers, rent billboards, or buy targeted online advertising.

Retail marketing includes designing merchandise displays. Designers, called visual merchandisers, set up "rooms" on sales floors and dress store windows to attract customers and motivate purchases. Both window and interior displays need to be changed frequently to avoid looking stale, to coordinate with seasons and holidays, and to showcase sale pieces. Freelance visual merchandisers may work for a number of noncompeting businesses.

Sales and marketing occupations may include the following:

- Marketing Director
- Sales Manager
- Sales Representative
- Market Research Analyst
- Visual Merchandiser
- Advertising Executive
- Advertising Assistant
- Account Executive
- Account Associate

Facilities and Security

Facilities and security personnel maintain buildings and keep them clean and safe. A facilities manager oversees housekeeping and janitorial, maintenance, and security staffs. This manager is also responsible for interacting with contractors who perform outsourced facility-related work, such as landscaping, snow removal, and pest control.

Maintenance is a major concern in factories and in corporate or regional headquarters. Machinery used in production must be kept in good repair for both efficiency and safety. Regular maintenance can prevent equipment breakdowns that would not only be costly to repair but also interfere with filling orders on time. Maintenance personnel also keep things running smoothly in offices and warehouses. They include electricians, plumbers, general repair workers, heating and air-conditioning specialists, and carpenters, who perform preventive maintenance and general repairs.

Security personnel must not only guard the safety of personnel, consumers, and physical property but also guard against corporate espionage. In large stores, they make sure customers enjoy safe shopping experiences. Surveillance cameras monitor stores' interiors and parking lots. Alarms protect property from burglars and vandals outside of business hours. Though shoplifting is not likely in a furniture store, robberies and burglaries can occur. Employee theft is costly but easily prevented.

Facilities and security occupations may include the following:

- Facility Manager
- Housekeeping Director
- Cleaner
- Custodian/Janitor
- Maintenance Manager
- Electrician
- Plumber
- Heating, Ventilation, and Air-Conditioning (HVAC) Specialist
- Industrial Engineering Technician
- Carpenter
- Chief Security Officer
- Investigator
- Plainclothes Operative
- Security Guard

Technology, Research, Design, and Development

Computer technology drives many aspects of business, and information technology (IT) personnel oversee, maintain, and repair computer systems and equipment. IT directors and computer support technicians are involved in equipment purchase recommendations and personnel training, and they must be on call to address problems whenever they arise.

A company can stay competitive only as long as its products appeal to the buying public. For that reason, new home furnishings products are constantly introduced, and they are developed by product designers. After initial consultations with management, designers create designs and then submit them for final approval. After selections have been made, designers and the new product developers work together to build prototypes. Any problems are fixed, and then industrial production engineers design machines and processes to manufacture the products on a mass scale. The pieces are then put into production.

Many factors go into deciding which products to add to existing lines. These include profitability, sustainability and other material-related issues, and whether the product fits into a company's existing line and public image. New products are introduced to replace those that are slow sellers and to keep up with the competition.

Technology, research, design, and development occupations may include the following:

- Information Technology Director
- Computer Support Specialist
- Network and Systems Administrator
- Computer Programmer
- Industrial Engineer
- Industrial Engineering Technician
- Mechanical Drafter
- Commercial/Industrial Designer

Production

Production personnel make furniture and home furnishings. They include self-employed craftspeople who create unique pieces alone in their workshops, as well as team assemblers working on assembly lines to manufacture thousands of identical products.

In most factories, strict hierarchies determine the division of labor, particularly in union shops. A typical production department operates under the leadership of a vice president of manufacturing. Reporting to the vice president is a superintendent, who handles day-to-day operations. Department supervisors are responsible for the various steps in the process, from the first assembly to the finishing to the addition of drawer pulls or other hardware. The supervisors bring potential problems or concerns to the attention of superintendents.

Unskilled workers operate machinery and produce bare-bones pieces. Then, skilled workers apply artistic embellishments, such as carvings or painted designs. Finishers complete the products,

Workers spray paint furniture parts in an assembly line. (©Thor Jorgen Udvang/Dreamstime.com)

A young joiner works on a piece of furniture. (©Dreamstime.com)

which are inspected by quality control personnel at various stages of production. After the final application, products are prepared for shipment.

Production occupations may include the following:

- Owner/Craftsperson
- Vice President of Manufacturing
- Plant Superintendent
- Department Supervisor
- Team Assembler
- Cabinetmaker/Bench Carpenter
- Coating, Painting, and Spraying Machine Setter and Operator
- Woodworking Machine Operator
- Sawing Machine Operator
- Furniture Finisher
- Sewing Machine Operator
- Upholsterer
- Quality Assurance Manager
- Inspector

OCCUPATION PROFILE

Upholsterer

Considerations	Qualifications
Description	Makes new furniture, reconditions old furniture, restores antiques, and repairs broken furniture.
Career clusters	Human Services
Interests	Things
Working conditions	Work inside
Minimum education level	On-the-job training; high school diploma/technical training; apprenticeship
Physical exertion	Medium work
Physical abilities	Unexceptional/basic fitness
Opportunities for experience	Apprenticeship; part-time work
Licensure and certification	Usually not required
Employment outlook	Slower-than-average growth expected
Holland interest score	RCS

Note: See volume 1, "Publisher's Note," for an explanation of the Holland interest score.

OCCUPATION PROFILE

Woodworker

Considerations	Qualifications
Description	Cuts, shapes, and assembles raw wood to make household furnishings and components, recreational items, and many other products.
Career clusters	Manufacturing
Interests	Things
Working conditions	Work inside
Minimum education level	High school diploma or GED; high school diploma/technical training; apprenticeship
Physical exertion	Medium work
Physical abilities	Unexceptional/basic fitness
Opportunities for experience	Apprenticeship; military service
Licensure and certification	Usually not required
Employment outlook	Slower-than-average growth expected
Holland interest score	REI

Note: See volume 1, "Publisher's Note," for an explanation of the Holland interest score.

Distribution

Distribution personnel transport finished home furnishings from factories to warehouses, retail stores, and consumers' homes and offices. A traffic manager runs the department and arranges pickups with commercial carriers. The traffic manager may work alone or may have a staff, depending on the size of the company. The job requires contracting with carriers and preparing all the bills of lading and other relevant paper work. Some companies maintain their own delivery fleets and hire their own drivers. Those corporations need both drivers and truck mechanics to maintain their fleets.

Distribution occupations may include the following:

- Traffic Manager
- Shipping and Receiving Clerk
- Expediter
- Freight Loader/Unloader
- Truck Driver
- Mechanic
- Routine Truck Maintenance Worker
- Truck Washer/Detailer

Retail Sales

At a retail store, a store manager oversees all employees with the help of assistant managers, as long retail hours make it impossible for one person to be on site during all business hours. Larger stores have department managers as well. Sales associates serve customers directly.

Buyers visit markets and make informed decisions about which offerings will best appeal to their companies' clientele. Buying products at wholesale for retail sale requires extensive knowledge of the industry as a whole, as well as an understanding of what motivates a company's typical customer. A buyer must also be able to evaluate the compatibility between a given product and the public image or branding of the buyer's store.

There are behind-the-scenes jobs as well. Delivery personnel, including truck drivers, furniture movers, and delivery schedulers, handle the transport of goods from stores to consumers' homes. Stock clerks and pickers staff the warehouses of bigger companies and the back rooms of all stores.

Inventory control specialists maintain computerized databases of what has been received and what has been sold. If an item is out of stock in one store, it may be available in another. Databases also track sales to ascertain which items are most successful, providing valuable information to a company's buyers.

Retail occupations may include the following:

- Store Manager
- Assistant Manager
- Department Manager
- Sales Associate
- Store Clerk
- Buyer
- Warehouse Manager
- Stock Picker
- Freight Loader/Unloader
- Delivery Truck Driver
- Inventory Specialist

INDUSTRY OUTLOOK

Overview

The outlook for the furniture and home furnishings industry shows it to be stable. The industry enjoyed a particularly robust year in 2006, but it has declined since then, experiencing lackluster growth of 2.0 to 2.8 percent per year. Growth is projected to increase between 2011 and 2015, however. Some companies have not been able to survive the recession of 2007-2009 and have ceased

PROJECTED EMPLOYMENT FOR SELECTED OCCUPATIONS

Furniture and Related Product Manufacturing

Employment		
2009	Projected 2018	Occupation
70,540	91,000	Cabinetmakers and bench carpenters
11,930	16,300	Carpenters
16,610	20,300	First-line supervisors/managers of production and operating workers
11,410	13,900	Furniture finishers
38,530	45,100	Team assemblers
15,380	18,800	Upholsterers
18,200	24,400	Woodworking machine setters, operators, and tenders, except sawing

Source: U.S. Bureau of Labor Statistics, Industries at a Glance, Occupational Employment Statistics and Employment Projections Program.

operations or have closed some stores or production facilities. Others may follow.

The home furnishing industry is closely tied to new home construction, so when the housing market rebounds, the furniture industry is expected to rebound as well. There will always be a market for nursery and children's room furnishings. More generalized products remain in demand as young people establish their first homes, apartment renters become home buyers, and downsizers decide their old furnishings do not reflect their new lifestyles. As more people opt to work from home offices, the market for suitable furnishings will grow proportionately. Also, American society is relatively mobile, and each move requires at least some new purchases.

What may change is where and how people shop. Companies such as IKEA and Value City Furniture may benefit from expected shifts, while sales at pricier chains, including Pottery Barn and Ethan Allen, are expected to suffer until the economy recovers. Shoppers are also more likely to shop in secondhand or consignment shops during a slow economy. Antiques are growing in popularity, but—as is true of secondhand stores—sales at such shops are difficult to track. While they take away from the production end of the industry, they enhance the retail segment. E-commerce is also growing in the furniture industry.

Though in past decades manufacturing has been increasingly outsourced overseas to take advantage of cheaper labor, this trend may be lessening. In 2009, IKEA opened its first American factory in Danville, Virginia. Other companies located abroad, but with large North American customer bases, may also find it necessary to establish manufacturing facilities in the United States or in other countries to which they export. This development would not change the global market, but it would enhance the domestic sector.

The industry is further driven by trends. Shelter magazines and programming such as the House and Garden Television Network (HGTV) influence taste and help drive consumer demand. Homemakers no longer remain loyal to a particular style but have bought into the makeover mindset that demands a periodic update, whether of a few accessories or an entire home.

Globally, the outlook is similar. Economies have become so intertwined that when one falters, the ripples are felt around the world. Here, as well, there is room for optimism. Developing economies provide growth that helps offset losses. Also, new stylistic trends increasingly originate in Asia or Europe, meaning they benefit those economies first before taking hold in North America.

Employment Advantages

The furniture industry is a good fit for anyone who enjoys interior design and has a gift for helping others furnish their homes. Many opportunities exist in retail businesses for professional decorators. Candidates will benefit from gaining degrees in the field and being able to design complete ensembles by working with others to coordinate window coverings, floor coverings, accessories, and furniture. The proliferation of shelter magazines and furnishing-related television programming indicates that people are still interested in home decoration.

Creative people are drawn to the artistic detailing and design portions of the production process. Potential carvers and other skilled craftspeople can learn through apprenticeship programs that place applicants with skilled workers to learn a given process from the ground up. While the number of factory jobs has dwindled, there are still viable companies with an ongoing need for good employees. There have been layoffs, but the industry is expected to pick up momentum in the years ahead. Shelter is a basic need, and anything associated with it will always be in demand, albeit with market fluctuations. The industry is highly competitive, however, so job seekers need to distinguish themselves from the field of candidates.

Annual Earnings

According to Market Research, the U.S. furniture, home furnishings, and home appliance industry earned revenues of $150.7 billion in 2008, and the global industry earned $685 billion. Because these figures include home appliances, electronics, and lighting, they are slightly misleading, but they provide a general idea of the scope of industry earnings. These earnings have slowed following the global economic crisis, but they are expected to begin to grow again between 2011 and 2015, beginning modestly and then gaining momentum. Growth may reach 5.8 percent in 2014. Should the production portion of the domestic industry grow more slowly, the retail portion may make up the deficit, as its product mix includes imports as well as domestically produced goods.

RELATED RESOURCES FOR FURTHER RESEARCH

Furniture Today Magazine
  P.O. Box 2754
  High Point, NC 27261-2754
  Tel: (336) 605-0121
  Fax: (336) 605-0131
  http://www.furnituretoday.com

National Home Furnishings Association
  3910 Tinley Dr., Suite 101
  High Point, NC 27265-3610
  Tel: (800) 888-9590
  Fax: (336) 801-6102

UPHOLSTERED FURNITURE COUNCIL
P.O. Box 2346
High Point, NC 27261
Tel: (336) 885-5065
Fax: (336) 885-5072
http://www.ufac.org

ABOUT THE AUTHOR

Norma Lewis is the author of four nonfiction books, one an account of the Yukon gold rush for young adults, and the other three pictorial histories of the Southwest Michigan area she calls home. She is a prolific magazine writer. During the twenty years she has been writing travel articles, she has covered destinations, escorted group travel, solo travel, and recreational-vehicle camping. She holds a bachelor of science degree in business administration from Aquinas College but left the corporate world for what she considers the best job in the world: freelance writing.

FURTHER READING

Bennington, Richard R. *Furniture Marketing: From Product Development to Distribution.* New York: Fairchild Books, 2003.

Dugan, Michael K. *The Furniture Wars: How America Lost a Fifty Billion Dollar Industry.* Conover, N.C.: Goosepen Studio & Press, 2009.

International Trade Centre UNCTAD/WTO and International Tropical Timber Organization. *International Wooden Furniture Markets: A Review.* Geneva, Switzerland: Authors, 2005.

Purdy, Warren G. *The Guide to Retail Business Planning.* Boston: Inc. Magazine Business Resources, 1997.

Schroeder, Carol L. *Specialty Shop Retailing.* Hoboken, N.J.: John D. Wiley and Sons, 2007.

Segel, Dick, CSP. *Retail Business Kit for Dummies.* Indianapolis: Wiley, 2008.

Taylor, Don, and Jeanne Smalling Archer. *Up Against the Wal-Marts.* 2d ed. New York: American Management Association, 2005.

U.S. Bureau of Labor Statistics. *Career Guide to Industries,* 2010-2011 ed. http://www.bls.gov/oco/cg.

U.S. Census Bureau. North American Industry Classification System (NAICS), 2007. http://www.census.gov/cgi-bin/sssd/naics/naicsrch?chart=2007.

U.S. Department of Commerce. International Trade Administration. Office of Trade and Industry Information. Industry Trade Data and Analysis. http://ita.doc.gov/td/industry/otea/OTII/OTII-index.html.

Wille, Stefan, ed. *Employment Conditions in the U.S. Furniture Sector.* Atlanta, Ga.: ATKRIN Furniture, 2004.

Hand Tools and Instruments Industry

©Dreamstime.com

INDUSTRY SNAPSHOT

General Industry: Manufacturing

Career Cluster: Manufacturing

Subcategory Industries: Cutlery and Flatware Manufacturing; Cutlery and Hand Tool Manufacturing; Fabricated Metal Kitchen Utensil Manufacturing; Hand and Edge Tool Manufacturing; Power-Driven Hand Tool Manufacturing; Saw Blade and Handsaw Manufacturing

Related Industries: Household and Personal Products Industry; Industrial Design Industry; Light Machinery Industry; Scientific, Medical, and Health Equipment and Supplies Industry

Annual Domestic Revenues: $5.9 billion USD (High Beam Research, 2010)

Annual International Revenues: $12.3 billion USD (Research & Markets, 2009)

Annual Global Revenues: $19.87 billion USD (MindBranch Market Research, 2010)

NAICS Numbers: 3322, 333991

INDUSTRY DEFINITION

Summary

From woodworking and chiseling to boring and sawing, hand tools serve many purposes for builders and crafters of all skill levels. Despite an ever-changing array of high-technology machinery available in hardware stores around the globe, for many, hand tools are preferred because they require less effort, maintenance, and know-how. Although they have evolved over the years, many hand tools—such as the chisel—have remained all-purpose and may be used for marking, measuring, striking, and scraping. With such a wide variety of instruments, hand tools are just as useful now as they were in the eighteenth century and will always be the desired choice of furniture makers, builders, and woodworkers who build for work or craft for fun.

History of the Industry

The use of hand tools is directly associated with the human species, and their invention is presumed to be one of the earliest events in human history. Since trade has existed, there has always been a market for tools.

Perhaps the golden age of American hand tools encompasses the decades between the Civil War and World War II. That period produced a huge va-

Hand tools serve many purposes for builders and crafters of all skill levels. (©Dreamstime.com)

riety of tools and many variations of the same tool in a range of qualities and materials. The mass industry for such tools, however, began booming in the late twentieth century, when the do-it-yourself (DIY) craze began. Since then, the hand tools industry has evolved dramatically, and the competitive market has become saturated with many products claiming to make home building, improving, decorating, and refurbishing easy. Hand tools went from being heavy and bulky to lightweight and sleek, making them appealing to both men and women.

During the industry's early days, hand tools were targeted to skilled, professional crafters. Today, housewives, mothers, and daughters know exactly where to go and what to buy when it comes to hand tools. Another change over the years relates to cost. Hand tools are more expensive than ever, and now there is something for every application—whether to build a birdhouse or renovate a bathroom. Hand tools were once used daily to build fences, cabins, furniture, barns, horse carriages, and bug-

gies. The simplicity of the same tools makes them attractive to modern people who simply like working with their hands.

The hand tool market has been dramatically expanded by the many avenues of guidance and assistance now available to amateurs. Many television networks broadcast programming that teaches viewers to use hand tools to complete specific projects. From Web sites to catalogs to home improvement stores in just about every community, the hand tools industry has become ubiquitous. This wide availability, as well as the streamlining of tools over the years, continues to increase hand tools' appeal.

Manufacturers of hand tools engage in branding wars, seeking to associate their products with quality and reliability in the minds of consumers. As with any other product, there are high-end hand tool makers that target serious users and more inexpensive manufacturers that appeal to more utilitarian users. Today's industry has changed, though, in that as a whole it no longer targets a specific audience. Instead, it appeals to anyone who may have any use for a tool, whether professionals, serious hobbyists, or simply homeowners who wish to have hammers and wrenches in their tool kits just in case they are needed.

The Industry Today

The U.S. hand tools industry faces challenges, especially in the face of globalization. The use of electronic business is also creating a problem for the industry. E-commerce is forcing the current hand tools market to adjust its activities and business practices around the globe.

Major products of the hand tools industry include wrenches, hammers, scissors, vises, clamps, screwdrivers, pliers, chisels, and measuring devices, to name just a few products. These items account for nearly 60 percent of the industry's revenue. Cutlery, including kitchen knives, sporting knives, razor blades, and flatware—table knives, forks, and spoons—accounts for about 15 percent of industry revenue. Saw blades and kitchen utensils account for about 13 percent each. Manufacturers use a wide range of fabrication processes, including forging, stamping, bending, forming, and machining, to turn purchased metal into final products.

Steel and steel alloys are the major raw materials used by the industry. Alloys have special properties, such as hardness or resistance to corrosion, that suit them well to tool manufacture. Outside the United States, hand tools are big business. China continues to be one of the biggest manufacturers of hand tools. The value of its exports of hand tools grew by 28 percent in 2004, from $493 million to $630 million, and has continued to rise, averaging around 20 percent growth. India has an advantage in the hand tool industry because of its easy access to raw materials and available qualified labor at low wages. The country has experienced and benefited from an average annual growth rate of about 17 percent in the hand tool market since 2003.

Not surprising, Taiwan has already turned to the production of digitally enhanced tools to drive growth of its own hand tools industry. Digital tools such as torque wrenches and screwdrivers have become an increasingly important category in the hand tools industry. They generate better margins but require more advanced production technologies that use electromechanical integration to ensure quality and reliability. Taiwan's advantages mean that digital tools can be an answer for Taiwanese hand tool makers who face an increasingly challenging global market for DIY tools. Competition from China has eroded these Taiwanese manufacturers' sales, as the former has dumped low-end and very cheap tools on the international market. Indeed, China is now the largest exporter of hand tools in the world, with Germany and Taiwan ranking second and third, respectively.

To enhance the functionality and value of digital tools, Taiwanese hand tool makers have developed digital modules that allow wireless data transmission using the Bluetooth protocol. Manufacturers believe that the use of Bluetooth is a major enhancement in the reliability of digital tools because it allows remote control of the torque force applied through each digital torque wrench that is properly equipped. As a result, improperly torqued fasteners can be detected quickly.

A simple electric drill makes woodworking easier. (©Wellford Tiller/Dreamstime.com)

Modules with built-in Bluetooth have already been completed and are expected to boost Taiwan's profile as a home of digital tool experts. Digital modules make it more feasible to mass produce digital tools, and they help assure the tools' quality. The modules are designed to meet most digital tool specifications. Thus, manufacturers can use them with their existing tool models, using modular production methods to boost their capacity and maintain quality.

Digital hand tools are quickly becoming a major force for Taiwan's hand tools industry. Even though the cost of manufacturing and distributing digital torque tools is about five times that of traditional hand tool models, torque tools are expected to replace only 5 percent of total exports of traditional hand tool models but to generate an export value ten times greater than those they replace. Among the foremost Taiwanese digital-tool mak-

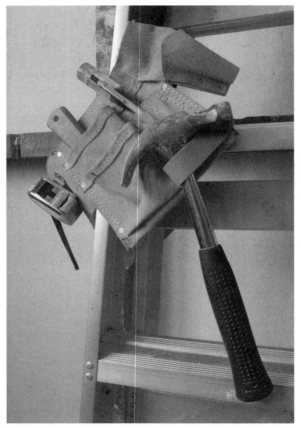

A hammer hangs from a builder's tool belt. (©Chris Hellyar/Dreamstime.com)

ers with their own brands in the global market is Eclatorq. The popular toolmaking company makes annual shipments of more than twenty thousand digital tools, including torque wrenches, screwdrivers, and pullers. The company claims that its torque wrenches are almost immune to stressful conditions and are especially cost-efficient because they need only one sensor instead of four strain gauges. Their simple design not only reduces defect rates but also enhances measuring accuracy.

There are more than fifteen hundred firms active in the U.S. hand tools industry, with a combined annual revenue of about $5.9 billion. These businesses range from small to major corporations. Some of the better-known hand tool manufacturers include Bostitch, Craftsman, Jennings, Plumb, Diamond, Disston, Rubbermaid, Marples, Starrett, Cooper Industries, Record, and Stanley. The hand tools industry has also become extremely energy-intensive, for the most part. In most economies all over the world, adoption of energy-efficient, green processes and technologies can yield energy savings between 30 and 50 percent. Hand tools' most common subindustries include hardware, lumber tools, cutlery, power tools, automotive tools, garden tools, plumbing tools, and carpentry tools. Automotive, construction, and home improvement are among the most common partnership industries.

INDUSTRY MARKET SEGMENTS

The hand tools and instruments industry includes facilities ranging in size from small mom-and-pop shops to large franchise stores. The industry serves a wide array of clients, from college students and housewives to newlywed couples and entrepreneurs looking to expand or improve their homes or work spaces. The following sections provide a comprehensive breakdown of each of these different segments.

Small Businesses

The demand for hand tools depends on the construction and building repair industries. Fortunately, small businesses in the hand tools industry are able to compete with larger businesses by making specialty products. Ongoing introduction of new hand tool products, especially improved cordless tools, will create gains in all markets.

Potential Annual Earnings Scale. The average earnings for an employee at a small company in the hand tools industry vary from state to state, but the salary range in the United States is from $16,000 to $35,000 a year for a clerk and $35,000 to $70,000 annually for a store manager. The salaries for employees that work in small hand tool businesses usually remain steady because of the nature of the business. Also, small establishments do not usually experience seasonal rushes, as do hand tool companies that are located in shopping centers such as malls or other highly populated shopping areas. Hand tool store employees that work in small businesses may not get regular pay raises or salary increases, but managers often provide other incentives, such as complimentary time off.

Toolboxes can be large and elaborate. (©Filip Miletic/Dreamstime.com)

Clientele Interaction. A lot of the clientele interaction in the hand tools industry is based on product demonstration and safety tips. Many of today's hand tools are advanced and updated versions of the hand tools of yesterday. Many sales professionals and even store clerks spend a few minutes with their customers to make sure they are well aware of how their new hand tools should be used, stored, and maintained.

Amenities, Atmosphere, and Physical Grounds. Small hand tools businesses tend to have few amenities. They do not offer the large-scale demonstrations available in some of the larger stores that specialize in hand tools, but there are intimate and often one-on-one interactions between customers and employees. The atmosphere, as is the case with most "mom and pop" companies, tends to be personal and nurturing, since many of the smaller stores want to make sure their customers are informed, safe, and happy with their products. Physical grounds may include a one-room facility with a small storage area, perhaps in the back of the store, for hand tool storage and incoming and outgoing shipments.

Typical Number of Employees. The typical number of employees in small hand tool stores can range from two employees to four. In small establishments, many stores can operate on less than ten employees. A clerk to greet customers and sell products and tools and an owner will suffice in many cases. One- to two-person shops are often successful, particularly in small rural communities. They usually have low turnover rates because many of the businesses are either family-owned companies or locally owned and operated.

Traditional Geographic Locations. Hand tool stores are located in every city in America. Whether it is a large chain like Home Depot, Lowe's, or Handy Dan's or a small family-owned store, hand tool businesses are rarely hard to find. Rural locations or hand tool stores in areas that have a small population are more likely to sell hand tools that are suitable for use on farms and in fields.

Pros of Working for a Small Business. Employees of small companies often know their regular customers by name and are often more knowledgeable about their products. This allows the employees to speak with their customers in detail about the projects they are working on and the tools they will need to complete those projects safely, effectively, and successfully.

Cons of Working for a Small Business. The cons of working in a small business include low pay and the possibility of wearing many hats. For instance, the owner of the establishment is usually also the receptionist, accountant, and clerk. Also, the products available in small businesses may not be as up-to-date or advanced as the tools available in larger stores. Shipments may be fewer for economic reasons. In addition, small hand tool store employees may not get paid sick time, vacation leave, or retirement plans because they simply may not be affordable for the business owner.

Costs

Payroll and Benefits: Small businesses that specialize in hand tools have both full-time and part-time staff, including salaried positions. Hand tool establishments with at least one employee but no more than nineteen employees must cover payroll, fringe benefits—including vacation, sick leave, and possible bonuses—health coverage, and benefit pension plans such as IRAs and 401(k) plans. There must also be a budget for temporary staff and leased employee expenses.

Supplies: Materials, parts, containers, shipping, packaging, and other essentials can cost $1,000 annually. In addition, fuel costs can be quite high. One way that small hand tool companies cut costs is by buying forgings or castings that are semifinished from external suppliers. Large hand tool makers usually manufacture their own.

External Services: Hand tool companies may contract accounting, advertising, cleaning, maintenance, computer support, or landscaping services, as necessary.

Utilities: Hand tool companies generally pay for electricity, water, sewage, refuse removal, telephone, gas or oil, and Internet access.

Taxes: Hand tool companies must pay local, state, and federal corporate and property taxes. Owners of very small companies may claim their income on their personal returns, in which case they must also pay self-employement taxes.

Midsize Businesses

Midsize hand tool businesses offer the same products and services as small businesses, but they offer more of them. They also have bigger budgets, but they often face the same challenges as smaller companies if the economy is in a recession. Imported hand tools from other countries also pose a threat to midsize businesses, just as they do to small hand tool companies.

Potential Annual Earnings Scale. The average earnings for an employee at a midsize company in the hand tools industry vary from state to state, but the salary range in the United States is from $17,000 to $35,000 a year for a clerk and up to $75,000 a year for a store manager or owner of a hand tool and equipment store. Unlike small hand tool companies, midsize establishments experience a seasonal rush during peak times of the year, such as the summer and spring months, when home renovation projects increase. Hand tool store employees that work in midsize businesses are likely to receive regular pay raises or salary increases, if budgets allow.

Clientele Interaction. In midsize hand tool companies, there is a lot of clientele interaction, which is beneficial for both employees and their customers. There are greeters, stockers, account managers, and employees who repair and maintain the supply of tools. There are dozens of employees in midsize businesses who perform a variety of tasks but can sometimes wear more than one hat. One of the benefits of patronizing midsize companies is that the customers are usually regulars who are somewhat familiar with the company's employees. This interaction allows the customers to receive one-on-one care when it comes to questions, product demonstrations, and follow-up visits regarding their tool purchases. Midsize companies also are likely to offer coupons, discounts, reward cards, and sales for their customers.

Amenities, Atmosphere, and Physical Grounds. Midsize hand tool companies may have multilevel facilities that house repair shops to work on damaged or malfunctioning hand tools. There may also be break rooms for members of the staff, as well as show rooms and several areas for certain tools; for example, power tool sections, modern hand tool sections, and sections for older hand tools. There may even be areas for refurbished hand tools.

Typical Number of Employees. The typical number of employees in midsize hand tool stores can range from twenty to forty. These employees are usually longtime members of the team who have benefits—job stability, retirement plans, paid vacation, and sick leave. Employees in midsize hand tool establishments often have opportunities for growth and advancement within the company.

Traditional Geographic Locations. Midsize hand tool stores are usually found in larger cities where there is plenty of room to grow and expand and flourish.

Pros of Working for a Midsize Business. Unlike small businesses, midsize hand tool stores do not have so few employees that they have a hard time keeping up with their regular customers and being familiar with what their patrons need. Midsize hand tool stores are able to deliver to their customers promptly, efficiently, and successfully. These companies are almost always fully stocked with the latest merchandise and receive frequent shipments to keep up with their customers' ever-changing needs.

Cons of Working for a Midsize Business. The cons of working in a midsize business include not having as much access to the latest tools as one would in a large business. Like any other business in any other industry, midsize hand tool companies are not immune to layoffs, downsizing, and taking financial hits when the economy is not booming.

Costs

Payroll and Benefits: Midsize businesses that specialize in hand tools have both full-time and part-time staff, including salaried positions. Hand tool establishments with at least twenty employees but no more than forty employees have to cover payroll, fringe benefits—including vacation, sick leave and possible bonuses—health coverage, and pension plans such as IRAs and 401(k) plans. There must also be a budget for temporary staff and leased employee expenses.

Supplies: Materials, parts, containers, shipping, packaging, and other essentials can cost $1,000 annually. In addition, fuel costs can be quite high. Midsize hand tool makers usually manufacture their own forgings or castings, which can save them money in the long run, though they may still buy forgings or castings that are semi-finished from external suppliers.

External Services: Hand tool companies may contract accounting, advertising, cleaning, maintenance, computer support, or landscaping services, as necessary.

Utilities: Hand tool companies generally pay for electricity, water, sewage, refuse removal, telephone, gas or oil, and Internet access.

Taxes: Hand tool companies must pay local, state, and federal corporate and property taxes.

Large Businesses

American demand for hand tools depends a great deal on the construction and building repair industries. The profitability of individual companies depends on marketing and efficient production. Large companies have economies of scale in purchasing and production.

Potential Annual Earnings Scale. The average earnings for a manager or owner of a large hand tools company can be as much as $100,000 or more annually. An entry-level employee at a large hand tools business can earn anywhere from $10 to $14 an hour or $20,000 to $25,000 a year. The salaries for employees that work in large hand tool businesses usually remain steady because of the nature of the business. Some large hand tool stores may also include bonuses and commissions as part of their employees' salaries, based on their performance and sales. Also, large establishments usually experience a seasonal rush during the holiday season and hurricane and tornado seasons, when repairs and renovations are needed. Hand tool store employees that work in large businesses get full benefits, including bereavement, sick, holiday, personal, and holiday time off.

Clientele Interaction. There is not much clientele interaction in large hand tool stores. Much of the interaction that takes place happens at checkout when the customer is actually making the purchase. Large hand tool stores are often crowded, and customers who need assistance do get the assistance they need, but they may not get as much time with a store employee simply because of the volume of customers in the store at any given time.

Amenities, Atmosphere, and Physical Grounds. Large hand tool companies are usually complex, multilevel establishments. There are acres of land for storage facilities, repair shops within the facility, and loading and unloading docks for outgoing and incoming shipments. There is usually plenty of room for expansion, and there is usually more than one location, since many large hand tool facilities are part of a franchise or chain.

Typical Number of Employees. The typical number of employees in a large hand tool store can range anywhere from forty employees to hundreds of workers. There are several clerks to greet customers as they walk into the store and sales clerks who sell products and tools to customers.

Traditional Geographic Locations. In large metropolitan areas, there are usually well-known store chains such as Lowe's and Home Depot, which specialize in hand tools and equipment for building and maintenance. There are also general stores like Walmart that have departments within the store that feature the latest in hand tools. In smaller communities, there are also stores that are part of a retail chain, but there is usually only one per community.

Pros of Working for a Large Business. Employees of large companies often get frequent shipments of the latest products that the hand tool industry has to offer. Employees are usually stable in their jobs and have plenty of opportunities for professional growth, development, and advancement. In addition, employees of large hand tool companies enjoy full retirement, medical, and other benefits. Employees who work in a large hand tool store often have access to top-of-the-line items that many of the smaller hand tool stores cannot afford or of which they may simply be unaware.

Cons of Working for a Large Business. The cons of working in a large business include serving thousands of different customers each week. This leaves little opportunity for individual interaction with the customers, aside from checking them out at a register when finalizing the sale. Employees in larger hand tool stores also have to keep up with the ever-increasing and ever-changing demand that customers have for hand tools. Also, when the economy takes a downturn and layoffs happen, many employees may be terminated to cut costs.

Costs

Payroll and Benefits: Large businesses that specialize in hand tools have both full-time and part-time staff, including salaried positions. Hand tool establishments with at least forty employees have to cover tens of thousands of dollars in payroll, fringe benefits—including vacation, sick leave, and possible bonuses—health coverage, and pension plans such as IRAs and 401(k) plans. Such expenses can cost large hand tool businesses several million dollars a year. There must also be a budget for temporary staff and leased employee expenses.

Supplies: Materials, parts, containers, shipping, packaging, and other essentials can cost several thousand dollars a year. In addition, fuel costs can be quite high.

External Services: Hand tool companies may contract accounting, advertising, cleaning, maintenance, computer support, or landscaping services, as necessary.

Utilities: Hand tool companies generally pay for electricity, water, sewage, refuse removal, telephone, gas or oil, and Internet access.

Taxes: Hand tool companies must pay local, state, and federal corporate and property taxes.

ORGANIZATIONAL STRUCTURE AND JOB ROLES

The hand tools industry consists of many employee roles. The employees are responsible for the day-to-day operations of a successfully run hand tool business, as well as the management, maintenance, service, and payroll schedule at the establishment. From cashiers to accountants to managers to owners, a lot of hats are worn in the hand tool business. While small hand tool shops may only have one person who serves as the store cashier, mechanic, accountant, and office manager, large hand tool stores have hundreds of employees that can fill such roles as clerk, repairman, order filler, stock room clerk, and so on. There may also be several human resources representatives responsible for interviewing potential employees and hiring new workers. In addition, there are interns, apprentices, builders, product demonstrators, and safety experts on hand to make sure customers know what products they are getting, what the products should be used for, and why they are or are not necessary for their impending projects. These employees, regardless of their role at the hand tool business, all need to be properly oriented and trained in order successfully and efficiently to perform their assigned duties and tasks.

The following umbrella categories apply to the organizational structure of businesses in the hand tools and instruments industry:

- Business Management
- Customer Service
- Facilities and Security
- Production
- Distribution
- Human Resources

Business Management

The business management division centers around aligning all aspects of a company with the wants and needs of its customers. Some of the roles associated with business management include accountants, administrative assistants, receptionists, and secretaries. In larger businesses, roles may also be fiscal analysts, bookkeepers, purchase order clerks, bursars, and file clerks. There are also financial analysts and planners in this division. The business management division of the hand tools business must keep up with each and every transaction that occurs day to day. This department keeps financial order and makes sure that the company stays in the black. The business management department is also responsible for making sure that all taxes are paid at the end of the year; that all licenses are obtained, up to date and renewed regularly; and that all necessary fees are taken care of. The business management office consistently makes sure that all transactions are necessary and beneficial to the establishment. Business management employees at some of the larger companies, for example, work to ensure that the company's revenue is enough to cover regular expenses, including employees' salaries, health insurance costs, maintenance expenses, and unexpected emergencies. Smaller companies may be a one-man-shop that work to bring in just enough money to run the business day to day. Keeping up with the budget from year to year is important so that the company's expenses do not exceed the business's revenue and profits.

Business management occupations may include the following:

- Accountant
- President
- Vice President
- Executive Assistant
- Administrative Assistant
- Industrial Production Manager
- Engineering Manager
- General or Operations Manager

Customer Service

Customer service representatives are responsible for ensuring customer satisfaction from the moment customers enter the establishment to the time they make a purchase and leave the store. Customer service may also interact with customers long after the purchase is made. This follow-up customer service may be done through customer satisfaction surveys and follow-up postcards to the customer's home or even coupons or reward cards for discounts on future purchases at the hand tool store. Customer service positions include quality insurance specialists, the cashiers who actually make the sale, the greeters who are the first to interact with the customer upon entering the store, and even the manager or owner of the establishment, who may have some sort of communication with the customer at some point. Customer service

Many hand tools—such as the chisel—have remained all-purpose and may be used for marking, measuring, striking, and scraping. (©Claudio Fichera/Dreamstime.com)

representatives provide a valuable link between customers and the companies who make the products they buy and the services they use. Most customer service representatives are able to do their work by telephone or in call centers, but some interact with customers by e-mail, fax, or face-to-face. In some cases, a representative's main function may be to determine who in the organization is best suited to answer a customer's questions. In large shops, customer service employees route calls to the appropriate department or person. In smaller stores, customer service may consist of a smile and getting to know their customers on a first-name basis. These skills will come across when it comes to revenue, the number of patrons that visit a store, and certainly the number of patrons that recommend that their friends and family members visit the establishment. Great customer service will also result in patrons revisiting a store regularly, which will result in more business and financial gains in the long run.

Customer service occupations may include the following:

- Customer Relations Manager
- Customer Relations Representative
- Sales Manager
- Sales Representative
- Account Executive
- Account Associate
- Clerk
- Cashier
- Receptionist
- Switchboard Operator

Facilities and Security

Facilities and security staff provide services, technical support, and information for managers. This staff can offer support with regards to the selection of design professionals and contractors, space planning, design development and construction administration. Anything regarding security issues, technology, furnishings, fixtures, and related equipment can also be provided. Facilities and security workers are responsible for the maintenance and upkeep of the facilities and keeping the business safe and secure, yet presentable and professional. This particular division is essential because security keeps the peace and keeps the environment free from any disturbances and inap-

propriate activity. Security not only protects the property from outside disturbances but also controls internal issues such as unruly or disgruntled employees, altercations between employees and customers, and also disturbances caused by break-ins, burglaries, shoplifting, and theft. Such security measures are effective because they are almost always enhanced with hidden surveillance equipment and sensor technology to keep products from being taken out of the store illegally. Facilities workers are necessary for the complicated upkeep of any business. These employees keep lawns manicured, buildings freshly painted, restrooms clean, floors swept and mopped, windows clean, and hallways and walkways clear of clutter and debris. Facilities workers keep general store workers, such as clerks, managers, and customer service representatives, in larger companies, from having to maintain and service the grounds in addition to serving customers and selling equipment and hand tools to patrons. A list of associated roles in this division includes security officers, janitorial employees including landscapers, maintenance employees, and general groundskeepers.

Facilities and security occupations include the following:

- Groundskeeper
- Maintenance and Repair Worker
- Loss Prevention Specialist
- Inventory Clerk
- Security Supervisor
- Security Guard

Production

Production personnel have the task of producing and overseeing the producers of hand tools. These workers manufacture wrenches, hammers, scissors, vises, clamps, screwdrivers, pliers, chisels, and measuring devices. Manufacturers rely on an array of fabrication processes, including bending, forming, and machining, to transform metal into finished products. Production and operations roles include assembly-line workers, producers, operations managers, and production managers and assistants. Perhaps one of the most important roles is that of chief operating officer (COO). The chief operating officer is responsible for integrating production, inventory, logistics, and transportation activities; lowering manufacturing costs; innovating in new

OCCUPATION PROFILE

Machinist

Considerations	Qualifications
Description	Makes metal parts and goods in numbers too small to produce with automated machinery but that must still meet precise specifications, sets up and operates machines in order to make metal and nonmetal parts, and fits and assembles the parts into complete units.
Career clusters	Agriculture, Food, and Natural Resources; Manufacturing
Interests	Data; things
Working conditions	Work inside
Minimum education level	Apprenticeship
Physical exertion	Medium work
Physical abilities	Unexceptional/basic fitness
Opportunities for experience	Internship; apprenticeship; military service
Licensure and certification	Recommended
Employment outlook	Decline expected
Holland interest score	RIE

Note: See volume 1, "Publisher's Note," for an explanation of the Holland interest score.

production and service techniques and processes; building standardized and streamlined processes to provide stable, consistent, and quality products; eliminating unnecessary production activities; and identifying key drivers of cost, risk, expenses, business growth, competition, quality, and profits, to name just a few duties. All these workers help ensure that products in the hand tools industry are made safely, efficiently, effectively, and quickly.

Production occupations may include the following:

- Chief Operating Officer (COO)
- Industrial Production Manager
- Industrial Engineer
- Production Supervisor
- Team Assembler
- Computer-Controlled Machine Tool Operator
- Machine Operator
- Machinist
- Tool and Die Maker

Distribution

The distribution department's function is to generate and print a pick list, pull products from inventory, box up products for shipping, and create and send a shipping label and bill to the accounting department and freight company. Distribution centers are run by general managers and middle managers, who oversee direct labor staffs and indirect labor staffs. The direct labor staff executes the distribution processes, while the indirect labor staff supports the direct labor staff.

The associated roles of a warehouse can include unloaders, who unload trucks and break down pallets as needed; receivers, who inventory and tag unloaded pallets; haulers, who transport received pal-

OCCUPATION PROFILE

Robotics Technician

Considerations	Qualifications
Description	Installs, services, troubleshoots, maintains, and repairs robots and robot systems used in such jobs as spray painting, welding, assembly, die casting, machine loading and unloading, plastic molding, forging, and heat treating.
Career clusters	Manufacturing; Science, Technology, Engineering, and Math
Interests	Data; things
Working conditions	Work inside
Minimum education level	On-the-job training; high school diploma/technical training; junior/technical/community college
Physical exertion	Light work
Physical abilities	Unexceptional/basic fitness
Opportunities for experience	Internship
Licensure and certification	Recommended
Employment outlook	Slower-than-average growth expected
Holland interest score	REC

Note: See volume 1, "Publisher's Note," for an explanation of the Holland interest score.

lets with equipment from the receiving dock to the storage racks; putaway drivers, who put products into racks with forklifts; replenishment drivers, who pull products from the racks and place them into the "pick slot" with a forklift; order-fillers, who pick products from the "pick slot" by hand and move them with power equipment; and loaders, who wrap order-filled pallets and load trucks.

Distribution occupations may include the following:

- Warehouse Manager
- Distribution Manager
- Distribution Worker
- Freight Loader/Unloader
- Shipping and Receiving Clerk
- Heavy Truck Driver
- Delivery Truck Driver
- Dispatcher

Human Resources

Human resources (HR) workers are responsible for finding and retaining qualified employees in the hand tools industry. Traditionally, the role of the HR professional in many companies has been to serve as the systematizing, policing arm of executive management. In this role, the HR team member also served executive agendas, such as addressing complaints of sexual harassment, discrimination, criminal activity, or unfair treatment by another employee or supervisor. These employees post newly created and vacant positions, contact potential employees for job interviews, screening and interviewing potential applicants and setting up drug screenings and physical examinations if required to fulfill the duties of a job. Also, HR workers are responsible for making sure that newly hired employees fill out all necessary paperwork, including retirement papers, investment forms, federal paperwork, payroll deductions, and other new hire forms. Associated HR roles include assistants and managers, shared services employees, and HR generalists. HR specialists are essential to any business because they help companies maintain a full staff. HR workers also keep employee paperwork updated and filed in an orderly manner and also set up training and training seminars for employees who want to develop and enhance their job skills. HR workers also process payroll information and keep track of employees' sick time, vacation request forms, personal time off and any overtime hours accrued. More often than not, HR is the first department that potential workers and newly hired workers see, and are the initial point of contact for employees.

HR occupations may include the following:

- Human Resources Manager
- Human Resources Generalist
- Benefits Specialist
- Administrative Assistant

INDUSTRY OUTLOOK

Overview

The outlook for the hand tools and instruments industry shows it to be rising rapidly. Power and hand tool demand in the United States is predicted to increase by more than 3 percent per year through 2012. This projected increase in demand is partly due to the construction outlook, as building construction is expected to increase as well. DIY popularity will contribute to consumer demand, in addition to home renovation and refurbishment projects. Steady introduction of new products—particularly improved cordless tools—will also create gains in all hand tool markets.

Increased competition from imported hand tools has certainly had a negative impact on U.S. production. Asian countries are leading suppliers of power and hand tools because of low labor cost advantages compared to the price of labor in the United States. China has become the major source of American imports. U.S. production of electric tools has been surprisingly decreased by outsourcing of production to lower-cost countries across the globe. Maintaining established trends, power tool demand is forecast to outpace hand tool demand as a result of the continuing popularity of

cordless electric products such as chain saws, power drills, sanders, wood polishers, and grinders. Hand tool demand is limited by the durability of these newer and updated products.

One of the major advantages of hand tools that makes them particularly attractive to users is their durability. Hand tools such as hammers and wrenches very seldom break. This fact lowers the demand for replacements for such products. Another thing that is appealing about hand tools is that they are cheaper than power tools. The cost of hand tools plays a big role in consumer demand, especially in markets with older families and customers who are on fixed incomes or live in rural areas, where hand tools are needed often but pay raises are few. In addition, product innovation is less common than in power tools, limiting opportunities for value gains.

Cordless products will continue to post the best gains, benefiting not only from macroeconomic factors but also from performance advantages over plug-in models. The development of better battery technology, such as lithium-ion chemistry, has encouraged both consumers and professionals to use cordless technology. Consumer hand tool demand will grow faster than will demand for professional tools, benefiting from the ongoing popularity of DIY activities and the desire of consumers to trade up to power tools that boast many features. In addition, the tightening of mortgage markets in the United States will compel many homeowners to remain in their current homes rather than purchasing new ones. This trend will boost home remodeling and repair activity. Although growing more slowly than consumer demand, professional demand will continue to account for the majority of overall tool demand through 2012. Professionals use a greater variety of tools, most of which are also more expensive than those used by consumers.

Employment Advantages

Although the domestic hand tool industry is being challenged by foreign competition, the boom in power tool sales, and the new market for digital hand tools, there are plenty of advantages to working in the hand tool industry. Americans will always need and use hand tools, whether standard wrenches or new and improved chisels. There will always be a demand for such tools. Home improvements will always be made and so will renovations to tool sheds, farm houses, and other facilities. For these tasks, many Americans prefer hand tools because they require little maintenance. Hand tools also require little training. In today's DIY age, homeowners want to take control of their maintenance and building needs. There will always be a need for men and women who understand the importance of hand tools and their numerous uses. With new technology, there will be opportunities for growth, training, and advancement in the hand tools industry.

Annual Earnings

The domestic U.S. hand tool industry earned revenues of $5.9 billion in 2009. Annual international revenues were $12.3 billion, while annual global revenues were $19.87 billion, an increase of more than 4 percent from 2006. These revenues are expected to continue growing, as the economy improves and the market for hand tools grows and expands.

RELATED RESOURCES FOR FURTHER RESEARCH

ANTIQUE TOOLS AND TRADES IN CONNECTICUT
61 Hawthorne
Fairfield, CT 06825
Tel: (203) 453-4281
Fax: (203) 371-4701
http://www.attic-us.org

HAND TOOLS INSTITUTE
25 N Broadway
Tarrytown, NY 10591
Tel: (914) 332-0040
Fax: (914) 332-1541
http://www.hti.org

MISSOURI VALLEY WRENCH CLUB
7913 SW 24th St.
Halstead, KS 67056
Tel: (316) 283-5876
Fax: (316) 284-7345
http://www.mvwc.org

POTOMAC ANTIQUE TOOLS AND INDUSTRIES
ASSOCIATION
6802 Nesbitt Place
McLean, VA 22101

Tel: (301) 253-4892
http://www.patinatools.org

TOOLS OF THE TRADE MAGAZINE
1 Thomas Circle NW, Suite 600
Washington, DC 20005
Tel: (202) 452-0800
Fax: (202) 785-1974
http://www.toolsofthetrade.net

ABOUT THE AUTHOR

Ramonica R. Jones has more than ten years of professional experience as a general-assignment reporter and media-relations writer. She is a 1999 cum laude graduate of Huston-Tillotson University in Austin, Texas, and also attended Texas Southern University's Graduate School of Communications in Houston, Texas. Jones has written numerous articles about many industries, including city, county, and state business dealings, product manufacturing, and the American economy. Throughout her career, she has consulted with experts in both the public and private sectors.

FURTHER READING

Chuang, Steve. "Digital Tools to Drive Growth of Taiwan's Hand Tool Industry." China Economic News Service, November, 2009. http://cens.net/cens/html/en/news/news_inner_30792.html.

Chylinski, Manya. *Career Launcher: Manufacturing.* New York: Ferguson, 2010.

Korn, Peter. *The Woodworker's Guide to Hand Tools.* Newtown, Conn.: Taunton Press, 1997.

Leseure, Michel J. "Manufacturing Strategies in the Hand Tool Industry." *International Journal of Operations and Production Management* 20, no. 12 (2000): 1475-1487.

Mintel International Group. *DIY Review.* London: Author, 2008.

Trotman Real Life Guides. *Manufacturing and Product Design.* Richmond, England: Author, 2009.

U.S. Bureau of Labor Statistics. *Career Guide to Industries,* 2010-2011 ed. http://www.bls.gov/oco/cg.

U.S. Census Bureau. North American Industry Classification System (NAICS), 2007. http://www.census.gov/cgi-bin/sssd/naics/naicsrch?chart=2007.

U.S. Department of Commerce. International Trade Administration. Office of Trade and Industry Information. Industry Trade Data and Analysis. http://ita.doc.gov/td/industry/otea/OTII/OTII-index.html.

Vereen, Bob. *Surviving in Spite of Everything: A Postwar History of the Hardware Industry.* Indianapolis: Dog Ear, 2010.

Watson, Aldren A. *Hand Tools: Their Ways and Workings.* New York: W. W. Norton, 1982.

Health and Fitness Industry

©Lougassi Gilles/Dreamstime.com

INDUSTRY DEFINITION

Summary

The health and fitness industry comprises facilities that offer exercise and recreational activities. Considered part of the amusement and recreation sector, this industry includes small aerobic dance or body building studios and large clubs that offer exercise, racket sports, and skating opportunities. These facilities may be found in a variety of locations, including communities, hospitals, corporations, and hotels, as well as cruise ships. Although the industry operates predominantly in the more economically developed areas of the world, it can be found worldwide, employing people as fitness leaders, managers, clerks, and maintenance workers.

History of the Industry

The value of fitness dates back to prehistoric times, when physical abilities were important for survival. Fitness as an optional activity evolved in early civilizations throughout the world. Ancient Greece is well known for using exercise to promote aesthetics and health. Its fitness facilities were called palaestra and gymnasiums, and paidotribes—similar to a modern-day fitness trainers—led men and boys in gymnastics, running, jumping, and wrestling. In ancient China, gymnastics and wrestling were promoted, and in ancient India a popular form of gymnastics called yoga was developed.

In the United States, fitness grew slowly at first. During the colonial period, most people performed hard, physical labor on farms. They became fit without having to engage in exercise or fitness training. By the early 1800's, Europe had organized physical education programs for children, while the U.S. education system was still focusing on the mind. In the 1880's, the Young Men's Christian Association (YMCA, now known as the Y) began building gyms and pools in its buildings. These facilities were among the first in the health and fitness industry.

With the development of machines that reduced the amount of physical labor required by workers, more people became unfit. The value of physical activity became more apparent. At a time when more physical education programs were developed in the United States, sports were gaining popularity too. A debate started about whether physical education should be geared toward the development of general health or specific sport skills. Sport skills became the focus in the early years.

By the advent of World War I, the fitness industry had still not fully emerged in the United States. Evaluating data after the war revealed that one in three draftees had been physically unfit for battle. Efforts to increase physical education in schools were emphasized again. However, the Great Depression began, and physical activity continued to be a relatively low priority. When World War II began, the Americans who were drafted were still unfit as a group. After the war was over, the nation renewed its focus on physical fitness and health. Dr. Thomas K. Cureton at the University of Illinois began scientifically studying the effects of exercise on the human body. More specifically, he studied what type of exercise was needed to produce health benefits.

In the 1950's, two events had profound impacts on the emerging fitness industry. In response to the lack of fitness of soldiers in World War II, a large study was conducted on the fitness levels of school children. The results were troubling, and President Dwight D. Eisenhower created the President's Council on Physical Fitness and Sports. In

Larger health and fitness clubs offer studio exercise classes, including spinning classes. (©Andres Rodgriguez/Dreams-time.com)

the same decade, Jack LaLanne began a fitness television show in San Francisco that was eventually broadcast nationally by the American Broadcasting Company (ABC). LaLanne was a major player in taking the fitness movement nationwide. Prior to his television show, he opened his first health spa in 1936. His chain of health spas grew into the hundreds by 1980. He also developed exercise equipment whose designs are the basis of present-day exercise equipment.

Fitness in the United States boomed in the late 1960's, when Dr. Kenneth H. Cooper published his book, *Aerobics* (1968). The health benefits of exercise were becoming apparent to the masses across the nation. Further promotion of the President's Council on Physical Fitness and Sports by President John F. Kennedy also helped create a young generation of physically active people, accelerating the development of the U.S. health and fitness industry.

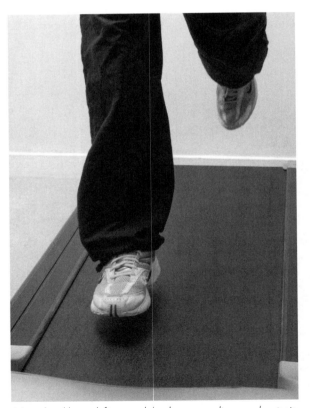

Most health and fitness clubs have cardiovascular training equipment, including treadmills. (©Adam Edwards/Dreamstime.com)

The Industry Today

Health and fitness facilities come in many sizes and are located both separately from and within many other industries. Some are small, individually owned facilities with limited programs, while others are large, national chains with extensive programs. Many health and fitness centers are distributed throughout communities and target the general populations of those communities. These include privately owned clubs, large national chains, hospital-owned and -operated complexes, municipal recreation centers, Ys, Young Women's Christian Associations (YWCAs), and Jewish Community Centers (JCCs). Other health and fitness centers target more specific groups. Corporations and other workplaces have facilities and programs for their employees. Retirement homes offer programs and facilities for older people. Many colleges and universities have recreational facilities for their students and employees that include health and fitness programs. Hotels, resorts, and cruise ships also operate health and fitness clubs for their guests. Any of these fitness centers may employ fitness trainers, aerobics instructors, managers, sales representatives, lifeguards, janitors, receptionists, and maintenance workers.

The largest health and fitness centers offer the most programs and services. They are more likely to have swimming pools, gymnasiums, racquetball courts, and running tracks. Some specialty clubs may have climbing walls, ice or roller skating rinks, turf fields, and wave pools. Most, however, have cardiovascular training equipment that could include treadmills, stationary bicycles, climbers, elliptical trainers, and rowing machines. There are many variations of these types of equipment, and the large centers usually have the most variety. Larger centers also have the most variety of weight training equipment, which may include free weights and selectorized, weight-stacked equipment.

Larger health and fitness clubs also offer many studio exercise classes. New types of classes are constantly being developed, and larger clubs are able to offer more options. Besides the original choreographed dance, some of the more popular classes include water aerobics, yoga, Pilates, boxing and other martial arts, step, weight equipment, and cycling or spinning.

Fitness assessments are commonly offered by health and fitness clubs. Assessments are beneficial

Personal trainers are fitness professionals who develop specific exercise programs tailored for individuals and then personally manage their clients' workouts. (©Dreamstime.com)

for determining a person's fitness level prior to beginning a fitness program or to periodically measure improvements (or lack of improvements) resulting from individuals' exercise programs. Such information is important to determine whether programs are accomplishing their intended goals or whether changes need to be made. Fitness assessments may include measurements of body composition, cardiovascular endurance, muscular endurance, strength, flexibility, balance, power, and agility.

An increasing number of consumers are employing personal trainers, either at health and fitness clubs or at home. Personal trainers are fitness professionals who develop specific exercise programs tailored for individuals and then personally manage their clients' workouts. They first assess clients' fitness levels. Then, trainers work with their clients to determine the specific goals of their exercise programs. Trainers develop exercise prescriptions with precise details for each exercise session.

In most cases, they direct exercisers throughout their sessions to verify proper technique and to motivate them to work hard. This one-on-one service is labor-intensive and therefore is more expensive than group training.

Many of the large health and fitness centers offer spa services. Spas focus on relaxing and healing. Many people find spa services appealing after hard workouts. The most common spa services in fitness centers include massage and skin care. Several types of massage can be offered, including Swedish massage, sports massage, aromatherapy massage, reflexology, and shiatsu. Standard skin services may include scrubs, wraps, peels, waxing, and moisturizing. Hydrotherapy can benefit both relaxation and skin. Some in-center spas also offer hair and nail care.

After exercise, people can be hungry and thirsty. Larger health and fitness clubs may have small restaurants or cafeterias. Generally, these establishments offer nominally healthy food and drink options in keeping with fitness centers' missions. Sport drinks, yogurt, low-fat soups, and sandwiches are most common. Light, healthy breakfast foods are also offered, since many people exercise early in the morning. In addition to prepared foods, many clubs sell nutritional supplements. Since exercisers tend to be health conscious, they are likely to purchase these products.

Some fitness centers provide towels and offer laundry service; others may have little more than drinking fountains. (©Lougassi Gilles/Dreamstime.com)

Some health and fitness facilities provide child care while parents exercise. These require dedicated child-care areas and staffs. Others offer towel services to their patrons. Others, although fewer, may also provide workout clothes. Therefore, some facilities also have laundries. Some clubs may use laundry services, but many have their own laundries to reduce costs.

Large, midsize, or small health and fitness centers must be prepared to change with the changing fitness market. New types of equipment are constantly being produced. New types of exercise programs are being developed. To keep members happy, health and fitness clubs must be willing to change to meet their members' new expectations. Interest in fitness is growing among people all around the world, making the outlook in the fitness industry very exciting for the organizations that stay creative and focus on the future.

INDUSTRY MARKET SEGMENTS

The health and fitness industry ranges in size from small spas to mega fitness centers that serve communities, employees, travelers, retirees, and students. While each of the larger health and fitness facilities offers many programs and services, the smaller facilities are more focused. Since they cannot offer as many programs and services as their larger competitors, smaller clubs target specific segments of the exercising community. Some may simply be studios that offer group fitness classes. Others may offer only free weights for building muscle. One national chain offers primarily a circuit training program for women. Midsize health and fitness clubs may offer several exercise options. The mega clubs can offer almost everything. Smaller clubs usually offer fewer services: Food services may be limited to sports drinks and nutritional supplements, and spa and laundry services may not exist. The different segments of the health and fitness industry are analyzed in the sections below.

Small Businesses

Privately owned spas and health and fitness clubs generally are single facilities that serve the same clientele as the larger organizations and national chains. While membership costs may not be significantly different at small clubs, each club specializes in a few types of exercise rather than offering a large selection. Self-employed personal trainers also fall into this business segment.

Potential Annual Earnings Scale. According to the U.S. Bureau of Labor Statistics (BLS), personal fitness trainers and aerobics instructors earned an average of $42,170 in 2009, while those employed by fitness and recreation centers earned an average of $36,710. In the United States, owners of well-run small health and fitness clubs can earn $100,000 per year and more.

Clientele Interaction. Small spas and clubs offer more intimate relationships between staff and clients than do larger centers. Since these clubs have fewer members and more focused program offerings, all people involved get to know one another better. Instructors are better able to understand the fitness needs and desires of their clients and can provide a personal touch that attracts certain individuals to their clubs. Depending on the focus of a club's offerings, certain amenities may be offered. The combination of limited but specific program offerings with complimentary amenities can be appealing to a specific niche market, resulting in a successful business operation.

Amenities, Atmosphere, and Physical Grounds. Small fitness facilities generally offer fewer amenities than their larger counterparts, so those offered are usually strategic. The major amenities are offered in locker rooms, where they exist. Quality showers with sinks and hair dryers are more standard than at larger facilities with more institutional locker rooms. Toiletries offered may include soap, shampoo, conditioner, shaving cream, disposable razors, skin creams, and lotions. Many fitness centers also offer entertainment during exercise, primarily cable television. Clubs may offer bottled water, water coolers, or simply drinking fountains.

Successful small spas and clubs generally serve small niche markets. Therefore, the atmosphere of such facilities is very important and designed to appeal to a smaller subset of exercisers. No two in a given area will be the same. The key is to create the right combination of atmosphere, programs, and amenities for potential clients.

Health and fitness businesses carefully design their indoor facilities and exercise programs. Many small operations are located in strip malls. Sometimes, outside exercise areas are offered. However, in the smaller facilities this is less likely to be the case. The most important aspect of exterior grounds is parking. Even though people are going to these clubs to work out, they do not want to spend time walking to and from their cars.

Typical Number of Employees. Small health and fitness businesses employ small full-time staffs, engaging part-time employees as necessary to ensure all necessary work gets done. Owners may be the only full-time workers in such businesses. They may manage all day-to-day operations and employ part-time workers to teach specific classes, staff front desks, clean and maintain equipment, and perform other duties that do not justify the expenses of full-time positions. Using this approach allows owners to staff their facilities fully only during peak hours and to engage few or no assistants during low-demand hours.

Traditional Geographic Locations. Small spas and health and fitness clubs can be found anywhere there are enough people to make them profitable. This includes large cities, suburban areas, and small towns. In large cities and suburban areas, smaller facilities cater to niche markets, while in small towns they may be the only facilities available—and offer more options than do small urban facilities.

Pros of Working for a Small Fitness Club. Small clubs provide their employees and owners greater autonomy than do larger clubs. Owners control hours of operation, programs offered, equipment available, decor, and other factors. Although they need to understand the fitness field and degrees in health and fitness are useful, owners of small clubs do not need to have the advanced degrees required by many larger organizations. Owners and managers also typically have a variety of responsibilities, including not only fitness operations but also business administration and facility maintenance. Some background in sales and marketing, accounting, and maintenance is therefore beneficial.

Cons of Working for a Small Fitness Club. Small clubs offer little or no opportunity for promotion. Employees can be limited to the same responsibilities for many years. Owners and managers can expand their roles only by adding new facilities, which can be expensive and risky.

Costs

Payroll and Benefits: Small health and fitness clubs typically pay employees hourly wages or pay instructors by the class. Benefits such as health care, retirement, sick leave, and vacation are typically limited and are offered at the discretion of the owner. Small-business owners and personal trainers pay themselves out of their profits, and their income is dependent on their businesses' consistent profitability.

Supplies: Health and fitness clubs require exercise equipment, maintenance tools, and cleaning supplies. They also need office materials such as paper, pens, phones, and computers. Some also provide toiletries such as soap, shampoo, towels, and other personal items. Personal trainers need vehicles and cell phones or other mobile communications devices.

External Services: Depending on the skills of their owners and managers, small clubs may need few external services. However, they may contract external, specialized fitness instructors, equipment maintenance, or business support services such as accounting, marketing, or legal counsel.

Utilities: Health and fitness centers typically require water, sewage, electricity, natural gas or oil, telephone, cable television, and Internet access.

Taxes: Small health and fitness facilities are required to pay local, state, and federal income taxes, as well as property taxes. Small-business owners may pay these as taxes on personal income rather than through their businesses. In many states, a sales tax is levied on membership fees and monthly dues, as well as on any retail products sold.

Midsize Businesses

Midsize health and fitness facilities offer multiple exercise options to their members. Typically, they include areas with cardiovascular machines, weight-training areas, and often group exercise rooms. Some may offer one or two additional specialized programs as well.

Potential Annual Earnings Scale. According to the BLS, fitness trainers and aerobics instructors employed by fitness and recreation centers earned an average of $36,710 in 2009, while massage therapists earned $41,830. General managers of fitness centers earned an average of $80,830.

Clientele Interaction. Personal contact between fitness trainers and their clients is always very important. Communication helps maintain members' commitment to a given club and gives trainers the opportunity to provide assistance, which can make exercise programs safer and more beneficial. As facilities increase in size, patrons interact less with management. Since managers are often busy handling many other issues, fitness trainers generally stand in for managers, routinely communicating with their clients and conveying any in-

formation that managers need to know about. As exercise trainers assume greater client-interaction responsibilities, managers must train and empower them to successfully perform this function.

Amenities, Atmosphere, and Physical Grounds. Locker rooms in midsize health and fitness clubs are generally more lavish than those in smaller facilities. Because they experience a higher volume of exercisers, midsize clubs find it feasible to expand locker rooms both in size and in amenities. Consumable amenities such as soaps and toiletries depend more on a given club's clients' desires and target market than on its size. Entertainment offered during exercise is often superior to that offered by smaller clubs. More television monitors and cable channels may be offered. Some of the more expensive exercise equipment can have an individual television built into each unit. Few midsize facilities offer food services. However, many have vending machines with healthy snacks, water, and sports drinks available for their members.

The atmosphere of health and fitness centers becomes less personal as the facilities grow in size and membership. At larger facilities with more employees and members, there is less likelihood of seeing the same people on a regular basis and developing personal relationships with them. However, it remains important for employees to make personal contacts, so members feel connected to their clubs and the employees get feedback on their exercise programs and techniques. Also, members must work harder to connect with others for exercise companionship. Fitness trainers need to help connect people with common interests to maintain a positive social atmosphere within their facilities.

Many health and fitness facilities are located in strip malls. Some are freestanding structures; however, there is generally limited value placed on the grounds. The important factor is good, convenient parking. In a few facilities, outside exercise is offered and exterior grounds are more important. If their locations are suitable, some clubs may provide running maps of their local areas for those who would prefer to run or walk outside as part of their exercise sessions.

Typical Number of Employees. Midsize facilities can employ up to fifty or one hundred people, and they generally employ more of their staffs full time than do small clubs. They rely less on contracted instructors since they offer enough classes to employ instructors full time. Some workers may still be employed part time to increase the flexibility of scheduling and to reduce costs.

Traditional Geographic Locations. Midsize health and fitness clubs are typically found in larger cities and suburban areas, where the population base is large enough to support them. Many are located on heavily traveled roads where their visibility is high. The cost of real estate in such locations is typically much higher, however, so some facilities are located on less-traveled streets.

Pros of Working for a Midsize Fitness Club. Midsize health and fitness facilities provide workers with more opportunities for full-time employment and professional advancement than do small businesses. Since these clubs offer a greater number of programs and exercise options, it is easier for them to fill full-time employees' schedules, provided employees have the right combination of skills. The varied nature of such schedules is also advantageous for employees who prefer to have variety in their work. Midsize clubs are large enough to employ staff at various levels of responsibility, providing opportunities for promotion.

Cons of Working for a Midsize Fitness Club. Midsize health and fitness facilities have more, and more diverse, members. Fitness trainers in particular must make an effort to get to know all the people exercising at their clubs. While doing so may be more challenging than it is at a small club, some employees may find this feature attractive. Midsize health and fitness centers also have more management issues. With more employees performing more specialized functions, more coordination is needed, and employees must often attend formal meetings.

Costs

Payroll and Benefits: Midsize health and fitness facilities hire many staff at hourly wages but also have some salaried employees. Benefits such as medical insurance, retirement, vacation, and sick leave are offered by some organizations.

Supplies: Health and fitness clubs require exercise equipment, maintenance tools, cleaning supplies, and audiovisual equipment. They also need office materials such as paper, pens, phones, and computers. Some also provide toiletries such as soap, shampoo, towels, and other personal items. Products for vending machines may also be needed.

External Services: Midsize health and fitness centers may contract equipment maintenance, custodial services, laundry, accounting, computer and audiovisual support, credit card processing, or vending machine stocking and maintenance.

Utilities: Health and fitness centers pay for water, sewage, electricity, natural gas or oil, telephone, cable television, and Internet access.

Taxes: Midsize health and fitness facilities are required to pay local, state, and federal income taxes, as well as property taxes. In many states, a sales tax is levied on membership fees and monthly dues, as well as on any products or special services that are sold.

Large Businesses

Large health and fitness centers are often chains, but a few are privately owned. They are very large operations that include cardiovascular fitness and weight training areas and a multitude of specialized programs. Many may also include specialized facilities such as racquetball courts, skating rinks, swimming pools, or turf fields.

Potential Annual Earnings Scale. According to the BLS, fitness trainers and aerobics instructors employed by fitness and recreation centers earned an average of $36,710 in 2009, while massage therapists earned $41,830. General managers of fitness centers earned an average of $80,830. At large businesses, salaries may be significantly above these averages.

Clientele Interaction. Large health and fitness centers have so many members that it is difficult for employees to maintain regular one-on-one interactions with everyone. Despite having many activities and exercise options, each member typically focuses on just a few. Therefore, fitness trainers in specific areas tend to see the same people often and may never see other members, who patronize other areas. It is important for trainers to establish working relationships with the members who exercise in their programs in order to encourage their continued participation and verify proper exercise techniques.

Amenities, Atmosphere, and Physical Grounds. Many amenities may be offered by large health and fitness facilities. Locker rooms are generally roomy and offer various toiletries and towel service. Some fitness centers have food service operations that include snack bars, cafeterias, or restaurants. They may sell exercise clothing and equipment in small retail shops. Others may include spas that offer massage and hair and nail care, as well as simple lounges for relaxation after exercise. Entertainment is generally available during exercise: Large televisions on walls or small televisions on individual exercise machines are common.

Large health and fitness centers are spacious and offer many options for their members. Their size, however, tends to make the atmosphere less personable. This poses a challenge for employees seeking to create a more intimate feel. Receptionists need to greet all members when they arrive and be ready to answer questions. Fitness trainers need to take the time to get to know the members who exercise in their program areas, so the members do not get lost in the large surroundings and so members get the personal attention needed to exercise safely and effectively. Customer service is an important component of all employees' jobs.

Large health and fitness centers may be located in high rises in major cities, or they may be self-contained suburban facilities with expansive lawns, woods, or gardens. Outdoor running trails, swimming pools, and tennis courts may be important parts of such complexes. Convenient parking or access on public transportation is required, and some facilities may offer valet parking.

Typical Number of Employees. Large fitness centers may employ more than one hundred people.

Traditional Geographic Locations. Large health and fitness clubs are usually found near large population centers. Those that have expansive grounds are generally outside or on the perimeters of large cities. Since these facilities have large memberships and tend to be destination clubs, they are often not located on highly traveled streets.

Pros of Working for a Large Fitness Center. A major benefit of large health and fitness clubs is variety. Because they offer many programs and services, employees have many different opportunities. To manage their large facilities, these clubs adopt compartmentalized structures, so employees can focus their work and training in specific ar-

eas. Since many of these facilities are part of chains, they offer significantly greater opportunities for promotion and other forms of career advancement. They may also enable employees to transfer among branches, allowing them to move without giving up their jobs. Employees also have opportunities to move laterally, from one department or program to another, enabling them to develop new skills and minimize the staleness of performing the same job functions for years. Furthermore, large organizations provide more training and development programs for their employees.

Cons of Working for a Large Fitness Center. Operating a large health and fitness club presents many unique challenges. Large facilities have more maintenance issues, and they experience significant changes in the volume of participants throughout the day that must be managed to maximize service while minimizing costs. Customer service is very important, and regular evaluations and trainings are required. Employees have a larger and more diverse clientele to understand and support. Club managers must administer a wide variety of programs and services that require a variety of skills.

Costs

Payroll and Benefits: Since there are many employees and job classifications in large health and fitness facilities, pay structures can be complicated. Managers at all levels are generally salaried. Receptionists, cleaning staff, retail personnel, and food service workers are usually hourly. Fitness trainers may be either salaried or hourly. Membership salespersons may work on commission. Benefits are offered at the discretion of management, with salaried personnel most likely to receive medical insurance, retirement plans, vacation time, and sick leave.

Supplies: Large health and fitness clubs require exercise equipment, maintenance tools, cleaning supplies, office supplies, toiletries, food products, audiovisual equipment, and communication and information technology. Those with grounds may need lawn mowers and other landscaping materials.

External Services: Large health and fitness centers may contract exercise equipment maintenance, custodial services, laundry, accounting, computer and audiovisual support, credit card processing, lawn and landscaping services, and vending machine stocking and maintenance.

Utilities: Large health and fitness centers typically pay for water, sewage, electricity, natural gas or oil, telephone, cable television, and Internet access.

Taxes: Large health and fitness facilities are required to pay local, state, and federal income taxes, as well as property taxes. In many states, a sales tax is levied on membership fees and monthly dues, as well as on any extra products and services that are sold.

ORGANIZATIONAL STRUCTURE AND JOB ROLES

The organization and job functions of health and fitness clubs vary with the size of the facility. A small club or spa may have only one full-time employee who manages the whole operation and performs many different tasks. As the size of the business increases there is a manager in charge who delegates responsibilities to other employees. All sizes of health and fitness clubs have similar job functions that must be completed by someone.

The following umbrella categories apply to the organizational structure of businesses in the health and fitness industry:

- Executive Management
- Sales and Marketing
- Fitness Operations
- Aquatics
- Recreation and Sports
- Reception
- Child Care
- Locker Room Attendants
- Personal Care
- Physical Therapy
- Food and Beverage Service
- Retail Sales
- Cleaning and Maintenance
- Groundskeeping
- Administrative Support

Executive Management

The general operations of health and fitness clubs are directed by executive managers. All facili-

ties have club managers, who are responsible for all the operations, planning, and supervision. In stand-alone clubs, managers are the chief executives. In chain facilities, club managers report to central offices that direct the operations of all clubs in the organization.

Club managers supervise all employees of their clubs. Larger clubs may employ department managers, who are supervised by club managers. Club managers are responsible for club operations, while department managers are responsible for the functions of their departments.

Club managers are generally the highest-paid employees of their clubs. Many have advanced degrees in fitness or business. To become a club manager, it is important to develop a good understanding of all operations in the health and fitness industry, as well as developing general business skills.

Executive management occupations may include the following:

- Owner-operator
- Club Manager
- Operations Manager
- Marketing Manager
- Food Service Manager
- Financial Manager

Sales and Marketing

One of the most critical functions in health and fitness club management is maintaining a solid membership base. Most club revenues come from initiation fees and membership dues. Other revenues depend on members being on the premises to purchase additional products and services. Therefore, membership sales is one of the most vital departments of a club.

Larger health and fitness clubs may have sales and marketing departments. Smaller operations may rely on their managers to handle marketing and sales functions. Marketing personnel typically have degrees in business. They develop marketing plans, including advertisements and promotions. Membership salespersons may have college degrees but must have good interpersonal and sales skills. Some clubs offer commissions on sales to their employees. Marketing and sales managers are among the highest-paid employees within the health and fitness industry after club managers.

Sales and marketing occupations may include the following:

- Marketing Manager
- Membership Sales Manager
- Advertising and Promotions Manager
- Retail Sales Manager

Fitness Operations

The primary operations of health and fitness centers are carried out by the employees who design and direct exercise programs and classes. Fitness trainers have a wide variety of responsibilities that include orienting new members, assessing fitness levels, writing exercise prescriptions, supervising cardiovascular and strength training areas, leading specialized classes, and training clients one-on-one. Some trainers may perform a variety of these functions, while others may focus on one or two.

Clubs prefer fitness trainers to have at least undergraduate degrees in the exercise and fitness area. Associate's degrees and certifications are also preferred. The average fitness trainer makes more than $35,000 per year. Entry-level positions pay closer to $20,000 per year. The highest-paid fitness trainers are usually personal trainers. Personal trainers can charge $60 or more per hour. However, those that work at health and fitness clubs must give a share to their billable payments to those clubs, up to 50 percent. The average income of personal trainers is over $42,000 per year. Nevertheless, personal trainers who have full client lists and who are willing to work long hours can earn more than $100,000 per year.

Aerobics instructors lead group classes in a specific type of exercise. Many different classes have been offered. Traditionally, these classes were dance oriented. However, now there are hundreds of different types. Classes include stepping, kick boxing, and spinning (stationary cycling), to name a few. Related group classes include various forms of yoga, Pilates, and tai chi.

OCCUPATION PROFILE

Fitness Trainer and Aerobics Instructor

Considerations	Qualifications
Description	Instructs individuals or groups in exercise activities, observes their progress, and helps them improve.
Career clusters	Education and Training; Hospitality and Tourism; Human Services
Interests	People; things
Working conditions	Work inside; work outside; work both inside and outside
Minimum education level	Bachelor's degree
Physical exertion	Medium work
Physical abilities	Unexceptional/basic fitness
Opportunities for experience	Volunteer work
Licensure and certification	Usually not required
Employment outlook	Faster-than-average growth expected
Holland interest score	ESR

Note: See volume 1, "Publisher's Note," for an explanation of the Holland interest score.

OCCUPATION SPECIALTIES

Dieticians and Nutritionists

Specialty	Responsibilities
Clinical dieticians	Plan and direct the preparation and service of diets prescribed by a physician.
Community dieticians	Plan, develop, administer, and coordinate nutrition programs and services as part of the health care services for an organization.
Consultant dieticians	Advise and assist public and private establishments, such as child care centers, hospitals, nursing homes, and schools on food service management, nutritional education programs, and nutritional problems.
Research dieticians	Conduct, evaluate, and interpret research to improve the nutrition of healthy and sick people.

Aerobics instructors need group leadership skills, and outgoing personalities are helpful. No college education is required for these positions, but many different specific certifications exist in the various types of aerobic activity, and such certifications may be helpful in securing employment. Many instructors work part time and get paid by the class. Pay averages $20 or more per hour, but few leaders can teach more than a couple of hours per day. Often, full-time fitness trainers can teach a class or two per day as part of their full-time jobs.

Fitness operations occupations may include the following:

- Fitness Manager
- Fitness Instructor
- Personal Trainer
- Aerobics Instructor

Aquatics

Health and fitness centers that have swimming pools must employ lifeguards and staff to maintain and ensure safety in their pool areas. Temperature, pH, and chlorine levels must be checked regularly and adjusted. The pool and decks must be kept clean. Lifeguards are required when anyone is in the pool area. Specialized water classes are also taught by aquatics personnel. To work in aquatics, certifications in lifeguarding, first aid, and cardiopulmonary resuscitation (CPR) are required.

Some aquatics director positions require college degrees.

Aquatics occupations may include the following:

- Aquatics Director
- Aquatics Instructor
- Lifeguard
- Pool Maintenance Staff

Recreation and Sports

Health and fitness centers with specialized program offerings, such as tennis or skating, employ workers with the skills to teach and supervise these programs. They may teach individual or group lessons. Recreation workers are also used in programs for children.

The educational backgrounds of recreation and sports personnel vary by their diverse job responsibilities. Most important are their specific teaching and sport skills. Compensation varies dramatically. Those who teach basic sports skills to children average $20,000 per year. Skilled coaches who train more elite athletes can earn significantly more, especially if they teach one-on-one. Recreation and fitness center coaches earned an average of $33,830 in 2009, while athletic trainers earned an average of $40,380.

Recreation and sports occupations may include the following:

- Recreation and Sports Director
- Recreation Worker
- Sport Skills Coach
- Athletic Trainer

Reception

The first contact members have with a health and fitness club is the front desk, where a receptionist greets them and checks their membership cards. This is a very important position from a public relations standpoint. Receptionists also answer phones, do clerical work, operate cash registers, and direct people to appropriate staff. They do not typically need college degrees but must have good interpersonal and organizational skills. Pay often starts near minimum wage.

Reception occupations may include the following:

- Reception Desk Manager
- Receptionist

Child Care

Child-care staff watch children while their parents exercise. Child-care centers are generally stocked with games and activities to occupy children. Depending on the size of the facility, there may be several different programs for children of different ages. Personnel entertain the children and maintain a safe environment for them. Child-care workers do not need college degrees but need to know how to supervise children and are typically paid minimum wage.

Child-care occupations may include the following:

- Child-Care Center Manager
- Child-Care Worker

Locker Room Attendants

Large health and fitness clubs with large locker rooms may employ attendants to keep them clean and dry, hand out towels, and refill toiletries. Since many people shower in the locker rooms, water is dispersed throughout them, and the potential for

Gyms, fitness clubs, and body-building studios offer weight training with free weights and equipment. (©Andres Rodriguez/Dreamstime.com)

bacteria to grow is high. Therefore, locker room attendants must constantly clean and dry these facilities. Attendants do not need college degrees and generally work at minimum wage.

Locker room attendant occupations may include the following:

- Locker Room Attendant
- Custodian/Janitor
- Cleaner

Personal Care

Massage, hair styling, and skin care are spa services offered at some of the larger facilities. Hard exercise and sweating create a market for services to revitalize the body. Massage therapists rub and manipulate muscles to soothe them. Hair dressers cut and style hair, while skin-care specialists provide facials, manicures, and pedicures. These employees must have training and certification in massage therapy or cosmetology. Wages vary but often depend on the type and amount of services provided, and they are commonly supplemented by tips.

Personal care occupations may include the following:

- Massage Therapist
- Cosmetologist
- Hair Dresser
- Manicurist
- Pedicurist
- Skin Care Specialist

Physical Therapy

Some of the larger health and fitness clubs have physical therapy units on-site. Often, these operations are contracted with local sports-medicine clinics. Having physical therapy on-site benefits the clinics by bringing their services closer to potential patients and increasing their visibility. Also, therapists and patients gain access to club exercise equipment, which gives them more options for rehabilitation therapy. Fitness clubs can gain new members from among a clinic's patients, since those patients see the club's facilities during their rehabilitation.

Physical therapists must have graduate degrees and be licensed to practice. This training qualifies them to develop specific exercise regimens to rehabilitate injuries. They are often assisted by athletic trainers, physical therapy assistants, or physical therapy aids. Athletic trainers must have bachelor's degrees and pass certification exams. Physical therapy assistants need associate's degrees, and aides require no formal education. Physical therapists' incomes at fitness and recreation centers averaged $67,150 in 2009. Athletic trainers averaged $40,380, while physical therapist aides averaged in the $24,790 range.

Physical therapy occupations may include the following:

- Physical Therapist
- Athletic Trainer
- Physical Therapist Assistant
- Physical Therapist Aide

Food and Beverage Service

Most health and fitness clubs offer some food and beverage service to their members. In smaller facilities, this service may be limited to vending machines or a few items sold by receptionists. Some large clubs may offer a full-service restaurant with bar. A wide range of food services can be found in various health and fitness clubs. Most tend to be limited to a food counter or nutrition bar and focus on healthier food and beverage options.

Food and beverage personnel generally sell bottled beverages and prepackaged food products. They may heat some food in microwave ovens, but their facilities are not typically stocked with deep fryers, grills, or conventional ovens. Therefore, these workers are easily trained on the job and do not require formal advanced education. They usually perform many functions that include greeting, serving, light food preparation, and cleaning.

Food and beverage service occupations may include the following:

- Food Service Manager
- Counter Attendant
- Cook

Retail Sales

Large health and fitness clubs may have small retail outlets or pro shops. Small clubs may offer limited merchandise sold by their receptionists. The merchandise sold is often limited to exercise clothing and sports equipment. Retail operations may constitute stand-alone departments if they are large enough, but they more commonly are part of larger departments. Some clubs may contract with retail companies to operate their shops. Retail salespersons may receive minimum wage or commission. They do not require college degrees, but knowledge of exercise clothing and equipment is needed.

Retail sales occupations may include the following:

- Retail Sales Manager
- Retail Salesperson

Cleaning and Maintenance

Keeping facilities clean is a very important requirement in the health and fitness industry. Since patrons routinely sweat, floors and equipment must be cleaned often. Also, exercise equipment has many moving parts and is used heavily at fitness clubs and centers. Therefore, the equipment breaks down regularly and must be repaired. In locker rooms, water is constantly tracked around and must be mopped.

Janitors and cleaners are responsible for most of the cleaning. Attendants can assist in the locker rooms, and fitness instructors can help with the equipment in the exercise rooms. Because of the risk of bacteria spreading among club members, equipment and floors must be cleaned many times per day.

Maintenance staff is assigned to repair broken equipment and building systems. A major concern is plumbing, which is a heavily used system in locker rooms. Large health and fitness centers can justify hiring their own maintenance workers. Smaller clubs may have to contract out such duties. Clubs generally provide so many different types of complex exercise equipment that their maintenance staffs may not be able to fix everything themselves.

Cleaning personnel do not need higher education and earn a little more than minimum wage. Maintenance personnel's qualifications vary widely, as do their wages. Some have vocational or higher education and earn higher wages than those with only experience.

Cleaning and maintenance occupations may include the following:

- Maintenance Manager
- Custodian/Janitor
- Cleaner
- Maintenance and Repair Worker

Groundskeeping

Most health and fitness clubs have no exterior grounds to maintain. Those that do, however, may have extensive grounds for aesthetic purposes and to provide venues for physical activity. Walking and running trails need to be maintained. Other outdoor facilities, such as tennis courts and swimming pools, may have landscaping around them. Mowing grass and caring for flower gardens are common responsibilities. In some geographical areas, snow removal is also required. Groundskeepers do not require higher education. They usually earn hourly wages based on their skills, which vary widely based on a property's characteristics.

Groundskeeping occupations may include the following:

- Head Groundskeeper
- Landscaping Worker
- Groundskeeper

Administrative Support

The size of the administrative support department varies with the size of the facility. Support staff answer phones, maintain files and records, manage data, and support managers in their responsibilities. They have many different skills and types of experience. The ability to adapt to and understand the fitness business is beneficial. These positions may be full or part time, and compensation is based on an individual's skills.

Administrative support occupations may include the following:

- Administrative Assistant
- Secretary
- Office Clerk

INDUSTRY OUTLOOK

Overview

The outlook for the health and fitness industry shows it to be on the rise. In response to growing obesity concerns in the United States and other developed countries, government and health organizations are strongly encouraging people to increase their participation in exercise and recreational activities. As a result, more people are taking control of their health by exercising regularly. The baby boomers make up the largest age group of fitness club members, and the increasing number of older individuals in the United States will support further growth. Increasing numbers of children and young adults are also expected, as families try to stay healthy and physical activity becomes more of a priority.

The arts, entertainment, and recreation sector is expected to grow faster than the average of all sectors combined between 2008 and 2018, with a sector growth rate of 15 percent. Overall industry employee numbers are expected to rise from 551,000 employees in 2010 to 610,000 employees in 2015. Within the sector, fitness and recreation jobs are expected to increase the most, by 37 percent. With 188,900 people in the workforce in 2008, an increase of 70,000 positions is expected by 2018.

The 2007-2009 recession presented challenges to the health and fitness industry. However, its impact was not as devastating as it was to some other industries. Customer loyalty helped minimize membership declines, and the development of creative nondues revenues along with cost-cutting minimized financial losses. Although club memberships dropped in 2009, they were expected to rebound shortly. The increase in memberships will increase revenues from monthly dues, as well as revenues from selling extra programs, services, and products to clients.

People join health and fitness clubs for a number of reasons. The major ones are to maintain or improve one's health, appearance, and social relationships. With increased media attention to health and obesity, more people are becoming aware of the health benefits of exercise. The media also continues to feature men and women with good muscle tone and physiques, increasing the desire of others to mimic their appearance. Also, health and fitness clubs are good places to meet others and to socialize while engaging in healthy activities. As more people begin to exercise, the demand for health and fitness services will increase.

Governments are also playing roles that could improve the future outlook of the industry. New York, New Jersey, and Oklahoma are considering legislation that would provide tax benefits to individuals or families who purchase health and fitness club memberships. If these bills pass and other states follow suit, citizens will have a financial incentive to join health and fitness clubs. The American Recovery and Reinvestment Act of 2009 provided $1 billion to the Department of Health and Human Services for prevention and wellness. These funds should help generate more demand for health and fitness facilities across the country. First Lady Michelle Obama has made childhood obesity in particular one of her primary areas of focus, and she has launched several initiatives—such as the Web site letsmove.gov—to convince young people to exercise, developing habits that should last into adulthood. The support of governments will only improve the future outlook of the industry.

The health and fitness industry is not as large as a function of total population in most other countries as it is in the United States. In 2006, Europe had slightly fewer health and fitness club members than the United States despite having nearly twice the population. Health and fitness clubs are growing internationally, but this growth in different countries varies with those countries' economic situations. Data from the International Health, Racquet, and Sportsclub Association reported in 2006-2007 indicated that Canada had the highest rate of health and fitness club membership, at 15 percent of its population. The United States closely followed at 14 percent. Australia and New Zealand had membership rates of 9 and 10 percent, respectively. Japan led Asian countries with 3 percent, while other Asian countries were below 1 percent. South America was led by Argentina with 3 percent membership and Brazil, Chile, and Mexico with

2 percent membership. The most developed countries had the highest membership rates, followed by those with emerging economies.

Employment Advantages

The health and fitness industry is among the fastest-growing industries in the United States. Its growth equates to future employment opportunities: It is expected that the number of available jobs will increase in the next five to ten years. Also, as the industry grows, there will be more opportunities for professional advancement.

The health and fitness industry is attractive to active people who enjoy exercise and sports. Fitness trainers can make a living doing the things they love. Since entry-level salaries and wages are below the national average of all jobs, professional advancement is desired by many. Fortunately, opportunities for promotions exist for individuals who are knowledgeable about health and exercise and have good business skills. Oftentimes, promotions entail spending less time working with clients and more time managing operations and employees.

For entrepreneurial fitness leaders who like to be more independent, personal training is an option. Personal trainers are the highest-paid health and fitness practitioners in the industry. They generally need to recruit their own clients and develop specific exercise programs to meet their clients' goals. This occupation is particularly attractive to people who like to work with clients one-on-one.

Annual Earnings

The health and fitness industry's earnings are influenced by the economy and people's desire to look good and be healthy. Because many people value their bodies and their health, the industry has continued to grow even when the economy slows. In 2009, memberships in the United States dropped for the first time in years, by 200,000 clients, and industry positions dropped by three thousand jobs. However, the number of health and fitness clubs increased by one hundred and revenues increased by $527 million, or 2.2 percent. As the economy slowly improves, employment is expected to increase by fifteen thousand jobs and memberships to increase by 700,000 people, easily erasing the drops in 2009. Revenues are also expected to increase by $775.5 million, or 3.2 percent.

Through 2014, sustained growth is anticipated.

Revenues are expected to increase by an average of 3 percent per year. Health and fitness club memberships should reach a record 45.9 million people in 2014. With more members and new higher-margin products and services, it is projected that profits will continue to rise at an annualized rate of 5.6 percent from 2009 to 2014.

RELATED RESOURCES FOR FURTHER RESEARCH

AMERICAN COLLEGE OF SPORTS MEDICINE
P.O. Box 1440
Indianapolis, IN 46206-1440
Tel: (317) 637-9200
Fax: (317) 634-7817
http://www.acsm.org

AMERICAN COUNCIL ON EXERCISE
4851 Paramount Dr.
San Diego, CA 92123
Tel: (888) 825-3636
Fax: (858) 576-6564
http://www.acefitness.org

INTERNATIONAL HEALTH, RACQUET, AND SPORTSCLUB ASSOCIATION
Seaport Center
70 Fargo St.
Boston, MA 02210
Tel: (800) 228-4772
Fax: (617) 951-0056
http://cms.ihrsa.org

NATIONAL STRENGTH AND CONDITIONING ASSOCIATION
1885 Bob Johnson Dr.
Colorado Springs, CO 80906
Tel: (800) 815-6826
Fax: (719) 632-6367
http://www.nsca-lift.org

ABOUT THE AUTHOR

Bradley R. A. Wilson has taught students in health and exercise at the university level for more than twenty-five years. He has coauthored three books on health and fitness management, published numerous articles on exercise-related topics, and conducted presentations on fitness topics internationally. As a student internship coordinator, he has visited hundreds of exercise facilities, including community for-profit and nonprofit health clubs, hospital and corporate fitness centers, and sports medicine clinics. His long career in the health and fitness industry also includes experience with the many types of exercise equipment found in these facilities.

FURTHER READING

American College of Sports Medicine. *ACSM's Health/Fitness Facility Standards and Guidelines.* 3d ed. Champaign, Ill.: Human Kinetics, 2007.

Bates, Mike, ed. *Health Fitness Management.* 2d ed. Champaign, Ill.: Human Kinetics, 2008.

Maguire, Jennifer Smith. *Fit for Consumption: Sociology and the Business of Fitness.* New York: Routledge, 2008.

Oakley, Ben, and Martin Rhys, eds. *The Sport and Fitness Sector: An Introduction.* New York: Routledge, 2008.

Tharrett, Stephen J., and James A. Peterson. *Fitness Management.* 2d ed. Monterey, Calif.: Healthy Learning, 2008.

Thatcher, Ron, and Andy Li. *Fitness Memberships and Money.* Victoria, B.C.: Trafford, 2004.

Thompson, Walter R. "Worldwide Survey Reveals Fitness Trends for 2010." *ACSM's Health and Fitness Journal* 13, no. 6 (November/December, 2009): 9-16.

U.S. Bureau of Labor Statistics. *Career Guide to Industries*, 2010-2011 ed. http://www.bls.gov/oco/cg.

U.S. Census Bureau. North American Industry Classification System (NAICS), 2007. http://www.census.gov/cgi-bin/sssd/naics/naicsrch?chart=2007.

U.S. Department of Commerce. International Trade Administration. Office of Trade and Industry Information. Industry Trade Data and Analysis. http://ita.doc.gov/td/industry/otea/OTII/OTII-index.html.

Heavy Machines Industry

©Dreamstime.com

INDUSTRY SNAPSHOT

General Industry: Manufacturing

Career Cluster: Manufacturing

Subcategory Industries: Automatic Vending Machine Manufacturing; Commercial Laundry, Drycleaning, and Pressing Machine Manufacturing; Construction Machinery Manufacturing; Farm Machinery and Equipment Manufacturing; Food Product Machinery Manufacturing; Industrial Machinery Manufacturing; Metalworking Machinery Manufacturing; Mining Machinery Manufacturing; Oil and Gas Field Machinery and Equipment Manufacturing; Paper Industry Machinery Manufacturing; Plastics and Rubber Industry Manufacturing; Sawmill and Woodworking Machinery Manufacturing; Textile Machinery Manufacturing; Tractor Equipment Manufacturing; Ventilation, Heating, Air-Conditioning, and Commercial Refrigeration Equipment Manufacturing

Related Industries: Construction Equipment Industry; Farming Industry; Mining Industry

Annual Domestic Revenues: $350 billion USD (Hoovers, 2009)

Annual International Revenues: $344 billion USD (Research and Markets, 2009)

Annual Global Revenues: $694 billion USD (Research and Markets, 2009)

NAICS Numbers: 33210-333112, 333120, 333131-333132, 333220, 333291-333294, 333298, 333311-333312, 333500, 333511-333516, 333921, 333991

INDUSTRY DEFINITION

Summary

Heavy equipment either reduces or replaces manpower to accomplish a task. It can be either mobile or fixed. A large portion of this industry is devoted to the manufacture of wheeled equipment for earth moving and manipulation, such as bulldozers and tractors. Other wheeled equipment has limited mobility, primarily for transfer from one location to another, such as cranes and drilling equipment. Mobile equipment requires specialized tires; thus, it supports a significant subindustry. Examples of fixed equipment include printing

A large portion of the heavy machine industry is devoted to the manufacture of wheeled equipment for earth moving and manipulation, such as this skip loader. (©Dreamstime.com)

presses, textile manufacturing machinery, and plastics and rubber manufacturing equipment. Heavy machines also encompass assembly lines, which can occupy an extensive area (for example, an automobile assembly line). Virtually every industrialized nation in the world has a significant heavy machines industry employing individuals in a wide variety of careers.

History of the Industry

Sectors of this industry either appeared or markedly expanded as a result of the Industrial Revolution, which began in the eighteenth century in the United Kingdom and then spread throughout Europe, North America, and the rest of the world. It was marked by major changes in manufacturing, mining, agriculture, and transport. This phenomenon had a profound impact on the economy and culture. However, the use of heavy equipment began in ancient Rome. In *De architectura* (c. 27 B.C.E.; *The Architecture*, 1771), the Roman engineer Marcus Vitruvius Pollio provided detailed descriptions of heavy equipment, cranes, and hoists, as well as war machines such as catapults and siege engines. He also described the aeolipile, a precursor to the steam engine.

In 1836, John Deere manufactured a polished-steel plow for use by pioneer farmers in the American Midwest. By 1870, the company was producing plows, cultivators, harrows, drills, planters, wagons, and buggies. In the 1880's, steam tractors appeared; they were replaced thirty years later by gasoline-powered tractors. In 1931, the first diesel-powered tractor rolled off the assembly line at Deere & Company in East Peoria, Illinois. By 1940, the U.S.-based Caterpillar Tractor Company was producing motor graders, generators, and a special tank engine used by the United States in World War II. In 1963, Caterpillar and Mitsubishi Heavy Industries formed one of the first joint ventures in Japan, Caterpillar Mitsubishi Ltd. The company is now known as Shin Caterpillar Mitsubishi and in 2010 was the second-largest producer of construction and mining equipment in Japan. In the early 1960's, Deere & Company also was taking steps to become multinational, opening small tractor plants in Mexico, France, Argentina, and South Africa.

Before 1900, machinery was produced at one location, one unit at a time. Although the origin of the assembly line often is associated with Henry Ford, Ransom Olds patented the assembly line concept and implemented it in his Olds Motor Vehicle Company factory in 1901. The concept was improved a few years later by Ford. Ford's version of the assembly line involved moving the work from one worker to another until each unit was complete; these units were then moved to a final assembly line, which produced the finished product. As a result of Ford's improvements, a complete automobile was produced every three minutes. Previous assembly lines produced a vehicle at a rate of about two an hour and required significantly more manpower. Furthermore, Ford implemented safety procedures that assigned workers to specific locations rather than allowing them to roam about the work area; this dramatically reduced the rate of injury.

Oil and gas field machinery also first appeared at the turn of the twentieth century. Prior to that time, drilling was done with muscle power—human or animal. Internal combustion engines revolutionized this burdensome task. In the early twentieth century, drilling rigs were semipermanent structures, often left in place after wells' completion. In the second half of the twentieth century, custom-built machines were developed that could be moved between drilling locations. Larger rigs required disassembly for the move. Before 1970, the drill bits were diamond-tipped; subsequently, faster and more efficient pneumatic reciprocating piston reverse circulation drills were developed.

Mining dates to prehistoric times. Tools made of stone, ceramics, and later metal were used to retrieve metals close beneath the Earth's surface. The ancient Romans employed hydraulic mining—diverting water to an area to wash the earth from mineral deposits. The introduction of the internal combustion engine dramatically transformed this industry. Other heavy machines industries, such as food product machinery and sawmills, rapidly evolved with the introduction of the internal combustion engine.

Textile manufacturing is one of the oldest human activities, dating back to 5000 B.C.E. Automa-

The heavy machines industry includes fixed machinery, such as this offset printing press. (©Moreno Soppelsa/Dreamstime.com)

tion of the textile industry began in the eighteenth century in England. James Hargreaves developed the spinning jenny, which replaced the work of eight hand spinners. In 1792, Samuel Slater opened a yarn spinning mill in Pawtucket, Rhode Island, the first successful business of its kind in the United States. In 1793, Eli Whitney and Hogden Holmes developed a simplified method of removing cotton lint from the seed. Their invention, the cotton gin, revolutionized the cotton industry in the United States and, subsequently, the rest of the world. The textile industry in the United Sates flourished until the 1990's, when lower-priced products from Asia replaced those made domestically.

South Americans first used natural rubber in the eleventh century; however, the plastics and rubber industry originated in 1839 when American Charles Goodyear discovered that combining natural rubber with sulfur greatly increased its flexibility. The development of motor vehicles by the end of the nineteenth century created high demand for tires. Plastics first appeared in 1909 when Leo Baekeland, an American chemist, developed phenoformaldehyde plastics (more popularly known as "phenolics"). Phenolics were the first plastics to gain worldwide acceptance. The use of plastics evolved in the 1940's and by the end of that decade, they were used in many products. Today, they are ubiquitous.

The Industry Today

Today's heavy machines industry is dominated by large, multinational companies that produce a wide range of products from industrial turbines to tractors. The industry supports major subindustries such as maintenance and repair, sales, leasing, engine manufacturing, and tire manufacturing. While some of these companies focus on one type of product (for example, Otis Elevator Company of Farmington, Connecticut), others produce machines for a variety of applications (such Mitsubishi Heavy Industries of Tokyo). Thus, some companies' products fall into more than one of the following categories. Furthermore, many companies not only manufacture products but also sell, lease, and repair the equipment.

A major segment of this industry is focused on construction and farming equipment. Products include graders, excavators, cranes, tractors, and cultivators. Some products—such as tractors—can be

Machines such as this excavator are used for construction. (©Dreamstime.com)

used for a variety of tasks, while others—pipe layers, for example—are designed for specific tasks. As of 2010, the top ten construction equipment companies were Caterpillar (Peoria, Illinois), Komatsu (Tokyo), Terex (Westport, Connecticut), Case New Holland (CNH; Amsterdam, the Netherlands), Volvo Construction Equipment (Götenburg, Sweden), Deere & Company (Moline, Illinois), Doosan Group (Bobcat Company; Seoul, South Korea), Hitachi Construction Machinery (Tokyo), Bell Equipment (Rochester, New York), and Hitachi Construction Machinery-Europe (Oosterhout, the Netherlands). These companies primarily produce earth-moving, construction, and farming equipment. Many manufacture their own engines, which are primarily diesel. Some, like Caterpillar, market their engines as separate products. Although the word Caterpillar brings to mind earth-moving equipment, the company also has a large presence in the marine engine industry.

Heavy equipment manufactured by these companies requires either continuous tracks or specialized tires. The equipment with more severe service requirements utilizes continuous tracks; however, tires are preferable when greater speed and mobility is required. Because of this need, the heavy machines industry is a significant source of revenue for the subindustry of tire manufacturing. Selecting the proper tire for the lifetime use of the equip-

The heavy machines industry is a significant source of revenue for the subindustry of tire manufacturing. (©Marian Mocanu/Dreamstime.com)

ment is important because it can have a major impact on per-unit production costs. The aforementioned companies are susceptible to the rate of economic growth. Much of the equipment is designed for construction; thus, when new construction experiences a slowdown, these companies are affected. Equipment produced for farm use is affected to a lesser degree because of the ongoing need for agricultural products worldwide.

In the early 1900's, textile manufacturing equipment was primarily produced in the United States and Western Europe; however, this production has shifted to Asia and Australia. Driving this shift is the fact that most textiles are now produced in Asia, including India. Textile manufacturing involves spinning natural or synthetic fibers into yarn, then weaving the yarn into cloth. This cloth is then processed to become fabric. The fabric may be dyed, printed, or embellished with colored yarns. Most textiles are machine-produced; however, many high-end textiles are produced by nonindustrial methods dating back centuries. Textile production is an essential industry for nations at all levels of development. Globally, the top five companies are Alok Industries (Mumbai, India), Bhavani Weavess (Erode, India), Bullivants (New South Wales, Australia), Manacol (Victoria, Australia), and Toray Industries (Tokyo).

The Machinery Manufacturing Industry's Contribution to the U.S. Economy

Value Added	Amount
Gross domestic product	$124.0 billion
Gross domestic product	0.9%
Persons employed	1.185 million
Total employee compensation	$84.5 billion

Source: U.S. Bureau of Economic Analysis. Data are for 2008.

Oil and gas field machinery and equipment manufacturers produce products for drilling rigs, such as this one in North Dakota. (©David Gaylor/Dreamstime.com)

Mining machinery manufacturing companies produce drills, ore crushers, loading machines, washers, mining cars, and quarrying machinery. Oil and gas field machinery and equipment manufacturing companies make products such as drill bits, derricks, and pipe assemblies. The equipment is produced for both land and offshore use. They also produce equipment for water drilling. Globally, the five leading companies that produce machinery for the mining, oil, and gas industries are Schwing Stetter (Tamil Nadu, India), Caterpillar (Peoria, Illinois), Katsushiro Indonesia (Bekasi, West Java), Komatsu (Tokyo), and Abu Dhabi Petroleum Company (London).

Plastics and rubber industry manufacturing companies produce machinery used to produce plastics, pipes and pipe fixtures, plastic bottles, and tires. They design and develop application-specific machinery, which must meet critical performance standards; often, these products are often produced in collaboration with their customers. Globally, the five largest companies (excluding tire manufacturing) are AVC Trading (Victoria, Australia), Faurecia Interior Systems South Africa (Uitenhage, South Africa), Amcor Limited (Victoria, Australia), Trelleborg (Trelleborg, Sweden), and Fletcher Wood Panels—Australia (Queensland, Australia). The top five tire manufacturing companies are Bridgestone Corporation (Tokyo), Compagnie Générale des Établissements Michelin (Clermont-Ferrand, France), Goodyear Tire & Rubber Company (Akron, Ohio), Pirelli (Milan, Italy), and Sumitomo Rubber Industries (Kobe, Japan).

Food product machinery manufacturing companies produce machines that cook, mix, chop, preserve, or otherwise process food products. Representative products include pasteurizing equipment, commercial ovens, distilleries, and juice extractors. As of 2010, the top five companies globally were Fuji Electric Retail Systems (Tokyo), Electrolux Lehel Hutogepgyar Korlatolt Felelossegu Tarsasag (Jaszbereny, Hungary), Enodis (London), John Bean Technologies Corporation (Chicago), and DeLaval International (Tumbla, Sweden).

Automatic vending machine manufacturing companies produce specialized vending machines for dispensing such items as snacks, ice cream, beverages, and stamps; they also manufacture change-making machines. Major companies include divisions of Coca-Cola (Atlanta, Georgia), Compass Group North America (Charlotte, North Carolina), Aramark (Philadelphia), and Sodexo (Issyles-Moulineaux, France). Of interest is the dominance of U.S.-headquartered businesses compared with other segments of this industry.

Inputs Consumed by the Machinery Manufacturing Industry

Input	Value
Energy	$3.1 billion
Materials	$174.6 billion
Purchased services	$48.1 billion
Total	$225.8 billion

Source: U.S. Bureau of Economic Analysis. Data are for 2008.

The ventilation, heating, air-conditioning, and commercial refrigeration equipment manufacturing industry segment manufactures climate-control machinery for residential and commercial buildings. In addition to heating and cooling equipment, this industry manufactures air purification equipment, which is extremely common in all new construction. The top five companies are Systemair (New Brunswick, Canada), Carrier Corporation (Farmington, Connecticut), Daikin Industries (Osaka, Japan), Ferguson Enterprises (Newport News, Virginia), and Kohler Company (Kohler, Wisconsin).

The metalworking machinery segment of this industry manufactures tools that form, cut, and shape metals. Because metal is a strong, durable material, it is difficult to form. This industry manufactures specialized molds, presses, rollers, grinders, and drills. Companies also produce the accessories used by these machines. Compared with the many large companies in the heavy machines industry, most metalworking machinery businesses are small—more than half of the businesses employ fewer than twenty workers.

Sawmill and woodworking machinery manufacturing companies produce sawmill and woodworking machinery (not including handheld tools), such as band saws, circular saws, drill presses, lathes, planers, sanders, shapers, and veneer forming machinery. Many companies that manufacture products for this industry also manufacture light machinery equipment and products for other industry segments. An example of a manufacturer in this segment of the industry is Schelling Anlagenbau (Schwarzach, Austria), which has subsidiaries based in North America, Great Britain, Poland, Slovakia, China, and Australia. This company manufactures woodworking machinery and precision saws for plastics, circuit boards, and nonferrous metals. It also manufactures sorting and stacking equipment, materials handling equipment, and packaging equipment and has a division that produces software to control production processes.

Commercial laundry, drycleaning, and pressing machine manufacturing companies manufacture commercial grade (nonhousehold use) washing machines, dryers, drycleaning equipment, and laundry pressing machines. Many companies that produce products for this industry also manufac-ture products for household use, light machinery, and products for other industry segments. For example, the Whirlpool Corporation, a global leader in this industry segment, markets Whirlpool, Maytag, KitchenAid, Jenn-Air, Amana, Brastemp, Consul, Bauknecht, and Gladiator appliances. Whirlpool, Maytag, KitchenAid, Jenn-Air, and Amana are familiar appliance brands in the United States and other parts of the world. Brastemp and Consul appliances are sold in Brazil. Bauknecht appliances are sold in Germany. Gladiator appliances are designed for the garage and the product line includes workbenches, tool storage, and cabinets. Whirlpool maintains headquarters in Michigan; São Paulo, Brazil; Comerio, Italy; and Shanghai, China. The company produces many models of each specific product. For example, as of 2010 it offers twenty different models of washing machines designed for home use.

INDUSTRY MARKET SEGMENTS

Although some smaller companies with fewer than one thousand employees compete in the marketplace, the heavy machines industry is dominated by large, international companies. The products manufactured by this industry are large and complicated, so large facilities are necessary for their production. The largest businesses are focused on producing construction, agricultural, and mining equipment. Companies producing machinery for commercial ventilation, heating, air-conditioning, and refrigeration also tend to be large. The metalworking machinery segment has the smallest businesses; half the companies have fewer than twenty employees.

Small Businesses

Small businesses in the heavy machines industry are concentrated in the metalworking machinery industry segment and the subindustry of maintenance and repair.

Potential Annual Earnings Scale. The average annual earnings for a small-business owner in the heavy machines industry vary from region to region and usually are less than $100,000.

Clientele Interaction. Small businesses tend to favor more interaction with customers, and the personal touch can foster consumer satisfaction. However, clientele interaction can vary widely. The owner might have direct contact with his or her customers or market products over the Internet with contact limited to the telephone and e-mail. A Web site is essential to a small business. A well-designed site can successfully compete with that of a large company. The Web site can not only market the product but also offer technical advice and serve as a vehicle for customer feedback.

Amenities, Atmosphere, and Physical Grounds. Amenities of small businesses often are limited. Inasmuch as the owner has extensive control over the business, the working environment can be tailored to personal taste and budget. An owner interested in a favorable working environment might have a facility with extremely pleasant working conditions; however, most facilities are utilitarian, no-frills structures.

Typical Number of Employees. The number of employees can range from one to several dozen.

Traditional Geographic Locations. Geographic locations of small businesses are unlimited. They usually are located near the owner's home.

Pros of Working for a Small Heavy Machines Business. The owner of a small business often is responsible for all operational decisions. The owner might consult with staff members regarding these decisions. A staff member usually has a closer working relationship with the owner than in a larger company. Part-time employment and flexible hours usually are easier to arrange than they would be in a larger company. A small-business owner can control waste and unnecessary expenditures to a greater degree than the owner of a larger company because all expenditures are subject to his or her approval.

If the company fosters teamwork and group decision making, an individual employee can be closely involved in the company's growth. In some cases, partnership opportunities exist for exceptional employees. If the company flourishes, the company might grow in size and revenue; this could lead to expansion or purchase by a larger company. In either case, the financial return could be significant. Some small-business owners are able to sell their companies for large profits, which might be shared among key or long-term employees.

Cons of Working for a Small Heavy Machines Business. Like most major industries, the heavy machines industry is extremely competitive. Even if a small company produces a good product, it might not be able to compete successfully with a large company that can produce a comparable product at a lower price. A small business is less resilient and can be bankrupted by an unexpected major expense such as a lawsuit or major equipment replacement cost. Also, the owner and staff of a small company generally will not have the variety of skills that the staff and management of a larger company possess. For example, the staff may have technical expertise but lack marketing skills. Furthermore, with a small staff, the owner and employees will be responsible for a wider range of duties. Loss of a key employee could slow or even halt production until a suitable replacement is found.

Costs

Payroll and Benefits: Small companies often pay all employees an hourly wage and usually do not provide the same level of benefits as do large companies; these benefits are at the discretion of the owner and include sick pay, health insurance, and vacations.

Supplies: Supplies usually cost more for small-business owners than for large businesses, which can negotiate lower prices for bulk purchases. Not only will supplies directly related to the construction of the machinery cost more per unit but also other office supplies necessary for the business will be more expensive.

External Services: Costs for external services for a small business are typically minimal and might include such things as Web site development and maintenance and billing services. If a small business becomes involved in a legal dispute, an attorney usually must be retained. In this situation, the small-business owner might incur significant costs.

Utilities: Utilities may be comparable to that of a home. The manufacturing of some equipment might involve significant usage of electricity or natural gas.

Taxes: Small businesses are obligated to pay local, state, and federal taxes.

Midsize Businesses

Midsize heavy machines manufacturing businesses tend to favor niche markets with limited product lines. These products might compete with those produced by large businesses; however, some midsize companies manufacture products that complement products made by large businesses. An example of a midsize heavy machines business is Technik Manufacturing. The company operates out of a single facility in Columbus, Nebraska, and employs fifty people. Technik manufactures automatic vending machines and vending machine kiosks. The company markets its products in more than forty-five nations. It offers online technical support and after-sales service, including replacement parts, of their products.

Potential Annual Earnings Scale. Salaries vary from region to region; however, the annual salary for a mechanical engineer is $32 per hour; sales representatives earn about $28 per hour and may receive commissions for sales; first-line supervisors/managers of production and operating workers earn about $26 per hour; tool and die makers earn about $21 per hour; machinists earn about $18 per hour; computer-controlled machine tool operators (metal and plastic) earn about $17 per hour; inspectors, testers, sorters, samplers, and weighers earn about $17 per hour; welders, cutters, solderers, and brazers earn about $16 per hour; cutting, punching, and press machine setters, operators, and tenders (metal and plastic) earn about $14 per hour; and team assemblers earn about $14 per hour. Incomes for managers in the manufacturing arm vary widely from more than $100,000 to less than $50,000 annually.

Clientele Interaction. Vendors can foster long-term relationships, which can generate repeat business. All midsize businesses will have a Web site for marketing and client interaction. The site will offer customer service, technical support, and often provide downloads of user manuals.

Amenities, Atmosphere, and Physical Grounds. Manufacturing facilities are customarily spartan and utilitarian.

Typical Number of Employees. A manufacturing facility consists of a management staff, assembly supervisors, and assemblers.

Traditional Geographic Locations. Manufacturers are typically in the industrial area of a city and are commonly located in areas near rail or ocean cargo service.

Pros of Working for a Midsize Heavy Machines Industry. The owner of a midsize manufacturing business often has more control over operational decisions than he or she would in a large company. Employee-management interaction often is more frequent and meaningful than at a large company. Midsize manufacturing businesses can employ individuals with a variety of skills; these employees include technicians, assemblers, and marketing personnel. Employees of a midsize company may have closer relationships with management than they would at a large company and may have a greater sense of being part of a team. Midsize businesses also may have one or only a few locations; thus, an employee who prefers to remain in one location usually will not be confronted with the threat of a transfer to another location as in a large, international company.

Cons of Working for a Midsize Heavy Machines Industry. Many midsize businesses produce a limited product line. In times of economic downturn, these companies are more susceptible to failure than larger companies. The limited number of management positions in a midsize company decreases opportunities for advancement, particularly for those commanding a high salary.

Costs

Payroll and Benefits: Midsize companies usually can offer benefits comparable to those of a large company; these benefits include sick pay, health insurance, and vacations.

Supplies: Midsize companies can often negotiate discounts from suppliers; however, the unit production cost may be higher than a comparable product produced by a large company.

External Services: Manufacturing companies often use accounting services and billing services; however, they might also maintain employees that can perform these services. They also often use outside legal services rather than in-house services.

Taxes: Midsize businesses must pay local, state, and federal income taxes, as well as applicable property taxes. Almost all businesses in the United States are incorporated; thus, they pay state and federal taxes at the corporate level. They also must collect state sales taxes for retail sales.

Large Businesses

Large heavy machines manufacturing businesses market their products internationally. The large companies in the United States are in direct competition with products manufactured by companies whose headquarters are in other nations. For example Deere & Company, headquartered in Moline, Illinois, maintains facilities in Canada, Europe, China, Australia, South America, and Russia. These companies often market a variety of products, including light equipment and products in other market segments (such as life insurance and televisions). They profit from brand recognition. Most consumers recognize these brand names when considering a purchase and will often favor a product that they deem to have a good reputation for reliability and features. Some equipment manufactured by non-American companies may have less brand recognition in the United States.

An example of a large, global company in the heavy machines industry is Mitsubishi Heavy Industries (Tokyo), one of the core companies of the Mitsubishi Group. The Mitsubishi Group markets an extensive variety of products, including automobiles, televisions, Nikon cameras, beer, and life insurance. A division of Mitsubishi Heavy Industries is located in the United States. Products marketed by Mitsubishi Heavy Industries include airplanes, shipbuilding/marine structures, steel structures and construction, power systems, turbochargers, forklifts, military combat tanks, wind turbines, air-conditioning/refrigeration systems, industrial machinery, paper and printing machinery, machine tools, and light rail vehicles.

An example of a large heavy machines company with a much narrower product range is Deere & Company, which primarily markets products for farm and construction use. At the heart of the farm product line is the John Deere tractor. Other farm equipment includes planting/seeding machines, combines, tillers, cotton harvesters, sugar harvesters, and cutters/shredders. The company markets a variety of construction products, including bulldozers, graders, and scrapers, as well as engines and drivetrains, forestry equipment, and golf carts. Deere & Company also markets smaller equipment for home use, such as lawn mowers (walking and riding), home workshop products, and snow equipment.

Potential Annual Earnings Scale. Salaries vary from region to region; the salaries for top management positions, such as chief executive officer (CEO), can be well over $1 million per year. The

annual salary for a mechanical engineer is $32 per hour; sales representatives earn about $28 per hour and might receive commissions for sales; first-line supervisors/managers of production and operating workers earn about $26 per hour; tool and die makers earn about $21 per hour; machinists earn about $18 per hour; computer-controlled machine tool operators (metal and plastic) earn about $17 per hour; inspectors, testers, sorters, samplers, and weighers earn about $17 per hour; welders, cutters, solderers, and brazers earn about $16 per hour; cutting, punching, and press machine setters, operators, and tenders (metal and plastic) earn about $14 per hour; and team assemblers earn about $14 per hour. Many large companies offer dealership franchises. A motivated individual with capital to invest has an opportunity to develop a dealership into a multimillion-dollar business providing tremendous personal financial benefits. These dealerships can operate with a high degree of autonomy, provided that they generate adequate revenues to the parent company.

Clientele Interaction. Vendors can foster long-term relationships, which can generate repeat business. All large businesses will have Web sites for marketing purposes and clientele interaction. A company's Web site can offer customer service, technical support, and often provides downloadable copies of operator manuals.

Amenities, Atmosphere, and Physical Grounds. Manufacturing facilities are customarily spartan and utilitarian. Dealerships range from utilitarian to luxurious. Corporate headquarters are luxurious and modern. The headquarters often have a large area devoted to displaying examples of the company's product line. For example, the Deere & Company World Headquarters in Illinois is located on 1,400 acres of manicured land, which is home to a variety of wildlife, such as deer, ducks, geese, and swans. Visitors can view displays of John Deere equipment, ranging from antiques to the company's latest offerings.

Typical Number of Employees. The number of individuals employed by many companies in the heavy machines industry dropped from 2009 to 2010 because of the widespread economic downturn. Deere & Company reported having 51,262 employees in 2009, down 10 percent from its 56,653 employees in 2008. Mitsubishi Heavy Industries initiated a plan in 2008 to reduce its average number of employees in Japan from 3,500 to 2,000 over two years. However, over that same period, the company planned to increase its workforce in overseas companies from 8,450 to 15,000 employees, particularly in growth businesses. The company predicts a consolidated workforce of 72,000 by March, 2015.

Traditional Geographic Locations. Corporate headquarters can be located in virtually any large or small city; large retail outlets also can be located in any area with a reasonable population density. Manufacturing facilities typically are found in industrial areas of large cities, near rail or ocean cargo services.

Pros of Working for a Large Heavy Machines Industry. A wealth of career opportunities exists within large manufacturing companies and their dealerships. Positions include high-paying management positions, technical/engineering opportunities, information technology, marketing, and sales. Upper management positions can be extremely lucrative in regard to salaries, bonuses, and retirement benefits. Even lower-level employees may be entitled to generous bonuses and retirement benefits. Large corporations offer summer internships for college students and training for those employees who wish to advance their careers. Lateral transfers are possible. For example, a marketing employee might have the opportunity to transfer to a management position in human resources. Large manufacturers offer a wide range of products at various price points; thus, they are more likely than smaller companies to survive an economic downturn.

Cons of Working for a Large Heavy Machines Industry. Despite efforts to foster good employee-management relations, an employee might have a sense that his or her opinion does not matter and that his or her position could readily be filled by another individual. Upper management personnel might be urged to relocate to another state or even another country at regular intervals to ensure promotion. Performance goals sometimes imposed on employees, even those in lower positions, also might be extremely stressful. These large businesses are profit-driven and must answer to a board of directors and shareholders. If a company loses market share or profitability, the CEO might be terminated. The same holds true for department managers if revenue drops.

Costs

Payroll and Benefits: Large companies usually offer many benefits, including sick pay, health insurance, vacations, and family leave.

Supplies: Large companies can achieve economies of scale because they purchase large quantities of goods. However, since they need constant replenishment of many items, a breakdown in the supply chain (for example, delays caused by weather, natural disasters, or strikes) can slow or halt production. Large companies often strive for just-in-time delivery of supplies (supplies arrive when needed to avoid maintaining a large inventory). This concept, however, increases the likelihood of a production slowdown in the event of a supply chain disruption. For example, the 2010 volcanic eruption in Iceland halted air shipment of many products.

External Services: Large companies usually have in-house departments for most services, which include accounting, payroll, legal, and even urgent-care medical services.

Utilities: Manufacturing of heavy equipment often entails high costs for utilities, particularly gas and electricity.

Taxes: Large heavy machines businesses—both manufacturing plants and dealerships—must pay local, state, and federal income taxes as well as applicable property taxes. These businesses are incorporated; thus, they pay state and federal taxes at the corporate level. They also must collect state sales taxes for retail sales.

ORGANIZATIONAL STRUCTURE AND JOB ROLES

A large business will have departments for each division of its organization. A midsize company often will have a department or at least one employee for each division.

The following umbrella categories apply to the organizational structure of businesses in the heavy machines industry:

- Business Management
- Customer Services
- Legal Services
- Medical Services

- Sales and Marketing
- Information Technology
- Facilities and Security
- Technology, Research, Design, and Development
- Production and Operations
- Distribution
- Human Resources
- Payroll

Business Management

Management of a heavy equipment company usually consists of hundreds of top-level individuals; some midsize companies might have a few dozen management positions. At a large company, the hierarchy is headed by the CEO; under the CEO are upper-management personnel who oversee operations for facilities in other countries or regions of the United States. Below these upper-management positions are middle-management positions and low-level managers. A large dealership may have a similar hierarchy. Individuals in the upper-management positions command high salaries ranging from several hundred thousand to more than $1 million a year. These individuals have college degrees and usually major in a business-related curriculum. Most also have master of business administration (M.B.A.) degrees. These high positions usually are achieved by motivated individuals who work their way up the corporate ladder. In some cases, after achieving a high-level position in one company, a manager will be recruited to work for a rival company or a company in a different industry. Included in management are assistants such as secretaries and clerks.

Business management occupations may include the following:

- Chief Executive Officer (CEO)
- Chief Financial Officer (CFO)
- Controller
- Administrative Assistant
- Secretary

Customer Services

Customer services are essential for both manufacturing companies and dealerships. Individuals working in this capacity must possess excellent people skills. When a customer issues a complaint, customer service personnel must handle it in a competent and pleasant manner. The customer may be an individual or a representative of another company that might purchase thousands of units annually. A large company may employ managers, assistant managers, and representatives who communicate with customers via the telephone or Internet. Customer services usually are augmented by automated telephone messages as well as Web-based services to handle common questions. It is imperative that these services be well designed and capable of handling many common customer service issues. These automated services can result in extreme customer frustration if the customer must invest significant time without getting an answer or being able to talk directly to a company representative. Customer services are a link between customers and the company and can therefore obtain valuable information about how a product is received.

Customer services occupations may include the following:

- General Manager
- Assistant Manager
- Supervisor
- Customer Service Representative
- Webmaster

Legal Services

Large companies incur significant expenses for legal services. Legal issues can arise with companies of any size and can include product liability, copyright infringement, employee matters, and disputes regarding business practices. Large companies are more vulnerable to large settlements because of their financial standing. Lawsuits ranging from the frivolous to multimillion-dollar cases all require the company's attention. Small and some midsize businesses must retain an outside attorney in these instances. Larger companies maintain in-house counsel consisting of one or more full-time attorneys. These attorneys must specialize in or have some expertise in the following areas: mergers and acquisitions, patents, contracts, and labor law. When a company is exploring a merger with another company or dissolution of a business segment, the in-house counsel is involved in the negotiations. These teams also include assistants such as legal secretaries and paralegals. Even large companies may be required to obtain additional legal services in the event of a high-profile case. Lawsuits have the potential to financially devastate even the largest corporations.

Legal services occupations may include the following:

- General Counsel
- Paralegal
- Legal Secretary
- Administrative Assistant

Medical Services

Large companies might maintain in-house health care professionals, who can handle urgent-care issues such as job injuries that arise during the workday. This department also might promote preventive health care including weight loss and smoking cessation programs.

Medical services occupations may include the following:

- Physician (usually a family practitioner, emergency medicine physician, or a physician with specialized training in industrial medicine)
- Nurse Practitioner
- Registered Nurse
- Physician Assistant
- Medical Assistant
- Administrative Assistant

Sales and Marketing

A manufacturing company maintains a staff of vendors—salespeople who call on businesses or individuals to promote the product line. These vendors often invite customers to lunches or dinners to explain and promote the company's product line; other incentives—which must comply with federal and state regulations—also might be offered. Dealerships maintain staffs of salespeople. Marketing is conducted by advertising in trade magazines and newspapers and on television and radio. Internet advertising also is a common way to promote products. Potential customers can obtain product specifications, compare products (including those of rival manufacturers), and purchase products (either on a company's Web site or by referral to a dealership). The marketing department includes graphic designers who can develop illustrations for a Web site, brochure, or magazine dis-

play. This department includes photographers and videographers. Photographers take pictures for sales brochures and advertisements. Videographers prepare video clips for television advertisements and the company's Web site. Writers also are employed to prepare text for publications. The marketing department also consists of public relations (PR) specialists. These personnel prepare press releases announcing new products. Large companies employ specialists in the aforementioned areas. Smaller companies typically contract for that work.

Sales and marketing occupations may include the following:

- General Manager
- Assistant Manager
- Secretary
- Administrative Assistant
- Webmaster
- Photographer
- Videographer
- Sales Representative

Information Technology

All heavy machines businesses will have individuals familiar with computer maintenance and operation. Computer networks are involved in many aspects of a business, including inventory, payroll, sales, and production. A breakdown in a computer network can bring production or sales to a halt. The information technology (IT) department consists of individuals with college degrees in computer science as well as technicians with lower levels of education. These employees usually receive their training in vocational schools or community colleges. Lower-level IT positions include installation, wiring, and maintenance of computer equipment.

Information technology occupations may include the following:

- General Manager
- Assistant Manager
- Information Technologist
- Technician
- Data Entry Clerk

Facilities and Security

Maintenance of large facilities requires housekeeping personnel, painters, and repairmen. A

838   Heavy Machines Industry

large manufacturing corporation also may have a large security department headed by one or more managers. Security personnel are responsible for preventing unauthorized entry to areas where research and development are being conducted. They also are responsible for ensuring safety of the company's personnel by guarding against entry by individuals who could pose a threat. Identification badges are commonly required for all personnel. Security staff often monitor surveillance equipment and electronic entry into restricted areas. Dealerships also often have video monitoring. Theft is a much greater problem for mobile equipment than it is for fixed equipment. The size and weight of these products limits theft; however, their per-unit value is high. Theft can be committed by employees as well as burglars. Larger establishments will maintain an on-site security force during nonbusiness hours.

Facilities and security occupations may include the following:

- General Manager
- Assistant Manager
- Security Guard
- Housekeeper
- Custodian/Janitor

Technology, Research, Design, and Development

Ongoing research and development is a vital element of a heavy machine construction company. Even midsize businesses must devote time in this arena to remain competitive. Although engineers and technicians are primarily responsible for the development of a new product, this department also includes a large number of support personnel. Before a new machine is ready for the production line, an extensive process of creation and testing must be completed. For complicated equipment, this process can take several years. Engineers with a variety of specialties are employed by this department. Mechanical engineers design the moving parts of the machine (for example, hydraulics, gears, levers, and engine pistons). They also oversee the work of technicians, who run tests on materials and parts before they are assembled into the final product. After assembly, this department tests products before they are released to the marketplace. Equipment is run through repeated duty cy-

cles, knobs are twisted, buttons are pushed, and doors are slammed. If a construction defect surfaces after a product is released, the company might incur a major expense in product recall. Electrical and electronics engineers are required for the development of machines with complicated electric or electronic systems; these engineers also assist in the design and testing process. The responsibility of industrial engineers is to optimize production of the product; they determine how to best allocate the factory's resources, both workers and equipment. Once the design process and testing are completed, draftsmen prepare the plans that production workers use for assembly of the machine. For each part, draftsmen provide specifications and diagrams; they also produce assembly instructions for the final product.

Technology, research, design, and development occupations may include the following:

- Engineering Manager
- Engineer (electrical, mechanical, and industrial)
- Manager
- Supervisor
- Technician
- Mechanical Drafter
- Production Worker
- Assembly Worker

Production and Operations

Production is overseen by managers, assistant managers, and supervisors. The bulk of the workforce consists of a hierarchy ranging from experienced workers with expertise in one or more production areas to inexperienced new hires. Large companies offer training programs to help workers advance. Large and many midsize companies assemble their products on a production line similar to that of an automobile company. Robots increasingly are being used in heavy equipment manufacturing. These devices replace workers, but personnel still are required to control them. A conflict often arises between management, which is interested in improving production with robotics, and labor unions, which are focused on preserving jobs. Employee safety is a major concern, and the production line is equipped with features to ensure safety. Special clothing and goggles may be required for workers. The primary responsibility of

OCCUPATION PROFILE

Heavy Equipment Service Technician

Considerations	Qualifications
Description	Maintains and repairs heavy equipment such as cranes and bulldozers.
Career clusters	Agriculture, Food, and Natural Resources; Manufacturing; Transportation, Distribution, and Logistics
Interests	Data; things
Working conditions	Work both inside and outside
Minimum education level	On-the-job training; high school diploma/technical training; junior/technical/community college; apprenticeship
Physical exertion	Medium work; heavy work
Physical abilities	Unexceptional/basic fitness
Opportunities for experience	Internship; apprenticeship; military service
Licensure and certification	Recommended
Employment outlook	Average growth expected
Holland interest score	REI

Note: See volume 1, "Publisher's Note," for an explanation of the Holland interest score.

some supervisors is to ensure employee safety. Small companies often have fewer than a dozen workers responsible for the entire production process. However, large companies often have a multistage production process, consisting of separate teams of workers for design and testing, parts manufacturing, and product assembly. Despite this segmentation, considerable interaction takes place among the teams. For example, to promote worker interaction, design offices often are located near the assembly line.

Production and operations occupations may include the following:

- Manager
- Assistant Manager
- Supervisor
- Assembly Worker
- Wireman
- Maintenance and Repair Worker

Distribution

Companies own or lease distribution centers to store and distribute products. Because many companies are global in nature, they have distribution centers located in various areas around the world. These centers typically are located near rail lines, ports, and interstate highways. Distribution centers are overseen by managers, who are in charge of a workforce consisting primarily of warehouse workers who move products in and out of the facility. Managers also must ensure that inventory remains at an appropriate level. A distribution center may employ truck drivers or contract with a trucking company to transport items.

Distribution occupations may include the following:

- Manager
- Assistant Manager
- Supervisor

- Dispatcher
- Warehouse Worker
- Truck Driver
- Freight Loader/Unloader

Human Resources

The human resources department of a manufacturing company or retail outlet is responsible for all personnel. It handles employee hiring and dismissal, employee relations, employee benefits (such as health care insurance, retirement plans, profit-sharing plans, and interdepartmental or interfacility transfer requests), and training. The human resources department is involved with recruiting employees via the Internet or personal contact at college campuses or job fairs. Managers typically are college graduates. Clerical personnel and assistants with less educational experience also can be employed in this department.

Human resources occupations may include the following:

- Manager
- Assistant Manager
- Administrative Assistant
- Secretary
- Interviewer

Payroll

The payroll department at a heavy machines company often is overseen by a certified public accountant (CPA) with management experience. Other CPAs, clerical personnel, and assistants also work in this department. Large companies have a computerized, automated system to generate paychecks; however, some daily human monitoring or input is required.

Payroll occupations may include the following:

- Manager
- Assistant Manager
- Administrative Assistant
- Secretary

INDUSTRY OUTLOOK

Overview

The heavy machines industry declined both in the United States and globally amid the overall economic downturn. However, *The Wall Street Journal* reported in September, 2010, that the Institute for Supply Management—which surveys U.S. purchasing managers—noted that its manufacturing index rose from 55.5 in July, 2010, to 56.3 in August, 2010. *The Wall Street Journal* also reported that new orders for factory goods rose in July, 2010, while the U.S. trade deficit decreased. In that month, exports increased by $2.8 billion and imports decreased by $4.2 billion. As a result, the trade deficit shrank from $49.8 billion to $42.8 billion. If this trend continues, hiring will increase. Many companies reduced their staffs between 2008 and 2010 through hiring freezes, layoffs, and incentives for early retirement. Augmenting this process was increased efficiency of operation via robotics and other technologies that reduced the demand for manpower. Even if a broad upsurge in hiring does not continue, many positions likely will become available because of the need to replace workers who retire or move to other industries. Production workers account for more than 50 percent of the workforce in this industry; those with greater technical skills will have a significant advantage in obtaining and maintaining work. Training beyond high school often is necessary for these positions.

Midsize and small businesses likely will see their numbers reduced. If the economic downturn continues further into the 2010's, smaller companies are more likely to become insolvent. These companies will either shut down or be acquired by other companies. Furthermore, mergers and acquisitions will result in an increase in size of the dominant companies. Large companies will increase not only in size but also in global reach. For example, Japanese businesses often require personnel to become fluent in English so that they can compete more successfully in the marketplace.

One sector of the industry will profit if an economic downturn continues: the repair sector. In this economic situation, consumers will be much more likely to have existing equipment repaired than replaced. The use of robotics will increase for manufacturing. This increase may be hampered by labor unions, which will fight to preserve jobs. A number of manufacturing plants outside the United States utilize robotics to a greater degree. The added efficiency increases their profit margin, thus giving these companies a competitive advantage over those in the United States. The industry also likely will continue to improve technology to add new features and increase the energy efficiency of heavy machines.

Considerable research is focused on increasing energy efficiency and reducing emissions. "Green" products often are more attractive to end users ranging from companies to individuals. An example of a machine that is being modified to be more eco-friendly is the diesel engine. Diesel engines are powerful, reliable, and yield significantly better mileage than gasoline engines; however, they release high levels of pollutants into the air. Engines are being designed to run on cleaner diesel fuel; emission-reducing techniques also have been developed.

Employment Advantages

According to the Bureau of Labor Statistics (BLS), "machinery manufacturing has some of the most highly skilled—and highly paid—production jobs in manufacturing." Even though this industry is in a decline, the industry is still a good career choice. Heavy equipment is an essential component of any industrialized nation. A demand for heavy machinery and its components and maintenance always will exist. Most of these companies are large, global, and produce a wide variety of products; thus, they offer a degree of stability not found in smaller companies and those that do not produce essential products. The industry can support a wide variety of careers including managerial, technical, and sales.

Annual Earnings

In the short term, the industry's growth potential is uncertain. Most companies reported a decline in net sales from 2008 to 2009. For example, net sales declined 26 percent for Deere & Company from 2008 to 2009. Komatsu also reported a 9 percent decline. The Doosan Group (Bobcat Company) bucked the trend and reported a 2 percent increase in net sales. The decline for most companies was attributed to a slowdown in both the United States and global economies as well as a slowdown in the U.S. construction, housing, and home improvement markets. Affecting the heavy machines industry is the stagnation of new home construction, which began in 2009. Some building resumed in the first quarter of 2010; however, the trend did not continue through the next two quarters. The economy also improved to a degree during the first quarter of 2010; however, consumer spending for all products in the United States fell 1.2 percent from April to May, 2010.

The relative stability of the United States economy also will benefit this industry. As of 2010, the American economy was faring somewhat better than the European economy. If this trend continues, the U.S. heavy machines industry will grow. However, the American industry is facing ever-increasing competition from Asian manufacturers. A large portion of the heavy machines industry is

PROJECTED EMPLOYMENT FOR SELECTED OCCUPATIONS

Machinery Manufacturing

Employment 2009	Projected 2018	Occupation
28,450	7,300	Computer-controlled machine tool operators, metal and plastic
16,990	4,800	Engine and other machine assemblers
71,090	16,700	Machinists
30,090	8,000	Mechanical engineers
115,470	27,000	Team assemblers
21,930	23,800	Tool and die makers
60,640	15,200	Welders, cutters, solderers, and brazers

Source: U.S. Bureau of Labor Statistics, Industries at a Glance, Occupational Employment Statistics and Employment Projections Program.

based in Asia. Japanese and Korean manufacturers hold a significant market share in the United States; however, a greater threat is that of China, which exports light machines. The heavy machines industry in the United States is likely to face major competition from China in the near future.

RELATED RESOURCES FOR FURTHER RESEARCH

CATERPILLAR
100 NE Adams St.
Peoria, IL 61629
Tel: (309) 675-1000
Fax: (309) 675-4332
http://www.cat.com

DEERE & COMPANY
Deere & Company World Headquarters
1 John Deere Place
Moline, IL 61265
Tel: (309) 765-8000
Fax: (309) 765-7283
http://www.deere.com

EQUIPMENT WORLD
3200 Rice Mine Rd.
Tuscaloosa, AL 35406
Tel: (800) 633-5953
Fax: (205) 349-3765
http://www.equipmentworld.com

INSTITUTE FOR SUPPLY MANAGEMENT
P.O. Box 22160
Tempe, AZ 85285
Tel: 480-752-6275, or 800-888-6276
Fax: 480-752-7890
http://www.ism.ws

KOMATSU
2-3-6 Akasaka, Minato-ku
Tokyo 107-8414
Japan
Tel: 81-3-5561-2616
http://www.komatsu.com

MARKETRESEARCH.COM
11200 Rockville Pike, Suite 504
Rockville, MD 20852

Tel: (240) 747-3000
Fax: (240) 747-3004
http://www.marketresearch.com

MITSUBISHI HEAVY INDUSTRIES
16-5 Konan 2-chome Minato-ku
Tokyo 108-8215
Japan
Tel: 81-3-6716-3111
Fax: 81-3-6716-5800
http://www.mhi.co.jp/en

TECHNIK MANUFACTURING
1005 17th St.
Columbus, NE 68601
Tel: (800) 795-8251
Fax: (402) 564-0406
http://www.technikmfg.com

ABOUT THE AUTHOR

Robin L. Wulffson, M.D., is a board-certified specialist in Obstetrics and Gynecology. In 1997, he transitioned to a writing career. He has written analytic reports on major corporations and industries. He has analyzed hospital systems and medical device manufacturers. He is familiar with the heavy machines industry in the United States, Europe, and Asia. For the past fifteen years, he has closely followed the business sector in the United States and abroad.

FURTHER READING

Dennis, Neil. "Economic Outlook: Measure of Manufacturing." *The Financial Times*, September 26, 2010.
Mitchel, Doug. *Anatomy of the John Deere.* Iola, Wisc.: Krause, 2007.
Orlemann, Eric C. *Caterpillar Chronicle: The History of the World's Greatest Earthmovers.* St. Paul, Minn.: Motorbooks International, 2009.
Rosen, William. *The Most Powerful Idea in the World: A Story of Steam, Industry, and Invention.* New York: Random House, 2010.
Stearns, Peter N. *The Industrial Revolution in World History.* 3d ed. Boulder, Colo.: Westview Press, 2007.

Supplier Relations U.S. *Farm Machinery and Equipment Manufacturing Industry in the U.S. and Its International Trade.* 2010 ed. http://www.marketresearch.com/product/display.asp?productid=2802962

U.S. Bureau of Labor Statistics. *Career Guide to Industries,* 2010-2011 ed. http://www.bls.gov/oco/cg.

_____. *Occupational Outlook Handbook,* 2010-2011 ed. http://www.bls.gov/oco.

U.S. Census Bureau. North American Industry Classification System (NAICS), 2007. http://www.census.gov/cgi-bin/sssd/naics/naicsrch?chart=2007.

U.S. Department of Commerce. International Trade Administration. Office of Trade and Industry Information. Industry Trade Data and Analysis. http://ita.doc.gov/td/industry/otea/OTII/OTII-index.html.

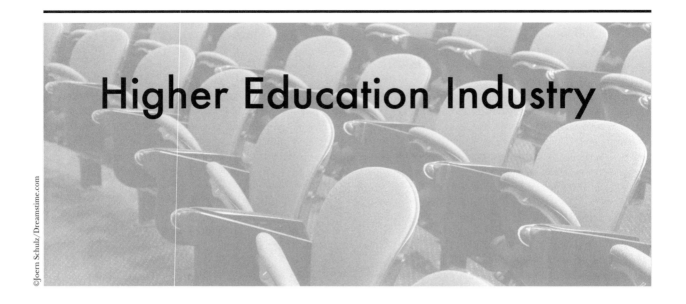

Higher Education Industry

©Joern Schulz/Dreamstime.com

INDUSTRY SNAPSHOT

General Industry: Education and Training
Career Cluster: Education and Training
Subcategory Industries: Business Schools; Colleges; Junior and Community Colleges; Music Conservatories; Professional Schools; Theological Seminaries; Universities
Related Industries: Private Education Industry; Public Elementary and Secondary Education Industry
Annual Domestic Revenues: $474 billion USD (U.S. Department of Education, 2006-2007)
NAICS Number: 6112-6113

INDUSTRY DEFINITION

Summary

The higher education industry serves students seeking postsecondary education—that is, education beyond the high school level. It includes colleges and universities with programs leading to undergraduate degrees such as associate's and bachelor's degrees, graduate degrees such as master's and doctoral degrees, and professional degrees such as medical or legal degrees. Higher education institutions may also offer other specialized degree programs, including a variety of academic and professional certificate programs. While the most obvious position within this industry is perhaps that of a professor, the industry also comprises numerous supporting roles across a variety of fields, including administration, management, marketing, and finance, all of which are essential to the operations of a postsecondary educational institution of any size.

History of the Industry

Higher education in the United States dates back to the seventeenth century, when its primary objective was to educate future members of the clergy. At that time, most higher education curricula were dominated by liberal arts subjects, particularly languages, literature, and religious studies. Faculties were small, and courses of study were often broad and designed on an individual basis depending on the interests of the student.

The nineteenth century saw significant change in the purpose of higher education, beginning with the Morrill Land-Grant Act of 1862. Signed by President Abraham Lincoln, the act included grants of land to states and territories to establish colleges devoted to agriculture, science, and engineering. This law sparked the growth of public colleges and universities, and it was an important step toward the explosive growth that would be experienced by the higher education industry during the twentieth century.

Demand for higher education programs in the early twentieth century was frequently driven by the needs of the Industrial Revolution. During this time, many schools expanded their engineering and science offerings, particularly in the fields of chemistry and physics, and specialization became more common. Programs that assisted in the manufacture of steel, rubber, chemicals, sugar, drugs, petroleum, and electricity generation grew in popularity. As specialization increased, faculty size grew, and the higher education industry experienced a fundamental change in both the way students were taught and the way departments were organized.

Following World War II, increased federal funding to public colleges, along with the GI Bill (officially, the Servicemen's Readjustment Act of 1944), made higher education affordable for a wider range of students. As a result, more young people started to attend college than ever before. This growth in scholarship was in large part directed toward public colleges and universities, as the tuition at such institutions was generally more affordable and the large number of students at public schools resulted in larger departments offering a wider variety of programs.

In the latter part of the twentieth century, programs such as affirmative action encouraged ethnic diversity within student bodies, and increased federal funding in the form of government-sponsored student loans and grants provided more indi-

The most obvious position within the higher education industry is perhaps that of a professor like this one; however, the industry also offers many positions in a variety of fields, including administration, management, marketing, and finance. (©Gualtiero Boffi/Dreamstime.com)

viduals with the opportunity to attend college. All these changes led to a more expansive and enriching experience in higher education, as well as an increased need for infrastructure and staff.

The Industry Today

Higher education in the early twenty-first century has grown to include a vast number of academic and vocational disciplines and a wide variety of delivery systems. Many schools now offer certification programs, as well as programs designed to help working adults enhance their existing careers. Additionally, many programs have moved away from traditional full-time day classes to include part-time and night programs, distance learning, online courses, and academic credit for employment experience.

The addition of new programs, as well as new loan and grant opportunities for students to fund their educations, has increased the number of individuals attending American colleges and universities. The U.S. Department of Labor projects that these numbers will continue to grow in the early twenty-first century. This growth is expected not only to increase the enrollment numbers at existing schools but also perhaps inspire the establishment of new ones, particularly in the for-profit sector. This growth bodes well for increased employment opportunities in the industry, although the nature of the jobs available may shift as institutions make changes to accommodate the early twenty-first century's lifestyles, demands, and economy.

Many schools, for example, are moving away from hiring full-time tenured professors and toward hiring part-time adjunct instructors in order to save money on salaries and benefits. This may have an unexpected up-side, however, in that these part-time instructors are often working professionals. As a result, they may be better able to relate to working adults returning to school and can help students of all ages integrate their academic experiences into the workplace upon graduation. On the other hand, adjunct instructors do not have the institutional service requirements that full-time faculty have. They are not required to serve on committees and are usually not asked to serve as advisers to students. As schools hire more adjuncts, then, the fewer remaining tenured and tenure-track faculty must pick up the slack, and each professor's workload outside the classroom increases significantly.

These changes have opened up higher education to a greater variety of individuals than ever before. While much debate remains within the academic community as to whether these changes have been a positive development or whether they are lowering the standards previously set for higher education, the increased diversity of students and programs can lead to a more enriching academic experience for everyone. The increased level of education among the U.S. workforce overall is likely to produce many positive changes in the years to come.

In response to their changing environment, many schools are also branching out with respect to their private industry associations. Historically, many schools (particularly large ones with science and medical programs) have affiliated themselves with hospitals and other research institutions to exchange facilities, equipment, expertise, and revenue. Schools are also increasingly seeking funding sources from private indus-

Many schools now offer certification programs, as well as programs designed to help working adults enhance their existing careers. (©Monkey Business Images/ Dreamstime.com)

tries to finance everything from research labs to programs that provide computers and other equipment directly to students. These affiliations can be of great benefit, as the schools may be able to obtain resources that they could not otherwise afford. However, such affiliations raise ethical questions about potential conflicts of interest if private industry becomes too closely associated with teaching methods within a school.

INDUSTRY MARKET SEGMENTS

Within the higher education industry, schools can range from small liberal arts or community colleges serving fewer than one hundred students housed in a single building to large universities with tens of thousands of students occupying as much space as a small city. The following sections provide details on different sizes of schools within the industry. Even within a particular size range, the specifics of a given institution are influenced by many factors, including the types of programs offered and the geographic location of the school.

Small Schools

Many small schools in the higher education industry are community colleges offering two-year associate degree programs, possibly along with some additional certification programs. However, there are some small schools that offer four-year bachelor degree programs and even some graduate-level programs. Small schools generally have fewer degree options than their larger counterparts, and their offerings are likely to be influenced by the types of jobs that are in high demand in the geographic area where the school is located. Smaller schools tend to attract local students, as well as older students who are returning to school after time spent in the workforce. Small schools generally have less than two thousand students and may have as few as twenty or thirty.

Potential Annual Earnings Scale. Salaries generally remain consistent throughout the higher education industry. According to the U.S. Bureau of Labor Statistics (BLS), the mean salary for office and administrative support occupations is $33,290 per year, although individual salaries will vary depending on the department and the position. Me-

dian salaries for middle-level managers and administrators, including the dean of students, registrar, and director of financial aid, range from $50,000 to $125,000. Median salaries for top-level management positions, including the chief academic officer and academic deans, range from $83,108 to $140,595. The mean salary for all management-level positions is $94,300. Salaries for any position at junior and community colleges are likely to be at the lower end of their respective ranges.

Clientele Interaction. The primary clientele of a higher education establishment are its students. Regardless of the position held, most employees at a small school interact with students at least occasionally. Positions that require the most interaction with students include any teaching position, library service positions, and customer service positions such as those in the registration office, financial aid office, or information technology (IT) department. Academic administration positions, such as a dean or certain supervisory positions, often involve some interaction with students, particularly when there is a difficult situation or problem to be resolved. The highest-level management positions may require very little student interaction.

Nonetheless, one of the perceived benefits of both working at and attending a small school is the increased opportunity for more interaction with students. Many students choose a small school because they want to receive personal attention that they believe they would not receive at a larger institution, so it is important to provide this personal touch when working in a small school environment. Additionally, many students at small schools are from the local area and may be working adults returning to school after time spent in the workforce. It is important for small schools to keep this background in mind when developing their educational programs, since these students may have significant experience in the employment industry but limited experience in an academic setting, and they may need some assistance making the adjustment.

Amenities, Atmosphere, and Physical Grounds. The atmosphere of a school will often depend on the size of its campus and whether the majority of its students live on campus or commute. Schools with predominantly on-campus students often have more of a community atmosphere than schools where most of the students commute

College recruiters sometimes ask current students to show prospective students around the campus. (©Lori Howard/ Dreamstime.com)

from their own homes. Similarly, schools where the staff consists mainly of individuals who live near the school may have more of a community feel than schools where much of the staff commutes from a significant distance. At many smaller schools, the staff tends to come primarily from the area immediately surrounding the school.

The smallest of higher educational facilities may be housed entirely in a single building. Commonly, small colleges are made up of several small buildings, either lined up on a city block or situated in a cluster to form a small campus. Amenities vary greatly, depending on the size and location of the school. Most schools will offer separate lounge areas for students, faculty, and other staff, and many schools provide a small library and possibly a cafeteria. Depending on the location (urban, suburban, or rural), there may be parking facilities or access by public transportation, making a school more or less commuter friendly for students and employees.

Typical Number of Employees. Small colleges typically have between two hundred and eight hundred employees. This number includes all full- and part-time staff, including professors and other instructors, deans, directors, managers, and administrators. Small schools may also directly employ workers in additional support positions, such as maintenance or cafeteria staff, but they may also contract those services out to an external company.

Traditional Geographic Locations. Small colleges can be found all over the country and in a variety of geographic areas, including quiet rural areas, suburbs, and large cities. The location of the school will have an impact on the feel of its campus. Often, rural or suburban locations feel more like college towns, where many of the local businesses cater to students and employees and many of the town's residents are transient students. Urban schools may have more of the character of the city where they are located, and the transient nature of the students will be balanced with the high number of permanent residents and non-education-related professionals in the community.

The size of a school's campus can also vary considerably. The smallest of schools may be located entirely within a single building, while others may include several buildings lining a city block or arranged in a cluster to form a campus. Small liberal arts schools may occupy quite large tracts of land that include athletic facilities, farmland, or other resources in addition to their academic buildings. The specific configuration will likely be dictated by the location of the school; for example, an urban school may be more limited in space than a suburban or rural school.

Pros of Working for a Small School. Small schools generally employ fewer people within each department, and with fewer fellow employees as competition, it may be easier to distinguish oneself professionally, as well as to develop personal relationships with colleagues and supervisors. There may be greater opportunities to take on leadership roles or to expand the scope of an employment position to include new responsibilities. There may also be less bureaucracy within smaller colleges, as there are fewer employees and fewer layers of management. Smaller schools also usually provide more opportunity for interacting with students, regardless of position, and instructors in particular may find that their smaller class sizes allow for more meaningful relationships with students.

Cons of Working for a Small School. Many smaller schools operate with a smaller staff, so any individual job description may expand beyond its expected scope. Even those occupying positions such as professor, dean, or upper-level management may occasionally need to perform their own administrative support tasks. With a smaller infrastructure, there may be less opportunity for advancement and fewer opportunities to develop new programs or courses. Smaller schools may also operate on smaller budgets, which could entail lower salaries than those paid for comparable positions at larger schools.

Costs

Payroll and Benefits: Salary and benefits vary widely depending on an individual's role in the organization and whether the college is a public or private institution. Benefit packages range from quite generous to nonexistent, again de-

pending on the position and employment status (full- versus part-time). Adjunct faculty often receive no benefits and are paid by the course taught, whereas tenured professors receive annual salaries and benefits. Potential benefits include health insurance, retirement packages or pension plans, paid time off, and reduced or free tuition for family members.

Supplies: Small schools require all standard office supplies, plus telecommunication equipment such as computer hardware, software, networking equipment, and telephones; classroom supplies such as desks, chairs, chalk- or whiteboards; audiovisual equipment; and common area supplies for lounges, such as study carrels, couches, tables, chairs, and refrigerators. Libraries require a variety of books, journals, and other research material, as well as subscriptions to computer-based academic research databases. Schools that offer laboratory facilities require benches and stools, fume hoods, glassware, chemicals, storage cabinets, and safety equipment, such as laboratory coats, gloves, and eye protection. Schools that offer athletic facilities require cleaning and maintenance supplies, as well as sporting and exercise equipment.

External Services: Common external services include landscaping of outdoor facilities and maintenance of athletic fields; cleaning of buildings containing classrooms, administrative offices, and common areas; and campus security services. Some smaller schools may also contract out telecommunication and computer network services, as well as dining-hall and other food-related services.

Utilities: Common utility costs include electricity, heat, air-conditioning, water, telephone, and Internet service for classrooms, administrative offices, common spaces, and dorms (although many smaller schools do not have such facilities).

Taxes: Applicability of state and local taxes depends on whether a school is a public, private nonprofit, or for-profit institution.

Midsize Schools

A midsize school in the higher education industry generally offers four-year bachelor's degree programs, along with some graduate-level programs and possibly a variety of certificate programs. Midsize schools will usually offer more degree options than their smaller counterparts but not the same variety as are available at large schools. A midsize institution may specialize in a particular area, offering a variety of degree programs within a single category (for example, liberal arts or science and engineering) and a limited number of programs in the other categories. Midsize schools have approximately two thouand to six thousand students across their various programs.

Potential Annual Earnings Scale. Salaries generally remain consistent throughout the higher education industry. According to the BLS, the mean salary for office and administrative support occupations is $33,290 per year, although individual salaries will vary depending on the department and the position. Median salaries for middle-level managers and administrators, including the dean of students, registrar, and director of financial aid, range from $50,000 to $125,000. Median salaries for top-level management positions, including the chief academic officer and academic deans, range from $83,108 to $140,595. The mean salary for all management-level positions is $94,300.

Clientele Interaction. Many employees at midsize schools have limited direct interactions with students, if any. Positions that require the most interaction with students include any teaching position, library service positions, and customer service positions such as those in the registration office, financial aid office, or computer help desk. Academic administration positions, such as a dean or certain supervisory positions, may require some interaction with students, but not as regularly and most likely only when there is a more serious problem to be resolved. Some positions, such as the highest-level management, financial services, or directorship positions, require very little, if any, student interaction.

Many students choose a midsize school because they want the amenities of a larger school but still wish to have a more focused and personalized experience than would be possible at the largest schools. Many students at midsize schools come from the geographic region in which the school is located (for example, New England), but there may be a significant number of students from outside the area who are likely to require some time to adjust to their new surroundings. Regardless of the position held within a midsize school, these issues will have an impact on any employee's relationship and interaction with students.

Amenities, Atmosphere, and Physical Grounds. The atmosphere of the school will often depend on the size of the campus, whether the campus setting is urban, suburban, or rural, and whether the bulk of the students live on the campus or commute. Schools with predominantly on-campus students often have more of a community atmosphere than schools where most of the students commute from their own homes. Similarly, schools where the staff consists mainly of individuals who live near the school may have more of a community feel than schools where much of the staff commutes from a significant distance or includes visiting professors.

As many students move to campus from outside the immediate area, most midsize schools have student dormitories. Off-campus housing is also generally located near these schools. As a result, many schools actively seek to develop a strong community surrounding the campus. The staff of most midsize schools tends to come primarily from the area surrounding the school. Depending on the location (urban, suburban, or rural), there may be parking facilities or access by public transportation, making a school more or less commuter friendly for students and employees.

Midsize colleges generally occupy a number of buildings grouped together, either lined up on a city block or situated in a cluster to form a small campus. Amenities vary depending on the size and location of the school, but schools generally offer separate lounge areas for students, faculty, and other staff. Many schools have a student union, which is typically a building set aside specifically for students to meet socially, study, and conduct meetings of various campus organizations. Midsize schools usually have a cafeteria and bookstore and often have a convenience store located on campus. Almost all midsize schools have libraries, although these vary in size and scope depending on the number of students and the types of programs offered. Many midsize schools, particularly those that cater to the study of science or engineering, will also have research laboratories and related facilities. Depending on the size and availability of space, midsize schools may also offer athletic facilities such as fields, gyms, and pools and may field a number of sports teams in lower divisions.

Typical Number of Employees. A typical mid-size college has between four hundred and two thousand employees. This number includes all full- and part-time staff, including professors and other instructors, deans, directors, managers, and administrators. Midsize schools may also directly employ workers in additional support positions, such as maintenance or cafeteria staff, but they may also contract those services out to an external company.

Traditional Geographic Locations. Midsize colleges can be found all over the country in a variety of geographic areas but will most often be found in suburban or urban locations. The location of a school will have an impact on the feel of the campus; often more suburban locations will feel more like college towns, where many of the local businesses cater to students and employees of the school (or schools) and many of the residents are transient students. Urban schools have more of the character of the city in which they are located, and the transient nature of the students is balanced by the high number of permanent residents and non-education-related professionals in the community. The size of the campus can vary depending on the number of students, the types of research facilities offered, and the geographic location. The configuration will likely be dictated by the location of the school, since an urban school is likely to be more limited in space than a suburban school.

Pros of Working for a Midsize School. Midsize schools are in many ways a happy medium between the smallest and largest schools. Each department is generally moderate in size, not only providing employees the opportunity for personal relationships but also allowing them to benefit from a more hierarchical management structure than at small schools. This structure may allow for upward mobility within the organization. There may be opportunities to take on leadership roles on certain projects or to expand the scope of a particular job to include new responsibilities. Midsize schools are likely to enjoy more funding than smaller schools and thus more opportunities to create or expand programs to better serve students.

Cons of Working for a Midsize School. Since midsize schools employ more people, their hierarchical management structure creates more bureaucracy than at a typical smaller school. More de-partments compete with one another for funds and students, and more people within each department compete for their particular resources and operations. Competition for full-time faculty positions is very competitive in midsize schools, and such positions often come with a requirement to conduct research and contribute to academic and scholarly publications to attract outside funding to the school.

Costs

Payroll and Benefits: Salary and benefits vary widely depending on an individual's role in the organization and whether the college is a public or private institution. Benefit packages range from quite generous to nonexistent, again depending on position and employment status (full- versus part-time). Potential benefits include health insurance, retirement packages or pension plans, paid time off, and reduced or free tuition.

Supplies: Midsize schools require all standard office supplies, plus telecommunication equipment such as computer hardware, software, networking equipment, and telephones; classroom supplies such as desks, chairs, chalk- or whiteboards; audiovisual equipment; and common area supplies for lounges, such as study carrels, couches, tables, chairs, and refrigerators. Since most midsize schools have dormitories, supplies for these facilities are needed as well, including beds, desks, lamps, and furniture for common areas. Libraries require a variety of books, journals, and other research material, as well as subscriptions to computer-based academic research databases. Schools that offer laboratory facilities require benches and stools, fume hoods, glassware, chemicals, storage cabinets, and safety equipment, such as laboratory coats, gloves, and eye protection. Athletic facilities require cleaning and maintenance supplies, as well as sporting and exercise equipment.

External Services: Common external services include landscaping of outdoor facilities and maintenance of athletic fields; cleaning of buildings containing classrooms, administrative offices, and common areas; and campus security services. Some midsize schools also contract out telecommunication and computer network services, as well as dining-hall and other food-related services. Others have teams of in-house specialists for these functions.

Utilities: Common utility costs include electricity, heat, air-conditioning, water, telephone, and Internet service for classrooms, administrative offices, common spaces, and dorms.

Taxes: Applicability of state and local taxes depends on whether a school is a public, private nonprofit, or for-profit institution.

Large Schools

Large colleges and universities offer a wide variety of degree programs across many disciplines, including associate's and bachelor's degree programs, graduate programs that offer master's and doctoral degrees, and possibly professional programs that offer medical, law, or business degrees, among others. These schools (which are often classified as universities) usually offer research facilities for a variety of fields. Large schools have more than six thousand students.

Potential Annual Earnings Scale. Salaries generally remain consistent throughout the higher education industry. According to the BLS, the mean salary for office and administrative support occupations is $33,290 per year, although individual salaries will vary depending on the department and the position. Median salaries for middle-level managers and administrators, including the dean of students, registrar, and director of financial aid, range from $50,000 to $125,000. Median salaries for top-level management positions, including the chief academic officer and academic deans, range from $83,108 to $140,595. The mean salary for all management-level positions is $94,300.

Clientele Interaction. As with all schools, the primary clients of a large university are its students, but many employees have limited or no direct interactions with students. Positions that require the most interaction with students include any teaching position, library service positions, and customer service positions such as working in the registration office, financial aid office, or computer help desk. Academic administration positions, such as deans or certain supervisory positions, may require some interaction with students but not as regularly. Some positions, such as higher-level management, financial services, or directorship positions, involve very little, if any, student interaction.

Many students choose a large school because they want the wide variety of amenities, as well as the name recognition, that comes with attending such a school. Many students realize that they will not receive the same personal attention that is possible at a smaller school. Nonetheless, they expect to receive the same high level of customer service that one would expect at a smaller school. Students come from all over the world to attend large universities, so a significant proportion of the student body is not from the local area, and these students may require some assistance to adjust to their new surroundings. Additionally, many students attend large colleges and universities immediately after high school and may need some additional assistance adjusting to life on their own. Regardless of which position one holds within a large school, these issues are likely to have an impact on student relationships and interaction.

Amenities, Atmosphere, and Physical Grounds. The atmosphere of a school often depends on the size of the campus, whether the campus setting is urban or suburban, and whether the majority of students live on the campus or commute. Large schools generally have many student dormitories and a large on-campus population, and they thus have a rich community atmosphere. Many other students choose to live in nearby off-campus housing, thus encouraging a strong community surrounding the campus. The staff for most large-sized schools tends to come from the area surrounding the school, although there may also be a significant number of visiting staff members (usually professors and researchers) from other areas. Depending on the location, there may be parking facilities or access by public transportation, making a school more or less commuter-friendly for students and employees.

Large colleges and universities occupy many buildings grouped together, either lined up on a group of city blocks or situated in a cluster to form a campus. These campuses range in size from several city blocks to the size of an entire town. Some universities situate various academic colleges or divisions in clusters within a city. This distribution might result in a university medical center being located alongside the city's larger medical community while the institution's school of study is located in an area that is less developed or where real estate is less expensive, allowing for future growth.

Amenities vary depending on the size and location of the school, but schools generally offer separate lounge areas for students, faculty, and other staff. Large schools have student unions, buildings set aside specifically for students to meet socially, study, and conduct meetings of various campus organizations. At universities where there are several or multiple campuses, an individual campus may contain amenities designed exclusively for that campus. Large schools have multiple cafeterias, one or more campus bookstores, and, often, convenience stores. Their libraries vary in size and scope, depending on the number of students and the types of programs offered, but are likely to be quite large and comprehensive and may offer private study or meeting areas.

Most large schools have significant research laboratories and other facilities related to their myriad academic departments. Research labs provide a number of important benefits to colleges and universities: They encourage important scientific breakthroughs, provide opportunities for students to engage in specialized advanced training, and create jobs connected to the newly developed technologies. High-quality research labs can also help a school attract top faculty, staff, and students to further develop its programs. Additionally, research labs can provide a significant source of revenue through private industry investment, government grants, and income generated from patents developed by the school.

Most large schools, particularly those in suburban settings with a lot of available space, have a variety of athletic facilities, including fields, gyms, and pools, and they usually field a number of sports teams, many of which may be upper divisional and high profile. Some programs, such as major conference football teams with national followings, can benefit their schools by providing a significant source of revenue through sales of tickets, merchandise, and concessions. Even sports teams that do not bring in a significant amount of revenue can raise the profile of their schools by providing positive media attention for the teams' accomplishments. However, financing such teams can also cost a great deal of money. Sports that do not bring in enough revenue to cover their own costs may be at risk when a school of any size cuts its athletic budgets in the face of economic hardship.

Typical Number of Employees. A typical large college will have anywhere from two thousand to more than ten thousand employees. This number includes full- and part-time staff, including professors and other instructors, deans, directors, managers, administrators, and numerous support staff positions.

Traditional Geographic Locations. Large colleges can be found all over the country and in a variety of geographic areas, but they are most often found in suburban or urban locations. The location of a school has an impact on the feel of its campus. Often, more suburban locations feel more like college towns, where many of the local businesses cater to students and employees of the school (or schools) and many of the residents are transient students. Urban schools have more of the character of the city in which they are located, and the transient nature of the students is balanced by the high number of permanent residents and non-education-related professionals in the community. The size of the campus can vary depending on the number of students, the types of research facilities offered, and the geographic location. The configuration will likely be dictated by the location of the school, since an urban school is likely to be more limited in space than a suburban school.

Pros of Working for a Large School. Large schools have far more amenities and a far greater amount of funding than their smaller counterparts. Because each department is larger, there are greater opportunities for advancement within the hierarchical management system. Because of the increased funding and increased availability of support staff, there are often more opportunities to create or expand programs to better serve students. For academics, research facilities at large schools encourage professional growth by providing equipment and funding for advanced study of highly specialized subjects. The greater number of faculty and graduate students provides a support system to better distribute basic tasks such as teaching lower-level courses and grading papers, which allows professors more time to conduct research. Additionally, supervising graduate students can be a rewarding experience, as it provides additional teaching opportunities and helps prepare the next generation of academics for careers in teaching and research.

Cons of Working for a Large School. Since large schools employ more people, the more hierarchical management structure creates more bureaucracy. More departments compete for funds and students. Competition for full-time faculty positions can be extremely competitive, and such positions often come with a requirement to conduct research and contribute to scholarly publications in order to attract outside funding to the school. While there is significant variation among schools, the research orientation of many large schools makes them poor fits for professors who see themselves primarily as teachers. Indeed, there may be fewer opportunities for people in all positions within a large school to work directly with students, and those interactions may not be as meaningful as they might be in a smaller setting.

Costs

Payroll and Benefits: Salary and benefits vary widely depending on an individual's role in the organization and whether the college is a public or private institution. Benefit packages range from quite generous to nonexistent, again depending on position and employment status (full- versus part-time). Potential benefits include health insurance, retirement packages or pension plans, paid time off, and reduced or free tuition.

Supplies: Large schools require all standard office supplies, plus telecommunication equipment such as computer hardware, software, networking equipment, and telephones; classroom supplies such as desks, chairs, chalk- or whiteboards; audiovisual equipment; and common area supplies for lounges, such as study carrels, couches, tables, chairs, and refrigerators. Since most large schools have dormitories, supplies for these facilities are needed as well, including beds, desks, lamps, and furniture for common areas. Libraries require a variety of books, journals, and other research material, as well as subscriptions to computer-based academic research databases. Laboratory facilities require benches and stools, fume hoods, glassware, chemicals, storage cabinets, and safety equipment, such as laboratory coats, gloves, and eye protection. Large schools have many different athletic facilities and require related supplies, including sporting and exercise equipment, as well as cleaning and maintenance supplies.

External Services: Common external services include landscaping of outdoor facilities and maintenance of athletic fields; cleaning of buildings containing classrooms, administrative offices, and common areas; and campus security services.

Utilities: Common utility costs include electricity, heat, air-conditioning, water, telephone, and Internet services for classrooms, administrative offices, common spaces, and dorms.

Taxes: Applicability of state and local taxes depends on whether a school is a public, private nonprofit, or for-profit institution.

ORGANIZATIONAL STRUCTURE AND JOB ROLES

Any size school within the higher education industry needs to account for activities in the following areas. In smaller schools, one person may hold several roles within several groups, and several of these functions may be combined into a single department. In larger schools, specialists often fulfill unique requirements in specific groups. Regardless of size and scope, the functions must be fulfilled.

The following umbrella categories apply to the organizational structure of institutions of higher education:

- Business Management
- Customer Services
- Sales and Marketing
- Facilities and Security
- Technology, Research, Design, and Development
- Production and Operations
- Human Resources

Business Management

All institutions of higher education employ significant staffs in a variety of areas, both academic and administrative. Even the smallest schools require a management structure that can support the wide variety of functions that a school needs in order to serve its students. On the academic side, individual departments are led by department chairs, who are often also full-time professors. These individuals generally have doctorates in their fields and may also have experience in managerial roles. Larger institutions have deans who lead groups of academic departments or schools within universities (for example, a dean of a school of engineering). These individuals may have doctorates in specific academic fields and often have degrees, or at least significant experience, in management specifically related to institutions of higher education.

On the administrative side, each department is led by a manager, who usually has at least a four-year degree in a subject relevant to his or her department and may have either a master of business administration (M.B.A.) or an additional degree in college administration. Larger institutions have deans who lead groups of administrative departments (for example, a dean of academic affairs or a dean of student affairs).

Members of a school's board of directors or trustees are often community leaders or individuals who have worked in private industry and have long-term ties to the institution. New members are generally appointed or elected into these positions by current board members. The members are responsible for setting general policies that are in line with the institute's mission and for ensuring its continuing financial health. The president or chancellor of the school is hired by the board and is responsible for executing tasks in a manner that aligns with the broader policy and fiscal guidelines set by the board. Depending on their specific role, these individuals are likely to have advanced degrees in business, management, law, or finance, as well as a great deal of experience performing these roles on behalf of an academic institution.

Business management occupations may include the following:

- College/University President or Chancellor
- Dean
- Department Chair
- Admissions Manager
- Member of the Board of Directors
- Member of the Board of Trustees

Customer Services

Students are customers of a higher education institution and require many administrative support services to assist them through their academic experience. Many positions within colleges and universities work directly with students, but some positions are more customer-service oriented in that they are specifically geared toward helping students get the most out of their college experience.

The most common departments to employ a large number of customer-service-related jobs are the admissions office, the registrar's office, and the financial aid office. Each of these departments deals with a large number of students and an even greater volume of paperwork on a daily basis and so requires employees who can maintain a friendly, upbeat, and helpful service-oriented nature, even when faced with a great deal of work.

Many of these positions are administrative in nature and require an ability to remain very organized when dealing with a high volume of paperwork, particularly in larger schools. Many positions require a four-year degree in a liberal arts field, and some require education and experience specifically in the area of college administration for advancement to supervisory positions.

Customer services occupations may include the following:

- Registration Office Administrator
- Financial Aid Officer
- Admissions Officer
- Career Development Counselor

Sales and Marketing

Within any given school, there are several different departments that can be categorized as sales and marketing. These include the admissions office, which recruits new students; the development office, which brings in funds and manages the school's image both professionally and within the community; and the alumni relations office, which raises funds to support the school's endowment through alumni donations and works to maintain an active community of graduates.

Schools of all sizes need to bring in new students each year to maintain their business. Although this function is often called admissions or recruitment, the reality is that the school is marketing itself to prospective students. The admissions office has two objectives: First, it seeks to recruit students to enroll in the school. Responsibilities in this area include developing marketing materials in print and online, as well as visiting high schools and hosting prospective students on campus. Employees who serve these functions in the admissions office usually have four-year degrees in public relations or communication, sometimes with a concentration in education or academic administration.

Second, the admissions office is responsible for selecting which students to admit to the school. This task requires reviewing application materials and possibly conducting interviews with individual students. Employees who serve this function in the admissions department generally have degrees in academic administration for higher education and often have experience working with postsecondary students either as an instructor or as an administrator.

For privately funded schools, the development office is responsible for seeking out funding sources in the form of contracts for research activities and donations. In larger schools, the development or alumni relations office may also be responsible for attracting investments from outside organizations and school alumni. They solicit contributions to capital and endowment campaigns that fund research and academic facilities, as well as scholarships and faculty chairs. Fulfilling these responsibilities requires employees to develop marketing materials that showcase a school's current facilities and potential for innovation in a particular field, as well as to cultivate relationships with business leaders and alumni. A typical employee in these areas has a four-year degree in a field such as public relations or communication, sometimes with a focus on academic administration or education.

Sales and marketing occupations may include the following:

- Admissions Director
- Gift Planning Director
- Development Director
- Treasurer
- Director of Foundation Relations
- Vice President of External Relations
- Public Relations Director
- Marketing Director
- Graphic Designer
- Copywriter
- Photographer

Facilities and Security

All higher education institutions, regardless of size or location, require some level of facilities maintenance and security. Smaller institutions require minimal maintenance and may have only a small permanent staff of such workers, preferring to contract out most services. Even schools housed within a single building require some security to ensure that only authorized individuals are allowed access to the building, for the safety of the students, faculty, and other staff.

Midsize institutions require more maintenance, addressing both indoor and outdoor facilities, and are likely to maintain a slightly larger staff of permanent maintenance workers. Other services may be contracted out. Midsize schools require more security staff to monitor access to buildings and the campus in general. Schools that house students in dormitories require some twenty-four-hour security services to ensure the safety of the students at all times. Many midsize institutions (and most large ones) also have athletic programs whose physical facilities require additional maintenance.

Large institutions require a great deal of maintenance, both indoor and outdoor, and often maintain a significant staff of permanent workers in addition to contracted labor. Large schools also require significant staff to provide around-the-clock security to students living on campus.

Employment requirements vary depending on position. Basic maintenance or janitorial positions may require no advanced education or experience, while more specialized facilities positions may require both a special license and relevant experience. Qualifications for security positions also vary but likely include at least some level of education or certification beyond a high school diploma.

Facilities and security occupations may include the following:

- Building and Grounds Facility Manager
- Building Maintenance and Repair Worker
- Building Security Manager
- Security Guard
- Emergency Services Crew
- Athletic Director

Technology, Research, Design, and Development

Most institutions of higher education rely heavily on technology to support their students' growth and development. The two biggest areas of technology most frequently used by schools of all sizes are computer networks and classroom audiovisual equipment.

Most schools maintain a campus network with both Internet and Intranet connections, and many have on-campus computer labs. The more extensive the network and the more students that rely on the network for their studies, the more support and assistance will be required to keep it functioning at all times. Depending on the size of the network, it may require a large staff of network and IT professionals to keep it functioning. A customer-service-oriented help desk may also be made available to answer students' questions at important times of the day.

The IT staff is in charge of maintaining not only a school's network but also the computers of its employees, including its administrative support staff.

Since most colleges now maintain all of their records on computers, this is an extremely important function; one seemingly small network failure could cause a far-reaching effect throughout all campus departments. As a result, these jobs are well suited for people who enjoy problem solving and who are not afraid to be on call to solve network problems at any time. IT staff often have four-year degrees in computer programming, computer systems engineering, or information technology, with concentrations in network systems.

Additionally, many classrooms are now equipped with audiovisual equipment such as SMART Boards, projectors, televisions, and digital video disc (DVD) players to allow instructors to make multimedia presentations in their classes. This equipment can require a great deal of support and maintenance to ensure that instructors know how to use it properly

OCCUPATION PROFILE

Research Assistant

Considerations	Qualifications
Description	Provides assistance and support to the work of a professor, including analyzing documents and data as well as conducting experiments.
Career clusters	Agriculture, Food, and Natural Resources; Business, Management, and Administration; Health Science; Manufacturing; Marketing, Sales, and Service; Science, Technology, Engineering, and Math
Interests	Data; people
Working conditions	Work inside
Minimum education level	Bachelor's degree; master's degree
Physical exertion	Light work
Physical abilities	Unexceptional/basic fitness
Opportunities for experience	Volunteer work; part-time work
Licensure and certification	Usually not required
Employment outlook	Average growth expected
Holland interest score	IER; ISE

Note: See volume 1, "Publisher's Note," for an explanation of the Holland interest score.

and to keep it in good working order at all times. Additionally, the presence of this type of equipment in classrooms may require more security personnel to ensure that it is secure and safe from theft. Audiovisual support staff may have two- or four-year degrees in computer programming, electrical engineering, or information technology.

Schools with significant research facilities have additional technology needs, depending on the type of research being conducted and the equipment involved. Research facilities have the same basic computer, network, and audiovisual needs as the rest of their university, but they also employ laboratory managers to operate and maintain specialized laboratory equipment, as well as to monitor safety conditions. Laboratory managers must at least have four-year degrees in science or engineering and often have graduate degrees in their subject areas. They may also be employed to conduct research in the labs they manage, or they may be currently enrolled graduate students supporting their studies with research assistantships.

Some large schools, particularly those that sponsor medical schools and are located in highly populated areas, may be affiliated with one or more local hospitals. These schools require managers to oversee the relationship between the hospital and the school, to ensure that the needs of both institutions are satisfied. This role is filled by a research administrator, who will generally have a four-year degree in business, administration, or finance.

Technology, research, design, and development occupations may include the following:

- Information Technology Manager
- Network Specialist
- Computer Support Specialist
- Audiovisual Support Specialist
- Research Laboratory Manager
- Laboratory Safety Manager
- Research Administrator
- Research Assistant

Production and Operations

Since the "customer" of a higher education institution is the student, the "production" role is that of the educators, including professors, researchers, and librarians. There are several categories of instructors within most higher education organizations and institutions. The most traditional is the full-time professor. Professors teach classes within their areas of expertise and may eventually fill the role of department chair. Many institutions of higher learning, particularly the larger ones, require full-time professors to conduct research and publish papers in addition to their teaching responsibilities. Professors are usually required to have a doctorate in their subject area.

Increasingly, colleges are relying on adjunct professors rather than hiring (and providing full tenure and benefits to) full-time professors. Adjunct professors typically teach only one or two courses per term, are not required to conduct research or publish papers, and receive few or no employment benefits beyond their salary. Adjuncts often teach basic first- and second-year courses, reserving the major-specific courses for full-time professors. Many adjuncts have doctorates, but some schools will hire adjuncts with master's degrees in the appropriate subject.

Some of the largest schools employ individuals solely to conduct research or run research labs at the institution, usually within scientific fields. This is not especially common; more often, researchers

Part-time adjunct instructors, often working professionals, teach classes in many subjects, including computer science. (©Dreamstime.com)

OCCUPATION PROFILE

College Faculty Member

Considerations	Qualifications
Description	Teaches students academic subjects at the college level; many faculty also must conduct research in their area of expertise.
Career cluster	Education and Training
Interests	Data; people
Working conditions	Work inside
Minimum education level	Master's degree; doctoral degree
Physical exertion	Light work
Physical abilities	Unexceptional/basic fitness
Opportunities for experience	Military service; part-time work
Licensure and certification	Usually not required
Employment outlook	Faster-than-average growth expected
Holland interest score	ESI

Note: See volume 1, "Publisher's Note," for an explanation of the Holland interest score.

are also professors, and they are required to teach at least an occasional class or supervise students conducting graduate-level research. Researchers have doctoral degrees in their specific fields and may have outside experience managing research laboratories.

Librarians and library staff also play a very important role in the academic experience at a college. Librarians are in charge of selecting materials for the library, maintaining an organized facility, and assisting students in finding the materials they need for their research and projects. Full librarians have master's degrees in library science, while other library support staff may hold bachelor's degrees in related fields.

Production and operations occupations may include the following:

- Professor
- Associate Professor
- Assistant Professor
- Adjunct Professor or Instructor
- Researcher
- Teaching Assistant
- Librarian
- Library Support Staff

Human Resources

Regardless of size, any institute of higher education is likely to employ at least one individual in a human resources role. The responsibility of human resources in an institution of higher education is to handle the paperwork required to hire new employees and to ensure that the needs of the faculty and staff are met. This can include anything from processing benefits paperwork to resolving disputes between employees and supervisors. Smaller schools may have only one or two individuals serving in the human resources function, and these employees must fill a variety of roles. Larger schools have entire departments dedicated to human resources and are thus able to hire individuals to specialize in specific areas within this field.

Human resources staff often have four-year degrees in business administration or management, possibly with a concentration or emphasis on higher education administration. Department managers may also have master of business administration degrees and significant related experience. Within larger institutions, individuals who specialize in benefits management may have a background in finance, while those that specialize in handling employee complaints and disputes may have a background in mediation or dispute resolution. The largest institutions may also have in-house employment law attorneys to ensure that all policies and procedures meet the requirements of the law.

Human resources occupations may include the following:

- Human Resources Manager
- Human Resources Generalist
- Benefits Specialist
- Mediation/Dispute Resolution Specialist
- Employment Attorney

INDUSTRY OUTLOOK

Overview

The BLS projects significant growth for the higher education industry, particularly in the private and for-profit segments. Much of this growth can be attributed to continued education, as many adults are returning to school to further their education or change careers. This new segment growth will be in addition to an expected increase in the number of students who pursue higher education immediately following high school.

As student enrollment increases, there will be an increased demand for individuals working in higher education across all occupations within the industry. In particular, this growth will create a greater demand for administrators to oversee the increased number of students, particularly as many smaller colleges expand their traditional enrollment numbers. Demand for course instructors will grow as colleges fill their classrooms and seek to expand their course offerings, although many institutions are choosing to meet this increased demand by hiring more part-time adjuncts, rather than creating additional full-time tenured professor positions. In addition, demand for the highest-level managerial positions—such as deans, directors, and trustees—may grow somewhat, but since so few positions are available in these areas, the growth will not be as significant as in other occupations within the industry.

Importantly, many of the new opportunities will come in less traditional forms, as many colleges and universities expand specifically to cater to working adults who might otherwise not pursue higher education. This expansion may include night and part-time programs, online and distance-learning programs, and programs that provide academic credit for on-the-job experience. Schools will need administrators, managers, and facilities directors with training and experience that are different from those traditionally expected in the field in order to adapt to these new educational models. There will be many opportunities, particularly for individuals with strong backgrounds in computers and technology, to play important roles in the development of these schools and their programs.

Higher education has become available to a wider range of people, including working adults. (©Joern Schulz/Dreamstime.com)

Employment Advantages

Most people choose to work in the higher education industry because they enjoy and gain satisfaction from working with young people and returning adult students. This field can be incredibly rewarding, as there are many opportunities to help individuals make a difference in their own lives through education. Individuals who enjoy working with people and who are willing to provide a high level of personalized service will succeed in this industry and will find they are able to make satisfying and lasting interpersonal connections with the students whose lives they influence in a positive way. For those individuals working in research areas within colleges and universities, much depends on the availability of funds to support that research. When university coffers are well stocked, the role of a researcher can be fulfilling and challenging. Even those who choose to work within the industry in support positions that require minimal direct contact with students often find the work to be satisfying because their efforts to maintain the required infrastructure ultimately support the goal of helping students of all ages meet their goals.

Annual Earnings

Revenue can be difficult to define in the higher education industry, as there are public and private institutions, nonprofit and for-profit institutions, and many different sources of funding for each of these combinations. The most common sources of revenue for higher education institutions include student tuition and fees, government grants and contracts, private gifts, and investment returns from prior endowments.

The U.S. Department of Education reports that the total domestic revenue from all sources for higher education in the United States was approximately $474 billion for the 2006-2007 academic year. This total includes revenue for public institutions ($268.5 billion), private nonprofit institutions ($182.5 billion), and private for-profit institutions ($14 billion). At public and private nonprofit institutions, only a small portion of this revenue comes from tuition and fees charged to students; at private for-profit institutions, the majority of the revenue comes from tuition and fees.

Colleges and universities in the early twenty-first century have come to recognize the importance of both capital campaigns to fund the construction of new facilities and endowment campaigns to fund operating budgets and student scholarships. Because of cuts in state and federal budgets, large universities have had to develop these campaigns in much the same way as private small and midsize colleges and universities have, by soliciting donations from business leaders and alumni. Duke University, for instance, funds 15 percent of its operating budget from endowment funds, while Harvard University, which boasts the country's largest endowment, funds about one-third of its operating budget from its endowment fund. Because nearly all investments lost significant value in the 2007-2009 fiscal crisis, many colleges and universities have implemented cost-saving measures to compensate for the loss in value of these endowment funds.

In 2006, the U.S. Department of Labor reported that there are approximately 13.2 million individuals employed in the educational services industry generally, of which around 32 percent—nearly 4 million people—are employed in the higher education sector. The U.S. Department of Labor predicted wage and salary employment growth of 11 percent across the entire educational services sector over the 2006-2016 period, with much of this growth occurring in the higher (postsecondary) education segment, as more high school graduates attend college and more adults return to schools to advance or change their careers.

RELATED RESOURCES FOR FURTHER RESEARCH

American Association of Collegiate
    Registrars and Admissions Officers
1 Dupont Circle NW, Suite 520
Washington, DC 20036-1171
Tel: (202) 293-9161
Fax: (202) 872-8857
http://www.aacrao.org

American Association of University
    Professors
1133 19th St. NW, Suite 200
Washington, DC 20036
Tel: (202) 737-5900
Fax: (202) 737-5526
http://www.aaup.org

APPA: Leadership in Educational Facilities
1643 Prince St.
Alexandria, VA 22314
Tel: (703) 684-1446
Fax: (703) 549-2772
http://www.appa.org

College Board
45 Columbus Ave.
New York, NY 10023
Tel: (212) 713-8000
http://www.collegeboard.com

National Association of Student Personnel
Administrators
1875 Connecticut Ave. NW, Suite 418
Washington, DC 20009
Tel: (202) 265-7500
Fax: (202) 797-1157
http://www.naspa.org

ABOUT THE AUTHOR

Tracey M. DiLascio is a practicing small business and intellectual property attorney in Newton, Massachusetts. Prior to establishing her practice, DiLascio taught writing and social science courses in Massachusetts and New Jersey colleges and served as a judicial clerk in the New Jersey Superior Court. She is a graduate of Boston University School of Law.

FURTHER READING

Belson, Ken. "Universities Cutting Teams as They Trim Their Budgets." *The New York Times*, May 3, 2009.

Bridges, David, et al., eds. *Higher Education and National Development: Universities and Societies in Transition.* New York: Routledge, 2007.

Buller, Jeffrey. *The Essential College Professor: A Practical Guide to an Academic Career.* New York: John Wiley & Sons, 2010.

Chen, Sheying, ed. *Academic Administration: A Quest for Better Management and Leadership in Higher Education.* Hauppauge, N.Y.: Nova Science, 2009.

Cohen, Arthur M., and Carrie B. Kisker. *The Shaping of American Higher Education: Emergence and Growth of the Contemporary System.* 2d ed. New York: John Wiley & Sons, 2010.

Duderstadt, James J. *A University for the Twenty-first Century.* Ann Arbor: University of Michigan Press, 2000.

Duesterhaus, Alan P. "College Board of Trustees and University-Structure and Composition, Governance, Authority, Responsibilities, Board Committees." Education Encyclopedia-StateUniversity.com. http://education .stateuniversity.com/pages/1793/Board-Trustees-College-University.html.

Farrell, Maureen. "Universities That Turn Research into Revenue." Forbes.com, September 12, 2008. http://www.forbes.com/ 2008/09/12/google-general-electric-ent-tech-cx_mf_0912universitypatent.html.

Goldin, Claudia, and Katz, Lawrence F. *The Shaping of Higher Education: The Formative Years in the United States, 1890 to 1940.* Working Paper No. W6537. Cambridge, Mass.: National Bureau of Economic Research, 1988.

Musselin, Christine. *The Market for Academics.* New York: Routledge, 2010.

National Center for Education Statistics. "Contexts of Postsecondary Education." In *The Condition of Education.* http://nces.ed .gov/programs/coe/2009/section5/ index.asp.

Ruiz, Joaquin. "Research Universities Enrich State." *Arizona Daily Star*, August 12, 2009.

U.S. Bureau of Labor Statistics. *Career Guide to Industries*, 2010-2011 ed. http://www.bls.gov/ oco/cg.

_____. "Education Administrators." In *Occupational Outlook Handbook*, 2010-2011 ed. http://www.bls.gov/oco/ocos007.htm.

U.S. Census Bureau. North American Industry Classification System (NAICS), 2007. http:// www.census.gov/cgi-bin/sssd/naics/ naicsrch?chart=2007.

U.S. Department of Commerce. International Trade Administration. Office of Trade and Industry Information. Industry Trade Data and Analysis. http://ita.doc.gov/td/industry/ otea/OTII/OTII-index.html.

Highway, Road, and Bridge Construction Industry

©Maria Isabel Villamonte/Dreamstime.com

INDUSTRY SNAPSHOT

General Industry: Architecture and Construction

Career Cluster: Architecture and Construction

Subcategory Industries: Airport Runway Construction; Bridge Construction; Highway, Elevated Highway, Causeway, and Parkway Construction; Highway, Road, Street, Bridge, and Airport Runway Repair and Resurfacing; Overpass and Underpass Construction; Public Sidewalk Construction; Road and Street Construction; Tunnel Construction

Related Industries: Building Architecture Industry; Building Construction Industry; Civil Services: Planning; Federal Public Administration; Landscaping Services; Local Public Administration

Annual Domestic Revenues: $376 billion USD (Datamonitor, 2009)

Annual International Revenues: $785.1 billion USD (Datamonitor, 2009)

Annual Global Revenues: $1.161 trillion USD (Datamonitor, 2009)

NAICS Numbers: 2373, 237990

INDUSTRY DEFINITION

Summary

The highway, road, and bridge construction industry is dedicated to new work, reconstruction, rehabilitation, and repairs of land-based infrastructure for land transportation. It builds and maintains airport runways, land-based bridges, elevated highways, roads and streets, public sidewalks, guardrails, and related structures. Industry crews also paint and repaint roads and fill potholes. The worldwide industry may be broken into several sectors because of significant differences in required equipment and skills, among other inputs.

History of the Industry

The first roads were paths created by animals that pushed and trampled through specific areas, creating clearings for humans to follow. The first stone-paved street is said to have been built in the Middle East around 4000 B.C.E. On the British Isles, corduroy roads or log roads were also built around 4000 B.C.E. Brick roads in India date from 3000 B.C.E. The Romans are considered to have had the best roadways of the ancient civilizations, inspiring the saying, "All roads lead to Rome."

The Roman army was responsible for the empire's road construction and maintenance. The workforce typically comprised slaves and convicts. Toward the end of the Roman Empire, construc-

The highway, road, and bridge construction industry is dedicated to new work, reconstruction, rehabilitation, and repairs of land-based infrastructure for land transportation. (©Ron Chapple Studios/Dreamstime.com)

tion ceased and maintenance became the primary concern, with the burden of maintaining roadways placed on private citizens.

Holy Roman Emperor Charlemagne (771-814 C.E.) helped develop European roadways and bridges. He appointed officials whose sole task was to organize road construction. Charlemagne required all citizens to work on road or bridge maintenance if there were insufficient slave laborers or prisoners of war. This system was known as *corvée*.

Road paving became a reputable artisan craft around the thirteenth century. Pavers were members of one of the earliest artisan guilds, the stonemasons. By 1502, apprentices were common. The English Highway Act of 1555 placed the obligation of road maintenance on parishes and required parishioners to devote four days a year to the corvée system. Workers were expected to have

their own equipment. Unpaid people in each parish were put in charge of inspecting the roads as surveyors. By 1570, the first official road construction and maintenance contracts were formed.

John Loudon McAdam revolutionized road making when he created macadam. Macadam stones could be broken into pieces and manipulated as necessary by women or children. Thus, road maintenance and construction ceased to be the sole province of strong men.

City roads in the 1700's were deplorable. The craft of stone paving was time-consuming, labor-intensive, and expensive. In the United States, slaves were often used for roadwork, and once emancipation occurred, convicts were used for roadwork instead. In the 1800's, the United States saw a move toward centralizing control of roadwork. In 1802, the Army Corps of Engineers was created and located at West Point. In the 1870's, Washington, D.C., established an asphalt-paving program that met with great success, and in 1891, the New Jersey Board of Agriculture was given authority to create roads connecting farms and markets. Massachusetts, in 1893, became the first state to create a road authority, when it created a highway commission. The next year, New Jersey followed suit, giving the power to create roads to the Commission of Public Roads. In 1912, the American Highway Association (AHA) was created out of the American Association for Highway Improvement (formed in 1910), but it disbanded in 1916 under the pressure of competition from the American Road and Transportation Builders Association. By 1920, all American states had highway organizations.

After World War I, American travel increased and roads deteriorated. The U.S. Highway Research Board was established. In 1921, the Federal Aid Highway Act gave each state funding for up to 7 percent of highway work and the federal government met half the cost. The act marked the beginning of the U.S. national highway system.

The Industry Today

The slice of the architecture and construction market of which the contemporary highway, road, and bridge construction industry is part allows for a great deal of competition, particularly in its ability to diversify and work in niche areas. Nonresidential construction brought in revenue of $330.4 billion and was the industry's most lucrative segment in 2009. The civil engineering segment earned $305.6 billion, approximately 48 percent of the industry's revenue.

Company sizes range from one-person operations—which are no longer required to belong to a guild, though there are unions—to companies with thousands of employees. There are very few clients in this industry—most of them are federal agencies or major private-sector buyers—but these clients often announce jobs for which companies must bid to win contracts. Companies are very dependent on the economic market, and there is little loyalty to a particular company except, perhaps, in the private sector, where a company's reputation and previous work are taken into account when a bid is made or announced.

Construction projects vary in size, from minor road maintenance to major highway construction.

Many times, subcontractors are hired by primary contractors, either because of their specialized skills or because the job is so large. One-person operations typically subcontract work, saving on expenses by renting necessary equipment and engaging labor as needed, instead of paying for constant upkeep, taxes, and salaries. Midsize companies may work from office buildings and typically have several full-time employees, allowing such companies to take on slightly larger or longer jobs. The largest of companies operate offices worldwide, with multiple employees from the administrative level down. These large companies bid on long-term and more complex projects.

Financing to pay transportation construction companies comes from one of three sources: public money raised through general taxes or borrowing in the form of bonds; private investors or landowners wanting to create a road to increase the value of their land; or tolls, fuel taxes, and vehicles taxes and licenses. The American Road and Transportation Builders Association (ARBTA), started in 1902, is one of the most well-known national transportation construction associations, and there are several associations made of lobbyists such as ARBTA that exist to cultivate and protect investment within the industry. Instead of guilds for industry interests, there are now multiple associations

Construction projects vary in size, from minor road maintenance to major highway construction. (©Tomas Kraus/ Dreamstime.com)

and boards. In 1991, the United States joined the Permanent International Association of Road Congresses (PIARC), an international group founded in France that represents government road authorities and acts as a forum for discussion on industry standards and issues.

"By April, 2010, at least 14,000 gained employment in the construction industry sector," according to *Industry Today*, and "these gains, which followed two years of dramatic losses, resulted from stimulus-funded projects now underway." Since February, 2010, the construction industry in general has added forty thousand new jobs. Without new jobs underway, there are still several million miles of existing highways and roads, as well as bridges, that need repair or maintenance work. According to the American Association of State Highway and Transportation Officials (AASHTO),

> federal road funding must increase by more than 80 percent by 2015 just to keep up with inflation. It estimates that the total cost to improve highway conditions and performance will reach $189 billion in 2015. Of the total, $83 billion needs to come from federal funds.

The Transportation Construction Coalition agrees with AASHTO and keeps track of current issues within the industry, from expired bills that remove funding from construction to congressional acts that need further support in order to create more jobs.

INDUSTRY MARKET SEGMENTS

The architecture and construction industry ranges in size from one-person operations to large global companies, and it serves a broad range of clients from the federal government to private consumers, such as a privately owned airport in need of runways. The following sections provide a comprehensive breakdown of each of these different segments.

Small Businesses

Small transportation construction businesses employ fewer than ten persons. Approximately 41 percent of them have one to four employees. They focus on maintenance, repair, reconstruction, ad-

ditions, and small-scale projects within narrow geographic markets. They often hire subcontractors to oversee work they cannot take on or perform themselves and often rent the equipment and tools necessary for a given job. Many times, small businesses are subcontracted themselves by larger firms or act as joint contactors with other firms, working on specific portions of larger projects. Typically, small businesses have fewer than five employees and can be found in rural and scattered areas, where there is less competition from larger firms.

Potential Annual Earnings Scale. According to the U.S. Bureau of Labor Statistics (BLS), the average annual income of an operating engineer or other construction equipment operator in the highway, road, and bridge construction industry was $48,450 in 2009. Highway maintenance workers earned an average of $34,560; paving, surfacing, and tamping equipment operators earned an average of $39,150; and general construction laborers earned an average of $37,290. Construction supervisors earned an average of $61,760, and construction managers earned an average of $93,340. Civil engineers earned an average of $74,930, civil engineering technicians earned an average of $50,550, and engineering managers earned an average of $99,520. These averages all assume full employment: Because of the nature of the industry, workers often are not paid if inclement weather or seasonal changes cause their projects to be delayed or canceled. This is particularly true of employees of small businesses, which may work on only a single project at a time.

Clientele Interaction. To compete for contracts, small businesses most often need to have proven themselves to be efficient and effective on previous jobs. They have a greater need to establish relationships with the appropriate local authorities in order to quickly learn about any upcoming contracts and to receive recommendations, and, depending on the size of the jobs or contracts they hope to receive, firms may have to impress clientele with their locations and images.

Amenities, Atmosphere, and Physical Grounds. A construction business operates temporarily on a given site until its work is completed. These sites can range from natural settings that need clearing in order to begin construction work to hazardous highways that need to be blocked off, with local police to help prevent cars from injuring or killing workers. If the weather becomes inclement, work often stops, so seasons can affect the progress of a job. Depending on the location of the site, there may be amenities for workers on location—either in a building or brought to them. Generally, the work is dangerous and workers are required to wear specific protective gear, such as hardhats or steel-toed boots, to protect them from burns or dropped heavy objects.

Typical Number of Employees. Because small construction companies are limited in geography and type of job they can complete, they also limit their staff size. In many cases, the owners are the companies' only full-time employees. Some small-company owners hire subcontractors for larger projects. In quickly developing areas, staff sizes may be significantly larger in order to take on more and bigger jobs.

Traditional Geographic Locations. Small companies are traditionally located outside the major cities where larger firms have already established themselves. These smaller companies are more willing to take on smaller and scattered jobs in rural areas where larger companies would earn less of a profit or would not be able to underbid a smaller company requiring less overhead.

Pros of Working for a Small Construction Company. Because owners of small construction companies act as both owners and employees, there is less overhead to be met—especially in a small company that does not use a store front—and more potential profit because there are fewer employees to insure and pay and no taxes to worry about if the employer subcontracts work. There is also a measure of independence in being one's own boss. There is often a greater efficiency level with a small firm as there are fewer layers of bureaucracy and a shorter chain of command. A small company is also able to fill niches, whereas larger companies already have established markets and clients. The few employees of a small company may often be friends or family. Owners of small companies do not typically need to acquire advanced de-

The equipment needed for construction, such as this tripod-mounted theodolite, used to measure angles, is often very expensive but usually can be rented. (©Wally Stemberger/Dreamstime.com)

grees in business, and most employees receive on-the-job training in many skills—with the exception of some that require certification. Apprenticeship is typical in the construction industry, with on-the-job training and sometimes classroom study in vocational schools. A small company may be more willing to take on novices because skilled laborers are more likely to work for larger companies that offer steady employment and higher wages.

Cons of Working for a Small Construction Company. When owners are also employees, they are responsible not only for the administrative operation and success of their businesses but also for performing necessary physical labor. When a company has few employees, the loss of a single one (temporarily or permanently) can jeopardize its ability to complete a job (on time or at all). Small companies may find it necessary to subcontract jobs, even if they must rely on subcontractors they do not know. One-person companies may work only with subcontractors in order to cut overhead, placing the overhead burden on the subcontractors. Furthermore, the type of work a small company can obtain can be mundane and lack excitement. Small companies are more likely to gain contracts to maintain roads rather than to build skyscrapers, for instance. Their narrow geographic scopes may limit small companies in their outreach efforts, rendering them unable to travel to another country or across a state to cultivate business. The competition among small companies is often fierce because several bid on any given job, and underbidding by too much could lead to loss of profit. Furthermore, small companies often exist from contract to contract, without steady income, and they may hire only highly skilled, fully trained laborers if they are under pressure to complete contracts quickly, consistently, and reliably.

Costs

Payroll and Benefits: Very small companies may pay daily wages instead of hourly to avoid the cost of overtime, but even small companies may not be exempt from federal labor laws mandating overtime payments. Most pay hourly wages to their own employees, as well as paying subcontractors based on the terms of their contracts. Owners, similarly, receive pay based on the terms of their contracts with contracting entities. Small construction companies with few if any full-time permanent employees are unlikely to pay benefits.

Supplies: Smaller firms often rent the supplies and tools needed for a given job. They must purchase some supplies, however, such as office supplies and equipment and fuel to travel to construction sites.

External Services: Small construction companies routinely subcontract portions of their contracts that they cannot themselves fulfill cost-effectively (or at all). Subcontractors may supply additional skilled or unskilled labor, specialized skills that a contractor lacks, or both. Small companies also rent most of the heavy machinery, equipment, and tools they need to complete their contracts. They may also contract accounting or legal services as necessary, and if they own equipment, they may contract repair and maintenance services. They may also contract portable latrines for construction sites.

Utilities: Typical utilities include Internet and telephone service, including mobile phone service, as well as electricity, water, and oil or gas. Contractors working from home may pay a portion of their home utilities from their business accounts or treat them as business expenses on personal tax returns.

Taxes: Small businesses must pay income and property taxes. They must pay payroll taxes on direct employees but not on subcontractors. Owners may report business income on their personal tax returns, in which case they must also pay self-employment taxes.

Midsize Businesses

Midsize construction businesses are often established firms and have between ten and fifty employees. They take on a wide range of projects, from maintenance to larger construction jobs, especially with their ability to hire multiple subcontractors should they need more people to complete their contracts. Often, the projects such companies take on include construction of runways, toll roads, and similar structures. They are not quite equipped to handle such major construction jobs as highway or street construction. Midsize businesses may operate in specific market niches, and they often own their own machines and tools rather than renting them. They are usually found in more developed urban and suburban areas and are equipped to travel to reach jobs.

Potential Annual Earnings Scale. According to the BLS, the average annual income of an operating engineer or other construction equipment operator in the highway, road, and bridge construction industry was $48,450 in 2009. Highway maintenance workers earned an average of $34,560; paving, surfacing, and tamping equipment operators earned an average of $39,150; and general construction laborers earned an average of $37,290. Construction supervisors earned an average of $61,760, and construction managers earned an average of $93,340. Civil engineers earned an average of $74,930, civil engineering technicians earned an average of $50,550, and engineering managers earned an average of $99,520. These averages all assume full employment: Because of the nature of the industry, workers may not be paid if inclement weather or seasonal changes cause their projects to be delayed or canceled.

Clientele Interaction. Competition for new projects can be intense, and midsize companies rely on their reputations and on obtaining repeat contracts with their clients. Often, midsize companies have storefronts to showcase either their work or their reliability and to impress potential clients. It still behooves midsize companies to make professional contacts and friends within city management in order to be among the first to know about upcoming contracts and to have recommendations made on their behalf.

Amenities, Atmosphere, and Physical Grounds. A construction business operates temporarily on a given site until its work is completed. Depending on the location of the site, there may be amenities for workers on location. Generally, construction work is dangerous, and workers are required to wear specific protective gear. Midsize companies also have storefronts where managerial personnel are located, and these companies may offer such amenities as coffee or other beverages to clients. They may also offer brochures and photographic examples of completed work for prospective clients to examine.

Typical Number of Employees. The majority of establishments within the construction industry have fewer than ten employees, but midsize companies range between ten and fifty employees, including the owner and sometimes a manager, as well as any other managerial personnel who work within the storefront. Midsize companies also directly employ at least some of their physical laborers.

Traditional Geographic Locations. Midsize companies are traditionally located within suburban and urban areas, where there is greater competition for contracts and established jobs. These companies are better able to take on larger jobs that require some travel—with more employees the midsize companies can ideally work on more than one contract at a time.

Pros of Working for a Midsize Construction Company. Owners of midsize construction companies may limit themselves to managerial work, if they wish to do so. Midsize companies have greater profit potential than small companies because they can take on more than one contract at a time. They may also be more efficient than large companies because they retain relatively short chains of command. A midsize company often operates within a niche, whether it is building airport runways or constructing toll roads. The owner of a midsize company is more likely to have an advanced degree in business because of the competitive nature of the midsize segment and the high turnover. Employees of midsize construction companies may have college graduates working for them as they learn the trade at a lower wage and as they are apprenticed to more skilled workers. In a midsize

company, there is also some room for advancement, but advancing may require further education or certification.

Cons of Working for a Midsize Construction Company. Midsize companies see a high turnover because of the cost of overhead in keeping a storefront, full-time employees, and managerial personnel. The midsize segment of the transportation construction industry is highly competitive. Often, without a degree, certification, or experience, less skilled workers may be passed over for employment. Longer hours may also be required.

Costs

Payroll and Benefits: Midsize companies often pay hourly wages. Employees who belong to unions often enjoy greater benefits, such as vacation days and sick leave. Federal or state mandated benefits are offered usually as required. There is some chance for either bonuses or promotion.

Supplies: Midsize companies often own the supplies and tools they need. These include hand and power tools, heavy equipment and machinery, and construction materials. They also require transportation vehicles and fuel, as well as office equipment, furniture, and supplies.

External Services: Midsize construction companies routinely subcontract portions of their contracts that they cannot themselves fulfill cost-effectively (or at all). Subcontractors may supply additional skilled or unskilled labor, specialized skills that a contractor lacks, or both. They may also contract equipment maintenance and repair; equipment rental; facilities cleaning, maintenance, and repair; printing; site security; or legal, accounting, or tax preparation services. They may also contract portable latrines for construction sites.

Utilities: Typical utilities include Internet and phone service, water and sewage, and electricity.

Taxes: Midsize businesses must pay income and property taxes. They must pay payroll taxes on direct employees but not on subcontractors.

Large Businesses

Large construction businesses are well-established firms with more than fifty employees. A large construction company operates large-scale projects, such as highway construction. Each large firm

Two men work alongside an asphalt-paving machine. (©Dwight Smith/Dreamstime.com)

is located in multiple metropolitan areas in order to remain visible and competitive. Firms may also be located in multiple countries, and they take on a wide variety of construction projects, not just limited to highway and road construction. For example, Bechtel Corporation has offices in twenty-six countries, including the United States, employs over forty-nine thousand people, and performs highway and railway construction projects, as well as working on defense facilities and conducting environmental cleanup operations.

Potential Annual Earnings Scale. According to the BLS, the average annual income of an operating engineer or other construction equipment operator in the highway, road, and bridge construction industry was $48,450 in 2009. Highway maintenance workers earned an average of $34,560; paving, surfacing, and tamping equipment operators earned an average of $39,150; and general con-

struction laborers earned an average of $37,290. Construction supervisors earned an average of $61,760, and construction managers earned an average of $93,340. Civil engineers earned an average of $74,930, civil engineering technicians earned an average of $50,550, and engineering managers earned an average of $99,520. These averages all assume full employment: Because of the nature of the industry, workers may not be paid if inclement weather or seasonal changes cause their projects to be delayed or canceled. However, large corporations overseeing many simultaneous projects may be able to transfer workers among projects as necessary to ensure full employment. Moreover, managerial salaries at such companies may be well above these industry averages.

Clientele Interaction. It is important for large companies to maintain a visible presence worldwide because their competition is not just from local companies but from foreign ones as well. Therefore, large firms need to have multiple office locations in major cities, where potential clients can meet with contractors and administrative personnel. Furthermore, it is very important that clientele are duly impressed with the firms' offices, as well as with the people within them, since both make direct impressions influencing a client's choice of firms.

Amenities, Atmosphere, and Physical Grounds. Large companies have offices worldwide, as well as online presences, and may provide amenities for their employees such as on-site gyms, cafeterias, and other recreational facilities and executive perks. On project sites, the amenities, atmosphere, and physical grounds vary by location, as they do for employees of any size company.

Typical Number of Employees. Large firms typically employ thousands of persons. Bechtel, for example, has more than forty-nine thousand employees in twenty-six countries.

Traditional Geographic Locations. Large construction firms have offices in major cities worldwide. For example, Bechtel has offices in Abu Dhabi, Istanbul, and London. Work locations vary worldwide, though they are typically near large or growing cities that require construction work to support their growth and infrastructure.

Pros of Working for a Large Construction Company. Large companies often pay better than smaller companies, and they provide benefits such as 401(k) plans, health insurance, paid vacation, and sick time. Many larger firms offer mentoring opportunities, as well as the chance to travel worldwide to different office locations or job sites. Well-known companies are more likely to obtain larger and more lucrative contracts, providing employees with opportunities to work on landmark projects. They also provide greater opportunities for promotions and pay raises, and they often devote greater resources to maintaining employee safety in compliance with federal and state regulations. Working at large, well-known companies often increases employee prestige, which may be satisfying to employees while at such firms, as well as impressing potential employers if they choose to seek employment elsewhere.

Cons of Working for a Large Construction Company. Large companies are highly bureaucratic, and employees may experience frustrations arising from ineffective communication or confusion. Employees of a large company may also have fewer close relationships with their coworkers, and their interactions may be more structured and regimented. There is also a great deal more competition within large companies for raises and recognition; this competition and other such workplace politics can lead to added stress. In a stressful economic period, hiring freezes and layoffs are highly likely. Working in other countries can be difficult because of language and cultural barriers. A balance between personal and work life may be difficult to achieve. Employees may be required to relocate to another city or country. Working for large companies can make employees feel anonymous, and they may have a great deal of trouble being noticed or having a recognizable effect upon their employers. Managers must often deal with collective bargaining units, complicating their jobs.

Costs

Payroll and Benefits: Salary structures within large companies vary widely as there are many types of employees with various jobs and skills. Employees such as maintenance and other service personnel are often paid hourly wages, while managers and administrative assistants are typically paid yearly salaries and may receive performance incentives. Employees of large companies often receive benefits such as health insurance, vacation, and sick pay.

Supplies: Large construction companies require hand and power tools, heavy equipment and machinery, construction materials, transportation vehicles, and fuel, as well as office equipment, furniture, and supplies. Some companies also maintain amenities such as gyms or cafeterias and require the supplies necessary to operate and restock those amenities.

External Services: Many large companies have on-site staff to handle maintenance and similar duties, but others contract this work to external vendors. Large construction companies may also contract catering, audiovisual services, technical support, lobbying, auditing, security, maintenance, and other support and business services. They may also contract portable latrines for construction sites.

Utilities: Typical utilities for a large firm include water, sewage, electricity, telephone (including mobile phone service), Internet access, and perhaps cable television.

Taxes: Large businesses must pay income and property taxes. They must pay payroll taxes on direct employees but not on subcontractors.

ORGANIZATIONAL STRUCTURE AND JOB ROLES

The organizational structure and distribution of job roles throughout the highway, road, and bridge construction industry can vary greatly depending on the size and scope of a company and the services it provides. Although construction roles make up over 66 percent of the industry, numerous additional job roles are imperative to the successful operations of a company. In large businesses, each separate job role could be fulfilled by one or more individual specialists, whereas smaller companies may require one individual to serve more than one role. Each job role, though, must be fulfilled in each company to some degree, even if very few individuals must serve them all.

The following umbrella categories apply to the organizational structure of businesses in the highway, road, and bridge construction industry:

- Business Management
- Sales and Marketing

- Facilities and Security
- Technology, Research, Design, and Development
- Operations
- Distribution
- Human Resources
- Business and Financial
- Office and Administrative Support

Business Management

Business management is responsible for the overall direction of the company. Through the formulation of company procedures and policies, business managers guide the company and create its employment culture. These individuals are also responsible for supervising and managing specific areas and departments within the company, while determining the best use of human resources. They are generally the highest paid employees, earning mean annual salaries of $105,820 in 2009, and require the highest level of education. They are responsible for ensuring the fluid operation of all the company's departments and achieving company goals. Ultimately, they are responsible for their company's success or failure. Business management can take the form of a single employee or multiple employees, depending on the size of the company.

The most common position under this umbrella is the construction manager, who coordinates, budgets, and plans the personnel and activities required to complete a project. Construction managers oversee projects from beginning to end and are immediately responsible for their successful completion. These projects can be complex, multiyear efforts or simple construction jobs. Construction managers must be able to work in a team environment and able to work with little or no supervision. They often require multiple years of experience on the job and advanced education.

Business management occupations may include the following:

- Chief Executive Officer (CEO)
- General or Operations Manager
- Financial Manager
- Superintendent
- Construction Manager
- Program/Project Manager
- Human Resources Manager
- Business Manager
- Quality Assurance Manager

Sales and Marketing

Highway, road, and bridge construction companies sell services rather than products. A company that cannot sell its services will be unable to obtain revenue and continue its operations. A single job can employ a number of individuals for many months, or even years, and lead to a large amount of revenue, so the ability to sell one's services is crucial for this industry.

Often, construction companies are selling themselves in a way much different from the way a retailer sells a product. They can be very selective about the jobs they pursue and can refuse potential clients. A successful company can afford to be much more selective than a struggling company, but both need to be able to sell their ability to complete jobs efficiently, cost-effectively, and at a high quality.

Sales and marketing occupations may include the following:

- Sales Representative
- Business Developer
- Proposal Manager

Facilities and Security

Facilities and security personnel are responsible for the maintenance and security of not only outdoor work locations but also administrative buildings and offices. They do not represent a very large portion of the workforce, but their functions are important, especially at larger companies. Work sites may require groundskeepers to maintain them or crossing guards to guide and manage vehicular traffic in and around them. Office areas may require cleaners or janitors to maintain them. Both areas could require security guards, depending on the business, location, and job.

Facilities and security positions are generally the lowest-paid positions in the industry, but they do not necessarily require any specialized knowledge of the industry itself. It is possible for someone familiar with the job requirements to jump into one of these positions without having worked previously in the industry.

Facilities and security occupations may include the following:

- Custodian/Janitor
- Groundskeeper
- Security Guard
- Crossing Guard

Technology, Research, Design, and Development

The highway, road, and bridge construction industry relies heavily on technology. Construction companies that do not keep abreast of the latest technologies and methods for conducting their services may fall behind their competitors. Technology can apply directly to the equipment used or to the techniques and design plans for a highway, road, or bridge.

Research and design personnel are important in the preliminary stages of construction jobs and are often involved in bidding for prospective jobs. Without proper planning, a construction job can meet numerous problems or provide a faulty or unsafe final product. Technology personnel must provide information related to the locations, dimensions, shape, and contours of land and land features on and near work sites. They may also conduct engineering work related to the planning, design, and oversight of construction structures.

Technology, research, design, and development occupations may include the following:

- Construction Engineer
- Field Engineer
- Office Engineer
- Structural Engineer
- Resident Engineer
- Structural Designer
- Drafter

Operations

Operations personnel engage in the direct construction of highways, roads, and bridges, and they constitute the vast majority of the industry's labor force, over 66 percent. Because construction jobs can be large scale and complex, effective and efficient operations are necessary for success. The efficiency of an operations crew can greatly affect the amount of time and money a job requires. Companies that require the least amount of time and money to complete jobs are often awarded contracts. An inefficient operations crew can harm the reputation of its company and possibly prevent it from winning construction bids.

Operations personnel keep jobs on schedule, which can be a critical component of a construction job. Running behind schedule can have ripple effects, negatively affecting the company, the region surrounding the construction site, and future construction jobs.

OCCUPATION SPECIALTIES

Bulldozer Operators

Specialty	Responsibilities
Angledozer operators	Drive bulldozers equipped with special angled blades attached to the front.
Crawler-tractor operators	Drive tractors that are specially equipped to move over rough or muddy ground.
Fine-grade-bulldozer operators	Grade land to close specification.
Scarifier operators	Operate bulldozers for the purpose of loosening soil.
Scraper operators	Operate bulldozers for the purpose of scraping surface clay to determine the existence and types of clay deposits or to gather clay into piles in preparation for its removal to brick-and-tile manufacturing plants.

The most common position within this umbrella is that of construction laborer, which earned a mean salary of $37,290 in 2009. Construction laborers perform the majority of the physical labor required at job sites and may operate hand tools, power tools, and other equipment and instruments. Equipment operators, or operating engineers, use power construction equipment, such as bulldozers, scrapers, shovels, tractors, and other motorized equipment. They use heavy equipment to excavate or move earth, erect structures, and perform other related functions. Other positions are responsible for maintaining tools and equipment, pouring and smoothing concrete, placing and uniting iron or steel girders or columns, laying pipe, or performing other maintenance activities.

Operations occupations may include the following:

- Construction Worker
- Equipment Operator/Operating Engineer
- Heavy Equipment Mechanic
- Maintenance and Repair Worker
- Inspector
- Material Mover/Handler

Distribution

Distribution of materials is a critical component of the highway, road, and bridge construction industry. Highways, roads, and bridges can require large pieces of equipment and large amounts of construction materials, all of which must be delivered to the construction location. Without the requisite materials and equipment, operations workers cannot perform their duties. Efficient distribution and delivery of construction equipment and materials are important to the completion of a construction job on time and at a high quality.

The majority of positions under this umbrella are filled by heavy truck drivers. These employees are responsible for transporting and delivering machinery, equipment, or other materials to job

	OCCUPATION PROFILE
	Construction Manager
Considerations	*Qualifications*
Description	Plans, organizes, and budgets activities associated with the construction of structures or systems.
Career clusters	Architecture and Construction
Interests	Data; things
Working conditions	Work outside; work both inside and outside
Minimum education level	On-the-job training; junior/technical/community college; bachelor's degree
Physical exertion	Light work
Physical abilities	Unexceptional/basic fitness
Opportunities for experience	Part-time work
Licensure and certification	Recommended
Employment outlook	Faster-than-average growth expected
Holland interest score	ERS

Note: See volume 1, "Publisher's Note," for an explanation of the Holland interest score.

OCCUPATION PROFILE

Highway Maintenance Worker

Considerations	Qualifications
Description	Performs maintenance and repairwork on highways and other roads.
Career cluster	Architecture and Construction
Interests	Things
Working conditions	Work outside
Minimum education level	No high school diploma; on-the-job training; high school diploma or GED; high school diploma/technical training; apprenticeship
Physical exertion	Medium work
Physical abilities	Unexceptional/basic fitness
Opportunities for experience	Apprenticeship; military service; part-time work
Licensure and certification	Usually not required
Employment outlook	Average growth expected
Holland interest score	CRS

Note: See volume 1, "Publisher's Note," for an explanation of the Holland interest score.

sites. Heavy truck drivers often require specialized training and licensing.

Distribution occupations may include the following:

- Heavy Truck Driver
- Light Truck Driver
- Material Mover/Handler
- Loading and Unloading Machine Operator

Human Resources

Human resources personnel are responsible for the interests of a company's employees. They maintain personnel records regarding personal information, earnings, absences, performance evaluations, and so on. They also administer employee benefits, such as vacation and insurance, prepare and distribute evaluations, and facilitate new employee orientation. They recruit, develop, and retain employees.

Human resources positions do not make up a very large part of the industry. In small companies, human resources is one of many hats worn by a head manager, but larger companies employ individuals specifically to manage or otherwise work in the human resources department. Human resources managers require additional education but also earned mean salaries of $93,700 in 2009.

Human resources occupations may include the following:

- Human Resources Manager
- Human Resources Assistant
- Human Resources Specialist

Business and Financial

Business and financial personnel are responsible for monetary aspects of their companies. The construction industry relies heavily on job bids and estimating the cost for certain jobs, so responsible and successful financial operations are critical for a

The Hoover Dam Bridge under construction in March, 2010. (©Thaer Joseph/Dreamstime.com)

successful business. A company in this industry must balance job bids to be competitively priced but also profitable. A company delivering an underestimated job bid has a high chance of being awarded the project, but it will lose money. Contrarily, a company delivering an overestimated job bid in the hopes of realizing a large profit runs the risk of losing the bid to another company.

Accurate and intuitive estimates are critical for the success of a highway, road, or bridge construction business. Cost estimators, specifically, are responsible for preparing cost estimates for construction projects in order to aid management and administration in bidding on potential jobs. These positions generally require a degree, training, or experience, and earned a mean salary of $67,270 in 2009. Cost estimators must work well with deadlines, and they must have strong work ethics and strong attention to detail. They must investigate job sites, evaluate complex projects, and prepare detailed cost estimates for entire jobs. Other business and financial personnel help keep financial records and maintain efficient utilization of funds.

Business and financial occupations may include the following:

- Cost Estimator
- Accountant/Auditor
- Purchasing Agent
- Accounts Payable Clerk
- Accounts Receivable Clerk

Office and Administrative Support

Office and administrative support positions conduct the behind-the-scenes daily activities of highway, road, and bridge construction companies. These are the types of positions that conduct peripheral, yet important, tasks of the business, such as answering phones, filing and archiving records, organizing travel and meetings, and controlling documents. The positions are often clerical in nature and do not necessarily require advance knowledge of the industry. Advanced degrees are not necessarily a requirement for these positions, but it is important for individuals in these roles to have strong organizational and communication skills.

Office and administrative support occupations may include the following:

- Bookkeeping, Accounting, and Auditing Clerk

- Payroll and Timekeeping Clerk
- Receptionist
- Information Clerk
- Executive Assistant
- Administrative Assistant
- Office Clerk
- Document Control/Records Clerk

INDUSTRY OUTLOOK

Overview

The outlook for this industry shows it to be on the rise domestically as well as globally. The industry suffered significantly from the economic crisis of 2007-2009, but it was also a focus of the American Recovery and Reinvestment Act of 2009, so it has experienced an influx of government funding. U.S. infrastructure is in significant disrepair, so theoretical demand for the industry's services is extremely high. However, funding to repair the infrastructure is not always available, so practical demand often lags behind theoretical demand.

Because its services are needed but not always affordable, the transportation construction industry is an indicator of economic conditions, as well as of population growth, in the United States and worldwide. Federal Highway Administration research shows the relationship between the economy and the highway industry, suggesting that investment in highway, road, and bridge construction is important to economic growth. Worldwide, the industry facilitates surface transportation, which in turn facilitates mobility and is therefore an integral part of life: Providing jobs, permitting travelers to go further to consume and spend on products, and moving consumer goods increases productivity and supports the economy. Everyone uses infrastructure, from regular citizens to the military. Increased growth within the industry is expected, particularly in the areas of maintenance and repair.

Tourism is also intimately linked with infrastructure: The tourism industry offers taxes and other support to the highway industry as it is in the tourism industry's best interest to have maintenance and repairs ongoing in order to allow for easier and smoother access to specific destinations whose economies rely on tourists. Other intimately connected industries include construction equipment and materials.

As a large portion of industry workers retire or leave between 2010 and 2020, skilled and experienced trade workers will be in demand. Furthermore, as technology rapidly develops, those within the industry who have technological skills and are up-to-date with the latest developments will be in high demand. New entrants into the industry who have stable backgrounds, such as retired military personnel, can expect excellent job prospects. Certain skill sets, licenses, or experience will be needed for most jobs.

Employment growth within the office sector of

PROJECTED EMPLOYMENT FOR SELECTED OCCUPATIONS

Heavy and Civil Engineering Construction

Employment		
2009	Projected 2018	Occupation
27,220	30,900	Carpenters
184,470	229,900	Construction laborers
63,300	72,500	First-line supervisors/ managers of construction trades and extraction workers
109,550	22,000	Operating engineers and other construction equipment operators
38,250	45,300	Truck drivers, heavy and tractor-trailer

Source: U.S. Bureau of Labor Statistics, Industries at a Glance, Occupational Employment Statistics and Employment Projections Program.

the industry will continue to be limited, as automation replaces many of the human components. Overall, the number of available jobs fluctuates, as these jobs are dependent on the economy. Currently, there is a great deal of competition within the industry for jobs, particularly at the entry level. According to the BLS, those laborers with limited skills will experience the most competition,

> because of a plentiful supply of workers who are willing to work as day laborers. Overall opportunities will be best for those with experience and specialized skills and for those who can relocate to areas with new construction projects. Opportunities also will be better for laborers specializing in road construction.

Companies and individual employees familiar with green trends will be in high demand as a result of federal green initiatives.

Employment Advantages

According to the BLS, the highway, road, and bridge construction industry will see growth in wage and salary jobs of 19 percent between 2008 and 2018, or approximately 1.1 percent growth each year. This growth is higher than the average across all occupations of 11 percent growth. The U.S. Department of Commerce released data at the beginning of July, 2010, indicating that spending on construction in the industry overall was down 12 percent from 2009. However, highway construction specifically was at a "seasonally adjusted annual rate of $83.1 billion, 2.7 percent above the revised April estimate of $80.9 billion."

Jobs over the next decade are nearly assured with continued voting by citizens and legislators approving spending on road construction. Positions and employment for construction managers is an anticipated growth area resulting from the many new projects in development as well as because of the "increasing complexity of construction work that needs to be managed, including the need to deal with the proliferation of laws dealing with building construction, worker safety, and environmental issues."

Annual Earnings

The highway, road, and bridge construction industry is inextricably linked with the economy in its ups and downs. Budget pressures have forced an increasing number of states to cut funding for surface transportation projects. Over thirty states have cut their highway investments since 2009 according to Transportation for America and the American Road and Transportation Builders Association. However, revenue is expected to increase by 2.2 percent each year in the United States through 2015 as a result of federal funding. Globally, by 2014, the industry will have a forecasted value of $2.7585 trillion, which is a 23.3 percent increase since 2009.

RELATED RESOURCES FOR FURTHER RESEARCH

AMERICAN ASSOCIATION OF STATE HIGHWAY AND
    TRANSPORTATION OFFICIALS
444 N Capitol St. NW, Suite 249
Washington, DC 20001
Tel: (202) 624-5800
Fax: (202) 624-5806
http://www.transportation.org

AMERICAN ROAD AND TRANSPORTATION
    BUILDERS ASSOCIATION
1219 28th St. NW
Washington, DC 20007-3389
Tel: (202) 289-4434
Fax: (202) 289-4435
http://www.artba.org

ASSOCIATED GENERAL CONTRACTORS OF AMERICA
2300 Wilson Blvd., Suite 400
Arlington, VA 22201
Tel: (800) 242-1767
Fax: (703) 548-3119
http://www.agc.org

ASSOCIATION MONDIALE DE LA ROUTE/WORLD
    ROAD ASSOCIATION
AIPCR/PIARC
La Grande Arche
Pario North, Level 5
92055 La Defense CEDEX
France
Tel: 33-1-47-96-81-21
Fax: 33-1-49-00-02-02
http://www.piarc.org/en

ENGINEERING NEWS-RECORD
  2 Penn Plaza, 9th Floor
  New York, NY 10121
  Tel: (212) 904-3507
  Fax: (212) 904-2820
  http://enr.construction.com

REED CONSTRUCTION DATA
  30 Technology Parkway South, Suite 100
  Norcross, GA 30092
  Tel: (800) 424 3996
  http://www.reedconstructiondata.com

WORLD HIGHWAYS
  Route One Publishing
  Horizon House, Azalea Dr.
  Swanley, Kent BR8 8JR
  United Kingdom
  Tel: 44-1322-612-055
  Fax: 44-161-603-0891
  http://www.worldhighways.com

ABOUT THE AUTHORS

Michelle Marie Martinez is an assistant professor and librarian at Sam Houston State University. She is a 2007 graduate of the University of North Texas Graduate School of Library and Information Sciences and a 2005 graduate of Sam Houston State University, where she earned an M.A. Her research includes a wide variety of topics, including Shakespeare, feminist literature, and film studies. She has presented research and papers at multiple conferences, including "Incest, Sexual Violence, and Rape in Video Games," presented at Oxford University.

Tyler Manolovitz is the digital resources coordinator and an assistant professor at Sam Houston State University. He earned an M.A. from the University of North Texas Graduate School of Library and Information Science in 2006. His research interests are varied and have included classic and contemporary literature, mythology, film studies related to Alfred Hitchcock and John Hughes, and sexual violence in video games. Manolovitz continues to research, write, and present at conferences internationally on a variety of topics.

FURTHER READING

Associated General Contractors of America. "Construction Industry Adds Jobs (But with a Caveat)." *Industry Today*, May 17, 2010. http://www.industrytoday.com/article_view.asp?ArticleID=we250.

"Highway and Street Construction." In *Encyclopedia of American Industries*. Farmington Hills, Mich.: Gale Group, 2010.

Institute for Career Research. *Careers in Infrastructure Building—Engineers, Contractors, Skilled Heavy Construction Workers: Building Our Nation's Highways, Bridges, Tunnels, and Airports.* Chicago: Author, 2008.

_____. *Highway Building Careers: Working to Keep America Connected—Excellent Earnings Operating Heavy Machinery and Managing Huge Construction Projects.* Chicago: Author, 2005.

JobBank USA. "Jobs Outlook: Construction Laborers." http://www.jobbankusa.com/career_employment/construction_laborers/jobs_outlook.html.

Jones, Heather. "Industry Forecast II: Highways and Streets." *Construction Today*, September 25, 2007. http://www.construction-today.com/cms1/content/view/676/82.

Jones, Samantha R. *Highways: Construction, Management, and Maintenance.* Hauppauge, N.Y.: Nova Science, 2010.

Kelly, Anthony, and Kathleen Ripley. "IBISWorld Industry Report 23411a: Road, Street, and Highway Construction in the U.S." Santa Monica, Calif.: IBISWorld, 2010.

Khan, Mohiuddin A. *Bridge and Highway Structure Rehabilitation and Repair.* New York: McGraw-Hill, 2010.

LePatner, Barry B. *Too Big to Fall: America's Failing Infrastructure and the Way Forward.* New York: Foster, 2010.

Transportation for America et al. *Stranded at the Station: The Impact of the Financial Crisis in Public Transportation.* Washington, D.C.: Author, 2009. http://www.t4america.org/docs/081809_stranded_at_thestation.PDF

United Nations Centre for Human Settlements. *Policies and Measures for Small-Contractor Development in the Construction Industry.* Nairobi, Kenya: Author, 1996.

U.S. Bureau of Labor Statistics. *Career Guide to Industries*, 2010-2011 ed. http://www.bls.gov/oco/cg.

_____. *Occupational Outlook Handbook*, 2010-2011 ed. http://www.bls.gov/oco.

U.S. Census Bureau. North American Industry Classification System (NAICS), 2007. http://www.census.gov/cgi-bin/sssd/naics/naicsrch?chart=2007.

U.S. Department of Commerce. International Trade Administration. Office of Trade and Industry Information. Industry Trade Data and Analysis. http://ita.doc.gov/td/industry/otea/OTII/OTII-index.html.

U.S. Department of Transportation. Federal Highway Administration. "Productivity and the Highway Network: A Look at the Economic Benefits to Industry from Investment in the Highway Network." Washington, D.C.: Author, 2006. http://www.fhwa.dot.gov/policy/otps/060320b/060320b.pdf.

World Bank. *Indian Road Construction Industry: Capacity Issues, Constraints, and Recommendations.* Washington, D.C.: Author, 2008.

Home Maintenance Services

©Crystal Craig/Dreamstine.com

INDUSTRY SNAPSHOT

General Industry: Personal Services

Career Clusters: Human Services; Architecture and Construction

Subcategory Industries: Appliance Repair and Installation; Carpet, Upholstery and Floor Cleaning Service; Consumer Electronics Repair and Maintenance Services; Electrical Maintenance; Exterminating and Pest Control Service; Handyman Construction Service; Interior Design Service; Lawn and Garden Maintenance Services; Plumbing and Heating Maintenance Service; Residential Cleaning Service; Swimming Pool Maintenance and Service

Related Industries: Building Construction Industry; Electrical and Gas Appliances Industry; Landscaping Services

Annual Domestic Revenues: $27.4 billion USD (Freedonia Industry Market Research, 2009)

Annual International Revenues: $41.4 billion USD (Global Industry Analysts, 2009)

Annual Global Revenues: $68.8 billion USD (Global Industry Analysts, 2009)

NAICS Numbers: 236118, 2382, 54141, 5617, 8114, 8123

INDUSTRY DEFINITION

Summary

Owning or renting a home and surrounding property can require a great deal of work to ensure that the residence stays clean and in good repair. Even with regular maintenance, problems can develop and repairs will be needed. These repairs and maintenance may require expertise and equipment that are beyond the knowledge of the average resident. Home maintenance services provide assistance to residential customers with various tasks inside and outside their homes. The accessibility and affordability of outsourcing home maintenance has made it an attractive alternative to those who do not have the time, knowledge, or skill to perform household maintenance or repairs. This industry encompasses a wide range of cleaning, repair, landscaping, and maintenance services for the interior and exterior of the customer's home.

History of the Industry

It can be argued that the beginning of the home maintenance industry began with the first emergence of humankind and the need for shelter. *Homo habilis*, one of the first species of humans, was nicknamed "handyman" because it was the first to create tools.

Many home maintenance tasks, such as installing exterior lights, can be done by a handyman. (©Crystal Craig/Dreamstime.com)

The home maintenance services industry has its roots in several ancient occupations and traditional roles within a household. In ancient times, pharaohs, kings, and emperors would assemble workforces of hundreds or thousands of people to build, maintain, and protect their castles and empires. Residential maintenance service was something that only the noble, powerful, and wealthy had and it usually was performed by housemaids, servants, and slaves. Service providers often were born into lower or impoverished castes and had few or no other options beyond serving the wealthy. Strenuous work was diligently performed in exchange for food and basic accommodations. Until the development of labor laws in the twentieth century, service personnel had no protection under the law and often were considered property of their employers.

The Flatiron Cleaning Company, founded in 1893, was the first residential house and window cleaning service in New York. In contrast, the first home cleaning service company in the Republic of China was not started until 2002 in Taiwan. For most people, household skills were passed from mothers to daughters and fathers to sons. People built and maintained their homes to the extent of their skill and knowledge, using only materials that were readily available to them. With the introduction of modern conveniences, homes became much more complicated in their construction and amenities, which increased the potential for problems and need for skilled repair providers. In the 1880's, small electrical stations able to power a few city blocks were created based on the principles of Thomas Alva Edison's work. By 1930, most homes in American cities had electricity. Electricians and appliance repairmen had to be consulted to install and repair the new technology.

Experts in the delivery and drainage of water to buildings were described by the ancient Romans. These individuals were skilled in the installation and repair of pipe and related apparatus. Indoor plumbing became more common in middle-class homes in the mid-1800's, and plumbing services soon followed.

Wall-to-wall carpeting, nailed to the floor, was introduced after World War II. It was considered very luxurious but created a concern when the time came for it to be cleaned. Previously, when rugs in a home became soiled, they were rolled up and taken away to be cleaned. The need for in-home carpet cleaning fueled the development of mobile carpet cleaning technology and services beginning in the 1950's. By the late 1990's, there were more than nine thousand mobile carpet and upholstery cleaning services in the United States.

The Industry Today

It is estimated that almost 10 percent of households in the United States hire outside services to help with housecleaning. Businesses in this industry provide increasingly convenient, accessible, and affordable options to consumers who are unable or unwilling to perform cleaning and maintenance tasks in their homes. These services can include cleaning, repair, and maintenance of all areas of a home and property. Businesses in this industry are dominated by small establishments, operating in metropolitan areas, employing fewer than five people. However, many franchises and large, globally recognized companies with thousands of employees also exist.

Historically, people who performed cleaning

and maintenance services usually resided on the property, but this is no longer a common arrangement. Most services now are performed by a small team or individuals who visit regularly. Some cleaning services may be performed by professionals living in the home who also provide other services, such as child care or daily living assistance to seniors or disabled persons.

As a large segment of the population ages, home maintenance and cleaning services are expected to grow in popularity. The baby-boomer generation tends to have higher than average annual income and the desire to maintain an independent lifestyle in their homes, which will lead to increased outsourcing of home maintenance and cleaning. Home maintenance and improvement also has experienced growth because most homes in the United States are several decades old. Economic challenges have convinced many homeowners to spend available funds to improve and repair their current homes, rather than purchasing new homes. Another driving force in this industry involves the amenities and technology available to average households. People enjoy modern conveniences and high-tech devices but do not have the knowledge to install them or perform repairs should a problem arise. Modern amenities such as swimming pools, air-conditioning systems, underground sprinklers, and home entertainment systems require specialized care, repair, or regular maintenance.

This highly competitive industry is seeing increasing emphasis on services that use eco-friendly and nontoxic products. Consumers are demanding that products used in their homes for cleaning or pest control are safe for the environment, family members, and pets. This has led to research into more natural but equally effective products and methodologies. Large companies in this industry employ teams of chemists to develop superior cleaning agents.

Maintenance management companies are emerging as a popular choice for consumers.

An independent company can assess the customer's needs and arrange to have the required services performed by other companies. This is valuable for large jobs where different services need to be coordinated and when the customer prefers to have a single contact person for the duration of a long or complicated job. These companies often are the first choice for groups of homes, such as gated and seniors' communities. Large home improvement stores have begun to form partnerships with home maintenance companies to provide customers with materials and services for their homes. An example is Home Depot, which teamed with ServiceMaster, the nation's leading provider of home services, to test the sale of a wide range of co-branded residential maintenance and repair services to its retail customer base. ServiceMaster specializes in a range of home services, including professional lawn, tree, and shrub care, landscape installation and maintenance, termite and pest control, plumbing and drain cleaning, carpet and upholstery cleaning, and home warranties. These services complement Home Depot's existing product installation and home improvement services, which include carpet and flooring installation, kitchen cabinet and countertop installation, door and window replacements, and roof replacements. Real estate compa-

A man uses a pressure washer to clean an exterior deck. Cleaning, interior and exterior, is an important part of home maintenance. (©Crystal Craig/Dreamstime.com)

nies also commonly enter into collaborative partnerships with home maintenance businesses. Realtors can sell a property more easily if it is clean and in good repair, so they may suggest these services to homeowners or bring them in to assist with preparing a vacant property for sale. New technology and strategies see businesses in this industry continuing to emerge and grow as customers regard these services as increasingly convenient, affordable, and essential to their lifestyles.

INDUSTRY MARKET SEGMENTS

Small Businesses

Small businesses dominate the home maintenance industry: Most companies have fewer than twenty employees, and the majority of those started as sole proprietorships. Many small businesses provide service within a metropolitan area or specific neighborhood. Cleaning services can be provided as needed, but many customers arrange for recurring service. Service often is provided on a weekly basis, although frequency and level of service can vary greatly. Cleaning usually includes vacuuming, dusting, and general tidying, and can also incorporate services such as laundry, wall washing, and bed

A pool service employee cleans the filters on a pool. (©Dreamstime.com)

making. Specialty cleaning for items such as carpeting or drapery normally is arranged when needed. Maintenance services and repair services also tend to be contracted as problems arise. These small businesses can be contracted by larger businesses or management companies. Because services are provided at the customer's residence, the small businesses in this industry are mobile and often home-based.

Potential Annual Earnings Scale. The annual average earnings for small businesses in home maintenance vary widely by region and the type of service being provided. The annual average income for an independent small-business owner providing cleaning services, general home maintenance, or lawn services is $52,000. The salary for a nonowner employee of these small businesses usually starts at minimum wage and rises depending on work performance. Outdoor maintenance and cleaning can be seasonal in some regions, which can result in inconsistency of work available. Skilled tradespeople in this industry can earn significantly higher income based on experience. Annual salaries for independent or small-business plumbers and electricians start at approximately $48,000 and increase with experience. Many independent small businesses without regular contracts can see variability in the amount of work available, relying on responses to local advertising and marketing, making the business challenging to predict.

Clientele Interaction. Small home maintenance businesses have direct clientele interaction several times each day. Customers contact the service provider or dispatcher and normally arrange a time to meet the service provider at the residence. In some very small businesses or sole proprietorships, the dispatcher and service provider are the same person. Repeat business and recommendations from happy customers are keys to success, so all clientele interaction must be positive. Providing service in someone's home can be a delicate situation and personnel must appear capable and trustworthy. Employees often are required to maintain appearance standards and undergo drug testing, as they are representatives of the company.

Amenities, Atmosphere, and Physical Grounds. Small home maintenance companies might have a small office space, but most consider their vehicles to be their offices. Most of the actual service work is provided in a customer's residence or yard. A dispatch center may be located in a home office or in a vehicle, with calls managed by cell phone. Most small businesses do not maintain retail locations.

Typical Number of Employees. As in most small-business situations, the goal is to keep expenses low and revenues high. Depending on the service being provided, many businesses can be managed by a single individual or small group. For safety and security of employees, many businesses now have service providers work in pairs. The typical number of employees for a small home maintenance or cleaning service can range from one to twenty.

Traditional Geographic Locations. Most small businesses operate in urban centers and serve a specific geographic area, such as a single city, neighborhood, or district within a city. Fuel, time, and other transportation expenses make it difficult to serve large areas.

Pros of Working at a Small Home Maintenance Company. Independent service providers and subcontractors can decide how much and when they want to work. Small companies or individuals who have regular service contracts enjoy a familiarity with customers and the security of regular work. There usually is not a great deal of direct supervision for employees of small businesses; they most often work alone or in pairs. Many national labor unions have been established to provide guidance and protection to workers providing home maintenance services. Organizations such as the Association of Residential Cleaning Services International have been established to assist residential cleaning service owners and professionals in starting, promoting, building, and expanding their businesses. About 32 percent of all electricians are members of a union, such as the International Brotherhood of Electrical Workers.

Starting a business in the home maintenance industry is one of the most popular choices for emerging entrepreneurs. Many guides are available to direct people through the process. It is an attractive industry because start-up costs are relatively low and return on investment can be quite quick.

Cons of Working for a Small Home Maintenance Company. Within small companies, there is very little room for advancement. Seasonal fluctuations in business and a lack of regular service contracts can make income unpredictable. To generate income and keep existing customers satisfied, some work hours can be very long. For unskilled employees who are not owners or managers in the business, wages typically are low. Many workers find the circumstances and situations they encounter challenging and unpleasant. The work also can be physically demanding and may involve heavy lifting, moving of furniture, and prolonged bending, squatting, crouching, and fitting into tight spaces. Safety can be a concern for employees, as there is a certain level of uncertainty when entering into unknown premises.

Costs

Payroll and Benefits: Typically, small maintenance and cleaning companies pay their employees an hourly wage or employ independent contractors who are paid per completed job. Full-time employees usually receive the same benefits as other workers, at the discretion of the owner/manager; however, many independent contractors are not entitled to benefits.

Supplies: Transportation and the supplies used to perform the specific services can vary. Cleaning services travel to customers' homes, but some use cleaning supplies and equipment supplied by the customer. Most services provide their own supplies and equipment, including cleaning agents for a range of surfaces and mops, cloths, and dusters. Maintenance businesses need tools and materials specific to their service. A maintenance or trade worker may determine in advance what materials are needed for a repair, purchase them for the customer, and add the amount to the invoice for service. Pest control services require specialized equipment, such as traps and chemicals, depending on the problem being addressed.

The means of transporting workers, equipment, and supplies also is very important. A vehicle in safe, working order is necessary. A landscaping service, for example, may use a truck and tow a trailer carrying mowers and tools to a property. In many businesses, the transportation vehicles also serve as advertisements and are painted or decorated with company logos and contact information. An effective communication system among dispatchers and service personnel also must be maintained, such as cell phones, wireless devices, or two-way radios.

External Services: A small home maintenance business needs to maintain its vehicles and equipment. Fuel, repairs, and insurance costs can be considerable. In most regions, home maintenance businesses require licenses and insurance to protect themselves and their clients. In addition to insurance, many small businesses and individuals become bonded, which provides additional assurance to customers. Some services, such as landscaping, produce large amounts of material requiring disposal. Hauling and dumping fees usually are the responsibility of the service provider and are included in the overall fee charged to the customer.

Utilities: Many small businesses do not have central offices or service centers, so utilities are minimal. Services are provided on customers' properties, utilizing their water and electricity if required.

Taxes: Small businesses are required to pay local, state, and federal income taxes, as well as regional business and service taxes and permit fees.

Midsize Businesses

Midsize home maintenance services usually operate within larger geographic areas, have more employees, and may provide a broader range of services to residential clients than small businesses. Midsize businesses also may have centralized customer service and dispatch hubs to manage service requests and inquiries.

Potential Annual Earnings Scale. Midsize home maintenance businesses tend to have more employees and positions. Unlike at smaller companies, the owner or manager typically takes on a more administrative or supervisory role, rather than providing services directly to customers. Similar to small businesses, employees earn relatively low wages for unskilled positions. Trade and expe-

rienced workers earn significantly more. Some trades, such as electricians and plumbers, may have salary and pay increase structures outlined by local or national labor unions.

Midsize companies might have positions available in customer service, advertising and marketing, and a range of other supporting roles in addition to the service providers. Wages for these positions vary by region and job responsibilities. Nonowner supervisors earn an average hourly wage of $18, and these positions often are filled by individuals with previous experience who have been promoted within the company. Supervisory and management positions come with higher earnings, depending on qualifications and responsibilities. Customer service representatives and dispatchers earn an average hourly wage of $12. Many midsize businesses have incentive and bonus programs available to employees in addition to their hourly wages.

Clientele Interaction. As home maintenance service businesses get larger, they tend to have more positions that involve less direct clientele interaction. After a request for service, customers may be visited by a manager or estimator who will make arrangements for service and act as the contact person for future interactions. This position removes some of the clientele interaction from the actual service providers.

More administrative positions are required to maintain the smooth operation of a midsize business. As with any service industry, repeat business and recommendations from happy customers is key to success, so all clientele interaction must be positive. Employees often are required to wear uniforms and carry identification, as well as adhere to appearance standards, as they are representatives of the company.

Amenities, Atmosphere, and Physical Grounds. Midsize home maintenance service businesses often maintain an administrative office, central dispatch office, or warehouse space for equipment, supplies, and fleet vehicles. These businesses' high standards can create a highly organized but frequently stressful atmosphere. Most service providers spend a minimal amount of time at an office receiving their instructions for the day and collecting the required supplies before going out to customer residences to work. Depending on the job, a service provider might work at the same residence for a long period of time, on a regular schedule, or go to several residences throughout the day.

Typical Number of Employees. The typical number of employees for a midsize home maintenance service business depends on the service provided and geographic area covered. Businesses can have thirty to five hundred employees in a wide range of positions.

Traditional Geographic Locations. Midsize home maintenance services usually operate within larger geographic areas and have more services and employees than small businesses. They may have service hubs in several cities within a state or region. Most operate in urban centers and might also serve some rural customers, although that is uncommon.

Pros of Working at a Midsize Home Maintenance Company. Midsize companies tend to pay employees hourly wages or an annual salary, and many companies have established incentive or bonus programs. This results in more income stability. There also are more options for advancement or changes in position. Midsize companies often provide benefits and uniforms to their employees. They have their own equipment, supplies, and fleet of transport vehicles, so workers are not required to provide and maintain their own.

Cons of Working for a Midsize Home Maintenance Company. Midsize company employees usually are on a more structured schedule and receive more direct supervision than employees of small companies. The work can be unpleasant and physically demanding. Service providers might have to perform heavy lifting, move furniture, and spend prolonged periods of time bending, squatting, crouching, and fitting into tight spaces. Safety can be a concern for employees entering unknown premises. The geographic area a midsize company serves is typically larger than that of a small business, which may cause increased stress because of time commitments and customer calls.

Costs

Payroll and Benefits: Midsize home maintenance companies pay their personnel an hourly wage or per completed job or service provided. Full-time employees usually receive the same vacation and benefits as other workers, at the discretion of the owner/manager.

Supplies: Similar to small businesses, transportation and the equipment and supplies used to perform the specific services can vary. Cleaning services travel to customers' homes, but some use the customers' own cleaning supplies and equipment. Companies purchase their cleaning chemicals and supplies in large quantities from wholesalers. Most services bring all of their supplies and equipment with them, including cleaning agents for a range of surfaces and any mops, cloths, or dusters they need. Maintenance businesses need tools and materials specific to their service. These tools will need to be reliable and of good quality.

The means of transporting the workers, equipment, and supplies is very important. Safe, well-maintained vehicles are required. A landscaping service, for example, might use a truck and tow a trailer carrying mowers and tools to a property.

An effective communication system between dispatchers and service personnel also must be maintained, such as cell phones, wireless devices, or two-way radios. Some companies also have Global Positioning Systems (GPS) on their fleet vehicles to increase drivers' efficiency and allow dispatchers to track service personnel.

External Services: A midsize home maintenance business needs to maintain its transportation vehicles, communication equipment, and any tools or equipment required to provide the service. Insurance can be very expensive, but it is required to maintain the legal operation and safety of the business, employees, and customers and their property. Specific business and operating licenses will be required, as will certification and bonding of individual employees, depending on their position. Fleet vehicles must meet Department of Transportation and Federal Motor Carrier Safety Administration requirements. Advertising and marketing for midsize businesses may be managed within the company or outsourced to another company. Hauling and dumping fees for trash or landscaping materials usually are the responsibility of the company and will be included in the fee charged to the customer.

Utilities: Utilities depend on the physical space or property type maintained by a business. Warehouses and dispatching or equipment hubs re-

Home Appliance Repairer

Considerations	Qualifications
Description	Maintains and repairs appliances used in the home.
Career cluster	Manufacturing
Interests	Data; things
Working conditions	Work inside
Minimum education level	On-the-job training; high school diploma/technical training; junior/technical/community college; apprenticeship
Physical exertion	Medium work; heavy work
Physical abilities	Unexceptional/basic fitness
Opportunities for experience	Internship; apprenticeship; part-time work
Licensure and certification	Required
Employment outlook	Slower-than-average growth expected
Holland interest score	RES

Note: See volume 1, "Publisher's Note," for an explanation of the Holland interest score.

quire electricity, heating, water, and sewer services. Internet and telephone services are the key to communication with customers and within the business.

Taxes: Midsize businesses are required to pay local, state, and federal income taxes, as well as business and service taxes and permit fees as required by their specific region.

Large Businesses

Large home maintenance businesses are the best recognized in the industry and employ thousands of people. This highly competitive industry has revenues of more than $27 billion in the United States. ServiceMaster is the world's largest cleaning and service company. It is the umbrella organization for well-known businesses such as Merry Maids and Terminix and operates more than 5,100 franchises. ServiceMaster provides expertise in cleaning, lawn care, pest control, and home inspection. American Residential Services/Rescue Rooter is another of the largest home main-

tenance companies with more than sixty service locations in twenty-four states, providing plumbing, heating, and air-conditioning installation and repair. Sears remains a leader in the home appliance repair sector, providing almost 10 percent of all appliance and electronic repairs in the United States.

Potential Annual Earnings Scale. The annual earnings for employees of large home maintenance service businesses have tremendous variability, depending on geographic area, service provided, and job responsibilities. At ServiceMaster, for example, there are more than 160 different job titles. The majority of these positions have a salary range of $18,000 to $55,000 annually. Executive positions can exceed $250,000. Service provider salaries at large businesses are similar to those at midsize companies and average $18,000 to $24,000 for unskilled crew members. At large companies, there is greater potential for higher earnings, benefits, and job security.

Clientele Interaction. Larger home maintenance companies have many administrative and other behind-the-scenes positions that require little or no direct clientele interaction. Sectors for business management and operations are required in order to maintain the organization. Customer service representatives will accept telephone and online requests for service and provide information to potential customers regarding service and appointments. After a request for service, customers may be visited by a manager or estimator who will make all the arrangements for the service and act as the contact person for future interactions. These individuals often will follow up with the customer after the job has been completed. This position removes some of the clientele interaction from the actual cleaners or other service providers. Repeat business and recommendations from satisfied customers are key to success, so any clientele interaction must be positive. Employees often are trained in customer relations and required to wear uniforms and carry identification, as well as adhere to appearance standards, as they are representatives of the company.

Amenities, Atmosphere, and Physical Grounds. The physical grounds of large home maintenance companies can include warehouses or offices, but the majority of work still is done at the residential properties of the customers. The company structure and service being provided determine what facilities are needed. Large companies usually have one or more large warehouses within a designated area where employees start their day, receive the addresses where they will respond to service requests, and collect supplies and equipment that are required. Large companies also have large administrative headquarters with smaller satellite offices to manage specific areas. Most service providers consider their transportation vehicle their office. The atmosphere can be stressful when trying to accommodate a large number of customer requests during a specific time period. Larger companies tend to have more resources available to contribute to causes within the community they serve, promoting a positive profile and increasing employee morale. An example is ServiceMaster's employee and corporate involvement with Habitat for Humanity.

Typical Number of Employees. Large home maintenance companies typically have hundreds or thousands of employees. Most are full-time employees, although casual and part-time staff can be brought in to assist with seasonal services. ServiceMaster employs more than 32,000 people.

Traditional Geographic Locations. Large companies serve entire cities, states, or countries, some even expanding into neighboring countries. For instance, Davey Tree Expert Company provides landscaping and other services on a national and international level, including all fifty states and four Canadian provinces. ServiceMaster serves more than 6.5 million customers in thirty countries.

Pros of Working at a Large Home Maintenance Company. Employees at large companies often are part of labor unions, which provide collective bargaining for better wages and benefits. Benefits provided to almost all workers include overtime pay, health insurance, and pensions. Large companies have a greater focus on workplace health and safety management, protecting the employees and the corporation. Wages at large companies usually are above average for non-skilled workers. Employees at larger companies normally are responsible for specific jobs, rather than covering multiple roles as required by smaller companies.

Cons of Working for a Large Home Maintenance Company. These companies are a very popular career choice for many people, especially unskilled workers and new immigrants; therefore, hiring can be very competitive. The work can be unpleasant and physically demanding. It may involve heavy lifting, moving of furniture, and prolonged periods of time bending, squatting, crouching, and fitting into tight spaces. Safety can be a concern for employees, as there is a certain level of uncertainty when entering into unknown premises.

Large companies usually have higher levels of supervision and enforce standard operating procedures, which do not allow for flexibility or creativity by individual workers. Completing all service requests in a timely manner can be stressful. Many large companies provide twenty-four-hour emergency service, requiring some maintenance professionals to be on call overnight and on weekends and holidays.

Costs

Payroll and Benefits: Large companies employ thousands of people with varying skills and job descriptions. Large teams of people are employed solely to manage the payroll and benefits for employees.

Supplies: Costs for equipment, chemicals, and transportation are significant for large companies.

External Services: Large home maintenance companies tend to have internal personnel to cover all requirements for operations. Hauling and dumping fees for trash or landscaping materials usually are the responsibility of the company and will be included in the fee charged to the customer. Maintenance of facilities and equipment is often managed on-site by employees of the company. Communication (Internet, telephone, radio, GPS) services are provided by national carriers and need to be of the highest quality and reliability. Insurance costs involving vehicles, worker injury, and property damage can be quite substantial. Fleet vehicles must meet Department of Transportation and Federal Motor Carrier Safety Administration requirements.

Utilities: Large companies operate numerous offices, warehouses, and service hubs. Utilities for these facilities include water, sewer, electric, heat source, and communication services. Larger companies that have thousands of franchise locations do not pay the utilities for these locations; utility costs are the responsibility of the franchise owner.

Taxes: Large home maintenance businesses are required to pay local, state, and federal income taxes, as well as business and service taxes and permit fees as required by their specific regions.

ORGANIZATIONAL STRUCTURE AND JOB ROLES

The organizational structure of companies within the home maintenance services industry is usually based on the size of the company and the service being provided. Some small, independent companies may only have one or a few employees who take on numerous roles. Sole proprietors directly accept the service request from the customer, provide the service, collect the fee, and perform all administrative and operations tasks. Larger companies have thousands of employees with hundreds of distinct job classifications. Employees in this industry range from the unskilled or trade certified to corporate executives and scientists.

The following umbrella categories apply to the organizational structure of businesses in the home maintenance industry:

- Business Management
- Customer Service
- Sales and Marketing
- Facilities and Security
- Technology, Research, Design, and Development
- Production and Operations
- Distribution and Service Providers
- Human Resources

Business Management

Management and executive positions are the highest ranking positions within home maintenance corporations. This level normally comprises a small group of individuals, supported by a larger team of administrative and other professionals. The goal of this team is to make decisions that ensure that their company continues to generate maximum revenue, reduce costs, and improve service. A top executive at a large company in this industry, such as ServiceMaster, earns in excess of $950,000 annually. Executive assistants perform a wide range of administrative duties critical to business operations and earn an average annual salary of $40,000.

Business management occupations may include the following:

- Chief Executive Officer (CEO)
- Chief Operating Officer (COO)
- Chief Financial Officer (CFO)
- Chief Information Officer (CIO)
- Regulatory Compliance Executive
- Executive Assistant

Customer Service

Customer service is critical to success. Customer service workers often create the first and lasting impression a company has on its customers. Personnel must provide accurate information and assistance, respond to inquiries, resolve problems, and sell company services.

Customer service employees proactively provide answers and resolutions to any customer inquiry. This may include assisting customers to determine their residential service needs, tracking service personnel, providing rate quotes, setting up service appointments, and answering billing and/or invoicing questions. Positions in customer service often do not require previous training or specialized education. Employees must demonstrate excellent communication skills, professionalism, patience, telephone etiquette, and problem-solving and multitasking skills. Bilingual or multilingual customer service representatives are in particularly high demand. In larger companies, customer service representatives provide customer support twenty-four hours per day, so limited shift work often is required. Full-time customer service representatives earn an average annual salary of $24,000. Supervisors and executives in customer service can earn $40,000 to $70,000 annually.

Customer service occupations may include the following:

- Customer Service Representative (Telephone/Online)
- Customer Relations Executive
- Customer Service Supervisor
- Service Agent
- Estimators

Sales and Marketing

Home maintenance and cleaning is a highly competitive industry. Customers have many choices depending on their service requirements, and therefore brand recognition and a superior service reputation are critical. Sales and marketing departments ensure that advertising dollars are well spent, their particular brand remains at the forefront of customer choice, and exceptional relationships with customers are maintained.

All businesses, large or small, have a dedicated advertising budget with which they need to create imaginative strategies that best represent their services and influence customer perceptions throughout their area of service. Companies market their services primarily through advertisements in the yellow pages, direct mail, the Internet, television and radio advertising, print advertisements, door-to-door solicitation, and telemarketing. Additionally, some companies market their services through real estate brokerage offices in conjunction with the resale of single-family residences and through financial institutions and insurance agencies.

Marketing and communications personnel need to project their message to potential customers; they also need to protect the company's reputation by identifying and managing emerging issues that may be harmful to the corporation. Effective media relations and media monitoring are critical in the handling of a crisis. A key measurement of corporate success is revenue; therefore, sales of products and services are imperative. A sales team must contact customers and prospective customers to be certain that they are aware of current and upcoming products and services and are satisfied with current service. Sales and marketing analysts determine if the advertising funds have been well spent. They report whether proposed sales goals and targets have been achieved and develop recommendations for future sales opportunities.

Sales positions often are compensated by a base salary and commission structure based on performance. Key skills include communication, influence, negotiation, problem solving, and organization.

Marketing and communications positions usually require a college degree or training in the area. Salaries can start at around $25,000 annually for entry-level positions. Marketing directors and managers can earn $52,000 to $90,000. General marketing and sales positions earn an average annual salary of $52,000 and usually include a commission or bonus structure. Key skills include communication, organization, and knowledge of branding, promotions, trade shows and event planning, database marketing, telemarketing, promotions, advertising, and research.

Sales and marketing occupations may include the following:

- Sales Account Manager
- Sales Analyst
- Sales Clerk
- Corporate Communications Specialist
- Marketing Manager
- Media Relations Representative
- Business Liaison
- Marketing and Business Development Coordinator
- Market Research Manager
- Business Analyst

Facilities and Security

The security and protection of customer property is extremely important, as is the safety of maintenance employees. The maintenance of facilities and equipment also is critical to the operation of any maintenance company. Disruptions or security failures in the information technology systems could create liability or limit the ability to effectively monitor, operate, and control operations and adversely affect operating results. The failure to protect the security of personal information of customers could subject a business to costly penalties or private litigation, as well as harm the company's reputation.

Security services for large companies work with local and federal law enforcement to investigate thefts, acts of vandalism, misconduct, and other activities detrimental to the company, its employees, and its customers. They also may be required to perform security duties to protect management and executives in the corporation. Specialized security personnel normally require training and experience in law enforcement and transportation security and familiarity with theft detection and applicable technical devices.

Residential cleaning and maintenance companies require staff to clean and maintain their business facilities as well. It is not uncommon for larger companies to own or lease hundreds of properties that all need to be managed and maintained. Facilities positions cover a wide range of duties—anything that ensures the smooth running and maintenance of the larger operations. These employees are responsible for minor repairs and routine maintenance for office, shop, warehouse, and yard facilities. Basic knowledge of electrical work, plumbing, and carpentry are required. Specialized maintenance of equipment, tools, and vehicles often is contracted out to other companies; however, larger companies may keep individuals on staff to perform repair and maintenance of fleet vehicles.

OCCUPATION PROFILE

Plumber and Pipefitter

Considerations	Qualifications
Description	Plans, lays out, and installs pipe systems, particularly for water and sewage, and maintains and repairs such systems.
Career clusters	Architecture and Construction; Manufacturing
Interests	Data; things
Working conditions	Work inside; work both inside and outside
Minimum education level	On-the-job training; high school diploma or GED; high school diploma/technical training; apprenticeship
Physical exertion	Heavy work
Physical abilities	Unexceptional/basic fitness
Opportunities for experience	Apprenticeship; military service; part-time work
Licensure and certification	Required
Employment outlook	Faster-than-average growth expected
Holland interest score	RCE; REI; RES

Note: See volume 1, "Publisher's Note," for an explanation of the Holland interest score.

Facilities and security occupations may include the following:

- Security Specialist
- Security Guard
- Loss Prevention Specialist
- Risk Analyst
- Maintenance and Repair Technician
- Mechanic
- Electrical Engineer
- Cleaner
- Plumber

Technology, Research, Design, and Development

Technology is becoming increasingly important in the home maintenance industry. Programmers, analysts, and technical support staff are experiencing the greatest job growth. Customers want to be able to make service requests online, get instant rate quotes, and electronically pay for service securely and in real time. Technology design constantly is changing because the systems need to be extremely efficient and effective while remaining easy for customers and employees to use.

Positions in technology, research, design, and development require specialized training for specific roles, such as degrees in computer science and information systems. Programmer analyst and systems programmer salaries begin at about $35,000 and can reach $80,000 annually. Information technology project managers earn annual salaries of $75,000 to $88,000.

Science careers are becoming increasingly important in the home maintenance and cleaning industry. Companies employ research and development teams to create effective cleaning, restoration, and pest control chemicals that are less harmful to people, pets, and the environment. Customers are demanding more natural options but still want to maintain cleaning and service standards. Companies with large fleets of service vehicles are exploring more cost-effective transportation options, including cleaner-burning fuel, in order to combat rising fuel costs and answer environmental concerns with the industry. Companies are becoming more aware of the demand of their customers to provide service while doing less damage to the environment.

Technology, research, design, and development occupations may include the following:

- Programmer Analyst
- Systems Analyst
- Technical Analyst
- Application Manager
- Application Analyst
- Application Project Manager
- Technical Specialist
- Technology Consultant
- Technology and Application Support
- Technological Adviser
- Chemist
- Chemical Engineer
- Environmental Impact Analyst

Production and Operations

Operations constitutes the inner workings of a home maintenance company and may include offices, storage, warehouse, call center, and data processing space. Operations personnel also assist customer service in the management and investigation of customer claims and complaints. Dispatchers receive information from customer service representatives and serve as liaisons between customers and service providers. The dispatcher may be a single position in a small company or part of a larger dispatch center. A dispatcher collects service requests and assigns them to appropriate service providers. Dispatchers may communicate with customers in case of delays and also are the primary contacts for service personnel when they are on the road. Dispatcher positions normally do not require any specialized training or diplomas. These workers need to be extremely organized, patient, and good multitaskers. The annual salary for dispatchers is about $25,000.

Operations staff ensures that the service providers are well equipped with all the supplies, equipment, or tools they may need to effectively serve the customers. All equipment needs to be in excellent working order. Operations engineers oversee and apply standardization processes and improvement policies, to develop increased service and cost performance for operations. Annual salaries for operations engineers start at about $47,000. Operations supervisors coordinate the activities within a warehouse or service hub. This often involves the coordination of employees inside with those at loading

OCCUPATION PROFILE

Insulation Worker

Considerations	Qualifications
Description	Evaluates the appropriate insulating materials and installs insulation in structures.
Career cluster	Architecture and Construction
Interests	Things
Working conditions	Work inside; work outside; work both inside and outside
Minimum education level	No high school diploma; on-the-job training; apprenticeship
Physical exertion	Medium work
Physical abilities	Unexceptional/basic fitness
Opportunities for experience	Apprenticeship; part-time work
Licensure and certification	Usually not required
Employment outlook	Faster-than-average growth expected
Holland interest score	RCI

Note: See volume 1, "Publisher's Note," for an explanation of the Holland interest score.

and unloading docks, and the organization of the vehicles dropping off and picking up supplies and equipment at the site. They also may determine how many employees are required to complete a specified service.

Production and operations occupations may include the following:

- Operations Supervisor/Manager
- Operations Engineer
- Dispatcher
- Stock Clerk
- Equipment Repair Specialist
- Procurement Staff
- Claims Manager
- Accountant

Distribution and Service Providers

Distribution in a home maintenance company involves the providing of the actual service in the customer's home or property. Successful and satisfactory completion of a repair, cleaning, or other maintenance service is what customers expect. There are numerous career options as a service provider. Many of these careers overlap with customer service, as these individuals are often viewed as the face of the corporation and have a lot of direct interaction with customers. These positions can be physically demanding and may involve heavy lifting, moving of furniture, and prolonged periods of time bending, squatting, crouching, and fitting into tight spaces.

Residential cleaners provide a range of services in order to keep homes organized and clean. These may include dusting, vacuuming, sweeping, mopping, washing dishes, making beds, removing trash, and cleaning all household surfaces. The U.S. Bureau of Labor Statistics (BLS) predicts that the demand for housekeepers will increase by 13 percent through 2016, resulting in the development of 186,000 new jobs in this service sector. Usually, there is no educational requirement for this type of job, although many employees do need to provide character references or submit to a background check. Housekeepers earn an average of $25,000 annually for full-time work.

Handymen also are known as residential maintenance workers and perform a variety of services and small repairs. General maintenance tasks might include the repair of plumbing or electrical systems, appliance repair and installation, painting, and general upkeep of a home and surrounding grounds. They may be hired to perform a specific task at a single residence, or kept under contract to provide service to numerous homes in a community or office complex. These workers usually do not need any advanced education, although many have vocational training or certificates in certain technical fields. The average annual salary for residential maintenance workers is $48,000.

Interior decorators and designers help people create pleasing and functional spaces in their homes. They may work with carpenters, painters, electricians, plumbers, and other maintenance professionals. Designers must be licensed in most areas and need to be familiar with building codes and regulations. There is a great deal of variability in income in these professions, depending on service and geographic area. According to the BLS, in 2008 the annual median wage for interior decorators and designers was $44,950.

Plumbers, electricians, and carpenters provide specialized service and repair to specific areas of a residence. These careers usually require individuals to have completed high school as well as additional training at a junior college or a vocational school. This training is normally followed by an apprenticeship to provide further practical and theoretical training. Apprenticeships can last up to four years. Licensing is required by most jurisdictions for these career choices. These professionals can earn an average annual salary of $56,000. Residential repair professionals usually work a regular work week, although some may be required to be on call.

Distribution and service provider occupations may include the following:

- Housekeeper
- Carpet/Upholstery/Window Covering Cleaner
- Window Cleaner
- Plumber
- Handyman
- Electrician
- Appliance Repair Technician
- Carpenter
- Landscaper
- Gardener
- Pool Maintenance Technician
- Heating, Ventilation, and Air-Conditioning (HVAC) Specialist
- Chimney Sweep
- Pest Control Technician
- Interior Designer/Decorator
- Painter

Human Resources

The human resources department is responsible for a company's employees. Workers in this department ensure that all employees in the company have the tools and training that they need to be effective and productive in their positions. They

Gardeners at work in the backyard of an Irvine, California, home. (©Darrin Aldridge/Dreamstime.com)

manage a variety of tasks, beginning with the hiring of personnel, their training and development, compensation and benefits, retirement, and dismissal. Human resources also ensures that all employee relations and practices comply with legal requirements and corporate policies. In many smaller companies, the owner or manager also assumes human resource responsibilities.

Most positions within human resources require a college degree or equivalent experience. Managers in this field earn approximately $80,000 annually. This is often a challenging area and employee relations require patience, collaboration, negotiation, and conflict-resolution skills.

Human resources occupations may include the following:

- Human Resources Director
- Human Resources Manager
- Human Resources Coordinator
- Human Resources Analyst
- Administrative Assistant
- Human Resources Generalist

INDUSTRY OUTLOOK

Overview

The outlook for the home maintenance services industry appears to be improving. Several factors are contributing to this growth, including an aging population, more two-income households, and more single-parent households. Almost 10 percent of all American residences outsource some or all of their household cleaning. Many seniors are turning to home maintenance services when they find that they can no longer perform some of the tasks they used to, but still wish to live independently in their homes. Double-income families use home maintenance services because they can afford to pay someone else to do the things they do not have time or desire to do themselves. A growing number of single-parent homes consult with maintenance or cleaning services to help them with household jobs that they do not have the time, tools, or knowledge to complete. The rise in demand for services and relatively low start-up costs have led many people to become entrepreneurs in this industry. In 1998, there were more than 58,000 cleaning and home maintenance businesses in the United States, the majority being sole proprietorships or small businesses. Hiring professionals to perform home maintenance has become very accessible and affordable for customers. This highly competitive industry does limit the ability of businesses to raise their prices for service but also has led to creative solutions and service options to attract clientele.

Employment Advantages

Despite economic challenges, the home maintenance industry continues to experience growth. It is an attractive avenue for individuals with an entrepreneurial spirit to start their own business, with few materials and limited education necessary. The work can be challenging and physically demanding but also satisfying. Hard work and providing customers with quality service can lead to referrals and regular contracts. This also is a good industry for unskilled individuals seeking employment and experience. Employment within an established company can provide job security, benefits, and op-

Replacing a chimney may require the services of a mason or bricklayer. (©Wisconsinart/Dreamstime.com)

portunities for advancement, even for unskilled workers. Many large companies in this industry sell franchise opportunities, which provide an individual the independence of owning his or her own business with the brand recognition of a well-known and respected name.

Annual Earnings

Home maintenance services make up global revenues of almost $69 billion annually and are expected to experience annual growth of nearly 5 percent. The United States is the largest market for this industry, with domestic revenues of $27.4 billion. Residential cleaning services, which make up a large part of the industry, have projected revenue increases of 5.2 percent annually in the United States to $15.8 billion by 2013. These gains will be driven by ongoing increases in the number of older homes and aging residents, as well as the growing affordability and availability of services provided. More dramatic growth is expected internationally as economic development escalates in markets such as China and the outsourcing of home maintenance becomes more culturally acceptable. Residential maintenance is expected to experience average annual growth of 4.1 percent. The economic downturn also has seen more families opting to repair and renovate existing homes rather than purchasing new homes. Employment in appliance repair also is expected to remain steady, and good opportunities exist for trained individuals.

PROJECTED EMPLOYMENT FOR SELECTED OCCUPATIONS

Specialty Trade Contractors

Employment		
2009	Projected 2018	Occupation
232,280	320,800	Carpenters
287,190	429,600	Construction laborers
421,690	536,000	Electricians
199,930	260,900	First-line supervisors/managers of construction trades and extraction workers
292,890	392,500	Plumbers, pipefitters, and steamfitters

Source: U.S. Bureau of Labor Statistics, Industries at a Glance, Occupational Employment Statistics and Employment Projections Program.

RELATED RESOURCES FOR FURTHER RESEARCH

ASSOCIATION OF RESIDENTIAL CLEANING
SERVICES INTERNATIONAL
7870 Olentangy River Rd., Suite 300
Columbus, OH 43235
Tel: (614) 547-0887
Fax: (614) 888-9240
http://www.arcsi.org

BUILDING SERVICES CONTRACTORS ASSOCIATION
INTERNATIONAL
401 N Michigan Ave., Suite 2200
Chicago, IL 60611
Tel: (800) 368-3414
Fax: (312) 673-6735
http://www.bscai.org

CLEANING MANAGEMENT INSTITUTE
19 British American Blvd. West
Latham, NY 12110
Tel: (518) 783-1281
Fax: (518) 783-1386
http://www.cminstitute.net

PROFESSIONAL LANDCARE NETWORK (PLANET)
950 Herndon Parkway, Suite 450
Herndon, VA 20170
Tel: (703) 736-9666
Fax: (703) 736-9668
http://www.landcarenetwork.org

ABOUT THE AUTHOR

April D. Ingram is a writer and researcher in British Columbia, Canada. She is a graduate of the University of Calgary and has worked in varying capacities in the home maintenance and cleaning industry since 1992.

FURTHER READING

Barnes Reports. *U.S. Home and Garden Equipment Repair and Maintenance Industry Report.* Woolwich, Maine: Author, 2009.

Bewsey, Susan. *Start and Run a Profitable Home Cleaning Business.* North Vancouver, B.C.: International Self-Counsel Press, 1999.

Commercial and Residential Cleaning Services to 2013. Cleveland, Ohio: Freedonia Group, 2010.

Meany, Terry. *How to Start a Home-Based Handyman Business.* Guilford, Conn.: Globe Pequot Press, 2009.

Morrow, Beth. *How to Open and Operate a Financially Successful Cleaning Service.* Ocala, Fla.: Atlantic, 2008.

Price, Laurence. *How to Start Your Own Horticulture Business: Landscape Maintenance, Lawn Renovation, Landscaping Services, Home Nursery.* Bremerton, Wash.: Botany Books, 1983.

U.S. Bureau of Labor Statistics. *Career Guide to Industries,* 2010-2011 ed. http://www.bls.gov/oco/cg.

U.S. Census Bureau. North American Industry Classification System (NAICS), 2007. http://www.census.gov/cgi-bin/sssd/naics/naicsrch?chart=2007.

U.S. Department of Commerce. International Trade Administration. Office of Trade and Industry Information. Industry Trade Data and Analysis. http://ita.doc.gov/td/industry/otea/OTII/OTII-index.html.

Hospital Care and Services

©Dreamstime.com

INDUSTRY SNAPSHOT

General Industry: Health Science

Career Clusters: Business, Management, and Administration; Health Science

Subcategory Industries: Cancer Hospitals; Children's Hospitals; Extended Care Hospitals; General Medical and Surgical Hospitals; Maternity Hospitals; Osteopathic Hospitals; Psychiatric and Substance Abuse Hospitals; Rehabilitation Hospitals

Related Industries: Counseling Services; Insurance Industry; Medicine and Health Care Industry; Pharmaceuticals and Medications Industry; Public Health Services; Residential Medical Care Industry; Scientific, Medical, and Health Equipment and Supplies Industry

Annual Domestic Revenues: $575 billion (First Research, 2010)

Annual Global Revenues: $4.5 trillion (total health care expenditures; The Medica, 2009)

NAICS Number: 622

INDUSTRY DEFINITION

Summary

Hospitals provide medical, diagnostic, and treatment services that are delivered by physicians, nurses, and other medical services staff. Specialized accommodations required by inpatients are more costly to provide than are outpatient services, and they represent the primary expense for entities delivering these services. Hospitals have traditionally provided outpatient services as a secondary activity, but their focus has shifted in the twenty-first century (largely driven by cost). Hospitals admit fewer patients to beds, and they provide more care on a nonadmission basis, either through the hospitals proper or through their ancillary clinics. Contemporary outpatient, or ambulatory, services provide greater revenue opportunities than do inpatient services. This situation represents a distinct change that occurred over the first decade of the twenty-first century.

The American Hospital Association (AHA) defines a hospital as a facility in which at least six inpatient beds are available for admission and occupancy twenty-four hours a day, seven days a week. A hospital must have on staff fully licensed physicians and other medical professionals authorized to provide inpatient oversight

Most hospitals provide both inpatient and outpatient services. (©Ken Cole/Dreamstime.com)

and care. Diagnostic services, some invasive, ranging from pathology to radiology are delivered by physicians, nurses, and ancillary staff. Inpatient services are highly specialized and require substantially greater facility and equipment expenditures and highly trained nursing support. Hospitals, however, must also provide some ambulatory services, such as emergency care, in order to meet criteria required to call themselves hospitals.

There are three overarching categories of hospitals that admit patients for care: general hospitals, specialty (tertiary) hospitals, and psychiatric hospitals. Specialty hospitals provide higher-acuity services—specialized facilities, medical specialists, and enhanced technologies—that general hospitals do not. Private and public hospitals in the United States employed over 5.5 million people in 2006, according to the U.S. Bureau of Labor Statistics (BLS). Some 35 percent of the U.S. health care workforce works in a hospital setting. Of that number, 70 percent work in facilities with more than one thousand employees.

Health care reform and efforts to curb prohibitive costs have resulted in a push to deliver more services on an ambulatory basis. For example, years ago it was common practice to admit newly diagnosed diabetics to hospitals for at least several days to start insulin therapy and educate the patients about their condition and treatment. In the twenty-first century, an admission of this sort is likely to be denied payment by most insurers, who expect such patients to be treated in doctor's offices or clinics on an outpatient basis. Hospitals have become places where only the sickest and most resource-intense patients are admitted, leaving outpatient care to doctors' offices and clinics.

Many physicians (internists and specialists) establish relationships with hospitals so that when their patients are sick, they can send them to those facilities. Traditionally, doctors in private practice would communicate with relevant hospital staff to coordinate their patients' care, visiting the hospital either before or after their workdays to gauge their patients' progress and issue orders for patient care.

However, a new physician specialty, the hospitalist, has developed. A hospitalist works solely within a hospital and assumes care for patients during their course of treatment. While hospitalists consult with their patients' primary care physicians, the responsibility for those patients' care rests with their hospitalists.

History of the Industry

Hospitals, or communal places where the sick might go to receive treatment, can be traced back to ancient cultures in Sri Lanka, India, and the Persian Empire. Later, in Europe, the Roman Catholic Church, through monasteries staffed with monks and nuns, assumed responsibility for the care of the sick. In eighteenth century England, independent hospitals developed, usually through the efforts of wealthy benefactors.

The U.S. hospital system originated around the time of the Civil War, when sterilization and modern medical treatments were being developed. In these early years, hospitals were public or not-for-profit; they treated all comers and were staffed by physicians and nurses. By the 1920's, public hospitals were viewed in some circles as service providers for the working class. A transition occurred, as some not-for-profit hospitals began to offer limited services for those who could afford them. This transition represented a response to a social demand for services of a presumed higher quality than those offered by public hospitals. People who could afford these better and costlier health care services, and who were willing to pay for them, brought much-needed revenue streams to the limited-access not-for-profits.

In the 1950's, during the baby-boom generation's birth, American families were living more financially secure lives than they had during previous generations. People began to move away from the centers of towns and cities, taking their wealth with them. Public hospitals, located in the center of many communities, began to suffer even more fi-

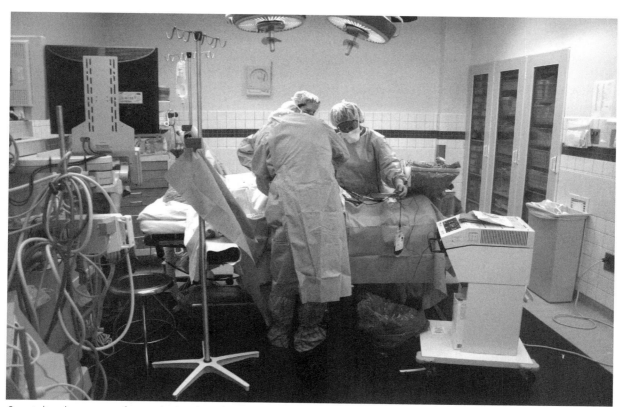

Specialized equipment for newly developed surgical procedures represents a major capital investment, but without such technological advances, a hospital can lose its competitive edge. (©Harold Riddle/Dreamstime.com)

nancial pressure, as their patients tended to be without means. It was not until 1965, though, with the passage of the Social Security Act that public hospitals began to have more secure sources of funding to treat the aged and the poor. As the years have progressed, public hospitals have not disappeared. In fact, public hospitals often play an important role as teaching institutions. Losing paying customers to not-for-profits, however, has presented an ever-growing challenge to the sustainability of these vital public institutions.

In the 1970's, federal legislation designated public hospitals serving a preponderance of poor and indigent persons as "disproportionate care hospitals." Both federal dollars and a commitment to the population that public hospitals serve have maintained the livelihood of these hospitals. Together with private and other not-for-profit hospitals, they provide a network of medical services to an American population that demands top quality, patient-centered care.

The Industry Today

There are nearly six thousand hospitals registered in the United States today. Over the years, hospital-delivered inpatient care has become more specialized, and designated units have been established to serve specific populations. These include pediatrics wards, cardiac care units, and neurology units specializing in seizure and epilepsy patients, among many others. Medical specialties started to emerge in the latter part of the twentieth century, and general practitioners who once took care of ev-

Inputs Consumed by Hospital, Nursing, and Residential Care Facilities

Input	Value
Energy	$9.7 billion
Materials	$96.7 billion
Purchased services	$215.6 billion
Total	$322.0 billion

Source: U.S. Bureau of Economic Analysis. Data are for 2008.

eryone in the hospital have began to specialize in any number of limited areas, such as orthopedics or emergency medicine. Nursing has begun to follow suit, as the medical community recognizes that consistency in care and highly skilled area-specific expertise results in better patient outcomes.

Hospital inpatient care has historically been paid by Medicare and other insurance companies under a formula based on a hospital's reported costs to deliver service. Today, most hospitalizations are paid on a per event basis, using a concept known as a "diagnostic related group." Physicians, nurses, and care managers—everyone involved in patient care—work toward one goal: to discharge the patient, either in an improved state or in a manner that allows for successful care at home.

People working in hospital care today face greater expectations for efficiency and economy, working with enough people to deliver quality care but, ideally, not so many as to cause financial hemorrhage to the organization. Registered nurses supervise direct inpatient care with support from nonlicensed patient-care technicians or licensed nursing assistants. Some hospitals employ licensed practical nurses (LPNs) for inpatient work, while some limit the LPN role to the ambulatory setting. Phlebotomists, radiology technicians, ultrasonographers, and respiratory therapists are just a few of the numerous professionals employed to care for patients in an inpatient setting.

The Contribution of Hospital, Nursing, and Residential Care Facilities to the U.S. Economy

Value Added	Amount
Gross domestic product	$419.2 billion
Gross domestic product	2.9%
Persons employed	7.656 million
Total employee compensation	$381.6 billion

Source: U.S. Bureau of Economic Analysis. Data are for 2008.

Hospitals, according to the BLS, constitute only 1 percent of health care establishments, despite being one of the largest employers in the industry. The majority of health care services revenue is driven by pharmaceutical utilization, the long-term care industry, and ambulatory care, not by inpatient hospital activity.

Common partnership industries to hospital care are primarily service driven. They include pharmaceutical companies and providers of medical technology for both patient care and information system infrastructure. Long-term care or rehabilitation facilities, which often serve those recovering from severe injury or illness, may be owned and operated alongside a parent hospital, or they may be privately owned. Transitioning patients too sick to go home but too well to stay in the hospital into such facilities is critical to medical professionals and their patients. Keeping patients in the hospital too long increases costs and can prevent the admission of patients needing immediate and more intense treatment by limiting bed availability.

INDUSTRY MARKET SEGMENTS

Hospitals may be small, community-based institutions that tend only to the needs of the local populations, or they may be large urban centers of treatment, research, and instruction of medical students. Some hospitals that specialize in a particular highly demanding service, such as cardiac or brain surgery, receive patients from all over the world seeking the best care available. Other, smaller hospitals may have no specialties to speak of, acting as general medical centers for relatively small populations.

Small Hospitals

The Internal Revenue Service (IRS) categorizes smaller hospitals as those in the gross revenue range of $25 million or less annually. Many smaller hospitals are not-for-profit institutions that closely manage costs. In the early twenty-first century, many rural and small hospitals have been purchased by larger hospital systems, often those centered in nearby metropolitan centers. For instance, University Hospitals in Cleveland, Ohio—a large

teaching institution affiliated with Case Western Reserve University Medical School—decided to expand its geographical reach. To that end, University Hospitals developed alliances with smaller hospitals outside the Cleveland area, expanding ambulatory services in these facilities. The benefit to smaller hospitals from such arrangements is an increase in the services they can offer, the ability to negotiate higher payments from insurers, and access to capital in order to purchase equipment and technology and to expand facilities.

Potential Annual Earnings Scale. Earnings for hospital staff vary greatly because there are hundreds of job types in hospitals. It can be noted, however, that smaller hospitals exist in more rural communities and provide services for inpatients who can be managed in a general hospital setting. Relatively simple diagnoses are usually managed by the community's private practice physicians or a small hospitalist group commonly employed by the hospital. Hospitalists are paid based on benchmarks compared to national benchmarks reported by the American College of Healthcare Executives or the National Medical Group Managers Association. Earnings for hospital-employed staff, including nurses and some physicians, are typically lower than those available in larger metropolitan hospitals. For those hospitals allied with larger health care systems, the earning potential can be greater. According to the Medical Group Management Association's Physician Compensation and Production Survey, the 2008 median salary for a primary care physician was $186,044, and the median salary for a specialist was $339,738. Physicians in small hospitals can be expected to earn less than those at larger institutions.

Clientele Interaction. Patients receiving services in a hospital setting, particularly during an inpatient stay, are in a highly vulnerable state and are often frightened, in addition to suffering the malady for which they are being treated. Patients rarely arrive alone, and employees of the hospital must be cognizant of extended family's pressures and fears. Financial worries, child care, lost wages, and social concerns for the patient and the family require providers of care to have compassion, understanding, a good sense of timing, and empathy. Hospital staff, from physicians to housekeepers, must maintain professional and respectful decorum; they should promote the hospital's quality to help allay fears and aid recovery, and they must always be aware of the need to protect patients' privacy and confidentiality.

Amenities, Atmosphere, and Physical Grounds. Cleanliness and a calm atmosphere are critical in hospitals. Entering the hospital should be made relatively simple, with such measures as sufficient parking and clear signage. Within the hospital, an attended receiving area should assist in allaying patients' anxiety. Probably the most important consideration within care-delivery areas is the comfort of patients. Controlled humidity and temperature, rigorous attention to modest noise levels, utmost attention to privacy and confidentiality, and minimal odors are all important. Employees in hospitals can expect to undergo an orientation that highlights these important patient-care factors.

Typical Number of Employees. Small hospitals employ up to one thousand staff members and often represent the largest employer in their small communities. These hospitals provide strong economic stability in their locales, offering positions from entry level all the way up to professional physician staff and chief operating officers.

Traditional Geographic Locations. Small hospitals are likely to be located in rural communities (with populations under fifty thousand). It is not uncommon to find these hospitals colocated with long-term care facilities (the next step for many patients no longer sick enough to be hospitalized in acute hospital settings or for those, such as the elderly, needing full-time care). While staff are drawn primarily from the immediate locale, specialty services and providers travel to small rural hospitals from other areas to provide services. Patient transportation to larger hospitals can be cost prohibitive, so many smaller local hospitals work hard to staff additional service deliverables for their consumers. These enhancements might include telemedicine, which leverages patients' ability to receive specialty services without leaving their hometown and can help smaller hospitals increase revenue and retain patients.

Pros of Working for a Small Hospital. Providing local care at a small, local hospital allows employees to work in a more intimate community atmosphere. Direct health care providers see many types of diagnoses and are exposed to variation in their work, providing them with learning opportunities. Working in a smaller setting will likely subject employees to less bureaucracy than they would encounter at larger hospitals. Larger hospitals have more pronounced cultures, or politics, which can be challenging to penetrate or change. Small hospitals provide full-service medical care, including emergency services, yet they rely on larger medical centers to treat complex patients who require specialty consultation and care.

Cons of Working for a Small Hospital. Many small hospitals do not have the financial resources of their larger counterparts. Capital investment in advanced equipment, facility enhancements, or structural expansion is limited. Smaller hospitals can have trouble recruiting and retaining trained staff, including physicians. Lack of resources and inability to match the salaries of larger organizations are two primary drivers behind these staffing challenges. The hospitals' purchasing power and negotiated prices for employee benefits are not as robust as those of larger institutions, which have better risk ratings and can likely offer employees more and better benefit options. In addition, small hospitals primarily provide general medical services, so health care providers working in this setting should not expect to see highly complex patients requiring specialty services. For some, this lack of specialty services may be limiting. These are the many reasons that smaller hospitals seek relationships with larger systems.

Costs

Payroll and Benefits: Hospitals employ both hourly and salaried employees, as well as doctors who often work on a fee-for-service basis. Benefits include health and dental insurance, possibly health savings accounts (HSA), long- and short-term disability insurance, and Family Medical Leave Act coverage. Continuing professional education time and dollars are usually provided, as are malpractice insurance, sick time, and earned time.

Supplies: Hospitals require medical supplies, disposables, pharmaceuticals, radiological products, surgical implants, and a plethora of patient-care-related items. Administrative and general operating supplies, such as cleaning, sterilization, and office supplies, are all required. According to Hoover's, small hospitals must have the same expensive equipment as midsize hospitals, so economies of scale are important, and controlling costs in small facilities is critical.

External Services: Small hospitals may engage outside legal and accounting counsel, grounds-keepers, biomedical supply and removal services, records storage and destruction services, and pharmaceutical services. These are just a few of a long list of possible external services necessary to keep a hospital open and functioning.

Utilities: Necessary utilities include electricity, heat, backup energy sources, telephone service, and high-speed Internet access. Temperature control and air-quality control are vital to successful patient treatment. Utility costs are often high for twenty-four-hour care facilities, and energy costs are volatile.

Taxes: Public hospitals may enjoy tax breaks; not-for-profits are tax exempt. Private for-profit hospitals act as private corporations and are subject to state and local tax requirements.

Midsize Hospitals

A midsize hospital's gross revenue is likely to be more than $100 million; net income after expenses, however, varies widely depending on the amount of charity care provided, the mix of insurance payers (including Medicare and Medicaid), expenses, and overhead. A hospital's profit margin can be very small after the impact of many factors, including the strength of the national and local economies. In terms of employee annual earnings, professional staff can expect to be paid on a salary basis at a level commensurate with similar positions in similar benchmark organizations. Some professionals work under a base salary with incentive opportunities for additional bonuses. Incentive drivers can include, but are not limited to, productivity or quality metrics for patient-care outcomes. Non-salaried staff members are paid hourly, and wages are generally competitive.

Potential Annual Earnings Scale. According to the Medical Group Management Association's Physician Compensation and Production Survey, the 2008 median salary for a primary care physician was $186,044, and the median salary for a specialist was $339,738. Staff members working in a midsize hospital, usually in a suburban location, are employed professionals. In these settings, professionals are salaried, their paycheck and benefits (if eligible) are guaranteed, and there may be an in-

centive salary available for meeting certain workload benchmarks. Contractual arrangements should address benefits such as employer-sponsored malpractice insurance coverage, professional membership dues, and travel. Nonprofessional (nonlicensed) staff are every bit as important to the viability of the hospital, and they are more likely to hold nonexempt (hourly) positions with a benefit structure similar to that of salaried staff.

Clientele Interaction. For the most part, hospitals' core function is fairly consistent: Providing inpatient hospital care and ambulatory services. Working purely in a service industry, staff must be customer-focused, possess excellent communication skills, and truly desire to be in a hands-on, interactive, and caring industry. Midsize hospitals are likely to be general-service facilities and have a critical need to provide service to referring physicians trying to admit patients to the facility. Maintaining positive relationships with those individuals and groups who refer their patients for care is critical to an organization's success.

Amenities, Atmosphere, and Physical Grounds. Usually located in suburbs or small cities, midsize facilities must have adequate parking, secure storage for medical records, privacy in the waiting area, an information technology infrastructure, sufficient support staff, and a commitment to quality patient care. Clinicians should have control over their own office area, and attention to patients' comfort and physical safety should be a priority.

Typical Number of Employees. The number of employees in a midsize hospital will vary by size and service lines offered. General hospitals, specialty hospitals, psychiatric hospitals, and rehabilitative hospitals vary by service line and number of beds. The staff can extend into the thousands depending on the facility. Though defining hospitals by size is challenging, there is evidence that those housing two hundred or more beds are considered to be midsize. If centralized functions such as billing, contracting, collections, and communications systems are contracted externally rather than in-house, the number of employees will be dramatically different.

Traditional Geographic Locations. Midsize facilities are typically located near more populated areas, though there are exceptions. A hospital-service-area population of fifty thousand or more in an urban setting would support a midsize facility. Referrals from medical providers are the lifeblood of these organizations. The closer they are to referring physicians, the greater the likelihood of visibility for such referrals. Professional engagement with the hospital's physician staff and private-practice physicians should be paramount. Socioeconomics in the area can play a role in a hospital's viability. The ability to access inpatient care without onerous travel for patients can contribute to the need for midsize facilities to situate in more populated locales.

Pros of Working for a Midsize Hospital. Well-established organizations provide employment security, and their purchasing power may allow them to offer better benefits at a more favorable rate for their employees that can smaller facilities. Midsize hospitals can provide the infrastructure for scheduling, human resource services, contracting, billing, managing day-to-day facility operations, and financial performance. Employees in this setting have access to health insurance for themselves and their families at group rates, which are more favorable than those a smaller hospital might be able purchase. Pay incentives may be available in these settings, usually based on productivity and expense controls. Shared responsibility for being on call at night and on weekends is more likely to be available than at smaller hospitals, given that more professionals are available to share this responsibility.

Cons of Working for a Midsize Hospital. Midsize hospitals are more complex organizations than their smaller counterparts. This greater complexity can entail more communication challenges and less autonomy, which can pose a challenge for professional medical service workers. Hours and work output are likely to be defined by employers with minimum expectations, even for professional staff. Round-the-clock staffing is required, so working weekends and holidays is likely to be required. The organizational structure of the hospital may require worthy individuals and units within the organization to compete for limited resources.

Costs

Payroll and Benefits: Midsize hospitals hire professional staff and pay on salary. Available benefits may include health insurance, dental coverage, short-term and long-term disability insurance, malpractice premium reimburse-

ment, continuing education funds (including money and time), employee assistance programs, and retirement/401(k) plans.

Supplies: Hospitals need both business (administrative) supplies and patient-care supplies. These include paper or electronic medical records, basic office supplies, computers, telephones, décor conducive to a health care setting, disposable medical supplies, uniforms, and other necessities far too numerous to list. Hospitals require a large number of supplies, and modern medical practice involves onetime use of most materials prior to either disposal or resterilization.

External Services: Midsize hospitals may engage outside legal and accounting counsel, groundskeepers, biomedical supply and removal services, records storage and destruction services, and pharmaceutical services. These are just a few of a long list of possible external services necessary to keep a hospital open and functioning.

Utilities: As is the case for small hospitals, necessary utilities include electricity, heat, backup energy sources, telephone service, and high-speed Internet access. Temperature control and air-quality control are vital to successful patient treatment. Utility costs are high for twenty-four-hour care facilities, and energy costs are volatile.

Taxes: Private for-profit institutions, as private corporations, are subject to applicable state and local taxes. Public and not-for-profit institutions enjoy certain tax exemptions.

Large Hospitals

According to an IRS study of over five hundred not-for-profit hospitals, the largest U.S. organizations accommodate over 100,000 visits annually, including inpatient, outpatient, and emergency services combined. An example of a large hospital is one housing sufficient inpatient beds to meet the needs of service and referral areas, a twenty-four-hour emergency department, and surgical and medical services. Typically, such an institution employs many thousands of people, ranging from physicians, nurses, and administrators to support staff, security, and housekeeping personnel. The organization may draw its business from patients within up to a one-hundred-mile radius, depending on competition and patient willingness to travel for services. Competition exists in the health

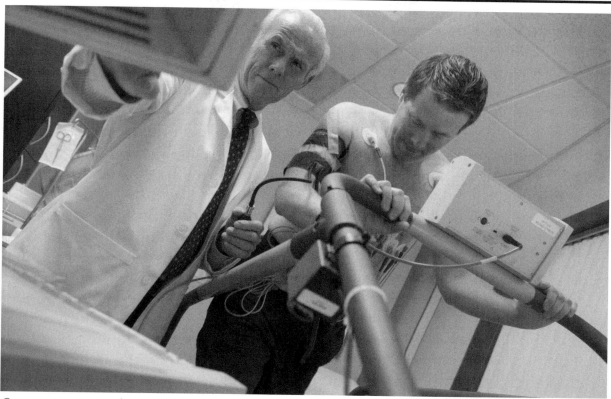

Outpatient services, such as cardiac fitness assessments, provide greater revenue opportunities than do inpatient services.
(©Monkey Business Images/Dreamstime.com)

care industry, and grappling for market share while maintaining sufficient staffing for a large hospital is a constant challenge.

Potential Annual Earnings Scale. According to the Medical Group Management Association's Physician Compensation and Production Survey, the 2008 median salary for a primary care physician was $186,044, and the median salary for a specialist was $339,738. Revenue from patient care services is in the tens of millions of dollars in large hospitals. These institutions target their revenue levels to maintain favorable operating margins in order to keep the hospitals viable and attract top-notch medical personnel. A favorable margin, depending on the legal structure of the organization, can result in profits for stakeholders or reinvestment into the entity. Not-for-profits, as a result of their legal structure, struggle for revenues and a sustainable bottom line because they are required to provide a certain level of charity uncompensated care. They may also experience the added expense of conducting medical education if they are associated with training programs.

Clientele Interaction. Larger organizations offer more diversity and opportunity for medical professionals. Concentrating on inpatient care, long-term care, or ambulatory care may be an option for professionals entering a large hospital setting. An example of a large organization would be an academic medical center with an embedded psychiatry department that offers both inpatient and outpatient services to adults, children, and employees. Daily interactions in such a hospital may involve patients and their families, as well as medical students, nursing students, insurance providers, social service providers, Medicare or Medicaid representatives, vendors, and myriad other stakeholders in the health care delivery system.

Each physician or nurse in this type of setting is part of a large group of similar professionals. All of them are expected to share in on-call (after hours and weekend) duties. Professionals represent their

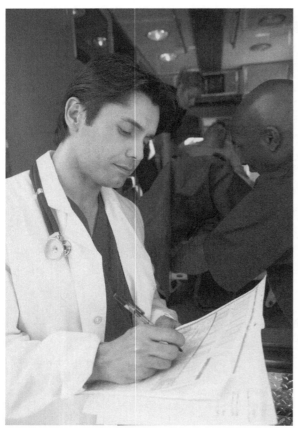

A physician takes notes as paramedics arrive with a patient. Emergency services are generally provided by larger hospitals. (©Monkey Business Images/Dreamstime.com)

organization and their colleagues whenever they interact with clients, so they are expected to be available and responsive when they are on call. Nonprofessional staff members play just as pivotal a role in supporting excellent and timely care and safety for patients, so they must have the utmost integrity when committing themselves to a career in the health services industry.

Amenities, Atmosphere, and Physical Grounds. Large organizations are typically freestanding, with sizeable grounds and many users. Open space, clear and visible signage, and friendly and helpful staff should be evident to make encounters favorable and stress-free for consumers and employees. Facilities maintenance is critical for patient health and continued patronage. Additionally, facility expansion (on-site or at a satellite location) is often desirable and necessary for large

institutions, as many expand their services within their campuses, within a larger urban neighborhood of medical facilities, or into suburban locations.

Typical Number of Employees. Large health care facilities employ thousands of people, including medical, administrative, financial, operations, and support staff. From the first phone call, to patient admission, to patient discharge and followup, hundreds of staff members representing the hospital come in direct or indirect contact with patients. It takes a synergistic, well-coordinated staff to meet the needs of the patients and fulfill the mission of the hospital.

Traditional Geographic Locations. Large hospital facilities, particularly academic ones, are generally located in metropolitan, highly populated areas. A sufficient population base with the promise of growth is critical to the livelihood of such a medical facility.

Pros of Working for a Large Hospital. Large health care facilities offer many people the opportunity for advancement. Throughout their careers, employees can work hard to develop leadership skills and move into growth positions, such as administrative or management roles, especially if they are motivated and committed to learning. Larger organizations tend to have the financial capacity to develop employee skills, particularly if their mission includes academic instruction or research alongside clinical care. The hospital industry, embedded in the overarching and mammoth health care industry, offers job security and opportunities for advancement.

Cons of Working for a Large Hospital. Employees of a large hospital can expect the bureaucracy and delays inherent to decision making within any large organization. Sometimes, it can take what seems a very long time to move initiatives forward. No area of the hospital is exempt from these challenges: Leadership and managers must advocate regularly for resources in order to receive them. Money plays a role in investments. Anyone searching for a position in a large hospital should pay close attention to the mission and vision of the organization and its current employees' satisfaction with their work. Potential employees should feel empowered to ask these questions when applying for a position.

The health care industry is somewhat more conservative than are other major industries: Hospitals do not tend to be on the cutting edge of progress when compared to large corporations or technology-based companies in other sectors. However, large hospitals with robust surgical and medical services need to remain competitive. Investment in organizational and facility growth is an ongoing expectation; information technology is exploding in hospitals, with patients demanding more immediate access to their medical information. Surgical and diagnostic advances represent major capital investments, but without them a hospital can lose its competitive edge. Computer and technology staff are always in high demand in this fast-paced environment.

Costs

Payroll and Benefits: Large organizations hire professional staff under a salary structure; salaried employees fall under the IRS category of "exempt," so overtime is not available for hours worked over what would be considered full time. The salary structure is built, presumably, to accommodate the peaks and valleys of the workload and to pay a fair, consistent rate. Benefits include insurance (health, dental, and disability), Family Medical Leave Act (FMLA) protection, retirement, malpractice coverage, continuing medical education (including reimbursements for travel, time, and registration for courses), and even tuition reimbursement for additional degree work. Benefits are generally prorated to the standard number of hours worked, with a minimum set for eligibility.

Supplies: Hospitals need both business (administrative) supplies and patient-care supplies. These include paper or electronic medical records, basic office supplies, computers, telephones, décor conducive to a health care setting, disposable medical supplies, uniforms, and other necessities far too numerous to list. Hospitals require a large number of supplies, and modern medical practice involves onetime use of most materials prior to either disposal or resterilization.

Administrative supplies are transitioning to an electronic world, and large hospitals with greater resources may be at the forefront of this trend. The need for typical "office" supplies is diminishing. For clinicians, their tools now include laptop computers, electronic medical records, virtual operators, pagers, billing software, and faxes. The size of larger institutions, and the intense volume of supplies they require, gives them better bargaining power than that enjoyed by small and midsize hospitals when negotiating with vendors.

External Services: Hospitals commonly outsource answering services, cleaning services, sterile supply services, uniform service, cell phone and pager service, waste disposal, medical records storage and destruction services, and risk management and legal counsel.

Utilities: Necessary utilities include electricity, heat, backup energy sources, telephone service, and high-speed Internet access. Temperature control and air-quality control are vital to successful patient treatment. Utility costs are high for twenty-four-hour care facilities, and energy costs are volatile.

Taxes: Many not-for-profit hospitals are 501 (c) (3) organizations, making them exempt from federal income taxes. Rigorous requirements for this status include quantifying and reporting community benefit offerings, as well as restricting senior leadership salaries. For-profit hospitals are responsible for all applicable taxes under state and federal guidelines.

ORGANIZATIONAL STRUCTURE AND JOB ROLES

Any size entity providing hospital services must function as a business, no matter what its nature and mission are. Particularly important in the hosptial industry is keeping patient care and safety paramount. The need to provide a positive operating margin to sustain the mission of a hospital drives its financial stewardship. It can be very challenging for administrative and financial professionals to keep their hospitals going concerns while maintaining favorable relations. Hospitals rely greatly on their primary revenue producers (physicians and medical staff) for financial viability. They are highly complex, integrated systems that require many key critical roles to be filled.

The following umbrella categories apply to the organizational structure of hospitals:

- Business and Operations Management
- Medical Staff
- Contracting and Reimbursement
- Human Resources
- Customer Service/Risk Management
- Marketing and Public Affairs
- Information Technology and Communication Systems
- Facilities and Security
- Housekeeping
- Nutrition

Business and Operations Management

Day-to-day operational management provides the infrastructure through which care is delivered to patients. Financial management—budgeting for revenues, expenses, and capital investments—keeps the doors open. Business and operations managers protect the jobs of everyone working in the hospital industry by assuring fiscal prudence and maximizing financial performance. Typical managers have undergraduate or graduate degrees. The business and operations group includes financial specialists, as well as on-the-ground managers who see to the smooth operation and delivery of services. Many of these positions are salaried or compensated at a higher hourly range than are entry-level positions. The BLS notes that the median annual salary for medical and health services managers was $80,240 in 2008.

Financial and operations staff must work hand in hand, as those two functions are inextricably entwined in the hospital industry. It is important to maintain relationships with stakeholders both within and outside the hospital. In most hospitals, financial services employees work for a centralized department. These white-collar professionals' work is intellectual in nature, drawing on their expertise in finance, operations, strategy, and relationships. In particularly large hospitals, a chief operating officer (COO) may direct them, setting the vision, strategy, and goals of the organization.

Business and operations management occupations may include the following:

OCCUPATION PROFILE

Health Information Technician

Considerations	Qualifications
Description	Organizes, prepares, and maintains medical records on hospital and clinic patients.
Career clusters	Health Science; Human Services
Interests	Data; people; things
Working conditions	Work inside
Minimum education level	Junior/technical/community college; bachelor's degree
Physical exertion	Light work
Physical abilities	Unexceptional/basic fitness
Opportunities for experience	Internship; apprenticeship; military service; part-time work
Licensure and certification	Recommended
Employment outlook	Faster-than-average growth expected
Holland interest score	CSI

Note: See volume 1, "Publisher's Note," for an explanation of the Holland interest score.

OCCUPATION SPECIALTIES

Medical and Health Services Managers

Specialty	*Responsibilities*
Chief dietitians	Direct institutional departments that provide food service and nutritional care. They provide direction for menu development, food preparation and service, purchasing, sanitation, safety procedures, and personnel issues.
Coordinators of rehabilitation services	Plan and direct the operation of health rehabilitation programs, such as physical, occupational, recreational, and speech therapies.
Dental services directors	Administer dental programs in hospitals and direct department activities. They are responsible for establishing training programs, setting up policies and procedures, and hiring and promoting employees.
Nursing services directors	Administer nursing programs in hospitals, nursing homes, or other medical facilities. They maintain standards of patient care and advise other medical staff about the nursing services provided.
Pharmacy services directors	Coordinate and direct the activities and functions of a hospital pharmacy. They implement policies and procedures, hire and train interns, and aid in the development of computer programs for pharmacy information management systems.

- Chief Operating Officer (COO)
- Chief Financial Officer (CFO)
- President
- Accountant
- Business Manager
- Legal Counsel
- Administrative Assistant

Medical Staff

Hospitals are defined by the quality and professionalism of those providing medical care, from surgeons to radiologic (X-ray) technicians. Successful organizations thrive on high standards of care, excellent communication, and a shared understanding of best practices in providing patient care. The range of medical staff is wide, including highly trained specialists, staff nurses, medical technicians, physical therapists, and nursing aides

or orderlies. Compensation is tied to training and expertise; according to the Medical Group Management Association's Physician Compensation and Production Survey, the 2008 median annual salary for a primary care physician was $186,044, and the median salary for a specialist was $339,738. The BLS notes that the median compensation for a registered nurse within a hospital in 2008 was $30.71 per hour, and nurse's aides or orderlies earned a median hourly wage of $12.03. Medical technicians, such as radiologic technicians, earned a median salary of $55,210 per year.

Medical staff occupations may include the following:

- Physician
- Specialized Physician
- Advanced Practice Nurse

- Registered Nurse
- Licensed Practical Nurse
- Radiologic Technician
- Phlebotomist
- Physical Therapist
- Laboratory Technician

Contracting and Reimbursement

Contracting, reimbursement, and billing departments are responsible for negotiating reimbursement contracts for all the services offered by a hospital, creating data sets for hospital-related billings, conducting actuarial analyses of financial risk, setting fee rates, and collecting fees owed. Responsibilities include working with legal counsel and with internal and external stakeholders to develop fair and reasonable contracts and working closely with operations to assure that the conditions of negotiated contracts are met. These job activities are white collar in nature and generally require a bachelor's degree or higher. Legal expertise may be required in the contracting arena. Compensation for jobs in this department varies widely, but the BLS reports that in 2008 the median salary of a hospital administrative services manager was $77,870.

Contracting and reimbursement occupations may include the following:

- Vice President of Finance
- Vice President of Contracting
- Revenue and Reimbursement Manager
- Contracting Director
- Financial Analyst
- Coding Manager
- Coding Analyst
- Charge Master Manager
- Denials Manager
- Data Entry Clerk

Human Resources

Human resources workers are responsible for recruiting, hiring, defining, and developing positions and for overseeing the compensation, benefits, education, and performance evaluation of employees. A growing area of responsibility within the domain of human resources is employee wellness. In larger organizations, professionals in human resources hold undergraduate or graduate degrees, sometimes with training in social work or counsel-

ing. Human resources professionals are responsible to managers and supervisors, providing them guidance in all functions of human resources and ensuring the fair and equitable treatment of employees. The human resources function is always centralized in hospitals, albeit with local autonomy within individual departments or business units. In 2008, hospital human resources managers earned a median annual salary of $91,580.

Human resources occupations may include the following:

- Chief Human Resources Officer
- Vice President of Human Resources
- Human Resources Director
- Recruiter
- Development and Education Specialist
- Benefits Manager
- Supervisor
- Payroll Clerk
- Health Coach
- Employee Health and Benefits Counselor

Customer Service/Risk Management

Customer service and risk management underpin the very livelihood of every hospital. Responsibilities of employees in this division include receiving and resolving customer concerns in a professional, prompt, and thorough manner, as well as overseeing front-line managers and employees with direct customer interface. Malpractice claims, injury, and other legal liability issues are managed within this area of responsibility, in collaboration with legal and senior medical counsel. Compensation within these occupations coincides with that of hospital administrators.

Customer service and risk management occupations may include the following:

- Patient Relations Manager
- Risk Management Manager
- Legal Counsel
- Service Recovery Specialist

Marketing and Public Affairs

Marketing and public affairs staff members are responsible for maintaining and growing a hospital's market share. Their responsibilities include advertising, integrating with customers inside and outside the organization, and developing marketing strategies alongside operations strategies. They must work closely with operations, overseeing and directing local departmental initiatives to grow their hospital's customer base. It is also the responsibility of public affairs professionals to be spokespeople for their hospitals generally, touting new discoveries by their researchers and defending the institution in the public eye against claims of malfeasance.

Advertising and outreach are a priority for hospitals, which get and retain business based on their reputation for quality, safety, and clinical outcomes. Public affairs professionals generally hold undergraduate or advanced degrees, and are paid roughly the same amount as hospital administrators, depending on their level of responsibility.

Marketing and public affairs occupations may include the following:

- Referring Physician Liaison
- Public Affairs and Marketing Director
- Vice President of Marketing
- External Relations Manager
- Marketing Manager
- Advertising Executive

Information Technology and Communication Systems

Computer hardware and networks, electronic medical records, and the related software are the responsibility of the information technology (IT) department. Hospitals require a plethora of advanced technologies, including communications, interconnectivity for programs supporting clinical care, and diagnostic technologies such as cardiac monitoring, radiology, and laboratory systems. As IT systems represent a major cost for hospitals and are critical to the quality of patient care, IT staff members are highly valued.

IT and communication systems occupations may include the following:

- Information Technology Manager
- Applications and Systems Manager

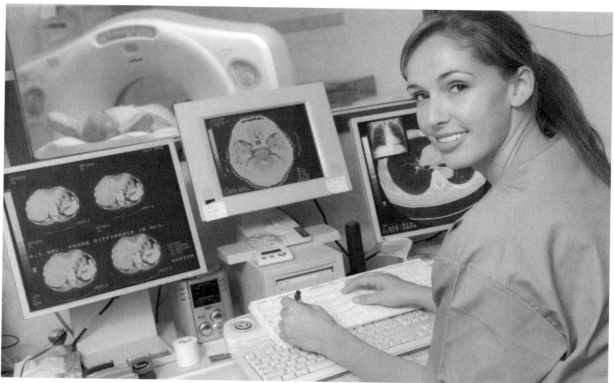

Diagnostic services, such as computed tomography (CAT) scans, are delivered by physicians, nurses, and ancillary staff. (©Monkey Business Images/Dreamstime.com)

- Telecommunications Manager
- Information Technology Training Manager
- Help Desk Officer
- Systems Analyst

Facilities and Security

Facilities and security personnel are responsible for the safety, structural integrity, and maintenance of a hospital's buildings, equipment, and grounds. Employees are valued for their consideration of personal responsibility, avoiding risk, and maintaining the safety and aesthetics of the facility. Maintenance personnel may have basic carpentry skills, some have plumbing and electrical training, and many have training in HVAC (heating, ventilation, and air-conditioning) systems. Their compensation may be hourly.

Hospital security professionals provide round-the-clock service and usually have law enforcement or similar backgrounds. Depending on their level of responsibility, high school or undergraduate education is required. Compensation may be a salary or an hourly wage, depending on the organization.

Facilities and security occupations may include the following:

- Security Director
- Facility Management Director
- Security Guard
- Parking Attendant
- Engineer
- Maintenance Contractor

Housekeeping

Housekeeping is responsible for maintaining a clean, safe environment for patients, visitors, and employees. This key role interacts with other staff and patients all day long. Hospital housekeeping staff generally receive specialized training, as their workplace holds many hazards particular to medical settings, including biological, chemical, and physical threats. Typical housekeeping staff members have high school or college degrees, depending on the level of their positions. Typically, wages are hourly and are paid at higher rates for evening and night shifts. Housekeeping positions must be staffed twenty-four hours a day, seven days a week.

Housekeeping occupations may include the following:

- Housekeeping Director
- Housekeeper

Nutrition

Nutrition and dietary workers are responsible for patient meals around the clock, seven days a week. They also are responsible for supplying and staffing employee and public-access food courts and cafeterias. Typically, their wages are hourly.

Nutrition occupations may include the following:

- Cashier
- Nutritionist
- Chef/Cook
- Dietician
- Meal Delivery Staff
- Dishwasher
- Kitchen Worker

INDUSTRY OUTLOOK

Overview

The outlook for the hospital care industry shows it to be on the rise. Demand for workers and career opportunities are favorable. Growth is rapid, with total health care expenditures representing 17 percent of the U.S. gross domestic product (GDP). With the largest aging population in the nation's history on the cusp of old age, growth in terms of services is inevitable, and with the passage of the Patient Protection and Affordable Care Act (2010), 34 million more Americans are projected to acquire health insurance and thereby gain greater access to health care services. By 2019, the health care sector is projected by the Department of Health and Human Services to represent 21 percent of GDP.

Challenges for those entering this industry will include greater competition for college-educated professionals, with a bachelor's degree as bare minimum. Those with advanced degrees will have greater prospects in this highly competitive service industry. The industry will look for those who are self-directed and have highly honed interpersonal skills. In the past, health care was not considered a business, so service, rather than finance, was its focus. Today, nurses and physicians are increasingly augmenting their education with finance and business operations training.

PROJECTED EMPLOYMENT FOR SELECTED OCCUPATIONS

Hospitals Industry

Employment		
2009	Projected 2018	Occupation
175,550	200,000	Licensed practical and licensed vocational nurses
102,050	101,600	Medical and clinical laboratory technologists
425,100	468,800	Nursing aides, orderlies, and attendants
130,230	140,900	Radiologic technologists and technicians
1,571,850	1,844,200	Registered nurses

Source: U.S. Bureau of Labor Statistics, Industries at a Glance, Occupational Employment Statistics and Employment Projections Program.

In terms of hospitals' financial stability, unemployment has led more customers to be covered under federal and state insurers (specifically Medicare and Medicaid), with insufficient reimbursement to hospitals to cover their costs. Pressures to reduce both the costs and the length of patient stays in the hospital, as well as to lower nurse-to-patient ratios, have occurred as a result of financial constraints on these health care facilities. The projected growth of the medical industry will make working in a hospital a secure career choice. The industry, however, is not immune to economic pressures. Difficult financial times can result in unexpected hiring freezes or reductions in force for "noncritical" positions. Direct patient care positions are mission-critical and are some of the most secure in the industry during economic downturns.

Academic excellence is a sure stepping stone for entry into this competitive market, particularly for skilled, white-collar positions in the hospital setting. Students should actively search for internship opportunities to gain hands-on exposure to the hospital environment during their academic train-ing. Early exposure is invaluable and a strong self-marketing tool.

Employment Advantages

People who work in hospitals will recognize job security as a strong attractor in a global economy that threatens other industries, such as manufacturing. Health care, particularly inpatient services, cannot be outsourced and demand for them will only grow over time. Health care professions are vast and disparate. In an industry of increasing federal oversight and legal compliance regulations, specialization in career avenues is inevitable. Hospital service offerings are increasingly focused on specific populations and medical conditions, such as geriatrics, adolescent care, mental health care, and other segments.

Because of growing specialization, and because the work of hospitals is to help people gain wellness, the opportunities for a rich, diverse career are numerous. Care and treatment of patients, as well as teaching and professional research in academic settings, are all intriguing opportunities for professionals to explore. Strong communicators who excel at helping others and who are emotionally competent will find themselves well-suited for health care careers. Working within a hospital provides great satisfaction to the professional who enjoys working face-to-face with customers and who enjoys being part of a vital community asset.

Annual Earnings

With an aging U.S. population, the hospital industry is seeing an increasing number of older patients demanding more intense and costly services. Technological and pharmacological advances continuously offer new treatments to meet this demand to extend quality of life well into patients' eighties and nineties, as well as the demands of an American public that has come to expect positive health outcomes.

Parsing out earnings in the hospital industry, nationally or globally, is speculative at best. Hospitals employ 35 percent of all people working in the health care industry, according to the BLS. Annual earnings in the hospital setting are no longer a metric of direct relevance to the BLS. Hospitals' gross revenues have historically been calculated based on what they bill insurers, and net revenues have been calculated based on what insurers actually pay, adjusted to reflect the hospitals' reported costs to render service. However, quality and medical outcomes have become the financial metric of success and are quickly becoming the core basis on which payment is made to hospitals for both inpatient and outpatient services. A unit of service is an admission, and payment is based not only on how patients fare in terms of health but also on how efficiently and cost-effectively the hospital rendered service. The BLS projects that health care and insurance revenues will grow by $547 billion by 2016. As the baby boomers continue into retirement, the demand for hospital services is expected to grow.

RELATED RESOURCES FOR FURTHER RESEARCH

AMERICAN ACADEMY OF MEDICAL MANAGEMENT
Crossville Commons
560 W Crossville Rd., Suite 103
Roswell, GA 30075
Tel: (770) 649-7150
Fax: (770) 649-7552
http://www.epracticemanagement.org

AMERICAN COLLEGE OF HEALTHCARE EXECUTIVES
1 N Franklin, Suite 1700
Chicago, IL 60606-3529
Tel: (312) 424-2800
Fax: (312) 424-0023
http://www.ache.org

AMERICAN COUNSELING ASSOCIATION
5999 Stevenson Ave.
Alexandria, VA 22304
Tel: (703) 823-9800
Fax: (800) 473-2329
http://www.counseling.org

AMERICAN HOSPITAL ASSOCIATION
155 N Wacker Dr.
Chicago, IL 60606
Tel: (312) 422-3000
http://www.aha.org

HEALTHCARE FINANCIAL MANAGEMENT ASSOCIATION
2 Westbrook Corporate Center, Suite 700
Westchester, IL 60154
Tel: (708) 531-9600
Fax: (708) 531-0032
http://www.hfma.org

MEDICAL GROUP MANAGEMENT ASSOCIATION
104 Inverness Terrace East
Englewood, CO 80112-5306
Tel: (303) 799-1111
http://www.mgma.com

NATIONAL ASSOCIATION OF PUBLIC HOSPITALS AND HEALTH SYSTEMS
1301 Pennsylvania Ave. NW, Suite 950
Washington, DC 20004
Tel: (202) 585-0100
Fax: (202) 585-0101
http://www.naph.org

ABOUT THE AUTHOR

Nancy Sprague holds a bachelor of science degree from Granite State College and a master of science degree in health policy from the Dartmouth Institute, Dartmouth College. She is a member of the National Medical Group Managers' Association, the Healthcare Financial Management Association, and the American College of Healthcare Executives. She is a fellow in the American College of Healthcare Executives, a registered nurse, and a health care operations consultant. Sprague has spent her career in medical practice and hospital operations, both in private practice and in a large academic tertiary hospital setting. She has extensive experience in physician and staff relations and is an expert in human resources, compliance, risk, billing, health care business management, hospital administration, and patient-centered care.

FURTHER READING

Cutler, David M., ed. *The Changing Hospital Industry: Comparing Not-for-Profit and For-Profit Institutions.* Chicago: University of Chicago Press, 2000.

Geisler, Eliezer, Koos Krabbendam, and Roel Schuring, eds. *Technology, Health Care, and Management in the Hospital of the Future.* Westport, Conn.: Praeger, 2003.

Gordon, Suzanne, John Buchanan, and Tanya Bretherton. *Safety in Numbers: Nurse-to-Patient Ratios and the Future of Health Care.* Ithaca, N.Y.: ILR Press/Cornell University Press, 2008.

Institute for Career Research. *Careers in Hospital and Health Services Administration: Healthcare Executives.* Chicago: Author, 2004.

Ohsfeldt, Robert L., and John E. Schneider. *The Business of Health: The Role of Competition, Markets, and Regulation.* Washington, D.C.: AEI Press, 2006.

Snook, I. Donald. *Opportunities in Hospital Administration Careers.* New York: McGraw-Hill, 2007.

U.S. Bureau of Labor Statistics. *Career Guide to Industries*, 2010-2011 ed. http://www.bls.gov/oco/cg.

U.S. Census Bureau. North American Industry Classification System (NAICS), 2007. http://www.census.gov/cgi-bin/sssd/naics/naicsrch?chart=2007.

U.S. Department of Commerce. International Trade Administration. Office of Trade and Industry Information. Industry Trade Data and Analysis. http://ita.doc.gov/td/industry/otea/OTII/OTII-index.html.

Hotels and Motels Industry

©Dreamstime.com

INDUSTRY SNAPSHOT

General Industry: Hospitality and Tourism
Career Cluster: Hospitality and Tourism
Subcategory Industries: Bed-and-Breakfasts; Casino Hotels; Innkeeping; Resorts; Rooming and Boarding Houses; Transient Accommodations; Vacation Rentals; Youth Hostels
Related Industries: Casino Industry; Food Services; Outdoor Recreation Industry; Restaurant Industry; Themed Entertainment Industry; Travel and Tourism Industry
Annual Domestic Revenues: $140.6 billion USD (Smith Travel Research, 2009)
Annual International Revenues: $344 billion USD (Research and Markets, 2009)
Annual Global Revenues: $484.3 billion USD (Research and Markets, 2009)
NAICS Numbers: 721, 62422

INDUSTRY DEFINITION

Summary

The hotels and motels industry is dedicated to providing temporary lodging accommodations to tourists, business travelers, and other transient guests. A segment of tourism, one of the largest industries in the world, it comprises small bed-and-breakfast establishments (B&Bs), inns, motels, hotels, resorts, and other room-rental properties. The industry is represented in virtually every country around the world, employing countless individuals who work across a broad spectrum of career paths.

History of the Industry

The practice of renting rooms to transient guests dates back to ancient times. During the Middle Ages, inns and other guesthouses were developed to accommodate religious pilgrims, and monasteries began their tradition of offering lodging for travelers. As Europe was approaching the early modern period in the fifteenth century, more and more inns were developing along stagecoach routes. Ordinaries, later known as inns or taverns, cropped up in colonial America during the seventeenth and eighteenth centuries, offering their guests not just rooms but meals as well.

The first hotel in the United States, the City Hotel, opened in 1794 in New York City. Twenty-five years later, the Tremont House in Boston became the nation's first luxury hotel, complete with a lock on each room's door. Nineteenth century America also witnessed an increase in the development of another type of hotel: the resort. Built at first around spas located on the East Coast, these kinds of accommodations quickly spread to seaside and mountain locations. The largest of the early resorts was built at the hot sulfur spa at Saratoga Springs, New York.

In 1908, the first hotel chain, the Statler brand, was introduced. Hilton followed suit in 1919 after Conrad Hilton purchased the Mobley Hotel in oil-rich Cisco, Texas. During the Great Depression of the 1930's, the first Sheraton Hotels were opened. It was also during this time that a small root-beer stand was transformed into the first hotel managed by what would become Marriott International.

The Depression era also saw America building on the tradition of B&Bs. The term, which was coined in England and Scotland before the American Revolution, applied to homeowners who of-fered rooms and meals to travelers. The concept expanded as boardinghouses opened during the Great Depression. These houses remained popu-lar during the 1930's, but they faded after the eco-nomic recovery and the advent of World War II.

In 1916, the Federal Aid Road Act spurred the development of a new form of lodging: motels. These lodging establishments were to be built alongside new highways and would provide rooms to travelers arriving in motor vehicles (the words "motor" and "hotel" were conjoined to form the name of this new type of lodging). After World War II, the number of motels increased signifi-cantly to parallel the number of automobiles on the roads. Most motels were located near highways and on the outskirts of towns, where land was less expensive. In light of their locations, their expen-ditures were considerably less than those of down-town hotels, and motels could therefore offer rooms to guests at much lower rates. Motels origi-nally offered minimal amenities for guests, but by

Motels and motor lodges, originally roadside establishments, also operate alongside larger hotels in urban areas and in resort and tourist communities. (©Oleg Ivanov/Dreamstime.com)

the 1950's many of them expanded to include cocktail lounges, pools, and other features.

The Industry Today

Today, hotels, motels, and other types of lodging establishments continue to offer a wide range of accommodations and services to their target clienteles. Some have thousands of rooms, while others have fewer than five. Many have in-house restaurants, pools, casinos, convention space, and other facilities and services that cater to the special needs of their particular clients. A single hotel may employ hundreds of people, from housekeepers and salespeople to security personnel and managers. The properties range in size from small, one- and two-bedroom B&Bs to massive convention hotels and resorts. They also operate across a broad spectrum of interests and themes, catering to specific clienteles and diverse guest populations alike.

B&Bs are the smallest hotels. These properties have only a handful of rooms available for guests

The Accommodation Industry's Contribution to the U.S. Economy

Value Added	Amount
Gross domestic product	$119.1 billion
Gross domestic product	0.8%
Persons employed	1.869 million
Total employee compensation	$65.0 billion

Source: U.S. Bureau of Economic Analysis. Data are for 2008.

and are often limited in terms of the amenities they offer. They typically have relatively small staffs, often comprising the proprietors themselves and perhaps a few others (such as housekeepers). In many cases, B&Bs are also the residences of their owners or operators. These properties offer alternatives for tourists and other travelers who prefer quaint, intimate settings over larger, homogeneous lodging establishments. They are particularly prominent in tourist-heavy areas such as historical sites, beachfront areas, and mountainous or wooded settings, and are often appointed with more personalized furniture, decorations, and bedding than one might find in a hotel or motel.

Larger than B&Bs, but still relatively small in terms of room numbers, are inns. Inns are frequently situated in historic areas, as well as picturesque and tourist-friendly regions. Some are attached to or contain restaurants or cocktail lounges, and many offer activities specifically designed for guests who appreciate the quaintness and antiquity of their settings.

Motels and motor lodges have undergone a significant evolution since the 1950's. Although many are still found along highways, twenty-first century motels also operate alongside larger hotels in urban areas and in resort and tourist communities. Many are independently operated, while others are franchised. Many more are part of national and even international chains, offering similarly appointed rooms and standard, recognizable building styles from one property to another to attract a steady and loyal patronage from frequent travelers who can depend on their consistency.

B&Bs are the smallest hotels, having only a handful of rooms available for guests. (©Dreamstime.com)

Hotels have also undergone a major transformation in the late twentieth and early twenty-first centuries. Some properties, located primarily in urban centers, cater largely to convention business. They contain hundreds or even thousands of rooms and offer such amenities as free Wi-Fi, exercise facilities, shuttle services, and meeting rooms of various sizes. Smaller hotels are also found in such areas, attracting tourists and business travelers. Boutique hotels represent a growing trend in U.S. lodging establishments: These smaller properties may be decorated in contemporary or thematic styles and cater to travelers with particular tastes and ideals. Most of the larger properties contain restaurants and lounges, although some, known as limited-service properties, may not have food and beverage services and may be near or attached to independently owned restaurants.

Unlike its historical relatives, twenty-first century lodging establishments seek to give their guests more than accommodations. Some contain casinos and entertainment facilities designed to keep guests in-house for the duration of their stay. Resorts remain enormously popular, with some owning adjacent theme parks, ski slopes, beaches, or wooded property—all dedicated to the sole use of the hotel's guests. Resorts and hotels are also catering to long-term guests, offering suites with kitchens and living rooms that are akin to apartments. A growing number also accommodate pets in-room.

A growing number of hotels and motels are adopting socially and environmentally conscious policies. For these properties, the use of green energy, recycling programs, low-flow faucets, and energy-saving lightbulbs not only reduces their carbon footprints but also attracts like-minded guests.

Modern technologies, such as the Internet, have also changed the hotel industry in the twenty-first century. Reservations, once made over the phone in the twentieth century, are now largely Internet-based, with an entire subindustry of online booking engines serving as one of the primary vehi-

Inputs Consumed by the Accommodation Industry	
Input	Value
Energy	$10.9 billion
Materials	$14.3 billion
Purchased services	$73.3 billion
Total	$98.5 billion

Source: U.S. Bureau of Economic Analysis. Data are for 2008.

cles for reservations and bookings. Similarly, as many hotels continue to be rated and chosen based on the availability and quality of their amenities, complimentary Internet access and related technologies have become sought-after amenities. In 2005, for example, the Rosewood Hotels made Global Positioning Systems (GPS) devices, instead of paper maps, available to guests. Moreover, the Internet itself has become a primary tool for generating and disseminating hotel ratings. Rather than seek the opinions of travel experts published in books and magazines, many travelers rely on Web sites with user-generated content (known as Web

Computers and the Internet have made reserving a hotel and checking in easier and faster. (©Andres Rodriguez/Dreamstime.com)

2.0 sites), in which a hotel's rating represents an amalgam of many individual ratings submitted by a consumer's peers.

Twenty-first century lodging establishments remain in a constant state of evolution, catering to the diverse needs of an increasingly diverse international population. With a multitude of internal and external staff and vendors, the industry remains one of the most powerful economic drivers in the global economy.

INDUSTRY MARKET SEGMENTS

The hotel industry ranges in size from small properties to large convention hotels, and it serves a broad range of clients, from business travelers to tourists. The following sections provide a comprehensive breakdown of each of these different segments.

Small Establishments

B&Bs and inns typically have fewer than fifty rooms. In a B&B, the owner often lives on the property and serves a continental or full breakfast to guests. Such properties generally charge less than do major urban hotels, although properties in tourist areas tend to charge higher rates during the tourist season.

Potential Annual Earnings Scale. The average earnings for a small property owner or manager vary from region to region. However, according to the U.S. Bureau of Labor Statistics (BLS), the range in the United States for such a position is between about $27,000 and $83,000 per year.

Clientele Interaction. Small properties rely on repeat patronage, and the treatment guests receive during their first stay strongly influences whether they will return. Small-property owners and managers have the unique opportunity to work closely with guests. In many cases, the innkeeper plays multiple roles in the property, managing the front desk, preparing food, and providing concierge services. Filling such roles allows the small-property owner or manager to develop closer relationships with guests and, as a result, foster repeat visits. Because of the relatively intimate nature of small properties, clients seek a more personal touch during their stays than they would expect at larger ho-

tels. Innkeepers must therefore be more communicative and attentive to the individual needs of guests. Small properties often offer special amenities and services in order to ensure that a guest's stay is comfortable.

Amenities, Atmosphere, and Physical Grounds. Although B&Bs and inns offer relatively few rooms, they usually offer a wide range of amenities, services, and comforts that are atypical of the average lodging establishment. Many innkeepers decorate each room themselves, selecting furniture, linens, and artwork according to their own tastes and ideals. The atmosphere of these small properties is akin to that of a large house, appointed with comfortable lounges, sitting rooms, and dining rooms.

Inns and B&Bs are designed largely for tourists. As such, they usually focus on fostering a relaxing atmosphere. Down comforters, operating fireplaces, four-poster beds, and antique furniture are prevalent, and a degree of informality among innkeepers and guests is typical. Breakfasts are casual, and many properties offer wine and other spirits for their guests.

The physical grounds of a small lodging property are usually simple in terms of real estate. Most inns and B&Bs are large houses (and in many cases residences) or small, renovated buildings. Some were constructed in the eighteenth and nineteenth centuries. Many have small yards, outdoor pools, and patios. A growing number of properties are offering technological amenities such as free Internet access and Wi-Fi services.

Typical Number of Employees. One of the largest issues facing innkeepers and small-property owners is expenses. In light of this fact, many inns and B&Bs have very small staffs. In many cases, the owners are the only individuals working on the property on a full-time basis. Some innkeepers hire additional staff to work at the front desk or perform housekeeping and laundry duties. In areas that receive seasonal guests, staff sizes often grow significantly for a few months to accommodate high demand and traffic during the peak season. On Cape Cod, Massachusetts, for example, large numbers of foreign workers and college students are hired during the summer months.

Traditional Geographic Locations. Small properties such as B&Bs and inns typically cater to vacationers looking to get away without sacrificing some of the comforts of home. They are usually located in picturesque communities and tourist-friendly areas—for example, along the shores of oceans or lakes or in regions of historic interest. Because they do not typically serve three meals per day, such properties are usually located near restaurants and taverns. Many of these properties appear in urban centers as well, providing less expensive basic alternatives for vacationers and business travelers alike.

Pros of Working for a Small Lodging Establishment. Because they operate as both owners and staff of inns or B&Bs, innkeepers have total control over their property. Room decorations and breakfast menus are tailored to their tastes, and all aspects of maintenance and upkeep are within their purview. If there is a staff, it generally comprises only a handful of people, many of whom may be friends or family. Innkeepers also do not necessarily need to attend business school or attain advanced degrees in hotel management to manage a small property. The best education an innkeeper can obtain is broad-based training in sales and marketing, property maintenance, accounting, food preparation, and the legal requirements of the municipal, state, or other government entity that oversees regulation in such fields.

Cons of Working for a Small Lodging Establishment. In many ways, the positive aspects of working on a small property are the same as the negative elements. For example, the fact that such a property owner can afford to hire few or no additional staff means that the innkeeper is responsible for virtually all operational duties, from cooking and dishwashing, to front-desk operations, to laundry and maintenance. Additionally, the innkeeper must take on the work of the business itself, from accounting to marketing. Hence, although a small operation may require only basic knowledge of these areas, it does require that the innkeeper fully grasp all areas necessary to running and maintaining the business, a requirement that entails training across a broad spectrum of vocations.

Adding to the challenges of a small property manager are the peaks and valleys of business. A large number of B&Bs and inns are located in tourist areas such as coastal regions or mountains, and the seasonal appeal of these areas results in a high rate of business during certain periods of the year and a low rate of business during off-peak seasons.

For example, tourist havens such as the islands Martha's Vineyard and Nantucket in Massachusetts see a very high volume of guests during the late spring and early summer months, but that volume drops precipitously during the fall and winter months. For innkeepers, the seasonality of their business may require them to locate alternative sources of revenue to remain open during off-season periods—or to shut down altogether during those periods.

Costs
Payroll and Benefits: Small properties generally hire staff at hourly wages. Because such small businesses usually employ very few staff, government-mandated benefits are often not required of these enterprises. Benefits such as vacation and sick time are therefore offered at the discretion of the innkeeper.

Supplies: Small inns, B&Bs, and similar properties require a wide range of items, including cleaning supplies, foodstuffs, linens, hardware (for maintenance), office supplies, information technology (telephones and computers), outdoor supplies (such as lawn mowers and snow shovels), bedding, and room amenities.

External Services: Although many have laundry facilities on site, some small properties employ laundry services to clean sheets, towels, and other linens. They may also use accounting services, computer maintenance services, credit card processing systems, and food vendors. Many employ local landscaping contractors.

Utilities: Typical utilities for a small property include water and sewage, electricity, gas or oil service, telephone, cable television, and Internet access.

Taxes: Small properties are required to pay local, state, and federal income taxes, as well as applicable property taxes. They must also collect state and local room or sales taxes from guests.

Midsize Establishments
Midsize hotels and motels typically have room counts of up to one hundred, although some are larger. Many motels and motor lodges are considered midsize properties, but some inns and smaller hotels also fall into this category. Some offer limited food and beverage services, among other amenities. Room rates for such properties are generally lower than those of larger properties and resorts.

Potential Annual Earnings Scale. Wages for senior managers at midsize properties depend largely on geography and the position itself. According to the BLS, the average salary of a front-desk clerk at such an establishment, for example, is about $18,000 per year, while hotel managers earn between $32,000 and $58,000 per year.

Clientele Interaction. Midsize hoteliers must maintain a delicate balance regarding interaction with their guests. Staffs are relatively small, which means that the hotelier must be easily accessible to guests. On the other hand, the hotelier may not be expected to tend to each guest personally, instead relying on a front-desk clerk, housekeeper, or sales manager to address guest needs.

Because many midsize properties cater to last-minute travelers who are primarily seeking basic bed and bath accommodations during their journeys, client interaction is often limited to check-ins and check-outs. However, hoteliers may still be called upon to oversee guest disputes, eject unruly guests, or address maintenance issues.

Amenities, Atmosphere, and Physical Grounds. Motels are the most prominent example of the midsize property. Motels traditionally differ from hotels in that many of their rooms have doors that lead outside, into a common courtyard or parking lot. This design is based on the premise that motels are convenient for those traveling by car, enabling suitcases to be moved readily from the vehicle to the room and back. In some cases, motels and similar midsize properties offer individual cabins for enhanced privacy.

Midsize properties have evolved since the mid-twentieth century to meet the changing demands of travelers. While pools, vending machines, and cable television are now generally considered standard features of motels, an increasing number of such properties now also offer limited meals, such as a continental breakfast or buffets, Wi-Fi access, meeting rooms, and other services. Although the traditional motel caters to travelers, a growing number market themselves as inexpensive alternatives to hotels in key tourist areas. As such, they also offer their guests tourist information, such as maps, coupons, and brochures.

Many midsize hotel and motel properties are part of larger chains. They therefore maintain the same external appearance, staff uniforms, and room designs of the parent company in order to generate repeat stays throughout all of the chain's properties. If repeat guests are more often than not families, this changes the atmosphere of the property from the traditional image of the "refuge for the road-weary traveler," replacing it with an image of a final destination for the cost-conscious tourist.

Typical Number of Employees. Midsize properties tend to have more full-time employees than do small properties, but staff levels tend not to exceed twenty to thirty people. However, seasonal employees may be brought in at properties in tourist-heavy areas during peak times.

Traditional Geographic Locations. Properties such as motels and other midsize lodging establishments have long been located in areas of high vehicular traffic, such as along highways and interstates. Because their prices are relatively low in comparison to those at other hotels, they also tend to be located outside downtown urban centers and on city outskirts. Many are also located near tourist areas, offering cost-effective alternatives to more expensive facilities in such areas.

Pros of Working for a Midsize Lodging Establishment. Midsize properties such as motels enjoy certain advantages over both small and larger properties. For example, because they offer few amenities and have smaller staffs, they are able to minimize expenditures and can market themselves to budget-conscious travelers. Additionally, many motel chains provide hoteliers with franchising opportunities, allowing some flexibility in decorations, human resources, and other aspects of property management. Furthermore, although they are considerably smaller than downtown hotels, resorts, and convention properties, midsize hotels and motels are able to accommodate larger numbers of guests than inns or B&Bs. In peak tourist seasons, this availability provides a theoretical advantage that can enhance job stability.

Cons of Working for a Midsize Lodging Establishment. Because midsize hotels and motels present themselves as budget-conscious alternatives to luxury hotels and other lodging houses, crime rates at such establishments are frequently higher than at more expensive properties. Other problems may be more common as well. Families with children, for example, may cause excessive damage to rooms or serve as sources of noise, prompting complaints from other guests. In addition, the fact that a midsize property still has a relatively small staff means that full-time workers, such as front-desk clerks and managers, must work longer hours. They must often assume multiple roles during their shifts as well, in order to address guests' needs and complaints.

Costs

Payroll and Benefits: Midsize properties generally hire staff at hourly wages. Benefits such as vacation and sick time are offered at the discretion of the owner or manager.

Supplies: Motels and other midsize properties require a wide range of items, including cleaning supplies, foodstuffs, vending machine items, linens, hardware (for maintenance), office supplies, information technology (telephones and computers), outdoor supplies (such as lawn mowers and snow shovels), bedding, and room amenities.

External Services: Although many have laundry facilities on site, some midsize properties employ the use of laundry services to clean sheets, towels, and other linens. They may also use accounting services to help manage the books, computer maintenance services, credit card processing systems, and vending machine companies. Many employ local landscaping contractors.

Utilities: Typical utilities for a midsize property include water and sewage, electricity, gas or oil service, telephone, cable television, and Internet access.

Taxes: Midsize properties are required to pay local, state, and federal income taxes, as well as applicable property taxes. They must also collect state and local room or sales taxes from guests.

Large Establishments

Large properties are generally considered hotels, although they may include some of the largest motels. Typically, a large hotel has more than one hundred rooms, if not several hundred rooms or more. Large properties often have limited or full food and beverage services, as well as other amenities, and their room rates generally are higher than those of similarly located motels or smaller properties.

Potential Annual Earnings Scale. The earnings of large-scale property employees vary considerably depending on their positions and the geographic location of the property. A sizable majority of positions in a given large property, about 64 percent, are service-oriented and hourly, paying minimum wage. Other employees, such as clerks, managers, and salespeople, are typically salaried, with some receiving performance bonuses and other incentives.

Clientele Interaction. At large hotels with many guests, hoteliers do not have much day-to-day interaction with their clients beyond casual greetings. Rather, an entire team will attend to a guest's needs, from doormen, to front-desk clerks, to restaurant servers, to concierges. Some of these positions are more functional, requiring merely prompt and polite service when requested. Others, such as concierges, are expected to cultivate relationships with guests, anticipating their requests and needs and perhaps suggesting activities the guests would not have thought of on their own.

Amenities, Atmosphere, and Physical Grounds. Large hotels and resorts offer a wide range of amenities that are often dependent on a business's location and the profile of guests it seeks to attract. Most have either an in-house restaurant or one that is independently operated and attached. Full-service hotels usually offer room service for guests seeking to dine in their own rooms. Additionally, many large properties have cocktail lounges and similar venues that cater both to overnight guests and to people attending functions or meeting friends at the hotel. Some large resort properties may have golf courses, discounted ski-lift tickets, and similar amenities, as well as athletic equipment rentals.

Large properties cater to a wide range of guests, from business travelers to tourists. Each property's atmosphere therefore stems from the type of clientele the property attracts. Large convention hotels, for example, may be predominantly visited by business travelers who seek access to the Internet, meeting rooms, and relative quiet during evening hours. Resort hotels, on the other hand, may have a more festive atmosphere, with staff focusing on encouraging both activities and rest and relaxation.

Physically, large properties tend to be multistory structures built for the maximum number of rooms and corresponding facilities. Some have swimming pools and parking lots with valets, and meeting rooms, ballrooms for large-scale events and receptions, and fitness facilities are quite prevalent. Some hotels are part of larger building complexes that are joined by commercial space and private condominiums, while others stand alone.

Typical Number of Employees. The number of employees a large property retains varies based on the size of the hotel, the number of rooms, the volume of guests, whether additional services (such as a casino, golf course, or theme park) are attached to the property, and other factors. New York's Waldorf Astoria, for example, has sixteen hundred employees, while the Bellagio in Las Vegas, in which the hotel itself is an attraction, employs ninety-seven hundred people.

Traditional Geographic Locations. Large hotels are found primarily in downtown urban environments, near or within tourist areas, and in other high-traffic locations. Some occupy multistory buildings in metropolitan centers, whereas others are constructed adjacent to beaches and ski resorts or near airports and other major transit centers. Many are situated at, or are part of, convention centers or, if located outside downtown areas, still offer easy access to them.

Pros of Working for a Large Hotel. More than smaller and midsize properties, large hotels rely heavily on a departmental, team approach to their operations. Employees may therefore spend the bulk of their time focusing on their areas of expertise rather than assuming multiple roles. For hourly employees, another benefit is the relative stability of pay, due in large part to collective bargaining agreements at union hotels. Additionally, because of the locations of large properties and their high guest demand, room occupancy tends to be relatively stable, barring a major downturn in the economy. Furthermore, a high percentage of large hotels are part of chains or networks, and opportunities exist for on-the-job training and career advancement within these companies.

Cons of Working for a Large Hotel. For many property managers, the sheer complexity of a large property, with its myriad working parts, can prove extremely vexing. Adding to the difficulty for managers is the high demand placed on hotel employees' energies during times of peak occupancy, such as events and conventions, as well as simple day-to-day check-ins and check-outs. For managers, the fact that many facets of hotel operations involve unionized workers adds the challenge of complying with regulations governing employee pay, ben-

efits, workloads, and staffing levels. Additionally, the fact that many chains buy and sell large properties means that employees may learn one operational system, only to have that system change fundamentally when a new corporation assumes control.

Costs

Payroll and Benefits: The salary structure of a large property can be complex, owing to the many positions and job types. Service personnel (such as housekeepers and servers) are generally paid on an hourly basis, while those in administrative or other positions (managers, administrative assistants, and salespersons, for example) are paid on a yearly basis with some performance incentives. Benefits such as vacation time and sick time are offered at the discretion of the hotelier or the chain of which the hotel is a part.

Supplies: Large hotels and resort properties require a wide range of items, including cleaning supplies, foodstuffs, dinnerware, vending machine items, linens, hardware (for maintenance), office supplies, information technology (telephones and computers), outdoor supplies (such as lawn mowers and snow shovels), bedding, and room amenities. Some, such as those that operate casinos, need entertainment supplies, such as playing cards, chips, and machine parts.

External Services: Although many large hotels have laundry facilities on site, many other large properties employ laundry services to clean sheets, towels, and other linens. They may also use accounting services to help manage the books, computer maintenance services, credit card processing systems, and vending machine companies. To accommodate receptions, events, and meetings, many subcontract with on-site or external audiovisual companies.

Utilities: Typical utilities for a large property include water and sewage, electricity, gas or oil service, telephone, cable television, and Internet access. Large hotels must also pay for sewer use and wastewater discharge, particularly in light of their significant use of such systems.

Taxes: Large properties are required to pay local, state, and federal income taxes, as well as applicable property taxes. They must also collect state and local room or sales taxes from guests.

ORGANIZATIONAL STRUCTURE AND JOB ROLES

The organizational structure and distribution of tasks within a hotel are typically based on its size. An innkeeper is likely to handle most of the major tasks because he or she is the only major employee, while the general manager of a large hotel will delegate tasks to the proper team. Nevertheless, the tasks themselves, in a general sense, remain similar throughout the industry.

The following umbrella categories apply to the organizational structure of businesses in the hotels and motels industry:

- Executive Management
- Sales and Marketing
- Reservations
- Front-Desk Operations
- Housekeeping
- Maintenance
- Security
- Food and Beverage
- Concierge
- Groundskeeping
- Human Resources
- Doorpersons/Porters/Valets
- Laundry Personnel
- Entertainment Workers
- Recreation and Fitness-Center Personnel
- Information Technology/Multimedia
- Administrative Support

Executive Management

Executive management handles the general operations of the hotel. These individuals help oversee major operations, goal setting, and the implementation of plans for the property. They also manage individual teams and departments (or, in the case of the general manager, oversee all departments). Many executive managers have advanced degrees, particularly in hospitality management, business, accounting, and similar fields. As with many industries, experience can sometimes serve as a substitute for advanced education.

Executive managers generally earn higher sala-

OCCUPATION SPECIALTIES

Hotel/Motel Managers

Specialty	Responsibilities
Convention services managers	Coordinate the activities of the large hotels' various departments for meetings, conventions, and other special events.
Executive housekeepers	Ensure that guest rooms, meeting and banquet rooms, and public areas are clean, orderly, and well maintained.
Food and beverage managers	Direct the food services of hotels.
Front office managers	Supervise front office activities and take care of reservations, room assignments, unusual requests, inquiries, and guests' complaints.
Lodging facilities managers	Supervise and maintain temporary or permanent lodging facilities, such as small apartment houses, hotels, trailer parks, tourist camps, and resorts.
Resident managers	Live in hotels and are on call twenty-four hours a day to resolve any problems or emergencies.

ries than anyone else in the business. Their job is to manage the overall functions of the property, address systemic issues, and ensure that all departments are functioning in a fluid fashion.

Executive management occupations may include the following:

- Chief Financial Officer (CFO)
- Hotel Manager
- General Manager
- Controller
- Sales Director
- Rooms Director
- Marketing Director
- Food and Beverage Director

Sales and Marketing

Sales and marketing personnel manage the solicitation and acquisition of corporate, tourist, and special events groups. Such groups purchase room blocks rather than single rooms. Groups, therefore, represent the largest revenue generator for a hotel. Sales and marketing personnel usually have at least undergraduate degrees in business management, marketing, or related disciplines. Their salaries are competitive, and their compensation packages often include performance bonuses and other incentives.

The primary task of sales and marketing personnel is to contact potential client companies that may require overnight accommodations, meeting or reception spaces, or both. They also help promote the company at trade shows, conferences, and other events. Because they are responsible for ensuring that room blocks and activities are satisfactory to their clients, they are closely connected with virtually every other department of the hotel. In many cases, marketing personnel serve as the advance communications representatives for properties that are under construction. In this capacity, they communicate with area media, trade associations, and other resources to ensure that the property's interests are met as development is ongoing.

Sales and marketing occupations may include the following:

- Corporate Sales Manager
- Sales Director
- Senior Sales Manager
- Administrative Assistant

- Catering Sales Manager
- Director of Catering

Reservations

Reservations personnel are charged with managing a hotel's reservation system and assigning rooms. They must consistently monitor the hotel's booking system to reconcile group sales, rooms reserved by individual guests, and room blocks reserved by online booking agencies and travel agents. They must also register incoming guests, assign keys and room cards, and collect payments from departing guests, as well as maintaining records of guest accounts. The average pay for a reservations agent is about $21,000 per year. An advanced degree is not required, but the ability to operate computer programs is expected, as are outstanding communications skills.

Reservations occupations may include the following:

- Reservations Manager
- Reservations Assistant
- Administrative Assistant

Front-Desk Operations

The front desk is the central receiving point for incoming, current, and outgoing guests. Front-desk personnel manage guests who are checking in and ensure that their needs are met. The average pay for a front-desk manager, who oversees the operations in this department, is about $42,000 per year. Advanced degrees are not typical, but front-desk personnel are expected to have excellent organizational and computer skills.

Front-desk occupations may include the following:

- Front-Desk Manager
- Front-Desk Assistant

Housekeeping

Housekeeping is charged with maintaining the general cleanliness of the hotel. Housekeeping personnel must change linens, vacuum, dust, empty trash and recycling bins, clean and sanitize bathrooms, and replace amenities (such as bar soap, shampoo, conditioners, shower caps, and glasses). Housekeepers are usually trained according to the hotel or hotel chain's standards. Hourly salaries and benefits are determined largely through collective bargaining, but most housekeepers work for minimum wage and, where applicable, tips.

Housekeeping occupations may include the following:

- Housekeeper
- Housekeeping Manager
- Executive Housekeeper
- Housekeeping Director

Maintenance

Maintenance and building-engineering staff repair malfunctioning building systems, such as air-conditioning, plumbing, electrical hardware, and similar devices. They may also play an important role in renovation planning and implementation. Building maintenance personnel are alternately called engineers, environmental services personnel, and facilities managers. Salaries are commensurate with experience. Most personnel in this department have vocational education and training, if not advanced degrees in engineering or related fields.

Occupations within this department include the following:

- Heating, Ventilation, and Air-Conditioning (HVAC) Specialist
- Plumber
- Apprentice
- Chief Engineer

Security

The safety of hotel staff and guests alike is charged to a security team. Hotel security personnel ensure that unruly guests are disciplined or ejected, that no illegal activity takes place in or around the property, and that emergency situations are addressed. Security personnel conduct periodic rounds, monitor surveillance cameras, and respond to relevant calls.

Hotel security personnel are expected to have training in public safety. They may obtain this training through undergraduate programs, vocational education, or by passing a variety of security certification programs. Many major hotels also require experience in military or professional law enforcement agencies. Additionally, security personnel may be required to obtain certifica-

tion in cardiopulmonary resuscitation (CPR) and other first-aid techniques. Salaries generally start at $35,000 per year for entry-level officers.

Hotel security personnel must maintain strong relationships not just with local and federal law enforcement but also with fellow security personnel at other properties. Good communication networks help track and defend against criminal activity directed against both the individual property and other properties in midsize and larger hotel chains.

Security occupations may include the following:

- Investigator
- House Detective
- Security Guard
- Chief of Security
- Technical Support

Food and Beverage

Food and beverage personnel (including caterers) often maintain strong relationships with employees in the sales and marketing departments. Their responsibilities include ensuring that meetings, receptions, and large events held at the property are successful. They work with sales teams to meet the meal and beverage needs of incoming guests, and they often play a central role in contract development.

Food and beverage personnel also provide food and drink service during such events, as well as setting up and breaking down event rooms before and after them. Catering managers often have educations in business or sales, while other food and beverage personnel may have limited educations but significant restaurant experience. Food preparers often have vocational training as well.

Other food and beverage personnel work within a hotel's restaurant, bar, or similar venues, serving guests, preparing food, and busing tables. Others work in room service, taking orders and delivering them to guests throughout the hotel. Because of the diversity of subgroups within a given food and beverage department, salaries range broadly. Managers generally earn between $30,000 and $55,000 per year, while bartenders, servers, and busboys typically earn minimum wage with tips. Chefs earn an average of about $45,000 per year, commensurate with experience.

Food and beverage occupations may include the following:

- Catering Sales Manager
- Director of Catering
- Administrative Assistant
- Server
- Greeter
- Executive Chef
- Line Cook and Chef
- Table Busser
- Room Service Personnel
- Dishwasher
- Bartender

Concierge

The concierge is responsible for providing hotel guests with information and for making useful services available to them. Guests approach the concierge for information about tours, local directions, and attractions. Often, the concierge will help guests make dinner reservations, locate tickets to shows and concerts, and assist with travel arrangements.

The concierge position varies in terms of the tasks performed from property to property. Qualified concierges have considerable training in the hotel and tourism industry and usually have undergraduate educations in hospitality. Concierges are also required to have strong organizational and communications skills. Normally, concierges are closely connected to virtually every aspect of their hotels, thereby ensuring that they will be able to provide every service to the guest that the property may offer.

Concierge occupations may include the following:

- Chief Concierge
- Concierge

Groundskeeping

The maintenance of the property surrounding a hotel, particularly a resort, falls to the establishment's groundskeeping crew. The groundskeepers maintain flower gardens and, where applicable, nature trails, golf courses, and other outdoor amenities. Groundskeepers must be familiar with the equipment necessary to maintain the hotel's horticultural features. They may not have advanced educations, but they generally have solid gardening experience, some ability to maintain sprinkler and other mechanical systems, and an eye for the aesthetic quality of the hotel's natural resources.

Although they need not possess a postsecondary education, groundskeepers are expected to be familiar with their property's external real estate. They may also be called upon to clear debris, snow, and other seasonal elements that may hinder guests' activity or the hotel's operations.

Groundskeepers are usually paid hourly, at a rate commensurate with their experience and skills. They work closely with those in the maintenance and engineering departments in order to ensure that they have the proper resources to tend to the hotel's grounds.

Groundskeeping occupations may include the following:

- Head Groundskeeper
- Landscaping Worker
- Assistant Groundskeeper

Human Resources

The human resources department is responsible for hotel personnel. It handles employee hiring, dismissal, relations, and benefits (such as insurance, retirement funds, and other employee incentives). The human resources department also assists employees with obtaining additional on-the-job training.

Human resources managers are well trained in their field through both experience and college-level education. Generally, human resources managers earn about $77,000 per year, although in many cases, depending on years of experience and level of responsibility, the salary is considerably higher.

Human resources occupations may include the following:

- Human Resources Director
- Human Resources Coordinator
- Human Resources Manager
- Administrative Assistant

Doorpersons/Porters/Valets

Usually, the first individual a guest encounters at a major hotel is a doorperson. This individual is assigned to stand in front of the property to greet guests and provide information about parking, the hotel, and nearby services. Doorpersons also signal for taxicab service and carry guest luggage into and out of the hotel.

OCCUPATION SPECIALTIES

Bellhops/Bell Captains

Specialty	Responsibilities
Baggage porters	Deliver luggage to and from guests' rooms and set up rooms for sales personnel.
Doorkeepers	Serve residents and guests by opening doors, hailing taxicabs, answering inquiries, and assisting guests into automobiles.
Head baggage porters	Supervise and direct the activities of baggage porters.
Room-service clerks	Deliver and remove packages, laundry, groceries, and other articles to and from guests' rooms and record all information pertaining to services rendered to guests.

Porters (also known as bellhops) are responsible for bringing hotel guests' luggage to their rooms. They usually remain in the hotel lobby until summoned by the front desk for guest assistance. In addition to transferring luggage, bellhops may assist guests in locating room amenities and operating the room's television, computer, and alarm system.

Hotel valets, where applicable, assist guests with personal services and are comparable to porters. In hotels that offer laundry or shoe-shining services, valets are often responsible for transporting guests' clothing to and from the hotel's laundry facilities. This category also includes parking valets, who are responsible for parking and retrieving guests' vehicles.

Doorpersons, porters, and valets are not required to have a postsecondary education. However, all are expected to have a strong understanding of the hotel and its environs and are required to be friendly and courteous at all times. Employees in these positions generally rely on tips for at least part of their income.

Occupations in this division may include the following:

- Doorperson
- Valet
- Parking Valet
- Chief Parking Attendant
- Parking Cashier
- Bellhop

Laundry Personnel

Laundry workers are responsible for cleaning, folding, and storing all bed and bathroom linens from guestrooms. Such services are usually located on a single floor or section of a lodging establishment. In full-service hotels, laundry workers are also charged with cleaning tablecloths, bar towels, and napkins. Laundry personnel do not typically have advanced educations. However, their education should be sufficient to allow them to comply easily with the hotel's rules on detergent usage, folding techniques, and other tasks.

Laundry staff occupations may include the following:

- Head of Laundry Services
- Linen Cleaner
- Guest Clothing Cleaner
- Laundry Worker

Entertainment Workers

In hotels and resorts that include such facilities as casinos and golf courses, personnel are required to perform such tasks as operating gaming machines and card tables, administering golf carts and equipment rental services, and driving shuttles and other service vehicles. Entertainment workers focus their attention solely on the casino, golf course, or other amenity in which they work. In many cases, they are employed by the facility and not directly by the hotel.

Entertainment workers appear in a wide range of capacities and organizational networks. Most do not have formal postsecondary educations but do have extensive training and experience in the areas in which they work.

Entertainment occupations may include the following:

- Card Dealer
- Stage Performer
- Pit Boss
- Golf Pro
- Caddy
- Gift Store Clerk
- Casino Security

Many hotels have full-service spas, complete with massage rooms. (©Inga Ivanova/Dreamstime.com)

Recreation and Fitness-Center Personnel

Many full-service and resort properties have on-site spas and fitness centers for health- and fitness-minded guests. Personnel working in such facilities are on hand to assist guests in their use. Most such individuals have training and certification in physical fitness, massage therapy, nutrition, cosmetics, or other fields. They also have first-aid and CPR training or certification. Salaries depend on the task performed, but most personnel in this field receive tips as well as an hourly wage.

Recreation and fitness-center occupations may include the following:

- Massage Therapist
- Personal Trainer
- Spa Facial Provider
- Nutritionist
- Tennis Pro

Information Technology/Multimedia

Hotels and other lodging establishments often have on-site personnel who manage computer systems, video technology, and sound systems. They are called upon to set up audiovisual devices such as microphones, laptops, projectors, speakers, and other hardware typically used during meetings and presentations. Information technology (IT) and multimedia personnel also help maintain the computer networks and systems that are in everyday use

at the property. They may help bring online and maintain computer networks in administrative offices, as well as at a hotel's business center.

These personnel must have training in computer and information technology, often obtained either at vocational institutions or at the undergraduate level. The average salary for IT managers is about $60,000 per year.

IT and multimedia occupations may include the following:

- Information Technology Director
- Information Technology Support Assistant
- Multimedia Technician

Administrative Support

Administrative personnel are located throughout the hotel, assisting each department in its overall operations. Administrative staff may be needed to assist at the front desk in answering phones during high-traffic periods, run errands for the concierge, make photocopies and send faxes for clients and guests, and perform other tasks. In many cases, they are the nucleus of each department, providing support to managers through scheduling, data entry, filing, and other activities as warranted by the particular department.

Administrative personnel have a wide range of backgrounds and professional training experience. Many are temporary employees, while others are brought in as entry-level staff for managers and other personnel.

Administrative support occupations may include the following:

- Administrative Assistant
- Executive Assistant
- Secretary
- Intern

INDUSTRY OUTLOOK

Overview

The hotels and motels industry has long been an indicator of economic conditions in the United States and around the globe. The close link between the health of this industry and that of the economy reflects demand for lodging across the spectrum of travelers, from business travelers and tourists to military personnel, political figures, public servants, and others whose jobs entail a high level of travel. Following the terrorist attacks of September 11, 2001, the impact of a receding economy sent the travel and tourism industry reeling. Virtually every type of lodging establishment saw significant losses during the 2001 recession. Hotel staffs were cut, and new hotel construction stagnated.

By 2007, the industry had largely returned to its pre-September 11 growth rate, as the number of rooms in major urban centers and in tourist-rich areas surged. This resurgence was largely due to the health of the global economy, as business travelers increased in great numbers. With the 2007-2009 global economic crisis, however, concern over the lodging industry returned. Given the broad impact of that economic downturn—felt by tourist travel and business travel alike—hotels saw major drops in room revenues, as well as in the food and beverage business. Such losses caused hiring freezes, layoffs, and a slowdown in the construction of new properties.

Several factors will contribute to the continued growth of the hotel industry over the long term. The first is the resurgence of corporate travel. When companies see opportunities for business development, they conduct more business travel. Corporate business is by far the largest contributor to a hotel's bottom line, and with a resurgence of conventions and business meetings, hotel growth will continue.

Accompanying the strengthening of corporate business is another key element for the hospitality industry: the return of vacationing guests. This clientele is essential to the survival of all lodging properties, large and small. With increased marketing and affordable rates, properties may see a return of steady tourist business.

One of the most important keys to the recovery of the tourism and hospitality industry is the government. Tourism, of which hotels are a major part, is the third largest industry in the United States and is essential to most economies. How governments facilitate the growth of this industry is pivotal, but government efforts toward economic recovery can have an adverse impact on hotels. For example, the near collapse of the banking industry in 2008 and 2009 fostered an enormous U.S. government bailout, albeit one with conditions. These included limits on perceived reckless spending, such as sending executives on wasteful junkets to resorts and casino hotels. However, in imposing such restrictions, the government also hindered the growth of the lodging industry, which relies on legitimate corporate travel.

Also invaluable to tourism is the attraction of foreign travelers. In 2007, nearly 56 million foreign travelers visited the United States, with a large percentage arriving from neighboring Canada and Mexico. Heightened security efforts in the post-September 11 environment may represent a challenge to would-be terrorists, but careful screening and security measures may also discourage foreign tourism. Encouraging foreign tourists and business travelers to spend their travel money in the United States during the new era of heightened security following September 11 is essential to the survival of the hotel and motel industry.

Much of the success of a reinvigorated hospitality industry relies on the ability of hotels and motels to manage costs and compete. The widespread impact of the global economic crisis has kept energy costs largely in check. However, the lack of federal aid to states—and, in turn, the lack of state aid to municipalities—has led governments on all levels to look at increasing commercial property taxes.

This is an added cost for hotels that include a great deal of taxable real estate. Additionally, the pursuit of additional revenues has led officials to seek higher taxes on room occupancy, sales, and meals. Such increased rates are passed along to guests, and unless properties lower room rates in an effort to remain competitive, potential guests may go to other areas or simply forgo travel.

The diversity and flexibility of the hospitality industry are among the main elements driving its continued growth, even in times of recession. To be sure, the significant drop in corporate travel and bookings during the economic recession of 2007-2009 had a severe impact on business at large urban and luxury resort properties. However, many tourist and seasonal areas continue to see strong numbers, largely because of the "drive" market (tourists who drive from shorter distances): As out-of-region guests have become increasingly reluctant to pay for airfare, more local tourists have taken their place.

Furthermore, the changing interests of the tourist and business markets have caused an evolution in the hotel industry. Increasing numbers of guests look for environmentally friendly hotels that minimize their use of water and energy and employ other green practices. Many properties also focus on certain demographics, such as pet owners or the gay and lesbian community. With a consistently evolving business approach and strong marketing campaigns, the hotel industry will likely continue to see growth in both the short and the long term.

Employment Advantages

According to the BLS, the lodging and hospitality industry will continue to grow well into the 2010's. Wages and salaries are expected to remain above the national average in terms of growth—14 percent versus the industry aggregate average of 11 percent—and industry-wide construction growth is also anticipated to continue.

The diversity of the industry in terms of the broad range of career paths it offers continues to be a great benefit to those seeking advancement. Most employees begin at a basic, entry-level position in a given hotel office, moving upward either within the hotel itself or at other properties owned by the hotel corporation. Most major hotels offer management training, certification, and other programs designed to give employees the opportunity to thrive in their current positions and advance in the future.

Additionally, those in the service sectors of the hotel industry, such as housekeepers, restaurant servers, and custodial staff, may see personal development in light of an ever-changing industry. For example, more programs in English as a second language (ESL) are being offered to foreign-born employees in order to enhance their communication skills and underscore the cosmopolitan image of a property.

Annual Earnings

In light of the widespread economic recession, it was believed that the hotel industry would continue to see drops in both room demand and revenues during the

PROJECTED EMPLOYMENT FOR SELECTED OCCUPATIONS

Hotels and Motels Industry

Employment		
2009	Projected 2018	Occupation
28,760	27,800	First-line supervisors/managers of housekeeping and janitorial workers
213,570	248,800	Hotel, motel, and resort desk clerks
28,970	30,600	Lodging managers
419,310	452,400	Maids and housekeeping cleaners
130,420	149,500	Waiters and waitresses

Source: U.S. Bureau of Labor Statistics, Industries at a Glance, Occupational Employment Statistics and Employment Projections Program.

period immediately following 2008. One U.S. industry expert predicted in 2008 that profits at American lodging establishments would decline as much as 8 percent in the following year or two. Another study, however, indicated that, although a significant decline in earnings was expected in 2009, a modest turnaround would begin in 2010.

Evidence bore out these predictions: One of the world's largest hotel chains, for example, saw a precipitous drop in earnings in the second quarter of 2009. Marriott International posted a 76 percent drop in earnings, from $157 million in the second quarter of 2008 to $37 million in the same period in 2009. Such major drops in earnings, coupled with stagnant growth, led to widespread layoffs and hiring freezes within an industry accustomed to posting more than $483 billion in global revenues. Though the drop in revenues represented a dramatic trend in the short term, it was expected to reverse slowly as the U.S. and other economies recovered.

RELATED RESOURCES FOR FURTHER RESEARCH

AMERICAN HOTEL AND LODGING ASSOCIATION
1201 New York Ave. NW, Suite 600
Washington, DC 20005-3931
Tel: (202) 289-3100
Fax: (202) 289-3199
http://www.ahla.com

AMERICAN RESORT DEVELOPMENT ASSOCIATION
1201 15th St. NW, Suite 400
Washington, DC 20005
Tel: (202) 371-6700
Fax: (202) 289-8544
http://www.arda.org

HOSPITALITY NET BV
Akersteenweg 31
6226 HR Maastricht
Netherlands
Tel: 31-43-362-6600
Fax: 31-43-362-6770
http://www.hospitalitynet.org

HOSPITALITY SALES AND MARKETING
ASSOCIATION INTERNATIONAL
1760 Old Meadow Rd., Suite 500
McLean, VA 22102
Tel: (703) 506-3280
Fax: (703) 506-3266
http://www.hsmai.org

INTERNATIONAL HOTEL AND RESTAURANT
ASSOCIATION
41 Ave. General Guisan (Lausanne)
1009 Pully
Switzerland
Tel: 41-21-711-4283
http://www.ih-ra.com

ABOUT THE AUTHOR

Michael P. Auerbach has more than sixteen years of professional experience in public policy and administration, economic development, and the hospitality industry. He is a 1993 graduate of Wittenberg University and a 1999 graduate of the Boston College Graduate School of Arts and Sciences. He has been associated with the hotel industry since 2006, both in Massachusetts and in other regions of the United States, and has worked closely with the American Hotel and Lodging Association and the International Society of Hotel Association Executives.

FURTHER READING

ASIS International. *Career Opportunities in Security*. Alexandria, Va.: Author, 2005. Available at http://www.asisonline.org/careercenter/careers2005.pdf.

Barrows, Clayton W., and Tom Powers. *Introduction to Management in the Hospitality Industry*. 9th ed. New York: John Wiley & Sons, 2009.

_____. *Introduction to the Hospitality Industry*. 7th ed. New York: John Wiley & Sons, 2009.

Brymer, Robert A. *Hospitality and Tourism*. 11th ed. Dubuque, Iowa: Kendall/Hunt, 2004.

Business Travel News. "STR Downgrades 2009 Hotel Forecast, but Sees Some Recovery." April 28, 2009. http://www.btnonline.com/

businesstravelnews/search/article_display .jsp?vnu_content_id=1003967053.

CareerBuilder.com. Salary Calculator and Wage Finder. http://www.cbsalary.com/salary-calculator.

Careers.org. Occupation Profiles: Descriptions, Earnings, Outlook. http://occupations .careers.org.

Dopson, Lea R., and David K. Hayes. *Managerial Accounting for the Hospitality Industry*. Hoboken, N.J.: John Wiley & Sons, 2009.

Internal Revenue Service. "Hotel Industry Overview: August 2007—History of Industry." http://www.irs.gov/businesses/article/ 0,,id=174494,00.html.

Larkin, Enda. *How to Run a Great Hotel: Everything You Need to Achieve Excellence in the Hotel Industry*. Oxford: How to Books, 2009.

Lee-Ross, Darren, and Conrad Lashley. *Entrepreneurship and Small Business Management in the Hospitality Industry*. Boston: Butterworth-Heinemann, 2009.

Medlik, S., and H. Ingram. *The Business of Hotels*. 4th ed. Oxford, England: Butterworth-Heinemann, 2000.

PayScale.com. "Salary Survey for Job: Catering Sales Manager (United States)." January 28, 2010. http://www.payscale.com/research/ US/Job=Catering_Sales_Manager/Salary.

PKF Hospitality Research. "PKF Revises 2009 U.S. Forecast." *Hotels*, October 28, 2008. http:// www.hotelsmag.com/article/CA6609097.html.

Rogers, Tony. *Conferences and Conventions: A Global Industry*. 2d ed. Tony Rogers. London: Butterworth-Heinemann, 2008.

Rutherford, Denney G., and Michael J. O'Fallon. *Hotel Management and Operations*. 4th ed. New York: John Wiley, and Sons, 2007.

SalaryList.com. "Manager of Information Technology Jobs Salary, Ranked by Salary." http://www.salarylist.com/all-manager-of-information-technology-real-jobs-salary.htm.

Smith Travel Research. "Hotel Industry Posts Record Revenue in 2008, Other Metrics Slide." Hotel News Resource, June 23, 2009. http:// www.hotelnewsresource.com/HNR-detail-sid-39541.html.

Stoessel, Eric. "Marriott Posts Steep Declines." *Lodging Hospitality*, July 16, 2009. http:// lhonline.com/news/marriott_second _quarter_0716.

United Nations World Tourism Organization. "Testing Times for International Tourism." *UNWTO World Tourism Barometer* 7, no. 2 (June 2009). http://www.unwto.org/facts/eng/pdf/ barometer/ UNWTO_Barom09_2_en_excerpt.pdf.

U.S. Bureau of Labor Statistics. *Career Guide to Industries*, 2010-2011 ed. http://www.bls.gov/ oco/cg.

_____. "Hotel, Motel, and Resort Desk Clerks." In *Occupational Outlook Handbook*, 2010-2011 ed. http://www.bls.gov/oco/ocos132.htm.

U.S. Census Bureau. North American Industry Classification System (NAICS), 2007. http:// www.census.gov/cgi-bin/sssd/naics/ naicsrch?chart=2007.

U.S. Department of Commerce. International Trade Administration. Office of Trade and Industry Information. Industry Trade Data and Analysis. http://ita.doc.gov/td/industry/ otea/OTII/OTII-index.html.

Venison, Peter. *One Hundred Tips for Hoteliers: What Every Successful Hotel Professional Needs to Know and Do*. New York: iUniverse, 2005.

Walker, John R., and Jack E. Miller. *Supervision in the Hospitality Industry: Leading Human Resources*. 6th ed. Hoboken, N.J.: Wiley, 2010.

Household and Personal Products Industry

©Monika Adamczyk/Dreamstime.com

INDUSTRY SNAPSHOT

General Industry: Manufacturing

Career Cluster: Manufacturing

Subcategory Industries: Polish and Other Sanitation Goods Manufacturing; Soap and Other Detergent Manufacturing; Soap, Cleaning Compound, and Toilet Preparation Manufacturing; Surface Active Agent Manufacturing; Toilet Preparation Manufacturing

Related Industries: Apparel and Fashion Industry; Chemicals Industry; Retail Trade and Service Industry

Annual Domestic Revenues: $102.7 billion USD in manufacturing (IBIS, 2010); $227.2 billion USD in sales (IBIS 2010)

Annual International Revenues: $441.4 billion USD (Datamonitor, 2010)

Annual Global Revenues: $492.4 billion USD (Datamonitor, 2010)

NAICS Number: 3256

INDUSTRY DEFINITION

Summary

The household and personal products industry manufactures and sells nondurable goods, from toilet-bowl cleaners and floor waxes to deodorants and lipstick. These items are sold through multiple retail and online stores, such as beauty supply stores and pharmacies. The industry exists worldwide and includes one-person firms as well as major corporations such as Procter & Gamble.

History of the Industry

Civilizations have been using and making household and personal products since ancient times. Makeup, for instance, in many ancient cultures such as Egypt, was thought to have magical properties, while perfumes initially had religious associations. Some cultures viewed them, as today, as enhancements or replacements for physical beauty or used them to decorate the dead. Beauty enhancement was not initially limited to women. For example, in ancient Egypt, men and women lined their eyes with kohl. Makeup could also indicate or hide social status or act as part of the preparation for war—to frighten opponents: Ancient Britons painted themselves with blue woad to frighten Romans.

Initially, many cultures relied on homemade products of locally available raw materials. One of

937

Selecting the appropriate shampoo may not be so easy. Procter & Gamble makes twenty-two varieties of Pantene and eleven of Head & Shoulders. (©Dreamstime.com)

the first factories for perfumes was found at Pyrgos, the southern end of Cyprus, dating back approximately four thousand years. Culturally, makeup was not necessarily accepted worldwide. For example, in ancient Israel, only prostitutes wore makeup. Other personal products such as soaps followed much the same pattern as makeup: They were homemade initially and culturally accepted in certain places while viewed with skepticism in others. Household products were also initially made the same way—from local materials and by hand, typically by the women in the household—and there was not necessarily one set recipe to concoct a product.

Traveling peddlers also sold personal and household items—sometimes these were items they had made themselves—that could be useful but more often than not were fake or, worse, dangerous. Eventually, guilds oversaw the processes and creation of certain products such as soap. Different sections of the household and personal products industry were overseen by various guilds or were left entirely in the hands of individuals. However, during the Middle Ages, wearing makeup became associated with low morals. During the Renaissance, pale skin was deemed attractive, and dangerous powders made of lead to whiten the face were used by both men and women. Mercury was another substance in the cosmetic registry used on women to brighten their cheeks.

The modern industry did not get its start until the Industrial Revolution, when the industry grew exponentially. There was a larger market for personal products as the middle class was created and grew, and there was a greater ability to create large amounts of product in a shorter time period, lowering the cost of such luxury items. With the growing concern for health, personal products such as soaps were successfully commercialized and sold. Major companies such as Clairol, L'Oreal, and Max Factor began industrial-scale operations. Initially, these companies had their own stores and chemists. Despite their creation, it was not until the 1920's that cosmetics were seen as an acceptable part of the fashion industry and successfully advertised in women's magazines. Until then, cosmetics, hair dyes, and the like were viewed as being worn only by women with low morals. They became more acceptable once they were popularized by movie stars.

By this time, the industry had expanded into fashionable department stores. Household products had also moved from the private homemaker's world into an industry where soaps, detergents, and other cleaners could be purchased through mail-order catalogs, as well as general goods stores. During World War II, many items were rationed, including products within the industry. Afterward, they became regulated in other ways. By the 1970's, laws limited permissible ingredients in household products. In addition, the use of animals to test products became public knowledge, and some consumers reacted by refusing to purchase products tested on animals. For much of its history, the personal products industry marketed primarily to middle-class white women. It was not until the 1980's that diversity became a keyword within the industry and products were developed for different ethnicities within the same company. With each decade, the marketing of household and personal products shifted with current political and social trends as well.

The Industry Today

Worldwide, cultural views and uses of makeup and household products are not the same, though with the advances in worldwide communications, there are very few places where advertising does not proliferate—whether online, on billboards, in magazines, on television, or on the radio. The major sectors of the industry own individual brand names that market not only specific products but also to specific cultures and cultural needs or desires. Skin-whitening products make up the sales for 60 to 65 percent of the female market in India, while in the United States antiaging personal products make up the bulk of sales to women.

Green products have become popular, and products with environmentally friendly packaging or that use natural elements—such as minerals and nutrient-rich muds—are growing rapidly in demand over chemically laden products. The market, though initially affected by the economic downturn of 2007-2009, is on the rise again. According to IBISWorld, it is expected to

experience only moderate growth over the five years from 2010 to 2015. This will occur in line with favorable long-term underlying economic, demographic and social trends. As with the previous five year period, the industry is expected to continue to benefit from an increasing awareness of health and wellbeing, which will see the development of more health-oriented products. Continued product development including in natural/organic, cosmeceutical or nutraceutical fusion products as well as environmentally friendly/green products and ultra-niche products will also help stimulate industry growth.

The generation that drives sales behind the household and personal products industry is the generation of aging baby boomers and their children. The first group is most responsible for the antiaging trends within personal products and requests. They also purchase chemical cleansers and brand names they grew up with, such as Comet or Lysol, while the following generation is equally interested in more natural, organic, and environmentally safe personal and household products.

Today, the industry is guided by government and other regulatory agencies, such as the Consumer Product Safety Commission, the U.S. Food and Drug Administration (FDA), and the FDA Center for Food Safety and Applied Nutrition. Reg-

A trend in household cleaners has been toward environmentally friendly, natural products, such as this line of non-toxic cleaners, safe for pets and children. (AP/Wide World Photos)

ulations ban certain types of ingredients outright, limit the uses of others, and govern how certain products can be created, tested, labeled, packaged, marketed, and advertised.

Companies within this industry vary in size and operation but typically fall into either the small or large business category. Smaller businesses include one-person operations that create their own products, selling them either at specialty stores, at farmers' markets, or online. These small companies are operationally limited: They do not have the financial backing or cash flow to order raw materials in bulk or to open and operate stores or factories worldwide. However, the Internet has helped them succeed. With online marketing, small operations such as Sweet Petula have been able to reach a wide audience on Facebook, Twitter, Etsy, blogs, and local business-support Web sites. Small companies rely most heavily on word-of-mouth and repeat customers. They have a unique position within the industry in that they can quickly change their product lines and cater to specific customers, even individual customers, for

Aging baby boomers are making antiaging products such as Olay's Regenerist popular. (AP/Wide World Photos)

product requests and suggestions. Large companies take much longer to change their products to meet changing demand.

Large companies are conglomerations of multiple brand names. Procter & Gamble, for example, is the leading manufacturer on the market, sells over three hundred brands, and has a 20.6 percent market share. SC Johnson is best known for household cleaning products such as Pledge, Glade, and Windex, operates in over seventy countries, and has approximately twelve thousand employees. Large corporations such as these had their start in the 1800's, when the industry was just beginning to grow. Even if the overarching corporation is not as well-placed in consumers' minds, the memories of brand names such as Pledge still stick, especially with the older generations. While large companies such as Procter & Gamble rely on brand loyalty, they have greater marketing reach and can sell their products at lower prices than can smaller companies. However, the major competitors of brand-name items have become value items, such as a store's in-house version of a brand-name product.

While sales of basic personal items such as soap, shampoo, and shaving products are generally not affected very much by economic trends, Standard and Poor's noted some consumers "trading down to 'value' brands and private-label products in 2009." Walmart is a large retailer of in-house brands. The most well known Walmart brands include Equate and Great Value, among nearly thirty others that compete in many industries. With conservative spending during the economic downturn, in-house brands saw a jump in sales. However, the market for brand-name items has a favorable outlook.

INDUSTRY MARKET SEGMENTS

The household and personal products industry ranges in size from one-person operations to large global companies and serves primarily individual consumers through storefronts that vary in size. There are no true midsize companies within the industry—all are either small or large. The following sections provide a comprehensive breakdown of each of these different segments.

OCCUPATION PROFILE

Online Merchant

Considerations	Qualifications
Description	Sells merchandise through the Internet.
Career clusters	Business, Management, and Administration; Human Services; Information Technology; Marketing, Sales, and Service
Interests	Data; people; things
Working conditions	Work inside
Minimum education level	On-the-job training; junior/technical/community college; bachelor's degree
Physical exertion	Light work
Physical abilities	Unexceptional/basic fitness
Opportunities for experience	Volunteer work
Licensure and certification	Usually not required
Employment outlook	Faster-than-average growth expected

Note: See volume 1, "Publisher's Note," for an explanation of the Holland interest score.

Small and Midsize Businesses

Small household and personal product manufacturers, according to the U.S. Small Business Administration, range from one to one thousand employees. Within the sales industry, a small business earns $7 million or less per year. At the lowest end of the spectrum, with only a handful of employees, these companies typically manufacture and sell their own products online or at farmers' markets. At the higher end of the spectrum, products may be sold wholesale to a small or specialty retail shop that in turn sells to the public at a markup. In the household and personal products industry, there is no true midsize business category. Either the companies are small, with one thousand employees or fewer, or they are large-scale.

Potential Annual Earnings Scale. According to the U.S. Bureau of Labor Statistics (BLS), industrial engineers in the household and personal products industry earned an average of $77,460 in 2009, and chemical engineers earned an average of $86,900. Chemists earned an average of $68,620, and chem-

ical technicians earned an average of $42,070. The combined average salary of all production workers was $32,630, while production supervisors earned an average of $57,220 and production managers earned an average of $96,190. Sales representatives earned an average of $71,310, while sales managers earned an average of $120,300. General and operations managers earned an average of $132,640.

Clientele Interaction. To compete for business, very small companies—such as one-person operations—have a greater need to be seen and known by the public, as the competition is exceedingly high within the industry at all levels. One-person operations need to have good interpersonal relationships with vendors and markets where they hope to sell their products, and they often reach out to consumers directly. One-person operations may also have good relationships with material manufacturers and vendors in order to get discounted products. Small companies with more employees at the production end of the industry need good negotiators in order to get contracts with those companies that will carry and sell their products because the product is not sold for free but for a fee. Small companies that act as the storefronts have more clientele interaction with consumers and need to be knowledgeable about the products they are selling on behalf of other companies or else the companies may not renew contracts and their sales figures may drop significantly.

Amenities, Atmosphere, and Physical Grounds. The manufacturing portion of the industry is likely to include a specific physical location where chemicals are handled under multiple precautions. There will be emergency aid kits in case of accidents as well as wash stations. Depending on the types of chemicals used, there may or may not be clean rooms. Typically, there will be restrooms and other amenities that offices generally have in order to support their employees. The sales section of the industry will have an organized layout with signage directing customer traffic. Ideally, the atmosphere will be friendly and conducive to shopping. There may or may not be public restrooms available. A one-person operation is most often a home business.

Typical Number of Employees. Because small companies are limited in the types and numbers of products they can produce and sell, they also limit their staff size. In some cases, the owners are the only full-time employees.

Traditional Geographic Locations. Single-person operations work locally, often on their own property, and sell their products through an online storefront or at a local farmers' market or specialty boutique. Small companies that sell household and personal care products are located in the remotest areas across the world, but they are not likely to own a chain of stores.

Pros of Working for a Small Business. Because owners of small companies act as both owners and employees, there is less overhead and more potential profit. However, there is often less product available because of the abilities of a small company. The small business can also neatly fill a niche and focus on a specific type of product such as all-organic and nonanimal tested. The few employees a small company might employ will often be friends or family. Owners of smaller companies do not typically need to acquire advanced degrees in business and most employees receive on the job training, especially for those working in the sales portion.

Cons of Working for a Small Business. For the sector of this industry working with chemicals, a degree or licensing will likely be needed to meet insurance needs or federal requirements of a small company. The hours may also be longer for those employees working in the chemical portion of production in this industry because once a chemical process has begun it cannot be stopped, and if there is only a single person they will be required, most likely, to remain to see the process through to the end. The company's product line will often be limited because of the inability to develop multiple products with few available employees or even the limited physical space of a small company. Also due to its size, the commercial outreach will be far smaller than a larger company though the Internet may take care of reaching a global market.

Costs

Payroll and Benefits: Smaller companies may offer federal or state mandated benefits depending on their size. To save money and time, smaller companies may not offer vacation or sick leave. Also, because of low product sales, employees earn less than their larger company counterparts.

Supplies: Small companies within this industry require a wide range of supplies, from chemicals to office supplies, depending on the products produced.

External Services: Small household and personal product companies may contract Web hosting, hazardous waste disposal, cleaning, accounting, legal counsel, marketing, or equipment maintenance and repair.

Utilities: Typical utilities include Internet and phone service, as well as electricity, water, sewage, and gas or oil.

Taxes: Small businesses must pay income and property taxes. Self-employed persons may report their business income on their personal returns and pay self-employment taxes.

Large Businesses

Large businesses are well-established companies with over one thousand employees, or over $100 million in annual profits. The top thirty personal and household products companies each earn more than $300 million per year in profits. A large company focuses on a variety of products from household cleansers to makeup. These companies have recognizable brand names, such as Procter & Gamble, which owns multiple brands including Tide laundry detergent and Covergirl cosmetics. Large firms are located worldwide. Unilever, the top British company within the industry according to Household and Personal Products Industry (HAPPI), has offices globally from Argentina to Zimbabwe. Large companies such as Unilever and Procter & Gamble often have in-house teams of chemists and producers that create and manufacture their products.

Potential Annual Earnings Scale. According to the BLS, industrial engineers in the household and personal products industry earned an average of $77,460 in 2009 and chemical engineers earned an average of $86,900. Chemists earned an average of $68,620, and chemical technicians earned an average of $42,070. The combined average salary of all production workers was $32,630, while production supervisors earned an average of $57,220 and production managers earned an average of $96,190. Sales representatives earned an average of $71,310, while sales managers earned an average of $120,300. General and operations managers earned an average of $132,640.

Clientele Interaction. The companies that own popular brands are very conscious of their public interaction because of potential earnings loss should their branding be damaged. If a brand were to be associated with unpopular practices, such as hiring undocumented immigrants or dumping pollutants into oceans, sales could suffer. Companies conscious of the importance of branding interact with the public online through cheerful Web sites that discuss company policies and standards. The

Crest toothpaste is one of many household and personal products made by industry giant Procter & Gamble. (AP/Wide World Photos)

brands owned by the large companies interact on a closer level with the public through television and print advertisements and spokespeople such as famous actresses and models for makeup brands such as Covergirl. On an even closer scale, employees of stores that sell a company's products interact on a personal level with consumers.

Amenities, Atmosphere, and Physical Grounds. Large-scale companies have storefronts worldwide, as well as an online presence, and may include amenities for their employees such as an on-site gym, a cafeteria, or other recreational facilities and executive perks. Different industry functions require different facilities. Some plants include laboratories for experimenting or animal testing, as well as emergency care facilities in case of accidents. The stores that sell the products, such as CVS or Target, offer some public amenities such as restrooms.

Typical Number of Employees. Large companies employ more than one thousand employees.

Traditional Geographic Locations. Large companies are often global. They typically have headquarters in major cities, as well as production and research facilities in industrial areas outside metropolitan centers. Retail stores are located in rural, suburban, and urban communities throughout the world.

Pros of Working for a Large Business. Large companies pay competitively and offer good benefits such as 401(k) plans, health insurance, paid vacation, and sick time. There is the potential for travel worldwide to different company offices. There is also a greater chance for promotion and pay raises. With a larger company there is often a safety program in order to meet federal, state, or a country's standards. Many large companies are able to give back to the community through large donations to charities or through scholarships to universities. For example, Procter & Gamble sponsors a scholarship for chemical engineering students at the University of Florida Foundation.

Cons of Working for a Large Business. Large companies are large bureaucracies, and employees may become frustrated by ineffective communication, confusion, or red tape. A large company may also be less personal with the employees and more structured and regimented when dealing with them. There is a high level of competition to enter into the industry and even from within the company for raises and recognition, which can lead to added stress. In a stressful economic period, downturns, hiring freezes, and layoffs are highly likely. Working in other countries can be difficult because of language and cultural barriers, and an employee must be prepared to move to a country not of their own choosing. The balance between personal and work life may be difficult to achieve. As a single employee within a very large firm, the job a single person would have to do in order to get noticed by management would need to outshine several hundred or thousands of other employees. For managers, there will be unionized employees, which can add another level of difficulty in trying to meet union rules such as staffing regulations and time schedules.

Costs

Payroll and Benefits: The salary structure varies widely, as there are many types of employees with various jobs and skills.

Supplies: Personal and household product companies require various supplies depending on the products they create. These may include chemical-handling and disposal equipment, industrial manufacturing machines and computers and software to control them, research laboratories, vehicles, and gasoline, as well as typical office supplies and equipment.

External Services: Large companies may contract cleaning, maintenance, landscaping, security, catering, audiovisual services, Web design, accounting or auditing, legal counsel, lobbying, hazardous waste disposal, or information technology support.

Utilities: Typical utilities for a large company include water and sewage, electricity, Internet, and perhaps cable television.

Taxes: Large companies must pay local, state, federal, and international income and property taxes, including sales taxes, tariffs, and import/export fees where applicable.

ORGANIZATIONAL STRUCTURE AND JOB ROLES

The household and personal products industry includes numerous job roles pertaining to the preparation, manufacturing, packaging, and selling of a variety of products. Some of these products include dishwashing detergents, soaps, toothpaste, laundry cleaners, polishes, waxes, perfumes, shaving creams, hair care products, beauty creams and lotions, sunscreen, cosmetics, bath salts, deodorants, nail care products, and toilet creams. Companies within this industry may be responsible for any combination of preparing, manufacturing, packaging, or selling of these products. Job roles, though, will be relatively similar whether as part of a small business or large business. Small businesses may require employees to fulfill multiple job roles, whereas large businesses will often employ specialists or employees who fill only a single role.

As a result of steep competition within the industry, businesses specifically involved in the manufacturing of soap and cleaning compounds reduced their employment by an average of 4.8 percent between 2005 and 2010. These companies are expected to further reduce employment by 5.3 percent each year through 2015. Also, as technology has advanced, much of the production of these products has become automated. In 2010, computers generally control the production equipment and manage the inventory.

The following umbrella categories apply to the organizational structure of businesses in the household and personal products industry:

- Business Management
- Sales and Marketing
- Facilities and Security
- Technology, Research, Design, and Development
- Production and Operations
- Distribution
- Human Resources
- Business and Financial
- Office and Administrative Support

Business Management

Business managers provide top-level leadership of their companies. They drive the direction of a company and create the culture and attitudes that it encompasses. Business managers develop procedures, policies, and goals that form the framework and foundation for their companies. Large companies have multiple departments and one or more business managers that are responsible for each area. Small companies may not have many separate departments as employees will serve multiple roles, but one or more business managers are responsible for each company. Business managers ensure that each department is functioning effectively and to the benefit of the company as a whole. Ultimately, those in business management are responsible for the success or failure of the company. Because of the high level of responsibility, business management jobs require the most experience and education, while also earning the highest salary.

Business management occupations may include the following:

- Chief Executive Officer (CEO)
- Chief Operating Officer (COO)
- Chief Financial Officer (CFO)
- Marketing Manager
- Sales Manager
- Account Manager
- Human Resources Manager
- Engineering Manager
- Product Manager
- Natural Sciences Manager

Sales and Marketing

Sales and marketing is one of the most critical components of the household and personal products industry. Products cannot be sold without successful marketing. Marketing can include media advertising, coupons, sponsorship, or Internet advertising. Although marketing is by its nature very fluid, there are some standard methods of sales and marketing throughout the industry.

The first sales and marketing technique is the movement into global markets in search for new product demand. Because most of the products in this industry are staples of the traditional household, there is little room to increase sales of a product in a saturated market. Purchasers in the United States are at the point where their only purchases are for replacing depleted products in the household. Sales and marketing departments, therefore, are refocusing their efforts on global markets that have not yet reached their saturation points.

Sales and marketing departments are also focusing their efforts on major core brands and letting peripheral products fail. Unilever, for example, has reduced its number of brands from sixteen hundred to four hundred in order to focus its efforts. This refocus allows the company to direct all of its resources to a central location, rather than spreading it to thinly amongst too many products.

Another development in the sales and marketing of household and personal products is the movement to more eco-friendly or green products. Sales and marketing employees have taken advantage of the global green movement in order to promote products that are created with organic or all-natural components and packaging. Companies have found that something as simple as new green packaging for an existing product can increase sales.

Somewhat related to the green movement is the importance of innovation in the creation of new products. Sales and marketing departments focus a large amount of effort into developing new products, creating a novel concept, or improving existing products or packaging. A stagnant product can quickly fade away in such a market, unless it has already been deeply established. Even these established products, though, are facing pressure to innovate and evolve in order to maintain their foothold.

The Internet has also changed the importance of marketing, as smaller niche companies are more able to reach target customers than ever before. Facebook pages for specific products have become increasingly utilized as a method to reach the consumer.

Employees within this area must be flexible, creative, innovative, and have excellent communication skills in order to develop strong relationships. They must know their customers and be able to devise methods for connecting with them. They create brand identity so that each product is unique and recognizable by the public.

Sales and marketing occupations may include the following:

- Art Director/Artwork Coordinator
- Graphic Designer
- Public Relations/Communications Coordinator
- Business Development Manager/ Coordinator
- Sales Consultant/Representative
- Brand Manager

Facilities and Security

The household and personal products industry includes businesses with facilities for any combination of preparing, manufacturing, packaging, or selling of products, in addition to corporate offices. These buildings require some level of maintenance and possibly security. Individuals in these job roles do not necessarily need specific expertise in the industry itself and instead require only knowledge of their job duties. These job roles do not make up a large portion of the industry and are among the lowest paid, but they also require the least amount of education.

Facilities and security occupations may include the following:

- Custodian/Janitor
- Maintenance Supervisor
- Maintenance and Repair Worker
- Security Supervisor
- Security Guard

Technology, Research, Design, and Development

Technology, research, design, and development are crucial components of the household and personal products industry. Research and development personnel create the products and product innovations that are so important for the sales and marketing department. The two departments often work in close collaboration in order to achieve success. For example, while the sales and marketing department is responsible for selling the idea of a green product, it is the technology, research, design, and development department that is responsible for developing products that are green. This type of innovation, in particular, has become important as a result of recent environmental and health concerns. The focus on green products is expected to continue through 2015.

The household and personal products industry is highly competitive, and technology, research, design, and development are the sources and keys of that competitiveness. Companies strive to become the first to release a new product so that they may gain footholds in new market segments. This competition has led to thousands of new products flooding the market each year, but only 15 percent of those new products succeed.

Research and development personnel develop

Lipstick and eyeshadow are available in many colors. For example, Revlon's Super Lustrous lipstick comes in seventy-two shades, and Ulta offers more than ninety shades of eyeshadow. (©Francisco Caravana/Dreamstime.com)

new products, which could be either brand new or modifications of existing products. Stagnant products can easily fade in the saturated contemporary market, and successful research and development departments are responsible for the evolution of the company's products. Many of the largest companies in the industry began with single products that evolved and expanded to help grow their companies into global entities.

Research and development job roles can be extremely specialized and require advanced expertise in technology, life science, pharmaceutical science, or social science. Employees may be required to hold engineering degrees, master's degrees, doctorates, or postdoctoral degrees. As a result, these positions are generally well paid.

Technology, research, design, and development occupations may include the following:

- Information Technology Specialist
- Computer Systems Analyst

- Systems Administrator
- Data Manager
- Chemist
- Biochemist
- Chemical Technician
- Raw Material Specialist
- Project Engineer
- Package Engineer
- Chemical Engineer
- Industrial Engineer
- Chemical Engineering Technician
- Industrial Engineering Technician

Production and Operations

Whereas the technology, research, design, and development area develops and invents products and the sales and marketing area pushes the products to consumers, the production and operations area manufactures and sells products. Individuals in these job roles are responsible for the products consumers see on the shelves and consume in their households.

Unfortunately, job roles in this area have been taken up by machines and computers as technology has advanced. As companies try to increase their efficiency and decrease their operating costs, this is the area that has been most affected. Just as the automotive industry was hit hard by mechanical and computerized automation, so, too, has the household and personal products industry. All of the major companies in this industry have cut jobs in this area while maintaining the same wage level.

Employees in this area may be required to work with raw materials in the creation of their products but are most often utilized in the operation of machinery. Although they will be working with very specialized products and components, employees in this area do not necessarily require special knowledge of the industry, instead requiring knowledge of machine and computer operations. Individuals are also required to maintain the heavy equipment and machinery.

Production and operations occupations may include the following:

- Plant Director
- Team Assembler
- Chemical Equipment Operator
- Mixing and Blending Machine Operator
- Packaging and Filling Machine Operator

- Industrial Machinery Mechanic
- Maintenance and Repair Worker
- Quality Inspector
- Production Worker/Shift Technician
- Store Manager
- Assistant Manager
- Retail Salesperson
- Stock Clerk

Distribution

Distribution personnel move products from manufacturing locations to selling locations. After products are manufactured and packaged individually, they must be packaged for shipping, generally on pallets or in crates. Much of this packaging is automated, but the loading and unloading of the materials is still manual. After a product is ready for distribution, it is picked up by an industrial truck for loading and shipping. This truck can be owned by the manufacturer, the seller of the product (if it is a secondary seller), or an independent trucking company. The product may be delivered to a distribution center for the manufacturing company or selling company, or directly to a retail store.

Employees in this area do not require specialized knowledge of the industry. In the case of some distribution methods, some employees, such as truck drivers, may not even be employed within the industry. These positions are generally not highly paid and do not require advanced education.

Distribution occupations may include the following:

- Industrial Truck and Tractor Operator
- Heavy Truck Driver
- Light Truck Driver
- Equipment Operator
- Material Mover/Handler
- Packer and Packager
- Warehouse Manager
- Shipping and Receiving Clerk
- Dispatcher

Human Resources

The human resources department is responsible for all the employees within the company. It does not work with the products in the industry, instead focusing on tasks related to the employees themselves. Human resources personnel prepare and distribute employment evaluations; facilitate new employee orientation, training, and education; and maintain employment records pertaining to personal information, earnings, absences, and performance. They also administer employee benefits, such as vacation and insurance, and are responsible for the recruitment of new employees.

Human resources positions do not make up a large portion of the industry, but they exist in nearly every company. Large companies have large departments focused only on human resources issues, but a small company may have a single person who managers human resources in addition to numerous other tasks. These positions do not generally require specialized knowledge of the industry, but can require advanced education, specifically for human resources managers, who earned an average of $91,570 in 2009.

Individuals in this area must work well with people and understand the workings of the company and its benefits. They must be patient and able to convey information in an effective manner.

Human resources occupations may include the following:

- Human Resources Manager
- Human Resources Assistant
- Human Resources Specialist
- Human Resources Professional
- Recruitment Officer
- Training Officer

Business and Financial

The business and financial department is responsible for all financial dealings within a company. Large companies, especially, have well-developed business and financial departments to handle the monetary activity of the company. Companies within the household and personal products industry perform complex financial transactions that can require a large department to execute and track.

Financial tracking and reporting are exceedingly important in informing future directions of the company and providing background for future transactions. Because of the variety of purchases that go into this industry (such as raw materials, equipment, buildings, staff, and trucks), the business and financial activities can become very numerous and complex.

Positions within this area generally require advanced education, but they also offer a generous pay scale. The average annual wage for someone in this department was $64,780 in 2009.

Business and financial occupations may include the following:

- Purchasing Agent
- Business Operations Specialist
- Accountant
- Auditor
- Financial Analyst
- Logistician
- Budget Manager
- Accounts Payable Clerk
- Accounts Receivable Clerk
- Tax Manager

Office and Administrative Support

Although these positions do not receive the recognition or salary of the more technical job roles within the industry, office and administrative support staff are crucial to the day-to-day functioning of businesses. Because of the numerous products involved, a large amount of paperwork and tracking must be maintained. As a result, these positions make up a significant portion of the industry. A single large company may employ thousands of individuals to serve these roles alone.

Employees in these job roles can have a multitude of tasks, such as answering phones, filing, making travel reservations, organizing meetings, and processing paperwork. Employees must have strong organizational and communication skills, and pay attention to detail. The accurate retention of records within a company is a good indicator of its success.

Office and administrative support occupations may include the following:

- Bookkeeping, Accounting, and Auditing Clerk
- Customer Service Representative
- Receptionist
- Production and Planning Clerk
- Shipping and Receiving Clerk
- Stock Clerk
- Executive Assistant
- Secretary
- Office Clerk

INDUSTRY OUTLOOK

Overview

The outlook for this industry shows it to be on the rise domestically and globally. However, this industry has oversaturated certain markets, and to continue to generate revenue, more targeted marketing and group-specific products are needed, such as products designed for men only or teenagers. Furthermore, the market experienced a minor downturn in 2009 caused by economic fluctuations domestically and globally, with people purchasing value items instead of brand-name items. However, it is projected that growth will resume shortly. Globally, import and export levels have been inconsequential to the market over the last five years. According to IBISWorld, "in 2008 exports at $6.79 billion were at their highest level since 1997 but even then accounted for just 13 percent of industry revenue." In the wake of the recession, export revenue declined to $6.30 billion, and the market did not regain its lost ground in exports in 2010. Local manufacturers have begun to target more specific international markets in an attempt to boost production and sales.

Within the industry, there are multiple jobs, ranging from cashiers at storefronts who need no advanced degrees and receive on-the-job training to cosmetic chemists who need advanced degrees to work in labs that work on testing and developing new products. According to the BLS, the industry has higher earnings on average than other manufacturing industries, with over half the jobs going to workers "involved in production and in installation, maintenance, and repair." There are multiple segments within the chemical manufacturing industry, which is where most of the household and personal product industry resides.

Production occupations range from plant operators to machine maintenance to packing and product movers. Some 12 percent of the workforce is in professional or related occupations, which include chemists, researchers, chemical engineers, and the like—those people who are most closely associated with product research and development. Some 11 percent of industry workers fill positions in office and administrative support, while 10 percent work in management, business, and financial occupations, including engineering managers and sales managers.

While the market is expected to make a comeback and is on a slight rise, employment is not expected to improve within the industry and is in fact in decline. There will be a great deal of competition for these jobs. The decline is due to the global economic slump. Furthermore, with rapid advancement and improvement in production technology, there is a reduced need for workers in the areas of production, installation, maintenance, and repair. However, it will be important to have an understanding and level of comfort with technology in order to work in this field. Meanwhile, overall, companies, to save costs, are merging or consolidating to remove duplicate tasks and to move overseas where production and operating costs are lowest. East Asia and Latin America are the expected recipients of many U.S. companies.

Employment in this industry will be difficult to obtain, especially for those who are entering this industry for the first time. According to the BLS,

> For production jobs, opportunities will be best for those with experience and continuing education. For professional and managerial jobs, applicants with experience and an advanced degree should have the best prospects. In addition, some job opportunities will arise from the need to replace workers who transfer to other occupations or who retire or leave the labor force for other reasons.

Employment Advantages

Even though the household and personal products industry is facing declining employment, despite the industry itself being on the rise, individuals who have higher education, especially doctorates in chemistry or cosmetic chemistry, and who are also interested in environmentally safe and healthy products and production should consider joining this industry. The trend on the rise for the foreseeable future will be for sustainable production and environmentally friendly products. The decline in hiring means competition will be high for positions, and those students who excel academically and who are capable of thinking outside the box and being creative will have better chances for employment within this industry: The industry is always looking for new products to sell to old and established markets, as well as to new demographics. Training and advancement within the industry vary based on the categories of occupations.

Annual Earnings

Globally, the household products portion of the industry has a forecasted value of $95.1 billion in 2013, which represents a 15.1 percent increase in the market since 2008, while the personal products sector is forecast to be worth $424.1 billion by 2013, which represents an increase of 17.4 percent since 2008. Domestically, the industry's value is forecasted to increase from $51.75 billion in 2010 to $60.55 billion in 2015.

RELATED RESOURCES FOR FURTHER RESEARCH

AMERICAN CLEANING INSTITUTE
    1331 L St. NW, Suite 650
    Washington, DC 2005
    Tel: (202) 347-2900
    Fax: (202) 347-4110
    http://www.cleaninginstitute.org

COSMETIC NEWS, COMMUNICATIONS INTERNATIONAL GROUP
    12-14 rong-point des Champs Elysees
    75008 Paris
    France
    Tel: 33-1-53-53-16-67
    Fax: 33-1-53-53-14-00
    http://www.cosmeticnews.com

COSMETICSDESIGN.COM, DECISION NEWS MEDIA
    Le Belem
    355, rue Vendemiaire
    34 000 Montpellier
    France
    Tel: 33-4-99-53-28-70
    Fax: 33-4-99-52-28-75
    http://www.cosmeticsdesign.com

HAPPI
    Rodman Publishing
    70 Hilltop Rd.
    Ramsey, NJ 07446
    Tel: (201) 825-2552
    Fax: (201) 825-0553
    http://www.happi.com

ABOUT THE AUTHORS

Michelle Marie Martinez is an assistant professor and librarian at Sam Houston State University. She is a 2007 graduate of the University of North Texas Graduate School of Library and Information Sciences and a 2005 graduate of Sam Houston State University where she earned an M.A. Her research includes a wide variety of topics including Shakespeare, feminist literature, and film studies. She has presented research and papers at multiple conferences, including "Incest, Sexual Violence, and Rape in Video Games," presented at Oxford University.

Tyler Manolovitz is the digital resources coordinator and an assistant professor at Sam Houston State University. He earned an M.A. from the University of North Texas Graduate School of Library and Information Science in 2006. His research interests are varied and have included classic and contemporary literature, mythology, film studies related to Alfred Hitchcock and John Hughes, and sexual violence in video games. Manolovitz continues to research, write, and present at conferences internationally on a variety of topics.

FURTHER READING

Betton, C. I. *Global Regulatory Issues for the Cosmetics Industry.* Vol. 1. Norwich, N.Y.: William Andrew, 2007.

Boyd, Lydia. "Brief History of Beauty and Hygiene Products." Duke University Libraries Digital Collections. http://library.duke.edu/digitalcollections/adaccess/cosmetics.html.

Dowd, Timothy John. *The U.S. Market for Natural and Organic Personal Care Products.* New York: Packaged Facts, 2005.

Household and Personal Products Industry. "The International Top Thirty." http://www.happi.com/articles/2006/08/the-international-top-30.

Jones, Geoffrey. *Beauty Imagined: A History of the Global Beauty Industry.* Oxford, England: Oxford University Press, 2010.

Key Note Publications. *The Toiletries and Cosmetics Industry.* Teddington, Richmond Upon Thames, England: Author, 2010.

Packaged Facts and Netscribes. *The U.S. Market for Home Fragrance Products*. New York: Packaged Facts, 2004.

Purifoy, Jennifer. "History of Twentieth Century Fashion: Understanding the History of Cosmetics." http://www.digitalhistory.uh.edu/do_history/fashion/Cosmetics/cosmetics.html.

Richardson, Arna. "IBISWorld Industry Report 32562: Cosmetic and Beauty Products Manufacturing in the U.S." Santa Monica, Calif.: IBISWorld, 2010.

_____. "IBISWorld Industry Report 44612: Beauty, Cosmetics, and Fragrance Stores in the U.S." Santa Monica, Calif.: IBISWorld, 2010.

Snyder, Sophia. "IBISWorld Industry Report 32561: Soap and Cleaning Compound Manufacturing in the U.S." Santa Monica, Calif.: IBISWorld, 2010.

_____. "IBISWorld Industry Report 44611: Pharmacies & Drug Stores in the U.S." Santa Monica, Calif.: IBISWorld, 2010.

U.S. Bureau of Labor Statistics. *Career Guide to Industries*, 2010-2011 ed. http://www.bls.gov/oco/cg.

_____. *Occupational Outlook Handbook*, 2010-2011 ed. http://www.bls.gov/oco.

U.S. Census Bureau. North American Industry Classification System (NAICS), 2007. http://www.census.gov/cgi-bin/sssd/naics/naicsrch?chart=2007.

U.S. Department of Commerce. International Trade Administration. Office of Trade and Industry Information. Industry Trade Data and Analysis. http://ita.doc.gov/td/industry/otea/OTII/OTII-index.html.

Willett, Julie A. *The American Beauty Industry Encyclopedia*. Santa Barbara, Calif.: Greenwood Press, 2010.

Industrial Design Industry

©Dreamstime.com

INDUSTRY SNAPSHOT

General Industries: Architecture and Construction; Arts and Entertainment; Information Technology; Manufacturing; Science, Technology, Engineering, and Math; Entertainment

Career Clusters: Arts, A/V Technology, and Communications; Science, Technology, Engineering, and Math

Subcategory Industries: Commercial Art and Illustration; Product Design; Strategic Consulting

Related Industries: Advertising and Marketing Industry; Apparel and Fashion Industry; Automobiles and Personal Vehicles Industry; Computer Hardware and Peripherals Industry; Computer Software Industry; Furniture and Home Furnishings Industry; Household and Personal Products Industry; Motion Picture and Television Industry; Museums and Cultural Institutions Industry; Plastics and Rubber Manufacturing Industry; Scientific and Technical Services; Sports Equipment Industry; Textile and Fabrics Industry; Themed Entertainment Industry; Toys and Games Industry; Watches and Jewelry Industry

Annual Domestic Revenues: $59.2 billion (Access Engineering, McGraw-Hill, 2009)

Annual International Revenues: $20.8 billion (Access Engineering, McGraw-Hill, 2009)

Annual Global Revenues: $90 billion (Reina and Tulacz, Engineering News Record, 2006)

NAICS Number: 541

INDUSTRY DEFINITION

Summary

Industrial design is the professional service of creating and developing concepts and specifications that optimize the function, value, and appearance of products and systems. Industrial designers turn technological solutions into market products that delight the customer and meet end users' needs. The industrial design industry is at the interface between technology and human tastes, related equally to the arts and engineering in its focus on both the utility and efficiency of using the device or product for its intended purpose and the creativity of external appearance and expression. People in this industry exhibit creativity, flexibility, and the ability to turn ideas into pleasing and practical forms. The portfolios of industry-leading companies include projects in urban construction, manufacturing, industrial plant and project design, and often in strategic redesign of entire corporations.

History of the Industry

The idea of adding aesthetic value to functional tools has existed for several thousand years. From prehistoric times, weapons, tools, pottery, metal vessels, lamps, and furniture have displayed features that were added to make the items look better, as well as to provide functional improvements over prior versions. The artistic talents of the designer were integrated with the skills of the producer. Early patronage of the arts was mostly from royal or ruling families, including kings and religious leaders such as popes. The Renaissance in Europe brought a tradition of adding ornamental features to machinery. By the eighteenth and nineteenth centuries, the Industrial Revolution had brought mass manufacturing, replacing large numbers of artists and craftspeople with machines. Captains of industry realized that, all else being equal, the most artistic product would win in the market, and they added ornamental features to machinery to provide a distinctive look for competitive advantage. The School of Design at Lyons, France, was cited as an influence that gave French industrial products an advantage in the marketplace.

By the middle of the nineteenth century, the British government had funded several schools of art and galleries. At the same time, a school of thought arose that held that the addition of art to machines often reduced their functionality. By the beginning of the twentieth century, the British government sought to establish common standards for product design, integrating functionality with aesthetic objectives. Scandinavian and German reactions to the ornamental style of machine design drove designs toward functionality and simplicity. American approaches to design combined elements of the British and German approaches.

In the early twentieth century, the automobile, electrical appliances, and a flurry of new inventions provided opportunities for industrial designers to make these products more attractive to buyers. The Great Depression cut the price of labor and resulted in a great deal of creative genius, like that of mechanical engineer Frederick Winslow Taylor,

being applied toward improving the efficiency of products. In the 1930's and 1940's, increasing aircraft speeds and the idea of drag reduction by streamlining caught the public fancy. Products ranging from railway engines and automobiles to toasters and fountain pens exhibited streamlining. The advent of metal-plating methods and of plastics made from inexpensive fossil hydrocarbons enabled low-cost, mass-produced durable forms to make machinery look highly polished.

Raymond Fernand Loewy (1983-1986) is one of the most famous personalities in American industrial design. His contributions can be seen in cigarette packaging, refrigerators, buses, locomotives, and the livery of the Air Force One presidential aircraft. Richard Teague (1923-1991) and Charles Eames (1907-1978) and Bernice "Ray" Eames (1912-1988) are famous for their creations in the automobile industry, and Jonathan Ive (born 1967) for his in the computer industry. In Europe, Alvar Aalto (1898-1976) designed furniture, textiles, and glassware.

The need for standardization and international recognition spawned professional societies. The International Council of Societies of Industrial Design (ICSID) was formed in 1957. In 1965, the American Society of Industrial Design, the Industrial Design Education Association, and the Industrial Designers Institute merged to form the Industrial Designers Society of America. The World Intellectual Property Organization (WIPO) was created in 1967 and serves to encourage creativity by promoting the protection of intellectual property throughout the world. It is useful to note that WIPO protects the intellectual property of industrial designers because this is the part of the design that contributes to the aesthetics, not the function, of the product.

In the 1960's and beyond, electronics products made in Germany and then in Japan began to dominate the marketplace, gaining a reputation for top quality. Sony Corporation's Yasuo Kuroki (1932-2007) and Norio Ohga (born 1930) led the design efforts for cofounder Akio Morita. Soichiro Honda (1906-1991), son of a weaver and a blacksmith and rejected for military service because he was color-blind, brought his experience of bike repair, racing, education in metallurgy, and a philosophy that "engineering without personality does not have much value" to one of the world's great automobile companies, known for tasteful designs and superlative quality. Japanese automobiles, popular in the East but initially viewed as cheap alternatives to large and luxurious American cars in the United States, eventually gained a well-earned reputation as attractive, functionally refined, and mechanically reliable vehicles as fuel efficiency became important and customers recognized their value. The quality movement, which started with American industrial engineering research, was heartily adopted by the Japanese kaizen (continuous improvement) movement and led to amazing advances in product quality, combined with excellent robotics engineering.

American manufacturers, focused on aesthetics and advertising, and Europeans, focused on hand-worked exclusivity, could not match the quality of highly automated but well-run Japanese production. Tasteful Japanese designs such as those applied to the products of Sony, Nikon, Canon, Seiko, and the major Japanese automakers left no doubt about the reasons these companies became world leaders.

In the 1980's, personal computing entered the world marketplace. Apple Computer invited revolutionary industrial designers to redesign the strategy for the whole corporation, applying lessons from Japanese electronics companies that had helped with early product components. These examples showed the value of industrial designers in developing not just the exterior forms of products but also the entire strategic plan and organizational structure of the corporation. Top industrial design houses became strategic consultants in addition to creating product designs under contract. Thus, modern industrial design became integrated into product design, starting with the conceptual planning stage.

Computer-aided design (CAD) and graphic design software tools made possible virtual reality simulations of form and visual surface texture, enabling designers to build and modify realistic soft-

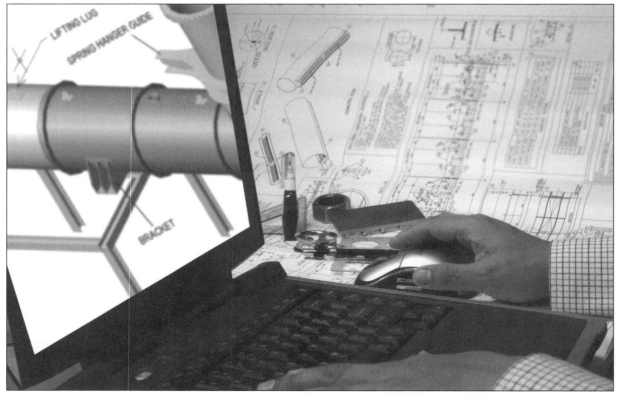

Computer-aided design and graphic design software tools enable designers to build and modify realistic software models of their creations. (©Dreamstime.com)

ware models of their creations. Color laser printers, computer graphics, and laser holography made presentations much more realistic. Computer-generated forms for numerical machines and injection molding made model building precise and repeatable. Stereo lithography, derived from a printing process in which successive layers were cured and laid over each other to form three-dimensional solid objects, revolutionized rapid prototyping. The first stereo lithograph was demonstrated in 1986. This methodology sharply reduced the time needed to make and refine models that were essentially generated from the same numerical mold as the final products. Although hand finishing and creativity based on hand-molded and sculptured models have certainly not disappeared, computer-aided methods have brought a large increase in the demand for technical skills as a part of the education of aspiring industrial designers.

The Industry Today

Industrial design has become a truly global enterprise. Since the automobile and electronics revolution in Japan and the economic boom in Asia in the 1980's and 1990's, technology-intensive manufacturing has grown in these nations. After the opening of trade with the People's Republic of China and as labor costs have risen along with the standard of living in Japan and the Asia-Pacific nations, mass manufacturing has shifted to China. The world trade agreements of the 1990's, combined with the growth of the Internet and mobile phone infrastructure around the world, have enabled the flow of products and ideas across continents. With this globalization comes the imperative of designing products using multinational teams, often working through Internet-based collaboration. It is common to find design teams working together in real time across continents and time zones, competing with other such teams to meet tight deadlines. Most successful industrial design companies in the United States and Europe participate heavily in international ventures, and many of the most successful design teams in Asia were able to expand their local ventures through collaboration with foreign enterprises.

The industrial design industry is spread out over the entire spectrum of the world marketplace. Therefore, it is not surprising that the numbers cited by various sources differ widely. The U.S. Bureau of Labor Statistics (BLS) estimated that more than 44,000 people were working as industrial or commercial designers in 2009. Of these, some 24,600 were industrial designers, working in more than 11,200 establishments. The Industrial Designers Society of America lists sixty-one schools accredited to teach industrial design. Europe has a very large base of industrial designers and schools. The People's Republic of China, Japan, South Korea, Taiwan, India, and Singapore have strong and growing presences in this field. Of the top two hundred international industrial design companies (rated by their 2007 revenue from outside their home countries), seventy-six are in the United States or Canada, fifty-seven are in Europe, forty are in Asia, and ten are in Australia or New Zealand. In the United States, more than 30 percent of industrial designers describe themselves as self-employed, working as consultants and independent designers. Many others are employed as in-house designers in large engineering corporations. In Europe, there are several large design houses, employing strong workforces of designers. The modern American school of design is thought to focus more on innovation and function, whereas the European school is associated with bringing art into industrial design.

Some of the largest customers of industrial design services have been in the Middle East. Some of these massive undertakings involved the design of entire urban neighborhoods and of industrial projects related to the petroleum and petrochemicals industry, the supply of drinking water, and wastewater and sewage treatment from the start to completion. However, Chinese industrial customers may be overtaking Middle Eastern customers as the demand for creative design in huge Chinese manufacturing enterprises grows rapidly.

University curricula in industrial design are often associated with colleges of arts and architecture rather than engineering. However, many people working as industrial designers have engineering credentials, and many people managing engineering divisions have industrial designer credentials. More than 50 percent of industrial design professionals have a bachelor's degree, 25 percent have an associate's degree, and fewer than 20 percent have some college experience but no degree. Modern industrial design education involves a strong grounding in mathematics and science, as well as

Smart phones are examples of devices subject to simplexity in design.
(©Dreamstime.com)

in art. Good problem-solving skills are expected of designers, and they must also have a good eye to predict what will be attractive to customers. Many industrial designers concentrate on a narrow area of specialization, but the people at the top of the major design houses are excellent generalists as well.

At the high school level, the student needs to study studio art, business, computer-aided drafting and design, physics, geometry, and other mathematics, at least to the precalculus level. The university curriculum for industrial design includes the history of the field, computer-aided design, marketing, materials and processes, packaging, visual communication, prototyping, and multimedia techniques. Design students exhibit their work at campus, local, national, and international competitions.

A number of trends are evident in the industrial design industry, as summarized by *Forbes* magazine. Some trends reflect the greater society and others target specific customers or employ particular design elements. One trend is designing for a cause, such as for environmental friendliness; green design must take into consideration the use of biodegradable or recyclable materials, efficient uses of energy that minimize carbon emissions during the production and lifetime of the device or system being designed, and the impact of the materials from which the item is made after its useful life has ended. For example, green lighting may use low-energy light-emitting diodes (LEDs), which consume only a fraction of the energy that incandescent lightbulbs consume.

The approach known as simplexity (a term highlighting the relationship between simplicity and complexity) entails devices that integrate many complex functions but are intuitive and approachable, meaning that users can learn to use them quickly and with minimal frustration. Handheld multifunctional, touch-sensitive communications and computing devices—such as smart phones—are examples of devices subject to simplexity in design. There is also a growing need for sophisticated home medical equipment for an aging population, devices that can accommodate or correct for physical tremors (such as shaking hands), arthritis, and declining eyesight.

Although simplexity makes a complex device seem simple, ornamentation makes a plain item appear more elaborate. Although the vogue for mechanical products with an exterior appearance that reflects a minimalist aesthetic has increased, home furnishings have trended in the opposite direction—moving toward increasing ornamentation made possible by high-quality computer graphics and printing.

Personalization and mass imperfection both seek to add individuality to mass-produced items. Personalization has the goal of allowing end users to apply a measure of their own individuality to mass-produced products such as shoes without incurring the steep cost of individually tailored designs. Personalized products give consumers a measure of freedom and an opportunity to exercise their creativity and express their individuality, and these products attract larger markets. In mass imperfection, some differences among items are deliberately introduced in an otherwise mass-produced batch in order to convey uniqueness. Such imperfections, as long as they do not affect functionality, can make the item appear handmade or custom crafted. A similar trend is the revival of artisan-crafted products, marketed as limited-edition pieces in a market flooded with mass-produced products.

Globalization—specifically, the participation of a broad variety of designers and their colleagues from around the world—has had a huge impact on industrial design. People from around the world can participate in the design, production, and distribution of a given product. For example, automobiles, despite their brand names, are impossible to identify as having been manufactured in any single nation. A General Motors (GM) automobile might have an engine designed and built in one country, an interior from another, tires from a third, and electrical equipment from a fourth; it may be assembled in a fifth. The United States—where GM is based—may be one, or none, of these participating nations. Globalization applies equally well to toy designers, who must consider family and diverse cultural values from around the world in designing their creations.

Several design trends strive to create products for specific groups of people. Pink design adapts products previously associated with male users to the tastes and needs of women. Polarization of design creates innovations to reach consumers in both the very high-priced and the very low-priced range of products rather than the middle-priced range. When designers "focus on the other 90 percent," they strive to create products that can reach the vast majority of the human population, whom are not reached by the middle-class consumer product array.

Professor Hartmut Esslinger of frog design (a leading design company with clients such as Apple Computer and Sony Electronics) classifies designers into four types. Classic designers, such as German Dieter Rams and Italian Mario Bellini, balance an appeal to the heart with an appeal to the mind. Artistic designers create products with spectacular visual appeal. Internal corporate design teams, probably best exemplified by those in major Japanese and American corporations, create products that can be identified because they have a particular look, however subtle. Strategic designers incorporate technologies as well as social and ecological needs into products

that can meet marketing goals and hence business realities.

Small Industrial Design Firms

Potential Annual Earnings Scale. In the United States, industrial designers working as employees in very small companies typically earn less than $50,000, although studio owners often are more highly compensated. In companies employing up to six hundred people, designer salaries can reach $67,000. However, in China, a starting designer may be paid the equivalent of $5,200. Salaries in Europe are comparable to those in America.

Clientele Interaction. Industrial designers must interact with clients, especially if they work for small businesses. Unlike most engineers or scientists, designers are at the mercy of subjective evaluations of their work. Small firms in particular must enter their creations in exhibitions or competitions to make themselves known to potential clients, generate new contacts, and gain new business. To win

Automotive design has been affected by globalization, one of the trends in industrial design. (©Dreamstime.com)

space at exhibitions and enter competitions, they must convince event organizers of the merit of their work. This requires excellent presentation and client interaction skills. Many small firms may depend primarily on local contacts, but others are specialized enough that they must seek business around the nation and across the world. They may win subcontracts to join international design teams working on major products. Because the primary assets in this industry are ideas and small businesses may not be able to afford teams of specialists in intellectual property agreements and other legal matters, employees must learn how to deal with clients coming from large organizations and successfully negotiate such issues.

Amenities, Atmosphere, and Physical Grounds. The workplace of a small industrial design company is likely to be a studio. This may be a loft apartment, a suite in an urban high-rise, or a small office in a commercial building or residence. Being near large potential customers and small businesses that can provide needed external services is advantageous, so the workplace is usually in the downtown area of a city or in an office park.

Typical Number of Employees. More than 50 percent of U.S. companies describing themselves as industrial design firms have revenues of less than $1 million per year and have ten or fewer employees. Another 40 percent have revenues under $10 million and have from ten to fifty employees. The national average revenue per employee in this industry is between $75,000 and $100,000.

Traditional Geographic Locations. Industrial design companies are typically located close to their largest customers because of the importance of frequent human interaction, although the increasingly global nature of design has substantially changed this tradition. For example, when Apple Computer selected the German firm frog design to help design its corporate strategy in the 1980's, one condition was that frog design relocate its headquarters from Germany to California's Silicon Valley, where it has remained. In the United States, concentrations of design firms correlate well with areas in which large corporations are headquartered and industrial manufacturing and artistic endeavor are concentrated. These include parts of California, Texas, Ohio, New York, Florida, Michigan, New Jersey, Illinois, Pennsylvania, Wisconsin,

North Carolina, Missouri, Indiana, Massachusetts, and Connecticut.

Pros of Working for a Small Industrial Design Company. It is not surprising that half of all American industrial design companies are small businesses, given the individualistic nature of designers and that the industry is idea based. One notable feature of this industry is that 74 percent of companies have been in business for more than ten years. Therefore, many of these firms offer the benefit of working with experienced teams in addition to the traditional advantages of being employed by a small business. In a small firm, an employee may work in a small team environment with familiar coworkers, gain experience in many aspects of the business (because of the need to fill multiple roles), participate to a greater extent in client interaction, and directly interact with top management. More often than not, the team is closely led by the company's top designer, which enables young employees to learn at an intensive pace. For those with immense creative drive and the willingness to take risks, the small business environment is a good fit because it affords much greater opportunity and freedom to propose one's ideas and even carry them out. Working in a small design firm often means coming into contact and working with a wide variety of people and companies because such collaboration is central to doing each project. This is an excellent experience for designers starting out in their careers because they can build a strong network that pays off richly if they decide to change employers or start their own firm. For instance, the designer in a small company may have a chance to discuss a design with a leading architect from another firm, who may have ideas for other projects and want to discuss other opportunities. The rewards of success can be substantially greater for an employee in a small design company than one in a large conglomerate.

Cons of Working for a Small Industrial Design Company. Much more than with other professions, the designer is judged by subjective rather than objective criteria. In a small business, this means that the demands can be intense. Pay scales are likely to be lower than in the larger companies, and routine financial benefits are substantially lower. Small companies cannot afford the same level of technical investment that large companies can, and therefore, the opportunity to work with new equipment and software will be less than in large companies, making it difficult to compete in projects in which expensive and specialized technology must be used to create models and prototypes. Although decisions to proceed along given directions may come swiftly, delays may result from having to send out work to shops that have equipment and skills not available in-house.

The small size of the company and direct participation by top management may mean that designers have less freedom than they might enjoy in a larger organization, unless they have the confidence and the ear of the owner, especially if the owner is an individualistic designer. Intellectual property and noncompete agreements may be more stringent than those used by a larger company, in that patent rights may be closely held by the company owner who is also likely to be part of the inventing team.

Costs

Payroll and Benefits: Pay scales in small companies are lower than in large ones. Payroll is a dominant expense, and benefit expenses are a large strain on company resources.

Supplies: Artwork and model building take many different types of materials and supplies. These constitute a substantial expense, especially since smaller companies usually have neither the storage space nor the money to maintain the large and diverse inventory that creative design demands.

External Services: Proposal preparation is a large expense for small industrial design businesses. It is crucial for small industrial design businesses to have access to many external services that can build models, try out processes and ideas, and produce high-quality graphics. Preparing presentations and advertisements may involve working with print media and video commercial production companies, which can be large expenses with no guarantee of payback.

Utilities: Typically, utility costs are not high because the primary facilities are offices. However, office leases may create a strain on the company's resources, especially in lean times.

Taxes: Taxes on small industrial design firms are primarily payroll social security taxes. One problem in design firms is that revenue, typically received after project completion, usually takes the form of lump-sum payments rather than installments, which can lead to sharp variations in income and therefore taxes unless multiyear averaging of revenue can be performed.

Other Expenses: Travel and presentation models and graphics are large expenses for small industrial design businesses.

Midsize Industrial Design Firms

Only about 5 percent of U.S. industrial design companies generate between $10 million and $100 million in annual revenue. The scarcity of these midsize companies suggests how hard it is for them to survive in this industry. Perhaps this is because such companies can neither move with the speed and flexibility of a small company nor bring to bear the immense and diverse resources of a large company. Many midsize companies are outgrowths of family-owned businesses that retained control of their intellectual properties and specialized in certain skills and types of markets. Others remain midsize because they are world-renowned specialists that have learned to succeed through collaboration with others. These firms maintain only a select team of experts and support staff as employees. Midsize industrial design companies have much in common with the industrial design department at a top research university. Facilities may include a machine room, an assembly room, a spray room, and a materials room. Metal-, plastic-, and wood-forming equipment are usually available, and a wide variety of model-making materials are also used. Designers have access to commercial design and graphics software packages. Other types of midsize companies where industrial designers work may be architectural firms or businesses producing some specialized product that employ a small in-house design team.

Potential Annual Earnings Scale. Salaries for industrial designers in midsize companies range from $40,000 to $70,000.

Clientele Interaction. Although the tasks performed by each employee are more narrowly defined at a midsize company than at a smaller company, each employee should still expect some level of client interaction. Midsize companies are likely to win contracts from very large commercial enterprises, which will insist on having in-depth interactions with the smaller company before and during the contract. Employees in the design department of midsize manufacturing companies must interact and often negotiate and debate with employees from other departments such as engineering and the production line to refine and articulate their ideas.

Amenities, Atmosphere, and Physical Grounds. Midsize industrial design establishments are usually in stand-alone buildings in business parks or large sections of high-rise buildings. They have studios, workshops for building models, computer-aided design and drafting workstations, graphics facilities, presentation/exhibit space, and conference rooms in addition to offices and cubicles. If the facility is the design department of a manufacturer, the designer potentially has access to excellent skills and equipment for making models that approach production versions.

Typical Number of Employees. Midsize industrial design companies have 250 to 1,000 employees. However, many designers working in midsize companies may be working for large engineering, manufacturing, and construction corporations. The automobile, computer, and consumer electronics industries are major employers and customers of industrial designers and consulting firms. A few midsize companies are specialized design houses in specific fields.

Traditional Geographic Locations. Midsize industrial design firms are likely to be located in major metropolitan areas such as Silicon Valley or the Los Angeles basin, Detroit, New York, Orlando, or Miami in the United States or in Berlin, Stuttgart, London, Paris, Marseilles, Tokyo, Osaka, Kobe, Shanghai, Singapore, Seoul, Taipei, Mumbai, New Delhi, Chennai, Bangalore, and Sydney.

Pros of Working for a Midsize Industrial Design Company. Midsize industrial design companies are mostly global in their business reach and work with clients who are at the top of their fields. The products that they design often have markets worth billions of dollars and are recognized by people all over the world. Because contracts come from all over the world, employees should expect some interaction with people from different cultures and a certain level of travel. Midsize companies must invest heavily in technology to be competitive, so workers can expect to work with leading-edge equipment and software. One very strong advantage of working as a designer inside a manufacturer is that one can refine one's ideas quickly and ensure that they will work in the production environment. Many companies, especially after the quality revolution of the 1990's, place their designers in close proximity to the production line for better integration and communication.

Cons of Working for a Midsize Industrial Design Company. The industrial design business at every level is extremely competitive and subject to intense pressures. Often projects will be canceled because of circumstances unrelated to the merits of the projects or the people working on them. Demand for industrial design services is correlated with consumer demand, and new design efforts often suffer first when large companies cut back.

Costs

Payroll and Benefits: Payroll and benefits are the dominant costs of a midsize industrial design business.

Supplies: Artwork and model building require numerous types of materials and supplies. Midsize companies may stock some materials and supplies and may even have an employee who takes care of the stockroom, but they have neither the storage space nor the money to maintain all materials required by designers. However, a midsize company engaged in production of goods may offer its designers access to various supplies that are on hand for other purposes or easily available.

External Services: Proposal preparation is a large expense. Midsize industrial design businesses may prefer to use their in-house resources for many services that a small or large business might outsource, such as building models, trying out processes and ideas, and producing high-quality graphics. To prepare presentations and advertisements, midsize firms are likely to work with companies that specialize in producing presentations or advertisements in various media, including print, film, and television. These types of expenses can be substantial and may never result in revenue generation.

Utilities: The cost of utilities usually is not high because the primary facilities are offices, with some workshops. Certainly, if the design division is part of a larger company engaged in manufacturing, there will be high utility costs.

Taxes: Taxes are primarily payroll social security taxes, real estate taxes, and local corporate taxes.

Other Expenses: Travel, presentation models, and presentation graphics are large expenses for all industrial design businesses. Getting new business usually involves making presentations at the corporate offices of potential customers using detailed solid models of proposed concepts presented in an attractive environment, along with informational multimedia presentations. Preparing these presentations is often done under extreme time pressure and consumes many hours of work by skilled experts.

Large Industrial Design Firms

Potential Annual Earnings Scale. In large companies, industrial designers' salaries range up to $80,000. The corporations that employ industrial designers can be large, dedicated industrial design firms but usually are large companies with a small design division that handles in-house product design. Large corporations with in-house design departments include the automakers Honda Motor Company, Ford Motor Company, and General Motors. Industrial design is central to the success of these companies' products, and designers work on concepts that form the basis of future products. Sometimes large corporations, such as consumer electronics and computer companies, hire design consultants from specialized design houses to work with their in-house employees. Large industrial design firms are much rarer but do exist.

Clientele Interaction. In large industrial design businesses, there is substantial compartmentalization. Generally, designated employees handle all interactions with clients. Designs are closely held secrets, and some companies may wish to shield designers from too much direct interaction with clients, although designers often interact with internal departments and divisions. For example, they may use market data generated by the company's research department to create their designs. Developed concepts may be displayed only to very select audiences for business or advertisement purposes or at industry exhibitions, where carefully controlled concepts are unveiled to gauge or create public and media reaction.

Amenities, Atmosphere, and Physical Grounds. Large industrial design businesses have well-established facilities and nicely appointed workplaces; however, these may be located inside heavily industrial areas or, in the case of stand-alone design firms, in downtown high-rise buildings. These businesses are able to provide environments tailored to the needs of highly creative individuals and teams, enabling them to function at their fullest potential. Although many companies and employees still favor the cubicle-maze approach to design departments, some have unusual layouts. The quality revolution of the 1990's advanced the idea of open workplaces without walls as a means of enhancing the flow of ideas. Some companies have adopted the notion of active walls to promote an exchange of ideas. Employees record their ideas and draw sketches on paper-covered walls or dry-erase boards, and the expressed ideas are discussed and recorded. Some large companies, reputedly including Hewlett-Packard, have placed their designers in a glass-walled, sound-insulated complex surrounded by the company's production lines to encourage real-time communication and relevance to the realities of production.

Many large design firms are capable of numerous design functions and seek the lucrative role of being the system integrator. Therefore, they have projects and resources in architecture, construction, engineering, business analysis, and market research in addition to traditional artistic and industrial design functions. These work environments vary substantially, but because designers often work in different departments and at client work sites, they can expect to experience many of these environments.

Typical Number of Employees. Large industrial businesses have one thousand to ten thousand employees and annual revenues from $250 million to more than $1 billion.

Traditional Geographic Locations. Large industrial design businesses have their headquarters in major metropolitan areas. However, they establish local offices near major clients, and often, the workplace that an employee commutes to may be that of a client.

Pros of Working for a Large Industrial Design Company. Young employees in the design departments of large manufacturing companies can expect intensive training in their first years, followed by the experience of working on projects that have immense significance. Large businesses specializing in industrial design are elite establishments. Employees can expect to work on projects that have global significance, but they must generally undergo fairly long periods of something similar to an apprenticeship, as part of a small team, before being allowed more freedom. However, as proposals are constantly being generated and presentations continually being made, new employees will quickly find themselves part of teams that go out to meet potential customers and hence have considerable responsibility. Experience in a large firm usually means formal training in the standards, practices, and expectations of the profession, which will help employees in later life if they choose to become independent or obtain a faculty position at a university. They may find much more opportunity to participate in the activities of professional societies and in fact to move up to positions of recognition in these societies through association with their employer's high profile. They may also find themselves working closely with world-famous designers. Large businesses have substantial in-house research operations and are able to get the best equipment and tools for their design teams. The workplace is likely to be global. Vacation time and other benefits may be much better than what a small company can offer.

Cons of Working for a Large Industrial Design Company. A large business is by nature more impersonal than a small business, and this may be especially difficult for the highly individualistic, independent, artistically sensitive, and creative people who aspire to become industrial designers. A general observation is that large companies become large by learning to be good at turning whatever they do into a commodity; they reduce everything to a standard, predictable network of operations that results in products reaching the largest number of customers with the greatest speed and efficiency at the lowest cost to the company. This is not an environment that tolerates much experimentation, radical change, or numerous different ways of doing things. Therefore, although large companies often state that they value innovation, employees often find that cost reduction takes precedence over everything else, and most ideas are rejected as being too expensive to try. A rule of thumb used in the American automobile industry in the 1980's was that if an innovation added more than $5 to the total cost per automobile of a model year, it would be rejected. Each car produced added $5 to the cost of the innovation, and

with so many cars being produced, few innovations could generate enough revenue to justify the costs.

In large businesses, young employees may expect a longer period of apprenticeship, during which they have limited freedom and authority. Although they may find themselves nominally responsible for project segments worth several million dollars, they will have several layers of management above them. Young designers are also likely to experience frustration because of the time required to get approval from multiple layers of management, especially in a subjective area such as design, where the opinions of successively higher levels of management may be based on different levels of understanding of the purpose, constraints, and philosophy of the design. What a young employee proudly considers a brilliant design and what receives the endorsement of colleagues and immediate superiors may languish for months without anyone in upper management giving an opinion or taking action, or it may be suppressed by middle managers.

Costs

Payroll and Benefits: Payroll and benefits are the dominant costs of a large industrial design business.

Supplies: Artwork and model building require various types of materials and supplies and constitute a substantial expense. The large business will spend heavily on materials and supplies and have stockrooms with substantial inventory because they assign high cost to the delay incurred if creative employees have to wait for supplies. Clients tend to expect large design houses to be able to respond very quickly, and competitors often compete on the basis of speed.

External Services: Proposal preparation is a large expense. Large industrial design businesses have substantial in-house resources and usually prepare for presentations entirely in-house. Sometimes, they bring in top-notch outside service providers to build models, test processes, or produce high-quality graphics. If media or film-television production companies become involved in production of presentations or advertisements, the expense can be substantial, and these costs may never be recovered.

Utilities: The cost of utilities usually is not high because the main facilities tend to be offices. If the company is primarily engaged in manufacturing and design is a division, utilities can be a large expense.

Taxes: Taxes are primarily payroll social security taxes. One issue is that income is likely to take the form of lump-sum payments received as projects are completed, and this can lead to sharp variations in income and therefore taxes due unless multiyear averaging can be performed.

Other Expenses: Travel and presentation models and graphics are large expenses for all industrial design businesses. Taking models across national boundaries usually is expensive because of customs duties and the cost of completing the complex paperwork and obtaining the required approvals, as well as legal expenses.

ORGANIZATIONAL STRUCTURE AND JOB ROLES

There are two types of organizations in which people can pursue careers in industrial design. The first, which accounts for the vast majority of such positions, is a company that is engaged in the design, development, and production of some product but is not primarily a design company. In these companies, the design department is a small but vital component, one among many. The organizational structure of such a company is specific to its field of business. For instance, a software company such as Microsoft may be very different in structure and job roles from companies such as General Electric or United Technologies, which offer a variety of products and services, or an automobile company, which focuses on specific model lines. Industrial designers can find rewarding careers in any of these corporations, as well as in smaller companies in many different fields.

The second type of company is one that specifically focuses on industrial design. These companies offer products and services to a wide array of corporate customers. The discussion of organizational structure and job roles that follows refers to such specialized industrial design companies and is based on the practices of some of the leading companies in this field. Such specialized design houses are increasing in number globally because design has become a worldwide, connected team activity,

and it is becoming beyond the reach of even the large manufacturers to do everything in-house.

The departmental organization of a large industrial design firm may be along the following lines of specialty: concept and research; financial, accounting, and purchasing; consumer electronics; media and entertainment; construction; communications; medical; consumer software; brand identity; Web site strategy and development; consumer products; retail; environmental; energy; business software; and computer products.

The typical career paths in the industrial design industry have been categorized by the School of Industrial Design at the Georgia Institute of Technology.

- **Design academics** obtain doctorates in design at an institution of higher learning; they work on the history, theory, trends, and future possibilities of the industry and teach others the rigorous core of knowledge in the field.
- **Design researchers** pursue social, technical, and design research. They seek to better understand, organize, and improve how industrial design is performed as well as to stay ahead of developing trends. Observing human behavior and understanding tastes is a part of design research.
- **Design educators** teach design at the college level. This role may vary substantially between design schools that are part of art and trade schools and research universities.
- **Corporate designers** work within a corporation as in-house experts designing products. Examples include people working in the design departments of automobile, electronics, media, or toy companies.
- **Consulting designers** work within consulting firms but undertake projects for client companies or government organizations.
- **Design entrepreneurs** embark on starting a business, typically a design firm.
- **Design advocates** are designers who promote design and make advocacy their primary mission. They may work closely with artists and exhibitors, industry leaders, and media personnel.
- **Social designers** are designers who dedicate themselves to solving social problems through design.

The range of services provided by designers, according to the Carnegie Mellon School of Industrial Design, includes consumer and recreational product design, medical equipment design, transportation design, information technology design, industrial/manufacturing equipment design, materials/color consulting, design research and design education, and human factors (ergonomic) design.

The following umbrella categories typical of many other industries apply to the organizational structure of industrial design companies as well:

- Business Management
- Customer Services
- Sales and Marketing
- Facilities and Security
- Technology, Research, Design, and Development
- Production and Operations
- Distribution
- Human Resources

Business Management

A design company has the usual designations of corporate officers. It usually has a president or chief executive officer and may also have a chief financial officer, a chief operating officer, a senior vice president, and vice presidents of finance and human resources. However, the firm's main business consists of creative professionals who identify new opportunities and ways of marketing new concepts and solutions. To be good at this, they must have excellent research and development and market analysis departments. Accordingly, such a company might list position titles such as the following:

- Chief Creative Officer
- Chief Development Officer
- Chief Marketing Officer
- Vice President, Global Delivery (heading program management)
- Vice President of Creative (expanding into new markets)
- Executive Creative Director (for areas such as brand innovation, global user research, digital products, user experience strategy, or software)
- General Manager

- Executive Director of Program Management
- Senior Program Manager
- Account Director
- Executive Assistant
- Corporate Counsel
- Desktop Administrator
- Front-Desk Manager
- Associate Financial Controller
- Production Director
- Software Program Management Director
- Financial Analyst

Customer Services

Fundamentally, the business of an industrial design firm is to please the company for which it is creating the design of a particular device or system. The Mercedes-Benz slogan, Only the Best, applies to the expectations of its customers as well as everything that is done by the company. The services of the customer services department can include conceptualizing long-term strategy for the customer and developing implementation plans, developing brand logos and identity, setting up Web pages, developing advertisement programs, assisting in designing products, choosing materials, planning for product safety, and developing end-user feedback that leads to product improvement. In addition, the company must have excellent points of contact for resolving problems in projects, products, and contracts. These are handled by customer service professionals or passed on to specific program and account managers.

Unique job titles that indicate the central role of customer service include the following:

- Principal Strategist
- Senior Strategist

Sales and Marketing

Sales of products from industrial design companies are usually handled as contracts following specific products. Accordingly, the title of vice president of creative shows the level at which sales and marketing are planned. The most significant long-term relationships with major corporations are set up through interactions at the very top of the company, at the chairman or mentor level. Below this are a number of client interaction positions, proposal development positions, and contract execu-

OCCUPATION PROFILE

Industrial Designer

Considerations	Qualifications
Description	Conceptualizes and develops products and systems that maximize function, appearance, and value.
Career cluster	Arts, A/V Technology, and Communications
Interests	Data; people; things
Working conditions	Work inside
Minimum education level	Bachelor's degree; master's degree
Physical exertion	Light work
Physical abilities	Unexceptional/basic fitness
Opportunities for experience	Internship
Licensure and certification	Usually not required
Employment outlook	Average growth expected
Holland interest score	AES

Note: See volume 1, "Publisher's Note," for an explanation of the Holland interest score.

tion positions. Marketing involves a considerable amount of travel to potential customer sites and conferences, along with making polished presentations and answering questions.

Facilities and Security

Apart from the usual concerns about the physical security of facilities, the major concern of design companies is the protection of intellectual property. Accordingly, several positions are filled by patent attorneys. Industrial designs qualify for intellectual property protection because of the unique, mainly aesthetic features of the design. Therefore, every new design must apply for a design patent or other mechanism of protection. This process requires a tremendous amount of paperwork and attention to detail. Likewise, major design houses must protect not only their own design ideas but also the plans, ideas, and technology prototypes given to them by their customers to develop proposals. Therefore, security of their data and models is a growing concern.

Technology, Research, Design, and Development

The core function of the design company is executed in research, design, and development. Typical tasks executed by employees in these areas include preparing sketches of ideas, making detailed drawings and illustrations, and talking with engineering, marketing, production, and sales departments and with customer organizations to evaluate design concepts for products. Employees may coordinate fabrication of models or samples and draft working drawings and specification sheets from sketches. They then evaluate the feasibility of designs, considering safety in addition to functionality and the cost of production. Once the concept is developed, it has to be presented to customers for approval or modification. The work environment is intensely competitive, as it depends on preparing proposals that win customer approval over competing proposals from other designers. One special position is that of an interaction designer, who applies a range of skills in user research, consensus building, prototyping, and balancing business requirements. This type of designer focuses on a human-centered design process, which answers real human needs in the context of everyday living.

Occupations within the technology, research, design, and development area may include the following:

- Principal Industrial Designer
- Creative Director
- Senior-Level Creative Leader
- Associate Creative Director
- Senior Visual Designer
- Visual Designer
- Senior Interaction Designer
- Technical Architect
- Associate Technology Director
- Technologist

- Program Analyst
- Mechanical Engineer
- Mechanical Designer
- Design Researcher
- Product Engineer
- Design Engineer
- Product Designer
- Product Development Engineer

Production and Operations

In companies whose focus is industrial design (as opposed to the industrial design departments of product-focused manufacturing companies in other industries), production lines are rare because the "product" is concepts, models, and demonstrations or presentation packages. Attempts to come out with shrink-wrapped software products to automate the creative process of industrial design have generally not been successful.

OCCUPATION PROFILE

Industrial Engineer

Considerations	Qualifications
Description	Designs and develops products and systems that maximize function, appearance, and value.
Career clusters	Agriculture, Food, and Natural Resources; Manufacturing; Science, Technology, Engineering, and Math; Transportation, Distribution, and Logistics
Interests	Data; things
Working conditions	Work inside
Minimum education level	Bachelor's degree; master's degree; doctoral degree
Physical exertion	Light work
Physical abilities	Unexceptional/basic fitness
Opportunities for experience	Internship; apprenticeship; military service; part-time work
Licensure and certification	Required
Employment outlook	Faster-than-average growth expected
Holland interest score	EIR

Note: See volume 1, "Publisher's Note," for an explanation of the Holland interest score.

Distribution

Like production, distribution is not mass scale but specific to each customer.

Human Resources

Finding and retaining top-notch creative talent, and people to support them in world-beating efforts, is a highly specialized task. Spotting creative talent itself takes substantial amounts of creative talent, which is not a trait typically associated with human resources departments. Recruiters in this field must also learn to deal with the large egos and insecurities, or the opposite extremes in attitudes, that are typical of many first-rate artists. In addition to dealing with the company's own employees, human resources professionals in industrial design companies may be called on to help recruit and manage the many people whom the company needs to model, sample, and test their designs. Sensitive dealings with such people call for special skills. Some job titles in this department are as follows:

- Talent Acquisition-Senior Recruiter
- Recruiter
- Human Resources Studio Partner

INDUSTRY OUTLOOK

Overview

A striking feature of modern design firms is that the leaders strive to expand out of specialty designing. They seek to become one-stop sources prepared to go into the highly lucrative and risky business of undertaking projects in totality, encompassing every aspect of the customer company if possible. Therefore, a large part of the revenue of the top firms comes not from traditional industrial design tasks but from major international projects undertaken on a turnkey basis, assuming responsibility for all aspects. The firms subcontract out the various specialized tasks, which in turn creates an immense project management and communications responsibility. Designers see creative freedom in this approach.

Americans spent nearly a trillion dollars a year on durable goods in 2004. In 2005 and 2006, the global construction boom was peaking and resulted in very large increases in business for indus-

trial designers. Strategic planners at many of the top firms already had predicted that the construction bubble would soon burst, as it did. Many large infrastructure projects were canceled after 2007. Even the petroleum-rich Middle East business economies have sharply reduced construction and consumer spending. At the end of 2010, consumer markets around the world were showing strong growth in several sectors, despite a prevailing economic downturn and economic distress in several nations that saw sharp spending booms in the prior decade.

The experience of the Great Depression shows that periods of economic downturn give birth to revolutions in creativity as it becomes harder to sell large numbers of the same product. These are followed by strong demand for innovative products that make the previous generations of consumer products obsolete. Thus, whether the economic distress of 2010 deepens or leads to recovery, there is a bright future for the creative designer in the coming decades. This future inevitably will be global, and every project in every country can conceivably be opened up to bidding from all over the world. On the other hand, every company in every country can conceivably benefit from all the resources that they can bring to bear from all around the world, and therefore, local companies with smart leadership should have a strong advantage in winning work in their own neighborhoods. This is an evolving situation, logically arising from the intensive efforts of Western leaders to force nations all over the world to open up their markets to imports from the West. In return, as communication technology advanced, nations all over the world found that they could conduct sophisticated technical and business dealings from offices within their own borders and still export services across the world. This is especially relevant to the design field.

Some major corporations reasoned that they could keep their own top technological capabilities to themselves and retain the highly lucrative business of doing the strategic planning and design integration while outsourcing tasks that were not cost-effective to perform in their home countries. This model, however, may come under increasing stress as the nations that are now doing the bulk of these tasks become more experienced in production and manufacturing. As the young people in these nations learn to succeed in the business of innovation and obtain formal credentials in industrial design, they will form local design houses that will move up the knowledge pyramid toward system integration and strategic planning. The examples of traditional family-held design houses in Europe and elsewhere that have formed alliances with local manufacturing firms to keep their local economies thriving demonstrate creative responses to such challenges. With the Internet and personal communication devices opening up the world and the mutual dependence of nations big and small through the World Trade Organization, it is unlikely that governments and political leaders will be able to regress to the age of national protectionism with closed economies and still be able to compete in the world.

The major feature of the industrial design industry in the twenty-first century is the explosive growth of the Asian sector. China's immense strength in manufacturing has translated to rising demand and opportunities for local creative design services. This is summarized by the idea that the proud Made in China label that became globally prevalent since the 1990's must change to Created in China. This drive has spawned sharp growth in the number of design schools in China; however, these are still under the control of the government and do not appear to have an open presence on the Internet outside China. The city of Shenzen, bordering Hong Kong, was designated as a United Nations Educational, Social, and Cultural Organization City of Design in 1980. By 2009, this city of 13 million people with an average age under thirty-one and more than two thousand square kilometers of creative industrial clusters had one-sixth of the total number of the people with doctorates in China, and more than six thousand design firms, employing more than 100,000 people. The city leads China in the design of light industrial products, as well as in packaging, graphics, architectural, fashion, and interior design. Surrounding nations in Asia are also experiencing growth in design services and education, driven by the growing demand and need to compete. India is transforming from a rapidly growing middle-class consumer market and outsourcing destination to becoming a creative design powerhouse, associated with several top companies and excellent engineering,

arts, and business schools. In Europe, many traditional design houses are moving to tighter integration with their production customers to keep their products competitive. This trend is likely to propagate worldwide as a counter to the Internet-spawned mass-outsourcing corporate culture of the early twenty-first century. Top design house experts point out that the greatest successes are produced by tightly knit teams of local designers and production companies. Thus it may well be that once the playing field is leveled somewhat by the new capabilities for global communications, some level of parochialism will return in the search for uniqueness.

The ability to commoditize a wide spectrum of products and services that were previously specialized or designer products is a feature of the early twenty-first century. Commercial success is predicated on the ability to flood the global market with a product much faster than any competitor can and thereby collect a large profit despite a rapidly declining profit margin per unit. Industry reports cite the extreme challenges of maintaining cohesion between teams spread out across the world, especially in tackling large and complex projects. Against this, small teams focused on excellence may come up with creative ways to generate products that use efficient manufacturing and distribution networks but win a competitive advantage by demonstrating some measure of exclusivity and thereby command high profit margins. As new schools of design traditions and philosophy from the previously ignored Eastern and African markets come up in global prominence, one may expect product design to undergo a huge change.

The revolution in materials technology predicts the advent of a wide range of innovations. This may drastically affect the size and shape of many products that have not changed substantially for decades. The familiar tube-and-wing shape of airliners is an example that may be headed for obsolescence. Robots may take over many human-powered and human-attended machines, including lawn mowers, vacuum cleaners, and even automobiles. Active materials could revolutionize even furniture. Another imminent revolution is in reducing energy use, adapting to low-power renewable resources, and cutting carbon emissions while enhancing standards of living.

Employment Advantages

The first advantage of working in the industrial design industry is that one is always engaged in creative endeavors. The second is that industrial design caters to the creative person who is good at the quantitative sciences but also has a great creative urge to do things differently. The third is that the designer gets to work on products that may have world-changing potential. Many jobs involve working with people across the world and often traveling to other countries.

Annual Earnings

On average, an American industrial design firm generates between $75,000 and $100,000 per employee per year. This is lower than the earnings per employee of major corporations in the defense, aerospace, medical, and other fields of mass production, but the environments are completely different. Given the relatively small number of employees who formally describe themselves as industrial designers, this accounts for less than 10 percent of the gross revenue of the industry. This is because industrial design firms employ many people other than industrial designers and also because firms engaged in industrial design now take on the responsibility for revenue-producing projects that extend beyond traditional industrial design.

Data from 2006 show several trends about the top one thousand firms that have international business, of which the top two hundred account for most of the revenue. The top firms earned $48.8 billion of revenue from domestic projects in their home nations, and $33.1 billion from international projects outside their home nations, for a total of $81.9 billion. They undertook diverse projects. Construction projects (such as shopping malls, urban areas, high rise buildings) accounted for 12.7 percent; projects for manufacturing companies, 2 percent; petroleum-related projects, 33.5 percent; water projects, 5.9 percent; sewer and waste treatment projects, 4.7 percent; electric power projects, 8.3 percent; and telecommunications, 0.6 percent. Formal industrial design projects were only 8 percent of the total. The companies that undertook these international projects were located in Canada, with 8.1 percent of the total revenue; United States, with 11.7 percent; Latin America, 4.3 percent, Caribbean islands, 6 per-

cent; Europe, 27.2 percent; Asia and Australia together, 20.4 percent; and Africa, 8.1 percent. A very important caution is that Western reports include only a few firms from the People's Republic of China. The Chinese domestic market must be huge, but numbers are not easily accessible.

RELATED RESOURCES FOR FURTHER RESEARCH

AMERICAN INSTITUTE OF GRAPHIC ARTS
164 5th Ave.
New York, NY 10010
Tel: (212) 807-1990
Fax: (212) 807-1799
http://www.aiga.org

THE DESIGN SOCIETY
University of Strathclyde
Design, Manufacture & Engineering
Management (DMEM)
75 Montrose St.
Glasgow G1 1XJ
United Kingdom
Tel: 44-141-548-3134
Fax: 44-141-552-0557
http://www.designsociety.org

INDUSTRIAL DESIGNERS SOCIETY OF AMERICA
45195 Business Ct., Suite 250
Dulles, VA 20166-6717
Tel: (703) 707-6000
Fax: (703) 787-8501
http://www.idsa.org

INTERNATIONAL COUNCIL OF SOCIETIES OF INDUSTRIAL DESIGN
455 St-Antoine Ouest, Suite SS10
Montreal, QC H2Z 1J1
Canada
Tel: (514) 448-4949
Fax: (514) 448-4948
http://www.icsid.org

ABOUT THE AUTHOR

Narayanan M. Komerath is a professor in the Daniel Guggenheim School of Aerospace Engineering at Georgia Institute of Technology. He heads the experimental aerodynamics and concepts group and teaches, among other courses, conceptual design of flight vehicles as a means of introducing aerospace engineering students to their field.

FURTHER READING

Esslinger, Hartmut. *A Fine Line: How Design Strategies Are Shaping the Future of Business.* San Francisco: Jossey-Bass, 2009.

Hiesinger, Kathryn B., and George H. Marcus. *Landmarks of Twentieth-Century Design: An Illustrated Handbook.* New York: Abbeville Press, 1993.

Kawasaki, Guy. *The Art of the Start: The Time-Tested, Battle-Hardened Guide for Anyone Starting Anything.* New York: Portfolio, 2004.

Meikle, Jeffrey L. *Twentieth Century Limited: Industrial Design in America, 1925-1939.* 2d ed. Philadelphia: Temple University Press, 2001.

Ōmae, Ken'ichi. *The Mind of the Strategist: The Art of Japanese Business.* 1983. Reprint. New York: McGraw-Hill, 1992.

Qu, Min, and Ran Li. "Industrial Design: Impetus from 'Made-in-China' to 'Created-in-China.'" In *Proceedings: 2009 International Symposium on Computational Intelligence and Design—Changsha, China, 12-14 December 2009*, by IEEE Computer Society, et al. Los Alamitos, Calif.: IEEE Computer Society, 2009.

Read, Herbert. *Art and Industry: The Principles of Industrial Design.* 1954. Reprint. London: Faber, 1964.

Reina, Peter, and Gary J. Tulacz. "The Top Two Hundred International Design Firms." *Engineering News-Record* 257, no. 4 (2006): 32-35.

U.S. Bureau of Labor Statistics. *Career Guide to Industries*, 2010-2011 ed. http://www.bls.gov/oco/cg.

U.S. Census Bureau. North American Industry Classification System (NAICS), 2007. http://www.census.gov/cgi-bin/sssd/naics/naicsrch?chart=2007.

U.S. Department of Commerce. International Trade Administration. Office of Trade and Industry Information. Industry Trade Data and Analysis. http://ita.doc.gov/td/industry/otea/OTII/OTII-index.html.

Welsbacher, Anne. *Earth-Friendly Design.* Minneapolis: Lerner, 2009.

Insurance Industry

©Dreamstime.com

INDUSTRY SNAPSHOT

General Industry: Finance
Career Cluster: Finance
Subcategory Industries: Agencies, Brokerages, and Other Insurance Related Activities; Claims Adjusting; Direct Life, Health, and Medical Insurance Carriers; Direct Property and Casualty Insurance Carriers; Direct Title Insurance Carriers; Insurance Carriers; Other Direct Insurance Carriers; Reinsurance Carriers; Third Party Administration of Insurance and Pension Funds
Related Industries: Banking Industry; Business Services; Medicine and Health Care Industry; Retail Trade and Service Industry
Annual Domestic Premiums: $1.24 trillion USD (Swiss Re, 2008)
Annual International Premiums: $3.03 trillion USD (Swiss Re, 2008)
Annual Global Premiums: $4.27 trillion USD (Swiss Re, 2008)
NAICS Number: 524

INDUSTRY DEFINITION

Summary

The business of insurance affects nearly every transaction that can be quantified in the world, as it offers protection to individuals and businesses from potential financial risks through automobile, casualty, disability, health, home, liability, life, and property insurance. In exchange for a sum of money—called the premium—policyholders receive the promise of reimbursement from insurers for small and large losses due to a variety of hazards, including car accidents, property theft, fire damage, medical ailments, and loss of income resulting from disability or death. The insurance industry is regulated in most cases by state governments rather than the federal government. The insurance industry offers full- and part-time employment in several occupations at different levels.

History of the Industry

Although the concept of risk management can be traced as far back as the third millennium B.C.E. among Chinese merchant traders attempting to encourage the safe arrival of goods, the practice of insuring officially began in the United States in the seventeenth century. Great Britain and its American col-

971

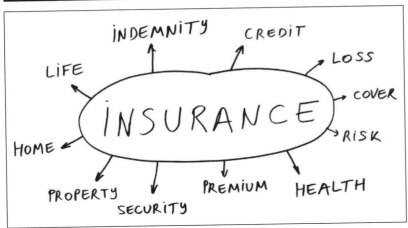

Insurance offers protection to individuals and businesses from potential financial risks through automobile, casualty, disability, health, home, liability, life, and property insurance. (©Alain Lacroix/Dreamstime.com)

onies were heavily involved in commercial trade of spices, tea, sugar, dyes, fabrics, and other goods. Given the treacherous seas, Britain developed a system of insuring the risks of loss of, or damage to, cargoes through Lloyd's of London.

In 1688, Edward Lloyd opened a coffee shop that attracted many shipowners and merchants. These traders began to transact business in the shop, so Lloyd also began offering marine insurance. By the end of the eighteenth century, Lloyd's had become the first modern-day insurance company. Today, Lloyd's is still a leader in the international insurance market, providing specialist services to businesses in more than two hundred countries and territories.

Another branch of the insurance industry also developed in Great Britain and America during the same period. Fire represented a growing danger in urban areas, where there was no running water and many structures were constructed of wood. In particular, the Great Fire of London, which devastated more than thirteen thousand houses in 1666, prompted a more serious interest in protecting buildings against this risk. Mutual fire protection services, in which residents and businesses pledged to help fight local fires, began to form.

In 1752, Benjamin Franklin and a group of prominent citizens started the Philadelphia Contributionship for the Insurance of Houses from Loss by Fire in South Carolina, which became known as the first property insurance company in the American Colonies. Franklin had personal experience with fire and wanted to ensure protection for others. The contributionship now includes five subsidiaries that still specialize in property insurance but cover much more than the loss of homes by fire. Franklin also organized the first life insurance company—the Presbyterian Ministers' Fund—in 1759.

From the eighteenth century forward, insurance companies became common business ventures in America. The industry diversified greatly in the United States during the nineteenth and twentieth centuries. For example, lenders required farmers to take out crop insurance when securing mortgages on their property to obtain crop loans. Additionally, the invention of the automobile led to the need for automobile insurance.

In many cases, purchasing insurance is not voluntary. Mortgage lenders require homeowners to insure their property as a condition of lending them money. Similarly, states require drivers to purchase automobile insurance. On the other hand, life insurance is usually voluntary.

Many societal factors have contributed to the evolution of the insurance industry, including the passage of workers compensation laws and the advent of the Industrial Revolution. Quite possibly the biggest growth area in the insurance industry has been in medical services and health insurance. Technology has prompted many developments in medicine, and the population has continued to grow. Both situations have increased the cost of health care, creating the need for a middleman to manage its utilization. Further, an aging population has sprouted new needs, such as long-term care insurance. Health insurance will continue to change as a result of the Patient Protection and Affordable Care Act (PPACA) of 2010 and the Health Care and Education Reconciliation Act of 2010.

Besides new coverage options, the standard policy language across most of the segments of the insurance industry has also changed through the years. Insurance coverage for some kinds of tangible losses is generally clear, but gray areas and exclusions remain that are decided on a case-by-case basis. So as long as there are transactions between members of society, there will always be insurance to minimize an individual's or a business's risk.

The Industry Today

There are a great many insurance companies in the United States today, and the insurance industry has grown to be one of the top five industry sectors in the twenty-first century. Some insurance companies have strong national presences, while others are regional businesses. Some offer all types of insurance, while others specialize. The industry is still mostly regulated at the state level, and even the PPACA designates the states as the primary regulators of the health insurance exchanges.

For the most part, the concept of insuring has not changed. An insurer agrees to shoulder a risk on behalf of an individual or business (the insured) for a set fee (a premium). Through the underwriting process, the insurer evaluates the circumstances surrounding the measurable risk and produces a policy, or contract, stating the risks it will insure against and how much it will guarantee as a reimbursement to the insured if the risk occurs. Policies also include lists of exclusions, or things that are not insured against, and these policies can be quite complex.

Another complicated aspect of insurance is calculating the premium. Insurers aim to profit overall, so total premiums received from all insured clients must be greater than the approved claims paid

Inputs Consumed by the Insurance Industry

Input	Value
Energy	$0.6 billion
Materials	$7.7 billion
Purchased services	$224.8 billion
Total	$233.1 billion

Source: U.S. Bureau of Economic Analysis. Data are for 2008.

out to those clients in a given year. Not all events are equally likely, so accurately determining the probability of a given event's occurrence is difficult.

The insurance industry includes insurance carriers, agencies, and brokerages, which together account for the majority of industry jobs. Insurance carriers are mainly the large companies that issue policies and assume their risks, often employing 250 workers or more. Agencies and brokerages sell individual polices on behalf of carriers and often employ fewer than 20 workers. Many agencies and brokerages are independent and sell a variety of policies, rather than working for only one carrier. Insurance companies come in all sizes, ranging from a handful of employees to thousands of workers. Many other establishments within the industry provide special insurance-related services, such as claims adjustment and processing. Insurance is a worldwide industry, and employment in the United States is not limited by geography.

The most common segments of the industry are property and casualty insurance (for automobiles, homes, and businesses), health insurance, and life insurance. Until the 1950's, each U.S. company was restricted to selling only one type of insurance. Today, firms can underwrite several insurance types each.

Beyond the main areas of coverage, insurance protection can be purchased for just about any measurable risk. Insurance companies generally fall into two catego-

The Insurance Industry's Contribution to the U.S. Economy

Value Added	Amount
Gross domestic product	$464.0 billion
Gross domestic product	3.2%
Persons employed	2.322 million
Total employee compensation	$192.9 billion

Source: U.S. Bureau of Economic Analysis. Data are for 2008.

ries—life insurance or nonlife insurance. Life insurers sell life insurance, annuities, and pension products, while nonlife companies sell all other types of coverage.

Disability insurance provides financial assistance to individuals when they are unable to work because of a disabling illness or injury. Similarly, workers' compensation insurance—purchased by employers—replaces all or part of emloyees' lost wages and accompanying medical expenses after job-related injuries. For businesses, disability overhead insurance reimburses for the overhead expenses experienced by businesses when their owners are unable to work.

Casualty insurance protects both people and property against unforeseen incidents, such as fraud and burglary. On properties, people can purchase supplemental protection policies tied to certain hazards, such as fire, flood, or earthquake. Liability insurance is another broad area. Individuals can purchase insurance to cover another party's losses and protect themselves against legal claims. Liability insurance is included in auto and property insurance policies, but there are other types of liability insurance.

Some other optional and specific types of coverage are pet and travel insurance. Travel insurance has been around since the 1950's, but it grew in popularity after the terrorist attacks of September 11, 2001. More than 30 percent of Americans used travel insurance in 2009. Pet insurance take-up rates, however, continue to be less than 1 percent.

A more unusual type of coverage, for example, is terrorism insurance, which also grew after September 11, 2001. Terrorism insurance was purchased by approximately 60 percent of U.S. businesses in 2005. Again, if a risk can be quantified and measured, it can be insured against.

Many insurance companies have expanded their traditional products and now offer services in partnership with financial firms, such as banks. A number of companies sell securities, mutual funds, and various retirement plans. This growth in services has contributed to industry and job growth. In fact, distinctions among the banking, investment, and insurance industries have diminished. Most major insurance firms refer to themselves as financial groups and offer a wide range of services to customers.

Reinsurance, the practice of sharing risks with other insurers, also has a large presence in today's industry. In exchange for a share of premiums, insurers agree to transfer portions of their risk portfolios to other parties, lowering the likelihood that the insurers will have to pay large claims. A party that diversifies its insurance portfolio is referred to

A car in flood waters. Casualty insurance protects both people and property against unforeseen accidents. (©Dreamstime.com)

Some insurance companies, such as Progressive, are offering pet injury coverage as part of auto collision coverage. However, this Jack Russell remains an authorized driver. (©Dreamstime.com)

as a ceding party, while a party accepting a potential obligation is a reinsurer.

Besides developments in society leading to greater coverage niches and industry opportunities, several outside factors have changed the modern-day insurance market. For example, technology has had both negative and positive effects on the insurance industry. Customers can use Web browsers to access account and billing information, submit claims, view insurance quotes, and purchase policies. Communication among sales agents, adjusters, and insurance carriers has also improved through the Internet. These functions may reduce paperwork and allow companies to keep better track of their customers, thus increasing productivity and decreasing costs. Claims adjusters may no longer need to visit the site of their customer's damage; instead, they can rely on satellite imagery to evaluate claims.

At the same time, the availability of information and services on the Internet has adversely affected some insurance occupations, such as insurance sales agents, who may be less necessary to businesses that can make sales online. Insurance offerings for property, casualty, and automobiles are relatively straightforward, and online resources allow customers to compare and purchase insurance products on their own. They thus eliminate the need to meet face-to-face with a live agent, although some customers still prefer to do so. Further, software upgrades have automated some jobs, such as that of an underwriter. The ability to compare rates online and identify the cheapest rate has also increased competition within the industry.

Jobs in the insurance industry range from agents and brokers to appraisers to underwriters to claims adjusters to actuaries, again working across several insurance coverage types. In addition to these industry-specific roles, there are administrative and executive opportunities in the industry. Overall job growth within the industry has been slowed by industry consolidation, corporate downsizing, new technology, and increasing direct mail, telephone, and Internet sales. In particular, the recession of 2007-2009 caused declining revenues, investment losses, and credit rating downgrades, as it did in many other industries.

In 2008, the insurance industry employed nearly 2.3 million wage and salary workers, mostly within insurance carriers. As of January, 2010, insurance employment was down to 2.2 million. However, the insurance industry is expected to stabilize and rebuild its capital. Demand for insurance will continue to increase, especially as the population keeps growing and aging, stimulating demand for all types of insurance and increasing claims.

INDUSTRY MARKET SEGMENTS

The mainstays of the insurance industry are property and casualty insurance, health insurance, and life insurance. Many companies sell several types of insurance coverage and may even fall into all three of these categories. To sell any insurance type, companies employ brokers or agents, or they work with independent contractors. Establishments range in size. Although the majority of insurance-related home and regional offices are located near large, urban cities, companies can be found all over the country and, agents and brokers spend much of their time working outside the office, meeting with customers or communicating via the Internet and telephone, so travel time varies depending on a person's role in the insurance industry. In addition to a state insurance license needed to work in the industry, some other special licenses may be required. Most workers specialize in one type of insurance, although there are multiline agents as well.

Property and Casualty Insurance

Property and casualty insurers offer protection against loss or damage to any property in the case of unforeseen occurrences, such as fire, theft, accident, or natural disaster. Many insurance products fall within the property branch of this segment, as individuals and businesses face a variety of catastrophic risks on a daily basis. The basic physical items protected under this umbrella are houses, cars, boats, airplanes, commercial buildings, and personal possessions as small as jewelry. However, the scope of coverage can be complex. Casualty and liability insurance protects policyholders from legal or financial responsibility for directly or indirectly causing loss or damage to other people, businesses, or their property. Legal liability falls under the casualty branch. Beyond these products, some insurers have begun offering financial planning products and protection.

Potential Annual Earnings Scale. On average, nonsupervisory workers in the property and casualty insurance sector earned $52,300 as of December, 2009. However, insurers are found in every part of the country—including small cities—so geography plays a role in earnings potential, as does business size and market presence. According to the U.S. Bureau of Labor Statistics (BLS), in 2009, insurance underwriters working in the direct insurance field, excluding life, health, and medical insurance, earned an average of $63,020. Claims adjusters, examiners, and investigators earned an average of $59,130. Financial managers earned an average of $122,300.

Clientele Interaction. Property and casualty insurance is a broad category, and an insurer may work with people or with businesses. Individuals usually deal with specific insurance agents or adjusters one-on-one, while complex business transactions may require a team of representatives from an insurer to meet with a team of representatives from a potential or existing insured. In general, insurance occupations are divided between those that have little or no interaction with clients and those that spend much of their workdays interacting with clients.

Amenities, Atmosphere, and Physical Grounds. Insurance companies are located in commercial offices. Small companies or branches may occupy offices within larger buildings, while large companies and main headquarters may occupy entire buildings. Agents and brokers provide minor amenities for clients, such as coffee or welcoming decorations, since they conduct sales in their offices. Carriers are likely to have more utilitarian facilities, and any amenities provided will be for the benefit of the staff rather than customers.

Typical Number of Employees. As of August, 2008, there were approximately 489,200 direct property and casualty insurers in the United States. A person can work independently as an insurance agent or can work in a company with thousands of employees, such as State Farm Insurance or Farmers Insurance Group.

Traditional Geographic Locations. Insurance companies exist nationwide. Headquarters of large companies are usually located in major cities, while branches and smaller companies are located in regional cities throughout the country. Some cities, such as Hartford, Connecticut, and New York City, are known as major centers of the insurance industry, where many headquarters are located. Offices also exist in rural areas, especially those that serve the insurance needs of agricultural businesses and workers.

Pros of Working in Property and Casualty Insurance. Most products in the property and casualty insurance category, such as auto insurance, are mandatory under state law. Thus, an agent need not convince a person to buy insurance; potential clients only need to be convinced to purchase their insurance through the agent. In addition, property and casualty insurers sell many different products, providing their employees with some variety in their jobs.

Claims adjusters, appraisers, and examiners are especially important in the property and casualty insurance segment. Persons interested in assessing damages on behalf of insurance companies may wish to specialize in such an occupation within this segment. Auto damage appraisers need not have college educations, but they need some formal technical training, such as that provided by vocational colleges. Some insurance companies have expanded their businesses by opening their own repair facilities, making appraisals easier. Because of advances in technology, too, adjusters can sometimes rely on satellite imagery to view the site of a customer's damage, decreasing the need for travel on the job.

Cons of Working in Property and Casualty Insurance. The variety of insurance products and exclusions within property and casualty policies can make insurance agents' jobs more complex. Unless an employer focuses solely on one type of insurance, employees may need to know about and understand several different types of policies. Additionally, laws and regulations governing this insurance segment vary by state, so employees serving clients in multiple states need to keep track of the differences among the states.

Insurance always deals with loss, but in this segment the loss can sometimes be devastating because of the personal connections between people and their property. Customers making claims on their insurance policies are typically emotional and can be dissatisfied with the results of their claims. Policies are generally complicated and incorporate many exclusions. Employees must break the bad news to clients when their claims are denied.

Another pitfall of working in property and casualty insurance is the unpredictability of natural disasters. Losses from catastrophic events can surge in particularly bad years, resulting in decreases in capital for most property and casualty insurers. Continued growth in the use of the Internet may affect property and casualty workers the most, since premiums for car insurance are the highest, and trends show that people are increasingly relying on the Internet to obtain the best prices.

Costs

Payroll and Benefits: Insurance companies may pay hourly wages or salaries, depending on the position. Sales employees may work on commission. Benefits are generally offered by large companies and include health insurance, sick leave, vacation, and retirement plans. Smaller companies may or may not offer such benefits. According to 2006 data, total annual payroll for all U.S. life insurance carriers was $34.33 billion.

Supplies: Insurance companies require standard office supplies and equipment, including computer hardware and software, copiers, telephones, fax machines, printers, and consumables. Field workers need cell phones or other mobile communication devices.

External Services: Insurance carriers may contract independent brokers, as well as payroll and pension services. They may also contract lobbyists, public relations firms, technical support, maintenance and cleaning services, landscaping and snow removal, and security as necessary.

Utilities: Insurance companies pay for general utilities, such as water, garbage, electricity, gas or oil, telephone, and Internet access.

Taxes: Insurance companies are required to pay local, state, and federal income taxes based on the net premiums they receive, as well as property taxes on their physical buildings.

Health Insurance

Health insurance covers the costs of medical care, as well as loss of income due to illness or in-

Insurance claim folders line the wall at this office. (©Darryl Brooks/Dreamstime.com)

jury. Dental care and long-term disability also fall under the umbrella of health insurance. Health insurance coverage varies from the most basic (covering only catastrophic events, or what used to be called "major medical") to the most comprehensive (covering preventive, inpatient, and outpatient care). The amount of coverage determines a person's premium, deductible, and coinsurance. Under the PPACA and its companion legislation, the Health Care and Education Reconciliation Act of 2010, health insurance will be required of most Americans beginning in 2014. Health insurance is offered through the private and public sectors and by both for-profit and nonprofit private entities.

Potential Annual Earnings Scale. A health insurer in a nonsupervisory position earned an average of $49,600 per year as of December, 2009. The BLS does not provide separate statistics for the health insurance segment. However, within the general category of insurance carriers that includes health insurance carriers, the average annual salary of an insurance underwriter in 2009 was $64,440. Claims adjusters, examiners, and investigators earned an average of $57,890 per year, and financial managers earned an average of $123,970 per year.

Clientele Interaction. In the health insurance business, a worker may deal with an individual purchasing insurance or a business purchasing coverage for its workforce. Many insurers specialize in either group policies or individual policies, in both the private and public sector. As the PPACA is implemented, the business of providing health insurance is bound to change. The act aims to make insurance more affordable and easier to purchase for both individuals and businesses.

Amenities, Atmosphere, and Physical Grounds. Insurance companies are located in commercial offices. Small companies or branches may occupy offices within larger buildings, while large companies and main headquarters may occupy entire buildings. Agents and brokers provide minor amenities for clients, such as coffee or welcoming decorations, since they conduct sales in their offices. Carriers are likely to have more utilitarian facilities, and any amenities provided will be for the benefit of the staff rather than customers.

Typical Number of Employees. As of 2008, there were 449,000 direct health and medical insurance carriers in the United States. A person can work independently as an insurance agent or can work in a company with thousands of other employees, such as Cigna or UnitedHealth Group.

Traditional Geographic Locations. Insurance companies exist nationwide. Headquarters of large companies are usually located in major cities, while branches and smaller companies are located in regional cities throughout the country. Some cities, such as Hartford, Connecticut, and New York City, are known as major centers of the insurance industry, and many headquarters are located there. Offices also exist in rural areas, especially those that serve the insurance needs of agricultural businesses and workers.

Lack of health insurance is more prevalent in poorer communities, including both rural areas and impoverished communities within major cities. As the PPACA is phased in, there may be greater demand for qualified health insurance agents in those locations. Also, while some large providers are national, others, such as Kaiser Permanente, are concentrated in specific geographic locations.

Pros of Working in Health Insurance. Growth is probably the biggest advantage in the health insurance segment. The PPACA will increase the market for health insurance by roughly 30 million people, opening a number of new opportunities for insurance agencies. The law's nationwide mandate to purchase health insurance will also increase sales. Industry reports indicate that approximately 5 percent of health insurers plan to increase the number of full-time employees on their payrolls by more than 20 percent.

Increasing life expectancy has had a positive impact on health insurance and will continue to do so in the future. This trend creates a greater need for health and long-term care insurance. Coupled with new discoveries and developments in medical care, the health insurance segment remains very dynamic.

Another pro is the niche found in the health insurance segment. As in the property and casualty insurance segment, claims examiners play an important and unique role, offering a specialty in the field. These workers review claims to see whether costs are reasonable based on their corresponding services and diagnoses. A second specialty is in the actuary career path. Actuaries help companies develop health and long-term-care insurance policies by predicting the likelihood of occurrence of heart disease, diabetes, stroke, cancer, and other chronic ailments among particular groups of people, such as those living in a certain area or sharing a family history of illness. Actuarial work can be beneficial to both consumers and companies because the ability accurately to predict the probability of a particular health event among a certain subgroup ensures that premiums are assessed fairly based on the risk to the organization.

Cons of Working in Health Insurance. The PPACA poses a number of challenges for the health insurance industry. Health insurance will become more regulated as the law is phased in. In addition to the individual insurance mandate and the mandate for companies to provide insurance, the law restricts the behavior of health insurance companies. Companies will no longer be allowed to deny coverage or charge higher fees because of preexisting medical conditions, and they will be required to offer particular levels of coverage if they wish to offer plans to individuals through insurance exchanges. All health plans will be required to cover preventive care. Although these changes are being phased in over a ten-year period, the industry will look very different at the end of the process than it did before the reforms were passed. Thus, working in the health insurance segment may become more complicated, especially in the short term.

Also, because medical care is always changing, coverage issues arise easily. Health insurance policies differ tremendously, and it is difficult for customers to read the fine print. It may be difficult even for insurance agents to keep up with all the changes.

Costs

Payroll and Benefits: Insurance companies may pay hourly wages or salaries, depending on the position. Sales employees may work on commission. Benefits are generally offered by large companies and include health insurance, sick leave, vacation, and retirement plans. Smaller companies may or may not offer such benefits. In 2006, health insurers paid a total of $27.09 billion in combined payroll.

Supplies: Insurance companies require standard office supplies and equipment, including computer hardware and software, copiers, telephones, fax machines, printers, and consumables. Field workers need cell phones or other mobile communication devices.

External Services: Insurance carriers may contract independent brokers, as well as payroll and pension services. They may also contract lobbyists, public relations firms, technical support, maintenance and cleaning services, landscaping and snow removal, and security as necessary.

Utilities: Insurance companies pay for general utilities, such as water, garbage, electricity, gas or oil, telephone, and Internet access.

Taxes: Insurance companies are required to pay local, state, and federal income taxes based on the net premiums they receive, as well as property taxes on their physical buildings. Beginning in 2018, an excise tax will be levied on all health insurance policies that cost more than a set amount (beginning at $23,500 for a family policy) that will increase annually with inflation.

Life Insurance

Life insurance protects against uncertainties in life, primarily death. Coverage provides money to beneficiaries, such as spouses and dependent children, upon the insured person's death, in order to cover the costs of a funeral, debts, and future living expenses. An insurer's liability is usually limited in cases of suicide and war. Generally speaking, the insured purchases either term insurance (coverage during a specified period) or whole life insurance (coverage lasting as long as premiums are paid, also known as ordinary or permanent insurance). Overall, while health and property or casualty insurance are seen as necessities, life insurance is generally seen as optional. Many employers offer some life insurance as part of their benefits packages. People typically accept this benefit as their only source of life insurance. However, some purchase additional coverage, either by augmenting their employer-sponsored benefits or by purchasing additional policies outside of those benefits. Those who are not offered coverage through a job often seek coverage for themselves and their families, while others have no life insurance at all. Overall, life insurance company employees need to be more sales-oriented and persuasive than employees in other segments.

Potential Annual Earnings Scale. Dependent on the location and size of the company, the average annual income for a life insurer was $52,000 as of December, 2009. The BLS does not provide separate statistics for the life insurance segment. However, within the general category of insurance carriers that includes life insurance carriers, the average annual salary of an insurance underwriter in 2009 was $64,440. Claims adjusters, examiners, and investigators earned an average of $57,890 per year, and financial managers earned an average of $123,970 per year.

Clientele Interaction. As with health insurance, a client may be a business purchasing a group policy for its workers, or it may be an individual seeking a life insurance policy.

Amenities, Atmosphere, and Physical Grounds. Insurance companies are located in commercial offices. Small companies or branches may occupy offices within larger buildings, while large companies and main headquarters may occupy entire buildings. Agents and brokers provide minor amenities for clients, such as coffee or welcoming decorations, since they conduct sales in their offices. Carriers are likely to have more utilitarian facilities, and any amenities provided will be for the benefit of the staff rather than customers. Traditionally, life insurance was sold door-to-door, but as with the entire insurance industry, much of the business is now conducted via the telephone and the Internet.

Typical Number of Employees. As of 2008, there were 804,000 direct life and health insurance carriers in the United States. A person may be employed independently as a life insurance agent or may work among thousands of other employees at large companies, such as Nationwide Mutual Insurance.

Traditional Geographic Locations. Insurance companies exist nationwide. Headquarters of large companies are usually located in major cities, while branches and smaller companies are located in regional cities throughout the country. Some cities, such as Hartford, Connecticut, and New York City, are known as major centers of the insurance industry, and many headquarters are located there. Offices also exist in rural areas, especially those that serve the insurance needs of agricultural businesses and workers.

Pros of Working in Life Insurance. The life insurance segment is a little more straightforward than the other segments of the insurance industry. While there is some variability among policies, they tend not to be too complex. Additionally, some career opportunities exist only in this segment. For example, life insurance actuaries help companies develop annuity and life insurance policies for individuals by estimating how long someone is expected to live. Insurance agents and claims examiners also have some special duties. For example, agents may help set up physical examinations to screen potential customers for policies, and examiners review causes of death and review qualifications within applications. Claims examiners need to investigate the details of insured persons' deaths.

Cons of Working in Life Insurance. As with the other segments, customers make claims while dealing with loss—in this case, the death of a loved one. Beneficiaries often first see the relevant policies after the holders are deceased, which can cause some confusion. In some cases, there may be conflict among family members about who the beneficiary of a policy is or should be. When insured persons die of causes not covered by their policies, such as suicide, employees must tell their beneficiaries that they cannot receive their benefits.

Life insurance is seen as more of a luxury than a need by many people. In contrast to automobile or homeowner's insurance, life insurance may be difficult to sell. While it has proven to be advantageous to those left behind to cover medical bills or funeral costs, people still do not readily seek out life insurance. Millions of Americans lack life insurance. Few even wish to discuss the matter, making an agent's job somewhat difficult.

Costs

Payroll and Benefits: Insurance companies may pay hourly wages or salaries, depending on the position. Sales employees may work on commission. Benefits are generally offered by large companies and include health insurance, sick leave, vacation, and retirement plans. Smaller companies may or may not offer such benefits. Payrolls of life insurance companies totaled $26.34 billion in 2006.

Supplies: Life insurance offices require computers, printers, copy machines, fax machines, and other general office supplies. Field workers need cell phones or other mobile communication devices.

External Services: Insurance carriers may contract independent brokers, as well as payroll and pension services. They may also contract lobbyists, public relations firms, technical support, maintenance and cleaning services, landscaping and snow removal, and security as necessary.

Utilities: Insurance firms with physical offices pay typical utilities, such as water, garbage, gas or oil, electricity, telephone, and Internet access.

Taxes: Life insurance companies pay local, state, and federal taxes on their net premiums and property taxes on their offices.

ORGANIZATIONAL STRUCTURE AND JOB ROLES

In 2008, the insurance industry employed 2.3 million wage and salary workers, up 2.9 percent from 2007. The jobs available in the insurance industry are similar across all types of insurance (property and casualty, health, and life). However, the knowledge, training, and functions needed for the varying roles may differ.

Some insurance workers work with only one type of insurance, while others work with multiple insurance products. Some 61 percent of industry jobs are within insurance carriers, while 39 percent are within insurance agencies and brokerages. Larger organizations often do business in more than one insurance segment, and they offer a wide range of position types, including office and administrative, sales, and management and executive-level jobs. Other companies provide insurance-related services, such as claims processing. Many individuals work independently as agents in the industry.

The most common jobs in the insurance industry, such as insurance agent positions, have no specific academic requirements, although state licensure is necessary. When seeking higher-level sales or management positions, a college degree or background in business or sales can be helpful. Local insurance offices and banks in rural areas are the best starting points for people interested in working in the insurance industry. Unlike other fields, there is no set path for advancement. Instead, workers control their own advancement, and many companies expect that their workers will seek further training on their own.

The following umbrella categories apply to the organizational structure of businesses within the insurance industry:

- Office and Administrative Support
- Management, Business, and Financial Operations
- Sales
- Medical, Legal, and Actuarial Staff
- Information Technology
- Human Resources

Office and Administrative Support

Office and administrative support roles account for 42.2 percent of jobs in the insurance industry. These personnel help make the overall business of insurance run smoothly. For the most part, they work traditional forty-hour workweeks, completing routine clerical functions, such as filing, and providing information to customers via telephone or e-mail. Some jobs allow more flexibility, such as temporary employment or part-time, evening, or weekend shifts.

Individuals who work in office and administrative roles possess at least a high school diploma and come from many professional backgrounds. Some of them have two-year postsecondary business degrees. On-the-job training to learn the mechanics of the insurance industry is important to continued success. Skill in communications, math, business, computer use, typing, and customer service are helpful. Duties can vary, but many support personnel spend a significant amount of time on the telephone with customers, entering data, and filing.

Bookkeepers and accountants handle a company's basic financial transactions. Insurance claims and policy-processing clerks have numerous duties, including processing new policies, making modifications to existing policies and claims, reviewing application forms for completeness, compiling customer data, reviewing insurance policies to determine coverage details, preparing forms, providing customer service for filing claims, keeping records organized, paying small claims, transmitting claims for payment, processing applications for, changes to, reinstatement of, and cancellation of insurance policies, corresponding with insured persons and agents, and letting agents know of policy cancellation.

Insurance companies offer internships to students and others seeking practical experience and training in return for labor. Often, interns take care of insurers' office and administrative duties. Annual salaries in this job category range from $32,000 to $41,000, according to 2008 data.

Office and administrative support occupations may include the following:

- Secretary
- Administrative Assistant
- Bookkeeper
- Accountant
- Auditing Clerk
- Claims and Policy-Processing Clerk
- Customer Service Representative
- Intern

Management, Business, and Financial Operations

Management, business, and financial personnel account for 29.1 percent of insurance jobs. These personnel are among the most important employees to an insurance company, and they require particular skills. In most cases, they require master's degrees in business administration or related fields. Some training programs offer certification in relevant areas that may substitute for advance degrees in some cases.

Claims adjusters, appraisers, and examiners (as

they are called in property and casualty insurance) determine coverage, investigate claims, and review settled claims. When negotiating claims settlements, they review the extent of their insurance companies' liabilities. In this process, claims adjusters must communicate with multiple parties—including medical specialists in the case of health claims and police and witnesses in the case of property or casualty claims—in order to gather all available information related to the claim. If a settlement cannot be negotiated, adjusters may recommend litigation. Adjusters look for overpayments, underpayments, and other irregularities. They require licensing by each state in which they are employed. According to the BLS, the median salary for claims adjusters, examiners, and investigators in 2009 was $57,130.

Insurance appraisers are unique to property and casualty insurance, particularly in the case of automobile damage. Appraisers calculate the value of damage done to vehicles, houses, and other property to determine the cost of repairs that will be paid in a claim settlement. They also calculate replacement value of property that has been stolen or damaged beyond repair. The median salary of automobile insurance appraisers in 2009 was $55,390.

Underwriters review applications to evaluate the degree of risk involved based on each applicant's financial standing and the condition of the property being insured. They determine whether to write a given policy, for how much, and under what terms. They decline excessive risks in order to preserve their companies' profits. Job prospects for underwriters are growing more slowly than some other industry positions because computer software has been developed to minimize the time it takes to assess risk. In 2009, the median salary of insurance underwriters was $57,820.

Management analysts, or loss control representatives, conduct studies and evaluations to assess various risks for insurers and make recommendations. They inspect the business operations of appli-

A claims adjuster examines a damaged car. (AP/Wide World Photos)

OCCUPATION PROFILE

Insurance Claims Adjuster and Examiner

Considerations	Qualifications
Description	Analyzes and investigates insurance claims and determines damages.
Career clusters	Business, Management, and Administration; Finance
Interests	Data; people
Working conditions	Work inside; work outside; work both inside and outside
Minimum education level	On-the-job training; high school diploma or GED; high school diploma/technical training; junior/technical/community college; bachelor's degree
Physical exertion	Light work
Physical abilities	Unexceptional/basic fitness
Opportunities for experience	Part-time work
Licensure and certification	Required
Employment outlook	Average growth expected
Holland interest score	ESC

Note: See volume 1, "Publisher's Note," for an explanation of the Holland interest score.

cants and look for potential hazards, such as unsafe conditions. The 2009 mean annual salary of management analysts in the insurance industry was $70,920.

Management, business, and financial occupations may include the following:

- President/Chief Executive Officer (CEO)
- Chief Financial Officer (CFO)
- Vice President of Compliance
- Vice President of Public and Government Relations
- General Counsel
- Marketing Manager
- Claims Director
- Claims Adjuster/Appraiser/Examiner
- Underwriting Manager
- Underwriter
- Insurance Investigator
- Senior Insurance Investigator

- Management Analyst/Loss Control Representative

Sales

As with all sales jobs, the abilities to persuade and promote are keys to success. Insurance salespeople sell services rather than goods. They may sell to individuals, or they may direct or manage the sale of business-related services. Sales personnel account for 16.5 percent of the jobs in the insurance industry.

Insurance sales jobs require college degrees—mainly in business, finance, or economics—and strong oral and written communication skills. Salespersons require licenses from each state in which they work. Frequently, insurance companies and brokerage firms send employees to obtain extensive training beyond their education. The insurance industry has also expanded its scope to include financial planning services. As a result, many

OCCUPATION PROFILE

Actuary

Considerations	Qualifications
Description	Predicts the likelihood of occurrence of heart disease, diabetes, stroke, cancer, and other chronic ailments among particular groups of people, usually for insurance purposes.
Career cluster	Finance
Interests	Data
Working conditions	Work inside
Minimum education level	Bachelor's degree
Physical exertion	Light work
Physical abilities	Unexceptional/basic fitness
Opportunities for experience	Apprenticeship; part-time work
Licensure and certification	Recommended
Employment outlook	Faster-than-average growth expected
Holland interest score	ISE

Note: See volume 1, "Publisher's Note," for an explanation of the Holland interest score.

insurance salespeople have also become licensed to sell securities, such as mutual funds or annuities.

Insurance agents work irregular hours, usually totaling more than forty hours per week. They work outside the office and travel often, and they must be available for clients experiencing emergencies twenty-four hours per day. Most sales agents and managers are assigned to specific territories—from a single metropolitan area to several states in size.

Approximately 50 percent of insurance agents work for agencies and brokerages, 21 percent work directly for insurance carriers, and 22 percent work independently. Independent contractors may perform work for two or more insurance firms. Individuals often specialize in the sale of specific insurance products, but they can cross-sell. The main role of an insurance agent is to assist customers (whether individuals or businesses) in selecting policies. Agents explain the details of the products they sell, help applicants fill out necessary forms, and write agreements between insured entities and insurers. Some agents may also be in charge of calculating premiums and receiving payments. Beyond working with current customers, agents must also seek out new business prospects and set up networking appointments for this purpose.

Insurance brokers also sell insurance but do not work for a specific insurance company. Instead, they review all the available policies and match each customer's needs with the appropriate company and product. Most agents and brokers work on commission. In 2009, the mean annual income of insurance sales agents was $61,210 for those employed by carriers and $61,660 for those employed by agencies and brokerages. Insurance sales managers earned an average of $113,710.

Sales occupations may include the following:

- Sales Manager
- Insurance Agent
- Insurance Broker

Medical, Legal, and Actuarial Staff

Some 11.4 percent of insurance personnel are members of companies' medical and legal staff. Lawyers represent their companies in litigation, responding to suits and bringing actions against clients and other companies as necessary. Doctors and nurses advise insurance companies in managed care health plans.

Actuaries represent a small portion of insurance employment but are essential. An actuary is an insurance professional who calculates probabilities for the purpose of setting policy premiums, providing statistical data for records, and developing new products for a company. This occupation is considered one of the top one hundred fastest-growing jobs. Actuaries have degrees in actuarial science, mathematics, statistics, or business-related fields and must take a series of national exams to attain full professional status, which takes five to ten years. Most actuaries work traditional workweeks of forty hours. In 2009, the mean annual salary for actuaries was $96,080 for those employed by carriers and $98,630 for those employed by agencies and brokerages.

Medical, legal, and actuarial occupations may include the following:

- Actuary
- Attorney/Counsel
- Title Examiner/Abstractor/Searcher
- Paralegal
- Nurse
- Physician

Information Technology

Information technology (IT) personnel provide technical support for insurance companies. They include computer system analysts and network administrators, as well as help desk workers who assist with day-to-day operations. IT personnel may start with associate's degrees and gain further certification and training, or they may already have professional experience working in IT departments in other industries. In addition to general IT jobs, insurance companies require specialists in medical records and health information, who work with electronic health records and design databases to organize them. In the insurance industry in 2009, the mean annual salary for computer support specialists was $51,900, while systems analysts earned

an average of $77,010 and database administrators earned an average of $78,160.

IT occupations may include the following:

- Chief Technology Officer (CTO)
- Chief Information Officer (CIO)
- Information Technology Manager
- Computer Systems Analyst
- Database Administrator
- Network Administrator
- Software Engineer
- Computer Programmer
- Computer Support Specialist
- Help Desk Staff

Human Resources

Human resources departments become more important in larger health insurance companies. Firms such as Progressive or Aetna, for example, employ a number of human resources personnel to handle the hiring and firing processes, oversee payroll, and administer benefits. However, in smaller firms, the administrative staff may be solely responsible for these duties, as is common in other industries as well. Insurance company human resources managers earned an average of $113,500 in 2009, while human resources assistants earned an average of $38,290.

Human resources occupations may include the following:

- Human Resources Manager
- Human Resources Director
- Human Resources Coordinator
- Human Resources Assistant
- Human Resources Generalist
- Payroll Clerk
- Benefits Specialist
- Administrative Assistant

INDUSTRY OUTLOOK

Overview

The outlook for this industry shows it to be on the rise. As with most industries, performance is linked to the economy and turmoil in the financial markets. In the wake of the recession of 2007-2009, the U.S. insurance market is expected to grow.

In some ways, the insurance industry is recession-proof, because the need for insurance coverage persists, and the need for some kinds of insurance—for example, health insurance—may increase in weak economies, in which consumers are less able to bear the direct costs of health care. In other segments, consumers may downsize to one car rather than two, or shy away from purchasing a new house, but most insurance needs still exist through a recession.

In 2008, the insurance industry employed approximately 2.3 million wage and salary workers. Employment in the industry is projected by the BLS to increase slowly from 2008 to 2018. Industry jobs will increase by 3 percent during that time, compared to an average across all industries of 11 percent growth.

Beyond economic conditions, another obstacle to long-term growth in the insurance industry is technology. Both the Internet and new software have increased the productivity of workers in the insurance industry, and this trend will continue. Greater productivity reduces the size of the neces-

sary workforce, as fewer employees can accomplish more. While the Internet prompts quicker automation of processes and better customer service, it could also reduce the need for insurance workers and increase competition for jobs. Most of the processes in the insurance business will never be completely automated, however. The Internet will affect property and casualty workers the most, since premiums for car insurance are the highest and consumers can use the Internet to determine the best price for their needs.

Other factors may fuel growth in the insurance industry. Health care reform and the changing face of health insurance will create new opportunities for health insurers. Advances in the medical and pharmaceutical fields will also affect health insurance, inspiring new coverage options. The aging of the American population will result in more people needing insurance for longer periods of time. The resulting greater demand will apply to all areas of insurance, including health and automobile coverage. In addition to growth, employment opportunities exist because of continuous turnover. Companies will always need to replace workers who leave or retire.

Another area of expansion for insurance companies is the ability to offer broader financial services. Consumers may appreciate the convenience of purchasing financial and insurance products at the same time from a single company, or of purchasing additional products from a company they already trust. Thus, bundling noninsurance services with insurance may help drive additional business to diversified companies.

In 2009, several occupations within the insurance industry were listed among the one hundred jobs with the most openings in the United States. Each year, on average, there are openings for nearly 64,500 insurance sales agents, 42,250 insurance claims clerks, and 42,250 insurance policy-processing clerks. Actuaries were named as one of the one hundred

PROJECTED EMPLOYMENT FOR SELECTED OCCUPATIONS

Insurance Carriers and Related Activities

Employment		
2009	Projected 2018	Occupation
198,140	220,300	Claims adjusters, examiners, and investigators
57,180	58,000	First-line supervisors/managers of office and administrative support workers
211,150	220,200	Insurance claims and policy processing clerks
309,360	366,800	Insurance sales agents
86,220	86,900	Insurance underwriters

Source: U.S. Bureau of Labor Statistics, Industries at a Glance, Occupational Employment Statistics and Employment Projections Program.

fastest-growing jobs in 2009, with a 23.7 percent growth rate.

From 2008 to 2009, earnings increased for most jobs in the insurance industry, except claims adjusters. In fact, according to a report by the Ward Group and the Jacobson Group, nearly 63 percent of insurance companies were expected to experience revenue increases in 2010, compared with 54 percent that expected such increases in 2009. Business growth was expected to foster job growth. In total, 44 percent of insurers said they planned to increase their staffs in 2010, up from 34 percent in 2009, while only 13 percent of firms said they expected staff decreases in 2010. Overall, the report predicted a 1.96 percent increase in insurance industry employment during 2010, translating to 26,500 new jobs.

Employment Advantages

The insurance industry is a good starting point for almost anyone entering the workforce, no matter where a person lives. Because many entry-level positions offer internal training and do not require college degrees, candidates can be hired with little education or experience and can begin to work their way up through the ranks and try out different roles. Insurance is not a difficult field to get into, especially since there are several types of insurance products across the nation, but advancing one's career requires persistence and determination.

Another advantage is the variety within the industry. Not only are there different insurance products but there are also diverse job functions. There is rarely a dull moment in the insurance industry because of all the tasks needed for daily operations. Flexibility is another high point in the industry. Many jobs can be part time or temporary, providing options to those who want to have a family or already have one. None of the jobs is overly demanding of time. Most full-time insurance workers complete their work in a traditional forty-hour workweek. Opportunities in the insurance industry exist nationwide and worldwide, in big cities and small towns, and they will continue to grow in the foreseeable future.

Annual Earnings

In 2008, insurance companies earned $1.24 trillion in premiums in the United States and $4.27 trillion globally. Allowing for some corrections

caused by the global financial crisis, these figures are expected to grow. Anticipated growth in domestic business volume is expected to translate to job growth for almost 50 percent of U.S. insurance firms. This growth will primarily be due to expansion of business and new markets. Further, there will be fewer staff reductions.

The international and global insurance markets are expected to experience similar trends. Competitive pricing, innovative services, and increasing regulation all play a role, as does the recovering economy. Among countries outside the United States, China and India appear to have the largest potential for industry growth.

RELATED RESOURCES FOR FURTHER RESEARCH

AMERICAN COUNCIL OF LIFE INSURANCE
101 Constitution Ave. NW, Suite 700
Washington, DC 20001-2133
Tel: (202) 624-2000
http://www.acli.com

AMERICAN INSURANCE ASSOCIATION
2101 L St. NW, Suite 400
Washington, DC 20037
Tel: (202) 828-7100
Fax: (202) 293-1219
http://www.aiadc.org

AMERICAN RISK AND INSURANCE ASSOCIATION
716 Providence Rd.
Malvern, PA 19355
Tel: (610) 640-1997
Fax: (610) 725-1007
http://www.aria.org

INDEPENDENT INSURANCE AGENTS AND BROKERS OF AMERICA
120 S Peyton St.
Alexandria, VA 22314
Tel: (800) 221-7917
Fax: (703) 683-7556
http://www.iiaba.net

INSURANCE INFORMATION INSTITUTE
110 William St.
New York, NY 10038

Tel: (212) 346-5500
http://www.iii.org

NATIONAL ASSOCIATION OF INSURANCE AND
FINANCIAL ADVISORS
2901 Telestar Ct.
Falls Church, VA 22042
Tel: (877) 866-2432
http://www.naifa.org

NATIONAL ASSOCIATION OF INSURANCE
COMMISSIONERS
444 N Capitol St. NW, Suite 701
Washington, DC 20001
Tel: (202) 471-3990
Fax: (816) 460-7493
http://www.naic.org

NATIONAL ASSOCIATION OF PROFESSIONAL
INSURANCE AGENTS
400 N Washington St.
Alexandria, VA 22314
Tel: (703) 836-9340
Fax: (703) 836-1279
http://www.pianet.com

SOCIETY OF ACTUARIES
475 N Martingale Rd., Suite 600
Schaumburg, IL 60173
Tel: (847) 706-3500
Fax: (847) 706-3599
http://www.soa.org

ABOUT THE AUTHOR

Patrice La Vigne is a health care writer who identifies the most important news and research across multiple therapeutic areas and writes educational summaries to be disseminated to physicians, pharmaceutical representatives, patients, and other health care professionals. She has also written for newspapers and magazines and has worked as a career counselor for new graduates and low-income and homeless adults. She has a bachelor of arts degree in English and Spanish.

FURTHER READING

Grossman, Michael, Björn Lindgren, and Avi Dor. *Pharmaceutical Markets and Insurance Worldwide.* Bingley, West Yorkshire, England: Emerald, 2010.

Parker, Philip M. *The 2009-2014 World Outlook for Automobile Insurance.* San Diego, Calif.: ICON Group, 2008.

Preker, Alexander S., et al. *Global Marketplace for Private Health Insurance: Strength in Numbers.* Washington, D.C.: World Bank, 2010.

Swiss Re. "Sigma: World Insurance in 2008." http://media.swissre.com/documents/sigma3_2009_en.pdf.

Thomsett, M. *Insurance Dictionary.* Jefferson, N.C.: McFarland, 1989.

U.S. Bureau of Labor Statistics. *Career Guide to Industries,* 2010-2011 ed. http://www.bls.gov/oco/cg.

U.S. Census Bureau. North American Industry Classification System (NAICS), 2007. http://www.census.gov/cgi-bin/sssd/naics/naicsrch?chart=2007.

U.S. Department of Commerce. International Trade Administration. Office of Trade and Industry Information. Industry Trade Data and Analysis. http://ita.doc.gov/td/industry/otea/OTII/OTII-index.html.

U.S. Department of Labor. *The Big Book of Jobs.* 2009-2010 ed. New York: McGraw-Hill, 2010.

Ward Group and Jacabson Group. "Insurance Labor Market Study." February, 2010. http://www.wardinc.com/research-center/strategic-studies-detail.php?id=50.

Zevnik, R. W. *The Complete Book of Insurance.* Naperville, Ill.: Sphinx, 2004.

Internet and Cyber Communications Industry

INDUSTRY SNAPSHOT

General Industry: Information Technology

Career Clusters: Arts, A/V Technology, and Communication; Information Technology

Subcategory Industries: Application Hosting; Custom Web Page Design Services; Internet Entertainment Sites; Internet Publishers; Internet Service Providers; Social Networking Sites; Video and Audio Streaming Services; Web Hosting; Web Search Portals

Related Industries: Advertising and Marketing Industry; Broadcast Industry; Computer Hardware and Peripherals Industry; Computer Software Industry; Computer Systems Industry; Publishing and Information Industry; Telecommunications Equipment Industry; Telecommunications Infrastructure Industry

Annual Domestic Revenues: $23.4 billion USD (IT Facts, 2008; for Internet advertising)

Annual Global Revenues: $65.2 billion USD (IT Facts, 2008; for Internet advertising)

NAICS Numbers: 518, 517919, 519130, 541511

INDUSTRY DEFINITION

Summary

From businesses and schools to individuals and governments, the rise of Web sites, e-commerce, e-mail, and social networking has changed how humankind interacts and communicates. The Internet offers businesses and individuals instant access to digital information. Employees and entrepreneurs working in this industry create the content that, as of 2008, attracted 1.7 billion people worldwide according to Miniwatts Marketing Group. The number will only rise as developing countries continue to gain an increasing online presence. Internet advertising, paid online services, and online database publishing represent the leading revenue streams for the Internet industry.

History of the Industry

The evolution of the Internet represented an incredible leap forward in human interconnectivity. When programmers took their first tentative steps toward the information network that would become the Internet, there were only ten thousand computers in the entire world. In 1962, J. C. R. Licklider, head of the new military computer research program at the Advanced Research Projects Agency (ARPA), first envisioned an "intergalactic network" that would give people instant access to digital information. He began collaborating with scientists and researchers across the country to investigate the possibility of forming new communication networks.

By 1963, the National Aeronautics and Space Administration (NASA) had launched its first communications satellite. The development of communications satellites, first proposed by science-fiction author Arthur C. Clarke, played an important role in the development of the Internet. Meanwhile, scientists at the Massachusetts Institute of Technology (MIT), the RAND Corporation, and the National Physical Laboratory began researching ways to allow computers to exchange information in small units known as packets. This technology was called packet switching, and it remains the basis for most modern Internet communications.

By 1965, ARPA researchers were able to connect a computer in Massachusetts to a computer in California using a telephone line. This connection constituted the world's first wide-area network. Former NASA scientist Bob Taylor became head of ARPA's computer research department in 1966, and he quickly began working with researchers around the world to develop a communications network utilizing packet-switching technology. This network became ARPANET, the first real precursor to the modern Internet.

After years of experimentation, scientists at the University of California, Los Angeles (UCLA), ARPA, Stanford University, and the University of California, Santa Barbara, successfully connected to the ARPANET for the first time in 1969, and the Internet was born. Scientists quickly began to connect via the ARPANET, and by 1970, the network was growing by one new computer system, or "node," per month. As the ARPANET grew, researchers continued to experiment with new ways of exchanging information through the network. In 1972, Ray Tomlinson, a researcher at BBN Technologies, created the world's first e-mail program.

After years of testing and development, scientists unveiled the ARPANET at the 1972 International Conference on Computer Communication (ICCC). They attracted the attention of even more scientists, and by 1973, thirty nodes were connected via the ARPANET. New networks were also created, including Packet Radio, which utilized radio waves to connect seven computer systems in Hawaii. In Europe, scientists used satellite communication systems to connect two computers in Norway and the United Kingdom.

By 1977, ARPA had become absorbed into the U.S. Department of Defense and was renamed the Defense Advanced Research Projects Agency (DARPA). Vint Cerf and Bob Kahn, two researchers working for DARPA, become the first scientists to send information across multiple networks utilizing the APRANET, Packet Radio, and satellite communications. They called the process "internetting." This was an important precursor to the modern Internet, in which computers and digital devices are able to connect through telephone lines, mobile broadband networks, wireless access points, and satellite Internet services.

Once the ARPANET experiment was officially concluded in 1978, researchers at various universities continued to experiment with networking. By 1979, Steve Bellovin, a scientist at the University of North Carolina, developed USENET in an attempt to share information with his fellow researchers at Duke University. USENET allowed users to exchange e-mail, files, news, and information and attracted many new online visitors.

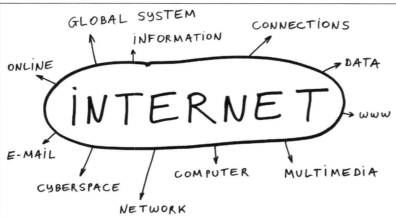

The evolution of the Internet represented an incredible leap forward in human interconnectivity. (©Alain Lacroix/Dreamstime.com)

At this time, the burgeoning growth of the earliest modern personal computers, led by Apple and International Business Machines (IBM), led to a revolution in computer technology. Governments, companies, universities, organizations, and individuals soon recognized the usefulness of connecting computers through a stable network, and the International Organization for Standards (ISO) created a universal standard for exchanging information over the Internet in 1982.

By 1984, universal standard domains such as .com, .org, .gov, .edu, and .net were adopted. However, it was not until Internet pioneer Tim Berners-Lee developed hypertext in 1989 that computers running different operating systems were able to connect easily via the World Wide Web. Working alongside collaborator Robert Cailliau, Berners-Lee created the world's first browser and developed the Hyper Text Markup Language (HTML), which is still used by millions of Web sites around the world.

Between 1962 and 1992, available network bandwidth increased by a factor of more than 20 million. By 2004, more than 873 million users were online, and by 2008 there were more than 80 million Web sites. Instant access to news, entertainment, and personal information has proven an extremely valuable commodity to people and organizations across the world. The Internet has created a robust and growing online economy, and low start-up costs have allowed savvy entrepreneurs to form many successful businesses. The Internet and cyber communications industry employs countless people worldwide, including Webmasters, graphic designers, and software engineers. Many others use the Internet to earn a second income, often through blogging, e-commerce, or running their own Web sites devoted to their personal interests and hobbies.

The Industry Today

Throughout the 1990's and into the early twenty-first century, the rapid rise of the Internet economy created a massive speculative bubble. The skyrocketing growth of Internet users led to a rush of new dot-com companies hoping to attract customers, with venture capitalists investing an estimated $106 billion in start-up Internet firms by 2000. By 2001, the bubble burst, as investors and shareholders rushed to abandon tech companies, many of which had never realized a profit. The collapse of the dot-com bubble left many thousands of people unemployed and many investors with significant—often devastating—losses.

Despite these challenges, some companies founded during the 1990's survived. These included eBay, Amazon, and Yahoo!. In addition, the Internet infrastructure set up during the dot-com bubble opened up Web access on a global scale, making it possible for the next generation of Internet companies to prosper. Internet companies formed after the dot-com bubble are usually founded with much more modest budgets, but many have been able to attract users and become profitable.

Many Web sites, including such well-known sites as Twitter and Facebook, can take years to earn a profit. However, Internet advertising can help bring in valuable revenues right from the start. Web sites can earn advertising revenues through several different methods. Google, for example, allows advertisers to bid for the right to appear in a

Many Web sites, including such well-known sites as Twitter, can take years to earn a profit. (AP/Wide World Photos)

The Web site for eBay claims it has 90 million active users globally. (AP/Wide World Photos)

small box labeled "Sponsored Links" that appears alongside certain search results. Thus, when users search for "sneakers," for instance, they see a selection of shoe stores and department stores beside their search results. Advertisers are charged every time a user clicks on a link. Sites can also earn revenues by selling banner ads. A Web site focusing on political news and commentary, for example, might sell banner ads to politicians running for office. Such sites may charge advertisers a flat rate or charge a fee every time a user clicks on an ad, a practice known as click-thru advertising.

Internet advertising has proven a reliable profit stream for many established Web sites, including Google, which made more than $1.65 billion in profits in the third quarter of 2009 alone. In fact, Google earned 97 percent of its total 2008 revenues through advertising. Some Web sites also charge users a premium to use certain services, while others collect donations and sell merchandise to offset costs.

There are many different ways Web sites attract visitors. Many new Web sites allow people to create their own content—a phenomenon known as "Web 2.0." YouTube, for example, has gained a significant following by allowing users to post their own videos. Social networking Web sites take this concept a step further, allowing users to share not just photos and videos, but also personal information about their lives. Other Web sites offer original content produced by employees, while some, such as Digg and Delicious (formerly del.icio.us), succeed by allowing users to collate and rank Web pages, providing users with centralized access to information, pictures, and videos that might interest them. Sites may also provide travel services, such as discounted airline tickets, car rentals, or hotel reservation rates, while others offer reviews of local businesses, including restaurants, repair shops, and doctors' offices.

Web sites such as Amazon and eBay have grown into thriving e-commerce companies with tens of thousands of employees. Meanwhile, hosting companies such as DreamHost offer customers easy, inexpensive ways to publish their Web sites online. In addition, there are many Web-based companies that focus exclusively on the business and financial needs of their customers, offering job postings, stock trading, accounting, or database services. In fact, most businesses, large or small, have their own Web sites and social networking accounts. Many outsource their Internet needs to Web designers and consulting firms, while others hire part-time or full-time employees to handle their online presence.

A new development in the Internet and cyber communications industry is the growth of cloud computing. Companies such as Apple, Microsoft, and Google all offer robust cloud computing services that allow businesses and individuals to access programs and documents from a decentralized system of servers. By dispersing data off-site, users can securely back up their data and easily collaborate across long distances. Businesses can also cut costs by outsourcing expensive server operations. According to a Global Study report, in 2009 more than half of businesses surveyed were utilizing cloud computing, an evolving technology that offers many new opportunities for growth.

Start-up costs for Web sites have become extremely low in recent years, in part because of the popularity of free open-source software. Entrepreneurs working from home have founded many successful Internet businesses. For example, Mark Zuckerberg launched Facebook from his dorm room while a sophomore at Harvard. First started as a hobby, Facebook has grown into one of the most popular sites on the Internet, with more than 300 million users worldwide as of 2009.

INDUSTRY MARKET SEGMENTS

The Internet and cyber communications industry includes small, midsize, and large businesses, as well as individuals engaged in full-time or part-time contract work.

Small Businesses

Since start-up costs for online business have fallen considerably, many new entrepreneurs are attracted to launching Internet businesses. Freelance consultants and Web designers also conduct much of their business through the Internet. In addition, community leaders with proven track records of founding successful Internet businesses often continue to launch small new start-ups or invest in promising new companies. Many entrepreneurs, freelancers, and small businesses in this industry attract visitors to their own Web sites, while others focus on providing Web advertising, Web design, Web hosting, database management, search engine optimization (SEO), or social networking services for other businesses and individuals.

Since most Internet-based businesses do not require physical warehouse space and server needs can easily be outsourced, even extremely high profile companies may have very small staffs of fewer than one hundred employees. Web-based businesses at this stage normally focus on providing new, often experimental features and attracting new visitors and clients.

Potential Annual Earnings Scale. Most small Internet start-ups do not earn a profit for the first few years. However, once a successful Internet company begins to sell stock or is purchased by a larger company, early employees can sometimes reap large financial rewards. Others launch their own Web sites as a hobby or a part-time second job, and in these cases, what revenue they earn may barely cover expenses. Many small businesses and freelance consultants also specialize in building Web sites, often for local businesses. According to the U.S. Bureau of Labor Statistics (BLS), such Web designers could expect to earn between $47,000 and $71,500 per year as of 2007.

Clientele Interaction. In small Internet companies, employees take a very hands-on approach to interacting with clients, often via e-mail or other means of cyber communication. Freelance Web designers and employees at small Web design firms usually meet directly with clients to ensure that their Web sites fulfill their expectations. Even top executives often interact directly with clients.

Amenities, Atmosphere, and Physical Grounds. Many Web sites are launched from home, often starting out as a hobby before earning a profit. Promising start-ups often attract investors and venture capitalists, allowing entrepreneurs to rent office locations, hire employees, and improve their Web sites' capabilities. The atmosphere at small Internet start-ups is normally much more relaxed than in other industries, often encouraging a sense of playfulness during late-night programming and brainstorming sessions. At small Web design and consulting firms, in contrast, a sense of professional decorum is usually required, since employees must frequently engage directly with business clients. Freelance Web designers and online consultants usually work from home, but they must also be prepared to visit clients in professional settings.

Typical Number of Employees. Freelance Web developers and consultants usually work alone, and most small Internet start-ups are launched by just one or two people. Even after gaining a significant client base, it is not uncommon for Web-based businesses and consulting firms to employ a staff of fewer than fifty. Well-known sites such as Craigslist and Twitter, for example, each had thirty employees or fewer as of 2009.

Traditional Geographic Locations. A Web-based business can be launched from anywhere in the world, and many Web designers and small consulting firms focus on local area businesses. However, many Internet companies are concentrated in major metropolitan areas, especially Silicon Valley in California's San Francisco Bay Area. Because Silicon Valley has a long history of supporting leading technology companies, many talented programmers, investors, and venture capital firms are located in the area. This can make it easier for Internet start-ups to obtain funding and compete for the most qualified employees.

Pros of Working for a Small Internet Company. Freelance Web designers, consultants, and entrepreneurs running their own Web sites have the freedom to pick which projects to work on and which clients to accept. They can also determine how much to charge for their services and set their own advertising rates, and they often make their own schedules. Employees for small firms may also enjoy greater creative input, since they can usually take their ideas directly to the owner or manager. Internet start-ups, in particular, offer a relaxed, laid back communal atmosphere with many new challenges and opportunities as the business grows. They may also enjoy generous stock options or other opportunities to invest in their companies, and early employees may reap great financial rewards if a company goes public or is bought up by a larger firm.

Cons of Working for a Small Internet Company. Since freelance Web designers, consultants, and entrepreneurs work for themselves, they are completely responsible for attracting new clients and Web site visitors. This can take a certain amount of luck, as well as tireless efforts and many long hours. They may hold down day jobs in unrelated fields for years before they attract enough clients or advertisers to make a living through their Web-based businesses. Income can also vary widely year-to-year, or even month-to-month, since online trends can change rapidly.

Employees at small start-ups may also face job insecurity, since many start-ups may take years to earn a profit and investors can abandon a company at any time. At small, established firms, employees are often expected to work long hours, with programming sessions that can last late into the night. At the same time, unexpected crashes may result from hacking attacks, server malfunctions, or simply too many people trying to log on at the same time. Employees at these companies are expected to continue working until the issue is resolved, no matter how long it takes.

Costs

Payroll and Benefits: Freelance Web designers and online consultants often work on a contract basis and usually receive no benefits. The same holds true for entrepreneurs first launching their own Web sites. However, established Web-based companies and start-up firms with sufficient capital usually offer generous benefits in order to attract talented employees. Benefits often include stock options, insurance, and paid sick days.

Supplies: Individuals and small Internet businesses require up-to-date computer systems, software, and other office supplies. Depending on the size and scope of the business, they may also have their own servers.

External Services: Small start-up Internet firms, freelance Web designers, consultants, and individual entrepreneurs launching their own Web sites typically outsource their Web hosting and server needs. They may also hire accountants on a contractual basis and sometimes hire external marketing firms to help grow their business.

Utilities: Individuals working from home typically have to pay for high-speed Internet access, as well as normal household utilities and expenses. Small businesses with office locations must pay rent, which may include water and sewage, as well as electricity, which may be a significant cost depending on the number of computers and servers located on the property. They also have to pay for high-speed Internet access and may require a dedicated T-1 line to handle high bandwidth requirements.

Taxes: Individuals and small businesses must pay all applicable local, state, federal, and property taxes.

Midsize Businesses

Most midsize businesses in the Internet and cyber communications industry are well established, with hundreds of thousands of regular visitors, significant investors, and profitable revenue streams. They usually maintain their own on-site servers and may have multiple offices. Since successful midsize Internet-based companies already enjoy large followings, employees must focus on introducing innovative new features, preventing outages, and ensuring visitors enjoy an extremely reliable level of service.

Potential Annual Earnings Scale. Midsize Web-based businesses hire people for many different kinds of positions, ranging from highly paid executives to Web developers, database administrators, programmers, and human resources workers, as well as public relations and marketing personnel. Database administrators can expect to earn between $70,250 and $102,000 per year, while programmers may earn between $55,250 and $90,250 per year, according to the BLS in 2007. Web developers earn between $54,750 and $81,500 per year.

Clientele Interaction. Most employees at midsize Internet companies do not physically interact directly with customers, although they may exchange e-mails with Web-site visitors or engage in conversations via forums, message boards, or instant messages. Company representatives may also attend conferences or conventions several times a year. In addition, employees focused on public relations and marketing will often meet with prospective advertising firms and business partners.

Amenities, Atmosphere, and Physical Grounds. Midsize Web-based companies usually have a single main headquarters, but they may also have satellite offices in various parts of the world. Satellite offices may contain Web-hosting servers, technical support operations, and sales and marketing offices. The atmosphere at companies in this industry varies greatly depending on the business, as well as the individual department. Programmers and Web developers, for example, often enjoy a more relaxed, easygoing environment than do employees working in sales and business development. Additionally, employees at midsize firms often enjoy many perks and amenities, including free food and beverages, child care, a casual dress code, and flexible working hours. They may also have the option of telecommuting.

Typical Number of Employees. By the time a Web-based business reaches a medium size, it may employ between one hundred and one thousand people. Employees normally work full time, although some midsize firms occasionally hire consultants, designers, or marketing firms on a contract basis.

Traditional Geographic Locations. Midsize Internet firms are highly concentrated in high-tech areas, especially Silicon Valley; Los Angeles, California; Portland, Oregon; and Seattle, Washington. Silicon Valley in particular has long been a home for many of the most well known midsize Internet businesses. Start-up Web sites launched elsewhere often move their headquarters to Silicon Valley in order to seek new investors and attract top talent. Facebook, for example, is a midsize business with more than nine hundred employees launched from a Harvard University dorm room in Cambridge, Massachusetts, by Mark Zuckerberg. In 2004, as the social media site began to attract new visitors and advertisers, Zuckerberg moved the company to Palo Alto, California, a high-tech hot spot in Silicon Valley.

Pros of Working for a Midsize Internet Company. Most midsize Internet companies are stable and well established. They often have multiple offices and may have international headquarters, which can give employees added mobility. They are also small enough that the companies can retain a sense of close camaraderie that may be lost in larger companies. Midsize companies may also offer employees more opportunities to experiment with new designs and features. Compared with smaller companies and Web-based start-ups, midsize firms may offer more job security and can often provide more generous salaries and benefits.

Cons of Working for a Midsize Internet Company. Midsize companies can be relatively stressful places to work. Employees may occasionally work late into the night in the case of outages or when rolling out new features. Midsize firms are also more likely to be purchased by larger companies, which can often result in layoffs as parent companies streamline operations after an acquisition. In addition, employees at midsize firms may not be able to obtain the generous stock options and investment opportunities offered to employees at small start-up companies.

Costs

Payroll and Benefits: Midsize companies usually offer employees generous salaries and full benefits, including health and life insurance, stock options, paid sick days, and optional telecommuting opportunities.

Supplies: Most midsize firms must purchase basic office supplies, and they usually require specialized high-end computer systems. They also usually own and operate their own Web-hosting servers, with multiple backup systems to prevent downtime or data loss.

External Services: While midsize firms usually hire full-time employees for most aspects of their core business, they usually contract out all cleaning and office-maintenance services, as well as catering services as needed. They occasionally hire consulting firms and often depend on contracts with advertising firms specializing in Web ads to bring in additional revenues.

Utilities: Since midsize firms frequently own and operate their own Web-hosting servers, electricity is often a major expense. They also normally require dedicated fiber optic data lines to handle high-bandwidth Internet operations. Additional utilities include telephone services and rent, which may include water and sewage.

Taxes: Midsize companies must pay all usual taxes, including state, local, federal, and property taxes. If they have a significant international presence, they may also pay additional taxes for their overseas operations.

Large Businesses

By the time an Internet company has grown into a large, established business, it normally receives millions of visitors every day, generating large advertising and sales revenues. Several of the world's most popular Web sites, social networking sites, search engines, and e-commerce companies are large enough to fit into this category, including Amazon, eBay, Google, and Yahoo!.

Potential Annual Earnings Scale. Large Internet companies often pay very competitive wages in order to attract top talent. They tend to hire experienced workers for full-time positions, including software engineers, Web designers, sales and marketing representatives, public relations specialists, and executive officers. According to 2009 BLS figures, highly qualified software engineers may earn up to $119,770 per year, while executives can expect to earn more than $145,600 per year, though some top executives can earn more than $1 million per year.

Clientele Interaction. Many employees at large Internet companies interact with clients. These firms often have significant technical support and customer service departments, where employees respond to questions and requests from Web site visitors, customers, and advertisers. They also employ public relations representatives, marketers, advertising executives, and sales representatives who interact with journalists, clients, and government workers. Although direct face-to-face interaction with customers is rare, large companies in this industry often participate in conventions and conferences.

Amenities, Atmosphere, and Physical Grounds. Large businesses often have luxurious, campus headquarters, such as the Googleplex in Mountain View, California, a part of Silicon Valley. The Googleplex serves as the primary headquarters for Google, one of the largest, most successful Internet search engines in the world. The campus features two swimming pools, several cafeterias, a full gym, and even a volleyball court, among other amenities. Large companies such as Google and Amazon may also have both domestic and overseas satellite offices and warehouses, often including large data-storage facilities, sales and advertising departments, technical support locations, and software development centers.

Typical Number of Employees. Large, established Internet-based businesses require many employees spread across various departments. They often employ tens of thousands of people in locations across the world. Many work as sales and marketing representatives, software engineers, technical support specialists, human resources officers, and Web designers. For example, Amazon, one of

OCCUPATION PROFILE

Electronic Commerce Specialist

Considerations	*Qualifications*
Description	Designs and analyzes Web sites to market products, produces online advertising, and analyzes online sales.
Career clusters	Business, Management, and Administration; Information Technology; Marketing, Sales, and Service
Interests	Data; people
Working conditions	Work inside
Minimum education level	Bachelor's degree
Physical exertion	Light work
Physical abilities	Unexceptional/basic fitness
Opportunities for experience	Volunteer work; part-time work
Licensure and certification	Usually not required
Employment outlook	Faster-than-average growth expected
Holland interest score	ECA

Note: See volume 1, "Publisher's Note," for an explanation of the Holland interest score.

the largest e-commerce sites in the world, was launched in 1995 and had a staff of more than twenty thousand as of 2009.

Traditional Geographic Locations. Most large Internet companies have multiple locations around the world. They often have international headquarters located in major cities overseas, as well as Web hosting sites, data centers, and off-site data-storage facilities. In addition, they usually maintain large campus headquarters in high-tech hot spots, especially Silicon Valley and Seattle, Washington.

Pros of Working for a Large Internet Company. Employees at large Internet companies often enjoy many benefits, including high salaries, increased job security, many opportunities for advancement, and the ability to transfer to other locations. Employees often have the chance to work on multiple projects and experiment with new ideas. They also benefit from having a large, creative team of coworkers, representing the best and the brightest in the industry. Working for large, well-

known firms is also very prestigious and may make it easier to find work in the future. Employees may also utilize the knowledge and business connections they gain at large, successful firms to later launch their own start-up companies.

Cons of Working for a Large Internet Company. Finding work at a large Internet company can be extremely challenging. Competition for open positions is fierce. Candidates need to have significant experience in the field and often have degrees from top universities such as Stanford, Massachusetts Institute of Technology, and Harvard. While employees have more opportunities to advance than they might have at smaller companies, they face significant competition, both internally and externally. The workloads at these companies can be extremely stressful and demanding, and with so many employees, the sense of camaraderie often experienced at smaller firms and Internet start-ups can be lost. In addition, since most of these companies already have established businesses models and a devoted following, it may be difficult to propose radical changes, although that may depend on the atmosphere of the individual company.

Costs

Payroll and Benefits: Employees at large Internet companies usually enjoy generous salaries and many benefits, often including health care, life insurance, vacation time, sick days, and stock options. They may also enjoy gym memberships, on-site exercise facilities, and even child-care services.

Supplies: Large Web-based companies usually have extensive on-site Web hosting servers and massive data storage facilities. E-commerce companies may also have warehouse facilities full of merchandise ready for distribution. Companies must maintain state-of-the art computer systems for their employees, especially those involved in Web design, software development, and content creation.

External Services: Full-time employees perform most duties at large Internet companies. However, these companies often hire external vendors to maintain their facilities, including cleaning and landscaping services. They may also occasionally sign contracts with external firms to handle advertising sales and sometimes hire consultants or outsource accounting, technical support, or Web-design duties, especially for their overseas operations.

Utilities: Large companies typically have extensive data storage and Web hosting facilities. These facilities have very expensive electricity requirements and require dedicated fiber optic data lines. Google's electricity needs are so great that the company has explored purchasing electricity wholesale from power plants and bypassing utility companies. Large businesses must also pay mortgages or rent for their facilities, as well as paying for water, sewage, and telephone services.

Taxes: Large companies in the Internet and cyber communications industry must pay all required local, state, federal, and income taxes. Since many large companies have a significant international presence, they may be required to pay additional taxes for their overseas operations. Depending on state and local laws, e-commerce companies may be required to charge sales tax.

ORGANIZATIONAL STRUCTURE AND JOB ROLES

Companies in the Internet and cyber communications industry share similar organizational structures, although in smaller firms a single person may handle many tasks that are overseen by several different departments in larger firms. In the case of a single freelancer or an entrepreneur launching his or her own site, one person may handle nearly every single aspect of the business while, outsourcing Web hosting and data storage needs to other firms.

The following umbrella categories apply to the organizational structure of businesses in the Internet and cyber communications industry:

- Executive Management
- Web Design and Development
- Software Development
- Sales and Marketing
- Information Technology
- Human Resources
- Technical Support
- Administrative Staff

Executive Management

Most Internet executives have advanced degrees. Entrepreneurs who launch successful online firms can reap large financial rewards once a company goes public or is purchased by a larger firm. In addition, many of the executives at today's largest Web-based businesses have previously helped launch online firms. Executives in this industry usually focus on leading employees and creating and promoting innovative ideas that will attract more Web-site visitors, sales, and advertisers. They are usually the highest-paid employees in their companies, often earning between $58,230 and $128,580 per year, not including stock options, bonuses, or other perks, according to the BLS.

Executive management occupations may include the following:

- Board Chair
- Chief Executive Officer (CEO)
- Chief Financial Officer (CFO)
- Chief Technology Officer (CTO)
- Chief Information Officer (CIO)

- Vice President
- Legal Counsel
- Project Manager or Managing Director

Web Design and Development

Web developers usually focus on testing and implementing new Web-site features and layout designs. They may engage in beta testing and usually work closely with software engineers, project managers, technical support specialists, and public relations personnel to ensure that new innovations match user expectations. They also focus on the day-to-day operations required to keep Web sites up and running.

Web design and development occupations may include the following:

- Web Designer
- Webmaster
- Graphic Designer
- User Interface Engineer
- Product Tester

Software Development

As opposed to Web developers, who focus on layout designs and user features, software engineers design the underlying architecture that allows Web sites to function on a more basic level. This usually involves writing the code to create the tools that Web developers and advertisers use to update content or implement layout changes or new features, as well as the programs and applications that individual users may utilize online or download to their computers. Web sites such as Facebook, for example, offer downloadable applications that help users more easily share photos or information, allowing programs such as iPhoto to upload photos directly from users' computers to their online profiles. Software engineers also play a major role at companies specializing in Web hosting, since they create the programs that allow users easily to upload their Web sites and make them available for online viewing. According to 2009 BLS figures, software engineers usually earn between $62,830 and $98,470 per year.

Software development occupations may include the following:

- Computer Applications Software Engineer

- Computer Systems Software Engineer
- Sales Engineer
- Data Analyst
- Database Administrator

Sales and Marketing

Employees in the sales and marketing departments of Internet companies are normally responsible for attracting new visitors, forming Internet advertising partnerships, and helping spread awareness about their companies. Public relations employees, meanwhile, usually interact with journalists and keep users informed about new developments. This may include launching viral marketing campaigns, buying and selling Web banner ads, collecting user comments on upcoming changes, and increasing e-commerce sales. According to 2007 BLS figures, advertising managers earn approximately $73,060 per year, while sales managers earn $91,560 per year, and public relations managers may earn $82,180 per year.

Sales and marketing occupations may include the following:

- Marketing Manager
- Sales Executive
- Sales Manager
- Marketing Strategist
- Public Relations Specialist

Information Technology

The information technology (IT) staff at companies in the Internet and cyber communications industry are responsible for maintaining the extensive computer networks and data-storage hardware facilities needed to ensure visitors have access to Web sites. Normally, they also provide technical support for employees. They are usually responsible for cyber security needs within an organization, which may include preventing hackers from accessing sensitive user information, protecting against viruses, fighting back against denial-of-service attacks, and securing both external and internal computer networks. They are usually highly trained, most commonly earning bachelor's or master's degrees at a minimum.

IT occupations may include the following:

- Network Specialist
- Computer Systems Analyst

OCCUPATION PROFILE

Computer Security Specialist

Considerations	Qualifications
Description	Plans, implements, and coordinates security for information systems to protect the data contained within them.
Career clusters	Information Technology; Science, Technology, Engineering, and Math
Interests	Data
Working conditions	Work inside
Minimum education level	Bachelor's degree
Physical exertion	Light work
Physical abilities	Unexceptional/basic fitness
Opportunities for experience	Military service; volunteer work; part-time work
Licensure and certification	Recommended
Employment outlook	Faster-than-average growth expected
Holland interest score	IRC

Note: See volume 1, "Publisher's Note," for an explanation of the Holland interest score.

- Information Technology Director
- Information Technology Support Specialist
- Computer Security Specialist

Human Resources

Human resources (HR) personnel are responsible for the well-being of employees. They recruit and train new employees and executives, facilitate their payment, and administer their benefits. In small companies, the HR department may consist of just a single employee, while larger firms may employ hundreds of HR representatives and recruiters. Most HR representatives and recruitment officers hold bachelor's or master's degrees in human resources or labor relations. HR managers can expect to earn between $67,710 and $114,860, according to the BLS.

Human resources occupations may include the following:

- Human Resources Manager
- Human Resources Representative
- Training Specialist
- Recruitment Officer

Technical Support

At Internet companies, most technical support representatives contact clients via e-mail, although they may also interact with customers over the phone, on message boards, or in chat rooms. They often work closely with Web developers, software engineers, and IT personnel in resolving customer complaints and assisting during service outages. They may answer hundreds of e-mails per day.

Technical support departments often offer entry-level positions. Since many firms promote from within, technical support employees may advance within their companies. They usually require an associate's or bachelor's degree or technical certification. Prospective employees must be adept at problem solving and providing excellent customer service. They usually earn between $32,110 and $53,640 per year, according to the BLS.

Technical support occupations may include the following:

- Technical Support Specialist
- Help Desk Specialist
- Customer Service Representative

Administrative Staff

The administrative staff is usually responsible for scheduling meetings and appointments, providing accounting services, keeping financial records, greeting visitors, and assisting executives. Small firms, freelancers, and individual entrepreneurs may outsource administrative services on a contractual basis, especially accounting. The education requirements for members of the administrative staff vary depending on the individual position. For example, it is not uncommon for accountants to earn advanced bachelor's or master's degrees, while receptionists or administrative assistants may have just a high school diploma. Income may also vary widely depending on the individual's position and training. According to the BLS, accountants can expect to earn between $42,520 and $71,960 per year, while receptionists may earn between $18,800 and $28,100.

Administrative occupations may include the following:

- Administrative Assistant
- Accountant
- Receptionist

Android, an operating system designed by Google and used on Motorola's Droid, allows smart phone users to easily access the Internet. (©Dreamstime.com)

Overview

Since the first researchers successfully connected two computers together through a simple phone line in 1965, the Internet has grown into a constantly evolving communications medium that continues rapidly to integrate countless aspects of society. As increasing numbers of people use the Internet as their primary source for information, older forms of media, including television, films, newspapers, and radio, are rushing to get their products online. This trend will only continue as the number of people with Internet access skyrockets on a global scale. While users in developed countries such as the United States switched to high-speed broadband service at a rate of 11 percent in 2008, the greatest number of new Internet users will be found in developing countries such as India and China. As of 2009, there are twice as many Internet users in Asia as in North America.

By 2008, the total number of Internet users worldwide reached more than 1.59 billion, with 14.7 percent of all users located in China. In fact, according to the *Computer Industry Almanac*, China boasts 860,000 more Internet users than the United States. Despite those impressive figures, only 22 percent of the Chinese population has access to the Internet, compared with 75 percent in the U.S. population. Such disparities are part of the reason that future overseas Internet growth is expected to far surpass domestic trends. Both Yahoo! and Google have launched many new services that allow overseas users to access the Internet in their native languages. In fact, new domain names featuring non-Latin characters, in such languages as Arabic and Japanese, have recently been approved for the first time by the Internet Corporation for Assigned Names and Numbers (ICANN), the main regulator of Internet protocols.

Analysts expect a surge of Internet access through cellular phones and other nontraditional devices. Mobile devices such as Apple's iPhone and Motorola's Droid, which features an operating system designed by Google, are revolutionizing the way customers use cell phones. The growth of reliable cellular broadband services allows customers to access the Internet while away from their computers. Many new mobile phones even allow users to connect their computers to the Internet wirelessly via their phones, a process known as "tethering."

The growth in the number of wireless access points at businesses, homes, schools, libraries, government facilities, and even entire cities and neighborhoods has made high-speed broadband freely available to more people than ever before. Hospitals, schools, and governments are all expanding their online services, allowing users easily to access medical records, school records, and government documents. These developments have helped exponentially grow the number of Internet users, creating many new opportunities for entrepreneurs to launch new businesses. By 2013, analysts predict there will be more than 600 million new Internet users, and people are expected to exchange eight times as many messages via e-mail, instant message, and social networking as they did in 2009. Meanwhile, the growth of cloud computing allows businesses and individual users to archive digital information such as pictures, documents, music, and programs online, often for backup purposes but also to gain access to these files from multiple computers or other devices capable of accessing the Internet.

Criminal activity on the Internet has also grown. According to Security Watch, criminal activity online had become a $1 trillion industry by 2009, surpassing even drug trafficking in total global revenues. Businesses, schools, governments, and individual users must focus on Internet safety as they become more dependent on the Web for their daily information needs. According to Carnegie Mellon University, there were 137,592 reported security incidents in 2008, including hacker attacks, denial-of-service attacks, and computer viruses.

The Internet is a constantly evolving marketplace of ideas and information, and this fluid environment allows users to create their own environments. Users at Twitter, for example, have created new tools to allow them to organize and repost information. In turn, the company has taken these ideas and incorporated them into its own designs for the site. Amazon allows users to create their own public online wish lists and write their own reviews for the products they own, and Facebook allows users to

review and comment on all major proposed privacy changes before they are implemented. Meanwhile, Web sites such as Second Life allow users to create their own virtual online worlds, complete with financial transactions and commercial property purchased by advertisers.

More people are launching their own Web sites than at any time in the past. While some of these are founded for business purposes, many more are launched to share information with family and friends or to support hobbies and connect with like-minded individuals. As people establish online identities, the amount of information exchanged through the Internet will continue to grow. This trend has helped raise demand for Web hosting services, software programmers, and Web designers.

Web pioneers with unique ideas have rapidly grown companies from start-ups to large, established businesses worth millions of dollars. Because of free open-source software, decreasing costs for computer hardware, and the rise of affordable Web hosting services, any idea has the potential to gain a strong following and, eventually, commercial success.

Employment Advantages

Internet usage has continued to expand, creating numerous opportunities for job growth. In addition, established businesses in every industry have increased their use of the Internet. From local businesses hiring Webmasters to build and maintain their sites to large, established companies hiring consulting firms to increase their Web presence, the future of businesses is on the Internet.

The BLS expects employment for computer specialists such as Web designers and database administrators to grow by 37 percent by 2016, which is much higher than the national average for growth in other industries. At the same time, significant competition for work in this field is expected. Prospective candidates should expect to earn a bachelor's or master's degree, depending on the position the are seeking. Since much of the growth of the Internet is expected to take place overseas, employees who speak other languages will also gain a considerable advantage.

Annual Earnings

As the number of Internet users grows, the amount of money exchanged through Internet transactions will continue to grow dramatically. Analysts predict that the Internet commerce industry will be worth $13 trillion by 2012, with more than twice the current number of users exchanging goods and services online.

Internet traffic is expected to continue its exponential growth, with experts predicting that users will exchange more than 1 trillion gigabytes of information through the Web by 2015. In addition, the cloud computing industry is still in its infancy, and as companies such as Apple, Microsoft, and Google enter this emerging field, Gartner expects 2009 revenues to grow by 21.3 percent to 56.3 billion, although IDC expects more modest growth of $42 billion by 2012. In contrast, by 2011, Merrill Lynch predicts soaring revenues of $160 billion.

As the Internet continues to become more fully integrated into daily life, it will continue to evolve and expand. The tremendous expected growth of the Internet and cyber communications industry will give future entrepreneurs many opportunities to launch new businesses and will also allow many established Internet firms to continue to attract new customers and advertising partners.

RELATED RESOURCES FOR FURTHER RESEARCH

ASSOCIATION FOR COMPUTING MACHINERY
2 Penn Plaza, Suite 701
New York, NY 10121-0701
Tel: (800) 342-6626
Fax: (212) 944-1318
http://www.acm.org

INSTITUTE OF ELECTRICAL AND ELECTRONICS ENGINEERS
3 Park Ave., 17th Floor
New York, NY 10016-5997
Tel: (212) 419-7900
Fax: (212) 752-4929
http://www.ieee.org

INTERNET CORPORATION FOR ASSIGNED NAMES AND NUMBERS
4676 Admiralty Way, Suite 330
Marina del Rey, CA 90292-6601
Tel: (310) 823-9358

Fax: (310) 823-8649
http://www.icann.org

INTERNET ENGINEERING TASK FORCE
48377 Fremont Blvd., Suite 117
Fremont, CA 94538
Tel: (510) 492-4080
Fax: (510) 492-4001
http://www.ietf.org

INTERNET SOCIETY
1775 Wiehle Ave., Suite 201
Reston, VA 20190-5108
Tel: (703) 439-2120
Fax: (703) 326-9881
http://www.isoc.org

SOFTWARE AND INFORMATION INDUSTRY ASSOCIATION
1090 Vermont Ave. NW, 6th Floor
Washington, DC 20005-4095
Tel: (202) 289-7442
Fax: (202) 289-7097
http://www.siia.net

ABOUT THE AUTHOR

Elizabeth Fernandez began working in the computer industry in 2002, serving as a Webmaster and a hardware and software repair specialist. For the past ten years, she has also worked as a writer and editor specializing in computer science and technology trends. She has been published online, in newspapers, and in local magazines, and she has edited several books focusing on the computer, aviation, and transportation industries. She graduated with a degree in journalism from the University of Central Florida.

FURTHER READING

Amazon.com. "About Amazon." http://www.amazon.com/Careers-Homepage/b?ie=UTF8&node=239364011.

Aspray, William, and Paul E. Ceruzzi, eds. *The Internet and American Business*. Cambridge, Mass.: MIT Press, 2008.

Campbell-Kelly, Martin, and William Aspray.

Computer: A History of the Information Machine. 2d ed. Boulder, Colo.: Westview Press, 2004.

Computer History Museum. "Internet History." http://www.computerhistory.org/ internet_history.

Discovery Institute. "U.S. Internet Traffic Projected to Grow Fifty-fold over Next Five Years." January 29, 2008. http://www .discovery.org/a/4444.

Kador, John. *Internet Jobs! The Complete Guide to Finding the Hottest Internet Jobs.* New York: McGraw-Hill, 2000.

Lacy, Sarah. *Once You're Lucky, Twice You're Good: The Rebirth of Silicon Valley and the Rise of Web 2.0.* New York: Gotham Books, 2008.

Singel, Ryan. "Google Profits up 27 Percent in Q3." *Wired,* October 15, 2009. http:// www.wired.com/epicenter/2009/10/google- profits-up-3q-200.

Sorid, Daniel. "Writing the Web's Future in Numerous Languages." *The New York Times,* December 30, 2009.

Stair, Lisa, and Stair, Leslie. *Careers in Computers.* 3d ed. Chicago: VGM Career Books, 2001.

Stibel, Jeffrey M. *Wired for Thought: How the Brain Is Shaping the Future of the Internet.* Boston: Harvard Business Press, 2009.

Twitter. "Working at Twitter." http://twitter .com/jobs.

U.S. Bureau of Labor Statistics. *Career Guide to Industries,* 2010-2011 ed. http://www.bls.gov/ oco/cg.

_____. "Computer and Information Systems Managers." In *Occupational Outlook Handbook,* 2010-2011 ed. http://www.bls.gov/oco/ ocos258.htm.

_____. "Computer Support Specialists and Systems Administrators." In *Occupational Outlook Handbook,* 2010-2011 ed. http:// www.bls.gov/oco/ocos268.htm.

U.S. Census Bureau. North American Industry Classification System (NAICS), 2007. http:// www.census.gov/cgi-bin/sssd/naics/ naicsrch?chart=2007.

U.S. Department of Commerce. International Trade Administration. Office of Trade and Industry Information. Industry Trade Data and Analysis. http://ita.doc.gov/td/industry/ otea/OTII/OTII-index.html.

Warman, Matt. "Macworld 2009: Apple's Cloud Computing Plans Will Threaten Google and Microsoft." *The Telegraph,* January 7, 2009. http://www.telegraph.co.uk/technology/ apple/4160043/Macworld-2009-Apples- cloudcomputing-plans-will-threaten-Google- and-Microsoft.html.

Landscaping Services

INDUSTRY SNAPSHOT

General Industry: Architecture and Construction

Career Cluster: Architecture and Construction

Subcategory Industries: Arborist Services; Cemetary Plot Care Services; City Planning Services; Garden Care and Maintenance Services; Garden Planning Services; Golf Course Planning Services; Industrial Land Use Planning Services; Interior and Exterior Plant Maintenance Services; Landscape Architectural Services; Landscape Care and Maintenance Services; Landscape Installation Services; Landscape Planning Services; Lawn Care and Maintenance Services; Lawn Supply Stores; Nurseries and Garden Centers; Seasonal Property Maintenance Services, Including Snow Plowing; Ski Area Planning Services; Tree Services

Related Industries: Building Architecture Industry; Building Construction Industry; Civil Services: Planning; Natural Resources Management; Real Estate Industry

Annual Domestic Revenues: $49.928 billion USD (IBISWorld, 2010)

NAICS Numbers: 444220, 541320, 561730

INDUSTRY DEFINITION

Summary

Landscaping services enhance the built environment, both commercial and residential. Landscaping may commence with design services. Exterior and interior landscaping services involve site preparation and installation of plant materials, including lawns, shrubs, trees, and gardens, followed by maintenance. During winter months, exterior landscape maintenance of plant materials and weed control may be unnecessary in areas with colder climates and landscaping service providers may plow snow and remove ice instead. Interior plant maintenance within buildings is required year-round. Landscaping services include ancillary activities, such as installation of irrigation and drainage systems; lighting planning and installation; and construction of outdoor structures, retaining walls, walkways, and built accents known as hardscape.

History of the Industry

Humans have tamed the natural landscape since ancient times. Early examples of such landscaping include the Hanging Gardens of Babylon, in which elaborate irrigation systems were maintained. In addition, Japanese gardeners have designed and maintained medita-

Landscaping may commence with design services. (©Dreamstime.com)

tive Zen gardens since the fifth century. Introduction of built features into the natural landscape was also a service provided by early landscapers, and the Great Wall of China is such a feature. Slaves often provided the labor necessary to complete such ancient landscaping projects.

The practice of landscaping began to evolve during the Roman era. Wealthy Romans and Greeks maintained formal gardens for decorative purposes that were based on rigid, geometric designs. Letters written by Pliny the Younger describe the landscape at his Tuscan estate as consisting of trimmed boxwood hedges maintained to segment the landscape into precise geometric shapes. In addition, archaeologists have found several examples of formal gardens that include landscaping features such as water fountains.

Although landscape design and services were of little consequence during the early part of the Middle Ages, the Renaissance of the sixteenth and seventeenth centuries prompted a reemergence of formal gardening in the West, especially in France and Italy. Many monasteries had gardens that were maintained by members of monastic communities.

Wealthy persons' gardeners, such as those employed to maintain the Tivoli Gardens or the classical French gardens of Versailles, sculpted plant materials into topiary animals and maintained elaborate water, walkway, trellis, arbor, and wall features to enhance the designs and further complement the surrounding architectural estates.

The English revived informal landscapes in the eighteenth century with English cottage gardens that often overflowed with flowers. As gardens became less formal and smaller, members the general populace provided their own landscaping services or began to engage gardeners to maintain agricultural plants, medicinal herbs, and fruit trees that not only served practical purposes but also enhanced aesthetics. The landscaping of grounds surrounding estates became more informal and natural, influenced by the Romantic movement and landscape art, and parklands were created for the public. The English gave birth to the profession of landscape architecture.

In the United States, lawn installation and maintenance emerged as a dominant component of landscaping services, influenced by nineteenth and twentieth century landscape and park designers such as Frederick Law Olmsted. Olmsted incorporated open lawns in many of his designs, including the 1869 layout of the Chicago suburb of Riverside. Public landscaping services to establish and maintain parks, cemeteries, golf courses, and related facilities were provided by municipalities, states, and the federal government. Urban planners encouraged the wedding of nature with the humanmade environment.

Edwin Budding invented the lawn mower in 1830, promoting the growth of landscaping in suburbs and increasing the need for landscaping services, which were no longer limited to the rich. Private landscaping services began to thrive as more private property owners designed lawns and planted other plant materials to beautify their homes. In addition, commercial landscaping services grew rapidly during the twentieth century, as owners of commercial and institutional buildings used plant materials and incorporated landscape features into their overall designs for aesthetic and marketing purposes. Maintenance of such plant materials and built landscape features is now a mainstay of the landscaping services industry.

The Industry Today

Twenty-first century landscaping serves many purposes, such as providing functional and relaxing living spaces, mostly outdoors; creating specific moods and first impressions through the deployment of plants and constructed materials; and enhancing property values. Landscapers and landscape architects improve many portions of the human built environment, including residential, commercial, and institutional buildings, such as educational facilities, hospitals, and museums; highways; airports; land subdivisions; and shopping malls. Public and private open spaces, including parks, playgrounds, recreational areas, golf courses, athletic fields, and cemeteries are also part of the constructed landscape developed and maintained through landscaping services.

Many of the twenty-first century's landscaping services are the same as those that have been employed in the past, but the methods for providing these services have been enhanced by technology and invention, starting with the lawn mower in 1830. Most landscapers use small hand or power tools and equipment to perform a variety of tasks that might involve digging, cutting, raking, water-

Exterior and interior landscaping services involve site preparation and installation of plant materials, including lawns, shrubs, trees, and gardens, followed by maintenance. (©Lisa Cora Reed/Dreamstime.com)

ing, and spraying. Shovels, rakes, saws, trimmers, clippers, pruners, loppers, shears, and blowers are typical tools used by landscape maintenance workers and groundskeepers. Landscapers, especially contractors, may also use larger equipment for installation and maintenance, such as tractors, grading implements, seeders, sprayers, sod cutters, trenchers, portable irrigators, and vacuums to remove water from playing fields. They may also work with dangerous chemicals, herbicides, pesticides, and fertilizers that require careful usage and training to prevent harm due to exposure.

Today's landscape practitioners plan, install, care for, and maintain landscaping features of exterior and interior spaces. Activities such as site preparation; planting of trees, shrubs, plants, vines, and flowers—including native, imported, and ornamental materials; seeding lawns; laying sod and turf; and hydroseeding to control erosion are part of landscape installation. In providing these services, a landscaper may need to engage surveyors to stake out the layout of a plan before installation. Installing plant materials also involves carefully preparing beds, pits, and other planting locations with proper soil, fertilizers, and drainage. It may require erosion control, staking of young plants until they are established, and construction of tree-protection grates, especially in urban areas.

Once plant materials have been installed, groundskeepers and gardeners see to their maintenance and care. They prune and trim exterior trees and shrubs; fertilize and spray to control insects and diseases; control weeds; mow, edge, thatch, and aerate lawns; mulch surfaces with bark, wood chips, and other natural materials; care for cemetery plots; maintain gardens, parks, playgrounds, and athletic fields; and care for interior plants and shrubs in places such as office buildings, hotels, commercial malls, and botanical gardens. Arborists may be called upon to maintain trees and larger shrubs through pruning and trimming. Because arborists have special knowledge of tree diseases,

Maintenance of plant materials and built landscape features is a mainstay of the landscaping services industry. (©Dreamstime.com)

they may also be required to clear diseased trees, remove diseased limbs and branches, treat tree wounds, and spray to control tree pests and diseases.

Landscaping service providers may also be called upon to remove plant materials to maintain rights of way through clear cutting and line slashing, mow along highways, and remove tree branches close to overhead utility lines. Modern sports arenas may employ groundskeepers to maintain playing fields and turf, whether natural or artificial. Landscaping may be a seasonal industry in many locales. During the spring, summer, and fall seasons, services may include cleanup after the winter, installation and maintenance of plants, and raking of leaves. During winter months, landscaping services may be limited to snow and ice removal.

A paver installs a walkway; paved walkways and similar elements are known as hardscape. (©Dreamstime.com)

Landscape service providers also introduce human-made features, known as hardscape, and some natural, nonplant materials into landscapes. In addition to designing such features, they may construct and install them. Hardscape and related landscape features include paved walkways and driveways; retaining walls; fencing; decks and outdoor living spaces; water features such as fountains and ponds; lighting; and other natural, structural, and masonry landscape elements, including rock walls, boulders, outdoor fireplaces, arbors, trellises, pagodas, gazebos, built-in furniture, garden art, containers, birdbaths, and birdhouses. Service providers may also be called upon to clean, paint, repair, and replace hardscape materials periodically; to turn on water features in the spring and winterize them in the winter; and to sweep walks and driveways.

Drainage and irrigation systems are also important features of landscape management. Landscape contractors, landscape architects, and related professionals analyze soils and water tables to determine the types of plant materials that can or should be installed in a given location and the irrigation levels necessary to sustain them. Some landscapers may use sophisticated equipment to obtain accurate readings of soil moisture, such as that involved in maintenance of golf courses. Some of the irrigation systems that might be installed and maintained by landscape service providers include sprinklers, drip or trickle systems, and newer technologies including subsurface irrigation distribution systems. Landscape management also includes control of water and proper drainage. Landscape workers may install and maintain drainage systems designed by civil engineers that include everything from drainage tiles to simple French drains.

The nursery industry is also a sector of the landscaping services industry. Landscape service providers may grow their own plant materials or create their own natural landscaping materials, such as wood chips and mulch, but they also partner with nurseries to provide such materials, and nurseries themselves provide advice and labor in addition to simply selling garden materials and supplies, thereby providing some level of landscaping service. A landscaper may also rely on a horticulturalist to provide information on the best plant materials for a particular climate or to resist locally prevalent diseases and pests.

Complex and even noncomplex landscape designs are typically provided by licensed landscape architects, who may be employed by architecture firms or by landscape services firms. In either case, architects work both with building architects and

Installing plant materials for a garden landscape such as this involves carefully preparing beds, pits, and other planting locations with proper soil, fertilizers, and drainage. (©Dreamstime.com)

contractors and with landscaping contractors to design and deploy features that meet the needs of clients and also fit well with the overall grounds of which they will be part. Some larger landscaping companies have begun to offer a more comprehensive range of services that include building maintenance and security in addition to landscape installation and maintenance.

INDUSTRY MARKET SEGMENTS

Landscaping services may be provided by self-employed individuals, such as gardeners, grounds-keepers, or sole practioner landscape architects, or they may be provided by large companies with multiple offices across the country. Indeed, large companies must spread themselves out geographically much more than companies in most other industries, because landscaping services by their very na-

ture cannot be centralized in the way many other businesses can be. Both large and small businesses may specialize in a specific component of landscape services, although large companies are better equipped to provide more comprehensive service than are smaller ventures. Small businesses may act as contractors, working on a portion of a larger project, or they may concentrate on tasks to which small concerns are well suited, such as residential lawn and garden maintenance.

Small Businesses

The thousands of small landscaping service companies account for the highest percentage of revenues in the overall industry. Small landscaping businesses are often owner-operated and offer limited services, mainly associated with plant material installation and maintenance for residential and commercial properties. Often, individuals who have worked as laborers for landscaping companies start their own businesses once they have obtained sufficient experience in the field. Many small business operations are seasonal and employ part-time workers. Small businesses are the most likely to include wintertime snow and ice removal among their services.

Potential Annual Earnings Scale. According to the U.S. Bureau of Labor Statistics (BLS), the average annual salary of a landscape architect in 2009 was $66,400, while the average salary of those employed specifically in the landscape services field was $59,580. Soil and plant scientists earned average salaries of $53,990. Landscaping and groundskeeping workers earned an average of $24,670, while tree trimmers and pruners earned an average of $30,830. In 2007, the total average annual earnings by a small landscaping business employing one to four persons was $133,011.

Clientele Interaction. Although marketing can be accomplished by placing advertising signs on completed landscaping projects, small landscaping companies rely heavily on referrals to grow their businesses. Moreover, repeat business, encouraged by providing quality service, is important to small landscaping businesses. Therefore, good client interaction is paramount.

The task of interacting with clients is usually carried out by the owner of a small business. Owners often have multiple roles within their companies, including management and sales. Because owners may spend significant amounts of time securing contracts and negotiating with clients, much day-to-day client interaction may fall to other employees. In conducting sales, a small-business owner normally negotiates with homeowners and owners of small commercial establishments, institutional facilities, and office buildings. Interaction involves not only making sales but also responding immediately to clients' questions and following up with clients upon job completion to ensure repeat business. Some small companies may have field supervisors to answer customers' questions on job sites, but all owners of small landscaping businesses should develop guidelines for employees to follow when working with clients to ensure they behave in a professional manner.

Amenities, Atmosphere, and Physical Grounds. For individuals who enjoy working mainly outdoors with plant materials and landscape features, owning and operating a small landscaping company provides a perfect opportunity.

The purpose of a small landscaping business is to beautify homes and businesses, so the work atmosphere is mostly pleasant. Landscaping work is physically strenuous, however. Outdoor work may involve uncomfortable heat during summer months and attacks by swarming and nesting insects. Small landscaping businesses may employ workers only part time as a result of the influence of the weather and other factors. Both owners and employees should be able to work with hand and power tools in a safe manner.

Those working for a small landscaping business spend most of their time installing and maintaining lawns and plant materials surrounding residential and commercial properties. Work activities include mowing lawns, digging and planting, raking grass and leaves, watering, mulching, and trimming hedges and trees. Some owners of small landscaping businesses have found a niche market in the installation and care of indoor plantings in office buildings and commercial facilities, such as malls and hotels.

All landscaping businesses require workers to travel to job sites. Travel may take place in employee vehicles, but businesses generally have at least one vehicle—owned by the company or its owner directly—to transport tools, equipment, landscaping materials, and employees. Thus, a driver's license and ability to drive a truck may be a requirement for obtaining a landscaping job, especially in a small company.

Typical Number of Employees. Most small landscaping businesses are run by their owners—and, in many cases, the owner's family members. Employees often include seasonal, part-time, contract, and day laborers who are employed on an as-needed basis to minimize costs. The typical small landscaping business has one to four employees.

Traditional Geographic Locations. Because landscaping mainly involves outdoor work, landscaping businesses are most often located in areas with year-round growing conditions, and the greatest number of U.S. companies are in the Southeast. However, landscaping businesses thrive throughout the globe, wherever residential and nonresidential development exists, albeit not always on a year-round basis, and almost all areas of the country have some landscaping businesses.

Pros of Working for a Small Landscaping Business. Landscaping providers work with plants and spend much of their time outdoors. In addition, most workers do not require training or college degrees to obtain entry-level positions, although they may need specialized training and licensure or certification if they are involved in tasks such as applying pesticides. Most training takes place on the job. In a small business, workers may have substantial responsibility for carrying out jobs on their own, as there may not be a supervisor on site. Workers, however, must be self-motivating, as timeliness is important in meeting contract obligations and ensuring that plant materials do not suffer damage from delays in replanting.

Landscape architects are able to exercise a great deal of creativity and may be relatively well compensated. While architects at small firms are unlikely to win major city-planning-related contracts, they may compete successfully for a wide range of other sorts of contracts, from residential remodeling and construction projects to planning and design of large commercial and nonprofit institutional properties.

Cons of Working for a Small Landscaping Business. Work in small landscaping businesses may be seasonal, is often part time, and can involve high rates of turnover due to factors such as the strenuous nature of the work. Wages for entry-level positions are low, and working conditions require substantial physical labor and repetitive bending and lifting movements. Based on BLS figures, landscaping laborers suffer an above-average rate of work-related injury and illness relative to workers in other industries.

Costs

Payroll and Benefits: Landscaping businesses usually pay manual laborers hourly wages. Because they are seasonal businesses, payrolls may be highest in the summer months, when the demand for landscaping services is at its peak. Landscaping workers, often part-time, rarely receive benefits such as vacation or sick leave. Owners of such businesses—including landscape architects at small or one-person firms—must pay themselves out of their companies' profits, after all other financial obligations are met. If a company has no profits in a given month, its owner or partners may receive no pay.

Supplies: Landscape maintenance crews require small hand tools and power equipment, as well

as seeds or seedlings; soil, compost, or fertilizer; and, usually, a company vehicle. Standard equipment includes lawn mowers, leaf blowers, power and hand saws, rakes, pruning shears, hedge trimmers, weed wackers, rototillers, and fertilizer spreaders. Contractors and installers may require heavier machinery, including tractors or bulldozers, as well as hardscape materials such as cement, asphalt, paving stones, and so forth. Landscape architects require drafting supplies, including professional-grade computer software.

External Services: Because contracting for services is an important component of any landscaping business and compliance with environmental laws may also be a factor, legal services are likely to be one of the main external service requirements of a small landscaping business. Landscapers may also contract accountants or tax preparation experts and computer support services. They may rent the equipment needed for a particularly large or unusual job, rather than purchasing equipment they are unlikely to employ regularly. Landscapers and landscape architects also frequently work with one another, and either one may represent an external vendor from the point of view of the other.

Utilities: Because landscaping work is completed on the property of others, there are not many utility costs directly assessed to the landscaping business. Costs that do exist, such as paying to move a utility line, are usually included in the contract. Businesses that maintain offices, however, require electricity and other standard utilities, including telephone and Internet service. Businesses run out of owners' homes may be able to pay a portion of the owners' utility costs, treating them as business expenses. Mobile phones are also necessary so owners and workers can communicate with one another and with clients while on, or traveling to, job sites.

Taxes: Landscaping businesses must pay payroll and unemployment taxes on employee income, as well as property taxes as appropriate. Small businesses may pay corporate taxes, or owners may instead pay personal income and self-employment taxes on their profits. Some states levy sales taxes on landscaping services, and businesses are responsible for collecting and paying those taxes as well.

Midsize Businesses

Midsize landscaping businesses are involved in many of the same residential and nonresidential installation and maintenance activities as are small companies. However, the scale of such services can be greater, encompassing larger sites as, as well as a greater number of clients per business. Midsize businesses may also offer more specialty services, such as those provided by arborists, horticulturalists, and landscape architects.

Potential Annual Earnings Scale. In 2007, the average midsize landscaping business earned revenues of $756,132. According to the BLS, the average annual salary of a landscape architect in 2009 was $66,400, while the average salary of those employed specifically in the landscape services field was $59,580. Soil and plant scientists earned average salaries of $53,990. Landscaping and groundskeeping workers earned an average of $24,670, and tree trimmers and pruners earned an average of $30,830, while their supervisors earned an average of $41,990.

Clientele Interaction. Professional client interaction is the driving force behind midsize businesses' success, as it is for small businesses as well. A midsize company is more likely to employ college-educated, dedicated sales and customer-relations personnel to manage and process contracts. Although the owner of a midsize business may still be involved in finding new customers, the tasks of following up on new leads and customer retention fall to other employees. Field supervisors are available on job sites to respond directly to customer questions and needs.

Amenities, Atmosphere, and Physical Grounds. Most midsize landscaping companies have autonomous commercial facilities separate from their owners' homes. These facilities include business offices, where management and support staff work, as well as storage and maintenance facilities for tools, equipment, and machinery. Some midsize landscaping companies produce their own plant or landscaping materials, such as mulch, and incorporate small greenhouse and nursery facilities into their business complexes.

The majority of employees work outside, stopping in their companies' offices only briefly or rarely to coordinate activities and interact with colleagues as necessary. In addition to their typical landscaping installation and weekly maintenance duties, on-site laborers may be involved in more complex landscaping work, such as grading and terracing property or installing and maintaining lighting, hardscape features, and irrigation systems. Some workers have certifications in pest and disease control and use larger equipment and machinery, such as small tractors, to carry out their tasks.

Typical Number of Employees. Midsize landscaping companies rely on more full-time employees than do small companies. Although lower-paid seasonal and part-time workers are employed during the busiest seasons, midsize businesses are better equipped financially to maintain a full-time core staff. Midsize landscaping businesses generally have between five and nineteen employees.

Traditional Geographic Locations. All landscaping businesses are located where there is sufficient residential and commercial development to establish a demand for their services. It is estimated that more than 25 percent of homeowners now utilize the services of a landscaping company, so areas experiencing residential growth, such as the southern United States, are prime locations for successful landscaping businesses. Midsize companies compete with smaller companies to provide landscaping services to residential homeowners and nonresidential business, institutional, and commercial properties. However, because midsize businesses often have more specialized staff, they are also able to secure contracts from utility companies and governmental entities to service public spaces. Thus, midsize companies may help maintain road and utility rights-of-way, parks, playgrounds, and recreational facilities, and they may be located anywhere such services are needed. Midsize landscaping companies may also fill specific niches, such as maintaining golf courses and athletic fields.

Pros of Working for a Midsize Landscaping Business. Midsize companies employ more full-time workers than do small companies, which rely on part-time labor, so they can offer their employees greater job stability. In addition, midsize businesses often employ foremen and other supervisors to coordinate workers in the field, so they are better able to maintain control of job sites. These supervisors reduce the amount of responsibility placed on low-wage workers and increase the level of service provided to clients. Midsize companies are also able to complete more ambitious projects than are small companies.

Cons of Working for a Midsize Landscaping Business. Landscapers working for midsize businesses must still perform strenuous physical labor outdoors in all types of weather conditions, and they still face the risk of injury or illness. They may also feel constrained by the presence of supervisors on site.

Costs

Payroll and Benefits: Midsize landscaping businesses pay most field workers hourly, and those employed on a part-time or seasonal basis are not likely to receive benefits. Support and management staff are likely to work full time and receive salaries. They usually receive at least some benefits, such as vacation and sick leave, and they may receive health insurance and bonuses as well.

Supplies: Landscape maintenance crews require small hand tools and power equipment, as well as seeds or seedlings; soil, compost, or fertilizer; and, usually, a company vehicle. Standard equipment includes lawn mowers, leaf blowers, power and hand saws, rakes, pruning shears, hedge trimmers, weed wackers, rototillers, and fertilizer spreaders. Contractors and installers may require heavier machinery, including tractors or bulldozers, as well as hardscape materials such as cement, asphalt, paving stones, and so forth. Landscape architects require drafting supplies, including professional-grade computer software.

Midsize businesses are better able to afford the cost of purchasing, maintaining, and repairing more power tools and larger equipment, including tractors and twin-axle vehicles, rather than renting or leasing such equipment. They are likely to have more than one company vehicle as well, facilitating workers' transportation to multiple job sites simultaneously.

External Services: Midsize landscaping businesses are more likely than small businesses to handle accounting and computer services in-house, but legal services typically remain external. As companies increase their supply and use of equipment and machinery, so too will their needs for external maintenance and repair services increase.

Utilities: Midsize companies, like small companies, require water, electricity, telephone, and Internet services. However, because midsize companies are more likely to have their own office and storage facilities, the cost of some utilities is part of such businesses' overhead expenses and is not included in customer contracts.

Taxes: Midsize companies are required to pay property taxes on any business offices or storage facilities they own, as well as local, state, and federal income, payroll, and unemployment taxes for employees. Landscaping contracts in some states may also include a tax on the price of the services provided.

Large Businesses

The fifty largest landscaping service companies generate about 15 percent of the industry's revenue. Although these large businesses provide services to practically all of the industry's largest customers, such as utility companies and recreational complexes, small and midsize landscaping companies are able to compete effectively with large companies because labor and equipment costs are mostly fixed, depending on the geographic location of the business. In fact, large, national landscaping companies need to establish small, local offices in order to compete with the smaller companies. Some of the large companies specialize in one service, such as the Davey Tree Expert Company, which provides mainly tree services, or TruGreen, which specializes in lawn care.

Potential Annual Earnings Scale. In 2007, the average annual earnings of large landscaping services companies ranged from $3,193,196 to $485,692,126. According to the BLS, the average annual salary of a landscape architect in 2009 was $66,400, while the average salary of those employed specifically in the landscape services field was $59,580. Soil and plant scientists earned average salaries of $53,990. Landscaping and groundskeeping workers earned an average of $24,670, and tree trimmers and pruners earned an average of $30,830, while their supervisors earned an average of $41,990. Company chief executives earned an average of $144,960, while general and operations managers earned $84,270.

Clientele Interaction. Retention of large accounts is necessary to sustain a large landscaping business. The owners of large companies have little day-to-day contact with customers, however, and rely on sales and customer-service employees to provide the bulk of client interaction. Large companies are usually compartmentalized, devoting entire departments to managing client relationships and contracts. Client interaction may include not only initially assessing customer needs but also following up at the end of a job to ensure satisfaction. Customer-service and other client-relations staff may administer customer satisfaction surveys as part of continuing quality control operations.

Amenities, Atmosphere, and Physical Grounds. Large landscaping companies often concentrate on one main service, such as tree or lawn care, pesticide control, or line-clearing for utilities. However, approximately 70 percent of their business still remains residential and commercial landscape installation and maintenance. Large landscaping firms must compete with small and midsize companies for this business.

Large landscaping companies have a greater number of support staff working out of central business offices than do smaller companies. The local branches of large companies, though, still employ mainly field laborers who provide exterior landscaping services. Large companies exercise greater control over job sites than do smaller companies, deploying supervisors and inspectors and using sophisticated computer software to manage jobs. Large landscaping businesses also have better-equipped facilities for storage, maintenance, and repair of equipment and machinery, and they are more likely to produce their own landscaping materials or to own subsidiary nursery and landscape-supply companies.

Landscape laborers in large companies may be involved in more complex landscaping tasks, such as following design plans for grading and terracing property; installing lighting, retaining walls, walkways, and patios; and implementing irrigation and sprinkler systems. Some workers have certifications in pest and disease control. Professional turf and field management is normally the purview of large landscaping companies and requires employees to conduct soil analysis, install proper drainage structures, aerate and vacuum sports fields, and periodically replace turf.

Typical Number of Employees. Large landscaping companies employ more than 20 people, and some employ more than 250. Although seasonal and part-time workers are still employed in local branches of large landscaping businesses, more employees work full time, especially in the main office.

Traditional Geographic Locations. Large landscaping companies have at least one central office to manage the work of several smaller branch offices, which may be located throughout the United States and even internationally. Branch offices operate in a manner similar to the single offices of small and midsize companies, with facilities located in areas where there is residential and nonresidential growth and a corresponding high demand for their services.

Large landscaping companies are more likely to secure long-term contracts for landscaping and related services, thus guaranteeing both seasonal and nonseasonal work. Their most profitable branch offices are located in affluent areas with temperate climates that require year-round residential and commercial lawn and landscaping services.

Pros of Working for a Large Landscaping Business. Some employees of large landscaping businesses are assigned specialized duties associated with landscape design, pest and disease control, plant hybridization, construction of sophisticated landscape features, or installation of complex irrigation systems and water features. Large companies are more likely to provide specialty employees with training and educational benefits. Large landscaping companies generally enjoy financial stability, increasing their ability to withstand economic downturns. They are able to provide greater job opportunities than are smaller companies, including full-time employment, higher wages, potential for job growth, and nonseasonal work.

Cons of Working for a Large Landscaping Business. Economic decline may have a substantial impact on a large landscaping business, especially one that is tied to the construction industry, resulting in numerous layoffs. With many branch offices, coordination of business activities becomes more complex and requires the additional expense of employing management personnel. Although specialists can be found in large landscaping companies, such companies also employ low-paid laborers who work at repetitive jobs and carry out overlapping duties, including performing strenuous tasks outdoors in all types of weather conditions.

Costs

Payroll and Benefits: Large landscaping companies employ more professional, full-time, salaried workers. These employees are likely to receive benefits such as health and life insurance, as revenues tend to be more stable in the larger companies, despite the seasonal nature of the landscaping industry. Hourly laborers are more likely to be full time as well and to receive vacation pay and sick leave. Many receive other benefits, such as health insurance.

Supplies: Large landscaping businesses have multiple inventories of basic tools and equipment, enabling them to serve many customers. Each branch office, however, is unlikely to have any more tools, equipment, or machinery than a small or midsize company, except when the local office is involved in specialty work. Specialty equipment might include graders, forklifts, bucket trucks, and turf vacuums. Large landscaping companies also maintain large fleets of company vehicles.

External Services: Large landscaping companies contract fewer services externally than do smaller companies. They have in-house professional staffs, including accountants, landscape designers, estimators, legal personnel, and computer technicians. They may still need some external services, such as legal and accounting services, as well as advertising services for major campaigns. Branch offices, moreover, may need to engage local professionals when central offices' staffs are unable to meet their needs. Large landscaping businesses are more likely to employ personnel to maintain and repair equipment, but in smaller branch offices this function may be outsourced.

Utilities: Job site utility needs for a large landscaping company are usually charged to or provided by customers. These include water and electricity. Utility services such as telephone and Internet access are part of business overhead. In addition, central offices and branch offices incur utility costs.

Taxes: Large landscaping businesses are required to pay property taxes on business offices and storage facilities. Labor costs present the greatest investment of a landscaping company, and these include payment of local, state, and federal income, payroll, and unemployment taxes for employees. Some states also have a tax on landscaping services sales related to maintenance.

ORGANIZATIONAL STRUCTURE AND JOB ROLES

The typical landscaping services company includes business management, sales, marketing, and customer relations personnel. The majority of employees, however, are the laborers who carry out the actual landscaping services. In smaller companies, many of which are family-owned, one person or a few family members may be responsible for most if not all of the job roles. Arborists, horticulturalists, and landscape designers, including landscape architects, are some of the specialists that might be involved in a landscaping services business.

Job categories within the landscaping services industry vary from highly paid management and marketing personnel, who are often college-educated, to unskilled laborers, who earn low wages and may be employed part time or on a seasonal basis. Not all landscaping services companies require personnel in all job categories, especially specialists. However, throughout the industry, the major tasks involved in running business operations remain largely the same.

The following umbrella categories apply to the organizational structure of businesses in the landscaping services industry:

- Business Management
- Customer Service
- Sales and Marketing
- Equipment, Facilities, and Security
- Technology, Research, Design, and Development
- Site Supervision
- Landscape Work
- Tree Trimming
- Pest Control
- Human Resources

Business Management

Landscape business managers must appreciate all aspects of the landscaping business, from familiarity with plant materials and the pests and diseases that affect them to knowledge of landscaping equipment and its operation. Management roles include supervising and directing employees directly or through field supervisors and coordinating all aspects of a business.

Contracting with clients is an important component of any landscaping services business, and management roles could include the preparation and review of contracts. Financial planning, budgeting, and asset management to keep a company solvent are also necessary tasks associated with landscape management. Because landscaping services involve some use of chemicals and pesticides, managers must also be familiar with governmental regulations and environmental laws that apply to the use and storage of such products. Managers remain current with industry advances through membership in professional associations and trade organizations.

Managers within the landscaping services industry usually have two- or four-year college degrees in landscape management or business fields, with course work in related fields such as horticulture and landscape architecture. A well-rounded manager should also have taken courses in finance, accounting, management operations, computer applications, business communications, and personnel management. Average annual salaries for landscape managers vary widely, from under $30,000 to over $60,000, depending on the size and location of the company.

Business management occupations may include the following:

- Owner/Company Manager
- Chief Financial Officer (CFO)
- Controller
- Department Manager
- Project Manager
- Production Manager
- General Counsel

Customer Service

Landscaping is a service industry, and customer relations is very important for sustaining a company. Customer service personnel assist management in preparing estimates and production budgets, writing specifications, conducting site evaluations, negotiating contracts, and, where necessary, ensuring contract compliance in a timely manner. Land-

scaping companies may need to engage the services of professionals, such as attorneys and accountants, to assist in contracting and budgeting tasks. Larger landscaping companies may employ some of these professionals.

Customer service personnel must be able to communicate and work with people, as often their jobs require addressing and resolving customer complaints. Employees need to coordinate with management, sales and marketing, and human resources staff to ensure that customers are satisfied. Although all landscaping companies must manage customer contracts, larger companies rely more heavily on computer software applications to support this task, which may be the responsibility of those in customer service.

In larger landscaping companies, most customer service employees have college degrees in areas such as business communications, consumer psychology, and English. Finance, accounting, and law degrees may also be valuable to those involved in contract processing and management. Small-business owners who have multiple responsibilities and no college degrees must learn how to manage customer service through experience. Wages within this category are dependent on the exact job title, with those involved in contract management and financial matters receiving average pay in excess of $50,000, while the average starting salary of a chief estimator in a midsize construction company is around $45,000.

Customer service occupations may include the following:

- Customer Service Manager
- Customer Service Representative
- Contract Supervisor
- Chief Estimator
- Cost Estimator
- Specification Writer

Sales and Marketing

Although some sales and marketing functions, such as advertising, may be outsourced to consultants, all companies must have personnel who sell their services, even if just on a part-time basis. In small landscaping companies, owners may conduct most of the sales and marketing. Because referrals are a main source of business in this industry, sales and marketing managers must ensure that their companies' work is of high quality by conducting site inspections. Moreover, salespeople may use finished landscaping projects as examples of their companies' work. They may keep portfolios of pictures and schematics of such projects, use them as locations for advertising shoots, or even take potential clients to the sites.

Sales and marketing employees may have several related functions, depending on the sizes of their companies. They may submit landscaping proposals to existing and potential clients and make bids to government agencies. They work with customer service staffs to maintain good working relationships with existing clients, and they use leads and client referrals to obtain new customers. Salespeople may also attend lawn and garden shows, and they may join and speak at community organizations and local service clubs and associations in order to promote their companies.

Sales and marketing personnel are likely to have college degrees in marketing and sales, especially in larger landscaping companies that cater to commercial enterprises. Many salespeople are paid on a commission basis, and marketing personnel and salespeople have high earning potential in larger companies in the industry. Although earnings vary widely depending on the location and size of the company, an average starting salary is around $30,000, before commissions.

Sales and marketing occupations may include the following:

- Sales Director
- Marketing Director
- Sales Representative
- Marketing Assistant
- Advertising Director
- Site Inspector

Equipment, Facilities, and Security

Landscaping companies need to protect the major investments they make in tools, equipment, and landscaping materials. Equipment, facilities, and security personnel purchase, operate, maintain, and provide security for company assets, mainly equipment and tools. Security staff may protect against destruction and theft of equipment, tools, and materials at job sites, in addition to guarding their companies' own facilities. Some companies outsource the maintenance of major equipment.

All landscaping companies require storage facilities for equipment, tools, and materials. Smaller landscaping companies that operate from home offices are not likely to hire separate personnel to provide security for storage facilities. Larger companies with business offices are more likely to employ personnel to provide building maintenance and security services, or they may outsource such services.

As landscaping services companies rely more heavily on computer software applications to manage landscaping contracts, the need for computer security personnel increases. Some security and procurement jobs may require two- or four-year college degrees. In most cases, jobs such as equipment operators and maintenance supervisors require only work experience and special training. Earnings in this category are not as high as for some jobs in this industry. The average annual wage for equipment maintenance and security personnel is about $35,000, and equipment operators earn an average of $30,000.

Equipment, facilities, and security occupations may include the following:

- Equipment Procurement Manager
- Equipment Operator
- Security Guard
- Computer Technician
- Building Maintenance Supervisor
- Building Maintenance and Repair Worker

Technology, Research, Design, and Development

Much of the technology and research in the landscaping services industry comes from universities. However, private chemical and equipment companies that cater to landscaping services also operate research facilities. Larger landscaping companies may have a few employees who act as liaisons to research and technology establishments, and specialists such as arborists and horticulturalists may be employed to improve soil conditions; develop disease-resistant plants, hybrids, and ornamentals; provide services to control landscape pests and diseases; and propagate existing and new plant materials. Smaller companies are unlikely to have job opportunities within this category and may contract for many of these services.

Landscaping design services are provided most often by licensed landscape architects, employed either by architecture firms or by landscaping service firms. Planning and design of landscaping features are crucial components of the industry, and any company that provides installation services must either employ or maintain business relationships with landscape architects so they will have projects to install. Subindustries within landscaping services, such as lawn and turf management, have spawned technological growth in the landscaping industry. Larger and specialty landscaping companies may be involved in the development of new products, application techniques, and equipment designs, especially related to pesticides, plant disease control, reliable automated equipment, or the greening of industry.

Specialists such as horticulturalists and arborists have the highest-paying jobs within this sector and usually have two- or four-year college degrees. The average annual wages for horticulturists are $36,000, and arborists can earn over $40,000 per year. Laborers who may assist in carrying out some of these specialties must have high school degrees and may need technical degrees, training, or some experience.

Technology, research, design, and development occupations may include the following:

- Horticulturist
- Horticulture Therapist
- Arborist
- Lawn Care Specialist
- Soil and Plant Scientist
- Landscape Architect
- Architectural Drafter
- Landscape Designer
- Chemical Technician

Site Supervision

First-line supervisors oversee on-site landscaping operations. Supervisors direct and coordinate

---

OCCUPATION PROFILE

Landscape Architect

Considerations	Qualifications
Description	Plans and designs parks, recreational areas, and land surrounding buildings and complexes.
Career clusters	Agriculture, Food, and Natural Resources; Architecture and Construction
Interests	Data; people; things
Working conditions	Work both inside and outside
Minimum education level	Bachelor's degree; master's degree
Physical exertion	Light work
Physical abilities	Unexceptional/basic fitness
Opportunities for experience	Apprenticeship; volunteer work; part-time work
Licensure and certification	Required
Employment outlook	Faster-than-average growth expected
Holland interest score	AIR

Note: See volume 1, "Publisher's Note," for an explanation of the Holland interest score.

landscaping and groundskeeping workers and other laborers as they plant and maintain plant materials; trim and prune trees and shrubs; apply pesticides and fertilizers; and develop hardscape amenities such as walkways, walls, patios, and irrigation systems. Supervisors should be able to read and interpret landscape design plans and contracts, as they are responsible for job management in the field. Necessary skills include the ability to organize and to motivate workers to ensure high-quality work.

First-line supervisors are also involved in scheduling; determining workforce needs; and customer relations, especially responding to customer questions and communicating with other company personnel should there be a need for contract changes. First-line supervisors in larger landscaping companies are likely to have degrees from two- or four-year college programs, but supervisors in smaller landscaping companies may have only high school educations with substantial experience. As of May, 2009, according to the BLS, the median hourly wage for landscaping field supervisory jobs was $18.77.

Site supervision occupations may include the following:

- First-Line Supervisor
- Foreman

Landscape Work

Landscape workers are the backbone of the landscaping services industry. Landscaping and groundskeeping laborers provide the demanding physical labor required to install landscape designs, both plant materials and hardscape, while groundskeepers maintain what has been installed. Personnel may use hand tools and power equipment in activities such as caring for lawns, laying sod, raking, digging, and watering.

Landscape workers do not need college educations and do not need any experience to obtain many entry-level jobs. Most landscaping companies require at least a high school education or

---

OCCUPATION PROFILE

Gardener and Groundskeeper

Considerations	Qualifications
Description	Installs garden and landscape elements and maintains them.
Career clusters	Agriculture, Food, and Natural Resources; Architecture and Construction
Interests	Things
Working conditions	Work outside
Minimum education level	No high school diploma; on-the-job training; apprenticeship
Physical exertion	Medium work; heavy work
Physical abilities	Unexceptional/basic fitness; strength may be required
Opportunities for experience	Part-time work
Licensure and certification	Required
Employment outlook	Faster-than-average growth expected
Holland interest score	CRS; RCE; RCI

Note: See volume 1, "Publisher's Note," for an explanation of the Holland interest score.

OCCUPATION SPECIALTIES

Gardeners and Groundskeepers

Specialty	Responsibilities
Landscape laborers	Assist landscape gardeners by moving soil, equipment, and materials; digging holes; and performing related duties.
Landscape specialists	Keep the grounds of city, state, or national parks and playgrounds clean and repair buildings and equipment.
Yard workers	Perform a combination of maintenance duties to keep the grounds of private residences in neat and orderly condition.

GED. As of May, 2009, the median hourly wage for landscaping workers was $11.23.

Landscape work occupations may include the following:

- Crew Chief
- Landscaping Worker
- Groundskeeper
- Gardener
- Irrigation Technician
- Interior Landscape Technician
- Cemetery Worker
- Golf Course Manager
- Greenskeeper
- Turf Manager
- Lawn Service Worker

Tree Trimming

Tree trimmers cut, trim, and prune plants. They use hand and power saws, shears, and clippers to conduct activities such as removing dead branches from trees, maintaining utility and road rights-of-way, creating topiaries in formal gardens, and working with arborists to control plant pests and diseases. Some of this work may take place from truck-mounted lifts. A high school education is usually all that is required for these jobs. As of May, 2009, the median hourly wage for tree trimmers and pruners was $14.18.

Tree trimming occupations may include the following:

- Tree Trimmer
- Plant Pruner

Pest Control

Pest control workers require the most specific training of front-line landscaping laborers, although a college education is usually not required. Their tasks may involve mixing, spraying, and applying chemical dusts and vapors to vegetation. These chemicals kill plant pests, insects, and fungi, and many pesticide handlers must obtain special state or federal certifications. Other pest control workers may specialize in organic pest control methods. These methods involve spraying plants with organic chemicals, including bacteria, that target or discourage common pests. They also commonly involve using natural predators, such as ladybugs and parasitic miniature wasps, to attack pests that harm plants. As of May, 2009, the median hourly wage for pest control workers was $12.43.

Pest control occupations may include the following:

- Pesticide Handler
- Pesticide Sprayer
- Pesticide Applicator
- Pest Control Worker
- Organic Gardener

Human Resources

Labor is the major cost within a landscaping services company, and human resources personnel spend much of their time advertising for new employees, reading resumes and interviewing, and providing employee training and fringe benefits, although most benefits are limited in smaller landscaping companies. Because of the high turnover rates and seasonal nature of the industry, human resources personnel are often kept quite busy finding and retaining qualified full-time and part-time employees. In addition, these personnel must understand the rights of employees, including those provided by federal and state laws and regulations governing minimum wages, overtime pay, privacy, family leave, discrimination, and workers' compensation. Human resources personnel also provide education and training to employees, such as sexual harassment training, and they must stay abreast of the latest personnel issues by completing certification courses in human resources.

Human resources personnel may have to terminate employees, and they usually conduct exit interviews for employees who are leaving or retiring. Other tasks include establishing wage ranges for various job categories, developing employee handbooks, and conducting grievance proceedings. Some human resources personnel also assist in conducting employee evaluations, develop programs to motivate employees, seek to reduce absenteeism, or work with security personnel to adopt and implement security measures to control theft of company tools and equipment.

Most human resources directors and managers have college degrees in human resources or related fields. Depending on the size and location of the company, the annual salary for human resources directors may start around $20,000 and reach an average wage of $60,000. Administrative personnel receive lower wages and may require only high school educations.

Human resources occupations may include the following:

- Human Resources Director
- Human Resources Manager
- Human Resources Generalist
- Payroll Clerk
- Benefits Specialist
- Administrative Assistant

INDUSTRY OUTLOOK

Overview

The outlook for the landscaping industry shows it to be on the rise. Although the recession of 2007-2009 and resulting growth in unemployment have resulted in a downward trend since 2007, and individuals and companies may have less disposable income for landscaping services, the landscaping services industry is expected to grow. This growth will be slow at first, but the rate will increase, both domestically and internationally, as the global economy continues to improve and building construction increases. The BLS projects that landscaping services will be one of the fastest-growing industries between 2006 and 2016. In addition, forecasters have placed the landscaping services industry in the development/growth phase of its life cycle, implying that there will be plenty of room for growth in the future. A good indicator of the favorable growth in the landscaping services industry is the fact that franchising of this industry in the United States and internationally is on the rise.

Approximately fifty large companies in the United States generate about 15 percent of the total revenue in the landscaping services industry. Worldwide, landscaping companies are highly affected by economic downturns. In addition, the landscaping services industry is very dependent on weather, and a company's revenues may vary depending on the weather conditions and the season of the year. The industry also suffers from higher-than-average turnover, the result of both its seasonal nature in some locales and also the physical demands placed on workers.

Owners of institutional facilities, commercial developments, shopping malls, and office buildings continue to recognize the importance of presenting a positive visual image through landscaping, so the demand for landscaping services will continue to rise in line with nonresidential development, some of which is increasing in nations with fast-growing economies, including China and India, and in major construction locales, such as Dubai. Moreover, the increase in the number of elderly homeowners who are no longer able to maintain the landscapes around their homes, the need for many working householders to hire landscapers because they lack the time to provide the labor themselves, the desire of homeowners to better utilize and beautify their outdoor living spaces, and the continuing development of suburbs are factors that will contribute to future growth in residential landscaping services.

Economic conditions in the United States and globally have hampered public funding for many government landscaping projects. However, once the economy recovers, governments are expected to continue to install and maintain plant materials to enhance urban environments and to develop additional public, landscaped open spaces. Utility companies also continue to provide ample growth opportunities for the landscaping services industry. Landscapers are engaged by public utilities not only to trim trees and prune plants to avoid power outages but also to prevent and control plant diseases and pests.

The greening of industry, also known as the environmental horticulture movement, has also favorably affected the growth of the landscaping services industry. In a study concerning the economic impact of the overall green industry in the United States, Hall, Hodges, and Haydu estimated that in 2002 the landscaping services sector had the greatest favorable impact on the economy in terms of employment, value added, and labor income. Thus, the landscaping services industry will continue to enjoy growth in the future, as more companies and individuals embrace the green movement and require the services of landscape workers and other related services.

Employment Advantages

The BLS has predicted that employment for groundskeeping and landscaping workers, which encompassed more than 1.2 million of the 1.5 million jobs in the landscaping services industry in 2006, will grow faster than the average rate of growth for all occupations during the period between 2006 and 2016. It has also been predicted that domestic groundskeeping jobs will increase by 27.43 percent between 2008 and 2018 and that overall employment for all occupations within this industry will increase by 26.74 percent during the same period. Although wages are low for entry-level positions and the work is physically demanding, this is the perfect job for individuals who enjoy outdoor work.

Most workers do not require training or college degrees, so younger workers may be able to find entry-level positions in the landscaping services industry. Moreover, because employment opportunities may be seasonal in some areas, the industry also provides part-time summer employment for students and others seeking seasonal jobs. Depending on the size of employees' companies, they may enjoy job diversity, from providing installation and maintenance services for commercial and residential properties, to managing public and private recreational facilities, to maintaining lines for public utility companies.

Annual Earnings

The economy, and for some locations the season of the year, have significant effects on earnings in the landscaping services industry. Even when the economy is good, earnings in this industry are low compared to those of other industries. In a 2007 study conducted by *Entrepreneur Magazine*, at a time of economic decline, the average revenue for a landscaping services company was $869,740, which represented a 2.4 percent decrease from 2004. However, the top-performing 10 percent of landscaping companies enjoyed average revenues of $2.7 million, representing a 27.8 percent increase from 2004. A 2010 study by IBISWorld showed revenues of $49.928 billion per year for U.S. companies in the landscaping services industry.

The average revenue generated by employees is another good indicator of an industry's earnings. Based on the *Entrepreneur Magazine* study, the average revenue generated per employee in the landscaping services industry declined between 2004 and 2007. In 2004, an employee in a top-performing company generated an average of $86,066, but in 2007 the average had fallen to $85,204. For an employee in a lesser-performing company, the average 2004 revenue of $87,403 decreased to $81,442 by 2007. A 2009 First Research study showed annual revenues per employee in the overall industry to be closer to $70,000.

RELATED RESOURCES FOR FURTHER RESEARCH

AMERICAN NURSERY AND LANDSCAPE
    ASSOCIATION
1000 Vermont Ave. NW, Suite 300
Washington, DC 20005
Tel: (202) 789-2900
Fax: (202) 789-1893
http://www.anla.org

AMERICAN SOCIETY OF LANDSCAPE ARCHITECTS
    636 Eye St. NW
    Washington, DC 20001-3736

Tel: (202) 898-2444
Fax: (202) 898-1185
http://www.asla.org

LAWN AND LANDSCAPE MAGAZINE, GIE MEDIA
4020 Kinross Lakes Parkway
Richfield, OH 44286
Tel: (800) 456 0707
Fax: (330) 659-0823
http://www.baumpub.com

PROFESSIONAL LANDCARE NETWORK (PLANET)
950 Herndon Parkway, Suite 450
Herndon, VA 20170
Tel: (703) 736-9666
Fax: (703) 736-9668
http://www.lawnandlandscape.com

TREE CARE INDUSTRY ASSOCIATION
136 Harvey Rd., Suite 101
Londonderry, NH 03053
Tel: (603) 314-5380
Fax: (603) 314-5386
http://www.treecareindustry.org

ABOUT THE AUTHOR

Carol A. Rolf has a bachelor of science degree in landscape architecture from Pennsylvania State University and more than twenty years of professional experience in landscape design and implementation. She has been a member of the American Society of Landscape Architects and has designed and assisted in the development of state parks for state governments, reviewed land subdivisions for municipal governments, and implemented residential and commercial landscape designs for private industry. With her law degree from Suffolk University, she has worked for over twenty years with private and public clients to ensure compliance with environmental laws that preserve the landscape.

FURTHER READING

Camenson, Blythe. *Careers for Plant Lovers and Other Green Thumb Types.* 2d ed. New York: McGraw-Hill, 2004.

_____. *Opportunities in Landscape Architecture, Botanical Gardens, and Arboreta Careers.* New York: McGraw-Hill, 2007.

Craul, Timothy A. and Phillip J. Craul. *Soil Design Protocols for Landscape Architects and Contractors.* New York: John Wiley & Sons, 2006.

Davidson, Harold, Roy Mecklenburg, and Curtis Peterson. *Nursery Management: Administration and Culture.* 4th ed. Upper Saddle River, N.J.: Prentice Hall, 1999.

Garner, Jerry. *Careers in Horticulture and Botany.* 2d ed. New York: McGraw-Hill, 2006.

Giles, Floyd. *Landscape Construction Procedures, Techniques, and Design.* 4th ed. Champaign, Ill.: Stipes, 1999.

Hall, Charles R., Alan W. Hodges, and John J. Haydu. *Economic Impacts of the Green Industry in the United States, Final Report to the National Urban and Community Forestry Advisory Committee.* Knoxville: University of Tennessee, Extension Service, 2005.

Hannebaum, Leroy G. *Landscape Operations: Management, Methods, and Materials.* 3d ed. Upper Saddle River, N.J.: Prentice Hall, 1998.

Hensley, David L. *Professional Landscape Management.* 2d ed. Champaign, Ill.: Stipes, 2004.

Hoovers. "Landscaping Services." http://www.hoovers.com/landscaping-services/—ID__194—/free-ind-fr-profile-basic.xhtml.

Ingels, Jack E. *Landscaping Principles and Practices.* 7th ed. Clifton Park, N.Y.: Delmar Cengage Learning, 2009.

_____. *Ornamental Horticulture: Science, Operations, and Management.* 3d ed. Clifton Park, N.Y.: Delmar Cengage Learning, 2000.

LaRusic, Joel. *Start and Run a Landscaping Business.* North Vancouver, B.C.: Self-Counsel Press, 2005.

Pigeat, Jean-Paul. *Gardens of the World: Two Thousand Years of Garden Design.* Paris: Flammarion, 2010.

Simonds, John O. and Barry Starke. *Landscape Architecture: A Manual of Land Planning and Design.* 4th ed. New York: McGraw-Hill Professional, 2006.

U.S. Bureau of Labor Statistics. *Career Guide to Industries,* 2010-2011 ed. http://www.bls.gov/oco/cg.

_____. *Occupational Outlook Handbook*, 2010-2011 ed. http://www.bls.gov/oco.

U.S. Census Bureau. North American Industry Classification System (NAICS), 2007. http://www.census.gov/cgi-bin/sssd/naics/naicsrch?chart=2007.

U.S. Department of Commerce. International Trade Administration. Office of Trade and Industry Information. Industry Trade Data and Analysis. http://ita.doc.gov/td/industry/otea/OTII/OTII-index.html.

Wasnak, Lynn. *How to Own and Operate a Financially Successful Landscaping, Nursery, or Lawn Service Business*. Ocala, Fla.: Atlantic, 2009.

Williams, George S. *Nursery Crops and Landscape Designs for Agribusiness Studies*. 2d ed. Vero Beach, Fla.: Vero Media, 1984.

Legal Services and Law Firms

INDUSTRY SNAPSHOT

General Industry: Law, Public Safety, and Security

Career Cluster: Law, Public Safety, and Security

Subcategory Industries: Corporate Law Offices; Criminal Law Offices; Estate and Tax Law Offices; Family Law Offices; Intellectual Property Law Offices; Labor Law Offices; Law Firms; Legal Aid Services; Notary Offices; Paralegal Services; Process Servers; Public Interest Law Offices; Title Abstract and Settlement Offices

Related Industries: Civil Services: Public Safety; Criminal Justice and Prison Industry; Environmental Engineering and Consultation Services; Federal Public Administration; Local Public Administration; Political Advocacy Industry; Public Health Services

Annual Domestic Revenues: $251 billion USD (U.S. Census Bureau, 2007)

Annual Global Revenues: Over $1 trillion USD (Harvard Law School Center on Lawyers and the Professional Services Industry, 2007)

NAICS Number: 5411

INDUSTRY DEFINITION

Summary

The law firm and legal services industry provides legal advice, assistance and representation to individuals, groups, and corporations. By engaging in legal research, preparing and filing legal documents, drafting contracts, giving advice, petitioning courts, attempting to persuade opposing parties, litigating, and appealing adverse judgments, lawyers use many diverse tools to help their clients. Law firms predominantly employ attorneys, paralegals, and administrative assistants and range in size from multinational corporations employing thousands globally, to solo practitioners doing business in small towns. Lawyers in private law firms usually charge clients for the legal services they provide, although some types of lawyers are paid only by opposing parties when they win judgements at trial that include legal fees, and many lawyers represent select clients for free (pro bono). A law firm's success is largely dependent on its financial stability. In this respect, it is very similar to any other private business.

The legal services industry is substantially similar in function to law firms. Hundreds of legal service organizations exist in the United States alone.

They range from small, local offices in rural areas to large international organizations with offices globally. Much like law firms, these organizations provide legal services for clients, but their fee structure and business goals are drastically different. Legal service organizations seek to assist individuals who otherwise may not be able to afford legal representation and, accordingly, legal service providers generally charge reduced fees. They may also provide pro bono legal representation. Instead of focusing on profits, many of these organizations are nonprofit; they solicit and accept donations from the public, the government, and business owners in order to cover their overhead costs.

History of the Industry

The legal industry has existed, in some form, for thousands of years. In ancient times, many countries and religions developed their own sets of rules, which were essentially common laws: laws that are not written out in books but that are implicitly adopted by society over generations of legal practice. In ancient Greece, common citizens argued legal matters on behalf of other citizens, notwithstanding the absence of formal training. They were not allowed, officially, to accept fees for their representation. Ancient Rome developed a much more comprehensive legal system under which attorneys practiced law as a vocation and could accept fees for their representation. This system was the genesis of the modern practice of law. Notably, however, neither Roman lawyers nor the judges they practiced before had formal legal educations.

The practice of law became more regulated in the first few centuries of the Byzantine Empire (330-1453). By the sixth century, a course of study

Trial lawyers spend most of their time outside the courtroom, preparing for trial by doing research and interviewing witnesses and clients. (©Rich Legg/iStockphoto.com)

was required in order to be admitted to the practice of law. By the thirteenth century, many other countries had followed suit, requiring some formal education and an oath of admission in order to practice. The United States developed many of its laws, as well as the traditions and customs surrounding the practice of law, based on the English model. By the time the United States had declared its independence from Great Britain, English legal scholars had drafted important treatises concerning, among other things, principles of property law, civil law, and criminal law. These treatises helped form both U.S. common law and, later, the country's statutory body of laws.

The first dedicated law school in the United States was the Litchfield Law School, established in 1784 in Litchfield, Connecticut, by American lawyer Tapping Reeve. At that time, no official law degree was required in order to practice law; to the contrary, individuals became lawyers by apprenticing with practicing attorneys. This form of appren-

ticeship existed into the 1890's, when the newly formed American Bar Association (ABA) strongly encouraged states to begin requiring potential lawyers to receive formal education in order to be considered attorneys. The first American law firms employing multiple attorneys appeared just prior to the Civil War (1861-1865). In 1906, the Association of American Law Schools (AALS) adopted a rule that law students must receive three years of study to earn their degrees. By 2008, there were approximately 199 ABA-accredited law schools, though a very small portion of those schools, most of them new, were only provisionally accredited.

In order to attend law school, most state laws require applicants to have completed undergraduate degrees, to have achieved satisfactory grade point averages (GPAs), and to have successfully completed the Law School Admissions Test (LSAT). In order to be admitted as an attorney, an applicant must satisfactorily complete law school, must fill out a comprehensive application (including a

Law books line the walls of this law office conference room. Increasingly, legal codes, cases, and forms are available in electronic versions. (©Lane Erickson/Dreamstime.com)

The Legal Services Industry's Contribution to the U.S. Economy

Value Added	Amount
Gross domestic product	$209.6 billion
Gross domestic product	1.5%
Persons employed	1.186 million
Total employee compensation	$112.8 billion

Source: U.S. Bureau of Economic Analysis. Data are for 2008.

complete job history and criminal background check), and must successfully pass the state's bar examination, which is traditionally administered twice each year.

A large proportion of newly admitted attorneys—approximately half—enter into private practice at law firms. Law firms may employ anywhere from one to thousands of attorneys and staff, located in one small office or spread throughout dozens of offices in major cities around the world. A small percentage of attorneys chooses to practice at legal service organizations, such as local legal aid offices or nongovernmental organizations (NGOs) such as Amnesty International. Much like law firms, these organizations run the gamut from operating as small businesses to, in the case of Amnesty International, functioning as national or multinational organizations with significant influence and lobbying power.

There are many other areas in which an attorney can seek employment. For example, attorneys are employed at nearly every corporation as in-house counsel. Similarly, federal, state, and local governments employ attorneys as prosecutors and judges. Furthermore, most every governmental agency employs staff attorneys who work on general legal matters within the agencies' spheres of influence, and legislatures employ legal counsel to aid in investigations and to produce the legal language from which new laws are crafted.

The Industry Today

A law firm is composed of a group of attorneys—anywhere from one individual to thousands

globally—who combine skills, resources, and revenue and who work under a shared name. Some law firms practice in only certain areas of law in which the attorneys have particular expertise. For instance, it is very common to find small personal injury litigation firms, or small plaintiffs firms, which are law firms that represent victims of car crashes, slip-and-falls, and other personal injury claims. The attorneys in this type of firm have particular expertise in plaintiffs' injury litigation, and they often provide very efficient and effective representation in this area of the law.

In contrast, many larger firms advertise themselves as full-service firms. This designation suggests that the firms are capable of handling any legal question or issue with which a client is concerned. Traditionally, individual attorneys at large firms retain expertise in one or two areas of the law, meaning that each attorney is not a general practitioner. When the attorneys and their diverse fields of expertise combine forces at a large firm, however, the firm is able to handle most legal issues. In general, particular legal practice areas include civil personal injury litigation, criminal cases, contract negotiation, property and real estate law and transactions, estate and probate law, intellectual property, patents and trademarks, mergers and acquisitions, administrative law, and appellate law.

At law firms, newly admitted attorneys are commonly referred to as first-year associate attorneys. Depending on the particular firm, they may carry that title for as little as one year or as many as eight

Inputs Consumed by the Legal Services Industry

Input	Value
Energy	$0.9 billion
Materials	$3.7 billion
Purchased services	$72.8 billion
Total	$77.4 billion

Source: U.S. Bureau of Economic Analysis. Data are for 2008.

years. After an associate's required service, the partners (part-owners) of the law firm vote to decide whether an associate will become a partner. The partners evaluate, among other things, associates' performance, work habits, and the amount of business they bring to the firm. Not only is the receipt of a partnership both a promotion and a recognition that an associate has performed well for the firm, but it is also financially rewarding. As a part-owner, the partner earns a share of the firm's annual revenue, rather than just a set salary with the potential for a bonus—simply stated, when the firm succeeds financially, so do the partners. Partners' shares at the largest American law firms can be several hundred thousand dollars per year. It is also important to note, however, that if the firm loses money, partners also share in the losses. In order to gain their part shares, moreover, the partners must buy into the partnership, so the promotion requires an outlay of capital on the part of the employee. In addition to partners and associates, law firms employ paralegals, administrative assistants, and a host of other employees to assist the firm.

Hundreds of legal service organizations exist in the United States alone. Although these organizations may receive some state or federal funding, many are private organizations. They seek to provide legal services for those who cannot ordinarily afford to hire an attorney. Commonly, legal service providers provide assistance in the following areas: civil and criminal law, property law (especially landlord-renter disputes and foreclosure cases), immigration law, administrative proceedings, and constitutional issues involving civil rights and liberties. An example of the latter might be assisting a high school student who wrote a controversial school newspaper article and was subsequently disciplined by school administrators in a freedom of speech case.

Some legal service providers are able to provide services free of charge for clients who satisfy certain financial eligibility rules. Others provide services and representation at rates that, when compared to comparable fees at private law firms, are drastically reduced. Traditionally, many legal service providers receive assistance from the federal or state government and seek donations from individuals and corporations to help cover overhead costs. Additionally, the operating costs of a legal service provider are significantly lower than those of a law firm, because the salaries paid to employees are often lower. Most legal service providers are local or operate within one particular state. Other legal service providers, such as the American Civil Liberties Union (ACLU) and the National Right to Work Legal Defense Foundation, operate on the national level.

INDUSTRY MARKET SEGMENTS

Both law firms and legal service organizations can range in size from individual practitioners to national and international entities. Many specialize in particular types of law. Even large, full-service firms have specialized departments or teams who concentrate on particular types of cases or particular levels. For example, litigators who represent clients at trial rarely represent the same client on appeal. Instead, appellate specialists take over the representation of the client in higher courts. If the appellate team is able to win a new trial for a client, the client may once again be represented by the original litigation attorney.

Small Law Firms and Legal Service Providers

Small firms generally employ between one and ten attorneys. They usually handle relatively few cases at a time, although some branches of legal practice require a heavier caseload in order to earn sufficient income. In addition, sole practitioners may be "of counsel" to firms, meaning that they are neither associates nor partners but they are contracted by the firms to help with specific cases as necessary.

Potential Annual Earnings Scale. A sole practitioner could earn, generally, between $30,000 and $100,000 per year. In 2004, the average annual income of a sole practitioner was $46,000 according to the American Bar Association Young Lawyer Division. A ten-attorney firm could generate well over $1 million in annual revenue. Many legal service organizations are nonprofit organizations and, accordingly, do not generate revenue in the sense that a private law firm does.

Clientele Interaction. One hallmark of small law firms is the importance of client interaction. When a firm employs only a handful of attorneys, the attorneys are generally very accessible to clients. To be sure, some small firms do not employ full-time administrative assistants or paralegals. When a client dials the main phone number or e-mails an attorney at such a firm, it is probable that the attorney him- or herself will answer the phone or personally respond to the e-mail. Thus, the degree of client interaction can be very high, as the buffer between the client and the firm is greatly reduced. Many clients feel reassured by this heightened interaction and believe that they can better track how their legal issues are being resolved. The buffer between client and counsel at a legal service provider is also relatively small, as these organizations seek to keep costs down while providing efficient and effective service.

Amenities, Atmosphere, and Physical Grounds. Small firms and small legal service providers often struggle to find office space suitable for their needs. Unlike major law firms, which typically occupy multiple floors or even entire buildings, small law firms operate like many small businesses—they seek to find affordable space sufficient for their needs. Accordingly, many small firms lack the aesthetics of large firms. Often, the proprietors of small firms finance their office leases and must consider rent or ownership as direct overhead costs that detract from the firms' profits. While waiting rooms for clients in large firms may have amenities such as coffee bars, plush leather sofas, and a bevy of magazines for perusal, the waiting room in a small firm may consist of no more than a small space with a few chairs.

In a small firm or in a legal service provider that operates as a nonprofit, the emphasis is on client contact and cost-effective representation, not glitz and glamorous surroundings. To that end, the physical grounds of a small firm could be a former house that has been converted into a law office, rented space in an office building, or simply an office with an administrative assistant that is shared by other solo practitioners. Whereas in large law firms, interior and exterior maintenance typically are outsourced to specialized businesses, the attorneys at small firms concerned with overhead costs may spend their Saturdays cutting their firms' lawns and attempting basic maintenance repairs, much as they might at their personal residences. It may also be common for attorneys to share office space in an effort to save rent. That being said, the physical grounds of most small firms generally present a very professional atmosphere, much like those of large firms.

Typical Number of Employees. Small firms and legal service providers may consist of only a solo practitioner or they may employ from two to ten attorneys. Aside from their attorneys, firms usually employ a few paralegals and administrative assistants to assist with the preparation and maintenance of files. Such firms are usually owned by just one or two individuals, so there exists an incentive to keep the number of employees relatively low. As long as the work is getting done in a timely and professional manner, hiring additional employees will only take away earnings from the rest of the office.

Traditional Geographic Locations. Small firms and legal service organizations may be found anywhere where people are in need of legal representation, and they can be found in most communities, both large and small, throughout the United States. Although there may exist a stereotype that small firms are only located in sparsely populated communities, this is not true, as small firms are just as likely to be located in large cities. Similarly, legal aid organizations often are located in cities because that is where the greatest need for low-cost or free representation is. If given a choice, proprietors of small firms may choose to locate their businesses near the courthouses in which they most regularly practice. Because the cost and time of travel to court hearings eventually gets passed on to the client, and because most small firms and legal service providers are concerned with keeping the costs of their representation competitive, it may be beneficial to be located within walking distance of court.

Pros of Working for a Small Firm. Small-firm owners are their own bosses, and they may not be expected to work the grueling hours that so-called big law attorneys are expected to work. Accordingly, many nights and weekends are free, and for some the job resembles a traditional forty-hour-per-week occupation, thus allowing attorneys to have lives outside of work. Additionally, for those who view client contact as particularly important, operating a small firm may be a great fit, as clients who can easily communicate with their lawyers are likely to feel that they are receiving better representation. Finally, small firms can be very successful financially. Like any small business, a small firm is built on trust and reputation; after establishing the trust of a community, life in a small firm can be emotionally and financially satisfying. Similarly, attorneys running small legal service organizations generally find the work to be both important and rewarding—both professionally and financially.

Cons of Working for a Small Firm. Although there are many benefits associated with running a small firm, there are also opportunity costs. First and foremost, the opportunity for financial success can be limited. Because the owner of a firm is responsible for paying salaries, rent, utilities, and a host of other bills, if the firm has a slow month, there may not be enough money left for the owner to pay her- or himself. Additionally, owners of small firms and legal service providers may find themselves working several hours per week on nonlegal matters, such as building maintenance or personnel issues, thus detracting from their ability to represent clients and build the business of their firms. Finally, the owners of small firms must decide what benefit packages to provide to their employees. Providing health care and a retirement plan can be very costly and can significantly detract from profit margins. Though an attractive benefit package can entice qualified employees into accepting offers of employment, the cost of providing benefits can be difficult for small businesses to afford. In legal service organizations, the benefits are generally very good, but often the attorneys in charge of these organizations sacrifice the potential for high salaries. Although they may love their work, they are often compensated at lower rates than those in the private sector.

Costs

Payroll and Benefits: The proprietors of small firms are responsible for paying the salaries of and providing benefits to their employees. This is likely to be the largest cost associated with operating a small business. In a legal service organization, it is possible that the state or federal government, or even individual private donors, may provide some funding to help offset the costs of providing salaries and benefits.

Supplies: Small firms and legal service providers must be equipped with, at a minimum, computers, Internet access, printers, fax machines, and telephones. In order to research legal issues for clients, they must also purchase law books or subscribe to an Internet-based legal research provider. These are costly investments, but they can save attorneys significant time. Additionally, most firms subscribe to law journals and trade magazines, as well as to newspapers and other periodicals, primarily for use by attorneys seeking to keep abreast of the law.

External Services: Small firms may contract lawn care and external building maintenance, as well as interior cleaning and maintenance services. Some attempt to take care of reasonable maintenance and lawn care on their own.

Utilities: Small firms must pay for electricity, heat, and sewage and trash-removal services, among other utilities.

Taxes: Traditionally, law firms pay their associates' state employment taxes associated with holding a license to practice law. If they own their office space, they must pay any state and local property taxes. Moreover, small firms must pay corporate income taxes. Legal service providers may be nonprofit entities, in which case their business tax liability, as well as other financial burdens associated with private practice, may be less significant.

Midsize Law Firms and Legal Service Providers

Midsize law firms generally employ between ten and fifty people. They are usually local or regional in nature, serving clients predominantly in one general locale. Midsize firms almost always have associates in addition to partners, whereas small firms may consist solely of partners.

Potential Annual Earnings Scale. According to the U.S. Bureau of Labor Statistics (BLS), the mean annual salary for a lawyer in 2008 was $124,750. The mean annual salary for a paralegal or legal assistant was $48,790. All other things being equal, employees of midsize firms can generally be expected to earn salaries in line with these averages.

Clientele Interaction. Midsize law firms and legal service providers place importance on client interactions. However, because there are more attorneys, paralegals, and administrative assistants in midsize firms than in small ones, there is likely to be less direct contact between attorneys and clients, as some of the client-relations tasks will be handled by these other employees. Additionally, corporations can also be clients of midsize firms, and it is often possible to handle certain legal needs of a corporation with less face-to-face contact than an individual client would expect. Consequently, depending on the nature of the services the midsize firm or legal service organization provides, there is likely to be a somewhat lower degree of interaction with clients than experienced at small firms and organizations.

Amenities, Atmosphere, and Physical Grounds. Midsize firms generally employ anywhere from ten to fifty attorneys, in addition to several paralegals and administrative assistants, whose services are often shared among attorneys. As a result, the office space needed by a midsize firm is greater than that needed by a small firm. In fact, some midsize firms may need two or more offices, especially if their clientele is spread across a larger geographic area. Depending on the size of the business, a firm may have its own freestanding building, or it may share space in a larger office building. Because the appearance of the building and grounds is important to generating business, larger firms may pay more attention to their physical grounds, amenities, and atmosphere. For instance, clients at a midsize firm may notice an elegant waiting room and may be offered coffee or tea as they await legal assistance.

In a ten-attorney firm, shared office space or a renovated single-family house may be sufficient for the firm's needs. With fifty attorneys, paralegals, and administrative assistants, however, a firm would likely need several thousand square feet of office space and may be inclined to have its own freestanding building or an entire floor in a large office building. Maintenance, including lawn work, plumbing, and electric repairs, is likely to be outsourced to private companies, as the larger a firm is, the lower the ownership interest is among the most senior attorneys.

Typical Number of Employees. Firms that employ between ten and fifty attorneys are generally categorized as midsize. If a firm has only ten attorneys, it may be able to get by with just a few paralegals and administrative assistants, as well as a receptionist. The total number of employees at a ten-attorney firm, then, might be somewhere between fifteen and twenty. If the firm employs fifty attorneys, the demand for legal and administrative support will be much greater. Such a firm might have a total staff of well over one hundred.

Legal service providers, such as legal aid offices, often operate under fixed budgets. Despite the great demand for their services, the resources often do not exist to hire all the personnel necessary to maximize the efficiency of the firm. In a legal service provider, attorneys may perform some of the same tasks that traditionally would be assigned to paralegals or administrative assistants at private firms.

Traditional Geographic Locations. As with small firms, midsize firms may be located anywhere there are clients and business to attend to. Cities, suburbs, and rural communities all host midsize firms.

Pros of Working for a Midsize Firm. With a sufficient number of attorneys, a midsize firm may truly be a full-service organization, effectively representing clients in nearly every type of legal dispute. Whereas sole practitioners and small firms often concentrate on one or two areas in the law, a midsize firm can practice in all areas, thus increasing both its clientele and its revenue. Additionally, because the firm is larger, each partner may carry fewer nonlegal burdens than they do at small firms. Midsize firms should generate more revenue and, consequently, have fewer cash-flow problems. Because their cash flow is generally higher, the opportunity for increased compensation should also exist. As with small firms, many midsize firms offer a good quality of life to their employees. Their benefit packages may be very competitive, but attorneys may not be required to work as many hours in order to succeed as are their counterparts at large firms or multinational corporations.

Cons of Working for a Midsize Firm. Although midsize firms and legal service organizations often provide excellent benefits and allow the attorneys to have a life outside the office, the potential earnings of managing partners pale in comparison to those of managing partners at large firms. Additionally, the owner or managing partner of a midsize firm often faces the same concerns as the owner of a small firm. Depending on the success of the firm, there could be cash-flow issues, employee termination issues, and issues affecting the firm's reputation in the community. Though these are important concerns, they are just as important as client responsibilities and the traditional day-to-day practice of the law necessary to generate revenue. Finally, as with small firms, the cost of providing benefits for employees and their dependents is difficult for many midsize firm owners. It is usually necessary to offer benefits (sometimes including paying the new associate's bar examination and study course fees) in order to attract top talent, but the return on investment for the firm may not be seen for some time.

Moreover, while attorneys at midsize firm may work fewer hours than those at major corporations, they still must work far more than forty hours per week. Because benefits and support staff represent significant expenses, many firms hire one new attorney instead of two, paying the attorney a high salary and expecting at least eighty hours of work per week in exchange. The firm thereby saves money by paying for only one benefits package and one secretary, even if the salary itself is equivalent to the combined salaries of two lawyers who are expected to work forty-hour weeks.

Costs

Payroll and Benefits: The single largest expense in a midsize law firm or legal service organization is payroll and benefits. Because associate attorneys typically earn higher salaries as the size of their firms increase, the overhead at midsize firms can be very high. Additionally, the benefits packages offered to these employees can be very attractive—but costly for the owner to provide.

Supplies: As the size of a law firm increases, so do the costs of supplying employees with the necessary day-to-day materials. Computers, software, paper, pens, and phones all combine to represent large costs that must be borne by the firm.

External Services: The larger a firm, the more likely it is to outsource services such as lawn care, maintenance, and even marketing or public relations, should those services be necessary. Additionally, as the number of attorneys increases, the degree of ownership or responsibility a managing partner may feel decreases proportionally.

Utilities: Just as with small firms, midsize firms and legal service providers are required to pay their electric, heat, Internet, mortgage or rent, and other costs.

Taxes: Law firms usually pay the yearly taxes and fees that their attorneys are required to pay in order to practice law in a given state. They also pay corporate income taxes, payroll taxes, and property taxes. Legal service providers may be tax-exempt nonprofit entities, but they must still pay payroll taxes on employee income.

Large Law Firms and Legal Service Providers

Large law firms employ more than fifty attorneys, sometimes far more. The largest are multinational for-profit entities and nonprofit NGOs that practice on multiple continents and represent the interests of their clients across national borders.

Potential Annual Earnings Scale. According to the BLS, the mean annual salary for a lawyer in 2008 was $124,750. The mean annual salary for a paralegal or legal assistant was $48,790. At large firms, each associate attorney earns somewhere between, generally, $90,000 and $160,000, and the highest-earning partners earn more than $1 million. *The American Lawyer* has reported that in 2007, the five largest law firms in the United States each reported revenues of between $1.38 billion and $2.17 billion.

Clientele Interaction. Attorneys at the largest law firms typically have less interaction with their clients than do attorneys at smaller firms. For example, it is common for associate attorneys to work on files for dozens of clients without ever meeting one. Traditionally, associates receive assignments from partners, complete the requested work, and then returns the relevant files to the partners who gave them the assignments. It is the partners who then meet with clients, if necessary, or attend court hearings. Because many clients are sophisticated entities, rather than individuals, it is sometimes not even necessary to meet face-to-face with clients or client representatives. At big firms, attorneys are paid solely to do legal work. There are hosts of paralegals, administrative assistants, and secretaries to do everything else. Additionally, when clients call, they reach attorneys' assistants, not the attorneys themselves.

Amenities, Atmosphere, and Physical Grounds. The largest law firms cater to the wealthiest and most sophisticated clients, who can afford to pay the highest fees in exchange for the best legal representation. Accordingly, most large law firms are lavish when compared to their small and medium counterparts. The grounds are well kept, the offices are large and well equipped with the newest technology, and it is not uncommon to find art adorning the walls. Because attorneys are paid to bill hours, on-site incentives exist to keep them inside, such as on-site coffee bars, dry-cleaning services, and even meal and car services for those attorneys who stay after hours to work.

The largest law firms and legal service providers require ample office space. Consequently, they often occupy multiple floors in skyscrapers or other defining buildings. Many of the firms are also multinational, and some individual locations may employ hundreds of people, taking into account all levels of attorneys, paralegals, and administrative support.

Typical Number of Employees. Firms employing fifty or more people are generally considered to be large firms. While fifty attorneys could be housed in one central in-state office, one thousand attorneys must be spread throughout several offices. Large firms and legal service organizations generally have the financial resources necessary to hire the proper number of attorneys and administrative personnel to enable the firm to operate at maximum productivity. A single big law firm may employ thousands of people worldwide.

Traditional Geographic Locations. The most successful law firms often have offices in large U.S. cities such as New York, Boston, Chicago, Los Angeles, and Washington, D.C., as well as in international metropolises such as London and Tokyo. Additionally, many firms have smaller offices in smaller cities that are commonly referred to as satellite offices. These regional offices do not employ as many attorneys and administrative support staff, but they help build and maintain the national and international presence of the firm. Large legal service providers, such as legal aid agencies, are traditionally located in large cities, as such locations provide the greatest service to the largest number of individuals in need of representation.

Pros of Working for a Large Firm. Those in charge of large firms are among the most well compensated attorneys in the world. They are partners and, accordingly, get a share of the success of an extremely large business. In the largest firms, most partners earn over $1 million annually, including bonuses. Partners are treated very well within the firm, as they have several associate attorneys working on their files and reporting to them; they have wealthy and successful clients; and they enjoy a high standard of living. For other attorneys, and even administrative employees, compensation at these firms is very competitive, as are the benefit packages. Though the work may be difficult and the hours long, employees are compensated for these sacrifices. In fact, large firms pay bonuses to associates and will even assist with bar exam fees, relocation expenses, and other professional fees associated with the practice of law.

Cons of Working for a Large Firm. The life of a partner in a large firm is not without sacrifice. The hours spent at the office can be grueling. As a general rule, attorneys at large firms are required to bill a minimum of eighteen hundred hours per year. The term "billing" does not refer to all time spent at work, however. Rather, this term describes only time that can legitimately be billed to clients; that is, time actually spent on files, including such activities as researching, writing, deposing a witness, or attending court. Furthermore, there are often limits for certain projects. As a result, while an attorney may spend ten hours working on a particular project, he or she may only be able to bill five or six of those hours toward his or her annual billable goal.

After vacation and holidays, a typical billable requirement averages around forty billed hours per week. Since not all time spent at work is billable, big firms' attorneys are at work many more than forty hours per week (seventy-, eighty-, and even one-hundred-hour work weeks are not unheard of in big firms). This leaves little time for a social life or a family. Additionally, the environment is often stressful. Attorneys' work products are carefully scrutinized and, if not satisfactory to their superiors, must be perfected. Finally, attorneys must wait several years at large firms before learning whether they will become partners. In large firms, the wait is often at least seven years.

Costs

Payroll and Benefits: Despite the requirement to bill a certain number of hours, most attorneys are paid salaries. They may also earn bonuses, however, and each employee at a large firm is offered a very competitive, and expensive, benefits package. In order to attract top graduates from the best law schools, firms will offer to pay many nonlegal expenses. For example, some firms offer a onetime bonus (up to $50,000) to reward and attract associates who, following their graduation from law school, served for a

Corporate lawyers ensure that business transactions are legal. According to PayScale.com, a little more than two-thirds of corporate lawyers are men. (©Endostock/Dreamstime.com)

year as a law clerk for a prominent judge or at a high-level appeals court.

Supplies: Large firms and multinational legal service providers must have an integrated network, through which an attorney in New York can communicate with an attorney in Tokyo. Accordingly, state-of-the-art computer and phone systems, printers, fax machines, and network capabilities for thousands of employees are necessities. Firms also require vast amounts of paper, pens, copiers and copying supplies, and other general office supplies and equipment. As technology changes, the largest firms must constantly adapt to keep pace with their competitors.

External Services: Big firms outsource almost everything unrelated to the practice of law. In addition to traditional services such as building maintenance and groundskeeping, these businesses may even outsource such functions as public relations and litigation management. They may also hire experts to help with such functions as jury selection or to act as consul-

tants in cases requiring expertise, such as those involving the precise effects of exposure to particular chemicals. Because many of these costs eventually are absorbed by wealthy clients—clients who expect their attorneys to work only on legal issues—big firms can afford to outsource and hire experts.

Utilities: Even multinational corporations must pay for building usage, electricity, heat, and other associated costs. With so many employees in several different buildings, such costs can be extensive. Before deciding to open new offices, firms must be sure that the demand for their services in that particular geographic area is sufficient to overcome the overhead costs.

Taxes: Like any other business, big firms and their employees must pay taxes on income. Further, it is almost a given in big firms that the firm pays the cost of its attorneys' employment-related taxes, such as bar licensure fees and any other mandatory fees attorneys must pay in order to practice law in a particular jurisdiction.

ORGANIZATIONAL STRUCTURE AND JOB ROLES

Any size law firm or legal services provider will need to account for activities in the following areas. In smaller companies and firms, one person often holds several roles within several groups. In larger companies, specialists generally fulfill unique requirements in specific groups. Regardless of size and scope, the functions must be fulfilled.

The following umbrella categories apply to the organizational structure of law firms and legal service providers:

- Legal Practice
- Business Management
- Customer Service
- Sales and Marketing
- Facilities and Security
- Human Resources

Legal Practice

Law firms and legal service providers exist primarily to practice law and to assist individuals or corporations in need of legal advice. At large firms, there may exist several categories of attorneys and administrative staff who do the work necessary to satisfy and retain clients and to earn revenue. Attorneys research the law, attend and argue at court hearings and trials, advise their clients, and draft documents, among other responsibilities. Administrative staff assist the attorneys in any number of ways, from helping keep files up to date to researching the law and drafting memoranda.

Legal occupations may include the following:

- Managing Partner
- Partner
- Senior Associate Attorney
- Associate Attorney
- First-Year Associate Attorney
- Staff Attorney

OCCUPATION SPECIALTIES

Lawyers

Specialty	Responsibilities
Corporate lawyers	Advise corporations on legal rights, obligations, and privileges in accordance with the constitution, statutes, decisions, and ordinances.
Criminal lawyers	Specialize in legal cases dealing with offenses against society or the state, such as theft, murder, and arson. They are responsible for preparing a case for trial, examining and cross-examining witnesses, and summarizing the case to the jury.
District attorneys	Conduct prosecutions in court proceedings for a city, a county, a state, or the federal government; also known as prosecuting attorneys, city attorneys, or solicitors.
Environmental lawyers	Specialize in the policies of environmental law and help their clients follow those statutes. They may help clients properly prepare and file for licenses and applications and represent parties such as interest groups and construction firms in their dealings with the U.S. Environmental Protection Agency.
Patent lawyers	Specialize in patent law and advise clients such as inventors, investors, and manufacturers on whether an invention can be patented, as well as on other issues, such as infringement on patents, validity of patents, and similar items.

- Of Counsel Attorney
- Law Clerk
- Intern
- Paralegal
- Administrative Assistant
- Legal Secretary
- Receptionist
- Volunteer (at nonprofit legal service providers)

Business Management

Business managers are responsible for the day-to-day operations of their firms. Typical responsibilities include directing the litigation in which the firm is involved, establishing the vision for the firm, maintaining relationships with important clients, and managing the employees and finances. Management at a firm is typically the job of the managing partner or partners, traditionally the most senior attorneys at the firm and those with particular expertise in the legal market in which the firm practices. Although managing partners are attorneys first and are still focused on the practice of law, a large portion of their time may be spent on nonlegal endeavors related to their firms' overall success.

Business management occupations may include the following:

- Managing Partner
- Partner

Customer Service

Unlike most industries, in which customers can call a 1-800 number to reach customer service, customer service at law firms is relatively individualized. There is not a dedicated team of employees fielding calls from across the world; rather, clients in need of service call the attorney or paralegal handling their matter directly.

Customer service occupations may include the following:

OCCUPATION PROFILE

Paralegal

Considerations	Qualifications
Description	Prepares legal documents under the direction of a lawyer.
Career clusters	Business, Management, and Administration; Law, Public Safety, and Security
Interests	Data; people
Working conditions	Work inside
Minimum education level	On-the-job training; junior/technical/community college; bachelor's degree
Physical exertion	Light work
Physical abilities	Unexceptional/basic fitness
Opportunities for experience	Military service; part-time work
Licensure and certification	Recommended
Employment outlook	Faster-than-average growth expected
Holland interest score	SEC

Note: See volume 1, "Publisher's Note," for an explanation of the Holland interest score.

- Attorney
- Paralegal
- Administrative Assistant
- Secretary
- Receptionist

Sales and Marketing

Because law firms are composed, for the most part, of attorneys and assistants who also have some degree of legal training, there often is not a dedicated sales and marketing department. Law firms in need of advertising and marketing assistance often enter into contracts with public relations or marketing businesses to provide those services. That being said, attorneys—and especially partners—bear a responsibility to bring in, and keep, clients. Commonly referred to in the legal industry as "making rain," the business of attracting clients is extremely important to the continued success of the firm. At some point, all attorneys bear a level of responsibility for helping their firms attract and retain clients.

Sales and marketing occupations may include the following:

- Managing Partner
- Partner
- Senior Associate Attorney
- Associate Attorney
- Of Counsel Attorney

Facilities and Security

Depending on the size and location of a given law firm, certain facilities and security services may, in part, be provided to the firm as part of a lease agreement if, for example, the firm rents one floor in a skyscraper owned by another party. Otherwise, facilities and security concerns for a law firm or legal service provider are no different from those for any other corporation. The firm or service provider will either directly employ security personnel, or it will outsource such services.

Facilities and security occupations may include the following:

- Security Manager
- Security Agent/Officer
- Building Maintenance and Repair Worker
- Heating, Ventilation, and Air-Conditioning (HVAC) Technician
- Computer Security Specialist

Human Resources

The scope and role of a legal human resources department depends on the size of a given firm or service provider and its needs. For example, many national and international law firms have a dedicated human resources department to review applications submitted by prospective employees. At small and midsize firms—and especially at non-profit legal service providers—managing partners and partners often act as de facto human resources officers. They typically solicit for, collect, and sort through applications, conduct the interviews, negotiate employment contracts, and assist new employees with issues related to their benefits packages. Occupations in this business area depend on the size of the firm and its status as either a for-profit business or a nonprofit legal service provider.

Human resources occupations may include the following:

- Human Resources Manager
- Human Resources Generalist
- Benefits Specialist
- Managing Partner
- Partner

INDUSTRY OUTLOOK

Overview

Like many other industries, the law firm and legal services industry rises and falls, to an extent, as the economy rises and falls. This was the case when the United States faced a significant economic downturn beginning in late 2007. As a result of larger national and global economic problems, attorneys at most levels noticed a negative change in the years 2008 and 2009. When significant numbers of clients and potential clients are themselves are being laid off or are having their wages and hours reduced, they are less inclined to seek legal counsel. With less money to spend, individuals are less likely to purchase property, enter into complex contracts, or engage in other activities that may traditionally require the service of lawyers. Similarly, corporations that have experienced financial losses and that have had to reduce their workforce are less likely to engage in mergers and acquisitions of new businesses, and they may be less likely to make complex employment decisions—ventures that traditionally would require the services of employment attorneys.

Attorneys may always be terminated for poor performance. Industry-wide layoffs, however, are usually relatively rare. In 2009, though, some of the largest—and traditionally the most successful—law firms undertook unusual measures aimed at surviving the tough economy. Some firms laid off attorneys, while others instituted pay cuts or froze wages. Finally, some firms delayed the traditional fall hiring of the new class of first-year associates. Though new attorneys still gained positions with these firms, they had to wait six months, or even a year, before beginning their employment and earning a paycheck.

Positions at legal services providers may be more stable than positions in law firms during economic downturns. Because many of the former entities are nonprofits, their bottom line is not associated solely with finances. Additionally, the salaries of attorneys, paralegals, and administrative assistants employed by legal service providers are traditionally lower than the salaries of those same positions at large law firms. To underscore this point, a staff attorney at a legal service provider, such as a legal aid agency, may earn approximately $60,000 annually. A first-year associate attorney at one of New York's largest law firms earns approximately $160,000 annually. When a for-profit firm struggles economically, it is an easier decision to lay off the attorney making $160,000, than it is for the legal aid agency to lay off an attorney making $60,000.

Nevertheless, the long-term outlook for both the legal services and the law firm segments of the industry is encouraging. In the period from 2006 to 2016, the BLS estimates that there will be an 11 percent increase in the number of lawyers in the United States, as well as a 22 percent increase in the number of paralegals and administrative assistants. The national average percentage increase for all occupations in the United States in this time period is projected to be 10.36 percent. When the numbers for the legal profession are compared to the national averages, it becomes clear that the need for attorneys will be both stable and growing and, equally as important, the need for administrative support positions and paralegals is expected to grow at more than twice the national average rate. For those considering a career in the law firm and legal services industry, these statistics should be encouraging.

Employment Advantages

The U.S. law firm and legal service industry has been consistently stable since the country's inception. Individuals who enjoy solving problems, interacting with people, conducting research, writing, and public speaking should consider a career in this industry. Moreover, becoming a licensed attorney does not limit one's employment prospects, should one decide later not to practice law in the traditional sense. Many people with law degrees work in business, marketing, academia, government, and many other employment sectors. Similarly, the skills of a paralegal and administrative assistant are easily transferable to other industries, and they provide excellent work experience for people who decide to attend law school and become attorneys.

Notwithstanding economic difficulties, as evidenced by the 2007-2009 global recession, there are always parties and corporations that need legal advice and assistance. This industry has persisted for centuries and is an ingrained segment of society, business, and the economy. For those who enjoy challenging and intellectually stimulating work, and those who desire to make a difference in their clients' lives, a legal career may be rewarding.

Annual Earnings

As of May, 2009, there were approximately 1,003,000 people employed nationally in the legal industry. This figure includes practicing attorneys, judges, paralegals, and other legal support workers. According to the U.S. Census Bureau, the industry's total U.S. revenues in 2007 were $251 billion. According to the BLS, the average wage in the profession in 2008 was $92,270 annually, while the average wage for lawyers in particular was $124,750. Approximately half of those in the legal profession worked as attorneys, while over 250,000 were paralegals and administrative assistants. The average wage of a paralegal or administrative assistant was $48,790 annually.

The outlook is strong for the law firm and legal services industry. The percentage increase output in terms of chained dollars (a method of adjusting real dollar amounts for inflation over the course of time) is expected to be 3.4 percent for the time period 2006-2016, slightly above the national average of 2.9 percent. Although no industry appears to be immune from economic downturns, the BLS expects the legal industry to outperform more than half the other industries in the United States in the long term.

RELATED RESOURCES FOR FURTHER RESEARCH

AMERICAN ASSOCIATION FOR JUSTICE
777 6th St. NW
Washington, DC 20001
Tel: (800) 424-2725
http://www.justice.org

AMERICAN BAR ASSOCIATION
321 N Clark St.
Chicago, IL 60654-7598
Tel: (800) 285-2221
http://www.abanet.org

AMERICAN CIVIL LIBERTIES UNION
125 Broad St.
New York, NY 10004
Tel: (212) 507-3300
http://www.aclu.org

AMNESTY INTERNATIONAL USA
5 Penn Plaza
New York, NY 10001
Tel: (212) 807-8400
http://www.amnestyusa.org

LEGAL AID SOCIETY
199 Water St.
New York, NY 10038
Tel: (212) 577-3300
http://www.legal-aid.org

NATIONAL ASSOCIATION FOR LAW PLACEMENT
1025 Connecticut Ave. NW, Suite 1110
Washington, DC 20036-5413
Tel: (202) 835-1001
http://www.nalp.org

NATIONAL ASSOCIATION OF CRIMINAL DEFENSE LAWYERS
1660 L St. NW, 12th Floor
Washington, DC 20036

Tel: (202) 872-8600
http://www.criminaljustice.org

NATIONAL LEGAL AID AND DEFENDER ORGANIZATION
1140 Connecticut Ave. NW, Suite 900
Washington, DC 20036
Tel: (202) 452-0620
http://www.nlada.org

ABOUT THE AUTHOR

Andrew Walter is an attorney licensed to practice in the state of Connecticut. He received a bachelor of arts degree in international management, with a minor in English, from Gustavus Adolphus College in St. Peter, Minnesota, and a juris doctorate from Roger Williams University School of Law in Bristol, Rhode Island. After having served as a law clerk for the judges of the Connecticut Superior Court, he is currently employed as an attorney at the Connecticut Supreme Court, engaging in a variety of civil and criminal issues before that court.

FURTHER READING

Anderson, Wayne, and Marilyn Headrick. *The Legal Profession: Is It for You?* Cincinnati: Thomson Executive Press, 1996.

Echaore-McDavid, Susan. *Career Opportunities in Law and the Legal Industry.* New York: Facts On File, 2002.

Feuer, Alan. "A Study in How Major Law Firms Are Shrinking." *The New York Times*, June 5, 2009.

Friedman, Lawrence M. *American Law in the Twentieth Century.* New Haven, Conn.: Yale University Press, 2002.

Furi-Perry, Ursula. *Fifty Unique Legal Paths: How to Find the Right Job.* Chicago: American Bar Association, 2008.

Harvard Law School Program on the Legal Profession. "Analysis of the Legal Profession and Law Firms." http://www.law.harvard.edu/programs/plp/pages/statistics.php.

Hazard, Geoffrey C., and Angelo Dondi. *Legal Ethics: A Comparative Study.* Stanford, Calif.: Stanford University Press, 2004.

Munneke, Gary. *Careers in Law*. 3d ed. New York: McGraw-Hill, 2003.

U.S. Bureau of Labor Statistics. *Career Guide to Industries*, 2010-2011 ed. http://www.bls.gov/oco/cg.

_____. "Lawyers." In *Occupational Outlook Handbook*, 2010-2011 ed. http://www.bls.gov/oco/ocos053.htm.

_____. "Paralegals and Legal Assistants." In *Occupational Outlook Handbook*, 2010-2011 ed. http://www.bls.gov/oco/ocos114.htm.

U.S. Census Bureau. North American Industry Classification System (NAICS), 2007. http://www.census.gov/cgi-bin/sssd/naics/naicsrch?chart=2007.

U.S. Department of Commerce. International Trade Administration. Office of Trade and Industry Information. Industry Trade Data and Analysis. http://ita.doc.gov/td/industry/otea/OTII/OTII-index.html.

Williams, Sean, and David Nersessian. *Overview of the Professional Services Industry and the Legal Profession*. Cambridge, Mass.: Harvard Law School Program on the Legal Profession, 2007. http://www.law.harvard.edu/programs/plp/pdf/Industry_Report_2007.pdf.

Libraries and Archives Industry

INDUSTRY SNAPSHOT

General Industry: Government and Public Administration

Career Cluster: Government and Public Administration Occupations

Subcategory Industries: Archives; Bookmobiles; Centers for Documentation; Circulating Libraries; Film Archives; Lending Libraries; Libraries; Motion Picture Film Libraries and Archives; Music Archives; Reference Libraries

Related Industries: Local Public Administration; Publishing and Information Industry

Annual Domestic Revenues: $1.9 billion USD (U.S. Census Bureau, Economic Census, 2007)

Annual International Revenues: $43.3 billion USD (International Federation of Library Associations, 2003)

Annual Global Revenues: $45.2 billion USD (International Federation of Library Associations, 2003)

NAICS Number: 51912

INDUSTRY DEFINITION

Summary

An archive is a repository of original documents, such as diaries, manuscripts, photographs, and letters. Historians and other researchers use this "raw material" to write books and articles for magazines; the "finished products" are then housed in libraries. Both of these institutions exist for the primary purposes of collecting and preserving materials, making these available to interested parties, and using them to answer questions. In addition, libraries offer such services as public use of computers and the Internet, borrowing privileges for a range of media (books, films, compact discs, and so on), and in-person classes, all of which are free of charge at public libraries.

History of the Industry

Archaeological evidence indicates that archives and libraries have existed since ancient times, with sites in what used to be the empires of Sumeria, Babylonia, and Assyria. The most important and well known of these early libraries was that of Alexandria in Egypt. Handwritten clay tablets and papyrus rolls, made from reeds, were typical of this era.

Literature arose with the Greek and Roman civilizations. Wealthy citizens amassed impressive private holdings of epics, poetry, and the like by such classical greats as Sophocles and Euripides, while

Libraries and archives may be one-person operations or may be institutions with hundreds of employees. (©William Britten/iStockphoto.com)

temples to the various gods contained public records and official histories. Reading materials consisted of scrolls of parchment, made from the skins of sheep or goats, and vellum, a more durable substance created from unsplit lambskin, kidskin, or calfskin.

The end of the Roman Empire in 476 C.E. brought with it marauding bands of Vandals, Goths, Huns, and other barbarian tribes, who burned and pillaged cities and the libraries they harbored. This destruction was offset by other developments, principally the rise of monasteries throughout Europe and especially in Ireland. The monks of these bastions of faith scoured the countryside for ancient manuscripts and laboriously copied them by hand.

Paralleling this trend was the establishment of universities, which, like the monasteries, were under the purview of the church. In large cities such as Paris, Oxford, and Heidelberg, with stable social structures and economies, more people were encouraged to matriculate, so the demand for books increased, and college libraries were established. By this time, paper had been introduced via the trade routes from China, and a primitive form of the book, known as the codex, was displacing parchment and vellum.

The Renaissance saw the advent of printing with movable type, when Johann Gutenberg of Mainz,

in what is now Germany, produced the now famous Bible of 1455. With mass production of books possible, their cost diminished considerably, giving rise to increased demand, which led to the establishment of private libraries. Members of royalty, not to be outdone, often donated their monumental collections to found public libraries. Influential individuals, such as Martin Luther, became advocates for libraries and encouraged their founding and maintenance.

The Enlightenment in the eighteenth century was a further impetus to the growth of libraries and archives throughout Europe and the British colonies in the new world. It was also at this juncture that archives and libraries became separate institutions. Up to this time, documents, records, books, and periodicals had been housed in single repositories. With the turmoil of the French Revolution, the value of preserving national heritage through historic documents and public records was recognized. In 1789, the Archives Nationales were founded in France. Their underlying model, in which the state is responsible for collecting and preserving important papers, was soon copied by other governments around the world.

With the nineteenth century came the establishment of national repositories, such as the British Library and the Library of Congress in the United States. Library and archive administration also became professionalized during that century. In 1876, the American Library Association was founded, and Melvil Dewey created his decimal classification system, which is still in wide use today. This period also saw the creation of specialized schools for the training of librarians and archivists. By the twentieth century, library construction and maintenance in the United States was furthered by such philanthropists as steel magnate Andrew Carnegie and by governmental foresight. The Library Services and Construction Act of 1964, for example, helped ensure that just about any school or town of any size had a library that it could call its own.

The Industry Today

Archives and libraries have evolved considerably from what they were in the past, namely, warehouses for papers and books run largely by clerks. Today, they reflect not only advances in technology but also the wishes of the clientele they serve, and they are administered by highly trained professionals. In the United States, the majority of librarians possess undergraduate degrees in the liberal arts and master's degrees in library science from schools accredited by the American Library Association. Archivists must also possess master's degrees, and, while a few institutions of higher learning offer archival studies or archival science programs, it is much more common for archivists to hold master's degrees in history or library science, with course work in such areas as records management, materials preservation, and so on.

Over time, libraries and archives have increased greatly in number and in the process have become quite specialized. According to the *American Library Directory, 2009-2010*, there are 29,880 libraries in the United States. Some of these are legal libraries at law firms, in which librarians must also be familiar with the law, oftentimes holding juris doctor degrees. Others are medical libraries at hospitals, where librarians need to understand medical terminology and procedures. Corporate libraries are located at the headquarters of Fortune 500 companies, and academic libraries exist on college campuses across the country. By far the most common type of library, however, is the public library, which can be found in the smallest towns and the largest metropolitan areas. Funded by appropriations from local governments, these institutions are often regarded as among the best uses of taxpayer dollars. The services they offer are many, varied, and generally free of charge.

Libraries today offer their visitors traditional services with a modern-day emphasis on conve-

Petaluma, California, is the site of a Carnegie library, built in 1906. Andrew Carnegie donated $12,500 of the $20,000 needed to build the structure, which served as a library until 1976, when it was converted into a museum. (©Richard Brookes/ Dreamstime.com)

nience and expediency. A cornerstone of public librarianship, for example, has been reference service. Traditionally stationed at a reference desk or information desk, reference librarians receive customers, known in the profession as "patrons," or sometimes as "users" or "borrowers." Patrons may ask for information on any topic, from the telephone number of a local business to how plants harness the rays of the sun in the process known as photosynthesis.

While patrons may pose their queries in person or over the telephone as they have in the past, alternative time-saving options now abound. Virtual reference allows patrons to communicate with librarians over the Internet via real-time chat software. This process allows patrons the luxury of receiving answers regardless of location or time of day, assuming that they have Internet access. The rise of the Internet itself and, more particularly, of freely available search engines such as Google, has been something of a double-edged sword for the profession, as many individuals now choose to do their own research, meaning that demand for this service has diminished somewhat. However, the questions posed, while fewer in number, have increased in complexity. For example, a patron may want to know if a book written in, say, French, has ever been translated into English and, if so, when it was published, whether it is available for loan, and from which library.

Archives, too, have harnessed the World Wide Web to enhance service to their customers. Historically, those who wished to view public records or other documents had to do so in person. Many archives have digitized their holdings or are in the process of doing so, allowing researchers to view items of interest at any time of the day or night, without the expenditure of time and travel necessary to visit the archive in person.

Today, archivists work in a variety of locations. Many are employed by government, such as those at the National Archives and Records Administration (NARA). Academia represents another generator of archivist jobs, as many college and university departments are responsible for preserving one-of-a-kind documents and objects. Some archivists are employed by private firms, while still others may make a living at state and local historical societies.

Classes on a variety of topics are held at libraries. Newly arrived immigrants may take English as a sec-

ond language (ESL), the unemployed may learn how to navigate the World Wide Web to search for jobs or polish their resumes, and senior citizens may learn new hobbies such as birdwatching or quilting. Because there has always been a teaching element to this profession, these classes are generally taught by librarians themselves, especially if they happen to have personal knowledge of the subjects. At the same time, librarians can recommend to their students relevant books, magazines, and other materials that their libraries have in their collections.

With the onset of the recession of 2007-2009, library usage increased dramatically, as people canceled magazine subscriptions, bought fewer books, and unplugged their home computers. Because library budgets remained flat or even declined, however, long waits for computer stations or for copies of popular novels became more common. Safety and security concerns at libraries have increased, especially at large facilities located in major metropolitan areas. Some libraries have resorted to having uniformed police officers patrol the aisles, while others have hired private security firms for this purpose. While violent incidents are still rare, the threat of unpleasant occurrences can dissuade people from visiting their local libraries, and managers are loathe to have unflattering coverage of their facilities appear in local newspapers or on television.

Libraries have been affected by a continuing shift from print to electronic and digital resources. Many reference books are now being purchased as part of electronic databases, which may be accessed remotely via the Internet. Novels have been available on compact disc for some time, and they are now becoming available as downloadable e-books, which can be read on personal computers; dedicated e-book readers, such as Amazon's Kindle and Barnes and Noble's Nook; or multipurpose mobile devices, such as tablet computers, handheld computers, and smart phones.

INDUSTRY MARKET SEGMENTS

Libraries and archives may be one-person operations or may be institutions with hundreds of employees, such as the Library of Congress or the National Archives. They serve patrons from all walks of life, from members of the public to academics pursuing professional research. The following discussion gives specifics about small, midsize, and large institutions.

Small Institutions

Libraries typically reflect their surrounding geographic and physical locations. Therefore, a rural community may have a single room set aside in its city hall as its designated library, with a single employee, known as a "solo librarian." A small library is defined as a facility serving a population of from ten thousand to twenty-five thousand. Libraries in this category generally have a minimal selection of materials and only a handful of public-access computers for Internet searching.

Potential Annual Earnings Scale. The average salary for a solo librarian varies with geographic location and the supply-to-demand ratio of librarians in the vicinity. The U.S. Bureau of Labor Statistics (BLS) reports that as of May, 2009, the median annual wage of all librarians was $53,710. The median annual wage of all archivists was $46,470. More precise figures can be found by consulting the most recent edition of the *American Salary and Wages Survey*, which is available in many libraries. For librarian positions specifically, the single best source of salary information is the *ALA-APA Salary Survey: A Survey of Library Positions Requiring an ALA-Accredited Master's Degree*, which is published annually by the American Library Association. According to this document, the median annual salary of a nonsupervisory librarian working in a small library is $43,519.

Clientele Interaction. Relationships between librarians or archivists and their patrons generally are informal and relaxed. At small libraries especially, patrons make weekly or even daily visits, and librarians get to know them on a first-name basis. Through long experience with these frequent visitors, librarians learn their favorite authors and literary tastes, and they begin to make suggestions to patrons regarding the arrival of new titles or up-and-coming writers whose work is in a similar vein to that of authors the patrons already enjoy. This kind of personal service, which is becoming increasingly rare in today's corporatized society, is very much appreciated on the part of the public. The goodwill engendered pays dividends in public advocacy of neighborhood libraries when elected

officials attempt to curtail hours or close library branches altogether.

Amenities, Atmosphere, and Physical Grounds. Small libraries come in a variety of guises. Some are almost invisible, as they are housed in buildings serving other functions. For example, a small-town city hall may have one room set aside for the community library, while other areas contain offices, meeting rooms, and the like. It is not uncommon for small libraries to be found in historic structures that have been rehabilitated for their new use, such as former churches, fire halls, or schools. Small archives, on the other hand, are usually found within the confines of college libraries or historical society basements.

As small libraries and archives invariably have small budgets, materials and equipment available for use by visitors are minimal and fairly basic. A small library may have only a handful of computer stations for Internet use, two dozen or so films on digital video disc (DVD), and perhaps a few hundred books available for checkout. All the traditional services of larger libraries or archives are generally available, but taking advantage of them may be less convenient, involving longer wait times for material to arrive as a result of the small library's distance from a main branch or urban center. Regardless of size or budget, maintenance of the building and grounds is almost always contracted out, so that private firms are responsible for snow removal, lawn care, and so forth.

Typical Number of Employees. Small libraries may have only one employee, but they will always employ full-fledged librarians or archivists. In some cases, a paraprofessional may also be on hand, such as a library clerk or page, to perform routine tasks, such as unloading books from book drops and putting out current copies of local newspapers. These clerks free librarians to answer reference questions and solve patron problems.

Traditional Geographic Locations. Small libraries are most frequently located in small towns and rural areas. They are stand-alone facilities serving the local population and most commonly are political subunits of the local government. However, large metropolitan areas can also have small libraries, although in such cases, they are small branches of larger library networks or systems. Such city-administered library networks generally have central or main branches located downtown.

Pros of Working for a Small Library or Archive. Librarians and archivists derive a deep sense of satisfaction from being able to answer questions or solve problems for their patrons. Because of the more intimate working relationship, helping someone find just the right book or document goes beyond merely doing one's job; on the part of both the professional and the patron, it seems more personal than that, as if the former were doing the latter a favor. The fact that the staff of a small library or archive is limited to one or two people generally makes service more responsive to requests, since patrons need not go through various levels of management or be shunted from one department to another, as might be the case at larger institutions.

Cons of Working for a Small Library or Archive. The one or two employees of a small library or archive must handle all necessary tasks related to running their institution, from shelving books and documents to fielding questions from visitors to opening the daily mail. The job may therefore involve a good deal of stress, as the workday is a constant balancing act between providing personal attention to users and still performing all requisite daily tasks.

Because small libraries and archives are not as heavily used as are larger institutions, they are often open fewer hours each week. They are generally open for business only during weekdays, and even then probably less than the standard eight hours per day. The resulting short shifts translate into reduced earning potential for their employees.

Costs

Payroll and Benefits: Librarians and archivists, by virtue of their professional education and job duties, are salaried. Some employees, such as assistant librarians and library clerks, are represented by unions, such as the American Federation of State, County, and Municipal Employees (AFSCME), as a majority of public libraries are governmental entities. Therefore, these employees are entitled to vacation and sick leave, prorated if they work less than full time.

Supplies: Libraries and archives require books and other media, as well as shelving on which to store them. They need computers, printers, photocopiers, consumables such as paper and toner, other basic office supplies, and some cleaning supplies.

External Services: Building maintenance, groundskeeping, and janitorial service are almost always provided by private contractors. Repair and maintenance of photocopiers and other equipment are managed by the companies leasing that equipment.

Utilities: Libraries must pay for broadband Internet service, telephone, electricity, water, and sewage service.

Taxes: The majority of libraries are local government entities and therefore enjoy tax-exempt status, although they must still pay employee payroll taxes.

Midsize Institutions

A midsize public library is defined as a facility serving a population of from 25,000 to just under 100,000. Midsize libraries typically are housed in buildings constructed for that specific purpose or are part of multifunction spaces, such as structures that also contain indoor parks, health and fitness centers, and community meeting rooms. These are often found in suburban areas.

Potential Annual Earnings Scale. Salaries vary with geographic location and the supply-to-demand ratio of librarians in the vicinity. The BLS reports that as of May, 2009, the median annual wage of all librarians was $53,710. The median annual wage of all archivists was $46,470. According to the *ALA-APA Salary Survey*, a department head or senior manager earns approximately $55,000 annually, while a manager or supervisory librarian earns $48,616 per year.

Clientele Interaction. Midsize libraries are often de facto community centers, the modern-day versions of town squares, where citizens come not just to acquire their reading material but also to meet friends, conduct business in a meeting room, or purchase coffee in one of the interior coffee shops that are becoming increasingly common in newer libraries. Therefore, librarians' interactions with individual patrons are likely to be limited to answering questions, checking out materials, and conducting other business that takes only a few minutes. In the world of academia, archivists are more likely to confer with department heads and professors on campus than with members of the public.

Amenities, Atmosphere, and Physical Grounds. The stereotype of the silent library, where a middle-aged woman with her hair in a bun tells people to be quiet, is a thing of the past. Today, midsize libraries are considered to be "working libraries." They host high-spirited high school students who talk as much as they study, mothers with squalling infants in tow, and other frenetic patrons of all ages. This level of chaos is akin to rush hour on the freeway and occurs about the same time, late afternoon. There is a definite rhythm to the workday, however, and lulls occur at mid-morning and after lunch. A varied selection of films on DVD, audio books, large print novels, current newspapers and magazines, and other materials is available to the public.

Typical Number of Employees. Midsize libraries can have variable staffing levels, depending on the square footage of the establishment and the gate count (number of people entering the premises). However, five to ten librarians, library clerks, and shelvers is typical for this category. Archives follow a similar pattern, sometimes hiring additional staff during busy periods. They may take on interns, who earn credits in lieu of a paycheck, as they gain on-the-job experience.

Traditional Geographic Locations. Midsize libraries are usually located in suburban areas surrounding cities and major metropolitan areas. Many are deliberately sited along or near major highways, freeways, or other arterial thoroughfares to make entrance and exit convenient for those who live in bedroom communities. Archives in this category can often be found on the campuses of colleges and universities, where their efforts support both the curricula and the missions of their host institutions.

Pros of Working for a Midsize Library or Archive. Employees of midsize institutions get to meet people from all walks of life. Dealing with such a diverse clientele helps them grow professionally, since the variety of questions and requests they receive almost invariably involves research and study. Thus librarians and archivists learn much in the course of their work. The fast-paced nature of the workday makes the time seem to go by quickly. Because there are more positions and job openings available at midsize facilities than at small facilities, there are greater opportunities for career advancement.

Cons of Working for a Midsize Library or Archive. The hectic pace of most days does not lend itself to forming lasting or meaningful relationships, such as may be formed at small libraries and archives. By the same token, there is usually little time to interact with coworkers. Library jobs can be hectic and stressful, involving people waiting in line at the reference desk, telephones ringing, and random interruptions such as photocopiers malfunctioning, all at once. Because facilities of this size are generally open evenings and weekends, librarians must expect to spend at least some of these hours away from home and family. Archivists may also work evening and weekend hours in order to accommodate students facing deadlines for term papers, reports, and other research projects.

Costs

Payroll and Benefits: Librarians and archivists, by virtue of their professional education and job duties, are salaried. Some employees, such as assistant librarians and library clerks, are represented by unions, such as the American Federation of State, County, and Municipal Employees (AFSCME), as a majority of public libraries are governmental entities. Therefore, these employees are entitled to vacation and sick leave, prorated if they work less than full time.

Supplies: Libraries and archives require books and other media, as well as shelving on which to store them. They need computers, printers, photocopiers, consumables such as paper and toner, other basic office supplies, and some cleaning supplies.

External Services: Building maintenance, groundskeeping, and janitorial service are almost always provided by private contractors. Repair and maintenance of photocopiers and other equipment are managed by the companies leasing that equipment.

Utilities: Libraries must pay for broadband Internet service, telephone, electricity, water, and sewage service.

Taxes: The majority of libraries are local government entities and therefore enjoy tax-exempt status, although they must still pay employee payroll taxes.

Large Libraries and Archives

Large libraries and archives can be state or federal government entities, such as the Library of Congress or the National Archives, both of which are located in Washington, D.C. Other large libraries serve as central or main branches of multibranch systems in major metropolitan areas. Generally speaking, a large public library serves a population of from 100,000 to just under 500,000. National libraries serve the entire nation, albeit in a less direct fashion.

Potential Annual Earnings Scale. Salaries vary with geographic location and the supply-to-demand ratio of librarians in the vicinity. The BLS reports that as of May, 2009, the median annual wage of all librarians was $53,710. The median annual wage of all archivists was $46,470. According to the *ALA-APA Salary Survey*, directors of a large facility earn median annual salaries of $102,871. Deputy or assistant directors earn median salaries of $73,219 per year, and department heads and senior managers earn median salaries of $59,635.

Clientele Interaction. Because large institutions are physically vast and employ a wide range of positions, many of their employees do not interact with the public. Many positions, such as catalogers, work behind the scenes in rooms reserved for staff. They enter and exit the building through employee-only doors and interact only with other library employees, vendors, and related professionals. The public face of a large library is presented by its circulation and reference staff. Circulation personnel assist patrons with checking out and returning library materials, setting up accounts for library cards, and other routine matters. Reference staff answer questions, help patrons find books and other materials, lend assistance with library equipment (such as public computer stations), and respond to other special requests. Because large libraries serve large populations, they are quite busy, and interactions between librarians and patrons are generally brief and businesslike.

Amenities, Atmosphere, and Physical Grounds. Large libraries tend to function as cen-

The ceiling of the Library of Congress. (©Nick Cannella/Dreamstime.com)

The main branch of the New York Public Library, the Stephen A. Schwarzman Building, is one of the city's eighty-seven branch libraries and four research libraries. (©Dreamstime.com)

tral or main branches of multibranch systems and are frequently located in the downtown cores of major metropolitan areas. The buildings they occupy may be historic structures of significant architectural value. The main branch of the New York Public Library, in New York City, is a prime example. Conversely, major architects may be employed to design new "library monuments" designed to impress the public and elected officials in order to increase patron traffic and operating budgets. The city of Minneapolis, Minnesota, caused a stir with its I. M. Pei-designed central library, which is notable for its glass curtain walls and silvery metallic "wing" jutting from the edge of the roof.

Ample square footage and hefty budgets ensure that the maximum amount of material will be available for patrons. Large libraries are destinations, in that patrons make special trips to these facilities, as it is well known that they have the best selections of books, films on DVD, audio books, and the like. Large libraries also have the greatest number of

public computer stations. Free Internet access is a major driver of traffic at all libraries, but this is especially true of large facilities, as many people cannot afford to purchase access for their own homes.

Large libraries also offer many special features and comforts that are beyond the reach of smaller facilities with limited budgets. Overstuffed chairs for comfortable reading, fireplaces to create warm and cozy corners, meeting rooms available for community groups or quiet study, and coffee shops for refreshment are just some of the amenities available in this market segment. Special events, too, play a role in large libraries, as well-known authors make appearances there to read from their latest novels and sign books. Classes on various topics are held at regular intervals for the edification of interested parties on such topics as gardening in cold climates or how to navigate the electronic databases that the library offers.

Typical Number of Employees. Large libraries employ ten or more people, sometimes many more. There is a wide range of staffing needs among these institutions, depending on factors such as square footage, location, and demand for services.

Traditional Geographic Locations. Most often, large libraries are located in the downtown cores of large cities, although suburban areas may also have them. It is not uncommon for these facilities to be part and parcel of historic quarters or otherwise be considered landmarks. Frequently nestled among theaters, museums, and other cultural attractions, these facilities help draw traffic to the downtown area and in return receive many visitors drifting in from other nearby destinations.

Pros of Working for a Large Library or Archive. The relatively large workforce of this type of establishment affords greater opportunities for career advancement, since there is more turnover in personnel and more positions of responsibility. Also, the many operational areas of large institutions, such as reference work, cataloging, information technology, and so forth, present learning opportunities for ambitious librarians. Pay tends to be higher and fringe benefits more generous, owing to larger institutional budgets and the bargaining power of unions.

Cons of Working for a Large Library or Archive. Employees of large institutions tend to have narrower, more specialized sets of duties. Many of their tasks can therefore become repetitive and routine, leading to on-the-job burnout. Contact with coworkers and members of the public may be perfunctory and impersonal as a result of employees' hectic work schedules and compartmentalization.

Costs

Payroll and Benefits: Librarians and archivists, by virtue of their professional education and job duties, are salaried. Some employees, such as assistant librarians and library clerks, are represented by unions, such as the American Federation of State, County, and Municipal Employees (AFSCME), as a majority of public libraries are governmental entities. Therefore, these employees are entitled to vacation and sick leave, prorated if they work less than full time.

Supplies: Libraries and archives require books and other media, as well as shelving on which to store them. They need computers, printers, photocopiers, consumables such as paper and toner, other basic office supplies, and some cleaning supplies.

External Services: Building maintenance, groundskeeping, and janitorial service are almost always provided by private contractors. Repair and maintenance of photocopiers and other equipment are managed by the companies leasing that equipment.

Utilities: Libraries must pay for broadband Internet service, telephone, electricity, water, and sewage service.

Taxes: The majority of libraries are government entities and therefore enjoy tax-exempt status, although they must still pay employee payroll taxes.

ORGANIZATIONAL STRUCTURE AND JOB ROLES

Administratively, libraries fulfill their duties to the public by allocating labor into three broad categories: User services include reference, reader's advisory (which provides help and advice on what to read), circulation, and interlibrary loan. Technical services encompass information technology (IT), acquisitions, and cataloging staff. Administrative services comprise library directors, managers, and other supervisory personnel who solve problems, create policy, and generally run their establishments. At small libraries, a single person may fulfill all of these tasks. Archives, on the other hand, being generally much smaller both physically and in terms of staff, are much more flexible in regard to organization and job roles. A hypothetical state historical society, for example, might have such job titles as collections assistant, government records specialist, and state archivist.

The following umbrella categories apply to the organizational structure of institutions in the libraries and archives industry:

- Management
- Reference Services
- Reader's Advisory
- Interlibrary Loan
- Circulation
- Information Technology
- Acquisitions

- Serials
- Cataloging
- Public Relations
- Administrative Support
- Children's Services
- Special Collections
- Government Documents
- Outreach Services

Management

Management has overall responsibility for the operation of a library or archive. Managers set policy, resolve and respond to disputes and complaints, supervise employees, establish budgets, solve problems, and plan for the future. In the case of new construction or the renovation and expansion of existing facilities, managers also act as contractors, in that they hire architects, approve plans, and manage the fund-raising and budgeting for these projects. In addition to holding master's degrees in library science (from institutions accredited by the American Library Association), managers oftentimes have taken additional course work in supervision, accounting, and other topics regarding the running of an operation.

Management occupations may include the following:

- Library Director
- Deputy Director

OCCUPATION SPECIALTIES

Librarians

Specialty	Responsibilities
Acquisitions librarians	Select and order books, periodicals, articles, and audiovisual materials on particular subjects.
Bibliographers	Work in research libraries and compile lists of books, periodicals, articles, and audiovisual materials on particular subjects.
Branch or department chief librarians	Coordinate the activities of a library branch or department; train, assign duties to, and supervise staff; and perform librarian duties.
Catalogers	Describe books and other library materials.
Children's librarians	Manage library programs for children and select books and other materials of interest to children for the library to acquire. They plan and conduct programs for children to encourage reading, viewing, listening to, and using of library materials and facilities.
Classifiers	Classify materials by subject.
Information scientists	Design systems for storage and retrieval of information and develop procedures for collecting, organizing, interpreting, and classifying information.
Reference librarians	Assist groups and individuals in locating and obtaining library materials.
Special collections librarians	Collect and organize materials on select subjects used for research.

- Library Manager
- Assistant Manager

Reference Services

Every library, regardless of size, offers reference service free of charge. Anyone may ask any question about almost any topic and expect to receive an answer. These services are provided by reference librarians, who by virtue of formal education and experience are familiar with all manner of reference books, Internet searching, electronic databases, and other information sources. Ethically, a reference librarian would refuse a request on how to construct an atomic bomb or anything else that might be construed as dangerous or illegal. Typically, librarians conduct what are known as "reference interviews" with requestors, whether the transaction is in person, on the telephone, or via virtual reference. Often, requestors are not entirely certain of what they want to know, so a series of questions is asked of them in order to arrive at the heart of the matter. It is not uncommon, especially in academic libraries, for reference librarians to be experts in specific subjects by dint of holding additional master's degrees beyond the master of library science.

Reference services occupations may include the following:

- Head of Reference
- Supervising Reference Librarian
- Reference Librarian

Reader's Advisory

Known as RA for short within the profession, reader's advisory staff provide consultation services to help patrons find and enjoy books they might not find on their own. RA staff may suggest authors whose work is similar to authors a patron already likes, or they may simply answer questions about titles in a series of which a patron has read only part.

Reader's advisory occupations include the following:

- Reader's Adviser

Interlibrary Loan

Interlibrary loan refers to the lending of books from one library to another for the benefit of patrons, so they need not travel about in search of the reading material they desire. Formerly taking up much time and paperwork, interlibrary loan has become largely automated with the advent of computers and the Internet. Closely allied to interlibrary loan is document delivery, which refers to the acquisition of photocopied individual articles from within periodicals in other libraries. Because the delivered documents are photocopies (or other facsimiles), they need not be returned.

Interlibrary loan occupations include the following:

- Interlibrary Loan Librarian

Circulation

Circulation is the library department responsible for handling the checking in and checking out of library materials, issuing library cards to patrons, levying fines for overdue or damaged materials, and ensuring that materials are returned to their proper place on the shelves. Many positions in this category are part time, also known as full-time equivalent, or FTE, positions. For example, two people each working twenty hours per week are considered equivalent to one full-time (forty-hour) worker.

Circulation occupations may include the following:

- Head of Circulation
- Library Clerk
- Library Technician
- Library Page
- Shelver

Information Technology

Computers and the Internet are integral parts of any library, regardless of size. Information technology, or IT, comprises computer acquisition, maintenance, and repair; firewall installation and maintenance; Internet connectivity; software upgrades; and automated equipment, such as self-checkout machines and receipt printers.

IT occupations may include the following:

- Systems Technician
- Chief Information Officer (CIO)
- Database Administrator

OCCUPATION PROFILE

Library Technician

Considerations	Qualifications
Description	Compiles records, sorts and shelves books, and issues and receives library materials, such as books, films, slides, and phonograph records.
Career cluster	Education and Training
Interests	Data; people
Working conditions	Work inside
Minimum education level	On-the-job training; high school diploma/technical training; junior/technical/community college
Physical exertion	Light work
Physical abilities	Unexceptional/basic fitness
Opportunities for experience	Part-time work
Licensure and certification	Usually not required
Employment outlook	Average growth expected
Holland interest score	CSE

Note: See volume 1, "Publisher's Note," for an explanation of the Holland interest score.

Acquisitions

Acquisitions staff oversee the purchase and receipt of library materials. In addition to acquiring newly released materials, libraries must regularly replace popular titles, which experience significant wear and tear through constant circulation, as well as being lost and stolen outright. Libraries are high-volume purchasers, so they often receive discounts from vendors.

Acquisitions occupations may include the following:

- Head of Acquisitions
- Acquisitions Librarian

Serials

Also known as periodicals, serials are magazines, journals, quarterlies, and other print materials that are published at regular intervals. With the advent of the Internet, many titles come with online versions bundled to physical subscriptions. Often, articles from back issues are also available online. Many libraries do not keep back issues for more than about two years because they take up so much shelf space and their content tends to become dated quickly. Others bind together each year's worth of a given periodical, providing those issues with hardcover protection.

Serials occupations may include the following:

- Serials Librarian
- Binding Technician

Cataloging

All incoming material must be classified, described, added to the library catalog, and processed, which entails applying protective material (such as a mylar cover over the dust jacket of a book), antitheft devices and stamps, and identification or shelf stickers. Catalogers typically work

OCCUPATION SPECIALTIES

Media Specialists

Specialty	Responsibilities
Audiovisual librarians	Coordinate the availability of audiovisual materials, such as films, video tapes, and cassettes, in a library, and they assist patrons in selecting materials. They evaluate materials, considering their technical, informational, and aesthetic qualities, and select materials for library collections.
Institutional librarians	Plan and direct library programs for residents and staff of extended-care facilities, such as mental institutions and prisons.
Music librarians	Classify and file musical recordings, sheet music, original arrangements, and scores for individual instruments.

in staff-only work areas and normally do not have contact with the public. However, the results of their labors are immediately apparent to anyone who uses the Online Public Access Catalog (OPAC), the modern-day electronic version of physical card catalogs. Catalogers typically take specialized courses in this field, as their work is considered a specialty of librarianship, just as cardiology and gastroenterology are specialties of medicine.

Cataloging occupations include the following:

- Cataloger

Public Relations

Every library needs to engage its public. This engagement can take the form of author readings, classes, special events, used book sales, other fundraisers, or any other modes of generating positive publicity. While flyers, banners, newspaper notices, and other traditional means are still used, the major forms of communication have become electronic. Libraries publish calendars of events on their Web sites, and they often send e-mail notifications or even full electronic newsletters to patrons who sign up to receive them.

Public relations occupations may include the following:

- Public Relations Librarian
- Webmaster

Administrative Support

Paperwork and forms are an ever present requirement of any organization, and libraries are no exception. Invoices must be paid, timesheets must be tabulated, and orders must be placed. These tasks are handled by administrative staff. Generally, such staff members' offices are housed in the main or central branch of a library system. In addition to clerical personnel, these areas also house the offices of library management teams and contain storage areas for office supplies, photocopiers, and other office equipment.

Administrative support occupations may include the following:

- Receptionist
- Clerk
- Secretary
- Office Manager

Children's Services

Most libraries have areas set aside just for children. These may include one corner of a small library or an entire wing of a larger facility. Children's areas are staffed by dedicated children's librarians, who are well versed in literature for young people. Special services include regularly scheduled story times, in which librarians read story books to children; show and tell sessions, in which various objects are presented for discussion; and furnishings built low to the floor for the comfort of youngsters. Very often, books are arranged by reading level, for ease of selection. It is also not uncommon for stuffed toys, puzzles, and other amusements to be available for those children who may have short attention spans.

Children's services occupations include the following:

- Children's Librarian

Special Collections

Special collections is an all-encompassing category that can include material not easily stored on shelves, such as pamphlets housed in file cabinets, or material of a significant nature, such as local history books, photographs, or artifacts. In a sense, a special collection is an archive housed within a library.

Special collections occupations may include the following:

- Special Collections Director
- Special Collections Librarian

Government Documents

While publications are produced by many political subdivisions, such as city councils and county boards, the majority of such documents come from the federal government. So prolific a publisher is the federal government, in fact, that a separate classification system has been devised to organize its documents, the Superintendent of Documents, or SUDOCS. Large libraries in the United States are known as "depository libraries," and these institutions automatically receive every book, pamphlet, map, or document printed by the government in Washington, D.C. Because of the amount and complexity of this material, special areas of large libraries are set aside for government documents, and librarians in charge of these areas must have specialized training.

Government documents occupations include the following:

- Government Documents Librarian

Outreach Services

Many people cannot physically come to the library, including disabled persons and incarcerated convicts. Libraries reach out to these persons in or-

der to serve their needs. Most libraries, for example, have homebound services, in which couriers deliver library materials to disabled persons' residences. Bookmobiles, essentially libraries on wheels, make regular stops in the neighborhoods of large cities. Libraries also have programs dedicated to loaning books and other materials to prisoners.

Outreach services occupations include the following:

- Outreach Services Librarian

INDUSTRY OUTLOOK

Overview

The outlook for this industry shows it to be stable. According to the 2010-2011 edition of the BLS's *Occupational Outlook Handbook*, employment for librarians is predicted to rise by 8 percent between 2008 and 2018, slightly less than the average of 11 percent for all industries. Two countervailing trends are at work: On one hand, the workforce is aging as the U.S. population as a whole ages. In a March, 2002, article titled "Reaching Sixty-Five: Lots of Librarians Will Be There Soon," *American Libraries* magazine warned of a possible shortage of librarians caused by impending retirements. On the other hand, the recession of 2007-2009 affected both the budgets of libraries and the retirement funds of librarians. As a result, fewer librarians will retire in the near term, and fewer retirees will be replaced, than would occur in a more robust economy.

Also affecting the industry outlook are younger librarians who are just entering the profession. The American Library Association runs an active recruitment campaign to entice college students to choose librarianship as a career. Anecdotal evidence suggests that many librarians made midcareer switches, having found that their bachelor's degrees in one of the humanities, such as English or history, led to less-than-satisfying career paths. While library careers may not be particularly remunerative, there are many positive factors that lead people to abandon their former occupations to become involved with books and people.

Entirely apart from the issue of incoming and outgoing individuals within the profession is the topic of funding. The vast majority of librarians work in public libraries and are therefore at the mercy of the political winds. During times of economic distress, elected officials look for easy targets to cut budgets, and libraries are usually at the top of the list of potential victims. The irony is that it is during these same periods that library usage spikes, as the unemployed flock to their neighborhood branches to use public Internet stations to look for work and to take classes in resume writing and other job-related skills.

Librarians are nothing if not innovative, however, and many are entering nontraditional employment. The more entrepreneurial are going into business for themselves as consultants and information brokers. They charge hourly fees to search for information and hard-to-find documents or to, say, analyze the competition for a particular business or industry. Still others engage in teaching at library schools, or in writing books on topics of interest to other librarians.

Employment Advantages

Those who enjoy literature and learning are able to indulge their twin passions as librarians, since to a large degree the profession involves being familiar with works of the past and present, from classics to contemporary best-selling novels. Librarianship is a helping profession, and in that regard it shares much with teaching and nursing. Librarians may derive satisfaction from matching people with the books they wish to read and from helping them discover new authors and works.

The work of librarians is intellectual, rather than physical. Librarians typically work in comfortable surroundings and are stimulated both by their association with patrons asking questions and by their interactions with colleagues who share their love of learning.

Annual Earnings

In the wake of the global financial crisis of 2007-2009, depressed conditions continue to be a drag on earnings for the libraries and archives industry. The industry's annual domestic revenues totaled $1.9 billion according to the 2007 Economic Census conducted by the U.S. Census Bureau. Some librarians, such as those covered by union contracts, will fare better than average, as collective bargaining has proven to be of benefit to workers generally.

According to the BLS, in 2009 the middle 50 percent of U.S. librarian salaries ranged from $42,980 to $66,750. The middle 80 percent ranged from $33,480 to $82,450. Librarians employed by the federal government, which tends to be highly unionized, earned substantially higher average salaries than those employed in other sectors: the mean annual salary of all librarians in 2009 was $55,670, while the mean annual salary of those working for the federal government was $79,550.

Salary figures for archivists are similar. The BLS reports that, for the same period, the middle 50 percent of U.S. archivist salaries ranged from $35,150 to $61,180, and the middle 80 percent ranged from $27,050 to $78,680. The mean annual salary of all archivists was $49,600, while the mean annual salary of federally employed archivists was $78,760—above the ninetieth percentile of earners.

Internationally, the library and archive industry would appear to be robust, having generated $43.3 billion in revenue in 2003, according to figures supplied by the International Federation of Library Associations (IFLA). Taken together with the United States, the annual global revenue totals $44.9 billion.

RELATED RESOURCES FOR FURTHER RESEARCH

AMERICAN ARCHIVIST
527 S Wells St., 5th Floor
Chicago, IL 60607
Tel: (312) 922-0140
Fax: (312) 347-1452
http://www.archivists.org

AMERICAN ASSOCIATION OF SCHOOL LIBRARIANS
50 E Huron St.
Chicago, IL 60611-2729
Tel: (800) 545-2433, ext. 4382
Fax: (312) 280-5276
http://www.ala.org/aasl

AMERICAN LIBRARY ASSOCIATION
50 E Huron St.
Chicago, IL 60611-2729
Tel: (800) 545-2433
Fax: (312) 440-9374
http://www.ala.org

LIBRARY JOURNAL
Reed Business Information
360 Park Ave. South
New York, NY 10010
Tel: (646) 746-6400
Fax: (646) 746-7431
http://www.libraryjournal.com

SOCIETY OF AMERICAN ARCHIVISTS
17 N State St., Suite 1425
Chicago, IL 60602-3315
Tel: (312) 606-0722
Fax: (312) 606-0728
http://www.archivists.org

ABOUT THE AUTHOR

Mike Bemis holds a master's degree in library and information science (2006) from the College of St. Catherine in St. Paul, Minnesota. His book reviews appear regularly in a number of professional publications, including *American Reference Books Annual*, *Reference and User Services Quarterly*, and *Library Journal*. A member of the American Library Association and the Reference and User Services Association, Bemis currently serves as chair of the latter association's Materials Reviewing Committee. He makes his living as a reference librarian at Washington County Library in Woodbury, Minnesota.

FURTHER READING

Battles, Matthew. *Library: An Unquiet History.* New York: W. W. Norton, 2003.

Bogart, Dave, ed. *Library and Book Trade Almanac, 2009.* 54th ed. Medford, N.J.: Information Today, 2009.

Camenson, Blythe. *Opportunities in Museum Careers.* New York: McGraw-Hill, 2007.

Cox, Richard J. *Archives and Archivists in the Information Age.* New York: Neal-Schuman, 2005.

Eberhart, George M. *The Whole Library Handbook 4.* Chicago: American Library Association, 2006.

Grady, Jenifer, and Denise M. Davis. *ALA-APA Salary Survey—Librarian—Public and Academic: A Survey of Library Positions Requiring an ALA-Accredited Master's Degree.* Chicago: American Library Association, 2009.

Information Today. *American Library Directory.* 62d ed. Medford, N.J.: Author, 2009.

International Federation of Library Associations and Institutions. "Global Library Statistics, 1990-2000." The Hague, Netherlands, 2003. http://archive.ifla.org/III/wsis/wsis-stats4pub_v.pdf.

Lynch, Mary Jo. "Reaching Sixty-Five: Lots of Librarians Will Be There Soon." *American Libraries* 33, no. 2 (March, 2002).

Simkin, Joyce P. *American Salary and Wages Survey.* 10th ed. Farmington Hills, Mich.: Gale Cengage, 2009.

Society of American Archivists. "So You Want to Be an Archivist: An Overview of the Archival Profession." http://www2.archivists.org/profession.

Spear, Martha J. "The Top Ten Reasons to Be a Librarian." *American Libraries* 33, no. 9 (October, 2002).

U.S. Bureau of Labor Statistics. *Career Guide to Industries*, 2010-2011 ed. http://www.bls.gov/oco/cg.

_____. "Librarians." In *Occupational Outlook Handbook*, 2010-2011 ed. http://www.bls.gov/oco/ocos068.htm.

U.S. Census Bureau. North American Industry Classification System (NAICS), 2007. http://www.census.gov/cgi-bin/sssd/naics/naicsrch?chart=2007.

_____. *Statistical Abstract of the United States: 2010.* 129th ed. Washington, D.C.: Author, 2009.

U.S. Department of Commerce. International Trade Administration. Office of Trade and Industry Information. Industry Trade Data and Analysis. http://ita.doc.gov/td/industry/otea/OTII/OTII-index.html.

Light Machinery Industry

©Dreamstime.com

INDUSTRY SNAPSHOT

General Industry: Manufacturing
Career Cluster: Manufacturing
Subcategory Industries: Lawn and Garden Tractor and
  Home Lawn and Garden Equipment Manufacturing;
  Office Machinery Manufacturing; Photographic and
  Photocopying Equipment Manufacturing; Power-Driven
  Handtool Manufacturing; Turbine and Turbine
  Generator Set Units Manufacturing
Related Industries: Hand Tools and Instruments Industry;
  Household and Personal Products Industry
Annual Domestic Revenues: $122.7 billion USD (U.S.
  manufacturing corporations seasonally adjusted after-tax
  profits; U.S. Census Bureau, 2010)
NAICS Numbers: 333112-333313, 333315, 333611, 333991

INDUSTRY DEFINITION

Summary

Light equipment either reduces or replaces manpower to accomplish a task. This equipment can be human powered, powered by electricity, or powered by an internal combustion engine (usually gasoline but rarely diesel). An example is the lawn mower, which can be hand propelled, gasoline powered, or electrically powered. Garden equipment such as lawn mowers, rototillers, and snow blowers also are produced by this industry. Office equipment, such as photocopiers and fax machines, also makes up a large segment of the light machinery industry. Many companies in this industry also produce heavy equipment as well as products for other industries. Virtually every industrialized nation on the planet has a significant light machinery industry employing individuals in a wide variety of careers.

History of the Industry

Sectors of this industry either markedly expanded or appeared during the Industrial Revolution, which began in the eighteenth century in Europe. It was marked by major changes in manufacturing, mining, agriculture, manufacturing, and transport; this phenomenon had a profound impact on socioeconomic and cultural conditions. However, the use of light equipment began in ancient times in Egypt, Greece, and Rome. In 1400 B.C.E., the lathe was developed. Two persons were required to operate this device: One would turn a length of wood with a rope while the other manipulated a pointed tool to shape the wood. The Romans improved the machine with the addition of a turning bow. The British, French, and Germans used similar lathes a few centuries later. In the middle ages, the addition of a foot pedal allowed the operator to propel the lathe while holding a carving tool in both hands. Mechanization of the lathe occurred during the Industrial Revolution; lathes were powered by water wheels and steam engines. By the end of the nineteenth century, electric motors appeared. Benjamin Franklin's investigations into the properties of electricity in the mid-nineteenth century served as a foundation for the accomplishments of his successor Thomas Alva Edison. Edison invented the electric lightbulb in 1879; in 1892, he established the first electric plant in New York City. Precursors of today's batteries also were developed in that century. In 1859, the lead-acid battery was produced; this type of rechargeable battery is used in today's automobiles.

Electric motors allowed for the development of stationary and portable power tools in the late nineteenth century. Robert Bosch (Stuttgart, Germany), founded by Robert Bosch in 1886, initially produced electrical components for automobiles. Bosch subsequently became a pioneer in the power tool industry; in 1932, the company introduced its first power drill. In 1923, the American inventor Raymond DeWalt introduced the first radial-arm saw. The Makita Corporation (founded in Japan in 1915) focused its attention on cordless, battery-powered tools; in 1978, the company introduced its cordless handheld drill.

At the heart of the garden equipment industry is the lawn mower. English engineer Edwin Budding developed the reel-type mower. Budding was working in a textile mill that used a shearing machine to trim the nap of velvet. He realized that the device could replace the scythe he used to mow his lawn. His mower, which consisted of a series of blades arranged around a cylinder, is similar to the hand-powered mower used today.

Office equipment, such as photocopiers and fax machines, makes up a large segment of the light machinery industry. (©Stephen Coburn/Dreamstime.com)

A mainstay of any business office is the copy machine. The device was invented by the Scottish inventor James Watt in 1779. His device physically transferred a special type of ink from a letter or drawing to a moistened piece of paper using a press. The American inventor Chester Carlson is credited with inventing photocopying in 1938. He produced multiple copies of a document using a zinc plate covered with sulfur. However, at that time, carbon paper was a more popular method of making copies. This industry segment began to flourish in 1949 when Xerox Corporation (Wilsonville, Oregon) introduced its first copier. Subsequently, the term "Xeroxing" became synonymous with "photocopying."

In addition to electricity, the assembly line fueled the development of the light equipment industry. Before 1900, machinery was produced at one location, one unit at a time. Although the origin of the assembly line is often linked with Henry Ford, Ransom Olds patented the assembly line concept, which he implemented in his Olds Motor Vehicle Company factory in 1901. The concept was improved a few years later by Ford, who moved the work from one worker to another until a product was complete; these units were then moved to a final assembly line, which produced the finished product. As a result of Ford's improvements, an automobile came off the line every three minutes. Previous assembly lines had produced vehicles at a rate of about two an hour and required significantly more manpower. Furthermore, Ford implemented safety procedures such as assigning each worker to a specific location rather than allowing them to roam about the work area; this dramatically reduced the rate of injury.

The Industry Today

The light machinery industry is dominated by large, multinational companies that produce a wide range of products for the home, workshop, and garden; these products are mainly powered by elec-

The lawn mower is at the heart of the light machinery industry. (©Dreamstime.com)

One large segment is power tools, such as electric hedge trimmers. (©Wisconsinart/Dreamstime.com)

tricity. An increasing number of battery-powered products are appearing on the market. Major sub-industries supported by the light machinery industry are maintenance and repair, sales, leasing, engine manufacturing (electric and internal combustion), and battery manufacturing. Many of these companies also manufacture products for other industries, such as the heavy machines industry, the office products industries, and the computer industry. In some instances, most of the products manufactured by a company are for another industry. For example, generators for home and recreational use represent a small percentage of generators available on the market. Most are large machines designed for industrial use. In addition to manufacturing their products, many companies sell, lease, and repair the equipment.

A major segment of this industry is focused on the manufacturing of hand and power tools. Products include chain saws, drills, impact wrenches, jigsaws, nail guns, riveting guns, routers (wood-shaping tools), sanders, buffers, and power-driven screwdrivers. Battery-powered tools are extremely popular for both contractors and nonprofessionals. They have proven to be extremely useful at outdoor work sites where electrical power is unavailable or unreliable. Major companies in this industry are Husqvarna (Huskvarna, Sweden), Stanley Black & Decker (New Britain, Connecticut), Techtronic Industries Company (New Territories, Hong Kong), Makita Corporation (Anjo, Japan), Bosch (Stuttgart, Germany), and Craftsman (a subsidiary of Sears Holdings Corporation, Hoffman Estates, Illinois). Companies such as these are highly susceptible to fluctuations in the rate of economic growth. Much of their equipment is designed for construction; thus, when new construction slows, the companies are affected.

Husqvarna has a similar product line. The company produces snow throwers, ice augers, and work clothing. Stanley Black & Decker has three product lines: construction and do-it-yourself (DIY) hand tools and power tools; industrial and automotive repair tools and infrastructure solutions; and secu-

Golf carts, as well as garden tractors and riding law mowers, are part of this industry's output. (©Dreamstime.com)

rity and health care products. Techtronic Industries Company produces power tools, outdoor products, and floor-care products. Techtronic is the parent company of Milwaukee Electric Tool Corporation (which produces heavy-duty power tools), AEG (power tools), Ryobi (power tools for the home market), Homelite (outdoor power equipment such as trimmers, chainsaws, pressure washers, generators, and water pumps), and three lines of floor-care products (Hoover, Dirt Devil, and Vax). Makita Corporation manufactures industrial power tools that run on rechargeable batteries. Bosch markets high-end power tools, automotive goods (for example, gasoline and diesel systems, brakes, electronics, and steering systems), home appliances, and many other products for the home and industrial markets. It also operates gasoline/diesel vehicle garages and diagnostic centers.

A well-known brand in the light machinery industry is Craftsman, which was launched by Sears (now Sears Holdings Corporation) in 1927. Craftsman tools have a reputation for quality and durability and are backed by a lifetime warranty. The company primarily manufactured basic hand tools such as hammers and screwdrivers before progressing to power tools. Today, Craftsman is one of the top-selling power tool producers. Craftsman tools are sold in Sears, Kmart, and Orchard Supply Hardware stores (all three are subsidiaries of Sears Holdings); they also are sold in Fastenal, U.S. military post exchanges, and Ace Hardware stores. Through the years, Craftsman tools have been produced for Sears by a variety of manufacturers, including New Britain, Moore Drop Forge, Stanley, Easco Hand Tools, the Danaher Corporation, and Western Forge.

While a number of the aforementioned companies market some products for the home garden and farm use, other companies focus primarily on those product lines. One such manufacturer is Deere & Company, whose main product line is focused on the agricultural and construction industry (such as tractors, combines, tillers, and harvesters). Another major portion of its product line is devoted to smaller equipment: golf carts, lawn mowers (walking and riding) and other home garden equipment, snow blowers, and home workshop products.

Photographic and photocopying equipment manufacturing is another significant segment of this industry. Products include aerial cameras, blueprint equipment, cameras (nondigital), developing equipment, film editing equipment, enlargers, light meters, and photocopiers. As of 2010, the five market leaders were Fujifilm Holdings Corporation (Tokyo), Canon Europa (Amstelveen, Noord-Holland), Olympus Corporation (Tokyo), Nikon Corporation (Tokyo), and Eastman Kodak Company (Rochester, New York). Although this segment of the light equipment industry comprises nondigital equipment, these companies have transitioned to the digital age and also market digital photographic products. Even venerable Eastman Kodak, a pioneer in film cameras, has embraced digital photography. Typical of global companies manufacturing light equipment, these companies have subsidiaries in related industries. Fujifilm Holdings Corporation is the holding company for three companies: Fujifilm Corporation, Fuji Xerox Company, and Toyama Chemical Company. Canon Europa primarily manufactures cameras, photocopiers, and optical equipment for both personal and industrial (including medical) use. The Nikon Corporation has a similar focus. In addition to digital products, these companies also market products for the computer industry. An example is the all-in-one printer, which combines a printer, photocopier, scanner, and fax machine into one compact piece of equipment.

In addition to photocopiers, many pieces of light machinery are designed for the business office. These include adding machines; binding and bundling equipment; calculators; cash registers; check writing machines; coin/currency counting machinery; coin wrapping machinery; collating machinery; dictating machinery; envelope stuffing, sealing, and addressing machinery; hole punchers; incoming mail handling equipment; letter folding, stuffing, and sealing machinery; postal machines; stenography machinery; typewriters; and word processors.

Most light equipment is produced by automated processes somewhat similar to automobile assembly lines. Small companies tend to be less auto-

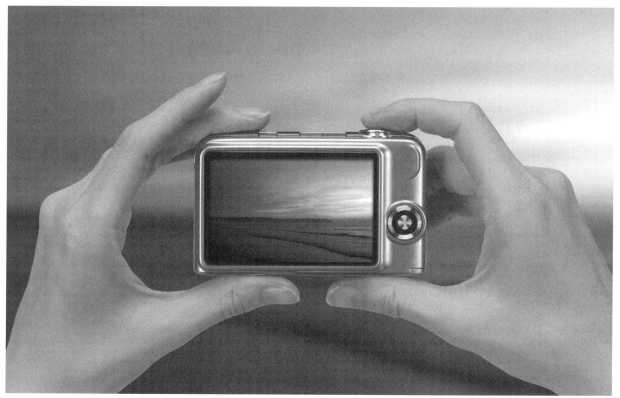

Photographic equipment makers have transitioned to the digital age with products such as this camera. (©Tezzstock/ Dreamstime.com)

mated than midsize or large companies. In many cases, the manufacturing process involves shaping metal (usually steel) into a framework, then assembling the components. Aluminum and plastic also are molded into housings and components for appliances. Painting often is part of the assembly process.

INDUSTRY MARKET SEGMENTS

While some smaller companies with less than one thousand employees compete in the marketplace, this industry is dominated by large, global companies.

Small Businesses

Small light machinery manufacturers usually offer specialty products designed for niche markets. They may offer a single product or a line of several related products. These products are primarily small appliances. Some small businesses produce unique products, while others manufacture products similar to those made by larger companies. Since the beginning of the twenty-first century, some small companies have flourished and experienced significant growth.

Potential Annual Earnings Scale. The average income for a small-business owner varies from region to region and usually is less than $100,000 annually.

Clientele Interaction. Small businesses tend to favor more interaction with customers, and the personal touch can foster consumer satisfaction. However, clientele interaction can vary widely. The owner might have direct contact with his or her customers or market the product over the Internet with contact limited to the telephone and e-mail. A Web site is essential to a small business. The Web site can not only market the product but also offer technical advice and serve as a vehicle for customer feedback.

Amenities, Atmosphere, and Physical Grounds. Amenities of small businesses often are limited. Inasmuch as the owner has extensive control over the business, the working environment can be tailored to personal taste and budget. An owner interested in a favorable working environment might have a facility with extremely pleasant working conditions; however, most facilities are utilitarian, no-frills structures.

Typical Number of Employees. The number of employees can range from one to several dozen. A small business could consist solely of an owner and family members who manufacture and market the product.

Traditional Geographic Locations. Geographic locations of small businesses are unlimited. They are usually located near, or even in, the owner's home.

Pros of Working for a Small Light Machinery Business. The owner is often responsible for all operational decisions. The owner might consult with staff members regarding these decisions or have complete autonomy. A staff member usually has a closer working relationship with the owner than in a larger company. Part-time employment and flexible hours usually are easier to arrange than they would be in a larger company. A small-business owner can control waste and unnecessary expenditures to a greater degree than a larger company because all expenditures are subject to his or her approval. If the company fosters teamwork and group decision making, employees can be more involved in the company's growth. In some cases, partnership opportunities exist for exceptional employees. If the company flourishes, the company might grow in size and profit margin; this could lead to expansion or purchase by a larger company.

Cons of Working for a Small Light Machinery Business. The light machinery industry is extremely competitive. Even if a small company produces a good product, it might not be able to compete successfully with a large company that can produce a comparable product at a lower price. A small business is less resilient when faced with an unexpected major expense, such as a lawsuit or major equipment replacement. This situation could bankrupt a small business. At a small company, the owner and staff generally will not have the variety of skills that the staff and management of larger companies will possess. For example, the staff may have technical expertise but lack marketing skills. Furthermore, with a small staff, the owner and employees are responsible for a wider range of duties.

Costs
Payroll and Benefits: Small companies often place all employees on an hourly wage and usu-

ally do not provide the same level of benefits as a large company; these benefits are at the discretion of the owner and include sick pay, health insurance, and vacations.

Supplies: Supplies usually cost more for small-business owners than for large businesses, which can buy in bulk and thus negotiate lower prices.

External Services: Costs for external services for a small business typically are minimal and might include such things as Web site development/maintenance and billing services. If a small business becomes involved in a legal dispute, an attorney must be retained. In this situation, the small-business owner might incur significant costs.

Utilities: Utilities may be comparable to that of a home; however, the manufacturing of some equipment might involve significant usage of electricity or natural gas.

Taxes: Small businesses are obligated to pay local, state, and federal taxes.

Midsize Businesses

Like small manufacturers in this industry, midsize light machinery manufacturers tend to favor niche markets and limited product lines. These products may compete with those produced by large businesses. Some produce products that complement the product lines of the large businesses. Midsize manufacturing businesses often started as small businesses and flourished and expanded. Other midsize companies are offshoots or former divisions of larger companies. Like small businesses, they tend to favor small appliances tailored to niche markets. Retail sales facilities consist of a single store or several facilities. An example of a small company that has grown into a midsize business is Bench Dog (Maple Grove, Minnesota). The company was founded by two people in 1995 and has grown to a midsize business that markets a line of router tables, tools, and accessories for contractors and nonprofessionals. The products are available from a number of retailers, including Amazon and Lowe's.

Potential Annual Earnings Scale. Salaries vary from region to region; however, a typical salary for a mechanical engineer is $32 per hour; sales representatives earn about $28 per hour and might receive commissions for sales; first-line supervisors/managers of production and operating workers

earn about $26 per hour; tool and die makers earn about $21 per hour; machinists earn about $18 per hour; computer-controlled machine tool operators (metal and plastic) earn about $17 per hour; inspectors, testers, sorters, samplers, and weighers earn about $17 per hour; welders, cutters, solderers, and brazers earn about $16 per hour; cutting, punching, and press machine setters, operators, and tenders (metal and plastic) earn about $14 per hour; and team assemblers earn about $14 per hour. Incomes for managers in a company's manufacturing arm vary widely from less than $50,000 to more than $100,000 annually.

Clientele Interaction. Vendors can foster long-term relationships, which can generate repeat business. All midsize businesses will have a Web site for both marketing and clientele interaction. The site will offer customer service, technical support, and often provide copies of user manuals for download.

Amenities, Atmosphere, and Physical Grounds. Manufacturing facilities are customarily spartan and utilitarian.

Typical Number of Employees. A manufacturing facility consists of a management staff, assembly supervisors, and assemblers.

Traditional Geographic Locations. Manufacturers of small appliances can be situated in a wide range of locations; however, their facilities typically are in industrial areas. Manufacturers of larger equipment such as riding lawn mowers are commonly located in areas near rail or ocean cargo service. Retail outlets can be located in any area with sufficient population to generate adequate sales.

Pros of Working for a Midsize Light Machinery Business. The owner of a midsize manufacturing business often has more control over operational decisions than he or she would in a large company. Employee-management interaction also often is greater than at a large company. Midsize manufacturing businesses can employ individuals with a variety of skills; these employees include technicians, assemblers, and marketing personnel. These companies typically have one or only a few locations; thus, an employee who prefers to remain in one location usually will not be confronted with the threat of a transfer to a distant location.

Cons of Working for a Midsize Light Machinery Business. Many midsize businesses produce limited product lines or specialty products. In times of economic downturn, these companies are more susceptible to failure. The limited number of management positions in a midsize company decreases opportunities for advancement, particularly those commanding a high salary.

Costs

Payroll and Benefits: Midsize companies usually can offer benefits comparable to those of a large company; these benefits include sick pay, health insurance, and vacations.

Supplies: Midsize companies often can negotiate discounts from suppliers; however, the unit production cost may be higher than the cost for a comparable product produced by a large company.

External Services: Manufacturing companies often use accounting services and billing services; however, they also might have employees on staff who can perform these tasks. Midsize companies also often use outside legal services rather than in-house counsel.

Utilities: Manufacturing of light equipment sometimes involves significant costs for utilities, particularly gas and electricity.

Taxes: Midsize businesses must pay local, state, and federal income taxes as well as applicable property taxes. Almost all businesses in the United States are incorporated; thus, they pay state and federal taxes at the corporate level. They also must collect state sales taxes for retail sales.

Large Businesses

Large light machinery manufacturers market their products internationally. The large companies in the United States compete directly with companies whose headquarters are in other nations. For example Deere & Company—headquartered in Moline, Illinois—maintains facilities in Canada, Europe, China, Australia, South America, and Russia; Makita Corporation—headquartered in Tokyo, Japan—maintains facilities throughout Asia, as well as in the United States, Canada, Australia, South America, the Middle East, and Russia. These companies often market a variety of products, including heavy equipment and products in other market segments. They profit from brand recognition.

Potential Annual Earnings Scale. Salaries vary from region to region and the salaries for top management positions, such as a chief executive officer (CEO) can be well over $1 million per year. The typical annual salary for a mechanical engineer is $32 per hour; sales representatives earn about $28 per hour and may receive commissions for sales; first-line supervisors/managers of production and operating workers earn about $26 per hour; tool and die makers earn about $21 per hour; machinists earn about $18 per hour; computer-controlled machine tool operators (metal and plastic) earn about $17 per hour; inspectors, testers, sorters, samplers, and weighers earn about $17 per hour; welders, cutters, solderers, and brazers earn about $16 per hour; cutting, punching, and press machine setters, operators, and tenders (metal and plastic) earn about $14 per hour; and team assemblers earn about $14 per hour. Many large companies also have franchised dealerships. A motivated individual with capital to invest has an opportunity to develop a dealership into a multimillion-dollar business. These dealerships can operate with a high degree of autonomy, provided that they generate adequate revenues to the parent company.

Clientele Interaction. Vendors can foster long-term relationships, which can generate repeat business. All large businesses will have a Web site for both marketing and clientele interaction. The site will offer customer service, technical support, and often provide copies of operator manuals for download.

Amenities, Atmosphere, and Physical Grounds. Manufacturing facilities are customarily spartan and utilitarian. Retail outlets range from simple to luxurious. Corporate headquarters typically are luxurious and modern.

Typical Number of Employees. The number of individuals employed in the light machinery industry declined from 2009 to 2010 amid the global economic downturn. For example, Deere & Company reported a 10 percent drop in its workforce from 2008 to 2009. However, some companies bucked the trend. For example, Stanley Black & Decker reported a 2.7 percent increase in employment from 2008 to 2009. As of early 2010, the company employed 16,700 people, nearly 8,200 of whom were in the United States.

Traditional Geographic Locations. Corporate headquarters can be located in virtually any large or small city; large retail outlets also can be located in any area with reasonable population density. Manufacturing facilities are typically in industrial areas near rail or ocean cargo service.

Pros of Working for a Large Light Machinery Business. A wealth of career opportunities exists within large companies in this industry. Positions include high-paying management positions, technical/engineering opportunities, information technology, marketing, and sales. Upper management positions can be extremely lucrative in regard to salaries, bonuses, and retirement benefits. Even lower-level employees may be entitled to generous bonuses and retirement benefits. Large corporations offer summer internships for college students and training for employees who wish to advance. Lateral transfers also are possible. For example, a marketing employee might transfer to a management position in human resources. Large manufacturers offer a wide range of products; thus, they are more likely to survive economic downturns than smaller companies.

Cons of Working for a Large Light Machinery Business. Despite a company's attempt to foster employee-management relations, an employee might have a sense that his or her opinion does not matter and that his or her position could be readily filled by another individual. Upper management personnel might be urged to relocate to another state or even another country at regular intervals to ensure a promotion. Performance goals sometimes imposed on employees, even those in lower positions, might be a source of extreme stress. Large businesses are profit-driven and top executives must answer to a board of directors and shareholders. If a company loses market share or profitability, the CEO might be terminated. The same holds true of the manager of one of the company's departments if revenue drops.

Costs

Payroll and Benefits: Large companies usually offer many benefits; these benefits include sick pay, health insurance, vacations, and parental leave.

Supplies: Large companies can achieve economies of scale because they purchase supplies in large quantities. However, because they need constant replenishment of many items, a breakdown in the supply chain can slow or halt production. Large companies often strive for just-in-time delivery of supplies (supplies arrive when needed to avoid maintaining a large inventory); this policy, however, increases the likelihood of a production slowdown in the event of a supply chain disruption. For example, the 2010 volcanic eruption in Iceland delayed air shipment of many products.

External Services: Large companies usually have in-house departments for most services, which include accounting, payroll, legal, and even urgent-care medical services.

Utilities: Manufacturing of light equipment often entails significant costs for utilities, particularly gas and electricity.

Taxes: Large businesses, both manufacturing plants and dealerships, must pay local, state, and federal income taxes as well as applicable property taxes. These businesses are incorporated; thus, they pay state and federal taxes at the corporate level. They must also collect state sales taxes for retail sales.

ORGANIZATIONAL STRUCTURE AND JOB ROLES

Large businesses have departments for each division of their organization. Midsize companies often have a department or at least an individual focused on each division.

The following umbrella categories apply to the organizational structure of businesses in the light machinery industry:

- Business Management
- Customer Services
- Legal Services
- Medical Services
- Sales and Marketing
- Information Technology
- Facilities and Security
- Technology, Research, Design, and Development
- Production and Operations
- Distribution
- Human Resources
- Payroll

Business Management

Management of a light equipment company usually consists of hundreds of top-level individuals; however, some midsize companies might have a few dozen top positions. A large company will consist of a hierarchy headed by the chief executive officer, below whom are upper-management personnel who are in charge of operations at regional facilities. Below these upper-management positions are middle-management positions and low-level managers. A large dealership may have a similar hierarchy. Individuals in the upper-management positions command high salaries ranging from several hundred thousand to well over a million dollars a year. These individuals have college degrees and usually majored in a business-related curriculum. Most also have master of business administration (M.B.A.) degrees. These high positions usually are achieved by motivated individuals who work their way up the corporate ladder. In some cases, after achieving a high level in one company, a manager will be recruited to work for a rival company or a company with another focus. Included in management are assistants such as secretaries and clerks.

Occupations in this area of the business may include the following:

- Chief Executive Officer (CEO)
- Chief Financial Officer (CFO)
- Controller
- Administrative Assistant
- Secretary

Customer Services

Customer services are essential to a company's operations. Individuals working in this capacity must possess excellent people skills. When a customer issues a complaint, customer service personnel must handle it in a competent and pleasant manner. The customer may be an individual or a representative of another company that may purchase thousands of units annually. A large company may employ managers, assistant managers, and representatives who communicate with customers via telephone or the Internet. Customer services usually are augmented by automated telephone messages and Web-based services. It is imperative that these services be well designed and capable of handling many common customer service issues.

Occupations in this area of the business may include the following:

- General Manager
- Assistant Manager
- Supervisor
- Customer Service Representative
- Webmaster

Legal Services

Large companies incur significant expenses for legal services. Legal issues can arise with companies of any size and can include product liability, copyright infringement, employee issues, and disputes over business practices. Large companies have more vulnerability to large settlements because of their financial standing. Small and some midsize businesses must retain outside attorneys when they face lawsuits or other legal matters. Larger companies maintain in-house counsel (a full-time attorney employee) or a team of attorneys. The attorneys must specialize or have some expertise in the following areas: mergers and acquisitions, patents, contracts, and labor law. When a company is exploring a merger or dissolution of a business segment, the in-house counsel is involved in the negotiations. The legal services department also comprises assistants such as legal secretaries and paralegals.

Occupations in this area of the business may include the following:

- General Counsel
- Paralegal
- Legal Secretary
- Administrative Assistant

Medical Services

Large companies might maintain in-house health care professionals who can handle urgent care issues such as job injuries. This department might also promote preventive health care including weight loss and smoking cessation programs.

Occupations in this area of the business may include the following:

- Physician
- Nurse Practitioner
- Registered Nurse
- Physician Assistant
- Medical Assistant
- Administrative Assistant

OCCUPATION PROFILE

Industrial Machinery Mechanic

Considerations	Qualifications
Description	Maintains and repairs production machinery, cranes, pumps, engines, conveyor systems, and other mechanical equipment used in factories.
Career clusters	Manufacturing; Transportation, Distribution, and Logistics
Interests	Data; things
Working conditions	Work inside
Minimum education level	On-the-job training; high school diploma/technical training; apprenticeship
Physical exertion	Medium work
Physical abilities	Unexceptional/basic fitness
Opportunities for experience	Apprenticeship; part-time work
Licensure and certification	Usually not required
Employment outlook	Slower-than-average growth expected
Holland interest score	REI

Note: See volume 1, "Publisher's Note," for an explanation of the Holland interest score.

Sales and Marketing

Manufacturing companies maintain a staff of vendors: salespeople who call on businesses or individuals to promote their product line. Vendors also meet with retailers to promote the company's products over those of competitors. Marketing is conducted by advertising in print, broadcast, and Internet media. The Internet is a particularly common vehicle for promoting products. Potential customers can obtain product specifications, compare, and purchase products (either on the company's Web site or by referral to a retailer). The marketing department includes graphic designers who can develop illustrations for Web sites, print advertisements, and other promotional materials. This department also includes photographers, videographers, and writers who prepare text for publications. Public relations (PR) specialists prepare press releases announcing new products and other news about the company. Large companies will employ specialists in the aforementioned areas. Smaller companies will outsource that work.

Occupations in this area of the business may include the following:

- General Manager
- Assistant Manager
- Secretary
- Administrative Assistant
- Web Designer
- Photographer
- Videographer
- Sales Representative

Information Technology

All businesses will have individuals familiar with computer maintenance and operation. Computer networks are involved in many aspects of a business, including inventory, payroll, sales, and production. A breakdown in a computer network can

---

OCCUPATION SPECIALTIES

Small Engine Mechanics

Specialty	*Responsibilities*
Gas engine repairers	Maintain and repair gas-driven, internal-combustion engines that power electric generators, compressors, and similar equipment.
Motorcycle repairers	Overhaul and repair motorcycles, motor scooters, and other similar motor vehicles. They may also repair or replace other parts of the motorcycle, such as the frame, brakes, spring fork, headlight, horn, handlebar controls, gas and oil tanks, mufflers, and wheels.
Outboard motor mechanics	Check out and adjust or repair electrical and mechanical systems of outboard motors. They may change or replace parts such as gears and propellers, or they may install and repair steering and throttle controls.
Power saw mechanics	Repair and maintain portable saws.

---

bring production or sales to a halt. The information technology (IT) department consists of individuals with college degrees in computer science as well as technicians with training from vocational schools or community colleges. These lower-level positions include installation, wiring, and maintenance of computer equipment.

Occupations in this area of the business may include the following:

- General Manager
- Assistant Manager
- Information Technologist
- Technician
- Data Entry Clerk

Facilities and Security

Maintenance of larger facilities requires housekeeping personnel, painters, and repairmen. Large manufacturing corporations often have large security departments headed by one or more managers. Security personnel are responsible for preventing unwanted entry to areas where research and development is being conducted. They also are responsible for ensuring safety of the personnel by guarding against entry by individuals who could pose a threat. Security personnel monitor video surveillance and entry into restricted areas. Dealerships also often have video monitoring. Larger establishments will maintain an on-site security force during nonbusiness hours.

Occupations in this area of the business may include the following:

- General Manager
- Assistant Manager
- Security Guard
- Housekeeper
- Custodian/Janitor

Technology, Research, Design, and Development

Ongoing research and development is a vital element of a light machine construction company. Even midsize businesses must devote time in this arena to remain competitive. Although engineers and technicians are primarily responsible for the development of a new product, this department also includes a large number of support personnel. Before a new machine is ready for the production line, an extensive process of creation and testing must be completed. For complicated equipment, this process can take several years. Engineers with a variety of specialties are employed by this department. Mechanical engineers design the machine's moving parts. They also oversee the work of technicians, who run tests on materials and parts before they are assembled into the final product. After assembly, this department tests products before they are released to the marketplace. Equipment is run through repeated duty cycles, knobs are twisted, buttons are pushed, and doors are slammed. If a mechanical defect is discovered after a product is released, the company might be forced to issue a costly recall. Electrical and electronics engineers are required for the development of machines with complicated electric or electronic systems; these engineers also assist in the design and testing process. The responsibility of industrial engineers is to optimize production of the product; they determine how to best allocate the factory's resources. Once the design process and testing are complete, draftsmen prepare the plans that production workers use for assembly of the machine. For each part, draftsmen provide specifications and diagrams; they also produce assembly instructions for the final product.

Occupations in this area of the business may include the following:

- Engineering Manager
- Engineer
- Manager
- Supervisor
- Technician
- Mechanical Drafter
- Production Worker
- Assembly Worker

Production and Operations

Production is overseen by managers, assistant managers, and supervisors. The bulk of the workforce consists of a hierarchy ranging from experienced workers with expertise in one or more production areas to inexperienced new hires. Large companies offer training programs to help workers advance. Large and many midsize companies assemble their products on a production line similar to that of an automobile company. Robots are in-

---

OCCUPATION PROFILE

Office Machine Repairer

Considerations	Qualifications
Description	Inspects, adjusts, and repairs office machines such as ATMs, digital copiers, and computer systems.
Career cluster	Manufacturing
Interests	Data; things
Working conditions	Work inside
Minimum education level	On-the-job training; high school diploma/technical training
Physical exertion	Light work; medium work
Physical abilities	Unexceptional/basic fitness
Opportunities for experience	Military service; part-time work
Licensure and certification	Recommended
Employment outlook	Decline expected
Holland interest score	RES

Note: See volume 1, "Publisher's Note," for an explanation of the Holland interest score.

creasingly being employed in light equipment manufacturing. These devices replace workers; however, personnel are still required to control them. Employee safety is a major concern. Specialized clothing and goggles may be required for workers. Small companies often have fewer than a dozen workers responsible for the entire production process. However, large companies often have a multistage production process, consisting of separate teams of workers for design and testing, parts manufacturing, and product assembly. Despite this segmentation, considerable interaction takes place between the teams.

Occupations in this area of the business may include the following:

- Manager
- Assistant Manager
- Supervisor
- Assembler
- Wireman
- Maintenance and Repair Worker

Distribution

Light machinery companies own or lease distribution centers to warehouse and distribute products. Because many companies are global in nature, they have distribution centers located in various areas around the world. These centers are often located near rail lines, ports, and the interstate highway system. Distribution centers are overseen by managers who are in charge of a workforce consisting primarily of warehousemen who move products in and out of the facility. Managers also must ensure that inventory remains at an appropriate level. The distribution center may employ truck drivers or contract with a trucking company for transporting items.

Occupations in this area of the business may include the following:

- Manager
- Assistant Manager
- Supervisor
- Dispatcher

OCCUPATION PROFILE

Mechanical Engineer

Considerations	Qualifications
Description	Researches, develops, designs, manufactures, and tests tools, engines, machines, and other mechanical devices.
Career clusters	Architecture and Construction; Manufacturing; Science, Technology, Engineering, and Math
Interests	Data; things
Working conditions	Work inside
Minimum education level	Bachelor's degree; master's degree; doctoral degree
Physical exertion	Light work
Physical abilities	Unexceptional/basic fitness
Opportunities for experience	Internship; apprenticeship; military service; part-time work
Licensure and certification	Required
Employment outlook	Slower-than-average growth expected
Holland interest score	RIS

Note: See volume 1, "Publisher's Note," for an explanation of the Holland interest score.

- Warehouse Worker
- Truck Driver
- Freight Loader/Unloader

Human Resources

The human resources department of a manufacturing company or retail outlet is responsible for all personnel. It handles employee hiring and dismissal, employee relations, benefits, and training. The human resources department is involved with recruiting employees through forums such as Internet job advertising and interviews on college campuses and at job fairs. Managers are typically college graduates. Clerical personnel and assistants with less educational experience also are employed in this department.

Occupations in this area of the business may include the following:

- Manager
- Assistant Manager
- Administrative Assistant
- Secretary
- Interviewer

Payroll

The payroll department often is overseen by a certified public accountant (CPA) with management experience. Other CPAs, clerical personnel, and assistants also are employed. Large companies have a computerized, automated system to generate paychecks; however, some human intervention on a daily basis is required.

Occupations in this area of the business may include the following:

- Payroll Manager
- Assistant Manager
- Administrative Assistant
- Secretary

INDUSTRY OUTLOOK

Overview

The economic downturn has adversely affected the light machinery industry. However, in September, 2010, *The Wall Street Journal* reported that the Institute for Supply Management, which surveys U.S. purchasing managers, had noted a slight increase in the manufacturing index from July to August, 2010. *The Wall Street Journal* also reported that new orders for factory goods rose in July, 2010, and the U.S. trade deficit decreased. Positive economic indicators such as these make it more likely that hiring will increase. Many companies reduced their number of employees between 2008 and 2010, through hiring freezes, layoffs, and incentives for early retirement. Augmenting this process were improvements in efficiency made possible by robotics and other technologies that reduced the demand for manpower. Regardless of the state of the economy, openings will occur because of the need to replace workers who retire or move to other industries. Production workers account for more than 50 percent of the workers in this industry; those with greater technical skills will have a significant advantage in obtaining and maintaining positions.

The presence of midsize and small businesses will most likely decrease. If the economic downturn continues, many of these companies either will disappear or be acquired by other companies. Furthermore, mergers and acquisitions will result in an increase in size of the dominant companies. Large companies also will look to expand their international reach to weather the instability.

One sector of the industry will profit if an economic downturn continues: the repair sector. In this economic situation, consumers will be much more likely to have existing equipment repaired rather than replacing it with a new one sporting state-of-the-art features.

Robotics will increase for manufacturing. This increase may be hampered by labor union representation, which will fight to preserve job positions. A number of manufacturing plants outside the United States utilize robotics to a greater degree. This situation increases their profit margin, thus giving these companies a competitive advantage over those in the United States. High-tech features will also increase with the introduction of new products. Power tool production is likely to increase in all industrialized nations because they are becoming more technology driven. Lighter, more powerful, and long-lasting batteries will appear on the market, thus increasing the popularity of cordless power tools. The charging time of these batteries, which initially was measured in hours, has been reduced to minutes.

Considerable research is focused on increased energy efficiency and reduced emissions for products such as the power lawn mower. Gasoline engines are being replaced by electric motors (particularly battery powered). As new "greener" products are released on the market, end users ranging from companies to individuals will be motivated to purchase machines that are more efficient and less polluting.

Employment Advantages

According to the Bureau of Labor Statistics, "machinery manufacturing has some of the most highly skilled—and highly paid—production jobs in manufacturing." Even though this industry has experienced a decline, it is still a worthwhile career choice. Light equipment is essential to any industrialized nation; demand for it always will exist, and over time, components will fail. Most light machinery companies are large, global, and produce a wide variety of products; thus, they offer a degree of stability not found in smaller companies and those that do not produce essential products. The industry can support a wide variety of careers, including managerial, technical, and sales.

Annual Earnings

The near-term outlook for the light machinery industry is unclear. Most companies reported a decline in net sales between 2008 and 2009. For example, net sales declined 16 percent for Stanley Black & Decker from 2008 to 2009. Deere & Company experienced a 26 percent decline during that period, while Makita Corporation experienced a 13 percent decline. Directly affecting the light machinery industry is the stagnation of new home construction since 2009. Some building resumed in the first quarter of 2010; however, the trend did not continue through the next two quarters. The economy also improved to a degree during the first quarter of 2010; however, consumer spending for all products in the United States fell 1.2 percent from April to May, 2010.

In 2010, the U.S. economy was faring somewhat better than the European economy. However, American companies face ever-increasing competition from Asian manufacturers. A significant portion of the light machinery industry is based in Asia. Japanese and Korean manufacturers hold a significant market share in the United States; however, a greater threat is posed by China, which not only exports light machinery but also manufactures products for American companies. The light machinery industry in the United States is likely to face increasing competition from China in the near future.

RELATED RESOURCES FOR FURTHER RESEARCH

DEERE & COMPANY
Deere & Company World Headquarters
1 John Deere Place
Moline, IL 61265
Tel: (309) 765-8000
Fax: (309) 765-7283
http://www.deere.com

EQUIPMENT WORLD
3200 Rice Mine Rd.
Tuscaloosa, AL 35406
Tel: (800) 633-5953
Fax: (205) 349-3765
http://www.equipmentworld.com

INSTITUTE FOR SUPPLY MANAGEMENT
P.O. Box 22160
Tempe, AZ 85285
Tel: (480) 752-6275 or (800) 888-6276
Fax: (480) 752-7890
http://www.ism.ws

KOMATSU
2-3-6 Akasaka, Minato-ku
Tokyo 107-8414
Japan
Tel: 81-3-5561-2616
http://www.komatsu.com

MAKITA USA
14930 Northam St.
La Mirada, CA 90638
Tel: (714) 522-8088
Fax: (714) 522-8133
http://www.makita.com

ROBERT BOSCH LLC
38000 Hills Tech Dr.
Farmington Hills, MI 48331

Tel: (877) 267-2499 or (248) 876-1000
Fax: (248) 876-1116
http://www.boschtools.com

TECHTRONIC INDUSTRIES NORTH AMERICA
1428 Pearman Dairy Rd.
Anderson, SC 29625
Tel: (864) 226-6511
Fax: (864) 226-9435
http://www.ttigroupna.com

ABOUT THE AUTHOR

Robin L. Wulffson, M.D., is a board-certified specialist in obstetrics and gynecology. In 1997, he transitioned to a writing career. He has written analytic reports of major corporations and industries. He also has analyzed hospital systems and medical device manufacturers. He is familiar with the light machinery industry in the United States, Europe, and Asia. For the past fifteen years, he has closely followed the business sector in both the United States and the international arena.

FURTHER READING

Abraham, Edward. *Competitive Assessment of the United States Power Tool Industry*. Washington, D.C.: Industrial Trade Administration, 1992.

Institute for Career Research. *Careers in the Machine Trades: Precision Machinist, Tool and Die Maker*. Chicago: Author, 2009.

Paz, Emilio Bautista, et al. *A Brief Illustrated History of Machines and Mechanisms*. New York: Sprinter, 2010.

Rosen, William. *The Most Powerful Idea in the World: A Story of Steam, Industry, and Invention*. New York: Random House, 2010.

Stearns, Peter N. *The Industrial Revolution in World History*. 3rd ed. Boulder, Colo.: Westview Press, 2007.

U.S. Bureau of Labor Statistics. *Career Guide to Industries*, 2010-2011 ed. http://www.bls.gov/oco/cg.

_____. *Occupational Outlook Handbook*, 2010-2011 ed. http://www.bls.gov/oco.

U.S. Department of Commerce. International Trade Administration. Office of Trade and Industry Information. Industry Trade Data and Analysis. http://ita.doc.gov/td/industry/otea/OTII/OTII-index.html.

Livestock and Animal Products Industry

INDUSTRY SNAPSHOT

General Industry: Agriculture and Food

Career Cluster: Agriculture, Food, and Natural Resources

Subcategory Industries: Bee Production (Apiculture); Beef Cattle Ranching and Farming; Dairy Cattle and Milk Production; Fur-Bearing Animal and Rabbit Production; Hog and Pig Farming; Horses and Other Equine Production; Poultry and Egg Production; Sheep and Goat Farming

Related Industries: Farming Industry; Fishing and Fisheries Industry; Food Manufacturing and Wholesaling Industry; Veterinary Industry

Annual Domestic Revenues: $154 billion USD (U.S. Census of Agriculture, 2007)

Annual International Revenues: $510 billion USD (Organization for Economic Cooperation and Development-Food and Agriculture Organization Agricultural Outlook, 2007-2016)

Annual Global Revenues: $664 billion USD (Organization for Economic Cooperation and Development-Food and Agriculture Organization Agricultural Outlook, 2007-2016)

NAICS Numbers: 1129, 1121-1124

INDUSTRY DEFINITION

Summary

The livestock and animal products industry produces farm animals and processes animal products for food. Livestock include dairy and beef cattle, hogs, sheep, horses, and poultry, as well as minor domesticated and farm animals such as rabbits, goats, and bees. Fish farms and other forms of aquaculture are included in the fishing and fisheries industry rather than the livestock industry. The animal products industry includes slaughterhouses and establishments that further process meat and other animal products. The industry has trended toward large production and processing firms, which are concentrated in distinct regions of the country and the world. Since the 1950's, farms with livestock have become more specialized as they have become industrialized, with a tendency to raise just one species of livestock.

History of the Industry

The world livestock industry had its beginnings when humans ceased to be hunters and gatherers, settled down into communities, and started agriculture. Sheep were domesticated between eleven thousand and fifteen thousand years ago in the mountains of southeastern Europe and central and southwestern Asia. They were raised for wool and meat. Cattle were domesticated around between ten thousand and fifteen thousand years ago near the boundary of Europe and Asia or southwestern Asia. Cattle were used for meat, milk, and draft labor. Horses were domesticated approximately five thousand years ago in eastern Europe and western Asia. Although originally used for meat and milk, horses became primarily useful as pack and draft animals. Goats were domesticated around eight thousand or nine thousand years ago in western Asia. Goats were used for meat and milk. Chickens were domesticated more than three thousand years ago in China and Southeast Asia. Chickens were raised for eggs and meat. Turkeys were more recently domesticated in middle North America and were raised primarily for meat.

The U.S. livestock industry had its beginnings with the European exploration of the New World. During colonial times, livestock was dependent on free grazing in forests and fields. Boston became a market town in the seventeenth century. The establishment of slaughterhouses provided an outlet for farmers' animals and for the purchase of fresh meat by residents. Other markets developed in Pennsylvania, New York City, and the Carolinas. When the United States expanded westward, the Ohio Valley became the center of the livestock industry, although the South and Northeast remained important livestock areas. Preservation of meat in the time before refrigeration was a major challenge, and much was wasted.

The livestock industry experienced a large expansion after the Civil War. As the western frontier opened, economics favored the production of large numbers of cattle, eventually reaching 5 million in the two decades after the Civil War. The Great Plains region, stretching north from Texas to the Canadian border, saw the establishment of huge cattle ranches to accommodate the equally huge demand for beef from eastern cities. The animals were driven to railheads to be transported by rail to slaughterhouses located in Chicago, Kansas City, St. Louis, and other midwestern cities. The development of refrigerated railcars helped in the distribution of meat products. Five companies dominated the meatpacking industry: Swift, Philip and Simeon Armor, Nelson Morris, Cudahy Packers, and Schwarschild and Sulzberger. This domi-

Cow dogs retrieve a wayward calf. Beef cattle businesses are still predominantly small family farmers and ranchers. (©Cynthia Baldauf/iStockphoto.com)

nance led the Department of Justice to conduct a series of antitrust investigations. Poor working conditions in the meatpacking industry also resulted in an active labor movement and the passage of the Fair Labor Standards Act of 1938.

Major changes in the livestock and meatpacking industry took place after World War II. Improvements in transportation and refrigerated trucks meant that slaughterhouses could be located closer to the places where livestock were raised. This decentralization led to the decline of the major slaughterhouses. Large numbers of cattle came to be fed in feedlots, since grain feeding resulted in higher-grade beef than pasture feeding. The dairy industry also experienced large changes in the 1940's. Automatic milking machines were invented, and milk was handled in bulk tanks. There was an astonishing increase in milk productivity per animal, so that dairy cattle numbers declined from 25.6 million animals in 1944 to around 9.2 million animals today, with no decrease in total milk produced.

The Industry Today

The current livestock and animal products industry is characterized by large operations, increased consolidation, and much greater productivity than was possible in previous years. Greater productivity results in fewer producers and fewer production jobs, but it also results in more jobs in other areas of the industry.

The beef cattle businesses are still predominantly small family farmers and ranchers, but the industry's activity is highly consolidated among the few large operations. Ranches with fewer than fifty cows constitute 63 percent of cattle owners but account for only 13.6 percent of the nation's cattle. Ranches with more than one thousand cattle, by contrast, constitute less than 1 percent of owners but account for 22.7 percent of cattle.

American beef productivity increased by 80 percent between 1955 and 2007. Currently, the total U.S. beef herd comprises 97 million animals at any given time and produces 26.4 billion pounds of beef per year. However, changes in consumer preferences resulted in a decrease in beef demand of nearly 50 percent between 1980 and 1988. Cow-calf operations graze cattle primarily on range or pasture. Cattle feedlots finish cattle. Feedlots are concentrated primarily in the Great Plains but are also important in the Corn Belt, the Southwest, and the Pacific Northwest.

More than sixty thousand dairy farms in the United States produce milk, cheese, yogurt, and other dairy products. Around 99 percent of all dairy farms are family owned and operated, but, similar to the situation in other livestock sectors, large farms produce the bulk of dairy products. The majority of dairy farms have less than one hundred cows, but farms with more than one hundred cows produce 77 percent of the milk. The top dairy-producing states are California, Wisconsin, New York, Pennsylvania, and Idaho. Cheese and fluid milk use most of the milk supply, but yogurt, butter, and ice cream are also made in processing plants.

Horses (and mules) have traditionally been considered livestock, although they are rarely used for meat in the United

More than sixty thousand dairy farms in the United States produce milk, cheese, yogurt, and other dairy products. (©Dreamstime.com)

Cowboys in Wyoming drive horses, assisted by a dog. More than 702,000 people are employed directly in the horse indus-try. (©David Mathies/iStockphoto.com)

States. They are used for recreation, showing, racing, farm and ranch work, carriage work, and polo. The American Horse Council states that the United States has 9.2 million horses and that almost 702,000 people are employed directly in the horse industry.

The swine industry continues to show steady improvements in pigs produced per sow. The number of hog farms declined from over 1 million in 1965 to around eighty thousand in 2001. Small hog farms of less than one hundred animals are rapidly disappearing. Large hog farms of more than five hundred animals, on the other hand, keep getting bigger. In 2002, nearly half of the hogs in the United States were owned by operations with more than fifty thousand head. Total U.S. hog inventory has remained stable at around 60 million head. It has become practically a necessity for a hog farm to be large in order for it to be profitable. Hog slaughterhouses are also showing a steady trend toward being larger and fewer in numbers. These trends are likely to continue.

The geographical area of hog production is shifting somewhat away from the Midwest toward North Carolina, which has developed a better system, and toward Oklahoma, Colorado, and Utah, which have the advantages of being away from rain and population centers. Hog production has increasingly adopted the vertical integration business model, increasing from 6.4 percent in 1994 to about 87 percent in 2010. In vertical integration, one company assumes control of all aspects of procurement, production, processing, and marketing of a product. In the hog industry, one type of vertical integration contract entails growers producing a given number of hogs in a company's facilities for a fee. These contracts accounted for 55 percent of all hogs produced in 2000.

Growing under contract raises total productivity by 20 to 23 percent. Although the size of hog operations is an important factor in lowering production costs, the managerial ability of individual hog producers is equally important. Since the 1970's, an increasing number of hogs have been raised in total

Small hog farms of less than one hundred animals are rapidly disappearing, while large hog farms are increasing in number. (©Martine De Graaf/ Dreamstime.com)

confinement. Hog production operations have become more specialized. Instead of growing hogs from farrow (birth) to finish on the same farm, more farms are specializing in just a portion of the growth cycle. Feed efficiency on hog farms improved by 20 percent from 1992 to 1998, while labor efficiency increased by 60 percent during this time period.

The number of sheep in the United States has declined, from a high of 56 million in 1942 to 6.2 million in 2007. Australia and New Zealand now provide 50 percent of the consumer lamb supply. Sheep are still grown largely on pastures, either unimproved in the West, or on improved pastures followed by feedlots in the midwestern and eastern states. Lamb meat is the mainstay of the industry, but milk for production of cheeses and yogurt is becoming important. Although wool was a primary reason to raise sheep, it is now of minor importance, as the market for wool has shrunk as a result of competition from other natural and artificial fibers.

The poultry industry did not develop significantly until the mid-1940's. Prior to that time, chickens and other poultry were raised on most farms primarily for eggs and only secondarily for meat, mostly for the farm families. New technologies and management methods permitted a rapid expansion and specialization of the industry. Currently, most chicken meat found in retail stores comes from young chickens, termed broilers in the industry. Broiler production is centered in the southeast states, with most growers under contract in the vertical integration system of management. Turkey production is similar in location and management, but with more independent producers and more production in the midwestern states. Egg producers use specialized breeds, with practically all flocks kept confined in cages.

Fur farming is in decline as a result of the activities of animal rights organizations and a decrease in demand. Worldwide, about 31 million mink and fox pelts are raised on fur ranches. Other animals raised for fur include chinchilla, fitch, finnraccoon, lynx, bobcat, and nutria. According to Fur Commission USA, in 2008 three hundred farms produced 2.79 million mink pelts with a total value of $115 million. Mink farming is concentrated in the northern states, as a cold climate is important to produce thick coats. The United States is the fifth greatest producer of minks. Rabbits as farm animals are raised primarily for meat, as their hides are of relatively poor quality. Roughly 2 million rabbits were slaughtered for meat in 2001, representing around $8 million in sales.

INDUSTRY MARKET SEGMENTS

Livestock and animal products businesses range in size from small producers that gain only a portion of their income from the enterprise to large, integrated firms that control all aspects of production and marketing. The following sections provide a comprehensive breakdown of each of these different segments.

Small Businesses

Small livestock and animal product businesses have gross sales of less than $100,000. Operators typically have other sources of income, either other farming activities or off-farm employment. Grazing animals such as beef cattle, sheep, and goats are the most common livestock, because they require low investment and labor expenditures. Recently, the growth of organic and value-added products has provided a new niche for small livestock producers.

Potential Annual Earnings Scale. Income derived from small livestock businesses can vary greatly depending on the type of operation and the objectives of the operator-owner. The U.S. Department of Agriculture (USDA) estimated in 2007 that the average small farm family income was around $63,000, quite similar to national family incomes. However, most of that income was not produced by farming: The average income derived from farm activities was only around $4,900. More than one-half of small livestock businesses have a negative profit margin. A small livestock producer cannot compete with large producers for standard products, since the small business lacks economies of scale and must accept a very low profit margin per unit of product. If profits are expected, a small livestock producer must produce a more valuable product for a specialty market. One example could be an organic, grass-fed approach in which livestock are raised without antibiotics or hormones. A consumer who adopts the organic philosophy might be willing to pay a premium price for meat, especially if it had a better taste. Another example of a value-added product is specialized breeding stock, such as miniature cattle.

Clientele Interaction. Most small producers sell their animal products to family and friends, rather than a traditional clientele. The nonmarket value of these products may be the main justification for an operation. Some products may be sold to consumers at farmers markets, to local grocery stores, or to restaurants. In these cases, producers and their employees interact with the managers and owners of retail outlets and with individual consumers at farmers markets. They must be able to communicate effectively the value of their products, to negotiate prices, and to deliver products at agreed-upon times.

Amenities, Atmosphere, and Physical Grounds. Small farmers and ranchers care not only for the animals on their land but also for the land itself. They often attempt to keep their property neat and attractive, in part so that its real estate value is maintained. They may improve the value of their property by clearing land, establishing neat pastures, exhibiting attractive livestock, and so on.

Consideration of physical grounds is essential before launching a small livestock business. The necessary infrastructure may already be in place if the business is located on an existing or prior farm. Physical facilities include pens, gates and shelters, and land for pastures and possibly for growing forage.

Supplying a niche market such as specialized dairy products could be a successful business approach. Dairy sheep and goats are smaller and require less space and maintenance than dairy cattle, and they can provide cheese and yogurt for a growing consumer market. A building appropriate for milking and processing dairy products would be necessary. If producers intend to sell fresh meats, they may have to slaughter animals themselves, as

Egg producers use specialized breeds of chickens, with practically all flocks kept confined in cages. (©Ryan Beiler/Dreamstime.com)

local slaughterhouses that accept small numbers of animals can be hard to find. The sale of farm-slaughtered meat is usually carefully restricted. Egg production may be an easy business to enter and can be profitable if there is no other local supplier of fresh, naturally produced eggs.

Typical Number of Employees. Small livestock and animal products farms and ranches usually draw all necessary labor from their owners and the owners' partners and family members. They do not usually hire full-time employees.

Traditional Geographic Locations. Small livestock and animal products businesses are located throughout the country, primarily in rural areas that have the necessary support businesses and markets to sustain them.

Pros of Working on a Small Farm or Ranch. For the health-conscious person, providing fresh, high-quality animal products is a major benefit of working in a small livestock business. The animals can be raised free of drugs, antibiotics, or feed additives. Most owners of these businesses like animals and the lifestyle associated with raising them. Raising livestock can be complementary to other farm or rural activities. Moreover, the USDA, through its "Know Your Farmer, Know Your Food" program, is providing funding to expand and develop the infrastructure necessary to support small and midsize farms. As a result, there may be funding available to those seeking to help build that infrastructure, such as by starting a small slaughterhouse, and the expansion of the infrastructure may increase the chances that a small business can be profitable.

Cons of Working on a Small Farm or Ranch. Small livestock businesses are noted for their low financial returns. Despite the expanding infrastructure, this situation is likely to continue. Livestock require care every day, so it is difficult to plan trips or vacations that require leaving one's property. Owners and producers must be adaptable and versatile in order to solve problems as they arise without recourse to outside consultants, and they must be creative in finding ways to keep expenses at a minimum.

Costs

Payroll and Benefits: Small family businesses may not pay standard wages. Instead, owners and workers share in any profits according to agree-ments worked out in advance. In such situations, workers also do not receive benefits.

Supplies: Livestock businesses require animals, feed, feeders, waterers, and medications. Dairies require equipment for milking and for processing milk, including bottling it for direct consumption and turning it into butter and cheese.

External Services: Livestock businesses may require the services of veterinarians, as well as county extension agents, who can provide low-cost assistance in subjects in which an owner lacks expertise. They may also require such maintenance experts as electricians or plumbers on occasion.

Utilities: Small farms and ranches require utilities for commercial facilities, as well as for owners' and other residences located on the property. These include water, electricity, and telephone service. Livestock usually do not need a heat source.

Taxes: Often, properties can be classified for agricultural use if they meet certain criteria. Such agricultural properties can receive a substantial reduction in local property taxes, but small livestock businesses may not qualify. In that case, they must pay full property taxes, and owners and their partners must pay income taxes, including self-employment taxes.

Midsize Businesses

Midsize livestock businesses have gross sales of between $100,000 and $250,000. These businesses, particularly the larger ones, are usually the primary source of income for their operators. They are typically family farms. Midsize businesses tend to be more diverse than large businesses in terms of the types of livestock raised, but the primary livestock kept are beef and dairy cattle.

Potential Annual Earnings Scale. As is the case with small farms and ranches, workers on midsize family farms do not necessarily receive regular wages. Instead, they share in profits, which can range from $15,000 to $100,000 per year, with an average income per business of $34,000. It is very difficult to estimate annual earnings for a livestock business because tremendous variables are involved. Size of farm, weather, health of the animals, overall economy, and many other factors can determine income in any given year. Midsize farms may be organized as sole proprietorships, partnerships, or family corporations.

Clientele Interaction. Most interactions with clients take place off the farm. Clients include agents, auction houses, retail store managers, and the like. At times, livestock buyers may visit farms, especially if they are purchasing breeding stock. Retail customers may visit farms to purchase specialty animal products, such as eggs, dairy products, wool, and garments made from the farm's wool. Midsize farms often have modest retail stores or rooms reserved for sales to visitors. Farmers that sell products at retail may also interact with customers at local farmers markets.

Amenities, Atmosphere, and Physical Grounds. Livestock must appear clean, healthy, and vigorous, and their housing and grounds should be clean, neat, and appropriate. The type of livestock being raised on a given farm or ranch determines the nature of the physical grounds needed. Grazing animals such as beef or dairy cattle, sheep, or goats require extensive pasture, as well as land for growing forage. Dairy cattle need more extensive housing that includes milking parlors and milk houses, while more simple housing can suffice for other grazing animals. Poultry and, to a lesser extent, swine are often kept largely in confinement, so housing is primary.

When a midsize livestock business is part of a diversified operation, its owner may have the resources needed to adopt an integrated farm management plan. Livestock being well cared for in a humane manner is an integral part of farm activities, which include crop nutrition and management, waste utilization, energy efficiency, and landscape and wildlife improvements. In this type of system, all components complement one another and little is wasted.

Typical Number of Employees. Often, all labor in a midsize livestock business is supplied by family members. Farmworkers may be hired, but only about 10 percent of the total labor hours in midsize livestock businesses come from hired labor.

Traditional Geographic Locations. Beef cattle are raised throughout the United States, typically on land that is not suitable for crop production. Sheep are raised on native or unimproved pasture lands in the western states and on smaller, improved pastures and in feedlots in the midwestern

or eastern states. Hog and poultry operations are most often large businesses. Midsize hog and poultry businesses are often diverse farms that raise hogs and poultry alongside other animals and crops, and they may be located almost anywhere that farms are located in general.

Pros of Working on a Midsize Farm or Ranch. Midsize family farms enjoy certain advantages over small and large livestock enterprises. A small business may not have all the components available to make an integrated farm management plan work efficiently, while large livestock businesses may demand more resources or generate more waste than can be supplied or used effectively by a complementary farm. People in the livestock business may enjoy working with animals and the outdoors environment. Producers have a lot of variety in their work, and time schedules are not too rigid.

Cons of Working on a Midsize Farm or Ranch. It has become increasingly difficult for midsize family farms to survive, as increasing costs of production have been coupled with lower prices received for livestock and animal products. Livestock production and income is always a risk, as it is prey to many unpredictable factors, including weather, diseases, and uncertain market prices.

Costs

Payroll and Benefits: Owners and family members working on midsize livestock farms generally share in profits rather than receiving traditional wages. Some midsize farms may hire one or two workers, who may be paid hourly, weekly, or monthly. Workers may receive benefits including health insurance, holidays, vacations, and even living quarters on the farm.

Supplies: Livestock businesses require animals, feed, feeders, waterers, and medications. Dairies require equipment for milking and for processing milk, including bottling it for direct consumption and turning it into butter and cheese. Farms may also require silos and grain storage structures, tractors and loaders, or trucks and stock trailers for transporting livestock.

External Services: Midsize livestock businesses may contract accountants or tax preparation experts, as well as veterinarians. Extension agents can serve as valuable resources for family farms.

Utilities: Midsize farms and ranches require utilities for commercial facilities, as well as for owners' and other residences located on the property. These include water, electricity, and telephone service. Livestock usually do not need a heat source.

Taxes: A property may be assessed for agricultural use if it meets certain criteria in terms of acreage, income generated, and number of livestock. Qualifying properties are taxed at lower rates than most residential and commercial properties. Regardless, farmers and ranchers must pay some property taxes, as well as personal income and self-employment taxes on their farm-related income. They must also withhold income and payroll taxes from any employees.

Large Businesses

Large livestock businesses have gross sales greater than $250,000. They include larger family farms and nonfamily farms run by corporations, cooperatives, or hired managers. Corporations often follow a business model employing vertical integration. These businesses usually specialize in one type of livestock, with hogs and poultry showing strong representation.

Potential Annual Earnings Scale. According to the U.S. Bureau of Labor Statistics (BLS), the average annual income of farmers and ranchers in 2009 was $52,050, although the relative standard error attaching to this estimate was nearly 20 percent, indicating a high degree of unreliability. The BLS provided a much more reliable estimate of annual salary for farm and ranch managers, whose average 2009 earnings were $63,140. Animal breeders earned an average of $36,770, while farmworkers handling farm and ranch animals earned an average of $23,250.

Clientele Interaction. Due to increasing risks in the marketplace, most poultry and swine producers sign contracts with vertical integration corporations. In these cases, company representatives visit farms to discuss contracts with producers. Sales and service representatives of integrated companies interact with distributors, retailers, and restaurant managers that purchase their animal products.

Amenities, Atmosphere, and Physical Grounds. Large livestock enterprises are characterized by large investments in buildings for confinement rearing of animals. Typically, only one type of livestock is kept and often only one stage of

production is managed. Examples would be farms producing only weaning piglets or stocker cattle. Some large operations still raise crops, but often the amount of waste generated can be greater than the capacity of the fields to effectively utilize it, leading to a waste problem.

The land required for a beef cattle business depends on the type of operation. Extensive operations grow cattle by grazing, so more land is needed. Often, especially in the western states, cattle can be grazed on public lands, reducing the investment cost to the producer. Feedlots are confinement operations that are used for the final growing and fattening phase prior to slaughter. Although less land is needed than grazing operations, an infrastructure is often needed for thousands of animals. Feedlots have no attached farms and often create significant waste problems. Vertical integration companies can have office buildings that are located away from production facilities, which have a typical infrastructure.

Typical Number of Employees. Over one-half of the labor is performed by hired labor. Two farm managers and five hired farm laborers is the average.

Traditional Geographic Locations. Most hogs have traditionally been grown in the Midwest, although North Carolina, Oklahoma, Colorado, and Utah have recently shown increases. Chicken meat (broiler) production is concentrated in the southeastern states, from Delaware to Arkansas. The top egg-producing states are Iowa, Ohio, Pennsylvania, Indiana, and Texas. The top turkey-producing states are Minnesota, North Carolina, Missouri, Arkansas, and Virginia.

Feedlots are common for finishing cattle in large operations. The cattle are fed grain and other concentrates to produce high-quality beef prior to slaughter. Feedlots are common in the Great Plains and are also important in parts of the Corn Belt, Southwest, and Pacific Northwest. The most important dairy states are California, Wisconsin, New York, Pennsylvania, Idaho, Michigan, New Mexico, and Vermont. Since milk is a perishable product, dairies are located within a convenient distance to retail stores (usually within one hundred miles).

Pros of Working for a Large Livestock Business. Large livestock businesses are often run by vertical integration corporations. These corporations can provide a large variety of specialized job opportunities. Employees who prefer to devote their energies and creativity in a specialized niche of the industry can thrive. Being an employee in a large corporation can provide income stability and job security.

Cons of Working for a Large Livestock Business. Managers of large corporations (particularly in the animal products industry) must remain keenly aware of government safety and quality regulations. Labor relations can also be an ongoing concern. It can be difficult to finance a large independent operation, since the typically low and variable returns can make it difficult to repay loans. Often, large livestock farms are family owned and result from the growth of midsize farms.

Costs

Payroll and Benefits: Large livestock businesses are more likely to hire managers and workers, who are usually paid on a monthly basis, often with benefits that can include housing. Vertical integration companies can have a large number of employees, who are compensated on an hourly or salary basis. Benefits typically include paid vacations and holidays, as well as health insurance.

Supplies: Livestock businesses require animals, feed, feeders, waterers, and medications. Dairies require equipment for milking and for processing milk, including bottling it for direct consumption and turning it into butter and cheese. Farms may also require silos and grain storage structures, tractors and loaders, or trucks and stock trailers for transporting livestock.

Large businesses' feeding systems are more likely to be automated, especially for poultry. Feedlots for cattle require extensive fencing, trucks, and distribution systems for feeding. Large dairy farms are normally not confinement operations, but they still require large additional investments in milking parlors and bulk milk handling. Egg farms require a room and machinery for egg handling and grading. Large companies have their own feed mills with their own requirements for feed grinding, mixing, and distribution. Poultry companies can have their own hatcheries, requiring incubators and other specialized equipment. Independent producers need to purchase foundation or replacement stock. Examples could be the purchase of calves or weaning piglets from breeders, or day-old chicks from hatcheries.

External Services: External services can include veterinarians, extension agents, representatives that service contracts, electricians, and plumbers.

Utilities: In addition to water, electricity, and telephone, large businesses need high-speed Internet and a source of heat, usually natural gas or oil.

Taxes: Large vertically integrated companies are most likely set up as corporations. They must pay corporate income taxes and property taxes, although properties where livestock are produced are likely to qualify for reduced rates as agricultural properties. Corporate offices must pay standard property tax rates.

ORGANIZATIONAL STRUCTURE AND JOB ROLES

Most livestock businesses must fulfill the same basic functions, regardless of size. Only large companies, however, are likely to engage in significant division of labor. Small family businesses generally assign most job roles to their owners, and any other employees may need to perform multiple tasks as well.

The following umbrella categories apply to the organizational structure of businesses in the livestock and animal products industry:

- Business Management
- Customer Service
- Quality Assurance
- Sales and Marketing
- Facilities and Security
- Technology, Research, Design, and Development
- Production and Operations
- Human Resources

Business Management

Business management personnel are concerned with the efficient and effective overall operation of their businesses. They plan, organize, direct, and control both individual departments and overall organizations. On small and midsize family farms, owners are the only managers. Larger companies may have extensive management staffs.

Accountants prepare financial reports, such as balance sheets and profit/loss statements, that are essential to evaluate the financial health of a company and to prepare budgets and plan future cash flows. Operations managers report to senior management about production and statistical data related to company operations. Financial analysts monitor financial documents and accounts to ensure their accuracy and report trends to management. They also perform credit investigations on new accounts, monitor credit status on existing accounts, and prepare and resolve any issues with invoices, payments, pricing, and proofs of delivery.

Procurement managers monitor and analyze trends in company spending and inventories in order to make future recommendations and to identify potential areas for cost savings. They also develop and implement purchasing policies for services and equipment. Purchasing agents work with members of other departments such as marketing and production in order to determine their needs. They must have in-depth knowledge of the goods and services their organizations need and how they will be used, and they negotiate prices with suppliers of necessary goods and services.

Business management personnel of large companies require at least a bachelor's degree in business administration or accounting. Many executive managers have a master of business administration, and accountants usually need to be qualified as Certified Public Accountants. According to the BLS, the average salary for an agricultural chief executive in 2009 was $161,700; the average salary for an agricultural operations manager was $94,130; the average salary for a farm or ranch manager was $63,140.

Business management occupations may include the following:

- Farmer/Farm Owner
- President/Chief Executive Officer (CEO)

OCCUPATION PROFILE

Meat Cutter

Considerations	Qualifications
Description	Reduces animal carcasses into small pieces of meat suitable for sale to customers.
Career clusters	Agriculture, Food, and Natural Resources; Human Services
Interests	Things
Working conditions	Work inside
Minimum education level	On-the-job training; apprenticeship
Physical exertion	Light work; medium work; heavy work
Physical abilities	Unexceptional/basic fitness; strength may be required
Opportunities for experience	Apprenticeship; military service; part-time work
Licensure and certification	Usually not required
Employment outlook	Slower-than-average growth expected
Holland interest score	RSE

Note: See volume 1, "Publisher's Note," for an explanation of the Holland interest score.

- Chief Financial Officer (CFO)
- Administrative Assistant
- Procurement Manager
- Financial Analyst
- Operations Manager
- Farm/Ranch Manager

Customer Service

Customer service representatives provide the primary communication link between companies and their customers. They attempt to handle requests or complaints from customers to their complete satisfaction. Representatives work closely with sales and marketing, and they must understand all products and programs that their companies offer in order to explain benefits to potential customers and create interest for company products. They must inform customers of the means by which their problems or concerns will be addressed. Customer service managers oversee their departments, review policies and procedures, and develop action plans to effect improvements. According to the BLS, agricultural customer service representatives earned an average of $33,890 in 2009.

Customer service occupations may include the following:

- Customer Service Representative
- Customer Service Manager

Quality Assurance

Quality assurance personnel ensure that government regulations and customer expectations regarding food safety and quality are met. Supervisors, in consultation with senior managers, establish and implement systematic procedures to meet both internal and external quality standards. They must be knowledgeable in animal product processing procedures and have management skills. Quality coordinators identify problems and issues involving these procedures and initiate actions to improve them. Process engineers evaluate production processes with an eye to improving them by reducing costs while maintaining or improving product quality. Starting salaries in quality assurance can range from $24,000 to $45,000, while supervisors can earn around $90,000.

Quality assurance occupations may include the following:

- Farmhand
- Quality Assurance Supervisor
- Quality Assurance Coordinator
- Process Engineer

Sales and Marketing

Marketing professionals analyze statistical data in order to develop strategies to increase market share of existing products and to identify and penetrate markets for new products. Marketing managers oversee all marketing, advertising, and promotional staff and activities. Sales personnel must understand their companies' products in order to communicate their uses and benefits to clients. They call on grocery supervisors and small, local customers and attempt to convince these potential customers to carry or purchase their companies' products. They perform sales activities at the store level, including merchandising, displays, set-ups, order writing, distribution, and stock management.

Directors of business development manage business relationships and keep attuned to market needs in order to identify new opportunities. Market research analysts and sales analysts monitor and coordinate statistical information relating sales achievements to sales goals and previous years' achievements. They assist in the sales planning process based on market intelligence. Packaging graphics specialists design appealing packaging. Marketing managers earn average annual salaries of $98,580 according to the BLS, while sales representatives earn an average of $63,810.

Livestock dealers work for farmers and ranchers, selling their livestock. Livestock brokers, on the other hand, work for packers, buying animals for meat products. The two jobs require the same skills but have opposing interests, as dealers seek the highest prices for farmers, while brokers seek the lowest prices for packers. Workers in either job need a complete knowledge of the type of livestock they work with and their grades and quality, as well as a keen sense of current market conditions. Dealers and brokers may work on commission or receive a portion of the purchase price. They typically earn between $40,000 and $90,000 per year.

Sales and marketing positions normally require bachelor's degrees and strong verbal and written communication skills. Specialization in animal science and marketing is a good academic background for these positions.

Sales and marketing occupations may include the following:

- Sales Manager
- Sales Representative
- Marketing Manager
- Pricing Director
- Business Development Director
- Market Research Analyst
- Field Sales Consultant
- Sales Account Manager
- Packaging Graphics Specialist
- Livestock Dealer/Broker

Facilities and Security

Security is very important to maintain animal health, particularly for large swine and poultry operations where thousands of animals can be kept in large buildings. Visitors and suppliers to these facilities are always asked if they have visited other farms that day and are not permitted to enter animal facilities unless they don protective clothing and footwear. They may even be required to shower. All of these procedures are designed to prevent the introduction of diseases that could have devastating consequences to herds or flocks. Guidelines and procedures are developed within each organization and assigned to production managers for implementation.

Facilities and security occupations may include the following:

- Live Production Manager
- Flock Supervisor

Technology, Research, Design, and Development

Research and development personnel identify new technological advances in meat, dairy, and egg production and determine whether their companies would benefit by adopting them. They seek to develop new products, to maintain and improve the quality of existing products, and to evaluate product shelf life and safety. Systems engineers seek continuous improvements to plants and businesses by optimizing system performance and product quality. Their goal is to maximize productivity and capacity of systems while reducing waste and costs. Systems engineers construct, configure, install, test, and maintain system software. They de-

velop technical design specifications, monitor system performance, and initiate corrective action when necessary. Package design engineers must have a thorough knowledge of the package development process, from concept through commercialization. Depending on the position, a degree in engineering or in food or dairy technology is needed. Agricultural engineers earned $70,100 on average in 2009, while food scientists and technologists earned an average of $47,900.

Technology, research, design, and development occupations may include the following:

- Food Technologist
- Dairy Technologist
- Systems Engineer/Analyst
- Packaging Design Engineer

Production and Operations

Personnel in production and operations are involved in livestock production on the farm and processing of meat and animal products. Livestock producers are the entrepreneurs who design, invest in, start up, and oversee animal product businesses. They are also known by such titles as rancher and herdsman. On small farms, they can assume the roles of manager and livestock worker.

Livestock managers must be very knowledgeable of the livestock operation, pay attention to detail, and have an innate sense of what is important. They invest in the people under their charge, empowering them to succeed and praising them when they do. Farm and ranch livestock workers perform a large variety of duties, including feeding, watering, herding, castrating, branding, debeaking, weighing, catching, and loading animals. They may maintain records, examine animals for diseases and injuries, assist in birth deliveries, and administer medications. They clean and maintain animal housing. Hired farmworkers make up less than 1 percent of all wage and salary workers. They make up 30 percent of all farmworkers (the remaining workers are family members).

Production managers supervise workers in processing lines in slaughterhouses and in the further processing of animal products. They require an essential understanding and control of the production process. These managers ensure that production resources, including materials, equipment, and human resources, are available as needed to

OCCUPATION PROFILE

Industrial Hygienist

Considerations	Qualifications
Description	Conducts health programs in industrial plants or governmental organizations to recognize, eliminate, and control occupational health hazards and diseases.
Career clusters	Manufacturing; Science, Technology, Engineering, and Math; Transportation, Distribution, and Logistics
Interests	Data; things
Working conditions	Work inside
Minimum education level	Bachelor's degree
Physical exertion	Medium work
Physical abilities	Unexceptional/basic fitness
Opportunities for experience	Internship; military service
Licensure and certification	Recommended
Employment outlook	Average growth expected
Holland interest score	IRE

Note: See volume 1, "Publisher's Note," for an explanation of the Holland interest score.

maintain production schedules. They are able to inspire teamwork, and they check daily production orders to ensure fulfillment of customer orders. They also ensure accurate shipments, rotation of inventory, and proper identification of products. They plan, organize, and direct preventive maintenance programs; monitor inventory and purchasing programs; and direct training and safety programs. They ensure that all product quality and safety processes are followed, and they define the best practices used in the production processes. Some positions may require foreign language skills, especially Spanish, in order to interact with workers. Managerial positions usually require a B.S. degree, particularly in animal science, although experience can be very important. Livestock managers receive a starting salary ranging from $25,000 to $37,000, increasing to around $50,000 for experienced managers.

Animal breeders apply principles of genetics to develop and improve lines or breeds of livestock. They must decide whether to have registered purebred animals or commercial animals. Although registered cattle are more valuable, they require more investments, care, and management. Breeders select and breed animals according to their genealogy, desirable characteristics, and offspring. They compile extensive data on animal characteristics that are used in the selection process. Livestock breeders should have bachelor's degrees in animal science, and often doctoral degrees in genetics are necessary to work at major breeding companies.

Poultry hatchery managers supervise the activities of workers and assign tasks. They monitor incubators and other equipment and maintain records. They interact with buyers for the sale of baby poultry and eggs.

Production and operations occupations may include the following:

- Farmer/Rancher
- Operations Specialist
- Supervisor of Processing
- Production Team Leader
- Plant Safety Manager
- Livestock Production Manager
- Livestock Producer
- Feed Mill Supervisor
- Poultry Hatchery Manager
- Animal Breeder
- Livestock Worker

Human Resources

The human resources staff recruits, staffs, trains, and develops employees. They administer payroll and benefits and oversee employee relations, including addressing employee grievances. Human resources managers predict hiring needs and monitor appraisal systems for promotions, transfers, and dismissals of employees.

The primary tasks of human relations personnel are to perform new employee orientation; assist employees when they become eligible for benefits; track employee activity (including vacation, sick leave, accidents, and attendance); and establish, track, and monitor employee training and development. They work with the top management staff to plan, develop, implement, and evaluate human resource activities.

The staff must be informed about equal employment opportunity and affirmative action policies, government regulations, and labor relations. Human resources managers can receive salaries of around $75,000.

Human resources occupations may include the following:

- Human Resources Manager
- Human Resources Specialist
- Human Resources Assistant

INDUSTRY OUTLOOK

Overview

The outlook for this industry shows it to be stable. Employment in the livestock industry is expected to experience little change between 2008 and 2018. Employment in all industries, however, is expected to increase, so the livestock industry's lack of growth will equate to a decline relative to other industries. Consolidation, resulting in fewer but larger farms, is expected to continue over that period, but at a slower pace than in previous years. The remaining farms will be more productive. As a result, the number of livestock workers will remain about the same. The number of livestock managers will rise, though, as more owners transfer their responsibilities to managers, particularly owners who do not live on their land. The number of livestock managers is expected to rise by only about 6 percent, however, which is still below the average growth projected for all professions.

U.S. meat and poultry production will show declines through 2011 because of declining consumer demand and higher grain and soybean-meal prices. The reduced domestic per capita consumption will continue through 2012. The result will be lower production at higher meat prices, resulting in improved net returns and incentives for moderate expansion. Poultry production will show the greatest growth over the 2010's, as poultry are the most efficient converters of feed to meat. Milk production will rise, but at a lower rate than it did at the beginning of the twenty-first century. Consumption of cheese will increase, while fluid milk consumption will decrease.

Livestock production in the United States is now often considered to be an agribusiness, as producers largely survive with very high volumes of product and very low profits per animal. The only way small livestock producers can survive in this environment is to supply a niche market with a value-added product. Increased awareness among consumers has allowed marketing features such as taste and texture differences, antibiotic-free status, and animal welfare issues, such as being raised on pasture. Natural and organic beef still represents only 1.4 percent of all fresh beef sold, so it is a small market. Retail organic beef products averaged $5.19 per pound in 2005, compared with $3.56 per pound for all beef products. However, for an animal product to be labeled "organic," there are stringent requirements. For animal products to be labeled "natural" requires fewer measures by producers. "Natural" refers only to the product, not to how the animal was raised. The product must contain no additives, artificial flavors, colors, or preservatives.

Large-scale vertical integration now provides 87 percent of the hogs produced, following a trend adopted much earlier in the poultry industry. With vertical integration, all aspects of hog production, from farrowing to final packing in retail counters, are controlled by one company. As a result of vagaries in the hog market, the majority of producers have felt compelled to sign contracts with vertical integration companies just to survive. Of the remaining 13 percent of hogs sold on the open market, the producers of only about 3 to 5 percent actually set the price for the commodity. This has resulted in a steady downward pressure in prices paid for live hogs.

The U.S. beef herd was 97 million head in 2007, producing 26.4 billion pounds of beef. The figure demonstrates a productivity increase of 80 percent since 1955, and the United States is now the most efficient producer in the world. Many factors have led to this increase in productivity, such as ionophore supplements, growth-promoting implants, genetic selection, and vaccinations for multiple diseases. Beef demand declined significantly during the global recession. People bought fewer high-end cuts and reduced their patronage of restaurants and other prepared food vendors outside the home. Although demand for hamburgers has remained high, this demand does not benefit the U.S. cattle industry, since the fast food industry relies heavily on beef imports. Beef and dairy production will need to double by 2050 to supply global demand.

Employment Advantages

According to the BLS, the number of self-employed farmers and producers is expected to decline moderately between 2008 and 2018, as technological advances lower profit margins and continue to favor large-scale production. However, opportunities are increasing for value-added and organic small farms. Moderate growth of 6 percent for farm managers is expected. Support services, such as farm labor contracting and farm management, will show a growth of around 18 percent as livestock farms grow larger. Vertically integrated corporations and very large farms will provide steady employment in a variety of positions.

Students with an interest and background in livestock will continue to have many employment and business opportunities. Students with a background in animal science could consider entering into production or development of new animal products. Students with communication skills can write for livestock publications, newspapers, advertising agencies, and public relations companies. Talented persons with advanced degrees can find rewarding careers in nutrition and disease research. Graduates in animal science can find openings teaching vocational agriculture at the secondary school level. Students with a farm background could find rewarding careers working as county agents with the Cooperative Extension Service.

Annual Earnings

The total value of livestock sales in the United States in 2007 was $154 billion, consisting of $61.2 billion in beef, $44 billion in broilers, $18 billion in hogs, and $31.7 billion in dairy products. Predictions for 2010 show an overall increase of $11.5 billion in livestock receipts, largely due to increases in processing of milk, beef, hogs, broilers, eggs, and turkeys. There will be declines in the number of dairy cows and hogs and small increases in veal, broilers, and eggs.

World exports of meat are predicted to increase by 1.8 percent per year. Rising per capita incomes combined with population growth will drive the global meat demand. World trade in major livestock products was around $664 billion in 2010, including $200 billion in beef, $192 billion in pork, $160 billion in poultry, $32 billion in lamb, and $77 in dairy products. The global recession of 2007-2009 resulted in a drop in U.S. exports of meat by more than 7 percent. As the economy grows, exports are projected to rise and to account for a growing share of U.S. meat use.

U.S. poultry and meat consumption is expected to decline through 2011, with modest increases through 2019. Global livestock numbers and value of animal products is predicted to rise around 10 percent by 2016. This would increase global trade earnings to around $73 billion. The increases would be due to increasing population and increasing affluence of developing countries.

RELATED RESOURCES FOR FURTHER RESEARCH

Food and Agriculture Organization of the United Nations
Viale delle Terme di Caracalla
00153 Rome
Italy

Tel: 39-6-5705-3625
Fax: 39-6-5705-3360
http://www.fao.org

NATIONAL INSTITUTE FOR ANIMAL
AGRICULTURE
13570 Meadowgrass Dr., Suite 201
Colorado Springs, CO 80921
Tel: (719) 538-8843
Fax: (719) 538-8847
http://www.animalagriculture.org

U.S. DEPARTMENT OF AGRICULTURE,
ECONOMIC RESEARCH SERVICE
1800 M St. NW, Room S2032
Washington, DC 20036
Tel: (202) 694-5100
Fax: (202) 694-5646
http://www.ers.usda.gov

ABOUT THE AUTHOR

David A. Olle holds a master of science degree in biochemistry, a bachelor of science degree in agriculture, and certificates in medical writing and editing. He has worked as a freelance writer since 1995 on a variety of projects, including more than sixty articles on cancer treatments, revisions of chapters for a medical text, essays for a medical encyclopedia, a review of an oncology text, and various online science writing projects. He has also worked as an animal nutritionist and on veterinary drug development.

FURTHER READING

Dunn, Barry. "Characteristics of Successful Ranch Management." *National Cattlemen: Producer Education* 22, no. 5 (Fall, 2007): 6. Available at http://www.beefusa.org/uDocs/NC_ProED _Fall_07.pdf.

Food and Agriculture Organization of the United Nations. *The State of Food and Agriculture.* Rome: Author, 2009. Available at http://www.fao .org/docrep/012/i0680e/i0680e00.htm.

Gegner, Lance. *Hog Production Alternatives.* Fayetteville, Ark.: ATTRA-National Sustainable Agriculture Information Service, 2004.

Available at http://attra.ncat.org/attra-pub/ PDF/hog.pdf.

Henkel, Keri, ed. *Occupational Guidance for Agriculture.* Minneapolis: Finney, 2002.

Key, Nigel, and William McBride. *The Changing Economics of U.S. Hog Production.* Economic Research Report Number 52. Washington, D.C.: U.S. Department of Agriculture, Economic Research Service, 2007. Available at http://www.ers.usda.gov/publications/err52/ err52.pdf.

McBride, William D., and Catherine Greene. "Organic Dairy Sector Evolves to Meet Changing Demand." *Amber Waves* 8, no. 1 (March, 2010): 28-33. Available at http:// www.ers.usda.gov/AmberWaves/march10/ PDF/OrganicDairySector.pdf.

McBride, William D., and Nigel Key. *Economic and Structural Relationships in U.S. Hog Production.* Agricultural Economic Report AER818. Washington, D.C.: U.S. Department of Agriculture, Economic Research Service, 2003. Available at http://www.ers.usda.gov/ publications/aer818.

MacDonald, James M., and William D. McBride. *The Transformation of U.S. Livestock Agriculture: Scale, Efficiency, and Risks.* Economic Information Bulletin EIB-43. Washington, D.C.: U.S. Department of Agriculture, Economic Research Service, 2009. Available at http://www.ers.usda.gov/Publications/EIB43.

National Academy of Sciences. *Changes in the Sheep Industry in the United States.* Washington, D.C.: Author, 2008.

Organization for Economic Cooperation and Development and Food and Agriculture Organization of the United Nations. *OECD-FAO Agricultural Outlook, 2009-2018.* Paris: Authors, 2009.

Perry, Janet, David Banker, and Robert Green. *Broiler Farms' Organization, Management, and Performance.* Agriculture Information Bulletin AIB748. Washington, D.C.: U.S. Department of Agriculture, Economic Research Service, 1999. Available at http://www.ers.usda.gov/ Publications/AIB748/.

U.S. Bureau of Labor Statistics. "Agriculture, Forestry, and Fishing." In *Occupational Outlook Handbook,* 2010-2011 ed. http://www.bls.gov/ oco/cg/cgs001.htm.

_____. *Career Guide to Industries*, 2010-2011 ed. http://www.bls.gov/oco/cg.

U.S. Census Bureau. North American Industry Classification System (NAICS), 2007. http://www.census.gov/cgi-bin/sssd/naics/naicsrch?chart=2007.

U.S. Department of Agriculture. Economic Research Service. *USDA Agricultural Projections to 2019*. Report OCE-2010-1. Washington, D.C.: Author, 2010. Available at http://www.ers.usda.gov/publications/oce101.

U.S. Department of Commerce. International Trade Administration. Office of Trade and Industry Information. Industry Trade Data and Analysis. http://ita.doc.gov/td/industry/otea/OTII/OTII-index.html.

University of California Cooperative Extension. *Structure of the Cattle Business*. Livestock and Natural Resources Publication 31-609. Berkeley: Author, 1996.

Local Public Administration

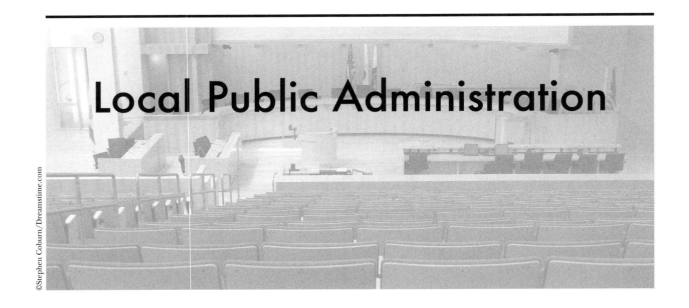

©Stephen Coburn/Dreamstime.com

INDUSTRY SNAPSHOT

General Industry: Government and Public Administration

Career Cluster: Government and Public Administration Occupations

Subcategory Industries: Combined Executive and Legislative Offices; Independent Administrative Agencies; Justice, Public Order, and Safety Activities; Legislative Bodies; State and Local Executive Offices

Related Industries: Civil Services: Planning; Civil Services: Public Safety; Federal Public Administration; Political Advocacy Industry; Public Health Services

Annual Domestic Revenues: Taxes only: approximately $1.28 trillion USD (The Tax Foundation, 2008)

NAICS Number: 921-926

INDUSTRY DEFINITION

Summary

Those working in the state and local public administration industry are responsible for the day-to-day operation of the executive, legislative, and judicial branches of state, county, and municipal governments. The industry encompasses millions of civil service employees employed by the various governmental levels and branches, who implement the policies and programs of their respective states and towns. Employees working for state and local government in a nonmilitary capacity are often referred to as "civil servants" and are employed in virtually every employment category. They advise governors and mayors concerning public policy issues, prosecute and defend lawsuits against cities and towns, research and collect data on important social issues, and formulate and manage state and municipal budgets and workforces.

State and municipal public administration is funded in large part by tax revenues collected by states and towns and paid by residents and landowners. Additionally, a portion of federal tax dollars is returned to states and towns to help fund local government programs. Goals associated with state and local public administration include serving members of the public in need of assistance, providing that assistance in a timely and efficient manner, and using resources to provide services utilizing the fewest tax dollars. Careers in state and local public administration are comparable to similar careers in the private sector and often offer competitive wages and benefit packages. However, some employees may find that both compensation and the opportunity for career advancement can be limited in the local public administration industry. Despite recent downturns in the U.S. economy, this industry as a whole has remained relatively stable and likely will continue to be a steady source of employment in the foreseeable future.

History of the Industry

Each state, county, and municipality has its own unique systems, rules, and procedures governing its public administration. These rules and regulations have developed over decades and, in some cases, centuries of trial and error, in an effort to maximize efficiency and minimize the waste of taxpayer dollars. States and towns must also follow certain uniform rules, such as paying employees the federally enacted minimum hourly wage set by the U.S. Congress, observing certain workplace safety standards that have been enacted by the U.S. Occupational Safety and Health Administration (OSHA), and adhering to federal employment discrimination laws when making hiring, disciplinary, and termination decisions. While other employment standards and rules differ greatly from jurisdiction to jurisdiction, states and towns share a common ancestry in terms of their public administration schemes.

Long before states, cities, and towns had established multilayered forms of local government and systems governing public employment, the U.S. federal government first enacted the system of civil service upon which nearly all state and local public administration systems are based. The federal system, however, was not the creation of the founding fathers. To the contrary, the federal system had its basis in ancient societies, some dating back thousands of years. Ancient Egypt and Greece, as well as the Roman Empire, all had forms of public administration. Centuries later, England became one of the first countries to require completion of a specialized course of education and passage of an exam in order to enter into a career in public administration. The U.S. federal government drew from these early public administration systems when enacting its own civil service system.

The early American public administration system, however, was not without its problems. Initially, the United States became mired in what is referred to as the "spoils system," a corrupted form of patronage. Under the spoils system, the vast majority of public administration positions were awarded to individuals that had supported a winning political candidate for office. As a consequence of the spoils system, individuals most qualified for a particular government position were unlikely to be hired unless they happened to support the candidate that gained, or kept, a public office. Patronage created at least two undesirable results: inefficient government offices operated by people who were not necessarily qualified for their positions and the frequent turnover of important positions when politicians either failed to win reelection or were unable to run again.

The Civil Service Commission, estab-

Inputs Consumed by State and Local Governments

Input	Value
Energy	$37.9 billion
Materials	$273.3 billion
Purchased services	$476.7 billion
Total	$787.9 billion

Source: U.S. Bureau of Economic Analysis. Data are for 2008.

State and Local Governments' Contribution to the U.S. Economy

Value Added	Amount
Gross domestic product	$1.275 trillion
Gross domestic product	8.8%
Persons employed	19.682 million
Total employee compensation	$1.103 trillion

Source: U.S. Bureau of Economic Analysis. Data are for 2008.

lished in 1883, and the Office of Personnel Management and the Merit Systems Protection Board, both established in 1978, were designed to remedy these perceived problems. They enacted a merit-based selection process for the vast majority of federal public administration positions to ensure that the most qualified applicants—and not political allies—were being considered and hired. Currently, the president has a direct role in appointing only approximately two thousand federal positions—most being high-level agency heads, federal judges, and other senior employees—out of a total of approximately 1.8 million federal civilian employees.

Both the federal government's early reliance on the spoils system and its subsequent move to a merit-based selection system are generally representative of the chronological journey of most states' public administration systems. For example,

Peoria State Hospital, closed in 1976, was one of many state hospitals charged with housing the mentally ill. (©Dreamstime.com)

the Illinois Civil Service Commission was established in 1905, but its initial jurisdiction extended only to employees working in the penal system, welfare organizations, and certain charitable institutions. It was not until 1957 that Illinois developed a personnel code and the Civil Service Commission became a watchdog for both the state and its employees, ensuring that state hiring procedures complied with relevant laws and regulations. To further its mission, the Illinois Civil Service Commission was composed of a bipartisan staff, helping depoliticize decisions.

Similarly, Louisiana was mired in the spoils system until the 1940's, when that state's first civil service legislation was enacted. In Louisiana, the Civil Service Commission consists of seven members charged with, among other duties, eliminating waste and inefficiency inherent in the patronage system, governing personnel practices, ensuring equal pay, and requiring that appointments be made on the basis of qualifications.

The Industry Today

According to the U.S. Census Bureau, in 2007 state governments employed approximately 3.7 million full-time workers and approximately 1.4 million part-time workers. The largest general employment categories within state service were education (accounting for 1.3 million employees), state-operated hospitals (381,000 employees), and the corrections system (464,000 employees). Local governments—including counties, cities, townships, special districts, and school districts—employed approximately 10.9 million full-time workers and approximately 3.2 million part-time workers in 2007. Within local government, the largest categories of employment were education (6.2 million employees), police protection (787,000 employees), and hospitals and related institutions (494,000 employees).

In total, state and local governments have approximately 14.6 million full-time employees and an additional 4.6 million part-time employees, considerably more than the federal government's 1.8 million workers. Indeed, state and local governments employ approximately seven times as many full-time workers as does the federal government.

State and local public administration careers offer benefits. First, the wages paid to state and municipal employees generally are competitive with wages earned by those performing similar work in the private sector. Additionally, many public administration positions offer set schedules, which is attractive to individuals with families. The benefit packages associated with state and municipal work are also competitive with—and often exceed—packages offered in the private sector. Categories of employment range beyond education, law enforcement, and health care. For example, hundreds of thousands of people are employed in areas such as parks and recreation, water supply, public welfare, and judicial and legal employment. Generally, if an occupational category exists in the private sector, there is a high likelihood that it also exists within state or local government.

Within the confines of state and municipal employment, several distinct agencies exist, all staffing civil service employees. For example, there are dozens of state agencies and offices in Minnesota. In 2007, Minnesota had approximately sixty-four thousand full-time state employees and seventy-eight thousand part-time employees, according to the U.S. Census Bureau. The largest categories of state employment in Minnesota were education, highways, and hospitals. Some of the larger state agencies include the Department of Agriculture, the Attorney General's Office, the Department of Commerce, the Department of Education, the Department of Employee Relations, the Office of Management and Budget,

The County of Los Angeles Fire Department not only fights fires but also performs swift water rescues during periods of flooding. (AP/Wide World Photos)

the Governor's Office, the Legislative Auditor, the State Lottery, the Department of Natural Resources, and the Public Defender's Office. One would expect to find comparable agencies in each state in the country.

There are also significant career opportunities at the municipal level. For example, the City of New York employs approximately 300,000 individuals in nearly seventy different agencies. Specific agencies in New York City include the Department of Transportation, the Department of City Planning, the Department of Environmental Protection, the Department of Buildings, the Campaign Finance Board, the Administration for Children's Services, the Department of Citywide Administrative Services, and the Civilian Complaint Review Board. Similarly, small towns employ civil service personnel to manage the business of the towns and to aid residents and members of the public in need of assistance. For example, in the small town of Simsbury, Connecticut, job categories exist within the Assessor's Office, the Engineering Department, the Finance Department, the Human Resources Office, the Police Department, the Public Library, the Probate Court, the Recreation Department, and the Office of the Town Clerk. As is evident from an examination of the employment categories at the state, city, and local levels, a wide variety of opportunities are available to individuals with many different educational and experiential backgrounds.

State and local agencies and offices differ in fundamental ways from their counterparts in the private sector. Primarily, these agencies perform public services and do not generate profits; public administration offices are not accountable to shareholders, as publicly traded companies are. Because they are not part of the private sector, competition does not exist as it does among private businesses. Aside from these operational and business differences, the similarities between the work performed in public administration and that performed in the private sector are strong.

Civil service positions exist for all employees, from entry-level hourly employees to high-level executives. With the exception of positions such as judges and agency heads, who may be appointed by governors or mayors, the vast majority of civil service positions are filled through a merit-based selection system. Under this system, the strongest candidate from the field is hired for the job. Because governmental agencies must comply with federal and state laws relating to the hiring, retention, and discipline of employees, the selection process is designed to be inherently fair to applicants. Federal and state laws prohibit discrimination on the basis of such immutable characteristics as race, gender, ethnicity, religion, national origin, disability, or age. Such offices also must provide reasonable accommodations for handicapped or disabled employees. Finally, most public administration positions are permanent or career-oriented

positions, and the benefits packages, including health care and retirement, are comparable to benefits packages offered to employees in the private sector.

INDUSTRY MARKET SEGMENTS

There is no individual ownership element associated with state and local public administration. The state or localized government is the entity that controls the means of production. The government sets the pay scales, the hours of operation, the duties associated with each position, and the benefits available to public employees. No one individual or professional organization can own or operate a government office. Additionally, unlike private businesses, which must generate profits in order to achieve financial success, profit is not a goal or a primary expectation of public administration. Public administration offices are funded largely through taxpayer dollars and, in some instances, through federal grants to aid in specific projects. These are important differences that separate local and state public administration generally from private businesses. Similarly, there are noteworthy differences that distinguish small, medium, and large state and local public administration offices or entities.

Small State and Local Agencies and Offices

Small agencies and offices may be rural offices of large state departments, or they may be the central governmental entities of small localities.

Potential Annual Earnings Scale. Potential earnings for an employee often depend on the type of work to be performed, not necessarily on the size of the office or the stature of the agency. Geographic location may also factor into an employee's pay scale; some governmental entities may compensate an employee at a slightly higher rate for work performed in a location that has a relatively high cost of living.

According to the U.S. Bureau of Labor Statistics (BLS), the average aggregate salary for all state employees in 2009 was $49,240, while the average aggregate salary for all local employees was $45,090. Those averages obscure a wide differential between various types of occupations, from municipal data entry clerks, who earned an average of $32,340; to civil engineers, who earned an average of $80,190; to state chief executives, who earned an average of $104,510; to state-employed crossing guards, who earned an average of $26,900.

Clientele Interaction. Clientele interaction varies widely on the basis of the position and the work to be performed. There are some positions that, by their nature, are individual and do not require much interaction. A state park ranger may interact with park visitors and campers but does not deal with nearly as many people as does a court clerk or receptionist at a small state or municipal courthouse. Notwithstanding this distinction, it may be generally said that smaller agencies' employees enjoy a greater level of interaction with the public than do larger agencies' employees. If there are fewer employees to carry out the work, more duties and responsibilities will fall on the shoulders of each employee. To be sure, a satellite office (the term used to describe smaller, oftentimes rural offices of larger agencies) may staff only a few employees, as the portion of the population to be served by that office is relatively small.

Amenities, Atmosphere, and Physical Grounds. The working atmosphere of a state or local public administration office is often not as appealing as those of any counterpart businesses in the private sector. Because the money necessary to update and renovate municipal buildings must be funded largely through taxes, buildings and offices sometimes are not updated until necessary. Further, legislation, such as a special act passed by a local governmental body, may be needed to release the funds necessary for renovation or for the construction of a new facility. There are also standards that must be complied with. For example, government buildings must provide access for handicapped or disabled employees and clientele.

Regardless, reasonable accommodations are made for the comfort of public administration employees regarding the performance of their jobs and their navigation of the office environment. Even small state and local public administration offices have the necessary technology and tools satisfactorily to perform their duties. Internet access and telecommunication technology, such as phone and fax systems, as well as other necessary office supplies are provided to most employees, and the technology is updated as necessary. In general, al-

though the buildings and grounds may be aesthetically lacking when compared to private businesses, the amenities will be suitable for the work that is to be accomplished.

The physical grounds of a small local public administrative agency range from a small section within a larger government building to leased office space owned by a private individual or business. The size of the office space depends on the work to be performed. A park ranger may need only a small office, whereas a physician employed by the state may require more space to accommodate necessary medical equipment. Grounds are properly maintained, including lawn care and building maintenance. These buildings are an official representation of the state, city, or town and are cared for accordingly.

Typical Number of Employees. Although parent agencies themselves may be large, totaling hundreds or thousands of employees, small satellite offices are designed to provide services to the public at the lowest cost to the taxpayers. In one extreme, for instance, the office of a town building inspector may comprise only that individual and an administrative assistant. Together, these two employees help residents obtain building permits and ensure that work has been satisfactorily and legally completed. On the other hand, small satellite offices of larger agencies or offices may employ several individuals, if necessary, to serve the public effectively. Even a rural medical office operated by a state likely will have at least one or two physicians, as well as physician assistants, nurses, and receptionists.

Traditional Geographic Locations. State, county, city, and town public administrations are located everywhere in the United States. Each state has its own civil service system, and each city and town has its own form of municipal government. Accordingly, all states, cities, and towns have offices that must be staffed by government employees. Even very rural areas must have some system of government to preside over local affairs and to manage important business. There is no state, city, or town—no matter how small—that does not have a system of government and government employees.

Pros of Working for a Small State or Local Agency. There are numerous advantages associated with careers in state and local civil service. First and foremost, most positions offer a competitive salary and excellent benefits. The majority of employees work a set schedule and, if overtime is occasionally required, they may be compensated for their extra effort. These positions generally offer an appealing work-to-life balance—that is, employees may find their careers fulfilling, but not at the expense of full, enriching lives outside the office. Moreover, salary information is made public to employees. They know in advance when they are scheduled for a raise, as well as the monetary value of that raise. There are few surprises in terms of compensation, which allows employees to plan their finances accordingly.

Small offices in particular may offer increased opportunities for advancement. If there are fewer employees in the office, one who performs well may quickly rise in stature when there are job openings. If one enjoys interacting with others, one may be well suited for small state or local employment, as employees in a small agency or office may have more direct contact with the public simply because there are fewer employees in the office. Additionally, in many state and local government offices, job openings often are posted internally—that is, they are posted to current employees—before they are posted to the public. Governments, and even private businesses, often engage in this practice, believing that current employees require less training and already are acclimated to the work environment, as compared to external candidates. If current employees are qualified for internal postings, they may have "first rights" to the jobs.

Cons of Working for a Small State or Local Agency. Some government employees may be compensated at lower rates than their colleagues engaged in similar work in the private sector. For example, a state attorney may earn a lower salary than an attorney employed by a small private practice law firm. Additionally, the opportunities for advancement and increased compensation may be limited. If employees are categorized as accountants, for example, after a certain period of years, their salaries may reach a maximum level. Aside from periodic cost-of-living increases, they will be ineligible to earn a raise until they progress to other positions or the published salary schedule of their employment changes. Conversely, in a private business, depending on the working environment and the success of the business, funds sometimes are available to give raises in recognition of

exemplary performance or just to prevent an employee from being tempted to seek employment elsewhere.

In a small office of a state agency in particular, employees may feel disconnected from the business that happens at the state level. The head of the agency likely will work in the state's capital, as it often is necessary for that person to remain in close proximity with other important state employees. If an employee reports to a small satellite office, that employee may feel disconnected from the agency (including its goals and mission).

Costs

Payroll and Benefits: State and local governments pay salaries to most full-time employees, as well as usually generous benefits. It is common for benefits to be above average relative to the private sector, while salaries may be above or below average, depending on the specific job category. Most salary grades are determined by legislative action at the appropriate level and require further action to be modified.

Supplies: State and local agencies require traditional office supplies and equipment, but they often do not require or obtain up-to-date equipment. Computer systems and software, for example, while required of all agencies, may be relatively old and even seem obsolete by the standards of private industry. In addition to these general requirements, specialized agencies may require highly specialized equipment, such as scientific testing supplies or secure communications devices.

External Services: State and local governments may contract a host of external services from a wide range of vendors, depending on the size of the government and its budget. For example, they may employ outside legislative consultants when seeking federal grants or awards, and they may even hire external security agencies to guard local buildings, rather than assigning city security officers. Custodial and maintenance services are often contracted, as are uniform services for uniformed personnel. Localities that do not have their own police forces typically do not engage paid forces. Rather, the county or state police force in whose jurisdiction such a town is located provides police and public safety services to its residents.

Utilities: Local and state governments consume all standard utilities, including electricity, gas, telephone service, and Internet access.

Taxes: State and local agencies are generally exempt from taxation by their own governments, but they may still need to pay some federal taxes, particularly employer-paid payroll taxes.

Midsize State and Local Agencies and Offices

Midsize agencies include many city agencies and offices, as well as some state entities. Smaller states' largest agencies may be midsize, whereas large cities may have agencies that far exceed those of such states.

Potential Annual Earnings Scale. Potential earnings for an employee often depend on the type of work to be performed, not necessarily on the size of the office or the stature of the agency. Geographic location may also factor into an employee's pay scale; some governmental entities may compensate an employee at a slightly higher rate for work performed in a location that has a relatively high cost of living.

According to the BLS, the average aggregate salary for all state employees in 2009 was $49,240, while the average aggregate salary for all local employees was $45,090. Those averages obscure a wide differential between various types of occupations, from municipal data entry clerks, who earned an average of $32,340; to civil engineers, who earned an average of $80,190; to state chief executives, who earned an average of $104,510; to state-employed crossing guards, who earned an average of $26,900.

Clientele Interaction. The nature of state and local civil service positions differs greatly. As a result, it is difficult accurately to gauge the degree of clientele interaction that one may expect in a midsize state or local public administrative agency. As the size of an agency or office increases, however, the degree of interaction between employees and the public may decrease. Certain state and local employees, as a result of their positions, must make their livings on the basis of their clientele interactions. Physicians and employees of a state's department of motor vehicles, for example, maintain constant patient and customer contact.

Amenities, Atmosphere, and Physical Grounds. Those working in midsize public administration agencies generally work in similar atmo-spheres as those working in small state and local public administration agencies. Because the agencies primarily serve the public, the amenities and atmosphere are substantially similar regardless of agency size. The services that must be provided to the public are the same.

As more employees and associated resources are required for the business of an agency, the special needs of the organization will increase accordingly. The headquarters of a state agency are usually located in the state's capital, while midsize satellite offices are often spread throughout the state. A good example of such a system is the state court system. A state's supreme court, traditionally located in the capital, is the head of its judiciary. Because it is necessary for citizens to have easy and open access to courts, courthouses are located in most midsize towns and cities. Many states and cities own large municipal government buildings that house several agencies and offices, and midsize offices and agencies may share office space.

Typical Number of Employees. Depending on the nature of the services to be provided, a midsize office of a state or local agency may employ approximately ten to fifty employees. Courthouses in midsize cities require judges, court clerks, bailiffs, law librarians, administrative assistants, and law clerks. Conversely, public libraries in the same cities may have only ten full-time employees and a few part-time employees. Finally, some agencies have unpaid student interns and volunteers to help with administrative work.

Traditional Geographic Locations. All states, cities, and towns have some form of government and, accordingly, opportunities generally exist in all locations for careers in local public administration.

Pros of Working for a Midsize State or Local Agency. Midsize agencies often have greater turnover due to retirement and resignations than do small agencies. As a result, their employees may have greater opportunities for advancement or promotion. Another important benefit sometimes associated with state and local public service is the retirement incentive package (sometimes referred to as a "golden handshake"). When governments need to cut costs, workers who are eligible to retire based on their years of government service may be offered financial incentives to do so. Retirement checks to former civil servants reflect a percentage of the employee's final salary, which is based on years of service. To motivate their most expensive employees to retire, agencies may offer the financial equivalent of additional years of service in their retirement paychecks as incentives. Retirement incentive packages exist in the private sector as well, but they are more common in the public sector and usually are highly publicized when they are proposed.

Cons of Working for a Midsize State or Local Agency. Some employees of local governments may find that their opportunities for advancement and salary increases are limited. In a midsize agency or office, employees may find that the level of bureaucracy is higher than in a small office. Additionally, when the economy is in a period of turbulence and it is necessary to downsize the workforce, layoffs in state and local government are carried out in a different manner than are layoffs in the private sector. Many civil service workers are members of unions, which often negotiate action plans with the government in the event that layoffs are necessary. In the private sector, underperforming employees generally may be the first to go, as their perceived value is relatively low. In the governmental context, however, employees with the least seniority are often the first to be laid off, regardless of their production or value. At such times, government employees may feel that they have little control over their own fates.

Costs

Payroll and Benefits: State and local governments pay salaries to most full-time employees, as well as usually generous benefits. It is common for benefits to be above average relative to the private sector, while salaries may be above or below average, depending on the specific job category. Most salary grades are determined by legislative action at the appropriate level and require further action to be modified.

Supplies: State and local agencies require traditional office supplies and equipment, but they often do not require or obtain up-to-date equipment. Computer systems and software, for example, while required of all agencies, may be relatively old and even seem obsolete by the standards of private industry. In addition to these general requirements, specialized agencies may require highly specialized equipment, such as scientific testing supplies or secure communications devices.

External Services: State and local governments may contract a host of external services from a wide range of vendors, depending on the size of the government and its budget. For example, they may employ outside legislative consultants when seeking federal grants or awards, and they may even hire external security agencies to guard local buildings, rather than assigning city security officers. Custodial and maintenance services are often contracted, as are uniform services for uniformed personnel. Localities that do not have their own police forces typically do not engage paid forces. Rather, the county or state police force in whose jurisdiction such a town is located provides police and public safety services to its residents.

Utilities: Local and state governments consume all standard utilities, including electricity, gas, telephone service, and Internet access.

Taxes: State and local agencies are generally exempt from taxation by their own governments, but they may still need to pay some federal taxes, particularly employer-paid payroll taxes.

Large State and Local Agencies and Offices

The largest state and local governments have budgets in the billions of dollars, and their largest agencies and offices may be massive by most standards, employing thousands of people to execute complex and crucial mandates.

Potential Annual Earnings Scale. Potential earnings for an employee often depend on the type of work to be performed, not necessarily on the size of the office or the stature of the agency. Geographic location may also factor into an employee's pay scale; some governmental entities may compensate an employee at a slightly higher rate for work performed in a location that has a relatively high cost of living.

According to the BLS, the average aggregate salary for all state employees in 2009 was $49,240, while the average aggregate salary for all local employees was $45,090. Those averages obscure a wide differential between various types of occupations, from municipal data entry clerks, who earned an average of $32,340; to civil engineers, who earned an average of $80,190; to state chief executives, who earned an average of $104,510; to state-employed crossing guards, who earned an average of $26,900.

Clientele Interaction. As the size of the office increases, the degree to which its employees interact with the public may decrease. At a state agency's headquarters, for example, one may find that more resources are devoted to intraoffice meetings and contact with other state departments than are devoted to contact with the public. Additionally, certain buildings—such as a state's legislative chamber, capitol building, and supreme court—may function as tourist destinations for citizens, travelers, and students. Groups commonly visit these buildings and receive guided tours. Accordingly, not only do important business and government transactions occur in these buildings, but they also serve as official representations of state agencies to the public.

Amenities, Atmosphere, and Physical Grounds. Large state and local administrative agencies are often headquartered in historic build-

ings, partly to underscore their importance and partly because it is costly to build new structures. Work spaces and amenities for average employees are usually substantially similar, regardless of whether the agency is large or small and regardless of whether the employee is working at a headquarters or a small satellite office. The services that must be provided to the public are the same in a large office as they are in a small office, and the amenities and atmosphere are likely to be substantially similar.

The physical grounds of an agency's headquarters may be aesthetically superior to those of a smaller office within that agency. Because the headquarters is the official representation of the agency to taxpayers, the media, and tourists, its grounds are likely to be very well maintained, including the landscaping and the building's exterior. These buildings are open to the public, host numerous events and meetings, and are photographed for books and postcards. Thus, agencies,

The Iowa state capitol building, built between 1871 and 1886, houses the governor's office as well as the state legislature and many other state offices. (©Walter Arce/Dreamstime.com)

as well as the governments they represent, have an interest in maintaining their grounds.

Typical Number of Employees. The number of persons employed by a large state or local government depends on the population that must be served. For instance, according to its Department of City Planning, New York City had a population of about 8.3 million people in 2008, and it employed nearly 300,000 people to serve them. This number does not take into account the thousands of state and federal employees who also work in New York City. At the state level, for example, the California State Controller's Office reports that the state employed 215,000 people full time in 2009. More than 11,000 of those employees worked for the California Highway Patrol.

Traditional Geographic Locations. Large state administrative agency headquarters are traditionally located in the state's capital. Having differ-

The California Highway Patrol employs 11,000 people. (AP/Wide World Photos)

ent agencies headquartered close to one another creates efficiency, as it often is necessary for key employees and heads of different agencies to meet with one another. Proximity reduces transportation costs and saves time. In large states, such as California and Texas, agencies have large offices spread throughout the state. Similarly, with respect to large cities, it makes sense to have key city employees work near one another—or even in the same large municipal building—so they can effectively collaborate when necessary.

Pros of Working for a Large State or Local Agency. Employees working at an agency's headquarters may find their work more rewarding or interesting. This is the building where the key employees report for duty, where important visitors come, and where crucial policy decisions are made. Moreover, because the number of employees in the agency's headquarters is very large, there may be an increased opportunity for advancement through internal job postings and the natural attrition of employees.

Cons of Working for a Large State or Local Agency. Large agencies and offices tend to have the greatest level of bureaucracy. In some agencies, promotions and prime work assignments are not always given to deserving employees but to employees who have good relationships with those making the employment decisions. An additional disadvantage to working in a state's capital or downtown in a large city is that the cost of living may be higher than it is in a smaller city or rural area. The government may compensate employees at a slightly higher rate to offset the higher cost of living, but this is by no means guaranteed.

Costs

Payroll and Benefits: State and local governments pay salaries to most full-time employees, as well as usually generous benefits. It is common for benefits to be above average relative to the private sector, while salaries may be above or below average, depending on the specific job category. Most salary grades are determined by legislative action at the appropriate level and require further action to be modified.

Supplies: State and local agencies require traditional office supplies and equipment, but they often do not require or obtain up-to-date equipment. Computer systems and software, for example, while required of all agencies, may be relatively old and even seem obsolete by the standards of private industry. In addition to these general requirements, specialized agencies may require highly specialized equipment, such as scientific testing supplies or secure communications devices.

External Services: State and local governments may contract a host of external services from a wide range of vendors, depending on the size of the government and its budget. For example, they may employ outside legislative consultants when seeking federal grants or awards, and they may even hire external security agencies to guard local buildings, rather than assigning city security officers. Custodial and maintenance services are often contracted, as are uniform services for uniformed personnel. Localities that do not have their own police forces typically do not engage paid forces. Rather, the county or state police force in whose jurisdiction such a town is located provides police and public safety services to its residents.

Utilities: Local and state governments consume all standard utilities, including electricity, gas, telephone service, and Internet access.

Taxes: State and local agencies are generally exempt from taxation by their own governments, but they may still need to pay some federal taxes, particularly employer-paid payroll taxes.

ORGANIZATIONAL STRUCTURE AND JOB ROLES

In small offices or satellite offices, one person may fulfill more than one role. In larger agencies and offices, specialists fulfill unique requirements in specific groups. Regardless of agency size and scope, all functions must be performed in order for the agency to operate efficiently.

The vast majority of state and local public administration employees work in the executive branch of government. The legislative and judicial branches, by contrast, employ comparatively few people.

The following umbrella categories apply to the organizational structure of state and local administrative agencies:

- Executive Management
- Legal/Legislative Affairs
- Information Technology
- Public Affairs
- Human Resources
- Facilities
- Security
- General Administrative Employment

Executive Management

Executive managers of a state or local agency bear ultimate responsibility for the success or failure of the agency. They are charged by law with carrying out the business of the agency and likely report to the governor, mayor, or county board of supervisors. Senior managers and other key employees report directly to department heads.

Executive management occupations may include the following:

- Governor
- Supervisor
- Mayor
- Commissioner
- Deputy Commissioner
- Administrator
- Secretary

Legal/Legislative Affairs

An office of legal and legislative affairs provides legal advice to agency heads and, in some cases, litigates matters to which the agency is a party. Day-to-day duties may include reviewing and drafting contracts, evaluating human resources issues, responding to right-to-know requests (per the Freedom of Information Act, or FOIA), or analyzing constitutional issues raised by prisoners. Legislative affairs professionals also liaise with legislative staffs and elected officials in state legislatures and city councils. They seek to represent the interests of their departments before these bodies and collaborate in drafting legislation.

Legal and legislative affairs occupations may include the following:

- Legal Affairs Director
- Attorney
- Human Resources Assistant
- Paralegal

OCCUPATION PROFILE

Public Administrator

Considerations	Qualifications
Description	Directs agencies engaged in developing monetary policy, collecting taxes, overseeing custody and disbursement of funds, and administering debts and investments.
Career clusters	Business, Management, and Administration; Government and Public Administration; Hospitality and Tourism; Transportation, Distribution, and Logistics
Interests	Data; people
Working conditions	Work inside; work both inside and outside
Minimum education level	Bachelor's degree
Physical exertion	Light work
Physical abilities	Unexceptional/basic fitness
Opportunities for experience	Military service; part-time work
Licensure and certification	Usually not required
Employment outlook	Slower-than-average growth expected
Holland interest score	ESA

Note: See volume 1, "Publisher's Note," for an explanation of the Holland interest score.

Information Technology

In an increasingly complex technological era, information technology (IT) personnel provide government employees with support in acquiring, designing, installing, and using computer, communication, and other technological systems. They may build proprietary systems or use off-the-shelf systems as appropriate, and they must ensure that personnel understand not only how their systems work but also the formal protocols governing their use of those systems.

IT occupations may include the following:

- Deputy Commissioner of Administration
- Information Systems Management Director
- Chief Technology Officer (CTO)
- Chief Information Officer (CIO)
- Information Technology Supervisor

- Information Technology Analyst
- Information Technology Technician
- Help Desk Staff
- Audiovisual Technician
- System Administrator
- Database Administrator
- Network Specialist
- Computer Security Specialist

Public Affairs

Public affairs employees communicate to the public the business of their agencies, responding to inquiries from the public and the media, and coordinating with other departments and offices as necessary. They seek to ensure that the public, department personnel, and other interested parties are accurately informed about department business in a timely manner. Positions in this area require communication skills, the ability to write and speak persuasively, and the ability to interact with other employees and departments concerning sensitive manners.

Public affairs occupations may include the following:

- Deputy Commissioner for Public/ External Affairs
- Public and Media Relations Director
- Legislative Liaison
- Freedom of Information Supervisor
- Standards and Policy Captain
- Audiovisual Production Technician
- Press Secretary
- Press Assistant
- Communications Director
- Web Designer
- Speechwriter

Human Resources

Any state or local department must have a dedicated team of human resources employees, who seek to attract, hire, and retain the candidates they believe can best assist their agencies in meeting their goals. Additionally, human resources personnel help evaluate, promote, train, and discipline most employees. They administer payrolls and benefits and respond to employee grievances. Some key employees of an agency may be outside the scope of its human resources department, as their hiring and termination may be coordinated by the head of the executive branch, such as a governor or mayor.

Human resources occupations may include the following:

- Deputy Commissioner of Administration
- Human Resources Director
- Principal Human Resources Specialist
- Human Resources Specialist
- Human Resources Assistant
- Payroll Clerk
- Benefits Specialist

Facilities

Any state or local department must efficiently manage its real estate and offices. Accordingly, facilities personnel design, approve, and supervise development projects, as well as overseeing the repair and maintenance of existing facilities. They also ensure compliance with standards set by the OSHA and certain environmental guidelines.

Facilities occupations may include the following:

- Deputy Commissioner of Administration
- Director of Engineering/Facilities Management Services
- Facility Manager
- Chief Custodian
- Custodian/Janitor
- Maintenance and Repair Worker

Security

Security personnel protect the employees, property, and proprietary information of their agencies and governments. They coordinate their activities with all relevant law enforcement agencies, as well as the attorneys general and district attorneys with jurisdiction over crimes they encounter, and they may aid in investigations of those crimes.

Security occupations may include the following:

- Security Director
- Warden
- Officer
- Security Guard
- Corrections Officer

General Administrative Employment

All agencies and offices require administrative support to fulfill their missions. Administrative employees, such as secretaries and receptionists, work actively with both agency employees and the public. These are important positions that must be performed properly in order for an agency to operate effectively.

General administrative occupations may include the following:

- Secretary
- Administrative Assistant
- Paralegal
- Receptionist
- Telephone Representative
- Customer Service Representative
- Intern
- Volunteer

INDUSTRY OUTLOOK

Overview

The outlook for the state and local public administration industry shows it to be stable. As with employees of businesses and industries in the private sector, civil service employees are not immune to economic downturns. The United States experienced a significant economic downturn beginning in 2007. Although civil service jobs are generally secure, some states and cities faced such severe financial trouble that they instituted layoffs, suspended hiring of new employees, and, in some cases, forced employees to take regular unpaid furlough days. Furlough days and hiring freezes are designed to protect existing jobs, while simultaneously saving states and cities money. Even the federal government decreased the rate of federal civil service pay raises for 2010.

Despite any short-term downturn in the national and international economies, statistical evidence supports the conclusion that the future for state public administrative service is stable, and the industry is expected to grow in certain areas. The BLS forecasts that, between 2006 and 2016, there will be a 0.2 percent increase in the number of state government employees. This rate of growth corresponds to the creation of approximately forty-three hundred jobs. Some sectors are projected to grow at very different rates than others, however. For instance, there is expected to be a 32.5 percent increase in the number of network systems and data communications analysts. Similarly, the number of correctional officers and jailer positions is expected to increase by 17.8 percent.

Other occupations are expected to experience large declines, including file clerks, telephone operators, and administrative support workers. Some tasks that once had to be performed by a person are now becoming automated, and specific administrative duties may be absorbed by other job classifications. Many of the occupations that are declining within the public sector are declining in the private sector as well.

The BLS projects substantially greater growth in local government jobs. Over the same 2006-2016 period, these are projected to increase by 11 percent, representing 612,300 new jobs. Particular occupations that are expected to increase dramatically include network systems and data communications analysts (which will grow by 51 percent), forensic science technicians (34.8 percent), and lawyers (34.8 percent). Specific occupations that are expected to decrease include word processors and typists, information and record clerks, meter readers, and file clerks. As with the state government projections, many forms of clerical work are expected to decrease in demand as a result of automation and improvements in technology.

Employment Advantages

Certain career categories in state and local public administration are expected to decrease by large margins through 2016. It is probable that some of these expected decreases do not represent a temporary reduction in demand but rather will begin a permanent trend toward the elimination of specific occupations that, largely as a result of technological developments, will no longer be necessary. Dedicated individuals seeking satisfying careers, interesting job responsibilities, the opportunity for growth, and the stability of working for a governmental entity likely will find state or local civil service careers rewarding.

One need not travel far to find a state or local agency or office seeking qualified individuals. Once hired, employees may choose careers in public service, receiving pay increases and promotions, or may choose to stay in public service only long enough to gain valuable skills before moving on to careers in the private sector. As the population ages, more public employees will become eligible to retire. Although it is impossible to forecast exactly when these employees will end their careers, a very large segment of the working population will reach the age of retirement over the next twenty years, give or take. As these workers retire, they will leave openings for new state and local employees to begin careers, as well as opportunities for current employees to be promoted to higher-level positions within the government.

Annual Earnings

Because the government operates based primarily on tax dollars paid by its citizens, the industry of government does not earn revenue in the sense that a private corporation does. State and local government earnings come directly through taxes and fees, as well as through grants made by the federal government to supplement local governments' budgets. Using figures provided by the federal government, the Tax Foundation has calculated that the total average state and local tax burden in the United States in 2008 was $4,283 per capita. With a population of roughly 300 million in that year, the total tax-generated revenues of all state and local entities were around $1.28 trillion. The federal government's revenues the previous year were $2.6 trillion.

Earnings for an individual employee vary according to the nature of the work to be performed, as well as the educational background necessary to qualify for a position. In some career areas, public sector and private sector employees are, on average, compensated similarly. For example, according to the BLS, in 2007, licensed practical nurses earned only 3.3 percent more working in the private sector than they did working for state governments—$38,033 compared to $36,349. Conversely, there are positions where an employee is, on average, compensated much better in the private sector. The average salary of all attorneys in 2009 was $129,020, while attorneys employed by state governments earned an average of $82,750.

Regardless of any temporary setbacks in the U.S. economy, careers in state and local public administration will continue to offer stable, rewarding careers for individuals of all backgrounds and degrees of education. Additionally, in uncertain times, careers in local and public administration offer a degree of security and stability that is second to none.

RELATED RESOURCES FOR FURTHER RESEARCH

AMERICAN SOCIETY FOR PUBLIC ADMINISTRATION
1301 Pennsylvania Ave. NW, Suite 840
Washington, DC 20004
Tel: (202) 393-7878
http://www.aspanet.org

ASSOCIATION FOR PUBLIC POLICY ANALYSIS AND MANAGEMENT
1029 Vermont Ave. NW, Suite 1150
Washington, DC 20005
Tel: (202) 496-0130
http://www.appam.org

CALIFORNIA STATE PERSONNEL BOARD
801 Capitol Mall
Sacramento, CA 95814
Tel: (916) 653-1705
http://www.spb.ca.gov

CITY OF HOUSTON
P.O. Box 1592
Houston, TX 77251
Tel: (713) 837-0311
http://www.houstontx.gov

NATIONAL ASSOCIATION OF SCHOOLS OF PUBLIC AFFAIRS AND ADMINISTRATION
1029 Vermont Ave. NW, Suite 1100
Washington, DC 20005
Tel: (202) 628-8965
http://www.naspaa.org

NATIONAL CONFERENCE OF STATE LEGISLATURES
444 N Capitol St. NW, Suite 515
Washington, DC 20001
Tel: (202) 624-5400
http://www.ncsl.org

ABOUT THE AUTHOR

Andrew Walter is an attorney licensed to practice in the state of Connecticut. He received a bachelor of arts degree in international management, with a minor in English, from Gustavus Adolphus College in St. Peter, Minnesota, and a juris doctorate degree from Roger Williams University School of Law in Bristol, Rhode Island. After serving as a law clerk for the judges of the Connecticut Superior Court, he became employed as an attorney at the Connecticut Supreme Court, dealing with a variety of civil and criminal matters.

FURTHER READING

American Federation of Teachers. *Compensation Survey: A Survey of Professional, Scientific, and Related Jobs in State Government Prepared by AFT Public Employees.* Washington, D.C.: Author, 2009. Available at http://archive.aft.org/salary/2009/PubEmpsCompSurvey09.pdf.
Baxter, Neale, and Mark Rowh. *Opportunities in*

Government Careers. Rev. ed. Chicago: VGM Career Books, 2001.

Frederickson, H. George, and Kevin B. Smith. *The Public Administration Theory Primer*. Boulder, Colo.: Westview Press, 2003.

Goldsmith, Stephen, and William D. Eggers. *Governing by Network: The New Shape of the Public Sector*. Washington, D.C.: Brookings Institution Press, 2004.

Lane, Jan-Erik. *Public Administration and Public Management: The Principal-Agent Perspective*. New York: Routledge, 2005.

Morgan, Douglas F., et al. *Foundations of Public Service*. Armonk, N.Y.: M. E. Sharpe, 2008.

Morphet, Janice. *Modern Local Government*. Thousand Oaks, Calif.: Sage, 2008.

Office of Citizen Services and Communications. "Statistics at the State and Local Levels." February 25, 2010. http://www.usa.gov/Government/State_Local/Statistics.shtml.

PublicServiceCareers.org. "Building a Professional Career in Public Service." http://www.publicservicecareers.org/index.asp?pageid=515.

U.S. Bureau of Labor Statistics. *Career Guide to Industries*, 2010-2011 ed. http://www.bls.gov/oco/cg.

U.S. Census Bureau. North American Industry Classification System (NAICS), 2007. http://www.census.gov/cgi-bin/sssd/naics/naicsrch?chart=2007.

U.S. Department of Commerce. International Trade Administration. Office of Trade and Industry Information. Industry Trade Data and Analysis. http://ita.doc.gov/td/industry/otea/OTII/OTII-index.html.